Experimental Philosophy

EXPERIMENTAL PHILOSOPHY

VOLUME 2

Edited by

Joshua Knobe
 and
Shaun Nichols

UNIVERSITY PRESS

OXFORD
UNIVERSITY PRESS

Oxford University Press is a department of the University of Oxford.
It furthers the University's objective of excellence in research, scholarship,
and education by publishing worldwide.

Oxford   New York
Auckland   Cape Town   Dar es Salaam   Hong Kong   Karachi
Kuala Lumpur   Madrid   Melbourne   Mexico City   Nairobi
New Delhi   Shanghai   Taipei   Toronto

With offices in
Argentina   Austria   Brazil   Chile   Czech Republic   France   Greece
Guatemala   Hungary   Italy   Japan   Poland   Portugal   Singapore
South Korea   Switzerland   Thailand   Turkey   Ukraine   Vietnam

Oxford is a registered trademark of Oxford University Press
in the UK and certain other countries.

Published in the United States of America by
Oxford University Press
198 Madison Avenue, New York, NY 10016

© Oxford University Press 2014

All rights reserved. No part of this publication may be reproduced, stored in a
retrieval system, or transmitted, in any form or by any means, without the prior
permission in writing of Oxford University Press, or as expressly permitted by law,
by license, or under terms agreed with the appropriate reproduction rights organization.
Inquiries concerning reproduction outside the scope of the above should be sent to the Rights
Department, Oxford University Press, at the address above.

You must not circulate this work in any other form
and you must impose this same condition on any acquirer.

Library of Congress Cataloging-in-Publication Data
Experimental philosophy. Volume 2 / edited by Joshua Knobe and Shaun Nichols.
   pages cm
Includes index.
ISBN 978-0-19-992740-1 (pbk. : alk. paper)—ISBN 978-0-19-992741-8 (hardback : alk. paper)
1. Philosophy—Research.   2. Psychology—Research.   I. Knobe, Joshua Michael, 1974–
II. Nichols, Shaun.
B52.E973 2013
107.2—dc23   2013008559

9 8 7 6 5 4 3 2 1
Printed in the United States of America
on acid-free paper

Contents

Preface vii
Credits ix
Contributors xi

PART I. METAPHILOSOPHY 1

1. The Rise and Fall of Experimental Philosophy 3
   Antti Kauppinen
2. Accentuate the Negative 31
   Joshua Alexander, Ronald Mallon, and Jonathan M. Weinberg
3. On Intuitional Stability: The Clear, the Strong, and the Paradigmatic 51
   Jennifer Cole Wright

PART II. CONSCIOUSNESS 75

4. Dimensions of Mind Perception 77
   Heather M. Gray, Kurt Gray, and Daniel M. Wegner
5. Two Conceptions of Subjective Experience 81
   Justin Sytsma and Edouard Machery
6. The Folk Psychology of Consciousness 111
   Adam Arico, Brian Fiala, Robert F. Goldberg, and Shaun Nichols

PART III. METAETHICS 137

7. The Psychology of Meta-Ethics: Exploring Objectivism 139
   Geoffrey P. Goodwin and John M. Darley
8. Folk Moral Relativism 169
   Hagop Sarkissian, John Park, David Tien, Jennifer Cole Wright, and Joshua Knobe

PART IV. THE IMPACT OF MORALITY ON JUDGMENT   193

9. Person as Scientist, Person as Moralist   195
   Joshua Knobe
10. Causation, Norm Violation, and Culpable Control   229
    Mark Alicke, David Rose, and Dori Bloom
11. Norms Inform Mental State Ascriptions: A Rational Explanation for the Side-Effect Effect   253
    Kevin Uttich and Tania Lomborozo

PART V. MISCELLANEOUS   279

12. The Vernacular Concept of Innateness   281
    Paul Griffiths, Edouard Machery, and Stefan Linquist
13. Gender and Philosophical Intuition   307
    Wesley Buckwalter and Stephen Stich
14. Expertise in Moral Reasoning? Order Effects on Moral Judgment in Professional Philosophers and Non-philosophers   347
    Eric Schwitzgebel and Fiery Cushman

Author Index   367
Subject Index   373

Preface

This is the second volume of *Experimental Philosophy*. It has been only five years since the first volume, but the field has moved quickly; the current volume collects a few of the many excellent papers that have been published since Volume 1.

The first volume covered what seemed at the time like a wide range of different philosophical issues. We had sections on cultural variation, intentional action, and free will—the three areas that comprised the bulk of the work in experimental philosophy at the time. Since then, however, there has been a burst of new studies across numerous areas, including everything from the philosophy of logic to the philosophy of race. Given this remarkable flowering of experimental research, it would be impossible for us to include all of the important work in the area. We have chosen just a few topics that are emerging as systematic research areas.

Experimental philosophy has also begun to draw on an increasingly rich set of experimental techniques. In the following pages, experimental philosophers draw on lesion studies, developmental studies, and reaction time studies. This diversification in method has been facilitated by the increasingly interdisciplinary and collaborative nature of experimental philosophy. In particular, a growing number of psychologists have begun working in the field, and several of the papers included in this volume are authored or coauthored by psychologists.

Finally, in addition to the more directly empirical research, there has been a flowering of inquiry into more metaphilosophical issues about the broader philosophical significance of experimental findings. The present volume includes a selection of papers on these issues, offering arguments both in favor of and opposed to experimental philosophy. (Readers looking for a more general introduction and defense of the field are referred to the manifesto at the beginning of the first volume.)

It has been a delight to see the growth of experimental philosophy over the last five years. We are grateful to Peter Ohlin for encouraging us to produce a second volume and to Chris Olivola for some excellent advice. We also thank Ker Medero and Christian Mott for help with the permissions. Finally, we are deeply grateful to all of the graduate students who have taken experimental philosophy in directions that we never could have anticipated.

Credits

Joshua Alexander, Ronald Mallon, and Jonathan M. Weinberg. 2010. "Accentuate the Negative." *Review of Philosophy and Psychology 1*: 297–314. Used with kind permission from Springer Science+Business Media.

Mark Alicke, David Rose, and Dori Bloom. 2011. "Causation, Norm Violation, and Culpable Control." *Journal of Philosophy 108*: 670–696. Used with kind permission from *Journal of Philosophy*.

Adam Arico, Brian Fiala, Robert F. Goldberg, and Shaun Nichols. 2011. "The Folk Psychology of Consciousness." *Mind & Language 26*: 327–352. Used with kind permission from John Wiley and Sons.

Geoffrey P. Goodwin and John M. Darley. 2008. "The Psychology of Meta-Ethics: Exploring Pbjectivism." *Cognition 106*: 1339–1366. Used with kind permission from Elsevier.

Heather Gray, Kurt Gray, and Daniel Wegner. 2007. "Dimensions of Mind Perception." *Science 315*: 619. Reprinted with kind permission from AAAS.

Paul Griffiths, Edouard Machery, and Stefan Linquist. 2009. "The Vernacular Concept of Innateness." *Mind & Language 24*: 605–630. Used with kind permission from John Wiley and Sons.

Antti Kauppinen. 2007. "The Rise and Fall of Experimental Philosophy." *Philosophical Explorations 10*: 95–118. Used with kind permission from Taylor & Francis Group (http://www.informaworld.com)

Joshua Knobe. 2010. "Person as Scientist, Person as Moralist." *Behavioral and Brain Sciences 33*: 315–329. Used with kind permission from the Cambridge University Press.

Hagop Sarkissian, John Park, David Tien, Jennifer Wright, and Joshua Knobe. 2011. "Folk Moral Relativism." *Mind & Language 26*: 482–505. Used with kind permission from John Wiley and Sons.

Eric Schwitzgebel and Fiery Cushman. 2012. "Expertise in Moral Reasoning? Order Effects on Moral Judgment in Professional Philosophers and Non-Philosophers." *Mind & Language 27*: 135–153. Used with kind permission from John Wiley and Sons.

Justin Sytsma and Edouard Machery. 2010. "Two Conceptions of Subjective Experience." *Philosophical Studies 151*: 299–327. Used with kind permission from Springer Science+Business Media.

Kevin Uttich and Tania Lombrozo. 2010. "Norms Inform Mental State Ascriptions: A Rational Explanation for the Side-Effect Effect." *Cognition 116*: 87–100. Used with permission of Elsevier.

Jennifer Wright. 2010. "On Intuitional Stability: The Clear, the Strong, and the Paradigmatic." *Cognition 115*: 491–503. Used with permission of Elsevier.

Contributors

JOSHUA ALEXANDER, Siena College
MARK ALICKE, Ohio University
ADAM ARICO, University of Arizona
DORI BLOOM, Ohio University
FIERY CUSHMAN, Brown University
JOHN M. DARLEY, Princeton University
BRIAN FIALA, Washington University in St. Louis
ROBERT F. GOLDBERG, Massachusetts Institute of Technology
GEOFFREY P. GOODWIN, Princeton University
HEATHER GRAY, Harvard University
KURT GRAY, University of North Carolina, Chapel Hill
PAUL GRIFFITHS, University of Sydney
ANTTI KAUPPINEN, Trinity College Dublin
JOSHUA KNOBE, Yale University
STEFAN LINQUIST, University of Guelph
TANIA LOMBROZO, University of California, Berkeley
EDOUARD MACHERY, University of Pittsburgh
RONALD MALLON, Washington University in St. Louis
SHAUN NICHOLS, University of Arizona
JOHN PARK, Duke University
DAVID ROSE, Rutgers University
HAGOP SARKISSIAN, Baruch College—The City University of New York

ERIC SCHWITZGEBEL, University of California, Riverside
STEPHEN P. STICH, Rutgers University
JUSTIN SYTSMA, Victoria University of Wellington
DAVID TIEN, National University of Singapore
KEVIN UTTICH, University of California, Berkeley
DANIEL WEGNER, Harvard University
JONATHAN M. WEINBERG, University of Arizona
JENNIFER COLE WRIGHT, College of Charleston

PART I

METAPHILOSOPHY

Philosophers often develop their theories by appeal to *intuitions*—spontaneous pre-theoretical judgments about cases. Intuitions about knowledge, morality, free will, etc., are taken to inform philosophical theories of knowledge, morality, free will, and so on. There is now a large body of evidence on people's intuitions about such cases. But it is a further question whether this kind of experimental work can shed light on philosophical problems. There has been a vigorous debate about the philosophical significance of experimental evidence on intuitions, and this section presents three very different views.

Alexander, Mallon and Weinberg defend the most radical approach. They distinguish two kinds of experimental philosophy: positive and negative. Positive experimental philosophy embraces the traditional view that intuitions are an important source of evidence for philosophy. However, positive experimental philosophy insists that empirical work on intuitions is needed to glean the evidential signal from the noise. Negative experimental philosophy launches a much more pervasive challenge to traditional philosophy. The negative view, which Alexander and colleagues promote, holds that the experimental results on the cultural diversity and intra-personal instability of intuitions provide strong reason to think that intuitions are not a trustworthy source of evidence. This view challenges both traditional philosophy and positive experimental philosophy, insofar as those approaches share the idea that intuitions provide good evidence for philosophical theorizing

Kauppinen argues that the experimental work cannot really undermine or replace traditional philosophical methods. Kauppinen maintains that philosophers are rightly interested in figuring out the commitments of our ordinary concepts—concepts like *free will* and *knowledge*. He argues, however, that experimental philosophy provides scant illumination on these matters. For the issues of interest to philosophy aren't what people *say*, but the fundamental competence involved in using philosophically important concepts. What matters for this competence is critically normative—what is the *right* way to apply the concept. No survey, Kauppinen argues, will tell you that.

In her article, **Wright** develops a very different defense of intuitions. One of the challenges to taking intuitions as evidence is that people's intuitions seem to be diachronically unstable: merely changing the order of presentation affects people's intuitions about cases. This instability does not apply to all cases. For instance, most people say that a lucky guess doesn't count as knowledge, regardless of the order in which that case appears. However, experimental philosophers have suggested that we can't tell from the armchair which cases are susceptible to order effects and which aren't. Wright's paper challenges this by investigating people's degree of confidence in their answers. She finds that when presented with cases, people have very different levels of confidence about their judgments for different cases. And, as it happens, people are much more confident about their judgments for cases that are resistant to order effects. This provides reason to think that there really is information, available from the armchair, that reflects the stability of our intuitions.

SUGGESTED READINGS

Cullen, S. 2010. "Survey-Driven Romanticism." *Review of Philosophy and Psychology* 1: 275–296.

Deutsch, M. 2009. "Experimental Philosophy and the Theory of Reference." *Mind and Language* 24: 445–466.

Nagel, J. 2012. "Intuitions and Experiments: A Defense of the Case Method in Epistemology." *Philosophy and Phenomenological Research* 85(3), 495-527.

Sosa, E. 2010. "Intuitions and Meaning Divergence." *Philosophical Psychology* 23: 419–426.

Stich, S. 2012. "Do Different Groups Have Different Epistemic Intuitions? A Reply to Jennifer Nagel." *Philosophy and Phenomenological Research*.

Weinberg, J. 2007. "How to Challenge Intuitions Empirically Without Risking Skepticism." *Midwest Studies in Philosophy 31*: 318–343.

Weinberg, J., Gonnerman, C., Buckner, C. & Alexander, J. 2010. "Are Philosophers Expert Intuiters?" *Philosophical Psychology 23*: 331–355.

Williamson, T. 2011. "Philosophical Expertise and the Burden of Proof." *Metaphilosophy* 42: 215–229.

1

The Rise and Fall of Experimental Philosophy

Antti Kauppinen

1. CONCEPTUAL ANALYSIS AND INTUITIONS

Conceptual analysis has made a sort of comeback in recent years. For a while, pressure from Quinean attacks on analyticity and Kripkean arguments for *a posteriori* metaphysical truths led many to keep a low profile about the aprioristic character of their claims, but the tide seems to be turning. Frank Jackson and his fellow Australians have made a strong case for the claim that you cannot do serious metaphysics unless you get clear on exactly what our ordinary talk of mental properties, for example, commits us to (Jackson 1998; Jackson, Pettit, and Smith 2004). In the same spirit, contextualists in epistemology have refocused their attention on the ordinary use of 'knows'—to the extent that Keith DeRose, for instance, now identifies himself as a practitioner of the once-despised ordinary language philosophy (DeRose 2005). In general, there is a growing recognition that the first step in resolving many philosophical problems is still laying out just what we talk about when we use the concepts we do, and this is just the business of conceptual analysis.[1]

Nonetheless, one might be sceptical about the prospects of success in such an endeavour. Whether it is the concept of free will or the nature of moral judgement, competing accounts have been slugging it out not just for decades, but for centuries, even millennia. If one philosopher says, for example, that it is a conceptual truth that an agent who sincerely makes a moral judgement is necessarily motivated accordingly, and another denies this, how is the argument to be settled? What counts as evidence one way or the other? The usual answer is to talk of *intuitions*: one account matches our intuitions or 'ordinary usage' better than the other.[2] Conceptual intuitions—or 'Socratic intuitions', as they are sometimes called (Margolis and Lawrence 2003)—are, roughly speaking, pre-theoretical dispositions to apply concepts to some particular cases or scenarios and refuse to apply them to others. There are countless examples of philosophers making claims to the effect that 'Intuitively, we...' or 'We would say...' or 'Ordinarily, we would not describe X as...' or 'It is a platitude that...', and so on. Often, intuitions are appealed to as counterexamples to a proposed analysis: 'Davidson's view would have the implication that X φ-s intentionally in S, but we would not in such and such a case of type S say that X φ-ed intentionally, so we must reject the analysis...'. Sometimes such claims are made in the language of possibility and necessity: 'Intuitively, it is not possible for water to be XYZ'. It is a matter of major metaphilosophical controversy whether these claims express modal intuitions that are distinct from conceptual intuitions; however that may be, I will only discuss concepts here.[3]

A remarkable feature of these claims is an appeal to a 'we'. It is rare to appeal to one's own judgement, and if one does so, the implication in context is that it is not only I who would judge this way, but other speakers would do so as well. For the appeal to intuition to serve its purpose, these others, the extension of 'we', must be those who are not partisans of this or that philosophical position. After all, the intuitions in question are supposed to serve as neutral data against which the competing analyses are assessed. So, it seems that the evidence that settles philosophical disputes about ordinary concepts is ultimately the particular judgements of non-philosophers.

Sometimes this is made explicit; John Hawthorne, for example, frequently appeals to what 'people are inclined to say' about particular cases of knowledge (e.g. Hawthorne 2004, 71). It is our shared, ordinary concepts that we talk about when we do conceptual analysis. Moral responsibility, for example, is not a technical notion, though some terms that philosophers use in explicating it may be. Indeed, why should anybody care about what philosophers do if they just argued about their own inventions? People want to know if they have moral responsibility or knowledge of other minds in the very sense in which they ordinarily talk about responsibility or knowledge, and to get at that sense one must work with the folk's own concepts. By and large, philosophers oblige; revisionism is a last resort, to be used only when one is convinced that the folk concept is hopelessly confused or too imprecise for one's purposes. To be sure, we are sometimes willing to discard individual intuitions in favour of theoretical unity to achieve a reflective equilibrium—perhaps, in the light of general considerations, we should after all agree not to call an agent in certain circumstances morally responsible, for example. But without a good understanding of folk concepts the whole process of reaching reflective equilibrium would and could not get going in the first place.

How, then, do we get at the intuitions that serve as evidence for the content of those shared, common concepts? The traditional view was that *a priori* reflection by a philosopher would suffice—conceptual analysis and aprioricity went hand in hand, and rejecting one meant rejecting both. It is this connection that is challenged by a new school of thought about philosophical methodology, sometimes called 'experimental philosophy'.[4] Experimentalists interpret claims about intuitions as straightforwardly empirical and therefore testable predictions about how ordinary people will answer when presented with actual or hypothetical cases. Experimentalists present themselves as providing much-needed hard, objective data, and consequently use detached, non-participatory social scientific research methods, above all surveys, to obtain it. They deny, at least implicitly, that reflective participation in concept-using practices yields knowledge about what people would say—otherwise, as we shall see, they would not have a case against *a priori* reflection. In recent years, a welter of survey-based studies has been published on such central concepts as knowledge (Swain, Alexander, and Weinberg 2008; Weinberg, Nichols, and Stich 2001), reference (Machery et al. 2004), moral judgement (Knobe and Roedder n.d.; Nichols 2002), intentional action (Knobe 2003, 2004, 2006; Nadelhoffer 2004), and free will (Nahmias et al. 2005; Nichols 2004). Other philosophers who have not themselves conducted polls, such as Frank Jackson, Gilbert Harman, and Brian Leiter, have expressed support for them in principle.[5]

So far, experimentalists have put the data generated by their studies to two different kinds of use. Some, like Weinberg and Stich, highlight the effect of cultural and socioeconomic background as well as framing of the questions on people's responses and their consequent variability and instability, raising doubts about the utility of appealing to intuitions in philosophy. Others, like Knobe and Nahmias, are more optimistic and find support for particular philosophical views in their results. To represent this division within the experimentalist school, I will separate the negative and positive theses of experimentalism:

- (EXPERIMENTALISM −) Armchair reflection and informal dialogue are *not* reliable sources of evidence for (philosophically relevant) claims about folk concepts.
- (EXPERIMENTALISM+) Survey studies *are* a reliable source of evidence for (philosophically relevant) claims about folk concepts.

Both pessimistic and optimistic experimentalists accept the negative thesis. However, while optimists embrace the positive thesis, pessimists reject it (at least the part about philosophical relevance).

The point of departure for my critique of experimentalism is that the proponents of this type of experimental philosophy,[6] whether pessimistic or optimistic, ignore the fact that typical philosophical claims of what people would say are elliptical. I identify three characteristic assumptions that philosophers implicitly make about the responses that count as revealing folk concepts—competence of the speaker, absence of performance errors, and basis in semantic rather than pragmatic considerations. I argue that in virtue of these assumptions, intuition statements cannot be interpreted as straightforward predictions, and therefore cannot, for reasons of principle, be tested through the methods of non-participatory social science, without taking a stance on the concepts involved and engaging in dialogue. For example, when philosophers claim that according to our intuitions, Gettier cases are not knowledge, they are not presenting a hypothesis about gut reactions to counterfactual scenarios but, more narrowly, staking a claim of how competent and careful users of the ordinary concept of knowledge would pre-theoretically classify the case in suitable conditions. The claim, then, is not about what I will call *surface intuitions* but about *robust intuitions*, which are bound to remain out of reach of the Survey Model of experimentalists, or so I will argue. Thus, I reject the positive thesis of experimentalism. This leaves the negative thesis. The key challenge for those who, like myself, reject the experimentalist epistemology of concepts, is to explain the source of our entitlement to make claims about laypeople's responses under possibly counterfactual conditions and thus about folk concepts. I argue that this authority is grounded in normative knowledge gained through reflective participation in ordinary concept-using practices. This knowledge is more like our knowledge of how far it is polite to stand from a conversational partner than like our knowledge of what percentage of people believe in angels. It explains the reliability of what I will call the Dialogue and Reflection Models of the epistemology of folk concepts.

2. TESTING INTUITIONS EMPIRICALLY

I will take the following as the canonical form of philosophical appeals to conceptual intuitions:

(I) S; In S, we would (not) say that X is C.

Here S is a description of a particular scenario or case, imaginary or real, X an element of that case, and C the concept that applies (or fails to apply) to X. Different concepts call for different grammatical constructions, but I will ignore such complications here, as well as modal formulations (such as 'Intuitively, it is not possible for X to be C in S'). Now, the main question is: how do we find out whether claims of type (I) are true or not? The general schema that experimentalists use in rephrasing intuition claims is something like the following:

(E) 'In S, we would (not) say that X is C' is a prediction that (most) non-specialists will (not) say that X is C if the case S is presented to them.

Appropriately filled in, a claim of type (E) is a hypothesis that is obviously empirically testable. If it is a correct operationalization of philosophical appeals to intuition, all that remains for a responsible researcher to do is to present a vignette of the case to a statistically representative sample of non-specialists and record their reactions. If a clear majority of the respondents answer as predicted, the intuition claim is (at least probably) true; if not, it is false. If responses are found to vary depending on background factors like socioeconomic class, the utility of appeals to intuition is placed in doubt, as pessimistic experimentalists argue. There's little reason to think that the truth or falsity of predictions of this kind could be reliably decided from an armchair.

How does this work in practice? I will take as my primary example an appeal to intuition that is typical in discussions of moral judgement internalism:

> (I-MJI) Suppose that George frequently says that everyone has a moral duty to make sacrifices during wartime. However, he lacks any motivation to make sacrifices himself, although he is well aware that the war is on, and goes on living just as he always did. In this situation, we would not say that George has made a sincere moral judgement.

The moral internalist uses such intuitions as data for a theory that postulates a necessary conceptual connection between making a sincere moral judgement and being motivated accordingly. The sort of situation in which George makes a judgement and fails to be motivated is not conceivable (in the relevant sense of conceivability). According to the moral internalist, the explanation for why we would not say that George has made a sincere judgement (or why it is not conceivable in this situation) is that the application conditions of our concept of moral judgement, and correspondingly the truth conditions of the thoughts or assertions of which it is a constituent, incorporate the agent's being motivated accordingly, at least to an extent.[7] In keeping with (E), the experimentalist transforms (I-MJI) into a testable hypothesis along the following lines:

> (E-MJI) '[In the case as described above in I-MJI] we would not say that George has made a sincere moral judgement' is a prediction that (most) non-specialists will not say that George has made a sincere moral judgement if the case is presented to them.

(E-MJI), obviously, can be tested by presenting a suitable version of the case to a representative sample of non-specialists. And indeed, something like it has been tested by Shaun Nichols (2002). He gave the following 'probe' to 'philosophically unsophisticated undergraduates':

> John is a psychopathic criminal. He is an adult of normal intelligence, but he has no emotional reaction to hurting other people. John has hurt and indeed killed other people when he has wanted to steal their money. He says that he knows that hurting others is wrong, but that he just doesn't care if he does things that are wrong. Does John really understand that hurting others is morally wrong? (Nichols 2002, 288)

According to Nichols, nearly 85 per cent of the subjects responded that the psychopath does really understand that hurting others is morally wrong (which Nichols takes to be the same as making the judgement that hurting others is morally wrong[8]), in spite of entirely lacking motivation. If this is the case, then (E-MJI) is (most likely) false; that is, non-specialists do not seem to think it is impossible to make a moral judgement while lacking motivation. That is, if (E-MJI) is the right way to construe (I-MJI), it is not a *platitude* the grasp of which is necessary for possessing the concept that genuine moral judgements have an internal connection to motivation or a conceptual *intuition* that someone counts as making a moral judgement only if she is motivated accordingly. If so, the thesis of judgement internalism in moral psychology is not a conceptual truth.

A more complex and ambitious variety of experimentalism uses polls not just to settle whether people really have the sort of intuitions that philosophers assume they do, but also to challenge conceptual assumptions that philosophers routinely make. Joshua Knobe's studies on folk psychological concepts are paradigmatic examples of this variety of optimistic experimentalism. Knobe's ingenious idea is to take two cases that differ from each other only with respect to a variable that prevailing views predict to be irrelevant to people's judgements, and then show that there is, in fact, variation in responses depending on changes in the variable. Thus, mainstream views differ about whether foreseen side-effects of actions are brought about intentionally or not, but agree that the applicability of the folk concept of intentionality depends exclusively on the agent's psychological states. Consequently, they predict that folk conceptual intuitions about particular cases of intentional action are not affected by factors external to the agent's psychology. To show that the assumption is problematic, Knobe has run a series of experiments pairing cases in which the side-effects brought about by the action are morally bad and morally good, respectively. Here is his first scenario:

> The vice-president of a company went to the chairman of the board and said, 'We are thinking of starting a new program. It will help us increase profits, but it will also harm the environment.' The chairman of the board answered, 'I don't care at all about harming the environment. I just want to make as much profit as I can. Let's start the new program.' They started the new program. Sure enough, the environment was harmed. (Knobe 2003, 191)

In this 'harm condition' in which the anticipated side-effect is bad, 82 per cent of Knobe's respondents (random people in Central Park) said that the chairman of the board harmed the environment intentionally. His second scenario differs from the first only with respect to the moral status of the side-effect:[9]

> The vice-president of a company went to the chairman of the board and said, 'We are thinking of starting a new program. It will help us increase profits, and it will also help the environment.' The chairman of the board answered, 'I don't care at all about helping the environment. I just want to make as much profit as I can. Let's start the new program.' They started the new program. Sure enough, the environment was helped. (Knobe 2003, 191)

In this 'help condition', 77 per cent of the people asked said that the chairman of the board did *not* help the environment intentionally. Thus, while prevailing views predict symmetry in people's responses to such cases, Knobe's studies suggest that the responses are in fact *asymmetrical*, driven by factors external to the agent's psychology, namely moral considerations. From this and other similar studies Knobe concludes, further, that moral considerations play a role in people's *concept* of intentional action (Knobe 2006).

The studies by Nichols, Knobe, and other experimentalists differ in details and aims, but all of them presuppose that something like (E) is the correct operationalization of appeals to intuition. For optimists, responses to surveys yield data against which competing philosophical views and analyses can be assessed. For pessimists, the fact that we can find ordering effects and cross-cultural variations in responses to surveys shows that the whole practice of appealing to folk intuitions is dubious.[10] Both subscribe, nevertheless, to the Survey Model of the epistemology of folk concepts, and endorse the claim that testing folk intuitions is an *a posteriori* enterprise on a par with empirical science. It promises to put philosophy on a path of progress and put an end to vain quarrel. This promise, surely, explains the rise of experimental philosophy.

3. ELLIPSIS AND THE IMPLICIT ASSUMPTIONS OF INTUITION CLAIMS

Where does the Survey Model go wrong? I believe that construing appeals to intuition as (E) is a natural mistake to make—it is one way to read literally what is often said. If what philosophers claim really was that people are inclined to say x in S, period, the experimentalist construal would be correct. But I will maintain that it is not what we do, in spite of the surface grammar. Instead, philosophical claims about intuitions are typically *elliptical*. Ellipsis is a common linguistic phenomenon; when it is taken to be obvious in the context, people say things like 'I love the City' instead of 'I love New York' (or London or Helsinki or whatever). Given the purpose of the discourse and shared background assumptions, there is no need to spell out explicitly what is being claimed—indeed, doing so would violate the Gricean maxim of not giving unnecessary information (see below). Similarly, when making claims about intuitions or platitudes, about what 'we would say', philosophers take for granted certain background assumptions that, when made explicit, show that (E) is *not* the right way to spell out what is asserted in (I). At least, this is how charity requires us to conceive of their claims. Moreover, as I will argue, these background assumptions are justified in light of the goals of conceptual analysis.

My alternative explication of (I) is the following:

> (A) 'In S, we would say that X is C' is a hypothesis about how (1) *competent users* of the concepts in question would respond if (2) they *considered the case in sufficiently ideal conditions* and (3) their answer was *influenced only by semantic considerations*.

It is central to my case against the positive thesis of experimentalism that requirements (1)–(3) rule out surveys as a method for accessing the semantic application conditions of folk concepts. In this section, I will discuss these requirements and the rationale for them, and address the issue of their testability in Section 4.

3.1. Surface Intuitions and Robust Intuitions

There are really two steps in the inquiry into folk concepts. First, if we are asking non-specialists, we want to find out what their individual representations of the concept (or whatever constitutes their grasp of it) are—what Larry's or Anne's or Lily's concept of knowledge is, for example. And we are interested in this because, second, we ultimately want to know what the folk's *shared* concept of knowledge is (or whether there is one in the first place). This latter step does not require that the linguistic behaviour of the folk is completely uniform, but only that they aim to conform their thought and speech to the same constraints as others.[11] We talk about *the* concept of knowledge or *the* concept of moral judgement, after all, and claims about conceptual truths are claims about how proper applications of such public concepts are related to each other.[12] What I will argue is that the sort of information that surveys yield does not warrant taking *either* step. A person's response does not reveal what the extension or intension of her concept is if it results from some other factor such as inattention or pragmatic considerations that surveys do not control for, and it does not, in addition, reveal what the public concept is if she has a poor grasp of it or if she simply makes a mistake in a certain (type of) case. This is why her 'intuitions' count only when the sort of conditions listed in (A) is met. One way to put this is to say that surveys can only inform us of *surface intuitions* that do not help us in the project of finding out the folk concepts. For that purpose, we need *robust intuitions* that are elicited only when conditions in (A) obtain—that is, when failures of competence, failures of performance, and influence of irrelevant factors are ruled out.

3.2. Competence and Normativity

It should be obvious that when philosophers appeal to 'us' in making their claims, the extension is limited to those who are competent with the concept in question. After all, what *incompetent* users of a concept say about a given case does not tell us anything about the concept we are interested in—someone who has no relevant pre-theoretical knowledge about the concept cannot manifest it. Nobody would test a Gettier analysis by asking a small child whether the person in the case described knows or not, or count the child's response as a counterexample. And children are only the most obvious example. On many theories of concept possession, competence with a concept is a matter of degree and context.[13] This is to deny that there is, strictly speaking, such a thing as a 'competent speaker of English', for example.[14] To be sure, normal speakers are able to latch on to patterns of proper use and extrapolate correctly to new cases, as long as the similarities and differences between the cases are salient enough. For many practical purposes such ability suffices for competence. But some will be less and some more successful at grasping the rationale guiding application to new cases and thus discriminating between scenarios. Some concepts will be harder to grasp than others—perhaps most people with normal physiological capacities will be able to tell, when presented with a visual scenario, whether an object is white or not, but it is not as easy to tell whether an argument is compelling or whether a person in a counterfactual scenario should be described as morally responsible or not, if one is to accord with the correct pattern of applications of the concept.

Importantly, as my talk of 'patterns of proper use' and 'correct extrapolation' already suggests, talk of competence brings in *normative* questions.[15] To say that someone is a competent user is to say that she is able to apply the concept correctly to a sufficient number of cases (where what counts as 'sufficient' will surely depend on context), and thus to take a stand on what counts as correct use. As discussions inspired by Wittgenstein's remarks on rule-following have shown, such normative claims about correct use (and thus competence) cannot be derived from facts about actual usage or (simple) dispositions to apply the concept. Meaning or conceptual content in effect lays down a rule dividing scenarios into those in which it is appropriate to apply the concept and those in which it isn't. In Kripke's example, to say that one means the addition function by '+' is to say that one *should* respond '125' when the task is to compute '57 + 68', not that one *will* or *would* so respond.[16] Without such normative constraints, the notion of content would vanish. If a person who applied *red* to pure fallen snow or a cucumber, for example, would not be making a *mistake*, her concept would not have the same content as ours, or perhaps no content at all—anything would equally fall in the extension of the speaker's concept *red*, provided that she was somehow led to apply it to an object.[17] For talk of mistakes to make sense, the concept must set some normative constraints for its use—there must be a distinction between what seems right and what is right.

It follows from the normativity of content that we cannot simply look at what situations someone applies a concept to and infer what the criteria or rules guiding her use are, since that would amount to excluding the possibility of making mistakes. What, then, determines which applications count as correct according to a speaker's grasp of a concept? A tempting response is to say that correct applications are those that one is *disposed* to give under suitable conditions. This allows for the possibility of mistakes, since it can be true that I am disposed to do something I do not actually do. It is, however, clear that at least simple forms of dispositionalism do not solve the problem, since, as Kripke points out, we can also be disposed to make mistakes. To take his example of following the rule for addition, he points out that there are some people who are disposed to forget to 'carry' when adding large numbers, so that their answers do not accord with the addition function. The simple dispositionalist will have to say that what these people mean by '+' is some other, more complex function (Kripke calls it 'skaddition'), with regard to which they make no computational mistakes. But this is most implausible. The correct description of the case is, as Kripke puts it, that 'for them as for us, "+" means addition, but for certain numbers they are not disposed to give the answer they *should* give, if they are to accord with the table of the function they actually *meant*' (Kripke 1982, 29). The question about what, if anything, makes it the case that the skadders actually meant to add thus remains open after we have considered their dispositions. Sceptics about meaning, like Kripke himself, say that there is, in the end, no fact of the matter; instead, when we say that someone means *addition* by '+' in spite of making occasional mistakes, we express acceptance into the community as an adder, as someone whose responses can be expected to 'agree with those of the community in enough cases, especially the simple ones' (Kripke 1982, 92).[18] Non-sceptics try to provide for a 'straight solution' that would show that there is, after all, some fact about a speaker or her community that makes it the case that she should give a particular answer, even if she does not actually do so.[19]

This is a live controversy, and I do not want to enter it here. What is important for my purposes is that the same points apply on the communal level, as many have pointed out. Communities can make mistakes by their own lights, and even be disposed to do so. Arguably, to make sense of the notion of normative constraint, we must allow for the possibility that the rules for our concept *red* determine whether or not it applies to a future case independently of what we will, then, judge—in other words, it may be that we should, by our rules, call something 'red' even if *everybody* in actual fact judges otherwise.[20] If this is the case, there is no way to derive the conceptual norms in force in a community, and thus standards of competence, from the responses or simple dispositions of a majority.

Let me recap the argument of this section. For the purpose of understanding a folk concept, only the responses of competent users count. Competent users are those whose application of the concept generally matches the conceptual norms prevailing in the linguistic community. To sort out incompetent users, one must therefore identify at least the most important norms governing the concept. These norms cannot be derived from either actual use or simple dispositions, individual or collective, since the very notion of normative constraint opens a gap between what people are inclined to say about a particular case and what they should, by their own lights, say about it. It is important to bear in mind that the norms in question are not imported from the outside by the philosopher—rather, they are rules that concept-users at least implicitly are committed to, even if they follow them 'blindly'. If you point out to the person who is systematically forgetting to 'carry' that she is not following the addition rule she thought she was and explain why, it is most unlikely that the response will be along the lines, 'But I'm not trying to add; I'm just skadding'. Given the potential gap between actual response and correct response, it will not be a simple task to determine which speakers are competent users.

3.3. Ideal Conditions

I argued in the previous section that appeals to intuition are appeals to the judgement of competent users of concepts. But competence is no guarantee of getting it right. Even competent users can make mistakes, and mistakes do not serve as support or counterexamples to proposed analyses. The conditions in which judgements are made must be conducive to avoiding performance errors. For short, I will call such conditions *ideal*. They are conditions in which there are no perturbing, warping or distorting factors or limits of information, access or ability (Pettit 1999, 32). There is no single substantively specified set of ideal conditions for applying concepts, since such conditions may vary with the concept in question. Rather, as Philip Pettit notes, we find these conditions implicit in the practices of resolving discrepancies across time or subjects—as we notice differences in responses and look for an explanation for them, we come to discredit judgements made under certain conditions (Pettit, 1999, 29–33). For example, we do not treat judgements about colours made in certain kinds of lightning or certain judgements about responsibility made in an agitated state as authoritative— we understand that there are circumstances in which people are tempted to blame somebody even if in a cool hour they themselves would acknowledge that nobody is to blame.

There are, to be sure, some general things to say about conditions that are favourable for intuitive judgements. When a philosopher says that competent speakers would say certain things, she does not predict that they will respond in a certain way off the cuff. Nor would such response support a philosophical thesis. Appeals to intuition are not appeals to gut reactions, but simply to pre-theoretic judgements that may require careful consideration. It is not always obvious whether a concept applies to a case, nor are users always attentive to relevant details. Giving the answer that reflects one's concept is, naturally, the more difficult the more unusual the case. Being asked to apply a concept to a hypothetical situation that is a remote possibility by ordinary lights can call for advanced skills in counterfactual reasoning—for example, what indeed would we say about responsibility if someone committed the same crime over and over again were the universe re-created over and over again with the same initial conditions and laws of nature?[21] In other cases, there may be considerations weighing in different directions that need sorting out. Concepts form webs and clusters, and it will often be necessary to look at several cases to find patterns, connections, and contrasts. To get it right by one's own lights can take hard thinking and time, and the attempt could be thwarted by passions or loss of interest. There is a general requirement to think through the implications of individual judgements—a hasty judgement or simply a judgement that fails to fit with one's other uses of the concept will not count as one's robust intuition about the case.

3.4. Semantic Versus Pragmatic Considerations

Even if we limited ourselves to responses by competent speakers in ideal conditions, what they would say about particular cases would not necessarily reveal to us what we are interested in, namely the *semantic* contours of the concept at hand or the contribution it makes to the truth conditions of sentences in which it is used. The core mistake of early ordinary language philosophy was assuming such a direct link between proper use and meaning (see Soames

2003, especially chap. 9). This is because the appropriateness of what we say also depends on various pragmatic factors that are not part of the meaning or semantic content of the expression. For example, some things are too obvious to say, others would give a wrong impression in the context. To take a classic example, Ryle claimed in *The Concept of Mind* that 'voluntary' and 'involuntary' are used only for actions which ought not to be done: 'We discuss whether someone's action was voluntary or not only when the action seems to have been his fault' (Ryle 1949, 69). Even supposing that this observation on ordinary use is correct—and there is certainly no reason to doubt Ryle's competence and attention!—the conclusion does not follow. For it is a solid Gricean pragmatic principle that cooperative speakers try to give just the right amount of information given the purposes of the conversation, no more and no less.[22] In most contexts it would be *unnecessary* to say, for example, that I voluntarily had lunch yesterday, unless there was something exceptional to it—as a result, it would typically conversationally implicate that I usually have lunch only involuntarily, or indeed that I accept whatever blame there may be forthcoming for having had lunch yesterday. Consequently, talk of voluntariness would be *misleading* in ordinary contexts, in which the implicatures do not hold, and therefore pragmatically inappropriate, something we would not ordinarily say. But that does not mean it would be *untrue* that I had lunch voluntarily; it would still be semantically appropriate to say so. In general, it is not easy to separate the contribution of semantic and pragmatic considerations to what people say (and what it is *proper* to say)—excellent, trained philosophers have made major blunders—and in surveys of amateurs it is practically impossible.

4. THE FAILURE OF THE POSITIVE THESIS OF EXPERIMENTALISM

In the previous section, I have argued that the correct explication of (I) is (A) rather than (E). As long as the requirements (1)–(3) above are not tested for, testing for (E) amounts, in effect, to testing for (E*):

> (E*) 'In S, we would say that X is C' is a prediction that (most) non-specialists who (1′) *appear to understand the question* will say that X is C if the case S is presented to them (2′) *however they consider it in whatever conditions they find themselves in* and (3′) *whatever kind of considerations influence* their response.

The truth or falsity of (E*) is surely quite irrelevant to whether our shared concept C properly applies to X, the question that the philosopher is asking. There is no support to be had from responses of those non-philosophers who only appear to understand the question, who may have an imperfect grasp of the concept in question, who may or may not think hard about the application of the concept in circumstances that may or may not be conducive to avoiding conceptual mistakes, who may or may not rush in their judgements, and who may or may not be influenced by various pragmatic factors. Nor do such surface intuitions provide data that is to be explained or explained away, since some of them may be mere noise that does not have to be accommodated in an account of the folk concept. Moreover, these responses are an unreliable guide not only to the public concept, but to the individual respondents' concepts as well, since they apply their own rules fallibly, and do not only respond to semantic factors. My first criticism of the positive thesis of experimentalism—that surveys are a reliable source of evidence for philosophically relevant claims about folk concepts—can then be formulated as follows: the *actual studies* conducted so far have failed to rule out competence failures, performance failures, and the potential influence of pragmatic factors, and as such do not yield the sort of results that could support or raise doubts about philosophical appeals to conceptual intuitions.[23]

The crucial question, however, does not concern the studies conducted so far. It is whether it would be, at least in principle, *possible* to test claims of type (A) empirically in the sense that experimentalists recognize, that is, in terms of non-participatory social scientific methods, and if so, how.[24] This is very doubtful. First, as I noted, the question about who is a competent user is a normative question, a question about who gets it right, and it is very hard to see how one could answer it from the detached stance of an observer. To begin with, it seems that experimentalists assume—and must assume—that meaning or conceptual content supervenes on actual use or simple response-dispositions of speakers. After all, that is what they are testing for. Taking polls is a more or less reliable way to discover facts about actual use, and thus, they implicitly assume, a more or less reliable way to discover facts about what people mean by their words or what their concepts are. But as I already noted, what counts as correct use for the folk cannot be derived from the folk's actual use of the concept in question, so that standards of competence cannot be established with reference to majority response. Further, though one may presume that respondents have general mastery of a language, that is not enough, given that there are local variations in competence. One may be a minimally competent user of a concept, having the sort of rough grasp that enables one to converse about central cases, but lack sufficient understanding to apply it to philosophically interesting cases. (Think about someone for whom subjective certainty is a central element in the concept of knowledge.) To be sure, it is possible to ask control questions to rule out, for example, the responses of people who identify knowledge with subjective certainty, as Weinberg, Nichols, and Stich (2001) did. But to make this commendable move is already to take a stance on what the folk concept of knowledge is—in this case, to distinguish between two different everyday senses of 'knowledge' and take one of them to be philosophically relevant. Control questions amount to presupposing that certain answers will not reflect the folk concept, and these presuppositions cannot, by definition, be justified by means of surveys. (I agree, of course, that they can often be otherwise justified, but that is to deny the negative thesis of experimentalism.) The burden is on the experimentalist to present a neutral test of who is a sufficiently competent user of the folk concept of knowledge or moral judgement, for example.

Second, testing for ideal conditions and careful consideration does not seem to be possible without engaging in dialogue with the test subjects, and that, again, violates the spirit and letter of experimentalist quasi-observation. What is needed is a way of checking whether the test subject is making a performance error by her own lights. We can imagine a researcher going through a test subject's answers together with her, asking for the reasons why she answered one way rather than another, making sure she really did correctly understand the counterfactual scenario involved and did not read more or less into it than described in the test, pointing out similarities and disanalogies with other cases of, say, knowledge or moral judgement, and trying to get her to reflect on whether her response is really what she wants to say in the case in point—whether she is really following her own rules. But this is no longer merely 'probing' the test subjects. It is not doing experimental philosophy in the new and distinct sense, but rather a return to the good old Socratic method (see below). Again, the burden is on the experimentalist to show how we could ascertain that ideal conditions obtain for each of the test subjects without leaving detachment behind. Otherwise, we might as well skip the superfluous and unreliable survey and go straight into dialogue.

Finally, testing for the influence of pragmatic considerations is no simple matter either, though here the problems seem to be practical rather than principled. The distinction between semantics and pragmatics is a matter of much contention in contemporary philosophy of language,[25] but one could perhaps roughly say that the semantic content of a sentence is determined by the standing meaning of the lexical items, syntactic rules for their combination, and those elements of the non-linguistic context that are needed to resolve the reference of lexical items in accordance with their standing meaning.[26] (The last clause allows indexicals, for example, to contribute to the semantic content of a sentence.) In short, semantic content comprises what is required for a sentence to express a truth-evaluable proposition in context. Depending on the context of utterance, a speech act may express a number of other propositions over and above its semantic content. Gricean conversational and conventional implicatures are at least a central class of these non-semantic—that is, pragmatic—contents. Now, while Grice provides criteria for what counts as an implicature and some tests for differentiating between what is said and what is meant, it is not at all clear how to apply them to a survey situation. For example, Fred Adams and Annie Steadman (2004) have suggested that in the Knobe study people say that the CEO brings about the side-effect intentionally in the harm condition because they want to blame the CEO and think that blaming and intentionality go together. In other words, saying that the CEO did *not* bring about the side-effect intentionally would implicate that he is not to blame for it. Adams and Steadman claim that this and the converse implicatures in the help condition show that pragmatic considerations explain the asymmetry in Knobe's results.[27] The question is how to test for this. On Grice's view, conversational implicatures are essentially such that they can be worked out, given the assumption of conversational cooperation and facts about the context, including mutual beliefs (Grice 1989, 31). But when a person responds to a yes/no survey question (or rates assent on a Likert scale), just what is the conversational context? Who is he or she conversing with, and how do we work out what he or she assumes about the hearer's beliefs? Frankly, this is a baffling task.[28] Once again, an actual dialogue would help, but it would mean leaving behind the Survey Model and its pretension to scientific objectivity.

4.1. The Argument from Disagreement

At this point the experimentalist may well say: 'But surely there is *something* about the test subjects' psychology that explains why most of them say psychopaths make moral judgements or why the moral status of side-effects makes such a dramatic difference to attributions of intentionality!' This is, of course, true as far as it goes. The question, however, is whether these results tell us something relevant about folk *concepts,* as experimentalists claim. So far, I have argued that for that to be the case, certain conditions would have to be fulfilled, and that experimentalist methods cannot test for them. But there is also a different reason to be suspicious about the inference from poll results to the contours of the folk concept. I will call it the Argument from Disagreement. Its starting point is that agreement and disagreement about a subject matter presuppose that both parties are talking about the same thing, and this in turn presupposes that they share the same concept. For the purposes of this argument, it does not matter what counts as sharing a concept, but for simplicity, I will say that the concepts of two people are identical if they make the same contribution to the truth conditions of claims involving that concept in all possible worlds.[29] Thus, if my concept of redness is the concept of a surface reflectance property R1 and your concept of redness is the concept of surface reflectance property R2, when I say that something is red and you say that it is not red, there is no disagreement between us; by calling the object 'red' I have attributed one property it and you another. We are merely talking past each other, and both our claims may be true at the same time. Agreement and disagreement thus both presuppose that our talk expresses a shared concept.

Now, let us consider the results of the surveys I mentioned. They are without exception *mixed*: a certain percentage of people are ready to apply the concept in question, while others will refrain. What can we say in such a situation? In the Nichols survey on moral internalism, 85 per cent of those surveyed answered that a psychopath with no moral motivation can still understand that hurting others is wrong, while 15 per cent disagreed. Nichols took this lopsided result to show that the internalist account of the folk concept of moral judgement is mistaken. But the argument from disagreement shows that this inference is illegitimate. It can be formulated as a dilemma. Either a test subject's response to a survey question reveals whether the case falls under her concept, or it doesn't. If it doesn't, the response is obviously uninformative and running the survey for this purpose is pointless. But what if it does? Then those who answer in the negative will not and cannot *disagree* with those who answer in the affirmative. Were this the case in the moral internalism survey, the minority's concept would incorporate the internalist motivation condition, so that attributions of moral judgement to people who are not appropriately motivated would be false, while the majority's concept would lack this condition and thus contribute differently to truth conditions of claims about moral judgement. In other words, there would be two distinct concepts at play, moral judgement-EXT and moral judgement-INT, the first employed by the majority and the second by the minority, and consequently no disagreement between the two groups—they would just talk past each other when using the phrase 'moral judgement'. But this is absurd. We know that in most such cases the people in fact disagree and consequently that they share a single concept, regardless of how they respond to the survey question. What, then, could we learn about the concept from asking the question? This is the argument from disagreement.

The obvious fallback position for the experimentalist is that the majority response reveals the correct application of the shared concept, and those in the minority are simply wrong in their application of the shared concept (that is, either lacking in competence or making a performance error). This is a step in the right direction to the extent that it acknowledges a gap between one's dispositions to apply a concept and the proper application of one's concept. But as we already saw, correctness is not a matter of going with the crowd—it is certainly possible that a majority is mistaken in the application of the shared concept. It is not *a priori* true that minorities cannot be more competent, more careful, or more aware of pragmatic influences in concept application than majorities. And why would the responses of those who happen to be in the majority not only reveal their concept but also that of those in the minority, while the responses of those in the minority would reveal nothing about anybody's concept? Whence the asymmetry? What entitles us to throw out the responses of the minority when we are trying to get at a concept shared by those in the majority and those in the minority? We need an explanation of why we should prioritize the majority's responses, and the mere fact that they are a majority is no such thing. Thus, we have another reason to believe that the experimentalist approach leads to a dead end. It cannot tell us what the folk's shared concepts are, because it cannot tell us which responses count as revealing them and which do not.

It may be worth pointing out that neither the argument from disagreement nor the conditions on robust intuitions show, or try to show, that the results obtained by experimentalists do not call for an explanation of *some* sort. There must indeed be a reason why people have the surface intuitions they do. That reason will no doubt be different in different cases. Some responses will indeed result from correct application of a shared concept. Others may be driven by a desire to blame, for example, and yet others by charity that leads test subjects to read more into vignettes than they explicitly state.[30] In some cases, the explanation may be philosophically interesting, even if not for the purposes of conceptual analysis. Mostly, however, the explanation will be psychological, and nothing I have said bears on the possibility of experimental *psychology*.

5. FROM SURVEYS TO DIALOGUE AND REFLECTION

In the previous sections I have argued that the Survey Model of the epistemology of folk concepts and with it the positive thesis of experimentalism fails, in spite of its initial promise and plausibility. This leaves the negative, sceptical thesis. How can we confirm or disconfirm appeals of the form (I), if not by running polls? How do we gain traction with the concepts of ordinary folk? How do we elicit robust intuitions instead of surface intuitions? I have argued that this is a question about assessing counterfactuals of type (A) about what competent, careful speakers would say in favourable conditions if they abstracted away from pragmatic considerations—in other words, what the semantic rules of our language say about the application of the concept in question. For example, when we ask whether genuine moral judgements conceptually involve corresponding motivation according to ordinary folk, we are in effect asking whether competent, careful speakers guided only by semantic considerations would describe someone who says he thinks something is wrong but is not disposed to refrain from doing it as having made a sincere moral judgement. This is why the fact, if it is such, that 85 per cent of those queried in a college classroom or a Manhattan park say a psychopath can make a moral judgement while being entirely unmoved does not contradict the strong internalists' claim about what non-specialists *would* say, since that claim is only about the folk's responses in the kind of conditions that I have outlined—about robust rather than surface intuitions, in the terminology introduced above. And there is no way for a philosopher to ascertain how people would respond in such a situation without breaking the fourth wall to create the relevant conditions—that is, without entering into dialogue with them, varying examples, teasing out implications, presenting alternative interpretations to choose from to separate the semantic and the pragmatic, and so on. I will call this approach the Dialogue Model of the epistemology of folk concepts.

5.1. The Dialogue Model

How and why does philosophical dialogue work? I will take a concrete example. In the moral internalism case, one might present non-specialists with the sort of scenario in which someone is trying to convince a friend to adopt a moral stance, say become a vegetarian, and ask if the friend has really become convinced of the wrongness of eating meat as long as he has no inclination of refraining from doing it. If they answer negatively, the philosopher could point out that this seems inconsistent with attributing genuine moral convictions to the psychopath, perhaps try to disambiguate in which sense one might be inclined to say the psychopath 'understands' something is wrong, and so on. If we want to get people to respond in ways that represent the rules they actually are committed to, we cannot pretend to be ignorant of common distorting factors—to use the Kripkean example, if we want to find out whether someone's concept of addition is the same as ours, we are surely entitled to point out an obvious failure to carry in a particular case and so perhaps get her to see the application as a mistake by her own lights. This process of making sure that a particular response genuinely reflects the respondent's concept is hard work, and never free of the danger of leading the witness in the direction favoured by the questioner. To engage in it is to give up the detached stance of the experimentalist observer and involve the folk in the fray of philosophical debate instead of reaching for a magic foothold outside of it. It is to do philosophy pretty much as it has always been done.

Suppose that through dialogue or otherwise one manages to create circumstances in which one can be reasonably confident that the conditions listed in (A) are fulfilled and the responses of competent non-specialists do in fact reveal their concepts. Perhaps the majority still responds to the original case in the same way. We could then say that the survey results have turned out to be robust, since they remain unchanged after potentially distorting factors have been pruned off. Robust intuitions, we might say, are represented by those responses of non-specialists that are *stable* under arbitrary increases in consideration of relevantly similar situations, ideality of circumstances, and understanding of the workings of language (centrally, the semantics/pragmatics distinction). In idealized terms, these responses are those that infinitely patient and focused respondents would give at the end of a dialogue with a Super-Socrates, who never misleads but engages in maximally skilful midwifery that consists in bringing about conditions (A). In practice, responses are more or less robust, depending on how closely the ideal dialogical situation is approximated. Since we use language to communicate with each other and sharing concepts is necessary for agreement and disagreement, there is strong *a priori* reason to believe that people's robust intuitions will line up with each other, at least in central cases.

Now, it is clear that as long as we are talking about the folk's own concepts, robust intuitions of competence speakers must count. This really is data that must be explained or explained away, but it is not obtained by surveys, at least not surveys alone, since they cannot discriminate between responses that are robust and responses that are not. Yet it is the only kind of data worth having. For example, if there are robustly varying patterns of response to a number of cases between, say, Americans and Southeast Asians, we can legitimately infer that there are two or more concepts at play and thus no straightforward agreement or disagreement between the groups.[31] And if a clear majority of robust intuitions support counterexamples to internalism, the internalist must withdraw his claim of having intuitive support and capturing the folk concept of moral judgement.[32]

5.2. The Authority of Reflection

Although I have defended dialogue as a privileged means of access to folk concepts, I do not think that it is strictly speaking necessary for philosophers to go around bothering their friends and acquaintances. In practice, assessing the truth of intuition claims can remain a relatively armchair business that begins with our own considered reactions to the case at hand. We are entitled to have confidence in such reflection, since we take a lot of real-life experience of using concepts to the armchair with us. Having participated in the relevant language games and having been corrected and sanctioned while we were learning the concepts under analysis, we have gained normative knowledge about criteria for their proper application to particular cases as well as about inferential relations among them. We know which moves are acceptable in our linguistic community (that is, acceptable by those who share our concepts), since we have received and given feedback to and from others. By the time we begin to do philosophy, we have accumulated years and years' worth of experience about what counts as proper application of concepts to different cases—we have, as it were, already done the sort of research I sketched above in connection with the Dialogue Model. This experience is what grounds the epistemic authority of the Reflection Model. Since dialogue and reflection do yield philosophically relevant evidence about folk concepts, the negative thesis of experimentalism fails as well. Pessimism about dialogue and reflection is no more warranted than optimism about surveys.

At this point, the experimentalist may reach for her last card: is not the long history of contentious appeals to conceptual intuitions by itself sufficient to show that armchair reflection leads nowhere? To see why this is not the case, we have to look at the practice of philosophical reflection on concepts more closely. To begin with, the normative knowledge that this reflection draws on, like similar knowledge of the rules of etiquette, for example, is implicit, and it is rarely easy to articulate and summarize it in an analysis. Some are better at making it explicit, some worse. There are connections between concepts to be missed and cases that are hard to fit in a pattern. There may be an unexpected but plausible pragmatic explanation for why something is inappropriate. Unbiased reflection is not easy, and the activity of reflecting itself may even destroy pre-reflective knowledge—many philosophers know how it feels to lack confidence in one's own reactions to particular cases. No wonder, therefore, that philosophers disagree among themselves both about appeals to intuition in particular cases and about the implications of particular cases for understanding concepts. But that is neither the end of the story nor a cause for desperation, for it is through mutual correction over time that explications of rules edge closer to the actual norms implicit in how we use terms. As examples and counterexamples mount, some intuitive judgements may well come to be widely accepted as data points that have to be accounted for, and may lead to theoretical convergence as well.

The moral internalism debate may serve as a case study of gradual convergence of intuitions through (philosophical) dialogue and reflection. In a classic article from 1937, Charles Stevenson presented a typical case of moral persuasion:

> When you tell a man that he oughtn't to steal, your object isn't merely to let him know that people disapprove of stealing...If in the end you do not succeed in getting *him* to disapprove of stealing, you will feel that you've failed to convince him that stealing is wrong. (Stevenson 1937, 19)

Here Stevenson appeals to his readers' intuitions to support his internalist contention that '[a] person who recognizes X to be "good" must *ipso facto* acquire a stronger tendency to act in its favour then [*sic*] he otherwise would have had' (Stevenson 1937, 16).[33] This 'magnetism' of moral judgement is a central plank of his argument for emotivism. Unsurprisingly, externalist critics challenged his contention. Here is Henry David Aiken:

> I may recognize, for instance, that the music of Tschaikowski is 'good,' since many honest and discriminating people have affirmed its power to move and to please, and yet not in the least be impelled to listen to it... Moreover, during periods of weariness or satiety, especially, 'goods' which we believe and gladly acknowledge to have the profoundest import to ourselves often leave us quite cold, and our judgment that they are 'good' has no magnetism or persuasive power whatever. (Aiken 1944, 461)

From such cases, call them *conventional* and *akratic* uses of 'good', respectively, Aiken drew the externalist conclusion that 'there is such a thing as the acknowledgement of truth or falsity of an ethical judgment when no "magnetism" is involved' (Aiken 1944, 461). Of course, internalists did not give up. But, importantly, their defence did not involve headbutting intuition against intuition or even outright rejection of the intuitive status of externalist claims like those of Aiken. R. M. Hare's *The Language of Morals* (1952) gave influential responses to both of the two intuitive challenges I have picked out. First, Hare argued that we sometimes, consciously or unconsciously, use 'good' and 'ought' in an inverted commas sense to indicate, for example, that something is considered to be good by most people or experts, without endorsing the evaluation ourselves (e.g. Hare 1952, 167). In other words, though Aiken and other externalists are right about what we would say in cases of conventional usage, these cases are not relevant to understanding moral judgement. Hare *accepts* the conceptual intuitions, but provides a different *theoretical* account of their status, appealing to a kind of pragmatic explanation.

In the case of akratic uses, Hare adopts a different strategy that amounts to solving the problem by a more complete description of the case. Here is what he says:

> If a person does not do something, but the omission is accompanied by feelings of guilt etc., we normally say that he has not done what he thinks he ought. (Hare 1952, 169)

The point that Hare is making is that, as the externalist points out, we do grant that someone may in some cases lack sufficient motivation to act as she thinks she ought, but, what the externalist fails to notice, we do so *only if* that person experiences guilt or some other residual feelings for failing to follow through on her judgement. We could say that Hare *refines* the case to draw out more clearly what is actually driving the intuitive judgement.

I lack the space to follow this dialectic all the way through to today, but I want to point out some important features of it. First of all, a number of judgements about particular cases have become broadly accepted data points that theories of moral motivation must accommodate. Externalists by and large accept that people are usually motivated by their judgements. As Russ Shafer-Landau, a prominent externalist, coolly puts it:

> There are two especially relevant items to be entered into evidence. Fact: everyone we know is motivated to some extent to comply with his or her moral judgements. Fact: we suspect the sincerity of someone who proclaims fidelity to a moral code, all the while showing no inclination to abide by it. (Shafer-Landau 2003, 156)

At the same time, internalists by and large accept that akratics, depressives, and certain kinds of amoralists may nonetheless make genuine moral judgements without being motivated by them (see e.g. Smith 1994, 133–36). So, there is a *convergence of intuitions*—not a perfect one, to be sure, but clearly noticeable. Second, disagreement in theoretical accounts still persists, suggesting that it is best explained by difference in auxiliary commitments in philosophy of language, philosophy of mind, or metaphilosophy. Externalists think they can explain away the internalist intuitions, or at least show that they are not robust, and vice versa. Correspondingly, there is no reason to think that experimental data, even if accepted on all sides, would take the debate forward any better than the data provided by dialogue and reflection. And finally, though disagreement in philosophical explanations indeed persists, there has been a significant degree of convergence on that front as well. Consider the position of Michael Smith, a leading contemporary internalist:

> [A]gents who judge it right to act in various ways are so motivated, and necessarily so, absent the distorting influences of weakness of the will and other similar forms of practical unreason on their motivations. (Smith 1994, 61)

Smith thinks that it is a conceptual truth that moral beliefs motivate agents insofar as they are rational, because, on his view, moral beliefs are beliefs about reasons and beliefs about reasons motivate rational agents (Smith 1997). Given that he postulates a non-contingent connection between judgement and motivation, his view is in one obvious sense an internalist one. Yet it allows for akratics, depressives, and even certain kinds of amoralists to make genuine moral judgements without motivation, if only at the price of irrationality.[34] For this reason, R. Jay Wallace in a recent article describes Smith as someone who *rejects* moral judgement internalism (Wallace 2006, 185).[35] Mutually accepted intuitions and counterexamples have here led to a situation in which insofar as the classification of a view is not a merely verbal matter, it hangs on theoretical considerations rather than on capturing cases. Philosophical progress has been made.

There is no reason to think that the debate about moral judgement is an exception. Of course, it does not show that reflection and dialogue will *always* lead to a convergence. But in many cases such failures will be explicable in terms of the nature of the concept in question. Perhaps the ordinary concept is simply too vague for philosophical purposes, so that there is no fact of the matter which of the competing appeals to what we would say better conforms to the rule implicit in everyday use. Or perhaps the use of the concept in question is subtly context-dependent, so that the intuitions that one side draws on are robust in one context and the intuitions of the other side in another, and the appearance of conflict is illusory.[36] Neither sort of case threatens the authority of reflection or the fruitfulness of dialogue.

In this final section, I have defended the epistemological authority of dialogue and reflection with respect to the content of folk concepts against the negative thesis of experimentalism, and provided a case study to undermine pessimism grounded in presumed lack of progress in debates about folk intuitions. I have charted the rise and fall of experimental philosophy to vindicate the self-confidence of traditional philosophers. In short, as philosophers, we continue to participate in ordinary linguistic practices, but do so reflectively, paying careful attention to what is appropriate and why and drawing on the insights of those who have explored the same paths before. Running a poll provides no shortcut in this business of reaching a better conceptual self-understanding. At best, survey results provide food for thought—but we are better nourished if instead of designing artificial setups we pay close attention to what is said in real-life situations of language use, as conscientious philosophers have done at least since Socrates.

ACKNOWLEDGEMENTS

In preparing this paper, I have benefited enormously from fair and generous feedback by philosophers who are sympathetic to or committed to the experimentalist approach, including Joshua Knobe, Thomas Nadelhoffer, Eddy Nahmias, Alfred Mele, and Jonathan Weinberg. In the same group belong, I suspect, the two anonymous referees for *Philosophical Explorations*. In addition, I want to thank for valuable comments Joel Anderson, Pekka Mäkelä, Alyssa Ney, Lilian O'Brien, Jussi Suikkanen, and the audience at the 2004 Brown Graduate Conference, where an earlier version of this paper was presented.

NOTES

1. There are, of course, some philosophers, like Jerry Fodor (1998), who believe that most or all of our (lexical) concepts are atomic and nothing like analysis is possible or necessary. These philosophers provide deflationary accounts of seemingly conceptual truths to explain these appearances away (see Margolis and Laurence 2003). I will simply ignore these views in the following, since the existence of conceptual truths is accepted on both sides of the debate I am addressing. I am afraid those who deny their existence will find little of interest here.

2. A related formulation is that the favoured account explains the *platitudes* involving the concept, the platitudes being those statements whose acceptance is necessary for competence with the concept. This is the 'Canberra' version of conceptual analysis (see

Jackson, Pettit, and Smith 2004). I will focus here on the intuition talk, though I believe most of what I will say could be formulated in the language of platitudes as well.

3. For a defence of the view that modal intuitions are cases of linguistically unmediated knowledge of metaphysical necessity and possibility, see Williamson (2005). For a view that links metaphysical possibility to conceivability in terms of two-dimensional intensions, see Chalmers (2002). My sympathies lie with linguistic approaches to metaphysical possibility (and I think Kripke and Putnam are ultimately in this camp as well), but for the purposes of this paper, it does not matter which meta-metaphysical view one adopts, as long as it is acknowledged that *some* questions about conceptual possibility are legitimate philosophical questions.

4. See e.g. the eponymous introductory article by Joshua Knobe (2011). 'Experimental Philosophy' is also the name of the blog devoted to these and related issues (http://experimentalphilosophy.typepad.com/, coordinated by Thomas Nadelhoffer).

5. Jackson talks about his readiness to take polls if needed, though he considers his own judgements as in fact representative (Jackson 1998, 31). Harman says that we make 'inductive and fallible' inferences from data of the form 'people P have actually made judgements J about cases C as described by D' and suggests that analyses are 'defended in the way one defends any inductive hypothesis' (Harman 1994, 44). Leiter calls experimental philosophy 'the most important recent development in philosophy' in his widely read blog (http://leiterreports.typepad.com/blog/2004/06/new_experimenta.html).

6. In practice, what is called experimental philosophy has been limited to the kind of surveys I discuss in this paper. Insofar as there could be other sorts of experiments yielding philosophically relevant data, my title is somewhat misleading. In the absence of a stable nomenclature, drawing a line between experimental philosophy and other forms of naturalistic, scientifically informed philosophy is somewhat arbitrary.

7. For varieties of internalist theories, see e.g. Hare (1952) and Smith (1994). Internalists go on to explain *why* our concept of moral judgement includes a motivational component. In short, the reason they offer is that the point of making moral judgements is making a difference to how we act.

8. The moral internalist thesis is not always clearly formulated in the literature, and the formulation of Nichols's question reflects this ambiguity. Properly understood, the thesis has two parts: a person who *understands* what it is to make a moral commitment *and undertakes* such a commitment will have some motivation to act accordingly.

9. At least, it is Knobe's goal to present a case that differs only in one respect. Finding a precise counterpart case is far from trivial, but I am going to grant here that it is possible.

10. For example, Swain, Alexander, and Weinberg (2008) present data that shows that people's responses to a putative reliabilist case of knowledge vary depending on what sort of cases they've been presented with before asking the question; Weinberg, Nichols, and Stich (2001) discuss various survey results showing a systematic divergence between responses of American and Southeast Asian as well as high and low socioeconomic status subjects to Gettier and other cases.

11. For an account of the sort of shared rule-following that makes 'commonable thought' possible, see Pettit (1996, 180–90).

12. In Frank Jackson's terms, this amounts to asking whether claims made in one vocabulary (such as that of justified true belief) are made true by the same facts as claims made in another vocabulary (such as that of knowledge) (Jackson 1998).

13. See, for example, Brandom (1994).

14. Here I disagree with Williamson (2005).

15. For this connection, see Kripke (1982, esp. 31 n22).

16. See Kripke (1982, 37) and *passim*. Kripke is, of course, developing a line of argument in Wittgenstein (1953). The distinction between linguistic content and mental content is not relevant to the issue of normativity, as Paul Boghossian (1989, 510) notes. I will use both kinds of examples for simplicity of exposition.

17. Better yet: *nothing* would fall into a concept's extension, if there were no normative constraints for its application.

18. This is Kripke's 'sceptical solution'; obviously, there could be sceptics who rejected that as well.

19. For important papers on the topic, see Miller and Wright (2002).

20. This is emphasized by McDowell, who argues that communitarians about rule-following cannot account for the crucial distinction between being out of step with the judgements of one's peers and failing to conform to the normative constraints set by the concept. This amounts to losing sight of the commonsense notion of objectivity, which requires that 'the patterns to which our concepts oblige us are ratification-independent' (McDowell 1984, 232). McDowell's dense paper aims to show that Wittgenstein provides a nonplatonistic vision of how we can grasp a pattern of application extending to future cases independently of the actual outcome of any future investigation.

21. This is the sort of case that Nahmias et al. (2006) ask people to consider in order to find out whether people find the compatibility of free will and determinism intuitive.

22. For example, Grice (1989, 26–27). Compare Mates (1971, 129).

23. It would not be fair to say that experimentalists are not at all sensitive to these issues, and some have tried to ensure that responses go beyond what I am calling surface intuitions. I will discuss some of these attempts shortly.

24. This question was pressed by anonymous referees for *Philosophical Explorations*.

25. See, for example, the papers in Szabo (2005) and Cappelen and Lepore (2005).

26. For an extended discussion on alternative ways of making the distinction, see King and Stanley (2005).

27. Knobe (2004) is an ingenious attempt to circumvent the problem by substituting an armchair-equivalent (!) phrase, 'in order to', that allegedly lacks the pragmatic implicatures of 'intentionally'; the obvious response is that if the phrase really has the same content as the original term, it is no surprise if it has similar implicatures. This is something to be settled case by case. Indeed, sharing implicatures is plausible in the case in question, since if there is a conversational implicature at play, it is a generalized rather than a particularized one—that is, if saying that A did not do something intentionally implicates that A is not to blame, it does so normally or in most contexts—and as Grice argues, generalized conversational implicatures have a high degree of non-detachability: 'Insofar as the calculation that a particular conversational implicature is present requires, besides contextual and background information, only a knowledge of what has been said (or of the conventional commitment of the utterance), and insofar as the manner of expression plays no role in the calculation, *it will not be possible to find another way of saying the same thing, which simply lacks the implicature in question*' (Grice 1989, 39, my emphasis).

28. In the case of conversational implicatures, one might be able to test for cancellability—that is, whether people regard it possible to say without contradiction that, for example, the CEO did not intentionally harm the environment, but he is still to blame for it, since he knew it was going to happen. If they agreed to this, and still went on to

say the CEO did what he did intentionally in the harm condition, this would support Knobe's case.

29. This is an extensional criterion, and in need of amendment to deal with necessarily coextensional but distinct concepts, if such exist.

30. I argue for a charity-based explanation of the results in Knobe and Roedder (n.d.) in my contribution to the first Online Philosophy Conference, 'Lovers of the Good: Comments on Knobe and Roedder' (http://garnet.acns.fsu.edu/~tan02/OPC%20Week%20Three/Commentary%20on%20Knobe.pdf).

31. This would indeed be the case if the results cited in Nichols, Stich, and Weinberg (2003) were robust—which we do not learn from their surveys alone, as I have argued.

32. However, lack of intuitive support does not yet mean that the moral internalist, for example, has to give up on her view or even modify it to accommodate legitimate counterexamples. It simply means that if she holds on to it, she will be to some extent a *revisionist* about moral judgement. This is to incur a cost, but if other alternatives are even more costly—say, they make no evolutionary sense—it is a cost that may be worth paying.

33. To keep the discussion focused on methodological issues, I will here ignore the difference in the motivational relevance of moral value judgements and ought-judgements, though I believe it is very important for serious moral psychology. I am also granting Stevenson that disapproval implies motivation.

34. Externalists like David Brink claim that principled, rational amoralists are conceivable, and Smithian internalism thus fails (Brink 1997, 18–21). Here there is a genuine open dispute about a particular case, but as it hangs on technical terms (who counts as rational?) it is not a counterexample to convergence in ordinary language intuitions.

35. Certainly Smith—as well as Simon Blackburn (1998, 61) and other recent defenders of internalism—counts as an externalist by Shafer-Landau's criterion, according to which externalists are those who accept 'the conceptual possibility of an agent who on a single occasion fails to be motivated by a moral judgment that he endorses' (Shafer-Landau 2003, 145).

36. I argue that this is the case with respect to the concept of moral responsibility in my 'Talk About Responsibility' (in preparation).

REFERENCES

Adams, F., and A. Steadman. 2004. Intentional action in ordinary language: Core concept or pragmatic understanding? *Analysis 64* (2): 173–181.

Aiken, H. 1944. Emotive 'meanings' and ethical terms. *The Journal of Philosophy 41* (17): 456–470.

Blackburn, S. 1998. *Ruling passions. A theory of practical reasoning*. Oxford: Oxford University Press.

Boghossian, P. 1989. The rule-following considerations. *Mind 98*: 507–549.

Brandom, R. 1994. *Making it explicit*. Cambridge, Mass: Harvard University Press.

Brink, D. O. 1997. Moral motivation. *Ethics 108*: 4–32.

Cappelen, H., and E. Lepore. 2005. *Insensitive semantics. A defense of semantic minimalism*. Oxford: Blackwell.

Chalmers, D. 2002. Does conceivability entail possibility? In *Conceivability and possibility*, edited by T. Gendler and J. Hawthorne. Oxford: Oxford University Press, 247–272.

Derose, K. 2005. The ordinary language basis for contextualism and the new invariantism. *Philosophical Quarterly 55* (219): 172–198.

Fodor, J. 1998. *Concepts. Where cognitive science went wrong.* Oxford: Oxford University Press.
Grice, P. 1989. *Studies in the way of words.* Cambridge, Mass.: Harvard University Press.
Hare, R. M. 1952. *The language of morals.* Oxford: Clarendon Press.
Harman, G. 1994. Doubts about conceptual analysis. In *Philosophy in mind. The place of philosophy in the study of mind*, edited by M. Michael and J. O'Leary-Hawthorne. Dordrecht: Kluwer, 43-48.
Hawthorne, J. 2004. *Knowledge and lotteries.* Oxford: Oxford University Press.
Jackson, F. 1998. *From metaphysics to ethics. A defense of conceptual analysis.* Oxford: Oxford University Press.
Jackson, F., P. Pettit, and M. Smith. 2004. *Mind, morality, and explanation. Selected collaborations.* Oxford: Oxford University Press.
King, J. C., and J. Stanley. 2005. Semantics, pragmatics, and the role of semantic content. In *Semantics vs. pragmatics*, edited by Z. Szabo. Oxford: Oxford University Press, 111-164.
Knobe, J. 2003. Intentional action and side effects in ordinary language. *Analysis* 63: 190-193.
———. 2004. Intention, intentional action and moral considerations. *Analysis* 64: 81-187.
———. 2006. The concept of intentional action. A case study in the uses of folk psychology. *Philosophical Studies 130* (2): 203-231.
———. 2011. Experimental philosophy. *Philosophers' Magazine.* (50), 72-73.
Knobe, J., and E. Roedder. N.D. The concept of valuing: Experimental studies. http://garnet.acns.fsu.edu/~tan02/OPC%20Week%20Three/knobe.pdf (accessed 17 June 2006).
Kripke, S. 1982. *Wittgenstein on rules and private language.* Oxford: Basil Blackwell.
Machery, E., R. Mallon, S. Nichols, and S. Stich. 2004. Semantics, cross-cultural style. *Cognition 92:* B1-B12.
Margolis, E., and S. Lawrence. 2003. Should we trust our intuitions? *Proceedings of the Aristotelian Society 103:* 299-323.
Mates, B. 1971. On the verification of statements about ordinary language. In *Philosophy and linguistics*, edited by C. Lyas. London: Macmillan. First published in *Inquiry* 1 (1958), 121-130.
McDowell, J. 1984. Wittgenstein on following a rule. In *Mind, value, and reality.* Cambridge, Mass.: Harvard University Press. 325-363.
Miller, A., and C. Wright, eds. 2002. *Rule-following and meaning.* Chesham: Acumen.
Nadelhoffer, T. 2004. Praise, side effects, and intentional action. *The Journal of Theoretical and Philosophical Psychology 24:* 196-213.
Nahmias, E., S. Morris, T. Nadelhoffer, and J. Turner.(2006). Is incompatibilism intuitive? *Philosophy and Phenomenological Research, 73:* 28-53.
Nahmias, E., T. Nadelhoffer, S. Morris, and J. Turner. 2005. Surveying free will: Folk intuitions about free will and moral responsibility. *Philosophical Psychology 18* (5): 561-584.
Nichols, S. 2002. How psychopaths threaten moral rationalism: Is it irrational to be amoral? *The Monist 85:* 285-304.
———. 2004. The folk psychology of free will: Fits and starts. *Mind and Language* 19: 473-502.

Nichols, S., S. Stich, and J. Weinberg. 2003. Meta-skepticism: Meditations on ethno-epistemology. In *The skeptics*, edited by S. Luper. Burlington, VT: Ashgate Publishing. 227–247.

Pettit, P. 1996. *The common mind. An essay on psychology, society, and politics.* Oxford: Oxford University Press.

———. 1999. A theory of normal and ideal conditions. *Philosophical Studies 96*: 21–44.

Ryle, G. 1949. *The concept of mind*. London: Hutchinson's.

Shafer-Landau, R. 2003. *Moral realism: A defence*. Oxford: Oxford University Press.

Smith, M. 1994. *The moral problem*. Oxford: Blackwell.

Smith, M. 1997. In defense of 'The Moral Problem'. A reply to Brink, Copp, and Sayre-McCord. *Ethics 108*: 84–119.

Soames, S. 2003. *Philosophical analysis in the twentieth century. Vol. 2, The age of meaning*. Princeton, N.J.: Princeton University Press.

Stevenson, C. L. 1937. The emotive meaning of ethical terms. *Mind 46* (181): 14–31.

Swain, S., J. Alexander, and J. Weinberg. 2008. The instability of philosophical intuitions: Running hot and cold on truetemp. *Philosophy and Phenomenological Research, 76*(1), 138–155.

Szabo Z., ed. 2005. *Semantics vs. pragmatics*. Oxford: Oxford University Press.

Wallace, R.J. 2006. Moral motivation. In *Contemporary debates in moral theory*, edited by J. Dreier. Oxford: Blackwell, 182-207.

Weinberg, J., S. Nichols, and S. Stich. 2001. Normativity and epistemic intuitions. *Philosophical Topics 29*: 429–460.

Williamson, T. 2005. Armchair philosophy, metaphysical modality and counterfactual thinking. *Proceedings of the Aristotelian Society 105* (1): 1–23.

Wittgenstein, L. 1953. Philosophical investigations. G. E. M. Anscombe and R. Rhees (eds.), G. E. M. Anscombe (trans.). Oxford: Blackwell.

2

Accentuate the Negative

Joshua Alexander, Ronald Mallon, and Jonathan M. Weinberg

1. INTRODUCTION

There are a number of different programs that fall under the umbrella of "experimental philosophy", and our interest here is to drive a wedge of contention between two of them. These two programs concern traditional analytic philosophy's practice of appealing to philosophical intuitions either as evidence for (or against) philosophical claims, or as data both about the nature of our folk philosophical concepts and judgments and about the nature of the domains in which we make those judgments.[1] According to what is sometimes called experimental philosophy's "negative program", experimental philosophy challenges the usefulness of this practice in achieving justified beliefs.[2] According to experimental philosophy's "positive program", experimental philosophy is (at least an indispensable part of) the proper methodology for this practice.[3] In this paper, we contend that the practice of appealing to intuitions, even as modified by the positive program, still faces significant challenges from the results of the negative program.

We identify four different positive programs: direct extramentalism, semantic mentalism, conceptual mentalism, and mechanist mentalism. Each of these positive programs share at least two commitments: that intuitions are a trustworthy source of evidence or data; and that intuitions about a particular hypothetical case will, by and large, be stable and shared. However, recent empirical work conducted by philosophers and psychologists has revealed significant (and surprising) inter- and intra-personal intuitional instability. As such, positive programs face the challenge of accommodating the results of negative experimental philosophy. Some positive programs (namely, the various forms of mentalism) seem, at first glance, to be well suited to meet this challenge. But we argue that these forms have their own problems, and so conclude that positive experimental philosophy seems to be almost as challenged by the results of negative experimental philosophy as is more traditional armchair analytic philosophy.

2. THE POSITIVE PROGRAM

In order to canvass the problems for the positive program, we begin by recognizing that there are a variety of positive programs extant in this still-young literature. These programs share—both with one another and with more traditional analytic philosophical programs—the view that intuitions provide an important source of evidence and data for philosophy. What distinguishes the various positive programs from more traditional analytic philosophical programs is the way in which we are supposed to go about gathering this evidence or data. According to proponents of more traditional philosophical investigation, we can determine what intuitions are (or would be) generated in response to particular cases simply by determining what our own intuitions are about those cases (e.g., Jackson 1998). Assuming that our own intuitions are appropriately representative, we need nothing more than our own intuitions about particular cases in order to determine what intuitions people would (or should) have about those cases. Proponents of positive experimental philosophy think that we would do better to actually empirically ascertain—typically employing survey methods—what intuitions people have about those cases.

While the positive programs share common views about the nature of philosophical evidence and appropriate methods of evidence collection, they can be distinguished according to what they take the immediate philosophical payoff of experimental philosophy to be. The most fundamental question for any program of positive experimental philosophy is whether it aspires to knowledge of "in-the-head psychological entities" or "outside-the-head nonpsychological entities"—positions Alvin Goldman and Joel Pust have called mentalist and extramentalist (Goldman and Pust 1998, pp. 183–4). Goldman and Pust introduced the distinction in terms of possible rationales for armchair deployments of intuition, but it applies equally well here: if the experimental results of positive experimental philosophy are meant to tell us something of philosophical import, what type of thing is it supposed to be? The answer one gives to this question will determine the most basic theoretical burdens that it must shoulder. We will consider four possible answers to that question here, corresponding to four different philosophical projects. We do not claim that this list is necessarily exhaustive, though we do think it covers almost all extant forms of positive experimental philosophy.[4] The four projects are direct extramentalism; conceptual mentalism; semantic mentalism; and mechanist mentalism.[5]

Direct extramentalist projects are those that draw conclusions about nonmental entities from premises that include empirical claims about folk intuitions or judgments but do not include premises about human psychology arrived at by those empirical claims. Direct extramentalists take a proposition's status as intuitive to be direct evidence for the truth of that proposition, even if perhaps not conclusive evidence. For example, they might take it that philosophical positions that are intuitive to a large majority of ordinary people and that are not matters of technical expertise should be given a significant default positive epistemic status. So, if most folks are intuitive compatibilists, then that is evidence for compatabilism, and perhaps incompatibilists should have the burden of proof in debates over free will—and vice versa, mutatis mutandis. A practitioner of this version of direct extramentalist positive experimental philosophy might hope that experimental psychological methods could then uncover which of those views has that argumentative burden (Nahmias et al. 2005, 2006).

But one may be concerned (as Goldman and Pust are) that direct extramentalism allows too ambitious an evidential role for intuitions. At best, one might argue, intuitions reflect facts about our minds, and it is only in virtue of our philosophical interest in these mental facts that intuitions can play their methodological role. The current positive experimental philosophy literature reveals a number projects that fall under this "mentalist" rubric albeit in a range of different ways.

Conceptualist mentalist projects take an interest in what actual conceptual structure is instantiated in people's heads, for various concepts of philosophical interest, such as INTENTIONAL (Knobe 2003a, b) or INNATE (Machery et al. 2009). Semantic mentalist projects are concerned to identify the meanings of our terms or concepts. For example, following the program of philosophical analysis of folk concepts that runs through David Lewis (1970, 1972) and Frank Jackson (1998), some positive experimental philosophers have insisted that the claim that some proposition is a folk platitude be empirically supported—or at least empirically scrutinized (see, e.g., Glasgow 2008; Ulatowski 2008). Finally, mechanist mentalist projects aim to understand the psychological structures and processes involved in our making judgments in a domain of psychological interest. Can our folk psychology be understood in primarily prediction-and-explanation terms, or is it deeply entwined with our moral and evaluative cognition as well? (Knobe 2003a, b, 2007b) To what extent do affect and rules contribute to the difference between normative evaluations that are moral and those that are not? (Nichols and Mallon 2006; Mallon and Nichols 2010).

Mentalist projects take knowledge of the mental to be not just the immediate philosophical payoff of surveying the intuitions of various subjects; a further subdivision is possible, according to whether that knowledge of the mental is the main philosophical payoff of the project, or whether instead such claims serve primarily as intermediate steps in a further philosophical argument. Joshua Knobe (2007a), for example, has argued persuasively for the philosophical legitimacy of the former sort of project. But some positive experimental philosophy offers the promise of speaking to philosophical questions beyond the mind itself; for example, a theorist may look to take an area of philosophy in which we have had conflicting intuitions, and deploy a psychological theory of those intuitions' production in order to help referee which should be trusted, and which merely explained away (e.g., Greene 2003; Nichols 2006).

3. THE PITFALLS OF POSITIVE EXPERIMENTAL PHILOSOPHY

3.1. The Empirical Challenge from Negative Experimental Philosophy

As we noted earlier, positive experimental philosophy shares with traditional armchair philosophy the commitment that intuitions about X are a trustworthy source of evidence or data for philosophical theorizing about X (or at least about "X" or the concept of X); and that intuitions about a particular hypothetical case will, by and large, be shared, at least by "the folk". But some recent empirical work conducted by philosophers and psychologists gives us reason to worry that philosophical intuitions might be neither trustworthy nor shared. They suggest that some particularly prominent, and commonly appealed to, philosophical intuitions are sensitive to facts about who is considering the hypothetical case (Weinberg et al. 2001; Nichols et al. 2003; Machery et al. 2004), the presence or absence of certain kinds of content (e.g. abstract vs. concrete; affectively neutral vs. affectively engaging) (Nichols and Knobe 2007; Uhlmann et al. 2009) or the context in which the hypothetical case is being considered (Swain et al. 2008; Petrinovich and O'Neill 1996). This sensitivity is problematic because such facts have not traditionally been thought to be relevant to the truth or falsity of the claims for which philosophical intuitions are supposed to provide evidence or data. Additionally, when these studies are coupled with our inability to either explain what it is about any of these intuitions that make them problematically sensitive or predict which other intuitions may or may not be problematically sensitive, they challenge the trustworthiness, not just of the class of intuitions that have so far been studied, but of the whole class of intuitions typically appealed to in philosophical discourse (Alexander and Weinberg 2007; Weinberg 2007).

In addition to calling into question the trustworthiness of philosophers' typical appeals to intuitions, these recent empirical studies also call into question whether there is, in fact, something like a shared intuition about a particular hypothetical case that can be appealed to either as evidence or data. These studies show that particular hypothetical cases can give rise to a number of different intuitions, thereby calling into question any claims as to what the folk intuitions are—a significant problem for positive programs, each of which views getting at the folk intuitions to be either a significant philosophical insight in its own right or a necessary step towards achieving a significant philosophical insight. It also raises the question of how we should proceed when confronted with conflicting intuitions. At a bare minimum, anyone who wants to select one from among those intuitions that are generated in response to a given hypothetical case needs to explain why the other intuitions should be discounted. The trouble is that determining just what to do when confronted with conflicting evidence or data is not especially straightforward, as the growing literature in the epistemology of disagreement demonstrates (see, e.g., Christensen 2007; Elga 2006; Feldman 2006; Feldman and Warfield 2007; Kelly 2005, 2007, 2008; White 2005).

These findings thus pose a significant challenge to positive experimental philosophy, inasmuch as positive experimental philosophy attempts to deploy intuitions as evidence or as data. In fact, we think that positive experimental philosophy may be almost as imperiled by negative experimental philosophy as is more traditional armchair analytic philosophy. Positive experimental philosophers need a way to accommodate the kinds of inter- and intra-personal differences discovered by negative experimental philosophers. Direct extramentalist projects appear lethally imperiled: they involve inferences from premises of the form "it is intuitive that P", but such premises now seem ill-formed, without specifying to whom it is intuitive, and under what circumstances.[6] However, the various mentalist positive programs may seem, at first glance, to be well situated to pull off just such a needed accommodation. But, as we shall see, these mentalist programs face equally challenging problems.

3.2. Conceptualist and Semantic Mentalism and the Machery-Quine Problem

Conceptualist approaches to positive experimental philosophy have proved popular, and are perhaps the most common sort of experimental philosophy today. Although conceptualists have not been motivated by the worries we reviewed in the previous section, conceptualist mentalism seems to hold out the prima facie promise of some resources that would make it better able to withstand the challenge from negative experimental philosophy. First, conceptualist mentalism allows for a modicum of relativization, which may go some way towards defusing the threat of cross-group differences in intuitions—if Asian and Western subjects have different intuitions, then perhaps they just have different concepts (though see Mallon et al. 2009). Relatedly, one may hope under conceptualist mentalism to be able to disregard some variation and instability of intuitions as mere noise, not reflective of the underlying concept. The two moves are related, as the first one is only possible if the second one can enable us to distinguish conceptually based differences in intuition from non-conceptually based differences.

Conceptualist mentalism thus relies on the idea that we can use empirical evidence to establish what is and what is not constitutive of a given concept of philosophical interest. But it is, in fact, far from clear how to do so—a point made in the context of experimental philosophy by Edouard Machery (2008) in his discussion of the debate over the so-called "Knobe-effect" or "side-effect effect". In probably the most famous finding of experimental philosophy, Joshua Knobe (2003a) showed that whether or not a foreseen side effect is judged to be intentional is influenced by whether or not the side effect is bad. Knobe presented subjects with two versions of the following vignette:

Harm Condition

The vice-president of a company went to the chairman of the board and said, 'We are thinking of starting a new program. It will help us increase profits, but it will also harm the environment.'
The chairman of the board answered, 'I don't care at all about harming the environment. I just want to make as much profit as I can. Let's start the new program.'
They started the new program. Sure enough, the environment was harmed.

In the second, Help Condition, the vignette was the same, except the word "harm" was replaced with "help". In each case, subjects were then asked whether or not the chairman harmed/helped the environment intentionally. But the conditions produced sharply divergent results. Most subjects in the Harm Condition said the chairman harmed the environment intentionally, while most in the Help Condition said the chairman did not help the environment intentionally. Knobe (2003b) concluded that this asymmetry was not a mistake by subjects, but rather reflected the structure of the concept INTENTIONALLY. Other commentators have disputed this, alleging that the effect emerges from considerations extrinsic to the concept, for example, a desire to blame the perpetrator of foreseen harm (see, e.g., Nadelhoffer 2004a, b; Adams and Steadman 2004a). Machery, however, rightly pointed out that the debate seems to hinge upon the appropriate individuation of the concept INTENTIONALLY and that there is simply no way to resolve this debate absent some specific idea as to how to individuate concepts. And positive program philosophers have not taken on the difficult task of defending such an idea and figuring out how to implement it in their methods.

Moreover, the most common criterion for philosophers for individuating a concept is semantic. That is, when faced with the question of whether an inference involving a bit of mental syntax, e.g. INTENTIONAL, does or does not figure as part of the concept, philosophers ask if the inference figures in constituting the meaning of "intentional"—and here conceptual mentalism gives way to semantic mentalism. But as Quine noted in "Two Dogmas," it is not at all clear in virtue of what facts we can adjudicate disputes about meaning (Quine 1951).

Thus, this one problem seems to us to bedevil both conceptualist mentalist and semantic mentalist approaches to experimental philosophy: semantic mentalists owe a way of distinguishing meaning-constituting facts from non-meaning-constituting ones; conceptualist mentalists owe either that or some other way of individuating conceptual structures from causally interwoven, but external, structures.

One option for either project might be to hope that sophisticated psychological inquiry might solve this problem. For example, "theory" theorist psychologists aim to discern deep principles of "core knowledge" or commitments that might pull apart confounding factors, perhaps revealing the semantic structure of ordinary concepts. For instance, there is now a widespread literature discussing folk essentialist construals of various natural kind concepts (e.g., Gelman 2003), and one might view these studies as revealing necessary or sufficient conditions for membership in the kind. Given important psychological research programs such as these it may seem presumptuous, and downright unQuinean, to try to use a philosopher's armchair argument to attack a scientist's way of arguing.

We confess to not seeing how even such sophisticated psychological inquiries distinguish, on empirical grounds, what properly belongs to a concept or a meaning, and what does not. But in large part we take this to be so because we also take it that one should not simply assume that the psychologists' projects and the philosophers' projects are the same. If, instead of trying to elucidate word meanings, psychologists are typically just trying to map out what are the psychological structures and processes that implement our abilities to categorize, with no attendant commitments to any aspect of those structures being conceptually discrete or meaning-constitutive, then this "Machery-Quine" problem just doesn't arise for them. Psychologists studying concepts do not seem to us to have been particularly interested in refereeing issues of which subtle differences in categorization represent real conceptual differences. Lexical semanticists, too, have seemed mostly interested in the behavior of whole classes of words (such as unaccusative vs. unergative verbs), and have not felt the need to develop the resources that positive experimental philosophers would need to, say, discern whether or when disagreement over Gettier cases would mean that East Asians and Westerners mean something different by "knows".[7] If we are right, then it does not follow from the success of empirical psychological work that psychologists have a solution to either concept or meaning individuation to offer philosophers (cf., Machery 2009, Chapters 1–2).

It may be objected that there are at least some instances in which scientists have employed machinery meant to distinguish properly conceptual or semantic from other psychological sources of behavior. Perhaps the most famous such machinery (though perhaps the only such machinery) for philosophers is the semantics/pragmatics distinction. And we do not wish to reject that distinction, or the wealth of tests (cancellability, etc.) that are available for making it in real scientific practice. And, furthermore, it is a distinction that has even been successfully appealed to in some debates within positive experimental philosophy (e.g., Adams and Steadman 2004a, b; Knobe 2004; Nichols and Ulatowski 2007). Nonetheless, we are not sanguine about the prospects of using this particular piece of theoretical machinery to handle the challenge advanced by negative experimental philosophy; the particular patterns of variability and instability in the negative experimental philosophy findings just do not look like the sorts of patterns one would expect, were they simply a matter of pragmatics. Nonetheless, we would certainly welcome attempts by positive experimental philosophers to do so, as a considered step in the right direction. And the richness of the theoretical background of the semantics/pragmatics distinction, with its attendant arsenal of tests for its proper deployment, just reveals how much really is required to even begin to develop tools that would begin to help answer this question of what experimental findings are truly semantic or conceptual.

Of course, as we mentioned above, a conceptualist mentalist may abandon semantic mentalism as a way of individuating conceptual structures, and offer some other, non-semantic criteria for distinguishing what does and does not properly belong to the concept or other relevant mental structure. Where meanings fail, perhaps appeal to the competence/performance distinction for, or the proper domain of, the relevant mental structure will do. We consider these in turn.

3.3. Competence, Performance, Marr, and the Limits of Surveys

Even as negative experimental philosophy has frequently demonstrated unexpected and unwanted variation in people's intuitions, this observed variation in intuition would no longer pose a problem if we possessed a means for discerning epistemic wheat from chaff. Shaun Nichols and Joshua Knobe (2007) have attempted to do just that, with regard to divergent intuitions concerning free will and determinism, by trying to argue that some of the observed variation is a matter of performance errors in one of the studied conditions.

To see how this might work, consider an example from linguistics. Linguists use intuitions about grammaticality as data to construct the grammar of a natural language, but they distinguish between the competence involved in producing judgments from the factors that influence performance. As Robert Cummins puts it: "competence is ideal...performance, that is, the performance that the system would exhibit but for resource limitations, physical breakdown, and interference from other processes" (Cummins 1998, p. 44). So, in one famous instance, subjects find multiply-center-embedded English sentences like

> The man the boy the woman saw heard left.

to be ungrammatical, but linguistic theory says that they comply with the syntax with which we work (viz., they are grammatical according to our competence). The apparent ungrammaticality of these sentences is often explained away in terms of limits on working memory in the parser (e.g., Marcus 1980). Thus, we take all the evidence we have and construct a model of the cognitive mechanisms that operate to produce judgments in a domain, and we determine the borders of a folk domain by looking at the mechanism in the model that produces the paradigmatic judgments we are concerned with. The workings of that mechanism determine the competence of the subject within that folk domain. Judgments that are influenced by factors outside that mechanism represent performance errors.

Although we are not troubled by many of the uses of the competence/performance distinction throughout cognitive science,[8] we do not think that it is a distinction that can—yet—do the work that some positive experimental philosophy practitioners have hoped to have it do. Simply put, experimental philosophy currently lacks the experimental and theoretical resources to make a good use of that distinction for its purposes.

First, most experimental philosophy has been (and continues to be) reliant on survey methods. Subjects are given a questionnaire, and their judgments are elicited regarding some range of scenarios, with the experimenters typically manipulating the substance of the scenarios but also possibly their order or other contextual elements. Such methods can generate a set of extensional and typically distributional data: given scenario x under conditions y, a certain percentage of subjects give answer z. Such data can, at best, operate only at the first of Marr's (1982) three levels, the theory of the computation—that is, an input/output account of what function the system computes. However, explanations in terms of performance error most plausibly operate at either the second or third of Marr's three levels of explanation—the level of the algorithm, and the level of the physical implementation. Without operating at those levels, the appeal to performance errors can be used, at best, to explain away small and unsystematic variation. But the negative experimental philosophy findings present a challenge precisely in virtue of their systematic nature.

To deploy the distinction as a response to those findings would, thus, depend on a construal of the actual workings of the system in question.[9] One cannot separate competence from performance with only input/output data; rather, one requires, at least in the background, some sort of account as to what the idealized operation of the system is supposed to be like, such that performance errors can be explained away in terms of the system falling short of that idealization in some way. In the absence of any processing or physical accounts, we just cannot know how the requisite idealization is supposed to go. Such explanations can only succeed, though, given a reasonably clear idea of what resources are being strained, and preferably also how that resource might be limited in the first place. This is why one standard performance error account of center embeddings works so well—working memory has a pretty good track record in both regards, as revealed in the general popularity of "cognitive load" as an experimental manipulation. But these are not questions at the level of which inputs produce which outputs, for they require some story about the inner workings of the system. They are therefore not the sorts of questions that can be addressed via survey methods.

It may be easier for positive experimental philosophy to apply a competence/performance distinction in terms of one process interfering with another, and this is indeed what we see with Nichols and Knobe (2007).[10] Nichols and Knobe explored two different factors that could influence subjects' willingness to attribute the possibility of moral responsibility in a hypothetical case: (i) whether or not the case was described as being in a deterministic universe or an indeterministic one, and (ii) whether or not the case was affectively engaging.[11] Unsurprisingly, Nichols and Knobe found that subjects were generally more willing to attribute the possibility of responsibility in indeterministic universes than in deterministic ones. Perhaps more unexpectedly, they found a similar increased willingness in high-affect cases over low-affect ones. So in a low-affect, deterministic case only a minority of subjects (23%) judged moral responsibility to be possible. A slender majority of subjects judged moral responsibility possible in the high-affect, deterministic case (64%), with more robust majorities in the low-affect, indeterministic case (89%) and most of all in the high-affect, indeterministic case (95%).

So we have some diversity of intuitions across different cases here. While philosophers may not worry about whether or not the determinism/indeterminism differences track a real difference in subjects' competence in attributing agency, they may worry about what to make of the influence of affect on these judgments. Nichols and Knobe consider two possible interpretations. On the "affective competence" interpretation, our emotions are properly part of our agency-attribution system, and their tendency towards compatibilism (as revealed by the majority response in the high-affect, deterministic case), thus, reveals a real commitment of our psychology of responsibility. On the "affective performance error" interpretation, our emotions interfere with the more properly incompatibilist judgments of agency. Here's how they argue for the latter interpretation:

> We think that the affective performance error model provides quite a plausible explanation of our results. What we see in the [low affect] case is that, when affect is minimized, people give dramatically different answers depending on whether the agent is in a determinist or indeterminist universe. On the performance error hypothesis, these responses reveal the genuine competence with responsibility attribution, for in the low affect cases, the affective bias is minimized. When high affect is introduced... the normal competence with responsibility attribution is skewed by the emotions; that explains why there is such a large difference between the high and low affect cases in the determinist conditions.
>
> Now let's turn to the affective competence account. It's much less clear that the affective competence theorist has a good explanation of the results. In particular it seems difficult to see how the affective competence account can explain why responses to the low-affect case drop precipitously in the determinist condition, since this doesn't hold for the high affect case. Perhaps the affective competence theorist could say that low affect cases... fail to trigger our competence with responsibility attribution, and so we should not treat those responses as reflecting our normal competence. But obviously it would take significant work to show that such everyday cases of apparent responsibility attribution don't really count as cases in which we exercise our competence at responsibility attribution. Thus, at first glance, the performance error account provides a better explanation of these results than the affective competence account. (p. 676)

Yet there is a problem here. To describe one process as interfering with another presupposes an individuation of the processes involved, which is again not something that can be done purely with the sort of survey data that Nichols and Knobe have (like almost all practitioners of experimental philosophy). If we already possessed a well-worked out account of the particular mechanisms operating in these domains and their various interactions, then such an account could maybe provide a framework within which such studies could do the required work. But no such account is currently on offer that can help tell us whether the affective influence on people's judgments is a component part of, or extraneous to, the system producing those judgments. In the absence of any individuation of mechanisms at either the algorithmic or the implementational level of explanation, we cannot tell. The question becomes particularly messy for Nichols and Knobe, as they want to opt for a "hybrid" account in which some of the affect is part of the competence, while other parts of it present an interfering factor. We are not arguing about the truth or falsity of that claim; but we are addressing whether positive experimental philosophy's survey methods are sufficient to establish such claims as true or false, and we are concerned that they cannot.[12]

One way to see this problem more sharply is to notice that the two hypotheses that Nichols and Knobe consider do not compete only with each other, but must also compete with a number of other hypotheses in which some set of the observed performance is produced by one system and some other set by a different, interfering system. They offer one way of carving things up, but the worry that we're articulating here is that it is extremely difficult, given only the sort of data that they have, to prefer any one of those ways over other possibilities. For example, a proponent of an affective competence model could suggest that people's answers in the high-affect cases are fine, but that some other mechanism interferes with people's judgments in the low-affect cases; perhaps the description of the determinist universe triggers some sort of explanation-detection system, which competes with the responsibility-attribution system, and produces improper interference. Or perhaps there is just one unified mechanism, and the profile of responses they report is simply the result of its computations, and there are no performance errors to be explained away at all! Such a result would be philosophically surprising, but there is no psychological reason, given only survey data, to rule it out.

3.4. The Proper Domain Problem

One way to get around the worries just articulated would be to already possess a mature theory of the computation for the system in question. Although such a theory tells us what the input-output function is for the system, it does more than that—it tells us what function it is that we should understand the system as computing. If we already had such a theory, then we could use it to help referee between at least some competing accounts at the algorithmic level. This could perhaps be put to use to separate conceptual from non-conceptual components of cognition, or to help underwrite an application of the competence/performance distinction to discern the boundaries of a computational mechanism.

Although such an appeal to the theory of the computation is theoretically possible, it will not help here. For we are considering cases in which positive experimental philosophy is supposed to help referee between conflicting accounts of a given domain. As such, these are cases in which the fundamental philosophical facts are dialectically up for grabs. To determine whether Nichols and Knobe's subjects' affect is interfering with their judgments, or is, instead, a manifestation of their competence at making those judgments, we need to know first what function it is that their psychological systems are trying to compute. If their systems are meant to judge their world along the lines of compatibilism, then the affect would be part of the competence; and if their systems are meant to judge the world along the lines of incompatibilism, then the affect would be an interference.

(Note that this worry, perhaps unlike the worry in the previous section, applies more generally than just to survey-based positive experimental philosophy. For example, it applies equally well to Joshua Greene's attempts to argue for utilitarianism based on his neuroimaging studies of subjects considering trolley cases (e.g., Greene et al. 2001). We fear that practitioners of positive experimental philosophy have overlooked the extent to which successful psychological appeals to a competence/performance distinction typically rely on key theoretical factors such as (i) substantial theories of the system in question, (ii) an account of the resources the system will need to draw upon, and (iii) a specification of the proper domain of the system. And when such theories are not in fact available, then appeals to that distinction are easily challenged (see, e.g., Stanovich and West 2000, Section 3). We unfortunately lack such theories in most areas of positive experimental philosophy.)

Practitioners of positive experimental philosophy might, thus, look around for other sources of evidence that could help determine what function it is that, say, our "moral responsibility" system is computing. But this will turn out to be difficult to do: there is no reason to think, even conceding that the mind is comprised of systems discrete enough to be assigned separate proper domains, that such systems will correspond closely enough with domains of philosophical interest (e.g., moral responsibility) to provide acceptable reductions of them. And to lose track of this fact is to distort both the philosophy and the psychology.

Philosophers are typically interested in psychological domains that correspond to philosophical concepts of interest, for example, responsibility, morality, knowledge, and so forth. But there is no reason to think that the cognitive architecture of our psychology neatly aligns with, rather than cross-cuts, the philosophical matters of interest. To see this, consider recent claims of a "linguistic analogy" for the moral domain—claims that moral cognition is underwritten by a domain-specific adaptation for morality, on a par with the linguistic faculty posited by Chomsky (e.g., Dwyer 1999; Harman 1999; Mikhail 2000; Hauser et al. 2007). One way of thinking about proper functions is in terms of evolution: the proper function of a mechanism is the function for which the mechanism was, or is, selected for—the function that computes solutions to problems in its proper domain (Sperber 1994). While there could be other ways of specifying what exactly determines or constitutes the proper function of a mechanism, the main point is that such proper functions may either be directed at problem domains that are more or less neatly coextensive with philosophical domain of interest like morality or they may not. Indeed, some proponents of a moral faculty are quite clear about this (see, e.g., Hauser et al. 2007): they mean to make the nontrivial claim that there is a species-typical, innate, and domain-specific mechanism whose proper function is moral judgment, and they understand such proper functions as produced by evolutionary pressures to solve moral problems.

But when we start thinking about natural selection, it suggests pressures that lead in quite different directions than moral reasoning. To choose a quick and straightforward example, it seems like sound evolutionary logic to think that evolution might favor mechanisms that systematically favor members of one's own family, or members of one's own group, or persons that might assist one's reproductive success, while it is at least plausible to think that these considerations are not morally relevant. At the very least, one cannot simply assume that the domain determined by the proper function of the mechanism or mechanisms that underwrite morality and the domain of morality are coextensive.[13]

Consider how losing track of the distinction between the domain of morality and the proper domain of the mechanism that implements morality can distort psychological inquiry. Much recent work in moral psychology, including work in the "linguistic analogy" tradition, has engaged in relatively straightforward appropriation of the philosophical technique of eliciting moral intuitions by presenting carefully constructed moral dilemmas (e.g., Mikhail 2000; Hauser et al. 2007). This appropriation, however, makes the substantial assumption that the kind of data of relevance to philosophers will also be relevant to psychologists. Notice, first, that philosophers carefully construct moral dilemmas as ways of eliciting intuitions of relevance to assessing competing theories of morality. For this reason, philosophers' dilemmas typically exclude factors that are widely considered to be morally irrelevant. For example, variations of the famous "runaway trolley" typically aim to probe the circumstances (if any) in which it is okay to bring about the death of one person in order to save five others. But such variations typically do not include versions in which we are asked to weigh the lives of relatives, out-group members, potential sex partners, and so forth, and (to repeat), this is precisely because whatever difference such factors might make is irrelevant to the moral questions at hand. But there's every reason to think that these factors are evolutionarily relevant and so considering them in computing moral judgments may be part of the proper function of whatever mechanism or mechanisms that underlie moral judgment.

When we deviate from this assumption and consider different factors, we may find different answers—answers that suggest a very different sort of faculty than a "moral" faculty is at work. In one of the earliest experimental investigations of trolley dilemmas, Petrinovich et al. (1993) report finding that subjects prefer the lives of relatives and friends over strangers in standard trolley scenarios, a finding they take to support sociobiologists' and evolutionary psychologists' suggestions that humans are designed, in part, to be concerned with their own inclusive fitness. Suppose that this data from Petrivonich et al. is correct. Suppose further that much of our moral judgment is underwritten by an evolutionarily designed mechanism M that computes using an internalized principle like:

> (K) The wrongness of an action resulting in an avoidable death is inversely proportional to the subject's relatedness to me.

Such a principle may well be morally irrelevant, but at the same time it may well be central to the operation of the faculty that underlies moral judgments about trolley cases. Hauser et al. (2007) indicate that, in contrast with such research that focuses on questions of "evolutionary significance", their research will probe "the computational operations that drive our judgments" (p. 127). But this begs a crucial question, viz. whether the computational processes driving our typical moral judgments are themselves biased by evolution in ways that are at odds with our intuitive sense of morality.[14] It is possible that our concept of morality may emerge only when an innate, domain specific mechanism is used in ways that are at odds with its design (e.g. when it is not allowed access to information such as the relatedness of a person to us).

If philosophical and psychological boundaries needn't be even approximately isomorphic, then it goes to show that inquiries into those borders are relatively autonomous. One cannot read the borders of philosophically interesting domains off of the psychology, and one cannot read psychological borders off of the philosophy.

4. CONCLUSION & PROSPECTS FOR THE FUTURE

Let us recap how the worries we have raised here can be seen to afflict the particular positive programs. Since all of the positive programs are committed to the view that intuitions are trustworthy and shared, each faces the challenge of figuring out what to do with the results of negative experimental philosophy. In particular, the positive programs owe us the same kind of story that traditional armchair philosophers owe: how do we discern which intuitions count? When different folks yield different intuitions, which one do we take to be likely to be tracking the philosophical truth?

This challenge can make some sort of mentalism attractive. One resource that mentalism offers is the legitimacy of some degree of relativism: maybe people with different intuitions just have different concepts, so everyone is still correct. (Here we see a clear case where positive experimental philosophy has an advantage over traditional armchair methods: the latter has no capacity to discern such demographic differences in intuitions, and hence concepts, whereas the former can commission as much cross-cultural research as is needed.) But, we are skeptical about just how attractive, or how helpful, such a move towards relativism is. Another resource that mentalism offers is some means for explaining away some of the variation, as due to factors other than the meaning-constitutive elements of the concepts themselves. But appealing to this resource entangles mentalism in Quinean difficulties that it has not (and, we worry, cannot) resolve. Finally, mechanist mentalism offers the possibility of accommodating the results of negative experimental philosophy by accounting for the various forms of inter- and intra-personal instability and variation in terms of performance errors. Mechanist mentalism, however, seems to require either a well worked-out architecture of the different systems involved, or some way of fixing the proper domain of those systems. Given the kinds of survey data typically gathered in current positive experimental philosophy research, though, and the problem of philosophical domains cross-cutting psychological domains, mechanist approaches seem to lack both the experimental and theoretical tools needed to advance their programs at this time.

At this point, the prognosis might seem rather grim for experimental philosophy's positive programs. Interestingly, their salvation might ultimately rest on their ability to become more experimental—or at least more like experimental psychology. The kinds of survey methods that experimental philosophers so frequently employ play little role in experimental psychology—and, for good reason: there are better methods available to answer the kinds of questions that are of interest to both experimental psychologists and philosophers (Scholl 2007).[15] Experimental philosophy's positive programs would do well, we think, to become more like experimental psychology. The hope of experimental philosophy's positive program was to use science to help do some of the work that traditional philosophy hasn't been able to do (or hasn't been interested in doing). Part of the challenge facing the positive programs is to become more scientifically sophisticated.

But doing more, and better, science will not be enough by itself to fully met the challenge—the positive programs must also do enough philosophy to see how to bridge the gap from empirical findings to philosophical payoffs. Positive experimental philosophy may face a situation now that Wittgenstein asserted once of psychology: "there are experimental methods and conceptual confusion...The existence of experimental methods makes us think we have the means of solving the problems which trouble us; though problem and methods pass one another by".[16] If we are right that neither psychologists nor linguists are really in the business of providing answers to the kind of meaning-constitutivity questions that semanticists and conceptualist philosophers are interested in, then philosophers will have to figure out for themselves how empirical results can speak to such questions. And we expect that attempts to draw a competence/performance distinction in such areas as moral or epistemic judgment, as many mechanist philosophers have been interested in doing, cannot succeed without drawing on at least some substantive philosophical claims about the nature of those domains. Compare, for example, how impossible a theory of 3-D vision would be without drawing on claims about the structure of the physical world about which vision gives us information, and in particular the way that visible light interacts with that world. Finally, we see no reason to think that appeals to the proper domain of a mechanism will gain much traction since there's no reason to think that, even granting that cognitive mechanisms are domain-specific, the proper domains of cognitive mechanisms will be isomorphic to domains of philosophical interest. Positive experimental philosophy may, in the end, be able to avoid some of the methodological pitfalls of its armchair predecessors. But it seems that some challenges are endemic to philosophy qua philosophy, no matter where one sits while one does it.

ACKNOWLEDGEMENTS

We would like to thank the participants in the 2008 Society for Philosophy and Psychology Workshop on Experimental Philosophy; the members of the Experimental Epistemology Laboratory (EEL) at Indiana University, especially Cameron Buckner and Chad Gonnerman; and two anonymous referees for this journal for valuable feedback on earlier drafts of this paper.

NOTES

1. In this paper, we will take as our target philosophical intuitions as they are standardly conceived of in current practice. According to this conception, philosophical intuitions are propositional attitudes generated in response to hypothetical cases in philosophy which are "minimally foundational" (a person may appeal to them as evidence without having to provide evidence for them), non-inferential, and fallible. We also think that most of these arguments will go through mutatis mutandis for other conceptions of such judgments and their place in philosophical methodology (see, for example, Williamson 2004, 2005, 2007; Alexander and Weinberg 2007).

2. The terms "negative" program and "positive" program are now in common use. We are unsure of their origin though they may have been introduced by Farid Masrour.

3. For additional discussions of experimental philosophy's positive and negative programs, see Alexander and Weinberg (2007); Kauppinen (2007); Nadelhoffer and Nahmias (2007); and Weinberg (2007).

4. One notable exception is the recent work of Stotz and Griffiths (2004). They document the varying intuitions of specialist populations regarding the concept of the gene, and they have a good reason for restricting their populations of interest. Moreover, there are a number of interesting examples of experimental philosophy that do not particularly concern intuitions (see, e.g., Nichols 2002; Schwitzgebel 2009), and that our arguments do not target.

5. See Nadelhoffer and Nahmias (2007) for an earlier but different elucidation of forms of positive experimental philosophy.

6. Perhaps some form of relativism or contextualism could be attempted. Different relativizations might have different degrees of plausibility (for example, see Glasgow 2008 on relativism and the concept of race). While such moves may be appropriate in some instances, we suspect that they will not prove generally attractive. For a discussion of why epistemic contextualism might not be particularly helpful, see Swain et al. (2008). For a discussion of relativizing intuitions about reference, see Mallon et al. (2009).

7. See, e.g., Johnson (2008). Note though that lexical semanticists might offer some resources that philosophers would find useful if the factivity of "knows" or other epistemologically interested verbs was under discussion.

8. In addition to its original home in linguistics, the distinction has also done important work in other parts of cognitive science, e.g., in the developmental folk psychology literature (Surian and Leslie 1999; Bloom and German 2000; Scholl and Leslie 2003).

9. It also presupposes at a minimum that it will be possible to decompose the relevant cognition into mechanisms with individually discernible functions. We note this commitment without taking issue with it here.

10. To our knowledge, no one has explored "physical breakdown" as a candidate source of performance errors in positive experimental philosophy.

11. We grant here, for the sake of discussion, that they have correctly characterized the way their experimental materials map into these distinctions.

12. See Scholl (2007) for a positive example of using implicit measures in experiments in the philosophical domain of the metaphysics of objects.

13. For further elaboration on this point, see Mallon (2007).

14. Hauser et al. make this same move more explicitly when they exclude gender as a relevant explanatory dimension, writing that "we find it clear that some distinctions (e.g., the agent's gender) do not carry any explanatory weight" (Hauser et al. 2007, p. 131). Here again, they make judgments that reflect a judgment about what sort of considerations are properly considered moral ones. But there seems little reason to think evolution would have respected such niceties in constructing us, so it is not clear why such exclusions are relevant to our underlying functional organization.

15. Scholl provides some excellent suggestions as to how philosophers and psychologists could do a better job of getting a handle on the mechanisms underlying various intuitions. However, it is not clear how to use his suggestions to help with the deeper sorts of problems discussed here. For example, he writes, "understanding the origins of our metaphysical intuitions in various psychological mechanisms could help us understand when they are worth revising or forfeiting in our philosophical theories, especially if there is reason to think that those psychological mechanisms may yield unreliable results in the particular contexts in which they are being asked to operate" (Scholl 2007, p. 586). But without knowing the proper domain of those mechanisms, it stands as an open question just what will count as reliable or unreliable operation.

16. Wittgenstein (1953), Part II, section xiv.

REFERENCES

Adams, F., and A. Steadman. 2004a. Intentional action in ordinary language: core concept or pragmatic understanding? *Analysis 64*: 173–181.

Adams, F., and A. Steadman. 2004b. Intentional action and moral considerations: still pragmatic. *Analysis 64*: 268–276.

Alexander, J., and J. Weinberg. 2007. Analytic epistemology and experimental philosophy. *Philosophy Compass 2*: 56–80.

Bloom, P., and T.P. German. 2000. Two reasons to abandon the false belief task as a test of theory of mind. *Cognition 77*: B25–B31.

Christensen, D. 2007. Epistemology of disagreement: the good news. *The Philosophical Review 116*: 187–217.

Cummins, R. 1998. Reflection on reflective equilibrium. In *Rethinking intuition*, ed. M. DePaul, and W. Ramsey, 113–128. Lanham: Rowman and Littlefield.

Dwyer, S. 1999. Moral competence. In *Philosophy and linguistics*, ed. K. Murasugi, and R. Stanton, 169–190. Boulder: Westview.

Elga, A. 2006. Reflection and disagreement. *Nous 41*: 478–502.

Feldman, R. 2006. Epistemological puzzles about disagreement. In *Epistemology futures*, ed. S. Heatherington. Oxford: Oxford University Press, 216–236.

Feldman, R., and F. Warfield. 2007. *Disagreement*. Oxford: Oxford University Press.

Gelman, S. 2003. *The essential child: Origins of essentialism in everyday thought*. Oxford: Oxford University Press.

Glasgow, J. 2008. On the methodology of the race debate: conceptual analysis and racial discourse. *Philosophy and Phenomenological Research 76*: 333–358.

Goldman, A., and J. Pust. 1998. Philosophical theory and intuitional evidence. In *Rethinking intuition*, ed. M. DePaul, and W. Ramsey, 179–200. Lanham : Rowman and Littlefield.

Greene, J. 2003. From neural "is" to moral "ought": what are the moral implications of neuroscientific moral psychology? *Nature Reviews Neuroscience 4*: 847–850.

Greene, J., R. Sommerville, L. Nystrom, J. Darley, and J. Cohen. 2001. An fMRI investigation of emotional engagement in moral judgment. *Science 293*: 2105–2108.

Harman, G. 1999. Moral philosophy and linguistics. In *Proceedings of the 20th World Congress of Philosophy*, vol. I: Ethics, ed. K. Brinkmann, 107–115. Bowling Green: Philosophy Documentation Center.

Hauser, M., L. Young, and F. Cushman. 2007. Reviving Rawls' linguistic analogy: Operative principles and the causal structure of moral actions. In *Moral psychology*, volume 1: The evolution of morality: Adaptations and innateness, ed. W. Sinnott-Armstrong. Cambridge: MIT (Bradford Books), 107–143.

Jackson, F. 1998. *From metaphysics to ethics: A defense of conceptual analysis*. Oxford: Oxford University Press.

Johnson, K. 2008. An overview of lexical semantics. *Philosophy Compass 3*: 119–134.

Kauppinen, A. 2007. The rise and fall of experimental philosophy. *Philosophical Explorations 10*: 95–118.

Kelly, T. 2005. The epistemic significance of disagreement. In *Oxford studies in epistemology*, vol. 1, ed. J. Hawthorne, and T. Gendler Szabo, 167–196. Oxford: Oxford University Press.

Kelly, T. 2007. Peer disagreement and higher order evidence. In *Disagreement*, ed. R. Feldman, and T. Warfield. Oxford: Oxford University Press, 187–217.

Kelly, T. 2008. Disagreement, dogmatism, and belief polarization. *The Journal of Philosophy 105*: 611–633.

Knobe, J. 2003a. Intentional action and side effects in ordinary language. *Analysis 63*: 190–193.

Knobe, J. 2003b. Intentional action in folk psychology: an experimental investigation. *Philosophical Psychology 16*: 309–324.

Knobe, J. 2004. Intention, intentional action and moral considerations. *Analysis 64*: 181–187.

Knobe, J. 2007a. Experimental philosophy and philosophical significance. *Philosophical Explorations 10*: 119–122.

Knobe, J. 2007b. Reason explanation in folk psychology. *Midwest Studies in Philosophy 31*: 90–107.

Lewis, D. 1970. How to define theoretical terms. *Journal of Philosophy 67*: 426–446.

Lewis, D. 1972. Psychophysical and theoretical identifications. *Australasian Journal of Philosophy 50*: 249–258.

Machery, E. 2008. The folk concept of intentional action: philosophical and psychological issues. *Mind & Language 23*: 165–189.

Machery, E. 2009. *Doing without concepts*. New York: Oxford University Press.
Machery, E., S. Lindquist, and P. Griffiths. 2009. The vernacular concept of innateness. *Mind & Language 24*: 605–630.
Machery, E., R. Mallon, S. Nichols, and S. Stich. 2004. Semantics, cross-cultural style. *Cognition 92*: B1–B12.
Mallon, R. 2007. Reviving Rawls inside and out. In *Psychology*, volume 2: The cognitive science of morality: Intuition and diversity, ed. W. Sinnott-Armstrong, 145–155. Cambridge: MIT Press (Bradford Books).
Mallon, R., and S. Nichols. 2010. Rules.. In *The Oxford handbook of moral psychology*, ed. J. Doris. Oxford: Oxford University Press.
Mallon, R., E. Machery, S. Nichols, and S. Stich. 2009. Against arguments from reference. *Philosophy and Phenomenological Research 79*: 332–356.
Marcus, M. 1980. *Theory of syntactic recognition for natural languages*. Cambridge: MIT Press.
Marr, D. 1982. *Vision*. San Francisco: W.H. Freeman.
Mikhail, J. 2000. Rawls' linguistic analogy: a study of the "generative grammar" model of moral theory described by John Rawls in "A theory of justice". Ph.D. Thesis. Cornell University, Ithaca.
Nadelhoffer, T. 2004a. On praise, side effects, and folk ascriptions of intentionality. *Journal of Theoretical and Philosophical Psychology 24*: 196–213.
Nadelhoffer, T. 2004b. Blame, badness, and intentional action: a reply to Knobe and Mendlow. *Journal of Theoretical and Philosophical Psychology 24*: 259–269.
Nadelhoffer, T., and E. Nahmias. 2007. The past and future of experimental philosophy. *Philosophical Explorations 10*: 123–149.
Nahmias, E., S. Morris, T. Nadelhoffer, and J. Turner. 2005. Surveying freedom: folk intuitions about free will and moral responsibility. *Philosophical Psychology 18*: 561–584.
Nahmias, E., S. Morris, T. Nadelhoffer, and J. Turner. 2006. Is incompatibilism intuitive? *Philosophy and Phenomenological Research 73*: 28–53.
Nichols, S. 2002. On the genealogy of norms: a case for the role of emotion in cultural evolution. *Philosophy of Science 69*: 234–255.
Nichols, S. 2006. Imaginative blocks and impossibility: An essay in modal psychology. In *The architecture of the imagination*, ed. S. Nichols, 237–255. Oxford: Oxford University Press.
Nichols, S., S. Stich, and J. Weinberg. 2003. Metaskepticism: Meditations in ethno-epistemology. In *The skeptics: Contemporary debates*, ed. S. Luper, 227–247. Burlington: Ashgate.
Nichols, S., and R. Mallon. 2006. Moral rules and moral dilemmas. *Cognition 100*: 530–542.
Nichols, S., and J. Knobe. 2007. Moral responsibility and determinism: the cognitive science of folk intuitions. *Nous 41*: 663–685.
Nichols, S., and J. Ulatowski. 2007. Intuitions and individual differences: the Knobe effect revisited. *Mind and Language 22*: 346–365.
Petrinovich, L., and P. O'Neill. 1996. Influence of wording and framing effects on moral intuitions. *Ethology and Sociobiology 17*: 145–171.
Petrinovich, L., P. O'Neill, and M. Jorgensen. 1993. An empirical study of moral intuitions: toward an evolutionary ethics. *Journal of Personality and Social Research 64*: 467–478.
Quine, W. 1951. Two dogmas of empiricism. *Philosophical Review 60*: 20–43.

Scholl, B. 2007. Object persistence in philosophy and psychology. *Mind & Language* 22: 563–591.
Scholl, B., and A. Leslie. 2003. Minds, modules, and meta-analysis. *Child Development* 72: 696–701.
Schwitzgebel, E.2009. Do ethicists steal more books. *Philosophical Psychology Volume 22, Issue 6: 711–725.*
Sperber, D. 1994. The modularity of thought and the epidemiology of representation. In *Mapping the mind*, ed. L. Hirchfeld, and S. Gelman, 39–67. Cambridge: Cambridge University Press.
Stanovich, K., and R. West. 2000. Individual differences in reasoning: implications for the rationality debate. *Behavior and Brain Sciences* 23: 645–726.
Stotz, K., and P. Griffiths. 2004. Genes: philosophical analyses put to the test. *History and Philosophy of the Life Sciences* 26: 5–28.
Surian, L., and A. Leslie. 1999. Competence and performance in false belief understanding: a comparison of autistic and normal 3-year-old children. *British Journal of Developmental Psychology* 17: 141–155.
Swain, S., J. Alexander, and J. Weinberg. 2008. The instability of philosophical intuitions: running hot and cold on truetemp. *Philosophy and Phenomenological Research* 76: 138–155.
Ulatowski, J. 2008. How many theories of act individuation are there? Ph.D. Thesis. University of Utah, Salt Lake City.
Uhlmann, E., D. Pizzaro, D. Tannenbaum, and P. Ditto. 2009. The motivated use of moral principles. *Judgment and Decision Making* 4: 476–491.
Weinberg, J. 2007. How to challenge intuitions empirically without risking skepticism. *Midwest Studies in Philosophy* 31: 318–343.
Weinberg, J., S. Nichols, and S. Stich. 2001. Normativity and epistemic intuitions. *Philosophical Topics* 29: 429–460.
White, R. 2005. Epistemic permissiveness. *Philosophical Perspectives* 19: 445–459.
Williamson, T. 2004. Philosophical "intuitions" and scepticism about judgments. *Dialectica* 58: 109–155.
Williamson, T. 2005. Armchair philosophy, metaphysical modality and counterfactual thinking. *Proceedings of the Aristotelian Society 105*: 1–23.
Williamson, T. 2007. *The philosophy of philosophy*. Oxford: Blackwell.
Wittgenstein, L. 1953. *Philosophical investigations*. Oxford: Blackwell.

3

On Intuitional Stability: The Clear, the Strong, and the Paradigmatic

Jennifer Cole Wright

1. INTRODUCTION

Intuition—what it is and how, when, and why it works—has recently received renewed attention in philosophy, cognitive science, and psychology. There has been much debate concerning the nature of intuition (Audi, 2004; Bealer, 1999, 2000; Claxton, 1998; Huemer, 2006; Kornblith, 1999; Laughlin, 1997; Osbeck, 1999, 2001; Parsons, 2000; Pust, 2000; Sosa, 1999, 2007a, 2007b; Williamson, 2007; Wisniewski, 1999), as well as what sort of cognitive process intuiting might be or involve (Cummins, 1998; Denes-Raj & Epstein, 1994; Dorfman, Shames, & Kilstrom, 1996; Epstein, Lipson, Holstein, & Huh, 1992; Gendler, 2007; Osbeck, 1999; Shafir, 1999; Sloman, 1996). There has also been debate about what role intuitions might play in logic and mathematics (Bealer, 2000; Bonjour, 1998; Casullo, 2003; Parsons, 1986, 2000; Sosa, 2006; Wright, 2004), epistemology (Alexander & Weinberg, 2007; Bealer, 1992; Brown, 2006; Nagel, 2007; Weinberg, 2007; Williamson, 2004), metaphysics (Bealer, 2002, 2004; Bonjour, 1998; Jackson, 1994, 1998; Pust, 2004; Sosa, 2000, 2006), morality (Audi, 2004; Bartsch & Wright, 2005; Dancy, 1991, 2006; Haidt & Joseph, 2004; Huemer, 2006 Jackson, 1998; Macnamara, 1991), and a variety of other areas.[1]

One such debate concerns the *epistemic*[2] status of intuitions. This debate centers around the following question: Is it legitimate, epistemically speaking, for individuals to form beliefs about matters of logic, mathematics, metaphysics, epistemology, morality, etc. on the basis of their intuitions about theoretical principles and/or concrete cases (involving actual or hypothetical examples)? In other words, do intuitions have some positive epistemic value?

While there are many who endorse an affirmative answer to this question (e.g., Bealer, 1992, 1999, 2000, 2004; Bonjour, 1998; Jackson, 1998; Pust, 2000; D. Sosa, 2006; E. Sosa, 1999, 2005, 2006; Williamson, 2004; cf. Osbeck, 1999, 2001), an increasing number of philosophers, cognitive scientists, and psychologists express a deep skepticism about intuition's epistemic value (see, e.g., Cummins, 1998; Denes-Raj & Epstein, 1994; Gendler, 2007; Hintikka, 1999, 2001; Machery, Mallon, Nichols, & Stich, 2004; Nichols & Knobe, 2007; Nichols, Stich, & Weinberg, 2003; Nisbett, Peng, Choi, & Norenzayan, 2001; Redelmeier & Shafir, 1995; Weinberg, 2007; Weinberg, Nichols, & Stich, 2001). In fact, whereas extreme skepticism about perception and memory might be considered somewhat 'academic' (D. Sosa, 2006), skepticism about intuition is thought by many (e.g., Machery et al., 2004; Nichols & Knobe, 2007; Nichols et al., 2003) to have serious implications for philosophical methodology.

This skepticism has recently been fortified by empirical research showing that concrete-case intuitions are vulnerable to irrational biases. Swain, Alexander, and Weinberg (2008), for example, found that people's responses to concrete cases were vulnerable to an 'order effect' (Tversky & Kahneman, 1974). Specifically, Swain et al. (2008) found that participants' concrete-case judgments about the *True-Temp* case (a much discussed thought-experiment in contemporary epistemology in which a man is unwittingly led, through a 'brain rewiring', to form true beliefs about the current temperature; see Lehrer, 1990) were significantly influenced by what case they had previously considered. Participants were more likely to say that True-Temp knew (as opposed to 'merely believed') that the temperature was 71° if they had just previously read the case about Dave, a man who formed the true belief that the next coin he flipped would land heads because he had a 'special feeling' right before he flipped the coin, and they were *less* likely to say that True-Temp knew if they had just previously read the case about Karen, a woman who formed a true belief about how to create a poisonous gas on the basis of reading an article about it in a top scientific journal.

Based on these findings, Swain et al. (2008) concluded that, to the extent that people's concrete-case intuitions are influenced by irrational biases such as one's previously elicited intuitions, they do not possess the sort of epistemic status that they have heretofore been taken to possess. They further concluded that the instability of intuitions demonstrated by their study (and others: e.g., Machery et al., 2004; Weinberg et al., 2001) brings into question our reliance on intuitions as sources of evidence for theoretical/philosophical positions, writing 'we contend that this instability undermines the supposed evidential status of these intuitions, such that philosophers [and others] who deal in intuitions can no longer rest comfortably in their armchairs' (2008, 1).

Is such a strong conclusion warranted? Some have argued that it is not, either due to a variety of methodological and conceptual difficulties (none of which will be touched upon here—for a discussion of some of these issues, see Laio (2008) and elsewhere) or on the grounds that Swain et al. (2008) hardly provide a definitive demonstration of intuitional instability, having found it in only one particular case. However, the true weight of the Swain et al. (2008) challenge is not that all (or even most) intuitions are unstable, but rather that we have no way of 'calibrating' our intuitions, no way of anticipating the conditions under which our concrete-case intuitions will be vulnerable to irrational biases, such as the order effect (for more on this worry, see Weinberg, 2007). This being the case, an adequate response to Swain et al.'s challenge needs to do more than simply demonstrate the stability of some (or even most) intuitions—it needs to identify a reliable method by which to track that stability and provide insight into why *certain* intuitions, but not others, are stable. In the absence of this, the epistemic legitimacy of consulting our intuitions remains open to skepticism.

The goal of the two studies reported here was to take up the challenge. Their guiding hypothesis was twofold: (1) that only *some* intuitions (that is, intuitions about *certain sorts* of cases) are vulnerable to intuitional instability and that people are implicitly aware of which cases these will be, and (2) that several potentially reliable methods for tracking intuitional instability exist—among them, the introspectively accessed confidence and belief strength of those doing the intuiting.

2. STUDY 1

2.1. Methods

2.1.1. Participants

One hundred and eighty-eight undergraduate college students (87 males, 101 females; dominantly Caucasian) from the University of Wyoming participated in this study. Participants were recruited through the Introduction to Psychology research pool and received research credit for their participation. Being dominantly college freshman, the assumption was that the participants had received little to no explicit philosophical training (though this question was not asked).

2.1.2. Materials and procedure

Participants received a randomized series of the Swain et al. (2008) cases as 'filler tasks' while participating in one of two larger, unrelated studies. The set included the *True-Temp* case, the *Coin-Flip* case, the *Fake-Barn* case, and the *Testimony* case (see Appendix), all four of which were presented to participants in a counterbalanced order. After reading each case, participants were asked whether the subject in the case *knew* a specific proposition (e.g., for *True-Temp*, whether the temperature was 71°), to which participants answered YES or NO. They were then asked to rate how confident they were about their answer (0 = not very confident to 5 = very confident).

2.2. Results

Preliminary note: There were no gender differences found and so all analyses to follow were collapsed across gender.

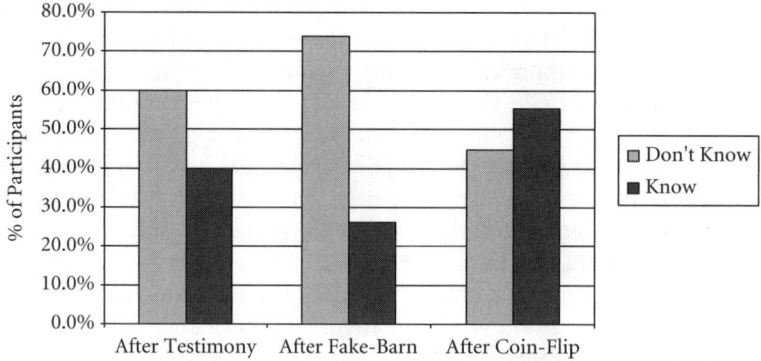

Figure 3.1. Attributions of knowledge in True-Temp.

Swain et al. (2008) had found that participants were *more* likely to judge that *True-Temp* really knew the temperature if the case was immediately preceded by *Coin-Flip* and *less* likely to do so if it was immediately preceded by *Testimony*. A similar pattern emerged in this study. Examining those cases in which *True-Temp* was the second case participants considered, being directly preceded by one of the other three cases (KTxx, DTxx, or STxx), the results revealed that participants were significantly more likely to attribute knowledge to *True-Temp* when it immediately followed *Coin-Flip* (55%) than when it immediately followed either *Testimony* (40%) or *Fake-Barn* (26%), χ^2 (2, $N = 143$) = 8.25, $p = .016$ (Fig. 1).

A similar trend emerged for *Fake-Barn*: participants were (marginally) less likely to count Suzy's mental state as knowledge when the case immediately followed either *Testimony* or *Coin-Flip* (40% and 39%, respectively) than when it immediately followed *True-Temp* (59%): χ^2 (2, $N = 144$) = 4.91, $p = .086$ (Fig. 2).

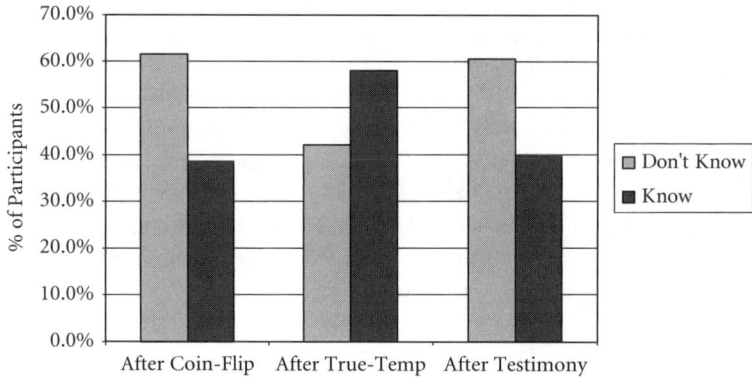

Figure 3.2. Attributions of knowledge in Fake-Barn.

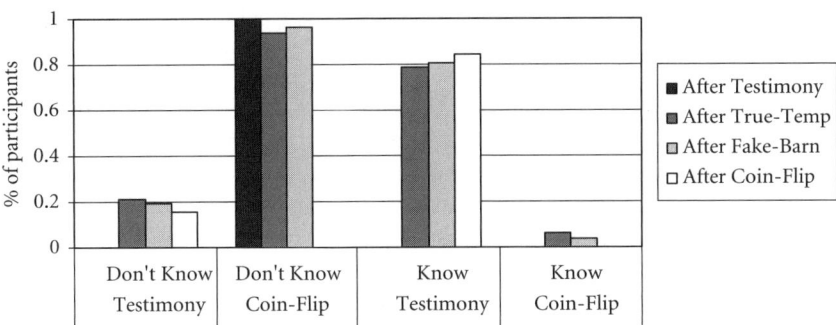

Figure 3.3. Attributions of knowledge in Testimony and Coin-Flip.

Participants' judgments about *Testimony* and *Coin-Flip*, on the other hand, did not display vulnerability to the order effect. Participants were equally likely to attribute knowledge in *Testimony*, regardless of which case immediately preceded (79–84%), χ^2 (2, N = 139) = .50, p = .77. Likewise, participants were equally likely to *fail* to attribute knowledge in *Coin-Flip*, regardless of which case immediately preceded (0–6%), χ^2 (2, N = 133) = 2.50, p = .29 (Fig. 3).

Of central importance is the fact that participants' themselves introspectively tracked this intuitional stability. Paired sample t-tests revealed that participants were significantly more confident in their judgments about *Coin-Flip* (M = 4.4, SE = .06) and *Testimony* (M = 4.5, SE = .06) than they were in their judgments about *True-Temp* (M = 3.9, SE = .09) and *Fake-Barn* (M = 3.9, SE = .08), ts(187) = 5.4 to 6.7, ps <.001, while their confidence did not significantly differ between the two stable and two unstable cases,[3] t(187) = 1.6, p = .11 and t(187) = .27, p = .79, respectively.

And this was true regardless of order in which the cases were presented. Participants expressed higher levels confidence in their judgments for *Coin-Flip*

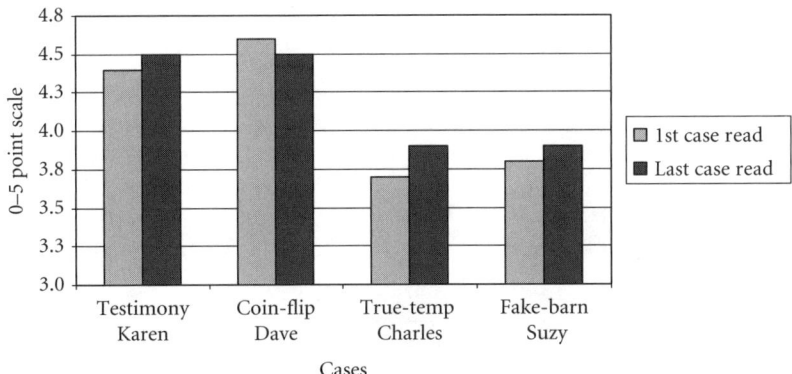

Figure 3.4. Reported confidence in judgments.

and *Testimony* than for *True-Temp* and *Fake-Barn* whether they were the first cases considered (M = 4.6, SE = .17 and M = 4.4, SE = .12 vs. M = 3.7, SE = .17 and M = 3.8, SE = .17, respectively) or the last cases considered (M = 4.5, SE = .12 and M = 4.5, SE = .12 vs. M = 3.9, SE = .20 and M = 3.9, SE = .18, respectively, Fig. 4). Thus, it would appear that participants' confidence served as an introspective indicator of intuitional stability.

To further explore the relationship between stability and confidence, nominal logistic regressions were performed to see if participants' confidence levels could be used to predict which case was being considered. Participants' confidence was regressed as a covariate over the cases (1 = *True-Temp*, 2 = *Fake-Barn*, 3 = *Coin-Flip*, 4 = *Testimony*), with each case functioning as the reference case. Each model revealed confidence to be a strong predictor of stable vs. unstable cases, $\chi^2(3, N = 188) = 26.8, p < .001$.

Specifically, the results show that confidence was a significant predictor of whether the case being considered was stable (*Testimony* or *Coin-Flip*) or unstable (*True-Temp* or *Fake-Barn*). For every 1 unit increase in participants' confidence, the odds of the case being *Testimony* (over *True-Temp*) increased by 203% (or a factor of 2.03), $\chi^2(1) = 9.6, p = .002$, and the odds of the case being *Coin-Flip* (over *True-Temp*) increased by 273%, $\chi^2(1) = 15.4, p < .001$. Changes in confidence did not distinguish between *True-Temp* and *Fake-Barn*, $\chi^2(1) = .134, p = .714$. Likewise, for every 1 unit increase in participants' confidence, the odds of the case being *Fake-Barn* (over *Testimony*) decreased by 53%, $\chi^2(1) = 7.7, p = .005$, but changes in confidence did not distinguish between *Testimony* and *Coin-Flip*, $\chi^2(1) = 1.24, p = .266$.

Framed in terms of probability, as participants' confidence increased, the probability that the case being considered was either *Testimony* or *Coin-Flip*

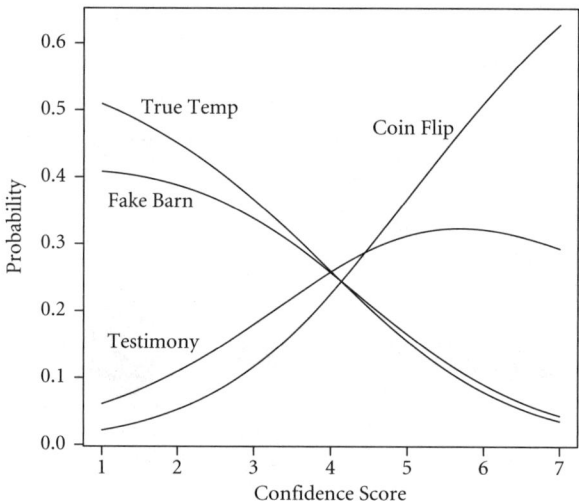

Figure 3.5. Case probabilities at each level of confidence.

increased significantly, from around 5% at a confidence of '1' to about 30% (*Testimony*) to 60% (*Coin-Flip*) at a confidence of '7', and the probability that the case being considered was *True-Temp* or *Fake-Barn* decreased significantly, from about 40% (*Fake-Barn*) to 50% (*True-Temp*) at '1' to around 5% at '7'. The case probabilities merged and became approximately equal at a confidence level of '4' (Fig. 5).

2.3. Discussion

In line with Swain et al. (2008), this first study found participants' knowledge attributions in the *True-Temp* case to be unstable and their fluctuation to be dependent upon which case had been previously considered. The same was true for the *Fake-Barn* case. And, also in line with Swain et al., both *Testimony* and *Coin-Flip* remained stable across the counterbalanced order in which they were presented.

Importantly, participants seemed to be introspectively tracking this instability, reporting significantly more confidence when considering cases that elicited stable judgments than when considering cases that elicited unstable judgments, regardless of order of presentation. As the results from the logistic regressions reflect, the lower participants' confidence, the more likely the case being considered displayed instability—the higher their confidence, the more likely it displayed stability.

Why would participants be vulnerable to bias in only two of the four cases? One reasonable explanation is that, when considering *True-Temp* and *Fake-Barn*, people's intuitions about them were less clear (if, indeed, they had any intuitions about them at all). If so, then it would make sense for participants to turn elsewhere, such as to the case that they had just previously considered, for information that would help to determine their judgment. For example, when considering whether or not *True-Temp*'s mental state should count as knowledge, perhaps participants who saw *Coin-Flip* first were more inclined to say 'yes' because it looks a lot *more* like knowledge than a 'special feeling'. On the other hand, it looks a lot *less* like knowledge than testimony from a top scientific journal. In short, under circumstances where our intuitions are not as clear, it would be natural for us to bring other information to bear on our judgments.

This could also explain why participants' knowledge attributions were not influenced by the preceding cases for either *Testimony* or *Coin-Flip*. As Swain et al. (2008) noted, these cases are 'clear cases'—or what we might call *paradigmatic* cases—of having (or failing to have) knowledge. Arguably, *Testimony* is the sort of case that most people (people with a reasonable degree of conceptual competence[4]) would agree is an instance of 'knowledge', just as *Coin-Flip* is the sort of case that most would agree *fails* to be an instance of 'knowledge'. It is not surprising to find that people's intuitions stabilize around paradigmatic cases—cases that are clear instances of our concepts—and so are not vulnerable to the sorts of biasing factors that Swain and colleagues argue undermines intuition's evidential status.

In order to investigate intuitional stability in more depth, a second study was conducted that expanded upon Study 1 in three ways. First, it introduced additional cases for participants to consider; second, it introduced belief strength as an additional introspective measure of stability. Research on attitude and belief strength has found strongly held beliefs to be more stable over time, more resistant to change, and less sensitive to contextual influences (for reviews see Krosnick & Petty, 1995; Petty & Krosnick, 1995). Thus it was hypothesized that belief strength might serve as another good introspective indicator of stability.

Lastly, perceived consensus was introduced as a (rough) proxy for 'paradigmaticity'. The hypothesis here was that participants would be likely to view clear (paradigmatic) cases as the sorts of cases everyone would agree upon—therefore, the more paradigmatic the case under consideration, the higher the degree of peer consensus they should report. The claim is not that perceived consensus would serve as a measure of *actual* paradigmaticity (which may involve factors outside of mere agreement), but rather that would provide important insight into how paradigmatic people *perceive* the cases they are considering to be.

3. STUDY 2

3.1. Methods

3.1.1. Participants

One hundred and eighty-one undergraduate college students (33 males, 148 females; dominantly Caucasian) from the College of Charleston participated in this study. Participants were recruited through the Introduction to Psychological Science research pool and received research credit for their participation. Ninety-three percentage of the participants had no philosophical training, 6% had taken or were currently were enrolled in Introduction to Philosophy, and 1% in some other undergraduate philosophy course.

3.1.2. Materials and procedure

This time participants were presented with three different sets of cases, nine cases in total (see Appendix). Two of the sets involved cases in epistemology, expanding upon the cases considered in Study 1 (Set 1: *Perception, True-Temp,* and *Coin-Flip*; Set 2: *Testimony, Farmer,* and *Guess*) and one set involved cases in ethics[5] (Set 3: *Break-Promise, Hide-Bombers, Sell-iPod*). Once again, the cases were presented to the participants in a counterbalanced order, though this time the counterbalancing occurred both *within* sets (e.g., Perception/True-Temp/Coin-Flip, True-Temp/Coin-Flip/Perception…) and *between* sets (e.g., Set1/Set2/Set3, Set2/Set3/Set1…). It was anticipated that six of these cases (*Perception, Coin-Flip, Testimony, Guess, Break-Promise,* and *Sell-iPod*) would elicit stable judgments and the other three would elicit unstable judgments.

After reading an epistemology case, participants were asked whether the subject in the case *knew* a specific proposition, to which participants answered YES or NO. After reading an ethics case, they were asked whether the action performed in the case was *morally wrong*, to which they answered YES or NO. Once again, participants were asked to rate on a Likert scale (this time, a 7-point scale in order to provide a neutral midpoint) how confident they were about their answer (1 = not very confident to 7 = very confident). Participants were also asked to rate on a 7-point Likert scale how strongly they believed their answer (1 = not very strongly to 7 = very strongly). Finally, participants were asked a perceived consensus question: If 100 other College of Charleston students were asked the same question, how many do you think would give the same answer you did? (1 = none of them to 7 = all 100 of them). The order of these questions was counterbalanced between participants.

3.2. Results

3.2.1. Preliminary note

There were no gender differences or differences between participants with vs. without philosophical training, so analyses reported below were collapsed across these groups. In addition, all analyses conducted with participants' confidence in Study 1 were replicated and participants' confidence and belief strength ratings were highly correlated across all nine cases (rs=.86 to.99, ps <.001), so for the sake of brevity analyses with confidence are not reported below.

Of the nine cases that participants considered, six (as anticipated) elicited stable intuitions. For *Perception, Coin-Flip, Testimony, Guess, Sell-iPod,* and *Break-Promise*, the order of presentation did not matter. Participants dominantly attributed knowledge in *Perception* (80–90%) and *Testimony* (84–87%) and failed to attribute knowledge in *Coin-Flip* (3%) and *Guess* (0–7%), regardless of order. Participants also dominantly judged the action to be morally wrong in *Sell-iPod* (100%) and not wrong in *Break-Promise* (0–3%), regardless of order. Examining the pattern of participants' answers when each of these cases was immediately preceded by the other cases in its set revealed no significant variation for any of them, $\chi^2 s(1, Ns = 57–61) = 0.0$ to 1.05, $ps = .31–.99$. All of these cases were perceived by participants as being highly paradigmatic (in the sense that participants reported a high degree of agreement in their peers): $Ms = 5.6–6.5$ ($SEs = .06–.09$).

Two of the remaining cases elicited unstable judgments: *True-Temp* and *Hide-Bombers*. Examining the cases in which *True-Temp* was directly preceded by one of the other two cases, the results showed that participants were significantly more likely to say that *True-Temp* knew the temperature immediately after reading *Coin-Flip* (84%) than after reading *Perception* (57%), $\chi^2(1, N = 61) = 5.4$, $p = .020$. Likewise, when reading *Hide-Bombers*, participants were marginally more likely to say that what Hilda did was morally wrong immediately after reading *Sell-iPod* (55%) than after reading *Break-Promise* (32%), $\chi^2(1, N = 60) = 3.2$, $p = .073$ (Fig. 6). These two cases were seen as significantly less paradigmatic than either the stable 'yes' or the stable 'no' cases: Ms. 4.9 and 5.2 ($SEs = .08–.09$), $ts(174–179) = 6.4–13.3$, $ps < .001$.

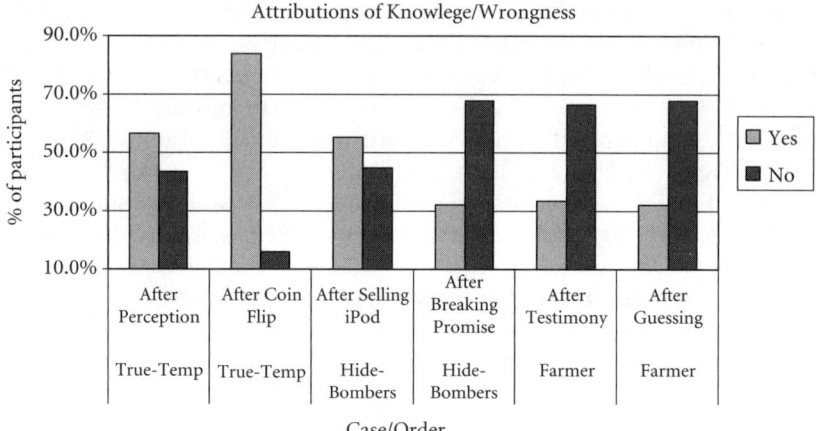

Figure 3.6. Attributions of knowledge/wrongness in True-Temp, Hide-Bombers, and Farmer.

The final case, *Farmer*, was an interesting case. Examining participants' knowledge attributions revealed that it was not unstable, in the sense of demonstrating an order effect, $\chi^2(1, N = 61) = .008$, $p = .93$, but neither was it paradigmatic—as with the unstable cases, participants were strongly divided over whether or not the Farmer knew his cow was in the field, approximately 1/3 saying he did know and 2/3 saying he did not (Fig. 6).

This fact was nicely reflected in participants' reports of paradigmaticity, which for *Farmer* fell significantly *in between* their reported paradigmaticity for the stable vs. unstable epistemology cases: paired-sample *t*-tests showed

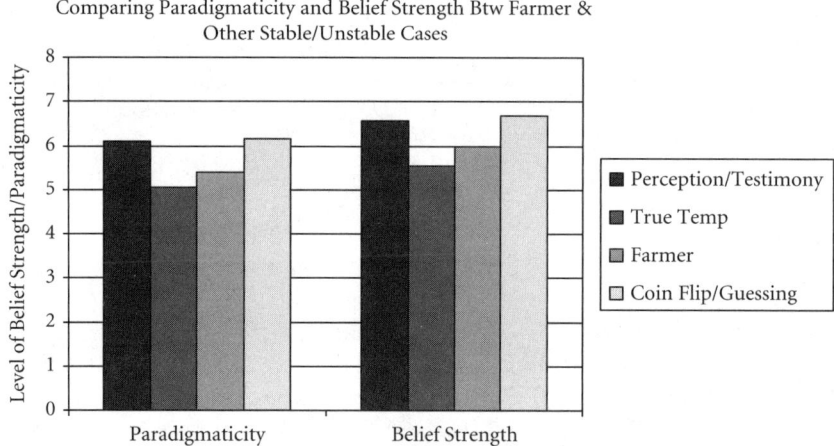

Figure 3.7. Paradigmaticity and belief strength between Farmer vs. Stable/unstable Cases.

perceived consensus for *Farmer* ($M = 5.3$, $SE = .09$) to be lower than their perceived consensus for the stable-yes (*Perception/Testimony*) and stable-no (*Coin-Flip/Guess*) epistemology cases ($Ms = 6.0/5.9$ and $5.6/6.4$, $SEs = .07-.09$, respectively), $ts(178) = 2.0-7.7$, ps from $.05$ to $<.001$, and yet higher than the unstable (*True-Temp*) epistemology case ($M = 4.9$, $SE = .08$), $t(177) = 5.2$, $p <.001$ (Fig. 7).

Interestingly, participants' belief strength showed a similar pattern: paired-sample t-tests revealed that participants' belief strength for *Farmer* ($M = 5.9$, $SE = .09$) was significantly lower than for the stable-yes (*Perception/Testimony*) and stable-no (*Coin-Flip/Guess*) epistemology cases ($Ms = 6.5/6.3$ and $6.4/6.7$, $SEs = .05-.07$, respectively), $ts(178) = 3.5-9.2$, $ps = <.001$, but also significantly higher than for the unstable (*True-Temp*) case ($M = 5.4$, $SE = .10$), $t(178) = 5.3$, $p <.001$ (Fig. 7). Given that participants' introspective judgments appear to be locating *Farmer* in between the stable and unstable cases, it will be heretofore referred to as an 'intermediate' case.

More generally, a within-subjects ANOVA with stability (stable-yes, unstable/intermediate, stable-no) and set (epist1, epist2, ethics) as within-subjects factors revealed that participants' belief strength was significantly higher for the stable cases than for the unstable/intermediate cases across all three sets, $F(2,346) = 87.7$, $p <.001$, $\eta^2 = .34$.

Importantly, this suggests that the same general relationship between stability and confidence also holds for stability and belief strength—and that it does so across multiple sets of cases, both epistemological and ethical. But does this mean that belief strength, like confidence, can be used to predict case? To investigate this, nominal logistic regressions (separate for each set) were performed with belief strength as the covariate over case (Set 1: 1 = *Perception*, 2 = *Coin-Flip*, 3 = *True-Temp*; Set 2: 1 = *Testimony*, 2 = *Guess*, 3 = *Farmer*; Set 3: 1 = *Sell iPod*, 2 = *Break-Promise*, 3 = *Hide-Bombers*).

For Set 1, belief strength was a strong predictor of stable vs. unstable cases, $\chi^2(2, N = 179) = 62.1$, $p <.001$. For every 1 unit increase in participants' belief strength, the odds of the case being *Perception* (over *True-Temp*) increased by 302% (or a factor of 3.02), $\chi^2(1) = 31.7$, $p <.001$, and the odds of the case being *Coin-Flip* (over *True-Temp*) increased by 272%, $\chi^2(1) = 28.7$, $p <.001$. As expected, belief strength was not predictive between *Perception* and *Coin-Flip*, $\chi^2(1) = .30$, $p = .584$.

Framed in terms of probability, as participants' belief strength increased, the probability that they were considering *True-Temp* dropped significantly, from almost 100% at a belief strength of '1' to around 10% at a belief strength of '7'. Likewise, as belief strength increased, the probability that they were considering either *Perception* or *Coin-Flip* increased, from almost 0% at '1' to around 45% at '7'. The case probabilities merged and became approximately equal between '5' and '6' (Fig. 8).

For Set 2, belief strength was a strong predictor of all three cases, $\chi^2(2, N = 180) = 31.5$, $p <.001$. For every 1 unit increase in participants' belief strength, the odds of the case being *Testimony* (over *Farmer*) increased by

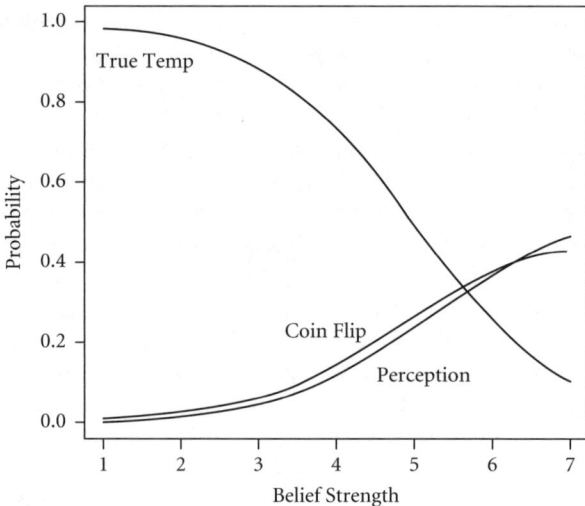

Figure 3.8. Set 1 case probabilities at each level of belief strength.

148%, $\chi^2(1) = 6.7, p = .010$, and the odds of the case being *Guess* (over *Farmer*) increased by 292%, $\chi^2(1) = 20.7, p <.001$. And for every 1 unit increase in participants' belief strength, the odds of the case being *Guess* (over *Testimony*) increased by 197%, $\chi^2(1) = 8.2, p = .004$.

As participants' belief strength increased, the probability that they were considering *Farmer* dropped significantly, from around 85% at a belief strength of

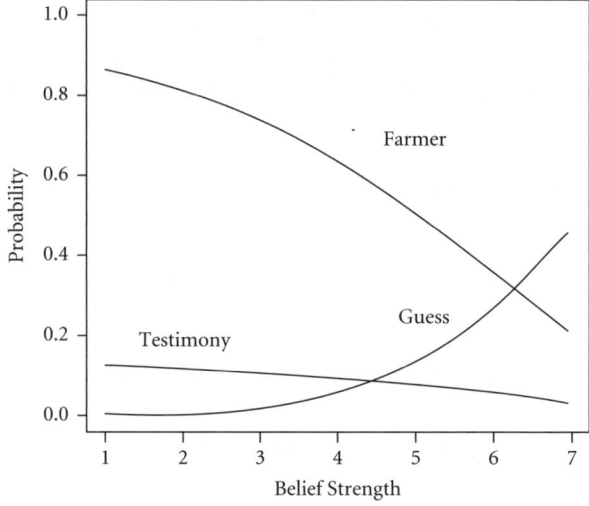

Figure 3.9. Set 2 case probabilities at each level of belief strength.

'1' to around 20% at a belief strength of '7'. Likewise, as belief strength increased, the probability that they were considering *Guess* or *Testimony* increased, from around 0% (*Guess*) to 15% (*Testimony*) at '1' to around 30% (*Testimony*) to 50% (*Guess*) at '7'. The case probabilities in this set never fully merged (Fig. 9).

Finally, for Set 3, belief strength was once again a strong predictor of stable vs. unstable cases, $\chi^2(2, N = 176) = 73.8, p < .001$. For every 1 unit increase in participants' belief strength, the odds of the case being *Sell-iPod* (over *Hide-Bombers*) increased by 903%, $\chi^2(1) = 21.0, p < .001$, and the odds of the case being *Break-Promise* (over *Hide-Bombers*) increased by 411%, $\chi^2(1) = 21.3, p < .001$. Belief strength was not predictive between *Sell-iPod* and *Break Promise*, $\chi^2(1) = 2.5, p = .110$. As participants' belief strength increased, the probability that they were considering *Hide-Bombers* decreased, from almost 100% at a belief strength of '1' to around 10% at '7', while the probability of the case being either *Sell-iPod* or *Break-Promise* increased from almost 0% at '1' to around 45% at '7'. The case probabilities merged and became approximately equal around '6' (Fig. 10).

Participants' perception of paradigmaticity was also predictive of case in all three sets. In Set 1, every 1 unit increase in peer consensus increased the odds that the case being *Perception* (over *True-Temp*) by 470%, $\chi^2(1) = 37.3, p < .001$, and increased the odds that the case was *Coin-Flip* (over *True-Temp*) by 195%, $\chi^2(1) = 10.5, p = .001$. It also decreased the odds that the case being considered was *Coin-Flip* (over *Perception*) by 42%, $\chi^2(1) = 15.7, p < .001$.

In Set 2, every 1 unit increase in consensus increased the odds of the case being *Testimony* (over *Farmer*) by 162%, $\chi^2(1) = 10.0, p = .002$, and increased the odds of the case being *Guess* (over *Farmer*) by 238%, $\chi^2(1) = 22.6, p < .001$.

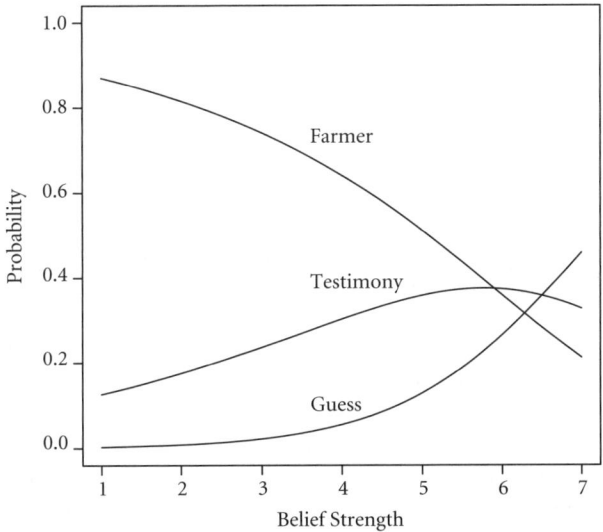

Figure 3.10. Set 3 case probabilities at each level of belief strength.

It also increased the odds that the case being considered was *Testimony* (over *Guess*) by 147%, $\chi^2(1) = 4.7$, $p = .035$.

Finally, in Set 3 every 1 unit increase in consensus increased the odds of the case being *Sell-iPod* (over *Hide-Bombers*) by 353%, $\chi^2(1) = 29.2$, $p < .001$, and increased the odds of the case being *Break-Promise* (over *Hide-Bombers*) by 413%, $\chi^2(1) = 32.6$, $p < .001$. Consensus was not predictive between *Sell-iPod* and *Break-Promise*, $\chi^2(1) = .44$, $p = .51$.

On a final note, when either confidence or belief strength are entered into logistic regression equations alongside paradigmaticity (multicollinearity issues make it problematic to enter confidence and belief strength together), each variable remains predictive of stable vs. unstable cases in Sets 1 and 3 (ps between $<.001$ and $.042$), while only paradigmaticity is significant in Set 2 ($p = .001$ for paradigmaticity, $p = .20$ for confidence; $p = .019$ for paradigmaticity, $p = .11$ for belief strength), perhaps because Set 2 contains the intermediate case. Thus, paradigmaticity, on the one hand, and confidence/belief strength, on the other, appear to be independently predictive of intuitional instability.

4. GENERAL DISCUSSION

The worry introduced by Swain et al. (2008) is that philosophers' reliance on intuitions in argumentation for/against particular theses and theoretical positions is problematic because at least some of those intuitions are epistemically vulnerable to irrational biases like the order effect. This worry gets its teeth not primarily because of the sheer number of intuitions that could be vulnerable, but more importantly because of our supposed inability to anticipate (and protect against) this vulnerability. The thought is that we lack reliable methods by which to track intuitional instability—and, therefore, we cannot know when our intuitions are being negatively impacted by it and when they are not.

Contrary to this claim, the studies reported here suggest that there *are* ways for us to anticipate intuitional instability—in fact, several different (though related) ways. For one, the participants in both studies clearly experienced more confidence in their answers when considering stable cases than when considering unstable cases, regardless of whether those cases involved the application of epistemological or ethical concepts. In addition, participants had significantly stronger beliefs (or, held their beliefs more strongly) about the stable cases than about the unstable cases.

Indeed, both confidence and belief strength were good predictors of whether the case being considered was stable or unstable. This is interesting because while confidence seems a more purely cognitive construct—the degree to which you experience conceptual clarity or certainty—belief strength is often treated as more of an affective construct, sometimes being employed in research paradigms as a proxy for things like 'attitude extremity' and 'emotional intensity' (e.g., Wright, Cullum, & Schwab, 2008). And it seems possible for a person to have a high degree of confidence in a belief they do not hold particularly strongly: my son and I could both be highly confident in our shared belief that the Pittsburg Steelers emerged as the best team in the NFL in 2009, but because he is such an avid football fan, he might hold that belief much more strongly (in the sense that it would be more important to him, etc.) than I. It also seems that people could be *very confident in x* and *believe very strongly in x* for different reasons: someone could be very confident in his belief that our country should make healthcare reform its top priority because of a variety of expert financial analyses he'd read, but then hold this belief very strongly because of a political/philosophical belief that people deserve equal access to healthcare. These potential differences between the two constructs aside, both clearly (and similarly) tracked with intuitional stability.

As mentioned above, one important factor behind the stability of particular cases may be their relative paradigmaticity—that is, the degree to which they represent clear instances of the concept(s) in question. In the epistemological cases participants considered, the concept in question was 'knowledge': whether the subjects *knew* or *did not know* some particular proposition. And some things strike us as clear examples of knowledge (e.g., beliefs gained through direct perceptual observation under ideal conditions), while some things strike us as clearly *not* knowledge (e.g., randomly guessing the answer to a question, even if you happened to guess the correct answer). In the ethical cases participants were asked whether or not an action was *morally wrong*. Here again, some things strike us as clearly morally wrong (e.g., stealing something of value that is not yours for frivolous reasons), just as some things strike us as clearly *not* morally wrong (e.g., breaking a promise involving a minor obligation because a loved one is in danger). When considering cases such as these, it is less likely that outside factors, such as cases previously considered, will influence our judgments than when we consider difficult borderline (or just otherwise confusing) cases.

Importantly, participants displayed awareness of paradigmaticity (at least insofar as perceived consensus serves as a legitimate measure). The degree of peer consensus that participants reported was strongly related to case stability and participants' peer consensus reports accurately identified between the stable, intermediate, and unstable cases. The stable cases were viewed as being the sorts of cases everyone would agree upon, whereas the unstable and intermediate cases were viewed as more open for disagreement (the unstable cases even more so than the intermediate case).

Collectively, these results suggest two things. First, they suggest that people are able to introspectively track—and thus potentially protect against—their vulnerability to (at least some forms of) bias. If those intuitive judgments people feel less confident and strongly about are more vulnerable to potentially biasing 'outside influences' (or if those cases that are vulnerable to bias are cases that people feel less confident and strongly about), then we can take care with the circumstances under which we elicit intuitions about those cases; we can control exposure to potentially biasing influences. We can also treat such intuitive judgments with caution, granting them less epistemic weight in philosophical/

theoretical discourse. Importantly, I would argue that most philosophers and scientists already do this, treating clear/strong intuitions (especially their own) more seriously than unclear/weak ones. Perhaps such efforts could be made more thoughtful and explicit, but I doubt that this would require any drastic changes to current philosophical/theoretical practice.

Second, the results suggest that the more paradigmatic the case, the less vulnerable it will be to (at least some forms of) bias. Again, this seems relatively unsurprising. Clear cases of any particular concept are precisely that: *clear* cases. Our judgments about them, barring substantial conceptual revolution, are unlikely to change. Of course, philosophy is often most interesting (and of most value) when it is working 'at the margins', wrestling with unclear and borderline cases. And this raises Swain et al.'s (2008) worry once again: does this render a potentially extensive area of philosophical debate epistemically vulnerable, philosophers being unable to rely on their intuitions without worry of bias?

This is an important consideration (especially when difficult, non-paradigmatic cases are often where philosophers' rely most heavily on their intuitions), but it seems unlikely to represent an insurmountable problem for several reasons. First, philosophers clearly can (and do) have clear/strong intuitions about non-paradigmatic cases. Such cases, while perhaps vulnerable to bias for the general population of reasonably conceptually competent people (such as the participants in the studies reported here), may nonetheless be stable for most philosophers. After all, philosophers receive extensive training designed specifically to refine and enhance their conceptual mastery. Such training gives philosophers a greater capacity for discrimination when it comes to concept application (e.g., whether something counts as an instance of knowledge) and, therefore, they may be able to see difficult cases more clearly, and more difficult cases clearly, than the philosophical novice—not unlike learning the difference between *Quercus rubra* (Northern Red Oak) and *Quercus alba* (Pin Oak), which thereafter gives one the ability to distinguish between trees that before that seemed indistinguishable.

What is more, the very process of engaging in philosophical discourse may ultimately *generate* new conceptual clarity where before there was conceptual confusion.[6] That is, the practice of philosophical and theoretical discourse itself may expand and refine our range of conceptual competence, both because of the learning that occurs in the individual and also because of the collective advancement that results for the discipline.

Of course, it is important to note that what confidence and belief strength track with is intuitional stability—not intuitional *accuracy*. Research suggests that people are notoriously overconfident in their judgments across a wide variety of contexts (Arkes, 2001; Einhorn & Hogarth, 1978; Kahneman & Klein, 2009). And, more to the point, simply having clear/strong intuitions does not guarantee that they are also veridical: intuitions are not infallible (and few, if any, philosophers think that they are). Thus, we must be careful not to mistake high degrees of confidence/belief strength as being indicators that we have gotten it right.

What is more, every scientist and philosopher must at some point encounter the line between looking for the theory that best fits one's data and looking at the data in a way that best fits one's theory. The latter is always a danger—and, likewise, there is always the danger that people's intuitions will be biased by the very training and theoretical advancement that resulted in their heightened conceptual clarity. But, this was not the problem for philosophical intuition that was raised by Swain et al. (2008)—and thus, not the problem the studies reported here were designed to address. And the good news is that whatever epistemically suspect reasons (e.g., unwarranted theoretical commitments) for intuitional stability that may exist, intuitional instability is *one* worry that we do not need to be too worried about.

APPENDIX A

A.1. STUDY 1 CASES

COIN-FLIP: Dave likes to play a game with flipping a coin. He sometimes gets a 'special feeling' that the next flip will come out heads. When he gets this 'special feeling', he is right about half the time, and wrong about half the time. Just before the next flip, Dave gets that 'special feeling', and the feeling leads him to believe that the coin will land heads. He flips the coin, and it does land heads.

TRUE-TEMP: One day Charles was knocked out by a falling rock; as a result his brain was 'rewired' so that he is always right whenever he estimates the temperature where he is. Charles is unaware that his brain has been altered in this way. A few weeks later, this brain rewiring leads him to believe that it is 71 degrees in his room. Apart from his estimation, he has no other reasons to think that it is 71 degrees. In fact, it is 71 degrees.

FAKE-BARN: Suzy looks out the window of her car and sees a barn near the road, and so she comes to believe that there's a barn near the road. However, Suzy doesn't realize that the countryside she is driving through is currently being used as the set of a film, and that the set designers have constructed many Fake-Barn facades in this area that look as though they are real barns. In fact, Suzy is looking at the only real barn in the area.

TESTIMONY: Karen is a distinguished professor of chemistry. This morning, she read an article in a leading scientific journal that mixing two common floor disinfectants, Cleano Plus and Washaway, will create a poisonous gas that is deadly to humans. In fact, the article is correct: mixing the two products does create a poisonous gas. At noon, Karen sees a janitor mixing Cleano Plus and Washaway and yells to him, 'Get away! Mixing those two products creates a poisonous gas'!

A.2. Study 2 Cases

A.2.1. Set 1: epistemic vignettes

> CLEAR YES (Perception): Pat walks into her kitchen during the day when the lighting was good and there was nothing interfering with her vision. She sees a red apple sitting on the counter, where she had left it after buying it at the grocery store the day before. As she leaves home, she tells her son, Joe, that there is a red apple sitting on the kitchen counter and to make sure to pack it with his lunch.
>
> CLEAR NO (Coin-Flip): Dave likes to play a game with flipping a coin. He sometimes gets a 'special feeling' that the next flip will come out heads. When he gets this 'special feeling', he is right about half the time, and wrong about half the time. Just before the next flip, Dave gets that 'special feeling', and the feeling leads him to believe that the coin will land heads. He flips the coin, and it does land heads.
>
> NOT CLEAR (True-Temp): Suppose Charles undergoes brain surgery by an experimental surgeon who invents a small device which is both a very accurate thermometer and a computational device capable of generating thoughts. The device, called a tempucomp, is implanted in Charles' head so that the very tip of the device, no larger than the head of a pin, sits unnoticed on his scalp and acts as a sensor to transmit information about the temperature to the computational system of his brain. This device, in turn, sends a message to his brain causing him to think of the temperature recorded by the external sensor. Assume that the tempucomp is very reliable, and so his thoughts are correct temperature thoughts. All told, this is a reliable belief-forming process. Charles has no idea that the tempucomp has been inserted in his brain, is only slightly puzzled about why he thinks so obsessively about the temperature, but never checks a thermometer to determine whether these thoughts about the temperature are correct. He accepts them unreflectively, another effect of the tempucomp. Thus, at a particular moment in time he thinks and accepts that the temperature is 71 degrees—and it is, in fact, 71 degrees.

A.2.2. Set 2: epistemic vignettes

> CLEAR YES (Testimony): Karen is a distinguished professor of chemistry. This morning, she read an article in a leading scientific journal that mixing two common floor disinfectants, Cleano Plus and Washaway, will create a poisonous gas that is deadly to humans. In fact, the article is correct: mixing the two products does create a poisonous gas. At noon, Karen sees a janitor mixing Cleano Plus and Washaway and yells to him, 'Get away! Mixing those two products creates a poisonous gas'!
>
> CLEAR NO (Guess): Laura's math teacher asks everyone to perform a difficult math problem. Laura realizes that she has no idea how to

do the problem and so she just sits there and doodles. After about a minute, the math teacher asks Laura to report to the class what answer she had gotten. Not knowing what else to do, Laura blurts out '35' as a completely random guess. As it turns out, this is the correct answer and the teacher congratulates Laura for a job well done.

NOT CLEAR (Farmer): Farmer Field is concerned about his prize cow, Daisy, whom he put out into a field to graze earlier that morning. In fact, he is so concerned that he goes out to the field to check on her periodically. Standing by the gate, he sees in the distance, behind some trees, a white and black shape that he recognizes as his favorite cow. He goes back home and tells his friend, the dairyman, that he knows that Daisy is in the field, grazing happily. Yet when the dairyman leaves to go home, he walks by the field and notices that even though Daisy is in fact in the field just as Farmer Field thought, she is actually napping in a hollow, behind a bush, well out of sight of the gate (and of Farmer Field). He then also spots a large piece of black and white cardboard that has got caught in a tree, making it look like Daisy is standing there.

A.2.3. Set 3: Ethical vignettes

CLEAR NO (Break-Promise): Fred promises his girlfriend that he will meet her for lunch at 12 pm on Wednesday at their favorite café. Wednesday at 11:45 am, on his way to the café, Fred runs into his grandfather, who is out for a stroll. They exchange hellos, and then suddenly Fred's grandfather clutches his chest and falls to the ground unconscious. An ambulance arrives minutes later to take Fred's grandfather to the hospital. Fred accompanies his grandfather to the hospital, even though he knows that doing so means that he will be breaking his promise to have lunch with his girlfriend.

CLEAR YES (Sell-iPod): Laura and Suzy are roommates. Laura asks Suzy if she has seen her new iPod, which she had worked an extra job over the summer to be able to afford. Suzy did recently see it under a pile of papers on the bookshelf. But Suzy lies to Laura, telling her that she hasn't seen it. She thinks that if Laura doesn't find it on her own in a day or two, she can take it down to the pawn shop and get $100 for it, which would provide her with beer money for the week.

UNCLEAR (Hide-Bombers): Martha hides her Jewish neighbors in her basement during the Nazi occupation of France. A German soldier comes to her door one afternoon and asks her if she knows where her neighbors have gone. Martha knows that her neighbors are wanted by the Germans for bombing a German-only schoolyard and killing several children, injuring others. Martha lies to the soldier, telling them no, she hasn't seen them recently, but she believes that they fled the country.

NOTES

1. For instance, intuition has been implicated in linguistics (Chomsky, 1988; Devitt, 2006; Hintikka, 2001), rapid judgment and decision making (Griffin & Tversky, 1992; Hammond, 1996; Kahneman & Tversky, 1982; Klienmutz, 1990; Plessner, Betsch, & Betsch, 2007; Sloman, 1996), insight and problem-solving (Bowers, Farvolden, & Mermigis, 1995; Bowers, Regehr, & Balthazard, 1990; Dorfman et al., 1996; Sternberg & Davidson, 1995), implicit learning (Reber, 1989, 1993), expertise (Dreyfus & Dreyfus, 1986, 1991), social cognition (Haidt, 2001; Osbeck, 2001; Seung, 1993), scientific theory-building (Goldman & Pust, 1997; Monsay, 1999), and even medicine (King & Appleton, 1997; Miller, 1995; Ubel & Loewenstein, 1997).

2. It is important to note that this concern about intuition's 'epistemic' status could be targeting several things, including intuition's rational, justificatory, and/or evidential status. Thanks to John Bengson for clarifying this issue.

3. Here I am using 'stable/unstable cases' as shorthand for cases that elicit stable vs. unstable intuitions—that is, strictly speaking, it is the intuitions that are stable (or unstable), not the cases.

4. It is important to distinguish here between conceptual *competence* and *accuracy*. While the hope is that most of the time these two will go together—that is, the competent use of our concepts will usually result in us getting things *right*—it seems nonetheless possible for them to come apart. We could envision two cultures, for instance (one whose beliefs about the nature of the universe are grounded by contemporary scientific/philosophical theory and another whose beliefs are grounded in ancient mythological lore) that might employ the concept 'knowledge' differently. Taking *Coin-Flip* as an example, while the first culture would hold that this clearly fails to count as an instance of knowledge, the latter might hold that it just as clearly counts, since Dave's 'special feeling' indicates the presence of a psychic ability (or something along those lines). While we may certainly want to say that the latter culture fails to adequately grasp the concept of knowledge (and, as such, their use of the concept in *Coin-Flip* is mistaken), we may nonetheless want to grant them conceptual competence, given that it seems reasonable to attribute knowledge to *Coin-Flip* when your belief system holds that psychic abilities (the presence of which is indicated by a 'special feeling') exist. Especially since what we are interested in here is people's intuitional *stability*, not accuracy, this issue seems important to keep in mind. Indeed, such variation in underlying belief systems may help to explain the cultural variability in intuitions found by Machery et al. (2004) and elsewhere.

5. Zamzow and Nichols (2009) found that confidence tracked instability in a set of classic ethical dilemmas (*Bystander, Scan, Transplant*) and so the inclusion of some ethical cases in Study 2 seemed prudent.

6. Perhaps philosophical training actually expands the range of paradigmaticity—that is, through philosophical and theoretical advancement, cases that were once non-paradigmatic become paradigmatic (or cases that are non-paradigmatic for some become paradigmatic for others).

REFERENCES

Alexander, J., & Weinberg, J. (2007). Analytic epistemology and experimental philosophy. *Philosophy Compass*, 2(1), 56–80.

Arkes, H. R. (2001). Overconfidence in judgment forecasting. In J. S. Armstrong (Ed.), *Principles of forecasting: A handbook for researchers and practitioners* (pp. 495–516). Boston: Kluwer Academic.

Audi, R. (2004). *The good and the right: A theory of intuition and intrinsic value.* Princeton, NJ: Princeton University Press.
Bartsch, K., & Wright, J. C. (2005). Towards an intuitionist account of moral development [commentary]. *Behavioral and Brain Sciences, 28,* 546–547.
Bealer, G. (1992). The incoherence of empiricism. *Aristotelian Society: Supplementary Volume, 66,* 99–138.
Bealer, G. (1999). Intuition and the autonomy of philosophy. In M. DePaul & W. Ramsey (Eds.), *Rethinking intuition: The psychology of intuition and its role in philosophical inquiry* (pp. 201–239). Lanham, MD: Rowman and Littlefield.
Bealer, G. (2000). A theory of the a priori. *Pacific Philosophical Quarterly, 811,* 1–30.
Bealer, G. (2002). Model epistemology and the rationalist renaissance. In T. Gendler (Ed.), *Conceivability and possibility* (pp. 71–125). Oxford: Oxford University Press.
Bealer, G. (2004). The origins of modal error. *Dialectica: International Journal of Philosophy of Knowledge, 581,* 11–42.
Bonjour, L. (1998). *In defense of pure reason.* Cambridge: Cambridge University Press.
Bowers, K., Farvolden, P., & Mermigis, L. (1995). Intuitive antecedents of insight. In S. Smith & T. Ward (Eds.), *The creative cognition approach.* Cambridge, MA: Bradford/MIT Press. 27–53.
Bowers, K., Regehr, G., & Balthazard, C. (1990). Intuition in the context of discovery. *Cognitive Psychology, 22,* 72–100.
Brown, J. (2006). Contextualism and warranted assertibility manoeuvres. *Philosophical Studies, 130,* 407–435.
Casullo, A. (2003). *A priori justification.* Oxford: Oxford University Press.
Chomsky, N. (1988). *The minimalist program.* Cambridge, MA: The MIT Press.
Claxton, G. (1998). Investigating human intuition: Knowing without knowing why. *The Psychologist, 115,* 217–220.
Cummins, R. (1998). Reflections on reflective equilibrium. In M. DePaul & W. Ramsey (Eds.), *Rethinking intuition: The psychology of intuition and its role in philosophical inquiry.* Lanham, MD: Rowman and Littlefield. 113–128.
Dancy, J. (1991). Intuitionism. In P. Singer (Ed.), *A companion to ethics.* Cambridge: Blackwell Publishing. 411–420.
Dancy, J. (2006). *Ethics without principles.* Oxford: Oxford University Press.
Denes-Raj, V., & Epstein, S. (1994). Conflict between intuitive and rational processing: When people behave against their better judgment. *Journal of Personality and Social Psychology, 665,* 819–829.
Devitt, M. (2006). Intuitions in linguistics. *British Journal for the Philosophy of Science, 57*(3), 481–513.
Dorfman, J., Shames, V., & Kilstrom, J. (1996). Intuition, incubation, and insight: Implicit cognition in problem solving. In G. Underwood (Ed.), *Implicit cognition* (pp. 257–296). Oxford: Oxford University Press.
Dreyfus, H., & Dreyfus, S. (1986). *Mind over machine: The power of human intuition and expertise in the era of the computer.* New York: The Free Press.
Dreyfus, H., & Dreyfus, S. (1991). Towards a phenomenology of moral expertise. *Human Studies, 14,* 229–250.
Einhorn, H. J., & Hogarth, R. M. (1978). Confidence in judgment: Persistence of the illusion of validity. *Psychological Review, 85,* 395–416.
Epstein, S., Lipson, A., Holstein, C., & Huh, E. (1992). Irrational reaction to negative outcome: Evidence for two conceptual systems. *Journal of Personality and Social Psychology, 62,* 328–339.

Gendler, T. (2007). Philosophical thought experiments, intuitions, and cognitive equilibrium. *Midwest Studies in Philosophy, 31*(1), 68–89.
Goldman, A., & Pust, J. (1997). Philosophical theory and intuitional evidence. In M. DePaul & W. Ramsey (Eds.), *Rethinking intuition: The psychology of intuition and its role in philosophical inquiry* (pp. 179–200). Lanham, MD: Rowman and Littlefield.
Griffin, D., & Tversky, A. (1992). The weighing of evidence and the determinants of confidence. *Cognitive Psychology, 243*, 411–435.
Haidt, J. (2001). The emotional dog and its rational tail: A social intuitionist approach to moral judgment. *Psychological Review, 108*(4), 814–834.
Haidt, J., & Joseph, C. (2004). Intuitive ethics: How innately prepared intuitions generate culturally variable virtues. *Daedalus, 133*(4) 55–66.
Hammond, K. (1996). *Human judgment and social policy.* New York: Oxford University Press.
Hintikka, J. (1999). The emperor's new intuitions. *Journal of Philosophy, 96*(3), 127–147.
Hintikka, J. (2001). Intuitionistic logic as epistemic logic. *Synthese, 127*(1–2), 7–19.
Huemer, M. (2006). *Ethical intuitionism.* NewYork: Palgrave Macmillian.
Jackson, F. (1994). Metaphysics by possible cases. *Monist, 771*, 93–111.
Jackson, F. (1998). *From metaphysics to ethics: A defence of conceptual analysis.* Oxford: Oxford University Press.
Kahneman, D., & Klein, G. (2009). Conditions for intuitive expertise: A failure to disagree. *American Psychologist, 64*(6), 515–526.
Kahneman, D., & Tversky, A. (1982). On the study of statistical intuitions. *Cognition, 11*, 123–141.
King, L., & Appleton, J. (1997). Intuition: A critical review of the research and rhetoric. *Journal of Advanced Nursing, 26*, 194–202.
Klienmutz, B. (1990). Why we will use our heads instead of formulas: Towards an integrative approach. *Psychological Bulletin, 1073*, 296–310.
Kornblith, H. (1999). The role of intuition in philosophical inquiry: An account with no unnatural ingredients. In M. DePaul & W. Ramsey (Eds.), *Rethinking intuition: The psychology of intuition and its role in philosophical inquiry* (pp. 129–142). Lanham, MD: Rowman and Littlefield.
Krosnick, J. A., & Petty, R. E. (1995). Attitude strength: An overview. In R. E. Petty & J. A. Krosnick (Eds.), *Attitude strength: Antecedents and consequences* (pp. 1–24). Hillsdale, NJ: Erlbaum.
Laio, M. (2008). A defense of intuitions. *Philosophical Studies, 140*(2), 247–262.
Laughlin, C. (1997). The nature of intuition: A neuropsychological approach. In R. Davis-Floyd & P. Arvidson (Eds.), *Intuition: The inside story* (pp. 19–38). New York: Routledge.
Lehrer, K. (1990). *Theory of knowledge.* Boulder, CO: Westview Press.
Machery, E., Mallon, R., Nichols, S., & Stich, S. (2004). Semantics, cross-cultural style. *Cognition, 923*, 1–12.
Macnamara, J. (1991). The development of moral reasoning and the foundation of geometry. *Journal for the Theory of Social Behavior, 212*, 125–150.
Miller, V. (1995). Characteristics of intuitive nurses. *Western Journal of Nursing Research, 173*, 305–316.
Monsay, E. (1999). Intuition in the development of scientific theory and practice. In R. Davis-Floyd & P. Arvidson (Eds.), *Intuition: The inside story* (pp. 103–120). New York: Routledge.
Nagel, J. (2007). Epistemic intuitions. *Philosophy Compass, 2*(6), 792–819.

Nichols, S., & Knobe, J. (2007). Moral responsibility and determinism: The cognitive science of folk intuitions. *Nous, 41*(4), 663–685.
Nichols, S., Stich, S., & Weinberg, J. (2003). Metaskepticism: Meditations in ethno-epistemology. In S. Luper (Ed.), *The skeptics* (pp. 227–247). Burlington, VT:Ashgate Publishing.
Nisbett, R. E., Peng, K., Choi, I., & Norenzayan, A. (2001). Culture and systems of thought: Holistic versus analytic cognition. *Psychological Review, 1082*, 291–310.
Osbeck, L. (1999). Conceptual problems in the development of a psychological notion of 'intution'. *Journal for the Theory of Social Behavior, 293*, 229–250.
Osbeck, L. (2001). Direct apprehension and social construction: Revisiting the concept of intuition. *Journal of Theoretical and Philosophical Psychology, 212*, 118–131.
Parsons, C. (1986). Intuition in constructive mathematics. In J. Butterfield (Ed.), *Language, mind, and logic* (pp. 211–229). Cambridge: Cambridge University Press.
Parsons, C. (2000). Reason and intuition. *Synthese, 1253*, 299–315.
Petty, R., & Krosnick, J. (Eds.). (1995). *Attitude strength: Antecedents and consequences.* Hillsdale, NJ: Lawrence Erlbaum Associates.
Plessner, H., Betsch, C., & Betsch, T. (Eds.). (2007). *Intuition in judgment and decision making.* Mahwah, NJ: Lawrence Erlbaum.
Pust, J. (2000). *Intuitions as evidence.* New York: Garland.
Pust, J. (2004). On explaining knowledge of necessity. *Dialectica, 58*(1), 71–87.
Redelmeier, D., & Shafir, E. (1995). Medical decision making in situations that offer multiple alternatives. *Journal of the American Medical Association, 273*, 302–305.
Reber, A. (1989). Implicit learning and tacit knowledge. *Journal of Experimental Psychology: General, 1183*, 219–235.
Reber, A. (1993). *Implicit learning and tacit knowledge: An essay on the cognitive unconscious.* New York: Oxford University Press.
Seung, T. (1993). *Intuition and construction.* New Haven, CT: Yale University Press.
Shafir, E. (1999). Philosophical intuitions and cognitive mechanisms. In M. DePaul & W. Ramsey (Eds.), *Rethinking intuition: The psychology of intuition and its role in philosophical inquiry* (pp. 59–74). Lanham, MD: Rowman and Littlefield.
Sloman, S. (1996). The empirical case for two systems of reasoning. *Psychological Bulletin, 1191*, 3–22.
Sosa, D. (2006). Scepticism about intuition. *Philosophy, 81*, 633–647.
Sosa, E. (1999). Minimal Intuition. In M. DePaul & W. Ramsey (Eds.), *Rethinking intuition: The psychology of intuition and its role in philosophical inquiry* (pp. 257–270). Lanham, MD: Rowman and Littlefield.
Sosa, E. (2000). Replies. *Nous, 10*, 38–42.
Sosa, E. (2005). A defense of intuitions. In M. Bishop & D. Murphy (Eds.), *Stich and his critics.* Blackwell Publishers.
Sosa, E. (2007a). Intuitions: Their nature and epistemic efficacy. *Grazer Philosophische Studien, 74*, 51–67.
Sosa, E. (2007b). Experimental philosophy and philosophical intuition. *Philosophical Studies, 132*, 99–107.
Sternberg, R. J., & Davidson, J. E. (Eds.). (1995). *The nature of insight.* Cambridge, MA: Bradford/MIT Press.
Swain, S., Alexander, J., & Weinberg, J. (2008). The instability of philosophical intuitions: Running hot and cold on true-temp. *Philosophy and Phenomenological Research, 76*(1), 138–155.

Tversky, A., & Kahneman, D. (1974). Judgment under uncertainty: Heuristics and biases. *Science, 185,* 1124–1130.
Ubel, P., & Loewenstein, G. (1997). The role of decision analysis in informed consent: Choosing between intuition and automaticity. *Social Science and Medicine, 445,* 647–656.
Weinberg, J. (2007). How to challenge intuitions empirically without raising skepticism. *Midwest Studies in Philosophy, 31*(1), 318–343.
Weinberg, J., Nichols, S., & Stich, S. (2001) Normativity and epistemic intuitions. *Philosophical Topics,29,* 429–460.
Williamson, T. (2004). Philosophical 'intuitions' and skepticism about judgment. *Dialectica, 58,* 109–153.
Williamson, Timothy. 2007. *The Philosophy of Philosophy.* Oxford: Blackwell.
Wisniewski, E. (1999). The psychology of intuition. In M. DePaul & W. Ramsey (Eds.), *Rethinking intuition: The psychology of intuition and its role in philosophical inquiry* (pp. 45–58). Lanham, MD: Rowman and Littlefield.
Wright, C. (2004). Intuition, entitlement, and the epistemology of logical laws. *Dialectica, 58*(1), 155–175.
Wright, J. C., Cullum, J., & Schwab, N. (2008). The cognitive and affective dimensions of moral conviction: Implications for tolerance and interpersonal behaviors. *Personality and Social Psychology Bulletin, 34*(11), 1461–1476.
Zamzow, J., & Nichols, S. (2009). Variations in ethical intuitions. *Philosophical Issues 19,* 368–388.

PART II

CONSCIOUSNESS

Intuitions about consciousness play a central role in philosophy of mind. One traditional question concerns the existence of the intuitions themselves. Consciousness is a paradigmatically private affair; why do we think others are conscious at all? This is part of the venerable problem of other minds. Philosophers also draw on intuitions about consciousness to try to determine the truth about consciousness itself. In contemporary philosophy of mind, some of the most famous arguments depend on our intuitions about consciousness in cases involving bats, sequestered neuroscientists, and zombies. To take one example, Ned Block asks the reader to imagine all the people of China contriving to replicate, en masse, the functional dynamics of a conscious human brain; in such a case, we find it counterintuitive that this collective—the nation of China—is a conscious entity. This is offered as a reason to reject the idea that functional dynamics can give a complete account of consciousness.

Although intuitions concerning consciousness are thus central to philosophy of mind, only recently has there been a concerted effort to investigate these intuitions empirically. Experimental philosophers have begun exploring the nature and basis of our intuitions about consciousness.

In one of the first forays into the experimental philosophy of consciousness, **Gray, Gray, and Wegner** report an experiment on people's judgments about the capacities of various entities. They found that people's judgments can be clustered into two categories, *Agency* and *Experience*. The *Agency* cluster includes the capacities for planning, action, and self-control; the *Experience* cluster includes the capacity for feeling pain, hunger, and embarrassment. People rate some entities (e.g., a frog) as very high on the Experience dimension but very low on the Agency dimension; other entities (e.g., God) elicit the opposite pattern—high on Agency but low on Experience.

Sytsma and Machery apply themselves more directly to a traditional philosophical debate. Philosophers often assume that their notion of 'phenomenal consciousness' reflects a commonsense notion of consciousness. In their experiments, Sytsma and Machery find that while ordinary people and professional philosophers are equally likely to deny that robots feel pain, ordinary people are more likely than philosophers to attribute visual perception to robots. This, Sytsma and Machery argue, suggests that the folk conceive of subjective experience as closely linked with valence, and this in turn, they argue, deflates the hard problem of consciousness.

While the previous essays focus on what kinds of judgments ordinary people make about consciousness, **Arico, Fiala, Goldberg, and Nichols** attempt to give an account of the psychological processes that give rise to the attribution of consciousness. They argue that the fundamental capacity underlying the attribution of goals (and other aspects of agency) also underlie the attribution of pain (and other aspects of consciousness). They suggest that the disposition to attribute conscious states to an entity is an automatic result of identifying an entity as an AGENT, and the identification of an entity as an AGENT is triggered by simple features like eyes and interactive behavior. The paper reports a reaction time experiment showing that participants were slower to deny conscious states to entities that possess those simple features. This fits with the idea that one must suppress an immediate inclination to attribute conscious states to such entities.

SUGGESTED READINGS

Fiala, B., Arico, A. & Nichols, S. 2012. "On the Psychological Origins of Dualism: Dual-Process Cognition and the Explanatory Gap." In E. Slingerland & M. Collard (eds.) *Creating Consilience: Issues and Case Studies in the Integration of the Sciences and Humanities.* Oxford University Press, 88–109.

Gray, K., Jenkins A. C., Heberlein A. H. & Wegner, D. M. 2011. "Distortions of Mind Perception in Psychopathology." *Proceedings of the National Academy of Sciences, 108*: 477–479.

Gray, K., Knobe, J., Sheskin, M., Bloom, P. & Feldman Barrett, L. 2012. "More than a Body: Mind Perception and the Nature of Objectification." *Journal of Personality and Social Psychology, 101*: 1207–1220.

Huebner, B., Bruno, M. & Sarkissian, H. 2010. "What Does the Nation of China Think about Phenomenal States?" *Review of Philosophy and Psychology, 1*: 225–243.

Knobe, J. & Prinz, J. 2008. "Intuitions about Consciousness: Experimental Studies." *Phenomenology and the Cognitive Sciences, 7*: 67–83.

Robbins, P. & Jack, A. 2006. "The Phenomenal Stance." *Philosophical Studies, 127*, 59-85.

Sytsma, J. & Machery, E. 2009. "How to Study Folk Intuitions about Consciousness." *Philosophical Psychology, 22*: 21–35.

4

Dimensions of Mind Perception

Heather M. Gray, Kurt Gray, and Daniel M. Wegner

What kinds of things have minds? Answers to this question often hinge on perceptions. Turing (*1*) held that a computer has a mind if a perceiver can't tell that it is not human, and Dennett (*2*) has proposed that every mind is defined as such in the eye of the beholder. But to date, it has generally been assumed that mind perception occurs on one dimension—things simply have more or less mind—and the dimensions of mind perception have remained unexamined. Studies testing whether chimpanzees perceive minds (*3*) and whether children or people with autism have this ability (*4*) use a variety of indicators but have not explored whether minds are perceived along one or more dimensions. We studied the structure of mind perception through 2399 completed surveys on the Mind Survey Web site (*5*).

Each survey called for 78 pairwise comparisons on five-point scales of 13 characters for one of 18 mental capacities (e.g., capacity to feel pain) or for one of six personal judgments (e.g., "which character do you like more?"). The characters included seven living human forms (7-week-old fetus, 5-month-old infant, 5-year-old girl, adult woman, adult man, man in a persistent vegetative state, and the respondent him- or herself), three nonhuman animals (frog, family dog, and wild chimpanzee), a dead woman, God, and a sociable robot (Kismet). So, for example, one such comparison involved rating whether a girl of 5 is more or less likely to be able to feel pain than is a chimpanzee. The survey samples were largely independent; 2040 unique respondents contributed data. Participants with many backgrounds responded but averaged 30 years of age and were modally female, white, unmarried, Christian, Democrat, and with some college education (*6*).

Mind perception dimensions were identified by computing character means for each mental capacity survey and submitting the correlations between

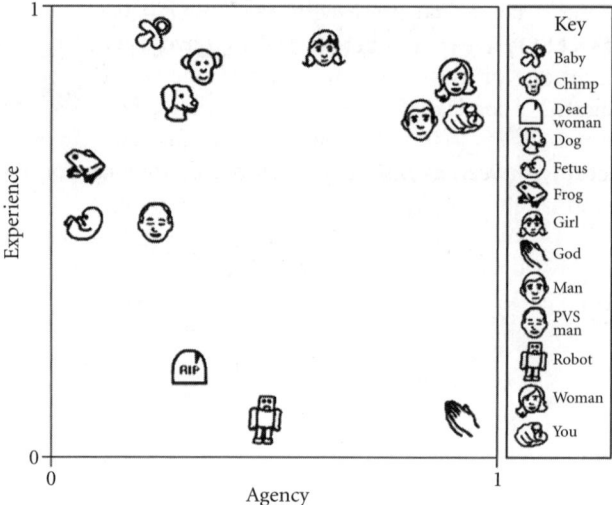

Figure 4.1. Adjusted character factor scores on the dimensions of mind perception. PVS, persistent vegetative state.

capacities across characters to principal components factor analysis (varimax rotation). The rotated solution accounted for all 18 capacities (extraction communalities ranged from 0.82 to 0.99), explained 97% of rating variance, and yielded two factors with eigenvalues over 1.0. A factor we termed Experience (eigenvalue = 15.85) accounted for 88% of the variance and included 11 capacities (from highest loading): hunger, fear, pain, pleasure, rage, desire, personality, consciousness, pride, embarrassment, and joy. A second factor, Agency (eigenvalue = 1.46), accounted for 8% of the variance and included seven capacities: self-control, morality, memory, emotion recognition, planning, communication, and thought. Characters' factor scores on these dimensions (Fig. 1) reveal interesting features; for example, God was perceived as having much Agency but little Experience.

Personal judgments of the characters were related to the mind perception dimensions. Some judgments were related to both Experience and Agency and suggest that, with the progression from no mind (bottom left) to adult human mind (top right), characters become more highly valued. Thus, both dimensions correlated with liking for a character, wanting to save it from destruction, wanting to make it happy, and perceiving it as having a soul (r ranging from 0.38 to 0.72). Such integrated use of the dimensions in valuing minds can account for the traditional conceptualization of mind as perceptible along a single dimension.

However, the remaining judgments showed differing correlations with the two dimensions. Deserving punishment for wrongdoing ("If both characters had caused a person's death, which one do you think would be more deserving of punishment?") correlated more with Agency ($r = 0.82$) than Experience ($r = 0.22$, $z = 2.86$, $P < 0.05$), whereas desire to avoid harming ("If you were forced to harm one of these characters, which one would it be more painful for you to harm?") correlated more with Experience ($r = 0.85$) than Agency ($r = 0.26$, $z = 2.10$, $P < 0.05$). The dimensions thus relate to Aristotle's classical distinction between moral agents (whose actions can be morally right or wrong) and moral patients (who can have moral right or wrong done to them). Agency is linked to moral agency and hence to responsibility, whereas Experience is linked to moral patiency and hence to rights and privileges. Thus, our findings reveal not one dimension of mind perception, but two, and show that these dimensions capture different aspects of morality.

REFERENCES AND NOTES

1. A. Turing, *Mind 59*, 433 (1950).
2. D. Dennett, *Kinds of Minds* (Basic, New York, 1996).
3. D. Premack, G. Woodruff, *Behav. Brain Sci. 1*, 515 (1978).
4. S. Baron-Cohen, *Mindblindness* (MIT Press, Cambridge, MA, 1995).
5. Mind Surveys, http://mind.wjh.harvard.edu/.
6. Materials and methods are available as supporting material on *Science* Online.
7. We acknowledge J. Bradshaw, J. Hromjak, K. Kassam, P. Piff, and B. Simpson and funding from National Institute of Mental Health grants MH-49127 and MH-71053 and from a Social Sciences and Humanities Research Council Fellowship.

5

Two Conceptions of Subjective Experience

Justin Sytsma and Edouard Machery

Our first goal in this article is to examine whether ordinary people (viz. people without training in philosophy or in consciousness studies) and philosophers conceive of subjective experience in a similar way. Philosophers see subjective experiences as including such diverse mental states as seeing red and feeling pain, treating them as having something in common, namely that they are phenomenal—viz. that they share the second-order property that there is "something it is like" (Nagel 1974) to be in these mental states. We provide suggestive evidence that the folk, by contrast, do *not* conceive of subjective experience in this way. Our second goal is to explore this folk conception for its own sake. We successively consider two accounts. We first examine whether the folk treat perceptual states differently from bodily sensations or felt emotions, taking the latter, but not the former, to be subjectively experienced. This might be phrased in terms of the folk distinguishing between those states that tell us about the world outside our skin (the products of the *external senses*) and those states that tell us about ourselves from the skin in (the products of the *internal senses*). Rejecting this first account, we argue for an alternative hypothesis: For the folk, subjective experience is tightly linked to valence.[1] As a result, people distinguish between states that essentially have a valence (such as feeling pain or anger), those that do not have a valence (such as seeing red), and those that have a valence as well as a prominent perceptual component (such as smelling banana).

While the folk conception of subjective experience is fascinating in its own right, it is also of substantial philosophical importance. Our third goal in this article is to investigate the philosophical implications of the divergence between ordinary people's and philosophers' conceptions of subjective experience. We argue, first, that our findings cast doubt on the claim that the philosophical concept of phenomenal consciousness is shared by the folk or is a part of folk psychology. Second, if our analysis of the folk conception is correct, then it raises serious doubt about whether there is a hard problem of consciousness to be solved. The hard problem is typically justified on the grounds that phenomenal consciousness is "the most central and manifest aspect of our mental lives" (Chalmers 1995, p. 207). Our findings challenge this justification: If the folk do not recognize that states such as seeing red and feeling pain are phenomenal, then it is hardly credible that phenomenal consciousness is central and manifest. This does not necessarily mean that there is no hard problem of consciousness, but it does call on philosophers to provide a better justification for the reality of this problem.

We begin in Sect. 1 by briefly characterizing the philosophical conception of subjective experience. In Sect. 2, we discuss the shortcomings of recent work in psychology, philosophy, and experimental philosophy that investigates folk intuitions related to consciousness. We conclude that this work is poorly designed to investigate whether philosophers and ordinary people conceive of subjective experience similarly. In Sects. 3–5, we aim to rectify this situation by examining people's judgments about perceptual experiences, bodily sensations, and felt emotions. In Sect. 6, we examine the philosophical implications of our findings about the folk conception of subjective experience.

1. THE PHILOSOPHICAL CONCEPTION OF SUBJECTIVE EXPERIENCE

For most contemporary philosophers, subjective experience is characterized by its phenomenality. There is, of course, much disagreement in the literature about what phenomenal consciousness is. Still, according to one standard line (and the one we will be interested in), mental states such as seeing red, feeling pain, hearing a C#, feeling anger, etc., all share the second-order property that it is like something to be in these states. What it is like to be in pain is distinct from what it is like to see red, but for both states, there is something it is like to be in them. "Phenomenal consciousness" refers to this second-order property. As Block puts it(1995, p. 227): "Phenomenal consciousness is experience; what makes a state phenomenally conscious is that there is something 'it is like' (Nagel 1974) to be in that state." Similarly, Searle (1994, p. xi) holds that it is one of the "simple and obvious truths about the mind" that "[w]e all have inner subjective qualitative states of consciousness." Finally, Chalmers writes eloquently (1995, p. 201; italics added):

> The really hard problem of consciousness is the problem of experience. When we think and perceive, there is a whir of information-processing, but there is also a subjective aspect.... This subjective aspect is experience. When we see, for example, we experience visual sensations: the felt quality

of redness, the experience of dark and light, the quality of depth in a visual field. Other experiences go with perception in different modalities: the sound of a clarinet, the smell of mothballs. Then there are bodily sensations...mental images...the felt quality of emotion.... *What unites all of these states is that there is something it is like to be in them.* All of them are states of experience.

Phenomenally conscious mental states are typically divided into a number of types in the philosophical literature. The most common type is *perceptual experiences* such as seeing, hearing, or smelling, followed closely by *bodily sensations* such as pain and hunger (Levin 1998). *Felt emotions* such as fear, rage, joy and *felt moods* such as elation, depression, boredom are typically added to this list (Tye 2003).[2] These four types of phenomenal states (perceptual experiences, bodily sensations, felt emotions, and felt moods) are typically contrasted with non-phenomenal intentional states like belief and desire.

Perceptual experiences of colors and bodily sensations of pains are easily the most frequently discussed in the philosophical and scientific literature. For example, Francis Crick describes qualia (the phenomenal properties of mental states) in terms of "the redness of red or the painfulness of pain" (1995, footnote 9). This strategy is typical—the concepts of phenomenal consciousness and qualia are generally drawn out through examples; as Papineau puts it, "the idea is best introduced by examples rather than definitions" (2002, p. 13; see also Block 1995). And the first examples are typically colors and pains; as Janet Levin opens her *Routledge Encyclopedia of Philosophy* entry on "Qualia":

> The term... [is] most commonly understood to mean the qualitative, phenomenal or 'felt' properties of our mental states, such as the throbbing pain of my current headache, or the peculiar blue of the afterimage I am experiencing now. Though it seems undeniable that at least some of our mental states have qualia, their existence raises a number of philosophical problems. (Sect. 0)

Given the illustrative centrality of perceptual experiences and bodily sensations to articulating the concept of phenomenal consciousness, if the folk and philosophers conceive similarly of subjective experience, we should expect them to treat perceptual experiences and bodily sensations analogously in these regards. In particular, we should expect the folk to deny that an entity, be it a simple organism, a simple robot, or a zombie, that lacks phenomenal consciousness can see red just as readily as they deny that it can be in pain. Dennett conforms with this expectation, for example, when he states that the robot Cog[3] "cannot yet see or hear or feel at all" (1996, p. 16).

2. PREVIOUS RESEARCH RELATED TO THE FOLK'S CONCEPTION OF SUBJECTIVE EXPERIENCE

In this section, we critically discuss three main lines of experimental research related to the folk conception of subjective experience. While this work is intriguing in its own right, we argue that none of the studies is adequate for determining whether the philosophical concept of phenomenal consciousness really coincides with what Block (2004, p. 785) has called the "common-sense conception of subjective experience."

2.1. Experience and Agency

Gray et al.'s fascinating study on "Dimensions of Mind Perception" (2007) reports empirical findings that people tend to distinguish between two broad aspects of having a mind. Gray et al. label these dimensions *Experience* (including hunger, fear, pain, pleasure, rage) and *Agency* (including self-control, morality, memory, emotion recognition). They had participants compare a host of characters (e.g., God, a 7-week-old fetus, the robot Kismet,[4] a frog, a corpse) on a range of mental capacities. For instance, participants were asked "whether a girl of 5 is more or less likely to feel pain than is a chimpanzee" (p. 619). They found a clear divide between experiential capacities and agentive capacities. The possessions of mental capacities like hunger, fear, pain (etc.) were correlated with each other, as were the possessions of mental capacities like self-control, morality, memory (etc.), while the possessions of mental capacities across these two groupings were poorly correlated. Thus, while a human baby scored low on Agency, but high on Experience, the robot Kismet scored very low on Experience, but had a moderate Agency score.

These findings are no doubt very interesting, but they fail to show that the philosophical concept of phenomenal consciousness coincides with the commonsense conception of subjective experience, in spite of what the term "Experience"—Gray et al.'s name of their second dimension of mind perception—might suggest.[5] As we have seen in Sect. 1, for philosophers, phenomenality is a second-order property shared by such diverse states as perceptual experiences, bodily sensations, and felt emotions. Perceptual states like seeing red are in fact the typical illustrative example of phenomenally conscious mental states. By contrast, the states Gray et al. tested (e.g., pain, pleasure, rage, etc.) were all non-perceptual. As a result, it remains unclear whether the folk think that mental states such as seeing red, feeling pain, and feeling rage have in common that they are phenomenally conscious, as they should if they conceive of subjective experience in the same way as philosophers.

2.2. Minds and Objects

In contrast to Piaget's (1929) claim that "children are adualistic rather than dualistic in that they fail to segregate two realms: the psychical and the physical, the subjective and the objective, the mental and the real" (Wellman and Estes 1986, p. 910), psychologist Bloom has argued that "even very young babies treat people differently from objects" (2004, p. 14). He holds that we have an "evolved capacity to understand and respond to the minds of other people" and "we also have the evolved capacity to perceive and reason about material objects" (p. 5). Bloom concludes that from an early age on, people are intuitive dualists in the sense that they naturally distinguish entities with minds from mere objects. Among other things, this corresponds with the fact that "empathy comes early and easily" (p. 114); from an early age people tend to empathize with some entities (those with minds), but not others.

Philosopher Robbins and cognitive neuroscientist Jack (2006) have drawn on Bloom's work to argue that a further stance, rooted in our evolved "capacity for empathy and moral understanding" (p. 74), should be added to Dennett's (1987) distinction between the intentional and physical stances: "The *phenomenal stance* corresponds to a component of social cognition that, like folk physics, is relatively independent of mindreading—namely, moral cognition" (p. 61; italics added). Moral cognition is then implicated in generating our "intuitive dualism" and specifically identified as "generating intuitions about the non-physical nature of consciousness" (p. 61).

Robbins and Jack's approach to the folk conception of subjective experience suffers from the same problem as Gray et al.'s. They hold that "regarding something as a locus of experience is a kind of emotional sensitivity" (p. 70). Thus they note that "it is usually pleasant to observe another's pleasure, and distressing to observe their distress" and state that "the capacity for such responses... is essential to the phenomenal stance" (p. 70). The problem is that not all phenomenal states are associated with pleasure or distress (think, e.g., about seeing a red patch). Robbins and Jack might be correct that "phenomenal states *typically* have some hedonic value for the bearer, either positive (e.g. pleasure, joy) or negative (e.g. pain, sadness)" (p. 70; italics added), but this is just to underline that the distinction between mental states that are associated with pleasure or distress is distinct from the philosophical distinction between phenomenal and non-phenomenal mental states.

2.3. Group Agents and Individuals

How the folk understand subjective experience has been investigated most specifically by Knobe and Prinz (2008). In their second of five studies, Knobe and Prinz asked people to evaluate how natural it is to ascribe a range of mental states to a group agent (Acme Corporation). They found that people seem to be unwilling to ascribe phenomenally conscious mental states (such as feeling depressed) to the corporation, while being disposed to ascribe mental states that are not phenomenally conscious, such as propositional attitudes, to it. In addition, in their fourth study, Knobe and Prinz provided some suggestive evidence that while people are willing to ascribe a mental state such as being upset or regretting to a group agent, they are reluctant to ascribe a mental state such as feeling upset or feeling regret to it. Knobe and Prinz interpret this body of evidence as showing that (i) the folk distinguish between phenomenally conscious mental states and mental states that are not phenomenally conscious and (ii) that in contrast to the latter mental states, the ascription of phenomenally conscious mental states does not depend merely on the functional properties of the ascribee's states.

In contrast to Gray et al.'s and Robbins and Jack's approaches, Knobe and Prinz's study seems to support the contention that philosophers' concept of phenomenal consciousness coincides with the common-sense conception of subjective experience (see also Huebner et al. 2010). Indeed, they conclude that "ordinary people—people who have never studied philosophy or cognitive science—actually have a concept of phenomenal consciousness" (p. 68).

Unfortunately, there are a few problems with Knobe and Prinz's study (Arico 2010; Sytsma and Machery 2009). Particularly, as we have argued elsewhere (Sytsma and Machery 2009), there is a confound inherent in this approach: Corporations differ in some significant behavioral and functional ways from individuals. A group agent like Acme Corporation is distributed; it does not have an individual body, although it is comprised of such bodies. As such, Acme cannot smile in happiness or grimace in disgust. It is thus difficult to determine whether people deny that Acme can experience great joy, feel excruciating pain, or vividly imagine a purple square because they believe that a group agent like Acme cannot have a phenomenal state or because they believe that a group agent like Acme does not have the proper functional organization for having mental states like joy and pain. For these reasons, we find that Knobe and Prinz's study of the ascription of mental states to corporations is inconclusive about the folk conception of subjective experience.

3. STUDY 1: SEEING RED AND FEELING PAIN

Previous research is by and large uninformative about whether philosophers' concept of phenomenal consciousness coincides with the common-sense conception of subjective experience. In this section, we provide and discuss some new evidence that the folk and philosophers conceive of subjective experience in markedly different ways.

The rationale behind our first study is straightforward. If the philosophical concept of phenomenal consciousness coincides with the folk's conception of subjective experience, we would expect their judgments about robots like Cog to be in line with Dennett's (Sect. 1): They would treat perception analogously to bodily sensations, tending to deny both to a simple robot. The Mental State Intuitions Study was designed to test this prediction. In the first experiment, participants were given a description of a relatively simple, non-humanoid robot performing tasks expected to elicit ascriptions of either a perceptual experience (seeing red) or a bodily sensation (feeling pain) in humans. Given the role of visual experiences and bodily sensations such as pain in spelling out the philosophical concept of phenomenal consciousness, we hypothesized that philosophers' attribution of the perceptual experience would not dissociate from their attribution of the bodily sensation. If the folk conceive of subjective experience in the same way as philosophers, they should give a similar pattern of answers.

A total of 671 participants completed surveys through the Mental State Intuitions Study website.[6,7] Participants were divided into two groups based on their responses to biographical questions concerning their philosophical training.[8] They randomly received one of four scenarios describing an agent manipulating a red object. The scenarios were varied along two dimensions. In half of the scenarios, the agent was a simple robot (Jimmy), while in the other half, the agent was a normal human male (Timmy). Moreover, in half of the scenarios, the manipulation was successful and participants were asked whether the agent (either the robot or the human) "saw red" on a 7-point scale anchored at 1 with "clearly no," at 4 with "not sure," and at 7 with "clearly yes." In the other half, the agent was electrically shocked and participants were asked whether the agent "felt pain" on the same 7-point scale. In each pair of vignettes the agents are described in behaviorally identical ways; in the first pair, the agents' behavior involves discrimination between colors, while in the second, the behavior is typical of a pain response.[9] The two robot scenarios read as follows:[10]

> Jimmy (shown below) is a relatively simple robot built at a state university. He has a video camera for eyes, wheels for moving about, and two grasping arms with touch sensors that he can move objects with. As part of a psychological experiment, he was put in a room that was empty except for one blue box, one red box, and one green box (the boxes were identical in all respects except color). An instruction was then transmitted to Jimmy. It read: "Put the red box in front of the door." Jimmy did this with no noticeable difficulty. Did Jimmy see red?
>
> Jimmy (shown below) is a relatively simple robot built at a state university. He has a video camera for eyes, wheels for moving about, and two grasping arms with touch sensors that he can move objects with. As part of a psychological experiment, he was put in a room that was empty except for one blue box, one red box, and one green box (the boxes were identical in all respects except color). An instruction was then transmitted to Jimmy. It read: "Put the red box in front of the door." When Jimmy grasped the red box, however, it gave him a strong electric shock. He let go of the box and moved away from it. He did not try to move the box again. Did Jimmy feel pain when he was shocked?

Participants were randomly ascribed to one of the four scenarios. After the participants read the scenario they were asked the target question ("Did Timmy/Jimmy see red?" or "Did Timmy/Jimmy feel pain?"), as well as a variation concerning other people: Participants were asked whether ordinary people

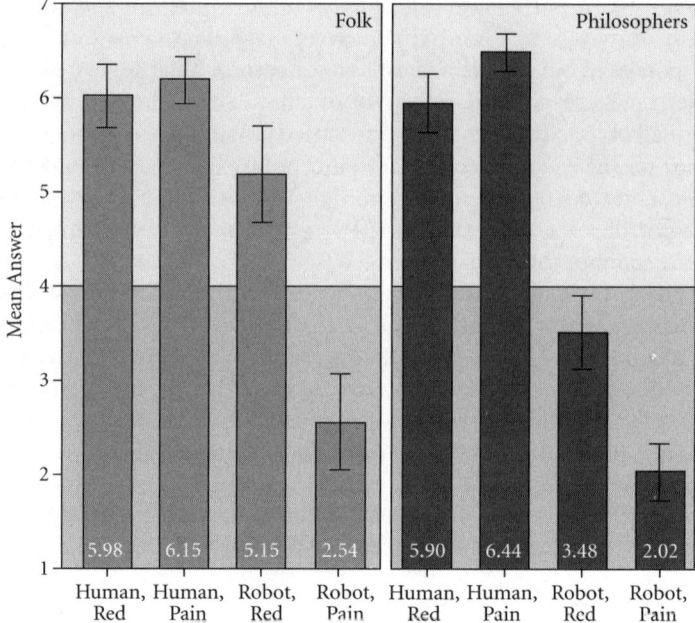

Figure 5.1. Results of Study 1 (error bars: 95% confidence interval)

would say that the agent (either the robot or the human) saw red or felt pain on the same 7-point scale. The questions were counterbalanced for order. Participants were then asked to explain their answers and to fill out a short biographical survey.

3.1. Results

Figure 1 and Table 1 summarize our results.

Consistent with our hypothesis, philosophers treated similarly feeling pain and seeing red. They were unwilling to ascribe either the perceptual experience of seeing red or the bodily sensation of feeling pain to the robot (the mean

Table 1 Results of Study 1

	Seeing red		Feeling pain	
	Folk	Philosophers	Folk	Philosophers
Human	$N = 55, 5.98$	$N = 92, 5.90$	$N = 62, 6.15$	$N = 84, 6.44$
	$(1.25)^{***}$	$(1.46)^{***}$	$(1.01)^{***}$	$(.87)^{***}$
Robot	$N = 52, 5.15$	$N = 96, 3.48$	$N = 59, 2.54$	$N = 100, 2.02$
	$(1.85)^{***}$	$(1.94)^{**}$	$(1.99)^{***}$	$(1.53)^{***}$

Number of participants per condition, mean answer, and standard deviation in parentheses; significance tests compare means to the neutral answer, 4

$^*p<.05;\ ^{**}p<.01;\ ^{***}p<.005$

answers are significantly lower than 4). By contrast, philosophers were willing to ascribe both states to a normal human male (the mean answers are significantly higher than 4). Contrary to the hypothesis that the folk and philosophers conceive of subjective experience similarly, however, ordinary people distinguished the perceptual state of seeing red from the bodily sensation of feeling pain. They were *willing* to attribute the perceptual experience to a simple robot that can effectively manipulate objects, but were *not* willing to attribute feeling pain to this robot. In addition, the folk's modal answer for feeling pain was 1 (like philosophers), while their modal answer for seeing red was 7 (unlike philosophers). By contrast, ordinary people did not differ from philosophers in their willingness to ascribe the perceptual state and the bodily sensation to a normal human male.

3.2. Discussion

In contrast to the prediction derived from the hypothesis that the philosophical concept of phenomenal consciousness coincides with the commonsense conception of subjective experience, the results show a clear divergence between philosophers and the folk: On average, the folk (but not philosophers) are willing to ascribe the perceptual state of seeing red to a simple robot. Given the illustrative centrality of the example of the redness of red to the philosophical concept of phenomenal consciousness, our results indicate that philosophers' concept of phenomenal consciousness is *not* how the folk understand subjective experience.

In addition, it is worth noting that philosophers are not aware that their conception of subjective experience differs from the folk conception. Remember that in addition to asking participants whether they thought that Jimmy was in pain and was seeing red, we also asked them how ordinary people would answer these same questions. Philosophers' answers are well calibrated for Timmy's pain, Timmy's perception of red, and Jimmy's pain. By contrast, for the robot's perception of red, philosophers' prediction about the ordinary people's answers is off the mark: They expected ordinary people to give only a neutral answer ($M = 4.18$; $SD = 1.81$), while ordinary people's mean answer was above 5 (Fig. 2).

Philosophers' expectation about ordinary people's evaluation of the robot's perception of red follows their usual pattern for estimating ordinary people's answer. Philosophers expected ordinary people to give approximately the same answer as themselves but to be a bit less skeptical (by giving a somewhat higher answer). In contrast to philosophers, non-philosophers' evaluation of whether ordinary people will ascribe seeing red to the robot is well calibrated. They expected ordinary people to give a mean answer of 5.38, while ordinary people's mean answer was 5.15.

3.3. Objections

We now turn to two possible replies to the claim that philosophers and ordinary people conceive of subjective experience differently. Our critic assumes

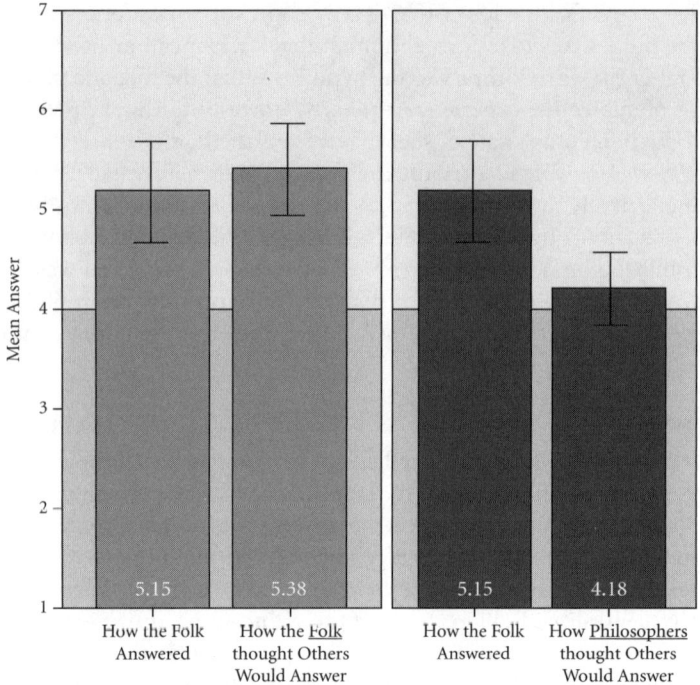

Figure 5.2 Comparison of the folk's mean answer for the question "Did Jimmy see red?", with how the folk and philosophers thought ordinary people would answer (error bars: 95% confidence interval)

that the folk understand subjective experience similarly to philosophers. She must then explain the folk's divergence from philosophers for the case of Jimmy seeing red in another way. The most obvious ways to do this are to argue that the folk understand the question "Did Jimmy see red?" differently than philosophers, or that the folk have divergent beliefs about Jimmy. We will consider each response in turn.[11]

First, it could be argued that "seeing red" is ambiguous.[12] On one reading (which our critic might call "informational"), a creature sees red if its behavior is responsive to the distinction between red things and non-red things or, to put the same point somewhat differently, if it can pick some information about red things from its environment and act on the basis of this information. In this sense, Jimmy certainly sees red (he performs the discrimination task). On a second reading (which our critic might call "phenomenal"), a creature sees red only if it has the appropriate phenomenal experience. In this sense, Jimmy does not see red, or so our critic maintains. The critic can then argue that in contrast to "seeing red," there is no informational reading of "feeling pain": one is in pain only if one has the appropriate phenomenal experience.

From this, our critic might argue that "seeing red" has the informational and the phenomenal readings both for the folk and for philosophers. However, the folk tend to understand "seeing red" according to its informational reading, while philosophers tend to understand it according to its phenomenal reading, which explains their divergent answers. Because "feeling pain" has only a phenomenal reading, philosophers and the folk give similar answers. If this proposal were correct, experiment 1 would not show that the folk understand phenomenal consciousness differently than philosophers, because for the folk as for philosophers, "seeing red" would still have a phenomenal reading. The folk would just interpret the question "Did Jimmy see red?" according to the informational reading of "seeing red," while philosophers would interpret it according to its phenomenal reading.

It should be noted that if the objection is to avoid being blatantly ad hoc, the critic owes us an explanation for the folk's divergence from philosophers in choosing the informational reading over the phenomenal reading of "seeing red." Regardless, the data simply do not bear out our critic's proposal. If she were right, we would expect that a reasonable proportion of the folk would answer negatively to the question "Did Jimmy see red?"—as philosophers do—while the remainder would answer positively. This is not the case, however. Figure 3 presents the distribution of answers for the folk: Almost all non-philosophers (84.6%) gave an answer equal or superior to 4.

This first objection is further undermined by the explanations that participants gave for their answers. Philosophers tended to refer to phenomenal consciousness (or to qualia, secondary properties, etc.) in explaining their denial that the robot saw red. A few typical philosophical explanations of an answer of 1 ("clearly no"—philosophers' modal answer) to the question ("Did Jimmy see

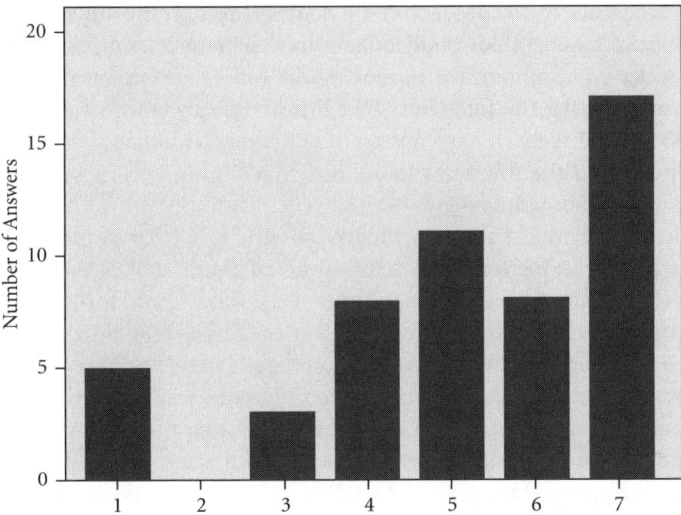

Figure 5.3. Distribution of the folk's answers for the question, "Did Jimmy see red?"

red?"), read as follows: "To actually see red requires experiencing the sensation of redness (qualia)"; "color is a secondary property"; "seeing red implies consciousness, not just ability to identify red"; "seeing is perceiving, and perceiving is conscious." In contrast, the three explanations given by non-philosophers who answered 1 to the question do not suggest a phenomenal reading; if anything they indicate a different analysis of "seeing"—an anthropocentric reading that restricts the term to humans and animals (see Bennett and Hacker 2003, for a related conceptual analysis of the term): "I'm not sure how color is understood by robots and computers"; "seeing is a human attribute"; "seeing is something which animals do."

Second, a critic could offer an alternative explanation of our results. Consider the following analogy. John and Joe might have the same concepts of right and wrong (say, both are utilitarian), but they might nonetheless disagree about whether the death penalty is wrong. They might disagree about the wrongness of the death penalty because they have different beliefs about the death penalty (for example, about its efficiency as a deterrent). Similarly, the disagreement between the folk and philosophers might not indicate that they conceive of subjective experience differently; rather, it might reflect that they have different beliefs about the robot Jimmy.

We have argued that if the philosophical concept of phenomenal consciousness coincides with the folk's conception of subjective experience, then we would expect them to treat seeing red and feeling pain analogously in denying both to a simple robot. The critic challenges this: Perhaps the folk do understand these states in the phenomenal sense, but unlike philosophers they believe that Jimmy is capable of having phenomenal visual experiences. Our argument assumes that the robot Jimmy (as described and pictured) is simple enough that if someone has the concept of phenomenal consciousness, then she will not feel that it applies to Jimmy. The critic denies this, arguing (in effect) that the folk are more lenient than philosophers in ascribing phenomenal consciousness. Besides an argument for supposing the folk to be lenient in this way, on the assumption that the folk really take Jimmy to be phenomenally conscious, the critic now owes us an explanation of why they deny that he feels pain. One possibility is that the folk tend to assume that Jimmy's visual system is more complex than his touch system.

While we feel that these are indeed possibilities (that could be explored through further experimental work), none of them strikes us as especially likely. As noted above, the explanations that the folk offered for their responses do not suggest a phenomenal understanding of "seeing red." Further, the details of the story do not support the assumption that Jimmy's visual system is significantly more complex than his touch system. Finally, while post hoc explanations of our data that are compatible with the assumption that the folk's understanding of subjective experience coincides with philosophers' can be given, our positive account of the folk's understanding of subjective experience suggests that this assumption is mistaken. We present this positive account in the following two sections.

4. STUDY 2: SMELLING BANANA AND FEELING ANGER

In Study 1, the folk deny that the robot Jimmy feels pain, but not that he sees red. What does this indicate about the folk understanding of subjective experience? One proposal that is suggested by the philosophical literature is that the folk's understanding of subjective experience is based on a distinction between the internal senses and the external senses: being subjective and being internal would be identified according to this proposal. As Newton put it, colors and pains "seem to lie at opposite extremes of internality and externality" (1989, p. 571). Thus, the folk might treat seeing red differently from feeling pain because the former is a product of an external sense while the latter is a product of an internal sense. If this explanation is correct, then we would expect the folk to be willing to ascribe other perceptual experiences (external) to Jimmy, but not felt emotions (internal).

To test the internal/external hypothesis, participants were given variations on the scenarios from the first experiment. If the hypothesis is correct, the folk should be willing to ascribe the perceptual experience of odor to the robot Jimmy in the same way they were willing to ascribe the perceptual experience of red to him in Study 1, while being reluctant to ascribe the felt emotion of anger to him. By contrast, they should ascribe both the perception of odor and the emotion of anger to the human Timmy.

Participants were randomly assigned to one of four scenarios. The scenarios were varied along two dimensions. In half of the scenarios the agent was a simple robot (Jimmy), while in the other half the agent was a normal human male (Timmy). Moreover, in half of the scenarios the agent successfully manipulated an object; participants were then asked whether the agent (either the robot or the human) "smelt banana" on the 7-point scale used in Study 1. In the other half the agent was prevented from successfully manipulating the object by a robot; participants were then asked whether the agent "felt anger" on the same scale.[13] The two robot scenarios read as follows:

> Jimmy (shown below) is a relatively simple robot built at a state university. He has a scent detector, video camera for eyes, wheels for moving about, and two grasping arms with touch sensors that he can move objects with. As part of a psychological experiment, he was put in a room that was empty except for one box of peeled bananas, one box of chocolate, and one box of peeled oranges. The boxes were closed, but had small holes to let the scent through (Jimmy couldn't see what was in the boxes). The boxes were otherwise identical. An instruction was then transmitted to Jimmy. It read: "Put the box of bananas in front of the door." Jimmy did this with no noticeable difficulty. Did Jimmy smell banana?
>
> Jimmy (shown below) is a relatively simple robot built at a state university. He has a video camera for eyes, wheels for moving about, and two grasping arms with touch sensors that he can move objects with. As part of a psychological experiment, he was put in a room with another simple robot; the room was otherwise empty except for one blue box, one red box, and one green box (the boxes were identical in all respects except color).

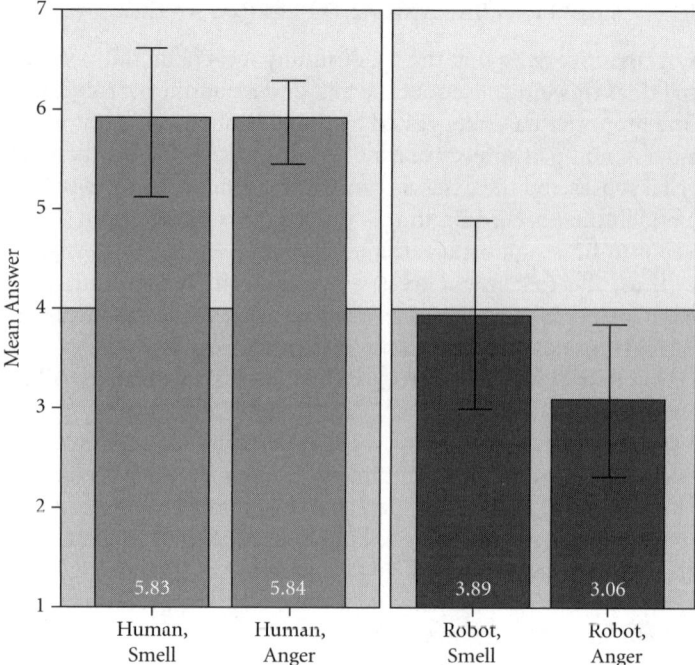

Figure 5.4. Results of Study 2 (error bars: 95% confidence interval)

An instruction was then transmitted to Jimmy. It read: "Put the red box in front of the door." When Jimmy went to move the red box, the other robot ran into him, preventing him from reaching the box. Jimmy tried again and again and each time the robot banged into him. Jimmy finally rammed the other robot; when the robot moved away from him, Jimmy chased after the robot. Did Jimmy feel anger?

4.1. RESULTS

Figure 4 and Table 2 summarize the results.

Unsurprisingly, participants were willing to ascribe both smelling banana and feeling anger to Timmy. By contrast, participants were reluctant to ascribe

Table 2 Results of Study 2

	Smelling banana	Feeling anger
Human	$N = 18$, 5.83 (1.46)***	$N = 25$, 5.84 (.99)***
Robot	$N = 28$, 3.89 (2.42)	$N = 35$, 3.06 (2.22)*

Number of participants per condition, mean answer, and standard deviation in parentheses; significance tests compare means to the neutral answer, 4

* $p < .05$; ** $p < .01$; *** $p < .005$

feeling anger to the robot Jimmy (their mean answer was significantly lower than 4) and were ambivalent about ascribing smelling banana (their answer was not significantly different from 4). Thus, in contrast to seeing red, people are not willing to ascribe smells to a simple robot. While most of the folk were willing to ascribe seeing red to the robot (more than 80% of participants gave a score of 4 or higher), they were more evenly split for the case of smelling banana (around 50% gave a score of 4 or higher).

4.2. Discussion

These results speak against the internal/external hypothesis as formulated: The folk do not appear to treat all external senses the same—they do not treat smelling banana analogously to seeing red. Our results suggest that the folk do not understand subjective experience in terms of a distinction between being internal and being external.

One possible response is to charge that our characterization of the division between the external and the internal is too coarse. For example, Newton (2000, p. 64) implies that not all the external senses are equally external: Where colors are seen as properties of external objects, she argues that this holds to only a lesser degree for sound. The folk might treat smell as yet more borderline between external and internal: While the sense of smell gives us information about external objects, the scent can seem to be located at or in the nostrils. A nuanced internal/external hypothesis would predict that the folk's willingness to ascribe perceptual states to a simple robot varies inversely with how external the sense is.

An alternative response is also suggested by Newton (1989), as well as the discussion of Robbins and Jack (2006) in Sect. 2—it might be that the folk conception of subjective experience is closely tied to those mental states that have a valence. Thus, Newton argues that experiences of colors and pains differ in that the latter has an "affective aspect" that the former lacks: "To have a pain is to have something that one does not like. Since not liking something is a psychological state, it has seemed as if pains, even if they are associated with our physical bodies, are also psychological in a way that e.g. colors, in this respect at least, fail to be" (p. 574). We hypothesize that it is not whether a mental state is the product of the external senses that matters for the folk understanding of subjective experience, but whether they associate that state with some hedonic value for the subject.

Note that there is much correspondence between the division between states with or without a valence and the internal/external division: the states explored in experiment 1 separate under each distinction; seeing a red box is both external and lacks valence, while feeling pain from an electric shock is both internal and has a valence. Nonetheless, not all external mental states lack valence; like feeling pain, but unlike seeing colors, tastes and smells are typically associated with hedonic value.

Thus, for a perceptual experience like seeing red that is neither liked nor disliked, the folk readily attribute it to the robot Jimmy. For non-perceptual mental states with clear valence like feeling pain or feeling anger, the folk readily

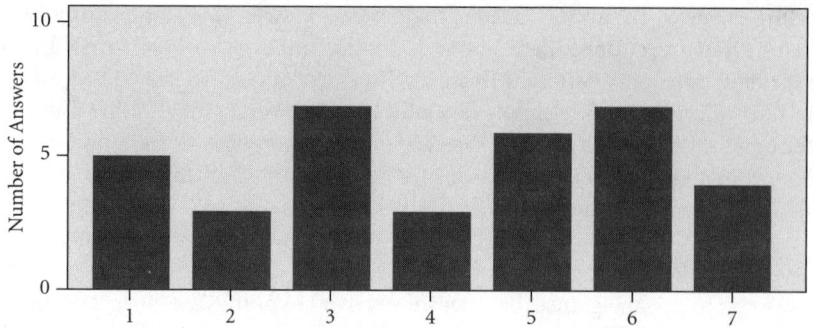

Figure 5.5. Distribution of the folk's answers for the question, "Did Jimmy smell banana?"

deny them of Jimmy. For a perceptual state like smelling banana that has an associated valence, however, the folk are divided. We conjecture that they are divided because they hold that while Jimmy is capable of perceiving the scent of banana, he is incapable of having the valence; he is incapable of *liking* the scent of banana. The folk are divided, here, because unlike pain where its valence is essential to it being pain, for smell they see the valence as potentially disassociating from the perceptual aspect. In other words, there is an ambiguity in the question "did Jimmy smell banana"—not between an "informational" and a "phenomenal" reading (see Sect. 3.3), but between a "perceptual" and a "valence" reading—that is not present for the questions about seeing red and feeling pain. This ambiguity is suggested by the wide distribution of responses (Fig. 5): 42.9% of the folk gave a negative response (a score below 4) while 48.6% gave a positive response (a score above 4).

If this explanation is correct, then we would expect that downplaying the valence reading for smell will increase the folk's willingness to attribute the state to the robot Jimmy. Specifically, we predict that for a "neutral" odor (an odor that participants are unfamiliar with and thus associate no valence with), participants will be more willing to say that Jimmy smells it than familiar odors like banana. Testing this prediction is the focus of our third experiment.

5. STUDY 3: THE VALENCE OF SMELL

That the sense of smell has strong connections to emotion and emotional memory is well recognized. It is obvious that we tend to find many odors distinctly pleasant or unpleasant. In recent years, a great deal of scientific work has been conducted on the emotional processing of olfactory stimuli. This work indicates that *in contrast with visual stimuli,* odors more readily elicit emotional responses and more readily call forth emotional memories (see, for example, Herz et al. 2004). Most recently, neuroimagining data has provided evidence that the emotional potency of memories elicited through smell are correlated with activation of the amygdala, a brain structure that is critical for processing emotive stimuli and for emotional memory (Winston et al. 2005). It is therefore not surprising that the sense of smell would be tied to valence since unlike the other sensory systems, the olfactory system projects directly to the amygdala.

Given this, it is reasonable to expect that participants associated each of the common olfactory stimuli described in experiment 2—banana, orange, and chocolate—with a valence. These are odors that most people are familiar with and find to be pleasant. We hold that this valence explains people's relative unwillingness to say that the robot Jimmy smelled banana in comparison to saw red.

To test this we ran a further variation on the Timmy/Jimmy probes. We tested folk responses for three sets of olfactory stimuli—familiar unpleasant stimuli (e.g., vomit), familiar pleasant stimuli (e.g., banana), and unfamiliar stimuli (e.g., isoamyl acetate). We predicted that the participants' willingness to attribute smell to the robot is sensitive to whether a valence is associated with the stimulus: Participants would be more willing to say that Jimmy could smell a stimulus that they did not associate with a valence than one that they did.

Participants were randomly assigned to one of six scenarios. The scenarios were varied along two dimensions. In half of the scenarios the agent was a simple robot (Jimmy), while in the other half the agent was a normal human male (Timmy). In each of the scenarios the agent successfully manipulated an object based on an olfactory cue. The scenarios were also varied with respect to the valence typically associated with the olfactory cue. In one-third of the scenarios, the olfactory cue was unfamiliar and thus associated with no valence (isoamyl acetate); in one-third, it was familiar with a positive valence (banana); in one-third, it was familiar with a negative valence (vomit). Finally, participants were asked whether the agent (either the robot or the human) smelt that stimulus on the 7-point scale used in previous studies. The first of the three robot scenarios reads as follows:

> Jimmy (shown below) is a relatively simple robot built at a state university. He is equipped with a microphone, scent detector, video camera, wheels for moving about, and two grasping arms with touch sensors that he can move objects with. As part of an experiment, three chemical compounds were placed under Jimmy's scent detector. The compounds were presented one at a time. As they were presented their names were transmitted to Jimmy: isoamyl acetate, 3-methylbutanal, and dipentene. The next day Jimmy was put in a room that was empty except for one box of isoamyl acetate, one box of 3-methylbutanal, and one box of dipentene. The boxes were closed, but had small holes to let the scent through. The boxes were otherwise identical. An instruction was then transmitted to Jimmy. It read: "Put the box of isoamyl acetate in front of the door." Jimmy did this with no noticeable difficulty. The test was repeated on three consecutive days with the order of the boxes shuffled. Each time Jimmy performed the task with no noticeable difficulty. Did Jimmy smell isoamyl acetate?

The other three scenarios varied only in the olfactory stimuli used. They were (the target is in italics):

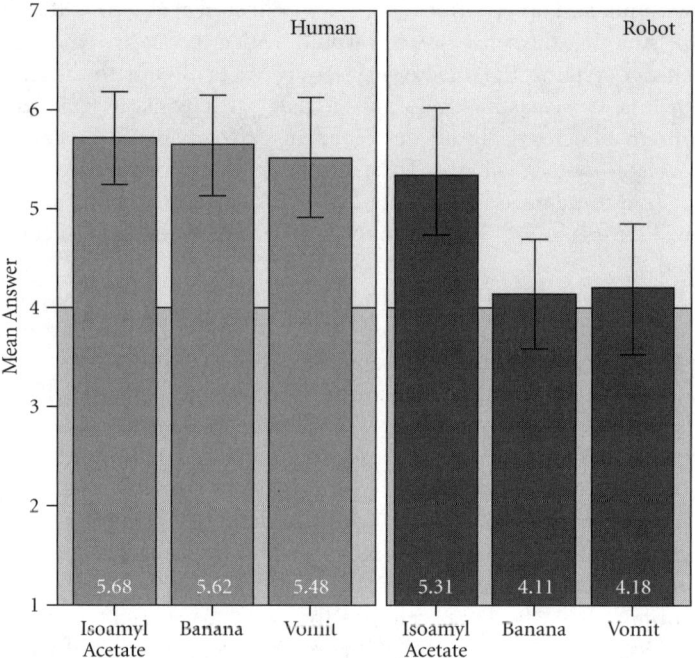

Figure 5.6. Results of Study 3 (error bars: 95% confidence interval)

Banana, Orange, Chocolate;
Vomit, Human Feces, Rotting Dog Meat.

5.1. Results

Figure 6 and Table 3 summarize the results.

Participants were willing to ascribe each smell to Timmy. They were also willing to ascribe the unfamiliar olfactory cue (isoamyl acetate) to Jimmy (the mean answer was significantly higher than 4), but not the two familiar olfactory cues (the mean answers were not significantly different from 4). Participants' answer to the unfamiliar smell was also significantly higher than their answer to the familiar smells and the latter were not different between each other.

Table 3 Results of Study 3

	Isoamyl acetate	Banana	Vomit
Human	$N = 25$, 5.68 (1.38)***	$N = 26$, 5.62 (1.56)***	$N = 25$, 5.48 (1.76)***
Robot	$N = 32$, 5.31 (2.13)***	$N = 35$, 4.11 (1.98)	$N = 34$, 4.18 (2.30)

Number of participants per condition, mean answer and standard deviation in parentheses; significance tests compare means to the neutral answer, 4

* $p < .05$; ** $p < .01$; *** $p < .005$

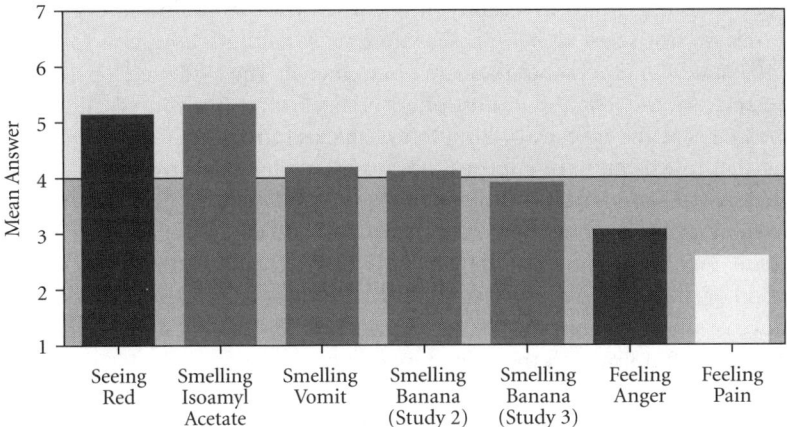

Figure 5.7. Folk's mean answers for mental state ascriptions to the robot Jimmy, within and across perceptual modality

5.2. Discussion

As we had predicted, people are more likely to ascribe the perception of an unknown olfactory stimulus to the robot than the perception of familiar smells associated with either positive or negative valence. The refined interior/exterior hypothesis discussed in Sect. 4.2 can hardly account for these findings, because we found that people's disposition to ascribe a mental state to the robot varied within a single modality. Because they are olfactory states, smelling banana and smelling isoamyl acetate are equally external. Thus, the refined interior/exterior hypothesis predicts that people should treat them similarly.

By contrast, the valence hypothesis predicts people's answers. Because people are unfamiliar with the smell of isoamyl acetate, they do not associate either a positive or a negative valence with it. Absent a specific valence, people focus on the perceptual reading of "smell" to decide whether Jimmy and Timmy can smell isoamyl acetate. By contrast, both the smell of banana and the smell of vomit are associated with valence. Because people tend to believe that only living creatures have likes and dislikes, they are relatively unwilling to ascribe these two smells to the robot. This is consistent with the proposal that the folk conceive of subjective states as states with an associated valence: People distinguish between different types of perceptual experiences, bodily sensations, and felt emotions depending on their valence.

6. PHENOMENAL STATES AND VALENCE

6.1. The Commonsense Understanding of Subjective Experience

The experimental studies reported on above offer preliminary evidence that the folk do *not* recognize the phenomenality of mental states such as seeing a color, hearing a sound, smelling, feeling pain, and experiencing some emotion.

To put the same point differently, in clear contrast to philosophers (Sect. 1), the folk do not seem to believe that there is something common to all these mental states—namely that they are phenomenal. The evidence for this difference between the folk and philosophers comes from three sources. First, Study 1 showed that the folk are willing to ascribe seeing red to a simple robot, but deny that it feels pain; in contrast, philosophers deny that the robot can be in either state. Second, unlike philosophers, the explanations given by those folk who deny that the robot could see red did not indicate that phenomenality was at issue. Finally, Studies 2 and 3 support our positive account of the folk conception of subjective experience: The folk's responses across modalities, and for a range of stimuli within the olfactory modality, correspond with the valence of those states, but not with their phenomenality.

We have seen that the folk are much more likely to ascribe mental states that lack valence (seeing red or smelling isoamyl acetate) to the robot than they are to ascribe a mental state with positive or negative valence (feeling pain, feeling anger, smelling banana, or smelling vomit). While each of these states is phenomenal, only those states that the folk were willing to ascribe to the robot Jimmy lacked a valence. Furthermore, people's relative willingness to ascribe the other mental states to the robot seems to correlate with traditional views about how essential valence is to that state. Valence is strongly associated with mental states like feeling pain or anger and the folk were unwilling to ascribe these states to Jimmy; in contrast, smelling banana and smelling vomit involve perceptual discriminations that can be carried out in the absence of any valence and participants were split in ascribing these states to Jimmy. For isoamyl acetate—an olfactory stimulus with no known valence for most people—however, participants were willing to say that Jimmy could smell it. Thus, across perceptual modalities, people's willingness to ascribe a mental state to a simple robot depends on the valence associated with the relevant perceptual modality and within the olfactory modality, people distinguish between mental states with and without a valence (Fig. 7).

Of the accounts of the folk understanding of subjective experience considered in this article, only our account predicts this pattern of answers. If people recognized the phenomenality of mental states such as seeing red and feeling pain, they would treat them similarly. But they don't. If people conceived of subjective mental states in terms of internal states (in contrast to the states produced by our external senses), they would treat similarly smelling banana and seeing red on the one hand and smelling isoamyl acetate and smelling banana on the other. But they don't.

6.2. Philosophical implications

What we have offered in this article in an initial empirical account of the commonsense conception of subjective experience. We have also presented preliminary evidence that it differs significantly from the philosophical concept of phenomenal consciousness. In contrast to philosophers' emphasis on the phenomenality of subjective mental states, for the folk, subjective states seem to be primarily states with a valence. We are aware that much work remains to be done to establish our hypothesis about the folk conception of subjective experience.[14] For the sake of the argument, however, we will assume in the remainder of the paper that it is by and large correct. We believe that the preliminary evidence reported here at least justifies taking seriously the hypothesis that philosophers' and ordinary people's conceptions of subjective experience differ in the way we proposed.

Understanding the common-sense conception of subjective experience is fascinating in its own right. It is also philosophically important. Although further research is needed to confirm the valence hypothesis, if correct it has some significant philosophical implications. First, some philosophers have claimed that philosophers and ordinary people conceive of subjective experience in basically the same way. Block (2004) likens the philosophical conception of subjective experience to the commonsense conception of subjective experience. Similarly, Dennett holds that the concept of phenomenal consciousness is part of "the lore" of our *folk theory of consciousness* that we pick up "in the course of our enculturation" (2005, pp. 26–27), Churchland talks of "the old folk notion of consciousness" (1988, p. 302), and Goldman writes about "the folk-psychological notion of phenomenal consciousness" (1993, p. 364). In line with such claims, we found in Study 1 that philosophers believe that ordinary people will give approximately the same answers as themselves. Our findings belie such claims.

Second, and more important, if further research supports our finding that there is a difference between the philosophical concept of phenomenal consciousness and the folk conception of subjective experience, it will have some significant implications for some central debates in philosophy of mind. We have particularly in mind Chalmers's hard problem of consciousness or Levine's explanatory gap.

For the sake of space, we focus on Chalmers's articulation of the problem. In substance, this problem is the following: supposing that one were able to describe all the functional properties of a mental state such as seeing red or feeling pain, something would remain unexplained, namely the phenomenal aspect of red (the redness of red) and the phenomenal aspect of pain (the painfulness of pain). Chalmers puts this problem as follows (1995, p. 203):

> [E]ven when we have explained the performance of all the cognitive and behavioral functions in the vicinity of experience—perceptual discrimination, categorization, internal access, verbal report—there may still remain a further unanswered question: *Why is the performance of these functions accompanied by experience?*

The sense of "experience" at issue is the philosophical conception of subjective experience, which unites perceptual experiences, bodily sensations, and felt emotions as each having a phenomenal aspect (see Chalmers's quotation in Sect. 1).

At this juncture, it is important to ask why we should believe that there is really a hard problem of consciousness. That is, why should we believe that there are experiences, as defined, such that an aspect of them is expected to be left unexplained even after we have thoroughly accounted for their functional roles? Chalmers's answer is characteristically limpid. As noted above, he suggests that phenomenal consciousness is undeniable because it is "the most central and manifest aspect of our mental lives" (1995, p. 207). In other words, on the basis of their introspective, first-person access to mental states such as seeing red or feeling pain, we are supposed to know that these mental states have phenomenal properties. As such, phenomenal consciousness has the status of an explanandum, but explaining it poses a hard problem: Chalmers holds that when we compare our first-person knowledge of the phenomenal properties of states such as feeling pain and seeing red to the functional accounts of these mental states, we will conclude that these accounts have failed to explain what had to be explained—viz. what it is like to be in pain and to see red.

Our findings cast some doubt on Chalmers's and others' justification of the hard problem of consciousness. If the account of the folk conception of subjective experience presented in this article is correct, then the folk do not find phenomenal experience manifest; their first-person experience with mental states such as seeing red and feeling pain does not lead them to judge that these mental states are united by each having a phenomenal aspect. But if most people do not judge that mental states such as feeling pain or seeing red have phenomenal properties in spite of their introspective experience with these states, then phenomenal consciousness can hardly be supposed to be "the most familiar and manifest aspect of our mental lives," as Chalmers puts it. It would be unclear whether these mental states have phenomenal properties at all. But, then, why should we view the hard problem of consciousness as a genuine problem?

It is worth contrasting the argument made here with the argument developed by Robbins and Jack (2006). Like us, Robbins and Jack link the commonsense conception of subjective experience to valence. They further argue that this commonsense conception is the source of the philosophical concept of phenomenal consciousness and of the resulting hard problem of consciousness. They conclude that while this problem is a pseudo-problem, "the gap intuition is psychologically real *and* deep" (p. 60). By contrast, we have argued that philosophers and ordinary people conceive of subjective experience differently. If this is correct, then the folk conception of subjective experience is *not* the origin of the hard problem of consciousness and cannot be used to underwrite it. Our skeptical challenge concludes that this undermines the usual justification for this supposed problem.

At this point, Chalmers and others might attempt to meet this skeptical challenge in two different ways. (Remember that for the sake of the argument, we are taking for granted that philosophers and ordinary people conceive of subjective experience differently.) First, they might argue that the fact that ordinary people do not conceive of subjective experience as being phenomenal does not undermine the claim that subjective experience is phenomenal.

Second, they might reformulate the hard problem of consciousness by focusing on the valence of pain and anger rather than on their phenomenality. We consider these two replies in turn, starting with the latter.

Our results suggest that the folk do not treat the diverse states at issue as being united by having phenomenal properties; rather they distinguish between them on the basis of valence. On this basis, we have asked, in a skeptical manner, why we should believe that there is a hard problem of consciousness. It is natural to reply that the valence of pain and anger raises a problem that is similar to the hard problem of consciousness: even if we knew all the functional and neural properties of pain and anger, one would not have explained why they have a valence.

This reply should be resisted. The hard problem specifically concerns phenomenal properties: It is the phenomenal properties that are thought to resist functional explanation. Valence, on the other hand, does not seem to raise this issue. It is far from clear why one would expect states with a valence to resist functional or neuronal explanation: the hedonic value of a stimulus or a bodily state seems to be an evaluation of its expected value to the organism. It might, of course, be conjectured that the folk understand the valence of states like feeling pain in such a way that they resist functional or neuronal explanation. Additional empirical work is needed to articulate how the folk actually understand the valence of states like pain, but in advance of such work we see little reason to expect that they understand valence in a way that would raise a problem that is similar to the hard problem of consciousness. Furthermore, even if it were to turn out that the folk understand valence in such a way, it is unclear that the resulting problem would have the philosophical force that the hard problem of consciousness has been thought to have, as opposed to being more akin to the problem raised by people holding a vitalist conception of life: Regardless of whether or not people hold that valence resists explanation, it is not clear why we should think that it actually does so.

Let's turn now to the other reply to our skeptical challenge. Chalmers and others might reply that justifying the hard problem of consciousness does not require that most people actually judge that mental states such as seeing red or feeling pain have phenomenal properties. It only requires that people who have carefully considered what it is like to be in such mental states make this judgment. Chalmers might then add that as our quotations illustrate, most philosophers have indeed done so.

It is currently unknown whether most people who have carefully considered what it is like to see red or feel pain do make this judgment. Artists, physicians, practitioners of various meditation practices, and so on, have presumably given due attention to such experiences, but we doubt that this introspection makes the philosophical concept of phenomenal consciousness any more obvious. Rather, we suspect that the proposition that subjective experience is phenomenal only becomes obvious as one is trained into a particular way of thinking about the mind.[15]

Now, if phenomenal consciousness only comes to seem obvious with philosophical training, then it is unclear whether the hard problem should be seen as raising a genuine challenge for philosophers, psychologists, and neuroscientists, as opposed to pointing out that there is a problem with the philosophical concept of phenomenal consciousness. The hard problem seems particularly cogent, because it is alleged that it is pretheoretically obvious that mental states like seeing red and feeling pain are phenomenal. Because this judgment is pretheoretical, it is difficult to challenge it on the ground that it is informed by one's philosophical perspective on consciousness. By contrast, if the judgment is not pretheoretical but is informed by one's philosophical perspective, then the hard problem can be rephrased as an argument against taking the theoretical concept of phenomenal consciousness to pick out an actual explanandum.

As an alternative reply to our argument, proponents of the hard problem of consciousness might argue that even though most people do not actually conceive of subjective experience as being phenomenal, they can *easily* be taught to conceive of them as phenomenal. It is important that this be easy if the hard problem is to remain cogent. Thus, the response concedes that while the folk do no spontaneously recognize phenomenal experience, it is nonetheless pretheoretical. Consider the analogy of pointing out to someone that their missing keys are in plain view. Like the keys, the proponent of the hard problem might argue that phenomenal experience is obvious, but that until it is pointed out to them many people miss it. To support this claim, they could appeal to their own experience of teaching undergraduates Nagel's notion of what it is like to have a conscious mental state or Levine's explanatory gap.

We are not convinced, however. We concede that if people could easily be taught to recognize the phenomenality of mental states such as seeing red and feeling pain, then the worry we have been raising would be alleviated. However, it is unclear whether the antecedent of this conditional is true. In our experience, many ordinary people either don't understand or don't take seriously the philosophical concept of phenomenal consciousness even after a lengthy explanation. It does not seem to us that the keys are in plain view.

7. CONCLUSION

We have provided some preliminary evidence that philosophers and ordinary people conceive of subjective experience in markedly different ways. Philosophers propose that subjectively experienced mental states have phenomenal properties: There is something it is like to see red, smell banana, feel anger, and be in pain. By contrast, ordinary people do not recognize that there is something common to all these states—viz. that they are phenomenal. Rather, they distinguish between the states that have a valence, such as pain, anger, and smelling banana, and the states that do not, such as seeing red and smelling isoamyl acetate. We have also argued that these empirical findings cast some doubts on whether there is really a hard problem of consciousness. The hard problem is typically justified on the grounds that we are acquainted with the phenomenal properties of states such as pain and seeing red and that functional accounts of mental states fail to explain how they can have such phenomenal properties. Our findings challenge the first premise of this argument. Because people do not seem to conceptualize their subjective mental life as phenomenal, it is at least unclear that we are pretheoretically acquainted with the phenomenal properties of our conscious mental states.

ACKNOWLEDGMENTS

The first author did most of the work on this article. We would like to thank Dave Chalmers, David Danks, Tony Jack, Joshua Knobe, Jonathan Livengood, Shaun Nichols, Peter Pagin, and Philip Robbins for their comments on previous versions of this article. We also would like to thank Eric Schwitzgebel for his reply to a talk based on this article at annual meeting of the Society for Philosophy and Psychology in 2008. Thanks also to the audiences in Santa Cruz, Stockholm, Lund, and Gothenburg.

APPENDIX

STUDY 1: SEEING RED AND FEELING PAIN

A total of 671 participants completed surveys through the Mental State Intuitions Study website. Sixty-eight participants were excluded because their biographical information was incomplete or because their comments indicated they misunderstood the probe. Biographical information was considered "incomplete" if we could not sort the participant into either the philosopher or the non-philosopher groups (see footnote 8). Participants were judged to misunderstand the probe mostly for the following reasons: they stated that the electric shock was not painful, they understood "see red" as meaning "is angry," or they stated that the robot was under remote control. Of the remainder, 61% were male; the mean age was around 33 (range: 18–68). There were 372 philosophers (71% male; mean age around 33) and 231 non-philosophers (46% male; mean age around 31).

A three-way ANOVA with type of agent, type of mental state, and philosophical training as between-participant factors yielded a main effect of the type of agent (Timmy > Jimmy), a main effect of the type of mental state (seeing red > pain), a main effect of philosophical training (non-philosophers > philosophers) and three-two-way interaction (type of mental state by type of agent; type of mental state by philosophical training; type of agent by philosophical training). Planned analyses showed that philosophers' mean answers for both feeling pain and seeing red were significantly above 4 for Timmy (red: $N = 92$, $M = 5.90$, $SD = 1.46$, $p < .005$; pain: $N = 84$, $M = 6.44$, $SD = .87$, $p < .005$) and significantly below 4 for Jimmy (red: $N = 96$, $M = 3.48$, $SD = 1.94$, $p < .01$; pain: $N = 100$, $M = 2.02$, $SD = 1.53$, $p < .005$); non-philosophers treated the states dissimilarly, the mean answers for Timmy being significantly above 4 (red: $N = 55$, $M = 5.98$, $SD = 1.25$, $p < .005$; pain: $N = 62$, $M = 6.15$, $SD = 1.01$,

p <.005), as was the mean answer for Jimmy seeing red ($N = 52$, $M = 5.15$, $SD = 1.85$, p <.005), while the mean answer for Jimmy feeling pain was significantly below 4 ($N = 59$, $M = 2.54$, $SD = 1.99$, p <.005). The difference between the average folk ascription of seeing red and of feeling pain is statistically significant [$t(109) = 7.12$, p <.001] and the effect size ($d = 0.87$) is large (Cohen 1992).

STUDY 2: SMELLING BANANA AND FEELING ANGER

253 participants completed surveys through the Mental State Intuitions Study website. Thirty-one participants were excluded because their biographical information was incomplete, because they had indicated they had already participated to the Mental State Intuitions Study, or because they were not 18 year old. Since this study was aimed at exploring the pattern of folk responses seen in our first experiment, an additional 63 participants were excluded based on their responses to biographical questions concerning their philosophical training (see footnote 8). Of the remainder, 38% were male; the mean age was around 30 (range: 18–75).

A two-way ANOVA with type of agent and type of mental state as between-participant factors yielded a main effect of the type of agent [Timmy > Jimmy; $F(1, 102) = 36.84$, p <.001] and no other main effect or interaction. Planned analyses showed that the mean answers for both smelling banana and feeling anger were significantly higher than 4 for Timmy (banana: $N = 18$, $M = 5.83$, $SD = 1.46$, p <.005; anger: $N = 25$, $M = 5.84$, $SD = 0.99$, p <.005); the mean answer was significantly below 4 for Jimmy feeling anger ($N = 35$, $M = 3.06$, $SD = 2.22$, p <.05) and neutral for Jimmy smelling banana ($N = 28$, $M = 3.89$, $SD = 2.42$).

STUDY 3: THE VALENCE OF SMELL

A total of 211 participants completed our survey in a classroom setting. Thirty-four participants were excluded because their biographical information was incomplete, because they were philosophers (see footnote 8), because they had already completed one of our surveys, or because they were not 18 years old. Of the remainder, 33.5% were male; the mean age was around 20 (range: 18–30).

A two-way ANOVA with type of agent and type of olfactory cue as between-participant factors yielded a main effect of the type of agent [Timmy > Jimmy; $F(1, 171) = 13.17$, p <.001] and no other main effect or interaction. Planned analyses showed that participants' mean answers for each of the three target smells for Timmy were significantly above 4 (isoamyl acetate: $N = 25$, $M = 5.68$, $SD = 1.38$, p <.005; banana: $N = 26$, $M = 5.62$, $SD = 1.56$, p <.005; vomit: $N = 25$, $M = 5.48$, $SD = 1.76$, p <.005); the mean for the unfamiliar smell (isoamyl acetate) for Jimmy was also significantly above 4 ($N = 32$, $M = 5.31$, $SD = 2.13$, p <.005), but the scores were neutral for the two familiar smells for Jimmy (banana: $N = 35$, $M = 4.11$, $SD = 1.98$; vomit: $N = 34$,

$M = 4.148$, $SD = 2.30$). Participants mean answer to the unfamiliar smell was significantly higher than either familiar smell [banana: $t(65) = -2.28$, $p = .02$; vomit: $t(65) = -2.08$, $p = .04$], while for the unfamiliar smells the mean answers were not different between each other [$t(67) = -.12$, $p = .9$].

NOTES

1. Throughout we will use the term "valence" as follows: mental states have a valence if and only if they have a hedonic value for the subject. That is, mental states have a valence if and only if they are pleasurable (they then have a positive valence) or disagreeable (they then have a negative valence). Not all mental states have a valence, and valenced states are more or less pleasurable or disagreeable. Typically, but perhaps not necessarily, disagreeable mental states motivate people to act as to discontinue these, while pleasurable mental states motivate people to act so as to perpetuate them.

2. While we follow convention in referring to mental states like seeing red and smelling banana as perceptual experiences, it is worth noting that some hold that mental states here classified as bodily sensations, felt emotions, or felt moods are also perceptual (e.g., Prinz 2006). We wish to thank an anonymous referee for *Philosophical Studies* for pointing this out.

3. See http://www.ai.mit.edu/projects/humanoid-robotics-group/cog/cog.html.

4. See http://www.ai.mit.edu/projects/sociable.

5. Heather Gray explicitly equated her Experience dimension with phenomenal consciousness at the 2007 Association for the Scientific Study of Consciousness conference.

6. http://www.JustinSytsma.com/MSIS.

7. See Appendix for demographical information and data analysis for each experiment.

8. "Philosophers" were defined as participants who indicated at least some graduate training in philosophy or either had already completed or were in the process of completing an undergraduate degree with a major in philosophy. Note that the results do not change when we count as philosophers only the participants who have some graduate training in philosophy.

9. We emphasize that the robot and the undergraduate behave in the same way. Thus, if participants were to ascribe differently pain and seeing red to the robot and the undergraduate, this difference could not plausibly be explained by reference to the functional and behavioral properties of the two agents; rather, it would result from participants focusing on the phenomenal properties of these states. This stands in contrast with Knobe and Prinz's (2008) comparison of an individual agent and of a corporation.

10. The complete set of probes is available at: http://www.JustinSytsma.com/MSIS/probes.html. The same image was used with each robot scenario in Studies 1, 2, and 3; an image of a typical undergraduate was used in each of the human scenarios.

11. We briefly mention a third possible reply (T. Jack, personal communication). A critic could argue that our hypothesis predicts that if we ask ordinary people whether Jimmy *experience red,* they would answer affirmatively. If they would answer *negatively* (as our critic suggests they would), then we would have to conclude that the folk conceive of subjective experience as philosophers do. In reply, we note that "experience" is a technical term and does not have the same meaning in ordinary English and in philosophy. In ordinary English, an experience typically is a significant interaction with an object (e.g., one might say "My encounter with the bear in the woods was a frightening experience"). For this reason, it is dubious that asking ordinary English speakers about a robot's experience would be of much relevance to study how they understand subjective experience.

12. See, e.g., Huebner (2009) for a related objection.

13. We replicated the experiment with the question "Was Timmy/Jimmy angry..." instead of the question "Did Timmy/Jimmy feel anger..." Since this variation had no effect on participants' answers, we present only their answers to the question formulated with "feel anger" to match the formulation used in Study 1 for "feel pain." For discussion of the construction "feeling + psychological predicate" see Sytsma and Machery (2009).

14. Particularly, one might argue that the fact that ordinary people have no difficulty understanding the classical thought experiments about consciousness, such as the inverted spectrum thought experiment, shows that the folk conception of subjective experience coincides with the concept of phenomenal consciousness. We are currently examining whether people really grasp these thought experiments.

15. While most philosophers seem to find phenomenal consciousness obvious, we suspect that this has not been the case for scientists. In fact, philosophers have often criticized psychologists and neuropsychologists for failing to see that their account of consciousness failed to solve the hard problem (see Chalmers 1995, Sect. IV, for example). We suspect that many psychologists and neuropsychologists have not failed in this respect by accident. Rather, it might be that like the folk, they do not conceive of subjective experience as being phenomenal, in spite of having plausibly carefully considered "what it is like" for them to see red, feel pain, and so on. For this reason, they might not recognize that there is a further aspect of these mental states that needs explaining.

REFERENCES

Arico, A. (2010) . Folk psychology, consciousness, and context effects. *Review of Philosophy and Psychology.* 1, 371–393.

Bennett, M., & Hacker, P. (2003). *Philosophical foundations of neuroscience.* Oxford: Blackwell.

Block, N. (1995). On a confusion about a function of consciousness. *Behavioral and Brain Sciences, 18,* 227–247.

Block, N. (2004). Qualia. In R. Gregory (Ed.), *Oxford companion to the mind* (2nd ed., pp. 785–789). New York: Oxford University Press.

Bloom, P. (2004). *Descartes' baby: How the science of child development explains what makes us human.* London: William Heinemann.

Chalmers, D. (1995). Facing up to the problem of consciousness. *Journal of Consciousness Studies, 2*(3), 200–219.

Churchland, P. S. (1988). Reduction and the neurobiological basis of consciousness. In A. J. Marcel & E. Bisiach (Eds.), *Consciousness in contemporary science* (pp. 273–304). Oxford: Oxford University Press.

Cohen, J. (1992). A power primer. *Psychological Bulletin, 112,* 155–159.

Crick, F. (1995). *The astonishing hypothesis: The scientific search for the soul.* New York: Simon & Schuster.

Dennett, D. (1987). *The intentional stance.* Cambridge, MA: MIT Press.

Dennett, D. (1996). *Kinds of minds: Toward an understanding of consciousness.* Cambridge, MA: MIT Press.

Dennett, D. (2005). *Sweet dreams: Philosophical obstacles to a science of consciousness.* New York: Basic Books.

Goldman, A. (1993). Consciousness, folk psychology, and cognitive science. *Consciousness and Cognition, 2,* 364–382.

Gray, H., Gray, K., & Wegner, D. (2007). Dimensions of mind perception. *Science, 315,* 619.

Herz, R., Eliassen, J., Beland, S., & Souza, T. (2004). Neuroimaging evidence for the emotional potency of odor-evoked memory. *Neuropsychologia, 42,* 371–378.

Huebner, B. (2009). Commonsense concepts of phenomenal consciousness: Does anyone care about functional zombies? *Phenomenology and the Cognitive Sciences,9,* 133–155.

Huebner, B., Bruno, M., & Sarkissian, H. (2010). What does the nation of China think about phenomenal states? *Review of Philosophy and Psychology 1*(2), 225–243.

Knobe, J., & Prinz, J. (2008). Intuitions about consciousness: Experimental studies. *Phenomenology and the Cognitive Sciences, 7,* 67–85.

Levin, J. (1998). Qualia. In E. Craig (Ed.), *Routledge encyclopedia of philosophy.* London: Routledge. Accessed 4 July 2007 from http://www.rep.routledge.com/article/V029.

Nagel, T. (1974). What is it like to be a bat? *The Philosophical Review, 83*(4), 435–450.

Newton, N. (1989). On viewing pain as a secondary quality. *Noûs, 23*(5), 569–598.

Newton, N. (2000). Humphrey's solution. *Journal of Consciousness Studies, 7*(4), 62–66.

Papineau, D. (2002). *Thinking about consciousness.* Oxford: Oxford University Press.

Piaget, J. (1929). *The child's conception of the world.* New York: Harcourt.

Prinz, J. (2006). *Gut reactions: A perceptual theory of emotions.* New York: Oxford University Press.

Robbins, P., & Jack, A. (2006). The phenomenal stance. *Philosophical Studies, 127,* 59–85.

Searle, J. (1994). *The rediscovery of the mind.* Cambridge, MA: MIT Press.

Sytsma, J., & Machery, E. (2009). How to study folk intuitions about phenomenal consciousness. *Philosophical Psychology, 22*(1), 21–35.

Tye, M. (2003). Qualia. In E. N. Zalta (Ed.), *The Stanford encyclopedia of philosophy.* Accessed 4 July 2007 from http://plato.stanford.edu/entries/qualia.

Wellman, H. M., & Estes, D. (1986). Early understanding of mental entities: A reexamination of childhood realism. *Child Development, 57,* 910–923.

Winston, J., Gottgried, J., Kilner, J., & Dolan, R. (2005). Integrated neural representations of odor intensity and affective valence in human amygdala. *The Journal of Neuroscience, 25*(39), 8903–8907.

6

The Folk Psychology of Consciousness*

Adam Arico, Brian Fiala, Robert F. Goldberg, and Shaun Nichols

1. THE PROBLEM OF OTHER CONSCIOUS MINDS

We find it so natural to think that other people and animals are conscious that it is easy to overlook a deep puzzle: *why* do we think anything else is conscious? Consciousness is widely regarded to be a paradigmatically private affair, something that could never be publicly observed. So what prompts us to think that others have conscious minds at all?[1]

The fact that we are inclined to attribute conscious states to other creatures has long been recognized as puzzling by philosophers (Augustine, *De Trinitate* 8.6.9; Reid, 1785/1969). We can think of this puzzle as the *descriptive* problem of other conscious minds.[2] Philosophers have made various speculations about what leads us to think that others have conscious states. J. S. Mill develops a version of the most famous answer to the puzzle: I come to believe in other minds by drawing an analogy with my own case. He writes:

> [B]y what considerations am I led to believe, that there exist other sentient creatures; that the walking and speaking figures which I see and hear, have sensations and thoughts, or in other words, possess Minds?...I conclude that other human beings have feelings like me, because, first, they have bodies like me, which I know, in my own case, to be the antecedent condition of feelings; and because, secondly, they exhibit the acts, and other outward signs, which in my own case I know by experience to be caused by feelings. (Mill, 1865, 208)

Mill's statement suggests the following procedure, which involves analogical reasoning: I know that my feelings come via my body, and I appreciate the analogy between my body and the bodies of others; I also know that certain behaviors of mine are caused by mental states; so when I see other analogous bodies exhibiting similar behaviors, I infer that their behaviors are also caused by mental states. It's easy to see why this view has been historically attractive. Analogical reasoning provides a sensible and familiar explanation for our belief in other minds.

Although the analogical theory has historical weight and a few contemporary advocates (e.g. Hill, 1991; Hyslop, 1995), the currently dominant view is that we believe in other conscious minds because it's the best explanation for what we observe. This approach has been developed in recent years by a number of people. For instance, Robert Pargetter asks, 'What is the nature of the inferences that we all so commonly, and rightly, make from certain behavioural evidence to the mental lives of other people?' He suggests that 'these inferences should best be viewed as being common scientific or hypothetic inferences, or arguments to the best explanation' (Pargetter, 1984, p. 158). The idea is that we come to believe in other conscious minds by using good inductive techniques—appealing to other conscious minds is the best explanation for the behavior we observe.[3] This basic approach has been widely adopted in recent philosophy. Indeed, it's promoted in standard textbooks in the philosophy of mind (Churchland, 1988, pp. 71–72; Graham, 1998, pp. 57–63).[4]

The philosophical appeals to analogy and best explanation are based on speculation and informal observation. But over the last several decades there has been an impressive body of empirical work on how children and adults attribute mental states across a broad range of conditions (for reviews see e.g. Goldman, 2006; Gopnik and Meltzoff, 1997; Nichols and Stich, 2003; Perner, 1991; Wellman, 1990). Some of the mental states that have been explored in this literature are, of course, conscious mental states (see e.g. Harris, 1989). This work has taught us a great deal, but very little of this work is focused directly on the traditional question, 'what leads us to think that particular individuals are bearers of *conscious* mental states'? That is, there is little work aimed at explaining what leads us to regard something as a candidate for having conscious states at all.

In addition to the intrinsic interest of the descriptive problem, solving the problem may also help us to evaluate whether the processes by which we gauge consciousness are in fact good processes. A familiar view in philosophy is that the way we in fact identify others as conscious is, in general, a rationally sound method (Mill, 1865; Pargetter, 1984). That is, the path by which we identify others as conscious is, roughly, a rationally appropriate path. However, it is an old and familiar philosophical worry that the basis for our thinking that others are conscious might be entirely spurious (e.g. Descartes, 1641/1986). To know whether such a worry is misplaced presumably requires determining the actual basis on which we come to think of others as conscious.

2. THE PROBLEM OF OTHER MINDS IN PSYCHOLOGY

The descriptive problem of other minds has a long history in philosophy. Over the last twenty years, cognitive scientists have been intensively exploring how people attribute mental states to others (see e.g. Goldman, 2006; Nichols and Stich, 2003; Perner, 1991; Wellman, 1990). As noted above, little of this work in cognitive science is focused directly at our question of what leads people to attribute *conscious* states—like pain—to others. However, there is one strand of work that provides a very promising framework. This research focuses on what generates the tendency to think that a certain object has mental states *at all*.

One of the earliest investigations on the topic is Heider and Simmel's (1944) study on how adults describe an animation involving geometric objects moving about in distinctive ways. They found overwhelmingly that adults describe the animation by adverting to mental states. For example, at one point in the animation, the big triangle repeatedly bumps up against the inside edge of a rectangle, and nearly all subjects say that the triangle wants to get out of the box. More recent work shows that children respond in much the same way to these sorts of stimuli. Like the adults in Heider and Simmel's study, when children are asked to describe what they saw, they advert to the goals, beliefs, and intentions of the triangles in a 2D animation (e.g. Bowler and Thommen, 2000; Abell et al., 2000; Dasser et al., 1989). If you've watched one of these animations, the results will come as no surprise. It's extremely natural to see these objects as having mental states because the motion trajectories of the triangles 'push the right buttons' to trigger mind attribution.[5] This becomes evident when one contrasts Heider–Simmel style animations with an animation of triangles moving about the surface in straight lines at constant speeds. In that case, there is no inclination to start attributing mental states to the triangles. Motion alone is not sufficient. But it remains possible that relatively simple motion cues suffice for agency attributions. For instance, change in speed plus change in direction might be sufficient to generate an attribution of a mind, even if nothing can be discerned about the goals or thoughts of that mind (Scholl and Tremoulet, 2000, p. 305). Of course, as adults, we don't cave to our first-blush intuitions of mentality here—we know, on slight reflection, that the images don't have minds. Nonetheless, there presumably is a mechanism that generates these powerful, if overridable, inclinations to attribute mental states, and this mechanism likely plays an important role in everyday attributions of mental states.

Susan Johnson and colleagues use very different techniques to discern the mechanisms underlying the attribution of a mind to an individual. There are several ways that a baby might reveal that she thinks an object has a mind: she might follow the 'gaze' of the object, try to communicate with the object, imitate the behaviors of the object, or attribute goals to the object. By exploiting this variety of indicators, Johnson provides evidence that infants attribute minds as a result of particular kinds of relatively simple cues. In a representative experiment, 12-month-old infants were shown a fuzzy brown object under a variety of different conditions (Johnson et al., 1998). In one condition, the fuzzy brown object (with no facial features) interacted contingently with the infant by beeping and flashing when the infant babbled or moved; in another condition, the fuzzy brown object exhibited an equivalent amount of flashing and beeping, but in this condition the activity was not contingent on the infant's behavior. In both conditions, children's looking behavior was measured when the fuzzy brown object 'gazed' at one of two objects by making a smooth, 45 degree turn towards the object and remaining in this orientation for several seconds. What Johnson and colleagues found was that infants were more likely to follow the 'gaze' of the fuzzy brown object when its beeping and flashing were contingent. In another set of conditions the fuzzy brown object did not flash or beep, but Johnson and colleagues found that babies were more likely to follow the 'gaze' of the fuzzy brown object when it had eyes than when it did not. In other experiments, babies were shown a stuffed orangutan that had a face and exhibited contingent interaction. Babies imitated the behavior of the stuffed animal and made communicative gestures toward it, indicating that the babies coded the object as having a mind (Johnson et al., 2001).

In more recent experiments, Johnson and colleagues devised a new object, the blob, a bright green object about the shape of an adult shoe that had no facial features but could beep and move around on its own. Again they explored contingent interaction, but in this case the contingent interaction was with a confederate rather than the baby herself. In one condition, a confederate engaged the blob in 'small talk', and the blob beeped contingently with the confederate; in the other condition the blob's beeps were not contingent upon the confederate's behavior. Again they found that babies were more likely to follow the 'gaze' of the blob in the contingent interaction condition.

Finally, and perhaps most impressively, the blob design has recently been coupled with Amanda Woodward's goal attribution experiment. Woodward (1998) showed babies an arm moving towards one of two locations, each containing one of two objects. Then the locations of the objects were switched. Babies looked longer when the arm reached to the same location that now held a different object, suggesting that the babies expected the arm to reach for the same goal-object. Shimizu and Johnson (2004) found something similar with the blob—babies looked longer when the blob moved in the same direction but towards a different object. But this effect only occurred when the blob had behaved contingently with the confederate.

Johnson suggests that this broad pattern of results is evidence that, by 12 months, the infant has a conceptual representation of *agent*. Characteristics like eyes and contingent interaction trigger this conceptual representation, and this representation then sets up the pattern of behavioral responses that we see in the experiments. As Johnson puts it, 'Those characteristics invoke an intermediary representation (intermediary in the processing stream between perception and action) of *intentional agent* that is available to support multiple behaviors' (Johnson, 2005, p. 254, emphasis added).

Johnson's suggestion that the concept of *intentional agent* is a critical intervening factor between the cues and the behavior can easily be expanded to accommodate the results from Heider and Simmel as well. The distinctive motion trajectories of the animation triggers the *intentional agent* concept, which in turn sets up the disposition to attribute desires, intentions, and so forth. Together, this generates the (partial) causal network depicted in Figure 1. 'Agent' as it is used in this network is obviously something of a technical notion. It is not clear that it corresponds to any term in vernacular English. We will use *AGENT* to denote this technical category.[6] If an entity exhibits one of the relatively simple features mentioned above, this will trigger the inclination to categorize the entity as an *AGENT*. Once an individual identifies an entity as an AGENT, this sets up certain dispositions in the person—e.g. the disposition to attribute goals, to imitate, and to anticipate goal directed behavior.

Now we can state our proposal. We maintain that, when it comes to the tendency to attribute mental states to an individual, there is nothing special about *conscious* mental states. Rather, once a person categorizes an individual as an AGENT, she will be inclined to attribute conscious mental states to the individual.[7] This account, which we'll call the 'AGENCY model', can be represented as a minor adjustment to the network characterizing the AGENCY concept, yielding Figure 2. The AGENCY model builds naturally on the work in developmental psychology to explain what leads us to think that others have conscious states. But there is a developing literature in philosophy and psychology that seems to challenge it.

3. AGENCY AND EXPERIENCE: A DISSOCIATION?

We have suggested that the attribution of agency suffices to dispose one to attribute conscious experiences. In a recent paper in *Science*, Heather Gray, Kurt Gray and Daniel Wegner have argued that agency and experience are independent dimensions of mental attributions. Gray and colleagues collected data from over 2000 respondents to an online survey. Participants were presented with 78 pairings of 13 different characters and then asked to rate (on a 5-point Likert scale) which character had a greater capacity for possessing a certain

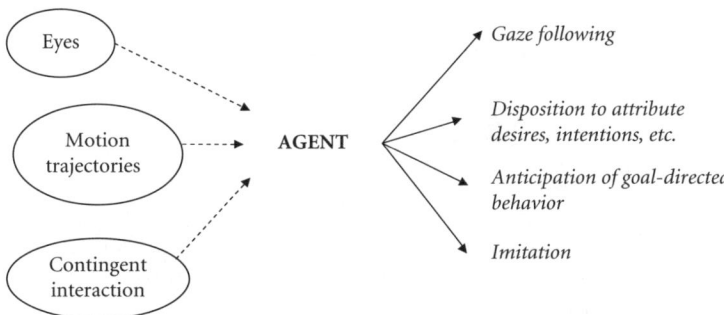

Figure 6.1. Network of A GENT concept

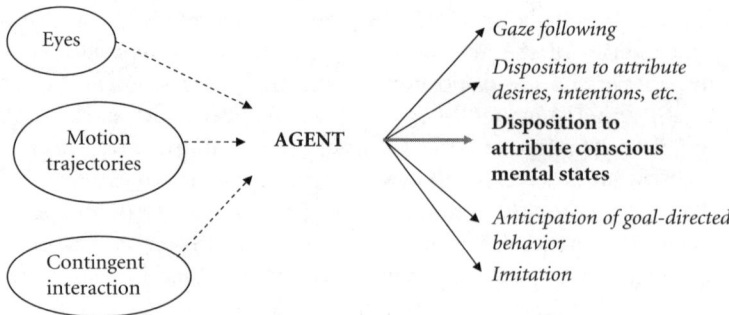

Figure 6.2. The AGENCY model

particular mental trait (e.g. 'Which character is more capable of experiencing joy?'). The researchers maintain that the responses reveal two quite different dimensions of mind perception: Agency and Experience (Gray et al., 2007, p. 619; see also Robbins and Jack, 2006). Moreover, Gray and colleagues conclude from the data that the two features, Agency and Experience, can be dissociated. God, for instance, rates at the top of the Agency scale, but at the absolute bottom of Experience; frogs and fetuses, conversely, rate high on the Experience scale while lacking any degree of Agency.

Although the work of Gray and colleagues might be thought to challenge our AGENT-based approach, there is a natural reply. The capacities that fall under the category of *Agency* in their study are relatively sophisticated: self-control, morality, memory, emotion recognition, planning, communication, and thought. Paradigmatic entities that would trigger AGENT in our sense, like frogs, are judged to lack many of those sophisticated capacities. Thus, while frogs are extremely low on 'agency' by the standards of Gray and colleagues, frogs would certainly trigger the AGENT category on our notion of AGENT. Frogs have it all—eyes, contingent interaction, and distinctive motion trajectories. Furthermore, the traits that fall under Gray and colleague's category of *Experience* also often involve sophisticated capacities, e.g. personality, pride, embarrassment, and joy. So, Gray and colleagues' results leave open the possibility that a minimal notion of agent of the sort we have in mind would produce a tendency to attribute minimal kinds of experience, like pain. The AGENCY model aims to capture the most basic features that generate the disposition to attribute the most basic conscious states. As a result, the model isn't threatened by the findings of Gray and colleagues.

Joshua Knobe and Jesse Prinz present a different kind of evidential argument for dissociating agency and experience, suggesting that people attribute agency while positively *resisting* consciousness attributions. Their studies focus on attributions of mental states to groups. In one study, Knobe and Prinz presented subjects with two sets of sentences; one set attributed non-conscious mental states to a group entity, while another attributed conscious mental states to that same entity. The non-conscious state attributions consisted of sentences like 'Acme Corp intends to release a new product this January' and 'Acme Corp wants to change its corporate image'. The conscious state attributions included such sentences as 'Acme Corp is now experiencing great joy' and 'Acme Corp is feeling excruciating pain'. Knobe and Prinz found that subjects rated sentences about Acme Corp's non-conscious mental states as sounding 'natural', while they rated sentences about Acme Corp.'s conscious mental states as sounding 'weird'. The moral of these experiments, they say, is that 'people are unwilling to ascribe to group agents states that require phenomenal consciousness' (Knobe and Prinz, 2008).[8]

Knobe and Prinz's work indicates that people might regard groups as agents in *some* sense, for people seem comfortable attributing desires and plans to groups. But it's possible that groups do not activate the *primitive* notion of AGENCY that we posit. Indeed, although this has not been studied yet, we suspect that there is a developmental pattern concerning the attribution of mental states to groups such that young children will be less likely than adults to attribute mental states to groups. If this turns out to be right, it would suggest that children are not identifying groups as AGENTS in our sense.[9]

Moreover, as argued elsewhere (Arico, 2010; Sytsma and Machery, 2009), there are methodological worries with the Knobe and Prinz experiments that call their conclusion into question. For instance, Knobe and Prinz found that subjects rated sentences attributing phenomenal mental states to groups as sounding 'weirder' (less natural) than sentences attributing non-phenomenal mental states to groups. However, Knobe and Prinz stimuli were not minimal pairs: sentences attributing non-phenomenal states included additional contextual information that phenomenal attributions lacked.[10] Though Knobe and Prinz interpret the difference in sentence ratings as evidence of the folk (tacitly) distinguishing between phenomenal and non-phenomenal states, Arico (2010) provides some evidence that the difference is actually produced by the disparity in contextual information between the two kinds of sentences.

It is important to note that neither Gray and colleagues nor Knobe and Prinz present a positive proposal about the descriptive question with which we started—what features trigger our attributions of conscious states? This is not surprising given that a central purpose of their accounts was to show the independence of *experience* and *agency*. But it does mean that their accounts do not yet give a full answer to the question, 'why do we believe that others have conscious mental states'? And of course that's exactly what the AGENCY model attempts to do. In what follows we will explain the model and its empirical commitments in more detail.

4. THE AGENCY MODEL

We suspect that a more fundamental notion of 'agency' does provide a sufficient basis for attributing conscious states. We have focused on the relatively simple features that serve as cues, which trigger the AGENT concept. But of course these sorts of cues are not the *only* way to activate the AGENT concept. For example, merely thinking about an acquaintance (who is not physically present) may trigger the AGENT concept. Relatedly, if a trusted source of testimony *tells* me that there is a person in the other room, then this will typically lead me to think that there is an AGENT in the other room. For our purposes, the role of the relatively simple features that serve as cues is especially important, since we are particularly interested in identifying a set of minimal sufficient conditions for attributing conscious states. The key idea is that relatively simple features (e.g. motion pattern, facial features, contingent interaction) will suffice to trigger AGENT categorization, and this will in turn produce an inclination to attribute conscious states to the individual. Hence, the core of the AGENCY model is a causal sufficiency thesis:

> *Sufficiency Thesis.* Typically, if an entity is categorized as an AGENT, then there will be an inclination for attributing conscious states to that entity.

We take the sufficiency thesis to be central to the AGENCY model. But we also want to promote a more specific view about the nature of the process that generates these attributions. The research on animations (e.g. Heider and Simmel, 1944) suggests that the distinctive motion trajectories lead to attributions of goals and intentions by a process that is *fast, automatic,* and *unavailable to introspection* (see e.g. Scholl and Tremoulet, 2000). Following Johnson (2005) we've suggested that this process is mediated by triggering the concept AGENT. On our AGENCY model, the disposition to attribute conscious states follows from triggering this concept. As a result, it's natural to maintain that the attribution of conscious states mediated by the AGENT concept is generated by a process that is fast, automatic, and unavailable to introspection. This is not, of course, the *only* way that an attribution of consciousness can come about. Our model allows for attributions of consciousness that do not involve these quick, automatic inclinations. The model thus aligns with various dual-process pictures, according to which, in addition to quick, automatic, low-level cognitive processes there are slow, deliberative, controlled, high-level reasoning processes capable of operating on the same domain (see, e.g. Chaiken and Trope, 1999; Sloman, 1996; Stanovich and West, 2000).

With the dual process framework in the background, we can now state a further, more ambitious thesis of the AGENCY model. We suggest that typically the only way to get the fast, automatic, gut-level inclination to attribute conscious states to an entity is by triggering the AGENT concept. That is, categorizing an object as an AGENT is causally necessary for a certain sort of inclination to attribute conscious states:

> *Necessity Thesis.* Typically, there will be a quick, automatic inclination for attributing conscious states to an entity *only if* that entity is categorized as an AGENT.

The claim is qualified to allow for the possibility that we might attribute consciousness to an entity on the basis of more deliberate, controlled processes. But to get the gut-level immediate inclination to attribute consciousness requires categorizing the object as an AGENT.

The *sufficiency thesis* suggests that if a person categorizes an object as an AGENT, then she will be disposed to attribute conscious states to that object. This produces the interesting prediction that even relatively simple features will generate an inclination to attribute conscious states to an object. The *necessity thesis* predicts that if a person rejects the categorization of AGENT for a given object, then she will typically not have the automatic inclination to attribute conscious states to the object.

Insects provide an intriguing real-world test case here. Insects are widely regarded among neuroscientists as incapable of experiences like pain, since they lack the relevant neural structures. Nonetheless, insects exhibit all of the simple features reviewed above—eyes, distinctive motion trajectories, and contingent interaction—that serve as cues for categorizing a thing as an AGENT. As a result, the AGENCY model predicts that insects should be categorized as AGENTS and, as a result, people should have a greater tendency to attribute conscious states to insects than to objects like clouds and rivers that lack the central cues of AGENCY and presumably do not get categorized as AGENTS.

5. EXPERIMENT

In order to test the AGENCY Model, we ran a reaction-time study in which subjects were presented with a sequence of Object/Attribution pairs. In the present study, we were interested to learn about the processes underlying folk attributions of states that psychologists and philosophers typically consider conscious or phenomenal rather than the folk's categorizations of certain states as 'conscious'. As such, the attributions we examined specified states or properties that we take to be paradigmatic of phenomenally conscious experience, such as 'Feels Happy' and 'Feels Pain'.[11] Objects were drawn from several categories, including Vehicles, Insects, and Plants.

Because the model we are proposing describes a low-level cognitive process that, we suggest, reacts automatically to simple features, we wanted to measure the mental chronometry for attributions of conscious states to various objects. Thus, for each Object/Attribution pair, subjects were asked to respond as quickly as possible (Yes or No) whether the object has the attribute. The AGENCY model makes predictions both about overt responses and about reaction times. For overt responses, the core of the AGENCY model, the sufficiency thesis, predicts that subjects should exhibit a tendency to attribute conscious states to objects that are likely to trigger AGENT categorization. Since insects exhibit the simple features that trigger the AGENT concept, and so are likely to be categorized as AGENTS, they are of particular interest. What will be especially telling will be to contrast the responses to insects with responses to objects that seem unlikely to trigger the AGENT concept, including individuals in the categories Vehicles, Natural Moving Objects, and Plants. The *necessity thesis* generates the further prediction that under speeded conditions, participants should not be inclined to make overt attributions of conscious states to objects that are not categorized as AGENT.

In a reaction time paradigm, faster response times suggest that the responses are dictated (largely, if not exclusively) by lower-level, automatic processes, while longer reaction times suggest that the responses are influenced by higher-level considerations, deliberations, associations, etc. Given this (standard) interpretation of response times, the *sufficiency thesis* predicts slower reaction times when participants *deny* conscious state attributions to objects that are typically classified as AGENTS (compared broadly with non-AGENTS). The idea is that even if someone were to overtly express the belief that insects don't feel pain (e.g. because they lack appropriate neural structures), she would still have a strong, automatic inclination to think that they do feel pain; she thus has to overcome that automatic inclination to get out her answer of 'no', and this will take some extra time.[12] Or, to put it more colorfully, when I am asked whether ants feel pain, there is a little guy inside of me saying 'yes'. And I need to repress that guy before I can get out my 'no' response.[13] By contrast, there's no little guy inside of me saying that trucks or rivers feel pain, so my denial in those cases should not be delayed in this way. Finally, the *necessity thesis* predicts that, for *anything* that is not counted as an AGENT, there will be no immediate inclination to attribute conscious states, so there should be no hesitation to respond 'no' for anything that does not trigger the AGENT concept.[14]

Method

Participants

Thirty-four participants (14 male, 20 female, mean age = 19.2) from the University of Pittsburgh volunteered for this study to fulfill course requirements.

Materials

Subjects performed a timed property-attribution task, in which they were asked to respond positively or negatively to a series of questions attributing different sorts of properties to different sorts of entities. Properties included 'Feels Anger', 'Feels Happy', 'Hunts', 'Made of Metal', 'Feels Pain', 'Feels Pride', 'Is A Living Thing', and 'Is Colored White'. Entities included fifteen word items for each of eight categories: Mammals, Birds, Insects, Plants, Artifacts, Vehicles, Inanimate Natural Objects (e.g. stone, mountain), and Moving Natural Objects (e.g. cloud, blizzard). All category items were matched for letter length, number of syllables, and lexical familiarity.

Procedure

The experiment used a within-subjects design. All stimuli were presented using E-Prime software (Psychology Software Tools, Pittsburgh, PA), which measured participants' response time for each trial. Participants were required to make a speeded response within two seconds before the next item was automatically presented and with a response the next item was presented. For each category (e.g. Insect, Plant), all subjects responded to 120 stimulus items (8 property attributions [e.g. feels pain, feels pride] × 15 entities [e.g. for Insect: bee, wasp]). Since our primary interest was in the attribution of simple conscious states, we collapsed responses to 'feels anger', 'feels happy' and 'feels pain' for our analyses. We preplanned comparisons for overt responses to attributions of these simple conscious states between the Insect category and the categories of Vehicles, Moving Natural Objects, and Plants. We also preplanned comparisons of reaction times of negative responses to simple conscious states between the category of insect and the categories of Vehicle, Moving Natural Objects, and Plants.

Results

As predicted, participants were significantly more likely (all p's <.001) to attribute simple conscious states (pain, happy, anger) to insects (70% of trials) than to Plants (10%) or items that exhibit motion, including Vehicles (6%) and Natural Moving Objects (6%) (see Figure 3). Also as predicted, participants were also significantly *slower* to reject the attributions of simple conscious states to insects (670 ms) than to natural moving objects (610 ms) ($t(33) = 2.17$, p <.05) or vehicles (616 ms) ($t(33) = 2.39$, p <.05). Contrary to our predictions, no significant difference in response times was found between insects and plants (651 ms).

In light of the failure to find a significant difference in RTs between insects and plants, we conducted additional analyses comparing Plants to Vehicles and Natural Moving Objects. To our surprise, we found that participants were also more likely to ascribe simple conscious states to Plants than to Vehicles ($t(33) = 3.28$, p <.01) and Natural Moving Objects ($t(33) = 4.79$, p <.001). Participants also demonstrated significantly slower RTs for denying simple conscious states to plants (651 ms) as compared to natural moving objects ($t(33) = 4.26, p$ <.001) and to vehicles ($t(33) = 4.73, p$ <.001) (see Figure 4).

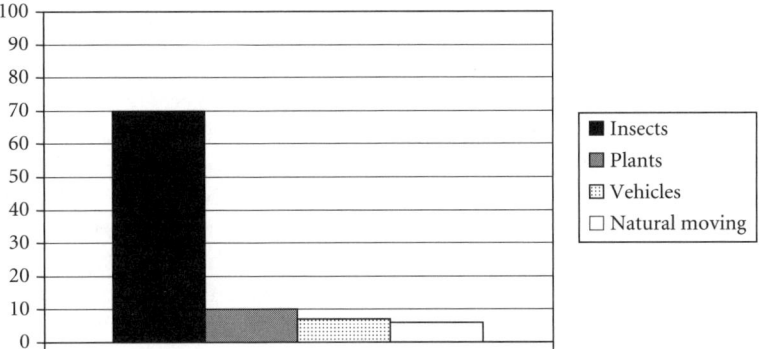

Figure 6.3. Percentage of 'yes' responses: simple conscious states (pain, happiness, anger)

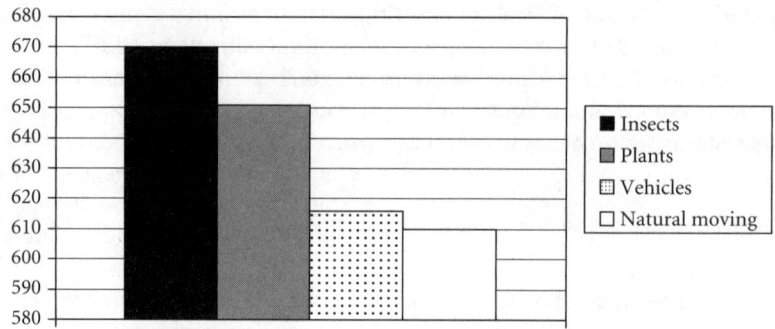

Figure 6.4. Reaction times (in ms) for denials of simple conscious states

To verify the generalizability of these effects across the items selected, item analyses (averaging across subjects, treating each item as a random variable in the analysis) replicated each of these effects (p's <.001). As a control on whether the effect with insect RTs was simply a general feature of how people respond to insects, we looked at the reactions times for denying a superficial property (e.g. *colored white*) to an object. No significant differences in response time were found between insects, plants, vehicles, and natural moving objects for these cases.[15]

6. DISCUSSION

The experiment supports the central hypothesis of the AGENCY model: that categorizing an entity as AGENT is typically sufficient for generating an inclination to attribute conscious states. The overt responses suggest that being identified as an AGENT generates strong inclination to attribute simple conscious states. In particular, insects, but not vehicles or clouds or rivers, were judged to have conscious states.[16] The reaction time data tell a similar story. Again, our prediction was that there would be a tendency to attribute simple conscious states like pain to insects, so denying that insects feel pain would require one to override an initial natural inclination.[17] As predicted, we found that denials of simple conscious states to insects were indeed much slower than denials of such states to vehicles and natural moving objects.[18]

The *necessity thesis*—the claim that AGENCY is necessary for the immediate inclination to attribute conscious states—also looks to get some support from the overt responses. Overall, items that lacked AGENCY cues were unlikely to be afforded the simple conscious states. Insects were overwhelmingly more likely to be granted simple conscious states than were the items that did not have paradigmatic AGENCY features. But the situation with RTs is more complex. Participants showed slower response times when denying simple conscious states to plants as compared with similar responses to vehicles and natural moving objects, and this seems to run contrary to the prediction generated by the *necessity thesis:* that *only* items categorized as AGENTS will generate the automatic inclination to attribute conscious states to the item.

As noted, the RT evidence on plants contravened our predictions, and this demands further consideration of how to model the role of AGENCY in the attribution of conscious states. There are a number of different models that can accommodate the data. We will not try to be exhaustive. Instead, we will review three models that we find especially interesting. First, though, we would like to note that in this experiment we also collected responses for each item on whether or not the object 'is a living thing'. In contrast to vehicles and natural moving objects, participants overwhelmingly judged insects and plants to be living things. So, throughout our discussion we will rely on the idea that plants (and insects) are coded as ALIVE.[19] The relevance of this fact will become more salient in the following discussion of the three explanatory models.

One possibility is to retain the AGENCY model and explain away the unexpected reaction times for plants. For instance, since many things coded as ALIVE are also AGENTS, ALIVE might have high cue validity—it might provide a good heuristic for thinking that an object has mental states. That is, if something is coded as ALIVE then that's a good cue that it's an AGENT, even though it remains possible for something to be coded as ALIVE but not as AGENT.[20] As a result, it takes some time to process the fact that plants fall into the class of things that are ALIVE but not AGENTS (this proposal is illustrated in Figure 5). The key point of this model is that people do not actually have a disposition to go all the way with attribution of conscious states to plants. Rather, they just need to do a bit more processing in order to exclude plants than they do for vehicles. Note that this would also explain why there were comparatively few overt responses in favor of plants having simple conscious states.

A second possible model holds that categorizing an object as ALIVE is actually a (previously unnoticed) cue, which then triggers the individual to categorize that object as AGENT. That is, perhaps activating the notion that a thing is ALIVE would also activate the notion of AGENT.[21] We'll call this the LIFE-to-AGENCY model (see Figure 6). On such an account, the presumed tendency to attribute conscious states to plants is mediated by the AGENT attribution.

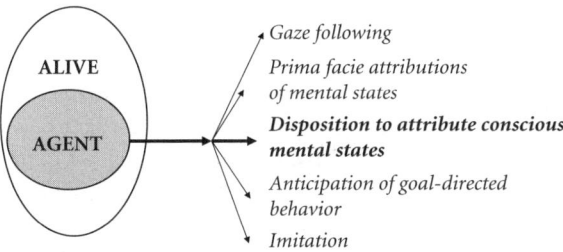

Figure 6.5. The AGENCY model, with ALIVE as cue

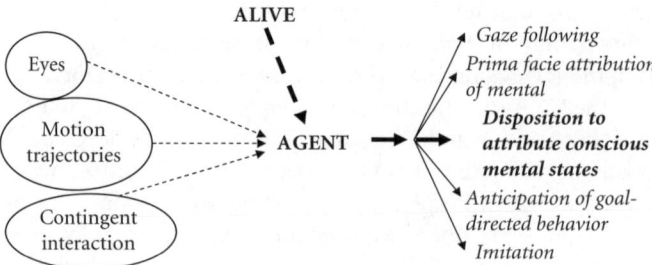

Figure 6.6. LIFE-to-AGENCY model

A third and much more dramatic possibility is that AGENCY is not the important category at all. Perhaps what really matters for attributing conscious states is categorizing an object as ALIVE (as depicted in Figure 7). This explanatory model provides a new way to defend the view that agency and experience are independent dimensions. An object, according to this explanation, can be regarded as something that is capable of having experiences even if it is not regarded as an AGENT. This approach would suggest that the deep conceptual link is not between AGENCY and consciousness, but rather between LIFE and consciousness. As such, we call this the LIFE model.

7. DEVELOPMENTAL QUESTIONS

The evidence from our experiment does not decide between the three positive models we've just sketched. Nonetheless, we can begin to adjudicate between them by considering data from related areas of inquiry. One critical source of evidence for deciding between the models is developmental. We know that in our experiment, adults tended to overtly deny that plants have conscious states. But given their reaction times, the question is whether there is an automatic inclination in favor of attributing conscious states to plants which then gets suppressed. If there is an automatic inclination to make such attributions, then we might find fully overt attributions of conscious states to plants if we look earlier in development, before children have acquired whatever it is that suppresses overt attributions in adults.

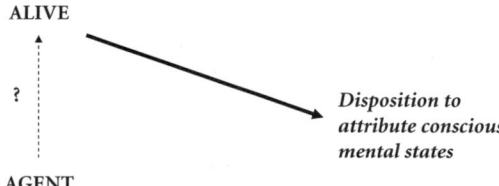

Figure 6.7. LIFE model

In a pair of classic studies, Inagaki and Hatano (1987, 1991) found that Japanese children attributed conscious states to tulips. Strikingly, they found that most children (72%) in their study said that tulips feel pain, but most (80%) deny that stones feel pain. The children also overwhelmingly (98%) denied that tulips *think* (1987, p. 1016). This is a significant data point in favor of the idea that attributions of LIFE are sufficient to generate the tendency to attribute simple conscious states. However, one (deflationary) explanation for the Inagaki and Hatano results is that the results are culturally specific to Japanese children.

Recent work by Jane Erickson and Frank Keil (2008) suggests that the attribution of mental states to plants is not isolated to Japanese children. Erickson and Keil offered American children different kinds of explanations for a variety of entities, including humans, plants, and non-living natural kinds. In one experiment, the child's task was to evaluate the quality of a psychological explanation for a behavior exhibited by different kinds of entities. The experimenters showed a picture of a plant growing toward the sun and offered the following psychological explanation: 'The flower grew towards the sun because it felt tired and hungry and knew that the sunlight would give it energy to make food'. Children regarded such a psychological explanation as apt for plants, but they rejected parallel psychological explanations for artifacts and non-living natural kinds. In addition, Erickson and Keil found a developmental progression—older children were less likely to allow psychological explanations for plants (though they continued to regard plants as exhibiting goal-directed behavior). All of this seems to fit with the possibility that the AGENCY model is completely misguided and should be rejected in favor of the LIFE model. For the data leaves open the possibility that LIFE is the operative categorization behind the immediate inclination to attribute conscious mental states.

Combined with our own evidence with respect to reaction times for plants, one might construe the evidence from Inagaki and Hatano and Erickson and Keil as thoroughly undercutting the AGENCY model. After all, one might take these studies to show that children are willing to attribute psychological states to plants based solely on the fact that plants are alive; if LIFE suffices to generate the inclination to attribute conscious states to an individual, then there seems to be no need to appeal to AGENCY to explain the inclination to attribute conscious states to people and insects. Although this looks very bleak indeed for the AGENCY model, recent work by John Opfer and colleagues motivates a much more favorable interpretation of the foregoing results. Opfer (2002) showed subjects—both children and adults—a series of videos in which irregularly shaped blobs moved along various paths. Among other things, the task required subjects to determine what the object was. In one condition, the videos included goal objects that corresponded to the blob's movement, while in the other condition, the videos did not include goal objects; they then presented subjects with a battery of attributions that included both psychological traits and biological traits. According to these studies, attributions of life themselves depend on the individual seeing the entity as a goal-directed agent. Even children as young as 5 years old, they say, relied on the blob's motion being goal directed in order to attribute to it either biological states (like being alive) or mental states (like being happy or feeling pain). Opfer observes, 'The goal-directedness appeared to be the decisive factor in these displays: identical blobs that moved identically but towards no goal failed to convince children and adults that they were living things' (p. 116).

In a separate study, Opfer and Siegler (2004) found that 5-year-olds did not initially take plants either to be alive or to behave in goal-directed manners. Indeed, Opfer and Siegler found that most children take animals to be only alive. Yet when told that plants move towards sources of nutrition, such as sunlight and water,[22] 5-year-olds inferred that these motions were goal directed. Importantly, Opfer and Siegler also found that the attributions of *life* seem to depend on attributing goal directedness to the entity:

> The changes in categorization by children in the teleology feedback group suggest that although 5-year-olds initially categorized only animals as living things, the preschoolers' concept of living things included capacity for goal-directed movement as an important property of life. After the preschoolers learned that plants, like animals, were capable of goal-directed movement, they quickly inferred that plants, like animals, are alive. Conversely, children who failed to revise their judgments about teleological agency also failed to revise their life judgments. (Opfer and Siegler, 2004, p. 321)

While most of the children in the study initially categorized animals—but not plants—as living things, the data from this study suggests that the exclusion of plants arises from the failure to recognize that plants display goal-directed behavior. Opfer and Siegler write, 'Once children conclude that plants can act in goal-directed, self-sustaining ways, they also conclude that plants are alive' (p. 329). This casts an entirely new light on the results concerning attribution of consciousness to plants. Although one might initially be inclined to interpret the data from Inagaki and Hatano or Erickson and Keil as undercutting the AGENCY models, this interpretation seems less plausible in light of the fact that the attribution of life itself seems to depend on the recognition of an entity *as a goal-directed entity*.

Moreover, considering the work by Opfer and colleagues, it now seems natural to interpret the Erickson and Keil data as providing some *support* for the AGENCY model. Erickson and Keil offered an explanation of plant behavior that was explicitly goal directed. To accept these explanations (as the children do) is to accept a goal-directed understanding of plants. According to the AGENCY model, AGENTs are, inter alia, the sorts of things that we are inclined to attribute goals to. That children approve of psychological explanations of goal-directed behavior attributed to plants just seems to show that, once children see plants as the sorts of entities that have goals and behave according to those goals, they are inclined to say that plants also can have psychological states. As such, Erickson and Keil's data seem to provide evidence that, once they are primed to categorize plants as AGENTs, children are inclined to attribute psychological states to plants. And that just is what the AGENCY model predicts.[23]

8. PHILOSOPHICAL IMPLICATIONS

Our proposed account has some relatively clear implications regarding the descriptive problem of other conscious minds. The picture on offer suggests that our cognitive systems are differentially sensitive to very specific features—eyes, distinctive motion trajectories, and contingent interaction—the detection of which is normally causally sufficient to bias the subject toward attribution of conscious states. Importantly, the cognitive processes that operate on these low-level cues appear to operate even when global considerations militate against the idea that the target has mental states. For example, my belief that a triangle from Heider and Simmel's animation is not a mentalistic agent does not stop me from seeing the triangle as 'wanting to get out of the box'. Similarly, my belief that insects are not conscious does not prevent me from having the inclination to attribute pain and anger to them. The simple features suffice to trigger the inclination to attribute conscious states. It is natural to think of the relevant cognitive process as exhibiting two central features of modularity: domain specificity and informational encapsulation (Fodor, 1983). The process is domain specific to the extent that a limited number of simple features are able to trigger that process. In the normal case, things like clouds, blizzards, cars and mountains do not exhibit the right sorts of features, and hence fail to trigger the process.[24] Since the relevant process fails to incorporate important information from the subject's broader set of beliefs (for example, the belief that that triangle is *literally* a two-dimensional figure), the process also seems, to that extent, informationally encapsulated. These points apply equally to the various models under consideration (whether they give a central role to AGENCY, LIFE, or both), for all models give special weight to a small set of relatively simple featural cues.

Consider again the two traditional answers to the descriptive problem of other conscious minds: analogy and inference to the best explanation. Both analogical reasoning and inference to the best explanation are thought to be paradigm cases of non-modular processing (Fodor, 1983, pp. 88–89, 107). First, neither process is domain specific: analogies can in principle relate anything to anything, and explanations can in principle target arbitrary explanatory domains. And second, neither analogical reasoning nor inference-to-the-best-explanation is informationally encapsulated; both are highly sensitive to information from all over the cognitive system (Fodor, 1983, pp. 104–107). If this assessment of the processes is correct, then there is a tension between the traditional answers to the descriptive problem of other conscious minds and the view that we are promoting. For unlike traditional accounts, on our account it is natural to view some of the mental processes responsible for the attribution of conscious states as modular.

The modularity hypothesis provides a familiar framework for articulating the difference between the AGENCY model and the traditional analogy and best-explanation models. But the important differences can still be drawn without adopting the modularity framework. The important point is that on the AGENCY model, the way we attribute consciousness to other things often involves simple cues (like contingent behavior) that quickly, automatically, and effortlessly trigger the AGENT concept, which in turn leads directly to an inclination to attribute conscious states. These operations differ radically from traditional intellectualist processes like analogical reasoning and inference to the best explanation. This point again resonates with various dual-process models that describe two distinct pathways for reaching the attributions. Kahneman provides a nice summary of dual-process architecture:

> The operations of System 1 are typically fast, automatic, effortless, associative, implicit (not available to introspection), and often emotionally charged; they are also governed by habit and are therefore difficult to control or modify. The operations of System 2 are slower, serial, effortful, more likely to be consciously monitored and deliberately controlled. (Kahneman, 2003, p. 698)

Regarding attributions of consciousness, we have essentially been developing an account of a System 1 or *low road* process involving automatic processing of relatively simple featural cues. But we also believe that people have another pathway for attributing conscious states, a *high road* process involving relatively slow, controlled and deliberative reasoning (see Fiala et al., 2012).

In addition to the implications for the traditional descriptive problem of other minds, the models we've sketched here might also have import for the status of particular intuitions about the consciousness (or not) of other entities. A number of prominent philosophers have built explicit theories of mind partly on the basis of our intuitions about what is conscious and what is not. One such case is Ned Block's famous example in which we are to imagine that all the residents of China are rigged up with radio transmitters so as to functionally mimic a living brain (Block, 1978). The intuitive reaction to this case is presumably that the nation of China (as a whole) does not have any mental states, and surely not any conscious states! This is then supposed to support the conclusion that merely getting a system to functionally mimic a brain does not make that system conscious. For intuitively, it seems clear that functionally organizing the residents of China to behave like a brain would not make the collective nation have conscious states.

Notice, however, that if our proposal is correct, there is a potential explanation for these intuitions that does not involve the denial that the nation of China enjoys conscious states. Instead, it may be that the example tends to provoke these intuitions because the sorts of featural cues that typically incline a subject toward attributions of consciousness are not salient with respect to the nation of China.[25] Each Chinese person, on the other hand, does possess the relevant cues (which are readily imaginable when considering Block's scenario). Hence, we have an inclination to attribute conscious states to individual Chinese people, but not to the nation of China. This is just one example, but it illustrates how the answer to the descriptive problem might influence the way the relevant intuitions are used in philosophical debate. For depending on what one thinks about the epistemic status of the relevant psychological processes, one might be led either to dismiss the intuitions, or to give them special weight.[26]

An answer to the descriptive problem might also bear on the idea that people intuitively embrace a 'folk dualism' (Bloom, 2004), according to which the mind is radically different than the body.[27] It's plausible that one aspect of such a dualism is the apparent gulf between consciousness and physical objects. For instance, when we think about a brain as a massive collection of neurons that has various chemical and physical characteristics, it is not at all intuitive that this mass has consciousness. Something similar can, of course, be said for other bodily organs. Even after we are told that the brain is the part of the body responsible for consciousness, this does not render it *intuitive* that the brain is where conscious experience occurs. We suggest that part of the reason for this is that when we consider brains as hunks of physical stuff, we are considering descriptions that exclude the sort of cues that tend to activate the low-level processes that generate the intuitive sense that an entity is conscious.[28] Hence, it's not surprising if we find some initial resistance to the idea that the physical brain is conscious.[29] In this light, it's somewhat ironic that, while people have difficulty thinking of the brain as conscious, they have no trouble at all thinking that *ants* are conscious. On the contrary, our experiments indicate that people have trouble thinking that ants are *not* conscious.

NOTES

* All authors made roughly equal contributions to the paper; the order of authors is alphabetical. We would like to thank the audiences at the Center for Consciousness Studies, Toward a Science of Consciousness 2008 Conference, Arizona's Experimental Philosophy Lab, the Experimental Philosophy Workshop at the 2008 meeting of the Society for Philosophy and Psychology, and the *Integrating Science and the Humanities* conference at the University of British Columbia for their comments. We are also grateful to Mike Bruno, Peter Carruthers, Yali Corea-Levy, Jane Erickson, Ian Evans, Jen Giesselmann, Josh Greene, Terry Horgan, Bryce Huebner, Tony Jack, Chris Kahn, Benji Kozuch, Uriah Kriegel, Trevor Kvaran, Theresa Lopez, John Pollock, Jesse Prinz, Philip Robbins, Deena Skolnik-Weisberg, Justin Sytsma, and especially Josh Knobe and Edouard Machery for suggestions.

1. For the purpose of this paper, we focus only on the cognitive process(es) underlying token attributions of conscious experience (e.g. pain) to different entities. We are not here concerned with the folk's metacognitive recognition that one's attribution is an attribution *of consciousness*. For one approach to answering the metacognitive question, see Sytsma and Machery, 2010.

2. We focus on the problem of why we are inclined to attribute conscious states to others. This can be thought of as part of a broader problem, 'the problem of other minds', which asks why we are inclined to attribute any mental states whatsoever to other beings. But for philosophers like Augustine, Reid, and Mill, the problem of other conscious minds would have been a critical part of the broader problem of other minds.

3. It should be noted, though, that Inference to the Best Explanation and Analogy need not be seen as mutually exclusive competitors. One could in principle take a particular argument from analogy to be the best explanation for certain kinds of behavior. In other words, one might reason along the following lines: 'well, the best explanation for that person's behavior, which is quite similar to my own, is that they are experiencing the same things as myself.'

4. Despite the enthusiasm for the best explanation approach, a number of philosophers have worried that it is inadequate for capturing why we attribute *consciousness* to others. The worry is that, while it is easy enough to see why the best explanation for behavior would require attributing information-processing states to others, it's much harder to see why the best explanation for behavior would require attributing *conscious* states (e.g. Melnyk, 1994).

5. It's possible that people regard the Heider–Simmel stimuli as fictional. But the point can also be made by adverting to natural reactions to the emerging class of robots—Roombas and Rodney Brooks' Mobots—that behave in goal-like ways. People even readily give names to these robots! Watching them just seems to trigger an attribution of mental states. Thanks to Bernie Kobes for these points.

6. Importantly, this technical category stands in stark contrast to the sophisticated concepts of agency put forth in philosophical theories of agency (cf. Korsgaard, 2008). Korsgaard, in the Kantian tradition, takes agents to be the sort of things that base their actions on principles of practical reasoning, including and especially principles of morality. This position is representative of the sophisticated theories alluded to above, in that they define agency in terms of the capacity to deliberate about reasons and principles when deciding how to behave. The notion of agency at play in the current discussion is significantly simpler and is, at best, a conceptual precursor to the more sophisticated notion under consideration in philosophical theories of practical rationality, free will, moral responsibility, etc. Whereas such theories concern themselves with the sort of agency necessary for moral responsibility, free will, rationality, and so forth, we are here concerned with a much simpler notion. Indeed, the technical category at work in the AGENCY model remains silent on such philosophical questions.

7. For present purposes, we are neutral on whether the AGENT concept is innate. However, comparative work by Mascalzoni et al. (2010) suggests that a similar mechanism may be in place in baby chickens. If the same mechanism is in place in both humans and chickens, one might argue for innateness on broadly phylogenetic grounds. If the concept is innate, then the view begins to look similar to Thomas Reid's solution to the problem of other minds (1785/1969). Our point is that, regardless of how the AGENT concept is acquired, once an entity is categorized as an AGENT, an inclination to attribute conscious states to the entity will be present.

8. One possible deflationary interpretation of Knobe and Prinz's results is that participants were speaking figuratively when attributing mental states to groups. We conducted pilot studies to investigate this possibility. To screen out those who fail to distinguish between literal and figurative language, we gave subjects a series of sentences, some clearly figurative (e.g. 'Einstein was an egghead') and some clearly literal (e.g. 'Carpenters build houses') and asked them to rate those sentences on a 7-point Likert scale of literalness (1 = 'Figuratively True' 7 = 'Literally True'). We also provided those subjects with sentences attributing different mental states to individuals (e.g. 'Some millionaires want tax cuts') and to groups (e.g. 'Some corporations want tax cuts') and compared their judgments regarding different types of mental states. We found that when subjects rated group attributions, they tended to rate non-conscious state attributions

as 'literally true' and gave significantly higher ratings for non-conscious than conscious mental state attributions ($t(66) = 7.735$, $p < .001$). For further discussion of Knobe and Prinz's experiments, see Arico (2010) and Sytsma and Machery (2009).

9. Bryce Huebner (2010) has suggested that folk psychology functions differently in attributions of beliefs (Agency, loosely speaking) than in attributions of pains and emotions (Experience). Huebner found that people attribute beliefs but not conscious states to robots. Furthermore, Sytsma and Machery (2010) have found that people are reluctant to attribute pain and emotion to robots even when the robots are described as exhibiting appropriate behavior. Once again, this suggests that there is an attribution of AGENCY with no concomitant inclination to attribute conscious states. But alternative explanations are available. One is that, as we suggested for Knobe and Prinz, the AGENCY category is not really triggered by the robots. However, given that Huebner's stimuli included a photo of a robot that possessed one of the relatively simple features that serve as cues mentioned above (eyes), this is not a satisfactory explanation. Another possible explanation is that the AGENT category *is* triggered in Huebner's subjects and does, in fact, generate the disposition to attribute conscious states, but that disposition is subsequently suppressed. Perhaps the disposition is suppressed by some generally held social schema about robots and sensations/emotions, or perhaps it is suppressed by higher-order deliberations about the robot's physiological makeup. Whatever the reason might be for suppressing the disposition, Huebner's results are problematic for the AGENCY model only in so far as it can be shown that subjects were not initially disposed to attribute phenomenology to the robots.

10. 'Acme Corp is upset about the court's recent ruling' versus 'Acme Corp is feeling upset'.

11. We follow philosophical tradition in taking pain to be a paradigmatic example of a phenomenally conscious state. For an alternative view, see Carruthers (2004). Also, Sytsma and Machery (2010) maintain that the folk conception of subjective experience is importantly different than the corresponding philosophical conception. Still, they recognize that a state like 'feeling pain' is traditionally taken to be a phenomenally conscious state. Whether the folk conceptualize it as such (tacitly or explicitly) has no bearing on the discussion at hand (cf. fn. 1).

12. A bit more fully, the prediction goes as follows. The presence of the cues biases the subject toward categorizing the individual as an AGENT with the consequent inclination to attribute conscious states to the individual; but competing processes defy these attributions. This creates an uncertainty that takes time to resolve, driving up RT times as a result. Since the whole issue here is about processing time, the way to investigate these matters is by testing performance under speeded conditions.

13. This tendency may be so strong as to persist even after extensive instruction and experiences in the domain. Goldberg and Thompson-Schill (2009) found that even biology professors made predictable, childish mistakes and slower reaction times on a speeded classification task of living/nonliving. Likewise, although neuroscientists might deny that insects feel pain, our bet is that they too would be significantly slower in those denials and be more likely to make mistakes (by their own lights) in speeded conditions.

14. The differences between the RT predictions flowing from the sufficiency and necessity theses is that the sufficiency thesis only says that we should expect faster denials (of conscious states) for at least some individuals that don't get categorized as AGENTs. The necessity thesis makes the stronger claim that we should typically expect fast denials for *any* individual that doesn't get categorized as AGENT.

15. One might take a deflationary stance toward the results of the experiment, holding that they do not call for the postulation of any specialized mental mechanism. Instead, the results might be explicable in terms of prior beliefs about the relevant categories. It might be that subjects take longer to respond to PAIN/INSECT stimuli because they do not have any prior beliefs about the presence or absence of conscious states in insects, and so they have to deliberate longer. By contrast, it might be that subjects *do* have prior knowledge that mammals, birds and so forth *do* have conscious states, and that artifacts, natural objects and so forth *do not* have conscious states. So responding to the insect stimuli requires some on-the-spot deliberation, whereas responding to the other categories does not. (Dave Schmitz and an anonymous referee have raised objections along these lines.)

There are a couple of reasons to doubt that this deflationary interpretation is correct. First, although the RTs for a No response to insects is significantly greater than RTs for other categories, the difference is on the order of 50 milliseconds. If the differential response reflected the necessity of conscious deliberation in the case of insects, one would expect a much larger difference. Second, we see no obvious reason for expecting people to have existing beliefs about the mental states of mammals and birds and plants but not insects. In the absence of evidence for thinking that subjects lack beliefs specifically and uniquely about insect consciousness, there seems little positive reason to adopt this interpretation of the data. Nonetheless, it is an empirically testable hypothesis that calls for further research on the matter.

16. The virtue of using familiar objects like insects, birds, and vehicles, is that the examples are ecologically realistic. We aren't using some completely artificial psychological construct. However, when using familiar objects, it's hard to exclude all effects of training and education even while the word items used were extensively controlled to minimize these differences. As a result, to make a persuasive case for the AGENCY model, it will be important to supplement our results. And perhaps the most important way to supplement the results is by using unfamiliar, novel objects. That, of course, is a central virtue of the work by Heider and Simmel and Johnson. To further explore the AGENCY model, it will be important to follow up that work by looking directly at attributions of conscious states. So, for instance, in the standard method developed by Johnson, infants will come to regard the blob (a very un-AGENT like entity) as an AGENT if it beeps contingently with a person's speech. This raises an obvious question about attribution of conscious states. Would infants in the contingent interaction condition be more likely to regard the blob as suffering pain if it were visibly damaged (as compared to a non-contingently interacting condition)? Our model predicts that they would, but the relevant experiments remain to be conducted.

17. There is a further question about why we attribute the particular states that we do (in this case, pain, anger, and happiness). Then there is the broader question of exactly what's included within the range of states that we are sometimes willing to attribute to AGENTS. We leave this as an important area for future research.

18. Because participants only had two seconds to respond to each item, it's unlikely that differences were caused by extended deliberations on each item. Rather, these response time differences are likely to reflect more immediate decision processes as shown in seminal and contemporary accounts of semantic processing based on these types of response time differences (e.g. McCloskey and Glucksberg, 1979; Smith et al., 1974).

19. Still, as noted above for the AGENT concept, we want to allow for the possibility that the ALIVE concept is not a perfect match for any word in English.

20. As we discuss in the following section, there is some evidence in the developmental psychology literature for thinking that categorizing plants as AGENTs is, in fact, a prerequisite for categorizing plants as ALIVE. That is, rather than merely seeing ALIVE as a highly valid cue for AGENCY, we might see ALIVE categorizations as being routed through AGENT categorizations.

21. It is also, of course, possible that categorizing an individual as an AGENT would bring with it the categorization of the individual as ALIVE. For instance, it might be that once the child identifies Johnson's blob as an AGENT, the child would also think of the blob as ALIVE. We set this issue aside for present purposes.

22. Opfer and Siegler label this group the 'teleology feedback' condition.

23. If categorizing plants as ALIVE requires categorizing them as AGENTs, then the *necessity thesis* is also preserved: the delayed responses for plants are no longer an obvious counter-example, since the initial inclination to attribute simple conscious states can plausibly be explained by attributions of LIFE tacitly depending upon attributions of AGENT.

24. However, such objects may *seem* to exhibit some of these features in unusual circumstances.

25. This is not to say that the *only* path to attributions of consciousness is via simple cues. Rather, the point is that if an entity fails to manifest the cues that trigger the AGENCY category, it will be significantly less natural to attribute conscious states to that entity. Instead, attributions of consciousness in such cases are likely to be the result of deliberate high-level reasoning.

26. Huebner, Bruno, and Sarkissian (2010) present some evidence that intuitions regarding the conscious states of group entities (like the Nation of China) are culturally diverse. They found that English-speaking students in Hong Kong treated consciousness ascriptions to groups and to individuals more similarly then did their U.S. counterparts. This cultural variance, they argue, undermines the epistemic status of (some) intuitions about groups and conscious states.

27. Cf. Chalmers (2003)[AQ: Please provide complete details of "Chalmers, 2002" in the reference list.] for a review of the gulf between consciousness and physical objects.

28. Though, as noted above, there might be other pathways that generate the judgment that an entity has conscious states.

29. For a more detailed treatment of dualist intuitions, especially 'explanatory gap' intuitions, see Fiala et al. (in press).

REFERENCES

Abell, F., Happé, F. and Frith, U. 2000: Do triangles play tricks? Attribution of mental states to animated shapes in normal and abnormal development. *Journal of Cognitive Development*, 15, 1–20.

Arico, A. J. 2010: Folk psychology, consciousness, and context effects. *Review of Philosophy and Psychology*, 1(3), 371–393.

Augustine. (2002)*On the Trinity*, trans. S. McKenna. Cambridge, UK: Cambridge University Press. Available

Block, N. 1978: Troubles with functionalism. In W. Savage (ed.), *Perception and Cognition: Issues in the Foundations of Psychology*. Minneapolis: University of Minnesota Press, 9: 261–325.

Bloom, P. 2004: *Descartes' Baby*. New York: Basic Books.

Bowler, D. and Thommen, E. 2000: Attribution of mechanical and social causality to animated displays by children with autism. *Autism*, 4, 147–171.

Carruthers, P. 2004: Suffering without subjectivity. *Philosophical Studies*, *121*, 99–125.
Chaiken, S. and Trope, Y. (eds). 1999. *Dual Process Theories in Social Psychology*. New York: Guilford.
Chalmers, D. (2003). Consciousness and its place in nature. In F. S. Stich and F. Warfield Blackwell Guide to the Philosophy of Mind. Blackwell, 102–142.
Churchland, P. M. 1988: *Matter and Consciousness: A Contemporary Introduction to the Philosophy of Mind*, rev. ed. Cambridge, MA: MIT Press.
Dasser, V., Ulbaek, I. and Premack, D. 1989: The perception of intention. *Science*, *243*, 365–367.
Descartes, R. 1641/1986: *Meditations on First Philosophy*, trans. J. Cottingham. Cambridge: Cambridge University Press.
Erickson, J. and Keil, F. 2008: The role of intention in teleological explanations. Poster at 2008 meeting of Society for Philosophy and Psychology ,University of Pennsylvania June 27.
Fiala, B., Arico, A. and Nichols, S. (2012) On the psychological origins of dualism: dual-process cognition and the explanatory gap. In E. Slingerland and M. Collard (eds.), *Creating Consilience: Issues and Case Studies in the Integration of the Sciences and Humanities*. Oxford: Oxford University Press, 88–109.
Fodor, J. 1983: *The Modularity of Mind*. Cambridge, MA: MIT Press.
Goldberg, R. and Thompson-Schill, S. 2009: Developmental 'roots' in mature biological knowledge. *Psychological Science*, *20*, 480–487.
Goldman A. 2006: *Simulating Minds*. Oxford: Oxford University Press.
Gopnik, A. and Meltzoff, A. 1997: *Words, Thoughts, and Theories*. Cambridge, MA: MIT Press.
Graham, G. 1998: *Philosophy of Mind: An Introduction*, 2nd ed. Oxford: Blackwell.
Gray, H., Gray, K. and Wegner, D. 2007: Dimensions of mind perception. *Science*, *315*, 619.
Harris, P. 1989: *Children and Emotion*. Oxford: Blackwell.
Heider, F. and Simmel, M. 1944: An experimental study of apparent behavior. *American Journal of Psychology*, *57*, 243–259.
Hill, C. S. 1991: *Sensations: A Defense of Type Materialism*. Cambridge: Cambridge University Press.
Huebner, B. 2010: Commonsense concepts of phenomenal consciousness: does anyone care about functional zombies? *Phenomenology and the Cognitive Sciences*, *9*, 133–155.
Huebner, B., Bruno, M. and Sarkissian, H. 2010: What does the nation of China think about phenomenal states? *Review of Philosophy and Psychology*, *1*(2), 225–243.
Hyslop, A. 1995: *Other Minds*. Dordrecht: Kluwer.
Inagaki, K. and Hatano, G. 1987: Young children's spontaneous personification as analogy. *Child Development*, *58*, 1013–1020.
Inagaki, K. and Hatano, G. 1991: Constrained person analogy in young children's biological inference. *Cognitive Development*, *6*, 219–231.
Johnson, S. 2005: Reasoning about intentionality in preverbal infants. In P. Carruthers, S. Laurence and S. Stich (eds.), *The Innate Mind: Structure and Content*. Oxford: Oxford University Press, 254–271.
Johnson, S., Booth, A. and O'Hearn, K. 2001: Inferring the goals of non-human agents. *Cognitive Development*, *16*, 637–656.
Johnson, S., Slaughter, V. and Carey, S. 1998: Whose gaze will infants follow? Features that elicit gaze-following in 12-month-olds. *Developmental Science*, *1*, 233–238.

Kahneman, D. 2003: A perspective on judgment and choice: mapping bounded rationality. *American Psychologist, 58,* 697-720.
Knobe, J. and Prinz, J. 2008: Intuitions about consciousness: experimental studies. *Phenomenology and the Cognitive Sciences, 7,* 67-83.
Korsgaard, C. 2008: *The Constitution of Agency: Essays on Practical Reason and Moral Psychology.* Oxford: Oxford University Press.
Mascalzoni, E., Regolin, L. and Vallortigara, G. 2010: Innate sensitivity for self-propelled causal agency in newly hatched chicks. *PNAS, 107,* 4483-4485.
McCloskey, M. and Glucksberg, S. 1979: Decision processes in verifying category membership statements: implications for models of semantic memory. *Cognitive Psychology, 11,* 1-37.
Melnyk, A. 1994: Inference to the best explanation and other minds. *Australasian Journal of Philosophy, 72*(4), 221-241.
Mill, J. 1865: *An Examination of Sir William Hamilton's Philosophy.* London: Longmans.
Nichols, S. and Stich, S. 2003: *Mindreading.* Oxford: Oxford University Press.
Opfer, J. E. 2002: Identifying living and sentient kinds from dynamic information: The case of goal-directed versus aimless autonomous movement in conceptual change. *Cognition, 86,* 97.
Opfer, J. E. and Siegler, R. S. 2004: Revisiting preschoolers' living things concept: a microgenetic analysis of conceptual change in basic biology. *Cognitive Psychology, 49,* 301-332.
Pargetter, R. 1984: The scientific inference to other minds. *Australasian Journal of Philosophy, 62,* 158-163.
Perner, J. 1991: *Understanding the Representational Mind.* Cambridge, MA: Bradford Books/MIT Press.
Reid, T. 1785/1969: *Essays on the Intellectual Powers of Man.* Cambridge, MA: MIT Press.
Robbins, P. and Jack, A. 2006: The phenomenal stance. *Philosophical Studies, 127,* 59-85.
Scholl, B. and Tremoulet, P. 2000: Perceptual causality and animacy. *Trends in Cognitive Sciences, 4,* 299-309.
Shimizu, Y. and Johnson, S. 2004: Infants' attribution of a goal to a morphologically unfamiliar agent. *Developmental Science, 7,* 425-430.
Sloman, S. 1996: The empirical case for two systems of reasoning. *Psychological Bulletin, 119,* 3-22.
Smith, E. E., Shoben, E. J. and Rips, L. J. 1974: Structure and process in semantic memory: a featural model for semantic decisions. *Psychological Review, 81,* 214-241.
Stanovich, K. and West, R. 2000: Individual differences in reasoning: Implications for the rationality debate. *Behavioural and Brain Sciences, 23,* 645-726.
Sytsma, J. and Machery, E. 2009: How to study folk intuitions about consciousness. *Philosophical Psychology, 2,* 21-35.
Sytsma, J. and Machery, E. 2010: Two conceptions of subjective experience. *Philosophical Studies, 151*(2), 299-327.
Wellman, H. 1990: *The Child's Theory of Mind.* Cambridge, MA: Bradford Books/MIT Press.
Woodward, A. 1998: Infants selectively encode the goal object of an actor's reach. *Cognition, 69,* 1-34.

PART III

META-ETHICS

The study of moral philosophy has traditionally been divided in two branches. The field of *normative ethics* addresses questions about how people ought to live their lives. The field of *metaethics* takes up second-order questions about how to understand the claims made within normative ethics. In other words, the field of metaethics is concerned with questions about the status of ethical claims. Are they just expressions of attitudes, or are they attempts to say something that might be true or false? Are they objective or relative? Can we ever know which ones are right, and, if so, how can we acquire this knowledge?

In the twentieth century, it was quite common to argue for metaethical theories by appealing to views about the role that moral claims play in ordinary life. In particular, a number of philosophers suggested that *people ordinarily see their own moral claims as being objectively true*. At least on the surface, this appears to be a straightforward empirical hypothesis, but it was widely believed that there was no need to explore it using systematic experimental methods. The assumption was that philosophers could assess views like this one on the basis of reflection alone.

More recently, however, the issue is becoming a more controversial one. Some researchers are beginning to wonder whether philosophical work within metaethics might benefit from experimental studies of people's ordinary metaethical views. As the papers collected here reveal, a number of such studies have now been conducted, and they reveal some surprising new facts about how people understand the status of ethical claims.

Goodwin and Darley present a series of systematic studies designed to determine whether people ordinarily think of ethical claims as objective or as relative. Their results suggest that people show a strong inclination to treat ethical claims as objective. Participants in their studies rated ethical claims as significantly more objective than claims involving taste or convention. Indeed, ethical claims were rated almost as objective as scientific facts.

Sarkissian, Park, Tien, Wright, and Knobe take up the very same question but offer a quite different answer. They report a series of studies that seem to point to a relativist element within people's ordinary understanding of morality. As long as the question is about disagreements within a single culture (e.g., between you and your neighbor), participants give apparently objectivist answers, but when the question is about disagreements across cultures (e.g., between you and someone living in the Amazon rainforest), participants seem to shift toward a more relativist view.

SUGGESTED READINGS:

Doris, J. M. & Plakias, A. 2007. "How to Argue about Disagreement: Evaluative Diversity and Moral Realism." In W. Sinnott-Armstrong (ed.), *Moral Psychology, Volume 2: The Cognitive Science of Morality*. Cambridge, MA: MIT Press, 303-331.

Feltz, A. & Cokely, E. T. 2008. "The Fragmented Folk: More Evidence of Stable Individual Differences in Moral Judgments and Folk Intuitions." In B. C. Love, K. McRae, & V. M. Sloutsky (eds.), *Proceedings of the 30th Annual Conference of the Cognitive Science Society* (pp. 1771-1776). Austin, TX: Cognitive Science Society.

Goodwin, G. & Darley, J. 2009. "The Perceived Objectivity of Ethical Beliefs: Psychological Findings and Implications for Public Policy." *Review of Philosophy and Psychology*, 1: 161-188.

Kelly, D., Stich, S. P., Haley, K. J., Eng, S. J. & Fessler, D. M. T. 2007. "Harm, Affect and the Moral/Conventional Distinction." *Mind & Language*, 22: 117-131.

Nichols, S. & Folds-Bennett, T. 2003. "Are Children Moral Objectivists? Children's Judgments about Moral and Response-Dependent Properties." *Cognition*, 90: B23-B32.

Wright, J. & Sarkissian, H. 2012. "Folk Meta-Ethical Commitments." In Fritz Allhoff, Ron Mallon, & Shaun Nichols (eds.), *Philosophy: Traditional and Experimental Approaches*. Oxford: Oxford University Press, 488-494.

7

The Psychology of Meta-ethics: Exploring Objectivism*

Geoffrey P. Goodwin and John M. Darley

1. INTRODUCTION

Debates about ethical issues commonly arise in everyday life. One sort of debate concerns the correct means to achieve an agreed upon end—for instance, is low taxation an efficient way to achieve a just and productive society? Another sort of debate concerns ethical ends themselves—for instance, is terminating the life of a terminally ill and pain-ridden individual morally defensible? The first sort of debate could in principle be resolved empirically. But the second sort of debate arguably cannot be resolved empirically. Here, instead, the focus is on foundational ethical principles. These sorts of disagreement are potentially irresolvable and are likely to be psychologically complex. And they are the focus of this paper.

Deep ethical disagreements are interesting partly because they give individuals occasion to think about how they would defend or justify their ethical beliefs. Reflective individuals might even be inclined to think about the epistemic status of their ethical beliefs, and what sort of ground they might have. Philosophers, of course, have spent a good deal of time on such "meta-ethical" issues. Some philosophers have argued that there are no moral facts, and that morality is not objective (e.g., Ayer, 1936; Blackburn, 1984; Hare, 1952; Harman, 1975; Mackie, 1977; Williams, 1985), whereas others have argued for the opposite position (e.g., Brink, 1986; Kant, 1959; Nagel, 1970; Railton, 1986; Smith, 1994; Sturgeon, 1985). This debate is real and not settled in the philosophical community. Indeed, within philosophy, "there are no dominant views" (Smith, 1994, p. 4).

But, how do ordinary individuals perceive and think about meta-ethics? Do they regard their ethical beliefs as factual and objective, or as more subjective and preferential? Curiously, this question has been largely unexplored. Most psychological investigations of morality to date have been concerned with questions of practical ethics, that is, with questions about the ethical beliefs and practices that individuals abide by (e.g., Baron & Spranca, 1997; Darley & Shultz, 1990; Haidt, 2001; Kohlberg, 1969, 1981; Maio & Olson, 1998; Piaget, 1965; Tetlock, 2003). The psychology of meta-ethics has been explored tangentially in the child development literature, which has focused on whether and at what age children are capable of distinguishing conventional from ethical rules. The evidence from this literature is extremely controversial (see e.g., Gabennesch, 1990a, 1990b; Helwig, Tisak, & Turiel, 1990; Shantz, 1982; Shweder, 1990; Tisak & Turiel, 1988; Turiel, 1978).

Moreover, psychological research that has specifically focused on meta-ethics, has not addressed questions concerning ethical objectivism. Instead, it has focused on the distinction between ethical universalism and ethical relativism—i.e., whether individuals treat their ethical beliefs as applying to all people, and all cultures (Nichols & Folds-Bennett, 2003). Participants in these studies are asked whether a particular moral belief they hold is shared by, or applicable to, all people or all cultures (e.g., Nichols & Folds-Bennett, 2003; Turiel, 1978), or whether ethics generally is dependent on the individual or on culture (e.g., Forsyth, 1980, 1981; Forsyth & Berger, 1982). However, the question of whether ethical standards should apply to all cultures is a question about the *scope* of ethical standards, and is independent of the question of whether such standards and beliefs are objectively or subjectively true (Sayre-McCord, 1986; Snare, 1992; Williams, 1972). Our interest centers on this second question, which concerns the *source* of such beliefs or standards—whether they derive their truth (or warrant) independently of human minds (i.e., objectively), or whether instead, their truth is entirely mind-dependent or subjective (Sayre-McCord, 1986).[1]

It is possible that the majority of people do not think about meta-ethics at all. However, we start from the assumption that individuals can be induced to think about meta-ethics. Certain civic or religious commitments may call for reflection on one's basic values and the source of those values. Indeed, one way that the question of how there could be objective moral facts might be answered is to view ethical statements as having a religious foundation—for instance, they are the word of God. As some have argued, those who ground their ethical beliefs in the notion of a divine being, are likely to view the source of morality as external and objective (e.g., Hunter, 1991). Conversely, those who do not are more likely to conceive of ethics as internal and subjective. Hunter (1991) views this distinction as one between "orthodox" and "progressivist" ideologies, and regards it as a more stubborn moral impasse than that between conservatives and liberals (pp. 127–128). Grounding ethics in religion does not appeal to everyone, of course, and it is by no means the only alternative for one who wishes to be an ethical objectivist. In sum, there may be a rich variety of meta-ethical positions that lay individuals report.

Accordingly, the three main questions guiding the present research were: (1) Do individuals tend to be objectivists or subjectivists concerning ethics? (2) How do they regard the objectivity of ethical statements alongside other sorts of statements such as scientific facts or statements of taste? (3) What factors predict individual differences in degree of objectivism?

To answer these questions, our method was to investigate individuals' responses to situations in which another individual ostensibly disagreed with them about a particular ethical issue. Our motivation for this strategy was twofold. First, we considered it inadequate simply to ask people whether they were objectivists or subjectivists with regard to a particular ethical issue. Put baldly like this, the question is so ambiguous that it could admit multiple differing interpretations, and we would have no control over, or knowledge of, the precise interpretation that any participant adopted. Second, although there are a variety of ways that philosophers have distinguished objectivism and subjectivism, one simple and respectable formulation is as follows: if an individual takes a particular ethical claim to be true, and regards situations of ethical disagreement as necessarily implying that at least one party is *mistaken*, then they are an objectivist (with respect to that statement), whereas if they instead allow that neither party need be mistaken, then they are a subjectivist (Smith, 1994; Snare, 1992).

With this in mind, we implemented the following general methodology across three experiments. We first presented individuals with a range of ethical and non-ethical statements in order to gauge how strongly they agreed or disagreed with them, and whether they regarded them as truths or mere opinions. We then told them that some individuals who we had previously tested (or in Experiment 3, hypothetical individuals) disagreed with them about certain statements. The key question concerned how our participants would regard such individuals—are they mistaken (indicating objectivism), or is it possible that neither party need be mistaken (indicating some form of subjectivism)?

Previous research suggests that participants will experience some tension in trying to gauge the objectivity of their ethical beliefs. On the one hand, we know that people can reliably distinguish ethical from social conventional violations (e.g., Turiel, 1978, 1983). There is also evidence that ethical values are akin to truisms in that they are widely shared and rarely questioned (Maio & Olson, 1998). On the other hand however, people's ethical values differ widely (see e.g., Schwartz, 1992), and individuals are liable to know that there is widespread disagreement about many ethical matters. Accordingly, we predicted that individuals would treat ethical statements as more objective than statements of taste or social convention, although not quite as objective as statements of plain or scientific fact. Moreover, we predicted that this pattern would obtain controlling for how strongly they agreed with the statements in the first place.

We also investigated the ways in which our participants *grounded* their ethical systems. Philosophically speaking, ethical objectivism can stem from multiple sources or groundings. Religious groundings tend to be objective (Hunter, 1991). Similarly, groundings which emphasize the *intrinsic* rightness or goodness of core ethical beliefs tend also to be objective. However, groundings which stress the *instrumental* utility of certain ethical beliefs are non-objective. These background observations allowed us to predict the following three factors to link to greater objectivism: citing a *divine being* as providing the foundation for one's ethical system, viewing the holding of certain ethical beliefs as important and universal constituents of being a *good person,* and viewing certain ethical beliefs as *self-evidently* true. However, we predicted that a pragmatic or instrumental justification—that society could not survive unless its citizens held these beliefs—would not predict greater objectivism.

2. EXPERIMENT 1

2.1. Method

2.1.1. Participants

Fifty undergraduate students (22 male, 28 female) from Princeton University participated for course credit.

2.1.2. Design, materials, and procedure

The participants acted as their own controls and completed two separate parts of the experiment. In the first part, they rated their level of agreement or disagreement with 26 statements (on a six-point scale ranging from 1: strongly disagree to 6: strongly agree), and whether they thought the statement was true, false, or an opinion. The statements were chosen to be prototypical instances of four main categories: ethical statements, statements of social convention, statements of artistic or aesthetic taste, and plainly factual or scientific statements.[2] The statements were selected on the basis of pilot testing as those that tended to produce either relatively strong agreement or disagreement. An illustrative factual statement was: *Boston (MA) is further north than Los Angeles (CA)*; an example ethical statement was: *Robbing a bank in order to pay for an expensive holiday is a morally bad action*; an example social convention statement was: *Wearing pajamas and bath robe to a seminar meeting is wrong behavior*; and an example taste statement was: *Frank Sinatra was a better singer than is Michael Bolton*. The full set of 26 statements is shown in Appendix A. Halfway through the experiment, statements 2 and 5 were changed, as shown in Appendix A (reasons for this change are discussed in Section 2.2). Each participant received the statements in the order shown in Appendix A. They were instructed as follows:

> We are interested in how people think about a range of issues. The first part of the experiment asks you to rate your agreement with 26 statements (on a scale from 1 to 6), and to indicate your opinion about the status of each statement whether it is true, false, or an opinion. Please read each statement carefully, and give each question your full consideration. Accept only the information given and try not to introduce additional assumptions

that go beyond the information as stated. That is, try to interpret the statements in as "normal" and non-exceptional a way as possible. If an event is described, assume that it occurs or occurred in the U.S.A. The second part of the experiment will ask several follow-up questions regarding the statements.

The instruction not to introduce additional assumptions and to interpret the statements in a "normal" way was included because the second phase of the experiment confronted participants with someone who disagreed with them. We wanted to curtail the range of possible interpretations of each statement, thereby reducing the ambiguity surrounding possible disagreement (i.e., to forestall the possible interpretation that a person who disagreed with the statement was simply thinking of a different situation or set of circumstances; see Turiel, Hildenbrandt, & Wainryb, 1991).

Participants marked their level of agreement on the six-point scale for each statement, and they then answered the question:

How would you regard the previous statement? Circle the number.

(1) True statement.
(2) False statement.
(3) An opinion or attitude.

After they had made both judgments for each of the 26 statements, participants performed a task for an unrelated experiment, allowing the experimenter to examine their responses and prepare the next phase of the experiment. During this time, the experimenter located five statements that the participants were to respond to in the second phase of the experiment: two ethical statements, and a single social convention, taste, and factual statement that the participant had indicated relatively strong agreement or disagreement with (the exact procedure is described later in Section 2.1.2). These statements were then entered by hand into an open-ended response sheet shown in Appendix B.

The purpose of this second phase of the experiment was to examine participants' reactions to another person who disagreed with them. Prior to completing this stage, participants were instructed as follows:

> Earlier you rated your agreement with a set of statements. We have done prior psychological testing with these statements, and we have a body of data concerning them. None of the statements have produced 100% agreement or disagreement. In what follows, you will be asked to indicate how you interpret disagreement with your own attitudes. Please give each question your full consideration. Accept only the information given and try not to introduce additional assumptions that go beyond the problem as stated. Remember also that the other people who rated these statements were instructed in the same way that you were i.e., they were instructed to interpret the statements in a normal and non-exceptional way, and not to introduce additional assumptions.

The principal question asked how participants interpret the information that another person disagrees with them. Each participant had to select one of the following options:

(1) The other person is surely mistaken.
(2) It is possible that neither you nor the other person is mistaken.
(3) It could be that you are mistaken, and the other person is correct.
(4) Other.

As previously discussed, some ethical philosophers (e.g., Smith, 1994; Snare, 1992) have often taken one of the hallmarks of ethical objectivism to be the implication that, in cases of genuine moral disagreement (i.e., a disagreement about moral ends, rather than a disagreement about the best means to pursue a particular end), at least one of the parties must be mistaken. We combined the truth versus opinion ratings at the first stage of the experiment with the responses to disagreement at the second stage to create a simple scale of objectivism. We distinguish three sorts of response in terms of their level of objectivism. The most objective response (which we term *fully objective*) is to regard a particular belief as true (or false), and to regard someone who disagrees with that belief as surely mistaken.[3] An *intermediately objective* response is to regard a particular belief as true (or false), but to see no need for either party to be mistaken if another person disagrees with that belief. Alternatively, a second type of *intermediately objective* response is to regard a particular belief as an opinion, but to regard a disagreeing other as surely mistaken. In terms of ethical beliefs, the first of these intermediate positions is consistent with philosophical subjectivism—a moral subjectivist regards their ethical beliefs as *true,* but only in a mind-dependent way, i.e., because of certain mental states that they (or perhaps the members of their group) have, and not because of something external to their own minds. Other people who have different minds can hold different ethical beliefs without either party necessarily being mistaken (see Sayre-McCord, 1986). Ethical truth on this view is thus a kind of personal or subjective truth. Although participants who respond in this way are unlikely to be self-conscious philosophical subjectivists, this response is philosophically defensible, and does at least capture the basic notion of a personal ethical truth. The second intermediate position seems more inconsistent, and may indicate oscillation (or possibly confusion) regarding a statement's objectivity. Yet, although quite different, both of these responses share a basic tension between trying to imbue certain beliefs (ethical or otherwise) with objective and subjective aspects, and so we classify them together as intermediately objective. Finally, the *least objective* response is to regard a particular belief as an opinion, and to see no need for either party to be mistaken if another person disagrees.

The procedure of the second phase of the experiment was as follows. Having inspected the participants' responses in the first phase of the experiment, the experimenter selected a set of five statements that the participant had expressed either strong agreement (responses 5, 6), or disagreement (responses 1, 2) with.

The set always included two ethical statements, one social convention statement, one statement of taste, and one factual statement. In choosing which statements were presented, we followed a procedure which prioritized keeping the strength of agreement scores as constant as possible across participants. This meant that participants did not always respond to the same statements as each other, since their agreement scores for any particular statement were not identical. However, the procedure kept the statement sets as constant as possible given the differences in agreement scores. The percentage of statements used for each category is shown in Appendix C. Participants were asked to fill out the questions presented in Appendix B for each of the five statements—the order of the statements was randomly determined for each new participant. Our main prediction was that on the three-point scale of objectivism that we have outlined, there should be a decreasing trend of objectivist responses across factual, ethical, social convention, and taste statements. In other words, we predicted that individuals would treat ethical statements as more objective than statements of taste or social convention on the one hand, although not quite as objective as factual statements.

Finally, at the end of the experiment, we asked another set of questions about the way individuals ground or justify their ethical positions. The participants could select as many of the groundings shown in Appendix B as applied to them. We predicted that individuals who ground their ethical systems in the notion of a divine being, or in the notion of a moral self-identity, or in the "self-evidence" of their ethical beliefs, ought to be more objective about ethics than individuals who do not ground their ethical systems in such a way. Moreover, we suspected that those individuals who viewed ethics as tightly dependent on religion, i.e., those who could not conceive of right or wrong acts without the existence of a divine being, would be particularly objective about ethics, although this idea was not tested until the second experiment. We did not predict that grounding one's ethical system in its pragmatic benefits would be associated with greater objectivism.

2.2. Results

Basic descriptive data for the first stage of the experiment are presented in Table 1. It indicates the mean agreement–disagreement ratings for each of the 26 statements and the overall frequencies of true, false, and opinion ratings.

Considering the ethical statements, it is noticeable that the assignment of truth to ethical statements varies considerably with the content of the statement. Participants generally agreed (on a six-point scale) with the goodness of anonymous donations (5.42), the badness of opening gunfire on a crowd (5.79), or of robbing a bank (5.77), and the wrongness of conscious racial discrimination (5.86) or of cheating on a lifeguard exam (5.72). But they varied considerably in how likely they were to regard these statements as true: 36%, 68%, 61%, 54%, and 58%, respectively. Perhaps more strikingly, although participants generally agreed (albeit not as strongly) with

Table 1 Mean agreement ratings and the overall percentages of true, false, and opinion responses for the 26 statements used in Experiment 1

Statement Category	Content	Mean agreement scores (s.error)	Percentage of "true" responses	Percentage of "false" responses	Percentage of "opinion" responses	Percentage of "other" responses
Fact	Geography	5.78 (.12)	98		2	
	Evolution	5.28 (.19)	68	4	28	
	Earth	5.58 (.15)	92		8	
	Exercise	5.68 (.09)	96		4	
	Mars*	1.54 (.18)	26	68	6	
	Mean	5.56 (.15)	84	6	10	
Ethics	Donate	5.42 (.10)	36		64	
	Gunfire	5.79 (.12)	68		32	
	Robbery	5.77 (.09)	61		39	
	Discrimination	5.86 (.06)	54		46	
	Cheating	5.72 (.09)	58		42	
	Abortion	4.12 (.25)	2	6	92	
	Euthanasia	4.36 (.20)	8	2	90	
	Stem cells	4.58 (.22)	2	4	94	
	Testimony*	1.90 (.19)	2	42	56	
	Mean	5.23 (.15)	37	2	62	
Convention	First name	4.58 (.14)	40		60	
	Pajamas	4.14 (.19)	18		82	
	Drive left	5.59 (.10)	86		12	
	Red light	5.54 (.12)	80		20	
	Talking*	1.70 (.14)	2	50	48	
	Mean	5.03 (.14)	55		44	
Taste	Writers	5.16 (.16)	16		84	
	Musicians	5.33 (.29)	16		79	
	Singers	4.87 (.14)	3		97	
	Speakers	5.52 (.10)	12		88	
	Schindler's	5.16 (.15)	6		90	2
	Music*	3.28 (.17)	0	2	98	
	Painters	3.56 (.14)		2	98	
	News	4.82 (.16)	12		88	
	B. Mind	3.74 (.21)			100	
	Mean	4.65 (.17)	7		91	

Note. Percentages do not always sum to 100 owing to some missing data. To compute the category averages, items which tended to produce disagreement (marked with an asterisk) were reverse coded. Missing cell values represent percentages of 0.

the permissibility of abortion (4.12), assisted death (4.36), and stem cell research (4.58) in the way we described them, they were highly reluctant to assign truth to statements expressing this agreement: 2%, 8%, and 2%, respectively. In other words, meta-ethical judgments about the truth of ethical claims appear to be highly sensitive to the content of the claims in question (i.e., robbery vs. abortion), and not merely to whether the claims are generally agreeable. Only 13 out of 50 participants applied the same category (truth vs. opinion) to the eight ethical statements they rated in the first part of the experiment.[4] The remaining 37 varied their assignment of truth/falsity versus opinion in some way.

We now turn to consideration of the data from the second and more important phase of the experiment. The primary question concerned how people would respond to the new knowledge that somebody else we had tested disagreed with them. To recapitulate our main predictions, we expected that on this measure there would be a decreasing tendency to view statements as objectively true across the following categories: factual, ethical, social convention, and taste.

We were wary of the fact that some individuals might interpret ethical disagreement as indicating that the disagreeing other person might have been thinking of extraordinary extenuating circumstances, or that they had misread the question, or that they may not have understood the words used in a conventional way, and so on (see Turiel et al., 1991). The list of such possible caveats to interpreting the prima facie ethical disagreement is large. However, for each disagreement, we asked people to further comment on the source of the disagreement that they were confronted with. When individuals did not interpret the disagreement in a bona fide way, as in the examples just mentioned, we excluded such data from all foregoing analyses.[5] In fact, only 7 out of a total of 102 responses were excluded on these grounds. The overall trend for objectivist responses is shown in Fig. 1.

Overall, considering the mean scores on the three-point scale of objectivism, the effect of statement content on degree of objectivism was highly significant in an ANOVA ($F(3,102) = 39.54$, $p < .001$).[6] Planned contrasts indicated that all of the adjacent comparisons were highly significant. Factual statements ($M = 2.91$) were treated as more objective than ethical statements ($M = 2.56$; $F(1, 34) = 9.62$, $p < .01$). Ethical statements were treated as more objective than statements of social convention ($M = 2.00$, $F(1, 34) = 9.62$, $p < .01$), which in turn were treated as more objective than statements of taste or preference ($M = 1.34$, $F(1, 34) = 15.17$, $p < .001$). For the ethical statements, the most common response (50 out of 100) was fully objective (3 on the scale of objectivism).[7] The next most common response was intermediately objective (28 out of 100; 11 of these were "true (or) false, but neither party need be mistaken"; and 17 were "opinion, but the other party is surely mistaken"), 11 responses out of 100 occupied the least objective position and the remaining 11 responses could not be categorized because participants chose to respond *other* to the question regarding disagreement.

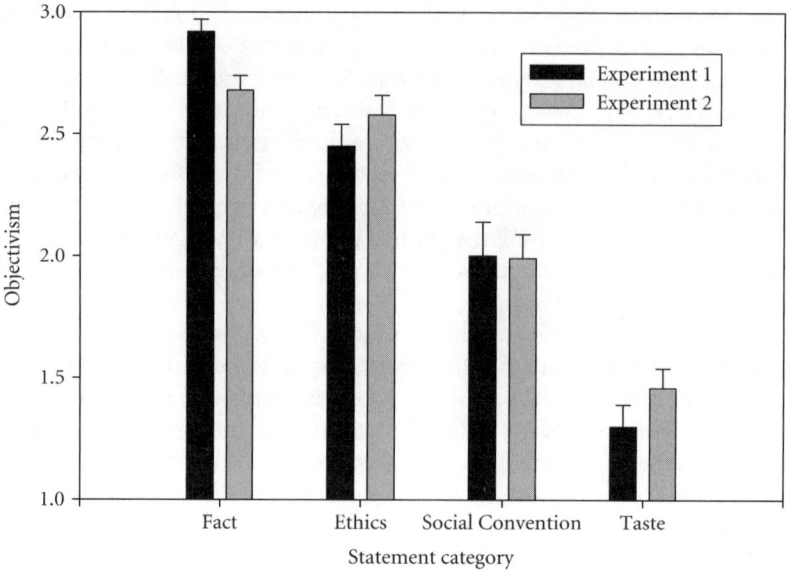

Figure 7.1. The level of objectivism shown for the four types of statement in Experiments 1 and 2.

The four statement categories differed in objectivism, as we have just demonstrated, but they also differed in strength of agreement ratings, $F(3,46) = 22.16$, $p < .001$. In order to control for this, we re-computed the ANOVA on four new within-subjects variables that were created by subtracting the strength of agreement ratings from the objectivism ratings (having rescaled the objectivism scores so that they were on the same 1–6 scale as the strength scores).[8] The resulting ANOVA was again highly reliable ($F(3, 102) = 39.57, p < .001$). On this analysis, planned contrasts indicated that factual statements ($M = -.11$) were treated as more objective than ethical statements ($M = -.83$; $F(1, 34) = 10.44$, $p < .01$). Ethical statements were not treated more objectively than statements of social convention although the trend was in that direction ($M = -1.34$; $F(1, 34) = 2.46$, $p < .13$). And statements of social convention were treated more objectively than statements of taste ($M = -3.00$, $F(1, 34) = 26.38, p < .001$).

We were interested in whether the ways individuals grounded their ethical systems might predict different levels of moral objectivism. For each of the four groundings that we presented (see Appendix B), a binary variable coded whether participants cited that grounding or not. In order to test for the independent effects of each of the four grounding variables, they were simultaneously entered as predictors of ethical objectivism in a multiple regression analysis. The resulting model was significant, $F(4, 44) = 3.30$, $R^2 = .23$, $p < .02$. As predicted, individuals who grounded their ethical beliefs in the notion of a divine being were more objective than those who did not, $\beta = .27$, $sr^2 = .25$, $p < .04$, one-tailed. Similarly, those who grounded their ethical beliefs in their importance to a moral self-identity ("every good person on earth holds these beliefs") were more objective than those who did not, $\beta = .25$, $sr^2 = .23$, $p < .05$, one-tailed. And surprisingly, individuals who cited a pragmatic grounding for their ethical beliefs ("society could not survive without its citizens holding these beliefs") were marginally more objective about those beliefs than those who did not cite such a reason, $\beta = .22$, $sr^2 = .22$, $p < .06$, one-tailed. Contrary to the prediction, individuals who claimed that their moral beliefs were self-evident were not more objective than those who did not.

The different groundings we examined were relatively independent. The only reliable correlation between them was that grounding ethics in a divine being was somewhat related to grounding in the notion of a moral self-identity, $r(50) = .31$, $p < .03$. Yet, the more groundings an individual cited (of the three that were shown to play some role in predicting objectivism: divine being, moral self-identity, pragmatism), the more objective about ethics they tended to be. This relationship was very clear-cut. Individuals who cited none of the three grounding reasons were the least objective about ethical statements (1.5). They were less objective than those who cited one grounding (2.42), who in turn were less objective than those who cited two groundings (2.65), who themselves were less objective than those who cited three groundings (2.81). The number of groundings an individual cited was a highly reliable predictor of objectivism in a hierarchical regression analysis in which strength of agreement was controlled for by entering it in the first block. Strength of agreement did not predict a significant proportion of variance in objectivism, $R^2 = .02$, $F(1, 47) = 1.08$, $p > .3$. After adding number of groundings into the regression, $R^2 = .29$, $F(2, 46) = 9.24$ ($p < .001$). The change in R^2 produced by adding number of groundings was highly reliable, $F(1, 46) = 17.23$ ($p < .001$).

Within the category of ethical statements, the final composite measure of objectivism significantly correlated with strength of agreement, $r(49) = .33$, $p < .02$.[9] One might therefore worry that participants were using the truth versus opinion distinction to represent degrees of certainty or confidence they had in each statement, rather than to mark an epistemic distinction between them. This objection cannot explain the fact that participants agreed very strongly with the taste statements that we gave them but did not treat them as objective (see Tables 1 and 2). They were able to differentiate between the strength of their attitude (or certainty) towards these statements and the statements' objectivity. This objection is further refuted by the results of Experiment 2, which we present next.

Experiment 2 was designed to replicate the findings of Experiment 1 using a different methodology. In the first stage of the experiment, rather than asking participants to assign truth, falsity or opinion to the various statements, we instead asked them a simple question: can there be a correct answer as to whether the statement in question is true? This question is very clearly concerned with the nature of the statement itself, and cannot be interpreted as asking for an assessment of confidence.

3. EXPERIMENT 2

3.1. Method

3.1.1. Participants

Seventy-one undergraduate students (29 male, 42 female) from Princeton University participated for course credit, and five students (3 male, 2 female) from Princeton's theological seminary participated for a payment of $10.[10]

3.1.2. Design, materials, and procedure

As in Experiment 1, participants acted as their own controls and completed two separate parts of the experiment. The materials and procedure for the both parts were almost identical to those in Experiment 1. In the first part, participants rated their agreement with the 26 statements shown in Appendix A on a six-point scale (rating the replaced versions for items 2 and 5). However, instead of judging whether they thought each statement was true, false, or an opinion, they were instead asked, "According to you, can there be a correct answer as to whether this statement is true?", and were given only the options *yes* and *no* to choose from. In the second part, the only difference was that after 18 participants, instead of assigning statement 6: "Boston (Massachusetts) is farther north than Los Angeles (California)," as the factual statement, we chose to assign statement 12 instead: "Homo sapiens evolved from more primitive primate species," which we still expected large agreement with.[11]

3.2. Results

We observed a broadly similar pattern of results as occurred in Experiment 1. Descriptive data for the 26 statements are shown in Table 2. We observed the same effect of the content of the ethical statements on individuals' tendency to regard them as objective. For instance, although participants tended to agree with the wrongness of robbing a bank (5.29), the goodness of anonymous giving (5.43), and the permissibility of assisted death (4.38), they were far more willing to say that there was a correct answer as to the wrongness of robbery (83%), than they were to say the same about the goodness of giving (52%), and highly unlikely to claim a correct answer as the permissibility of assisted death (17%). Across the eight ethical statements judged in the first part of the experiment, only 9 out of the 76 participants made the same response to the correct answer query for all eight statements. Thus, our participants' meta-ethical positions were again highly dependent on the specific ethical content that they were asked to judge.

We now turn to the data from the second phase, in which participants were asked to respond to disagreement. In the present experiment, unlike Experiment 1, there were no instances where the participants thought that the disagreeing other was conceiving of a different set of circumstances than they themselves were, so no responses were excluded on this basis. Objectivism scores were computed by combining responses to the "correct answer" and "mistake"

Table 2 Mean agreement ratings and the overall frequencies of correct answer and no correct answer responses for the 26 statements used in Experiment 2

Statement category	Content	Mean agreement scores (s. error)	Percentage of "correct answer" responses	Percentage of "no correct answer" responses
Fact	Geography	5.53 (.12)	97	3
	Evolution	5.43 (.12)	83	17
	Earth	5.64 (.09)	85	15
	Exercise	5.53 (.08)	84	16
	Mars*	1.79 (.17)	96	4
	Mean	5.47 (.12)	89	11
Ethics	Donate	5.43 (.08)	51	47
	Robbery	5.29 (.16)	83	17
	Discrim.	5.62 (.08)	79	21
	Cheating	5.63 (.08)	83	17
	Abortion	4.03 (.21)	22	78
	Euthanasia	4.38 (.14)	17	83
	Stem cells	4.84 (.15)	24	76
	False testimony*	2.14 (.16)	66	34
	Mean	5.01 (.13)	53	47
Convention	First name	4.08 (.15)	43	57
	Pajamas	3.88 (.16)	36	65
	Drive left	5.39 (.11)	83	17
	Red light	5.29 (.11)	86	15
	Talking*	1.83 (.11)	74	26
	Mean	4.76 (.13)	64	36
Taste	Writers	4.96 (.12)	25	75
	Singers	4.68 (.13)	17	83
	Speakers	5.37 (.10)	26	74
	Schindler's	4.75 (.12)	16	84
	Music	3.32 (.16)	4	96
	Painters	3.50 (.12)	4	96
	News	4.84 (.13)	34	66
	B. Mind	3.86 (.17)	9	91
	Mean	4.41 (.13)	17	83

Note. Percentages do not always sum to 100 owing to some missing data. To compute the category averages, items which tended to produce disagreement (marked with an asterisk) were reverse coded.

questions in the same way as in Experiment 1, to create a three-point scale of objectivism, ranging from 1 (least objective) to 3 (most objective). We again predicted that on the objectivity measure, ethical statements would fall between factual statements on the one hand and statements of social convention or taste on the other. This was largely what we found, as is shown in Fig. 1, with the exception that in this experiment, ethical statements were treated just as objectively as factual statements. Overall, statement content exerted a reliable effect on objectivism, as demonstrated in an ANOVA ($F(3, 198) = 58.18, p <.001$). Factual statements were treated the most objectively (2.70), although planned contrasts showed that ethical statements were in fact treated no less objectively (2.60; $F(1, 66) = 1.21, p >.2$).[12] However, ethical statements were treated more objectively than statements of social convention (1.97; $F(1, 66) = 25.12, p <.001$), which in turn were treated more objectively than statements of taste (1.43; $F(1, 66) = 19.34, p <.001$).

Concerning the ethical statements, 107 of the 152 responses (70%) were fully objective.[13] Sixteen of the 152 responses (11%) were intermediately objective (12 of which were "correct answer, neither party need be mistaken" and 4 of which were "no correct answer, other party is surely mistaken"); 21 of the 152 responses (14%) occupied the least objective position; and the remaining 8 responses (5%) were not able to classified.

As in Experiment 1, the four statement categories differed not only in objectivism, but also in strength of agreement ratings, $F(3, 73) = 21.15$ ($p <.001$).[14] We controlled for this in the same way as in Experiment 1, by rescaling the objectivism scores so that they were on the same scale as the strength of agreement scores, and then subtracting the strength of agreement scores from them. The resulting ANOVA was still highly significant ($F(3, 198) = 154.42, p <.001$), and the planned contrast results were unchanged.

We next investigated the same predictors of objectivism as those tested in Experiment 1. First, we entered these four variables into a multiple regression analysis to test for their independent effects. This model significantly predicted variance in ethical objectivism, $F(4,64) = 3.69, R^2 = .19, p <.01$. Replicating Experiment 1, individuals who grounded their ethical systems in the notion of a divine being were reliably more objective than those who did not, $\beta = .20$, $sr^2 = .19, p <.05$, one-tailed. Similarly, individuals who grounded their ethical systems in the notion of a moral self-identity were more objective about ethical statements than those who did not, $\beta = .32, sr^2 = .26, p <.02$, one-tailed. Unlike Experiment 1, individuals who grounded their ethical systems in their pragmatic consequences were not more objective than those who did not, $\beta = .15$, $sr^2 = .12, p >.14$, one-tailed. However, this is partly due to shared variance between the predictors: taken alone, the pragmatic grounding reliably predicts objectivism, $r = .29, p <.01$. The self-evident grounding was again not reliable.

The groundings were again relatively independent of each other. The only reliable correlation between them was that grounding one's ethical system in the notion of a moral self-identity was correlated with grounding one's ethical system in its pragmatic consequences, $r(71) = .52, p <.001$. As in Experiment 1, the more groundings an individual cited—of those that were predictive of objectivism (divine being, moral self-identity, pragmatic consequences)—the more objective they tended to be. Individuals who cited none of these groundings were the least objective (1.83). They were less objective than those who cited one grounding (2.58), who were in turn less objective than those who cited two (2.77) or three groundings (2.94). A hierarchical regression analysis in which strength of agreement was entered first showed that the number of groundings cited was a reliable predictor of objectivism. In this experiment, strength of agreement predicted a significant proportion of the variance in objectivism, $R^2 = .26$, $F(1, 71) = 24.28$, $p < .001$. Adding number of groundings to the regression equation, accounted for a higher proportion of the variance in objectivism, $R^2 = .37$, $F(2, 70) = 20.80$, $p < .001$, and this change in R^2 was highly reliable, $F(1, 70) = 13.16$, $p < .01$.

3.3. Discussion: Experiments 1 and 2

The findings from Experiments 1 and 2 are highly consistent and highlight several important facets of lay meta-ethics. First, how objectively individuals treat their ethical beliefs depends to a large extent on the content of those beliefs. Lay meta-ethical systems are not monolithic, but rather, are sensitive to specific ethical content. Second, individuals seem to treat core ethical beliefs as being almost as objective as scientific or plainly factual beliefs, and reliably more objective than beliefs about social convention or taste. Third, there was variation amongst individuals in terms of how objectively they treated their ethical beliefs. Individuals who grounded their ethical systems in the notion of a divine being, or in the notion of a moral self-identity, or in the pragmatic consequences of holding those beliefs, all tended to be more objective than those who did not. Moreover, these groundings functioned independently and additively. The more such groundings individuals cited the more objective they tended to be about their ethical beliefs.

The finding that individuals who grounded their ethical systems in the notion of a divine being tended to be more objective than those who did not led us to pursue one further hypothesis concerning religious belief. Grounding one's ethics in religious belief is the most obvious way that one could be an objectivist about ethics (although not the only way), and it may give rise to a particularly strong form of objectivism. To investigate this, at the end of both experiments we had asked participants: "According to you, is it possible for there to be right and wrong acts, without the existence of God?" We predicted that participants who did not believe that there could be right and wrong acts without a God, and who also grounded their ethical systems in a God, ought to be most objective about their ethical beliefs. We collapsed the data from Experiments 1 and 2 to create three groups. The first group (unreligious grounding) consisted of 84 participants who did not cite a divine being as part of the grounding for their ethical beliefs and were the least objective (2.43). The second group (religious grounding, but ethics not dependent on religion) consisted of 27 participants who cited a divine being but also thought that there could be right and wrong acts without the existence of such a being, and were somewhat more objective (2.65). The third group (religious grounding, ethics dependent on religion) consisted of 12 participants who cited a divine being and either thought that there could not be right and wrong acts without the existence of such a being or were not sure of their position on that issue. This finally group was almost maximally objective (2.95). The extent to which people saw ethics as dependent on religion exerted a reliable effect on objectivism, $F(2, 120) = 3.85$, $p <.03$. Moreover, this variable exerted a reliable effect on objectivism, even controlling for how strongly participants in each group held their beliefs. In a hierarchical regression analysis regressing ethical objectivism on strength of agreement and the dependence of ethics on religion (coding unreligious as 0, religious but ethics independent of religion as 1, and religious and ethics dependent on religion as 2), when strength of agreement was entered first, $R^2 = .19$, $F(1, 121) = 28.21$, $p <.001$. Adding the dependence of ethics on religion variable to this analysis accounted for more variance, $R^2 = .22$, $F(2, 120) = 16.41$, $p <.001$, and the increase in variance accounted for was reliable, $F(1, 120) = 3.93$, $p < .05$.

Experiments 1 and 2 used different methods to measure objectivism in the first stage of the experiment. Experiment 1 asked participants whether they thought various beliefs were true (or false), or alternatively, opinions, whereas Experiment 2 asked whether various statements could have a correct answer or not. A priori, this second question seemed less susceptible to being interpreted as asking for an indication of confidence. Converging with this general point, the question in Experiment 2 also produced more interpretable results for the ethical statements in terms of the intermediately objective responses. In Experiment 1, 39% of such responses were of the form "true, but neither party need be mistaken," with the remaining 61% being "opinion, but the other party is surely mistaken." Earlier, we remarked that this second response is harder to justify and may indicate oscillation between objective and subjective views of ethics (or possibly confusion), whereas the first is consistent with ethical subjectivism. In Experiment 2 however, the respective percentages switched markedly –75% of the intermediately objective responses were of the form "correct answer, but neither party need be mistaken" (which, despite the different question, can also be regarded as a philosophically defensible form of subjectivism), whereas only 25% of such responses were "no correct answer, but other party is surely mistaken." We take this as converging evidence for the greater felicity of the question asked in Experiment 2. Notably, a similar proportional increase in this more interpretable intermediate response was observed for all three remaining statement categories from Experiment 1 to 2 (facts: 50–80%; social conventions: 55–73%; taste: 25–57%).

4. EXPERIMENT 3

Experiment 3 aimed to further extend these findings by investigating the role of religiosity and political attitudes. It also generalized our initial findings on the grounding of ethical beliefs by using a different methodology. We were interested in testing two key hypotheses. First, does mere religious belief predict ethical objectivism, or is it the link between ethics and religious belief that is important, i.e., the grounding of ethics in religion? Second, is the difference between those who ground ethics in religion versus those who do not, subsumed by more general political or cultural differences—specifically differences between liberal and conservative attitudes (see e.g., Haidt & Graham, in press)?

4.1. Method

4.1.1. Participants

Two hundred and forty-seven Princeton University students participated in the experiment for the chance to win a $50 prize. Participants were solicited via an email which invited them to take part in a short web survey.

4.1.2. Design, materials, and procedure

Participants read three short scenarios which described three separate ethical decisions. One scenario concerned the decision of someone to donate 10% of their annual income to charity; a second concerned the decision of a woman to have an abortion due to the financial strain a child would cause; and a third concerned the decision of someone to provide a false alibi for a friend who is facing murder charges. The full description of each scenario is shown in Appendix D. Participants rated the extent to which they agreed with claims about the moral goodness, moral permissibility, and moral wrongness of each action, respectively (all scales in this experiment had six points). For each scenario, after making this initial agreement rating, participants were asked two further questions—first, the extent to which they thought there could be a correct answer as to whether each statement was true, and second, what they would conclude about someone who hypothetically disagreed with them on a scale that ranged from "neither of us need be mistaken" to "other person is clearly mistaken." Participants also rated how they grounded their moral beliefs, using the same groundings as in the previous experiments.[15] However, in this experiment, we asked participants to make ratings of the extent to which each of the four groundings provided support for their moral beliefs rather than simply checking those which applied. Additionally, we asked participants to indicate their degree of belief in the existence of a supreme being or God (or supreme beings/Gods) on a scale ranging from "not at all" to "very strongly."

The design involved two levels of counter-balancing. For half the participants, the three moral scenarios were presented first, in a randomly determined order, followed by the grounding and religious belief questions. For the other half of the participants, the reverse order was used. Within each of these two orders, the grounding question preceded the religious belief question for half the participants, whereas the reverse order was used for the remaining half. At the very end of the experiment, participants indicated their general political attitudes on a six-point scale ranging from "very conservative" to "very liberal."

4.2. Results and discussion

The data from two participants were removed because they failed to provide responses to the ethical questions. To aid interpretation, we dichotomized scores on all scales into those above and below the mid-point. No predictive power was lost in doing this. For each of the three ethical scenarios, ethical objectivism scores were computed as they were in the previous experiments. In this experiment, the inter-correlations between objectivism scores for the three separate ethical scenarios were low, so we treated each scenario separately. For none of the three scenarios (donating money, false alibi, abortion) did the counter-balancing of whether the ethical grounding and religious belief questions came before or after the ethics questions exert any effect on objectivism scores (p values >.5,.18,.97, respectively).

Our main analysis of interest was to regress objectivism scores on the four different groundings and on the religious belief and political attitudes questions. The results confirm the main conclusions of the previous experiments, and help answer the questions posed at the outset of the study. Whether or not participants grounded their ethical systems in the notion of a divine being was the only variable to reliably predict objectivism for all three scenarios. Grounding ethics in the notion of a divine being was a marginally reliable predictor of objectivism about the goodness of anonymous donations, and was the only predictor to approach significance (β = .12, sr^2 = .09, p <.08, one-tailed).[16] Similarly, it was the only reliable predictor of objectivism about the wrongness of providing a false alibi (β = .17, sr^2 = .12, p <.03, one-tailed). And grounding ethics in God was a reliable predictor of the impermissibility of abortion (β = .21, sr^2 = .16, p <.01, one-tailed), alongside mere belief in God (β = .25, sr^2 = .19, p <.01, one-tailed), and grounding ethics in the self-evidence of moral beliefs (β = .16, sr^2 = .15, p <.01, one-tailed). Political attitudes did not correlate with objectivism for any of the three scenarios.

These results confirm the findings of the previous two experiments, that grounding one's ethical beliefs in the notion of a divine being predicts greater objectivism. This variable appears to have greater predictive power than does mere religious belief, although in some cases (i.e., abortion) grounding ethics in God and mere belief in God do explain independent portions of variance. Grounding ethics in God also has greater predictive power than do simple political attitudes.

5. GENERAL DISCUSSION

Most current theorizing on the psychology of ethics has focused on identifying the actual ethical beliefs and practices that individuals subscribe to (see e.g., Baron & Spranca, 1997; Darley & Shultz, 1990; Haidt, 2001; Kohlberg, 1969, 1981; Maio & Olson, 1998; Piaget, 1965; Tetlock, 2003). Although very important, this sort of research does not answer questions about how individuals think more generally about their ethical beliefs—what sort of status they accord them, and in particular, how they think about them when they are challenged. In this paper, we develop a method that distinguishes ethical objectivists (i.e., individuals who take their ethical beliefs to express true facts about the world) from ethical subjectivists (i.e., individuals who take their ethical beliefs to be mind-dependent, and to express nothing more than facts about human psychology). According to this method, objectivism is measured by combining participants' judgments about the *status* of a particular belief that they hold (truth vs. opinion: Experiment 1; possibility of a correct answer: Experiments 2 and 3), with their judgments about the *mistakenness* of someone who disagrees with that belief.

The findings across all three experiments were very consistent. The first major finding was that individuals were not particularly consistent in their meta-ethical positions about various ethical beliefs and were instead highly influenced by the content of the beliefs in question. This finding suggests that unlike the meta-ethical systems of philosophers, which tend to be uniform in their treatment of a range of ethical beliefs, ordinary individuals' meta-ethical systems are highly nuanced. This finding is reminiscent of work in the deductive reasoning literature, which has shown that just as our participants did not make judgments as ethical philosophers would have, ordinary individuals do not reason as logicians. They are heavily influenced by content and not just by logical form. Perhaps the most famous demonstration of this in reasoning is in the effect of content in the Wason selection task (e.g., Cheng & Holyoak, 1989; Cosmides, 1989; Griggs & Cox, 1982; Johnson-Laird, Legrenzi, & Legrenzi, 1972), but the effect has also been shown repeatedly in the effects of belief on syllogistic reasoning (e.g., Klauer, Musch, & Naumer, 2000; Newstead, Pollard, Evans, & Allen, 1992), and in the pragmatic modulation of conditionals (Johnson-Laird & Byrne, 2002).

In the present context, the effects of content are likely to be multi-faceted. However, our data suggested one obvious cause—individuals' ratings of objectivism are influenced by how strongly they hold a particular ethical belief in the first place. This finding is arguably quite peculiar because there are clear instances where strength of agreement is disconnected from objectivism. For instance, our participants tended to strongly agree with the taste statements we presented, but viewed them as much less objective than each of the other three sorts of statements. Conversely, while one might be very uncertain whether Mars is bigger or smaller than Venus, one can still be fully confident that there is an objective fact about the matter. Although our participants clearly understood the difference between strength of agreement ratings and objectivism ratings, and decoupled them in some cases, the link between strength of agreement and objectivism was still strong: individuals were more objective about those ethical statements that they strongly agreed with. This finding was not confined to the ethical statements. But the fact that it occurs for ethical statements shows that, unlike philosophers of meta-ethics lay individuals are objectivists about some ethical beliefs but not others.

Content effects in reasoning have often been attributed to the reliance on semantic rather than purely syntactic processes. One version of this explanation is that reasoners build a specific mental model of the assertions they reason from and are thus pulled away from an abstract syntactic analysis based on the form of assertions (see e.g., Johnson-Laird & Byrne, 2002; Newstead et al., 1992). A similar process might be hypothesized in the present context. Individuals envisage the concrete ethical scenario they are presented with, and form a model of the relevant intentions and motivations at work. Their judgments of the objectivity of various moral claims are based on this particular and concrete model. Hence, they tend to treat each ethical judgment as unique, and any requirements of judgmental consistency across ethical scenarios are not considered (see relatedly, Kahneman & Lovallo, 1993).

The second major finding was that ethical beliefs were treated almost as objectively as scientific or factual beliefs and decidedly more objectively than social conventions or tastes. Individuals seem to identify a strong objective component to their core ethical beliefs and thus treat them as categorically different from social conventions. Arguably, many of our participants viewed their ethical beliefs as true in a mind-independent way. Such a view need not make ethical beliefs impervious to disagreement, but it does establish them as far less contestable than social conventions which can be considered somewhat arbitrary constructions. Moreover, it implies that there is an objectively true fact of the matter concerning whether ethical beliefs are true. This interpretation is vulnerable to the criticism that we only tested a very small range of beliefs and that one could easily construct counter-examples in which a social convention or taste would be treated more objectively than an ethical belief. Even within our own data, there are conventions that are thought to be true statements and to have a correct answer by the majority of participants. Participants tended to think that it was true that driving round a blind corner on the wrong side of the road and driving through a red light were wrong actions (86%, 80%, respectively, Experiment 1) and that there could be a correct answer as to whether these statements were true (83%, 86%, respectively, Experiment 2). We did not ask participants to respond to a disagreeing other for these statements, but it is likely that they would have tended to be highly objectivist about these sorts of conventional statements. However, this sort of conventional statement is not a prototypical social convention and is instead what has been referred to as a "high social utility rule"—i.e., a coordination rule that is essentially arbitrary but that is very important to observe once it has been set (Miller & Bersoff, 1988; Turiel et al., 1991). Transgressions of this sort of rule have been shown to be treated more seriously than transgressions of more prototypical social conventions (Miller & Bersoff, 1988). Moreover, the statements we presented to participants in the second phase of our experiments were deliberately chosen to be prototypical instances of each of the four different categories (factual, ethical, social conventional, taste). Hence, relevant counter-examples notwithstanding, our results support the claim that ethical statements are treated almost as objectively as facts and more objectively than social conventions and tastes.

The third major finding was that the way in which individuals grounded their ethical systems predicted how objective they were about their ethical beliefs. Those individuals who grounded their ethical systems in the notion of a divine being, in the concept of a moral self-identity, or in the pragmatic consequences of a society not adhering to that system all tended (to some extent) to be more objective than those who did not. These groundings were largely independent of each other, and the more groundings an individual cited, the more objective they tended to be, suggesting multiple routes to ethical objectivism.

The most robust of these predictors of objectivism was the religious grounding. Individuals who grounded their ethical beliefs in the notion of a divine being were more objective than those who did not across all three experiments. Moreover, the subset of individuals who very tightly connected ethics with religion by not admitting the possibility of right or wrong acts without the existence of a God, were almost maximally objective. Experiment 3 further emphasized the importance of the link between ethics and religion by showing that grounding ethics in God was a more powerful predictor of ethical objectivism than mere belief in God and more powerful than political conservatism–liberalism. This null effect for political attitude is consonant with Hunter's (1991) depiction of orthodox and progressivist ideologies as cutting across simple liberal and conservative divisions (p. 118).

It was a surprise that in Experiments 1 and 2 individuals who grounded their ethical beliefs in their pragmatic consequences for society tended to be more objective than those who did not. A pragmatic grounding makes reference to the external consequences of ethical beliefs rather than to their intrinsic truth or standing, and thus ought not to be objective. Respondents may have been reasoning that at the societal level the pragmatic consequences of certain ethical beliefs loom large enough to imbue such beliefs with an objective character.

Several potential criticisms of these findings about ethical groundings can be raised. We have described these findings as though the groundings that we assessed *gave rise* to the differing levels of objectivism. Of course however, this sort of causal account cannot be supported by our existing data. It may instead be that getting people to think about ethical disagreements first gave rise to their endorsing different sorts of ethical groundings. This possibility strikes us as unlikely, but it would require a more elaborate study to disentangle the direction of causation here. It may also be that a third variable explains both phenomena. A second criticism is that the amount of variance in the objectivism ratings that is explained by the different groundings is quite low. Evidently, the groundings that we have explored go only so far in explaining objectivism. Future research could aim to clarify which other variables are relevant to this explanation.

A question not pursued in the present research is whether meta-ethical differences in objectivism are associated with different ethical beliefs, behaviors, and practices. Philosophers have long noted that there is no logical connection between meta-ethics and practical ethics. Yet there may be some psychological connection. One hypothesis is that moral objectivism tends to be associated with a more strident ethical philosophy, for instance, one which is more inclined to endorse optional duties, such as say, the duty to give 10% of one's income to charity (see e.g., Singer, 1972). Accordingly, one potential benefit of holding an objectivist view of ethics is that it may lead to a more morally committed life. A different possible corollary concerns ethical dialogue. Some philosophers have argued that an objective view of ethics should make one more responsive to dialogue and more willing to listen to opposing sides of an ethical debate (e.g., Snare, 1992). According to this idea, since an objectivist believes that there is a truth to be discovered about ethics, she should therefore feel that ethical dialogue might expose her to new information which could change her mind. On the other hand, a subjectivist has his ethical preferences and can simply stick with them regardless of what new information comes to hand, since there simply is no truth to be uncovered about them. In contrast to this rather idealized sketch, we suspect that the opposite hypothesis is more likely to be true, and that objectivists are in fact less willing to engage in ethical dialogue and to listen to opposing views than subjectivists. Culture wars that are fought over fundamental ethical values may become more intractable to the extent that each side of the debate harbors an objective view of the truth of its own beliefs.

Our aim in this paper was to develop a method for assessing and predicting ethical objectivism. The present results represent only a first step towards a psychological understanding of this construct, and there is a need for further empirical investigation. Ethical disagreement and ethical conduct more generally may be elucidated by better understanding its nature and determinants.

APPENDIX A

The 26 statements that were used in Experiments 1 and 2 in the order they were presented to participants

No.	Statement category	Statement
1	Ethical	Anonymously donating a significant proportion of one's income to charity is a morally good action
2	Ethical	Opening gunfire on a crowded city street is a morally bad action/replaced by: robbing a bank in order to pay for an expensive holiday is a morally bad action
3	Convention	Calling teachers by their first name, without being given permission to do so, in a school that calls them "Mr." or "Mrs." is wrong behavior
4	Taste	Shakespeare was a better writer than is Dan Brown (author of "The Da Vinci Code")
5	Taste	Miles Davis was a better musician than is Britney Spears/replaced by: Frank Sinatra was a better singer than is Michael Bolton
6	Factual	Boston (Massachusetts) is farther north than Los Angeles (California)
7	Ethical	Consciously discriminating against someone on the basis of race is morally wrong
8	Ethical	Cheating on a knowledge section of a lifeguard exam, to obtain a job for which one is not qualified is morally wrong

No.	Statement category	Statement
9	Convention	Wearing pajamas and bath robe to a seminar meeting is wrong behavior
10	Taste	Bill Clinton is a better public speaker than George W. Bush
11	Taste	*Schindler's List* is a better film than *Police Academy*
12	Factual	Homo sapiens evolved from more primitive primate species
13	Ethical	Before the 3rd month of pregnancy, abortion for any reason (of the mother's) is morally permissible
14	Ethical	Assisting in the death of a terminally ill friend who is in terrible pain, and who wants to die, is morally permissible
15	Convention	Driving round a blind corner on the left hand side of the road (in the USA) is a wrong action
16	Taste	Classical music is better than rock music
17	Taste	Da Vinci was a better painter than was Monet
18	Factual	The earth is not at the center of the known universe
19	Ethical	Scientific research on embryonic human stem cells that are the product of in vitro fertilization is morally permissible
20	Ethical	Providing false testimony in court about the whereabouts of a friend who is being charged with murder (i.e., to protect that friend by offering an alibi) is morally permissible
21	Convention	Driving through a red light at a busy intersection because you are late for work is a wrong action
22	Convention	Talking loudly and constantly to the person next to you during a lecture is a permissible action
23	Taste	CNN provides better news coverage than does Fox News
24	Taste	*A Beautiful Mind* is a better film than *The Matrix*
25	Factual	Frequent aerobic exercising (i.e., running, swimming, cycling) usually helps people to lose weight.
26	Factual	Mars is the smallest planet in the solar system

APPENDIX B

The follow-up and final questions used in Experiments 1 and 2.

B.1. FOLLOW-UP QUESTIONS

Take claim ___: _____.
You circled ____ on the scale (1–6) which means that you strongly **agreed/disagreed** with this statement. A person who we tested strongly **agrees/disagrees** with this statement, which means that he or she sharply disagrees with you.

- What would you conclude about this disagreement? We are interested in what you would privately think about this —the question is **not** about what you would be willing to say to this other person. Please circle the number.

(1) The other person is surely mistaken.
(2) It is possible that neither you nor the other person is mistaken.
(3) It could be that you are mistaken, and the other person is correct.
(4) Other—please explain _____.

- Give us your thoughts about why it is that there is disagreement. What could be its source? _____

_____
_____
_____

B.2. FINAL QUESTIONS

- This is a general question about what we could call the "grounding," or "justification" for moral statements. People firmly believe certain moral statements (such as "do not commit murder"). Check as many of the following statements that you consider support for your moral beliefs. That is, that provide the reasons that you hold the particular set of moral beliefs that you do.

  – they are ordained by a supreme being;
  – every good person on earth, regardless of culture, holds these beliefs;
  – a society could not survive without its citizens holding these beliefs;
  – their truth is self-evident.

- According to you, is it possible for there to be right and wrong acts, without the existence of God?

  (1) yes;
  (2) no;
  (3) not sure.

APPENDIX C

The extent to which the different statement types were presented to participants in the second phase of Experiments 1 and 2

	Experiment 1		Experiment 2	
Factual	6. Boston location	92%	12. Homo sapiens	67%
	18. Earth orbit	8%	6. Boston location	20%
			18. Earth orbit	12%
			25. Exercise	1%

	Experiment 1		Experiment 2	
Ethical	8. Cheating on exam	84%	8. Cheating on exam	97%
	2. Robbery	60%	2. Robbery	89%
	2. Open fire on crowd	36%	7. Discrimination	13%
	7. Discrimination	10%		
	20. False testimony	8%		
	21. Assisted death	2%		
Conventional	3. First name	38%	9. Pajamas to seminar	46%
	9. Pajamas to seminar	36%	3. First name	21%
	22. Talking in class	26%	22. Talking in class	33%
Taste	10. Bill Clinton	38%	10. Bill Clinton	50%
	5. Frank Sinatra	30%	5. Frank Sinatra	47%
	5. Miles Davis	24%	4. Shakespeare	1%
	4. Shakespeare	4%	17. Da Vinci	1%
	16. Classical music	2%		
	11. Schindler's List	2%		

Note. The percentages sum to 100 for each category of statement except the ethical category where they sum to 200 because two statements were presented. This may not be exact in some cases owing to rounding error.

APPENDIX D

The three ethical scenarios presented in Experiment 3

1. DONATION

In the past, John has saved 10% of his income for vacations. But, after some deliberation, he decides that this money could be put to better use. He decides to change his savings plan so that he instead donates this saved income to charity, which he does so anonymously. Rate the extent to which you agree with the claim that John's actions are morally good.

2. FALSE ALIBI

One of Megan's best friends is being charged with murder. Megan is convinced that he is innocent, although she does not know what he was doing on the night of the alleged murder. Without having been asked, Megan provides a false alibi to the police for her friend, claiming that she was with him on the night of the alleged murder. Rate the extent to which you agree with the claim that Megan's actions are morally wrong.

3. ABORTION

Eve is 2 months pregnant. Despite Eve's wanting to have the child, she does not know who the father is, and after considering her financial situation she considers that having the child would be too big a burden. She decides instead to have an abortion. Rate the extent to which you agree with the claim that Eve's choice is morally permissible.

NOTES

* The first author thanks the Woodrow Wilson School, Princeton University for financial support. For their helpful comments, we thank Adam Alter, Sam Glucksberg, Adele Goldberg, Dena Gromet, Phil Johnson-Laird, Dan Osherson, Joe Simmons, and Erika Sloan.

1. This is not to deny that those who believe that an ethical statement is applicable to all people are more likely to consider the statement as objectively true, i.e., ethical objectivism and universalism are likely to be correlated psychologically. But, in theory they are distinct. One could, for instance, be an objectivist relativist (believing that it is objectively true that what is ethical varies by person or culture) or a subjectivist universalist (believing that although certain ethical standards are not true in any objective sense; they nevertheless apply to all persons and cultures).

2. We are aware that some ethical philosophers regard ethical statements as factual. Here we use the term *factual* to denote a relatively broad category of statements that are part of general knowledge, and which may be considered statements of empirical or scientific truth, and which are clearly not ethical.

3. An alternative and similarly objective response (both here and for the intermediately objective responses) is to say that the other person may in fact be correct and you yourself mistaken this indicates a view that the issue is one where mistakes are possible. This response, however, was exceedingly rare in our data.

4. For this analysis, we examined ratings of truth versus opinion for statements participants agreed with, and ratings of falsity versus opinion for statements participants disagreed with.

5. For instance, the following response was excluded for the gunfire version of question 2: "A difference in perception of a situation in which gunfire was opened on a crowded city street. I was thinking gunfire from terrorists/criminals; other person may have thought gunfire from police officers to catch a criminal." Responses in which participants said they needed more information about the context of the events were also excluded for this reason. However, responses in which participants said that perhaps the disagreeing other was operating with a different sense of "morally wrong/bad" were not excluded. Statements 2 and 5 were changed midway through the experiment (see earlier), because their original versions were more likely to allow disagreements of this non–bona fide sort.

6. There were some missing data, owing to the fact that some responses to disagreement were not interpretable. This meant that only 35 subjects were involved in this ANOVA, but the effect remained and was strengthened when each of the statement category means were substituted for the missing data.

7. Only 1 of these 50 fully objective responses was based on the participant having said: "It could be that you are mistaken (i.e., *the participant themselves*), and the other person is correct"; the remaining 49 were based on the participant having said: "The other person is surely mistaken."

8. This method presented itself as the simplest and best method of controlling for strength of agreement scores. There is no simple ANOVA procedure for controlling for a covariate (i.e., strength of agreement) which differs at each level of the repeated-measures variable (i.e., category of claim).

9. This correlation was also reliable for the three other statement categories.

10. We included the seminarians in order to increase the number of participants who grounded their ethics in the notion of a divine being. Circumstances precluded our including as many seminarians as we had planned, although indeed, 4 out of the 5 did ground their ethics in the notion of a divine being, compared with 18 out of 71 of the remaining participants. However, the seminarians who grounded their ethical beliefs in this way were not more objective about ethics than the other students who did so—in fact, they were practically identical on this measure (M = 2.75, seminarians; M = 2.74, non-seminarians, n.s.).

11. However, this statement was presented only in the second phase of the experiment to those participants who agreed with it. If participants did not agree with this statement, we presented an alternative factual statement.

12. As noted in the main text, for the majority of participants we used a more controversial factual statement in this experiment, "Homo sapiens evolved from more primitive primate species," than the uncontroversial geographical statement used in the last experiment (and for the first participants in this experiment). Within the present experiment, participants who received the evolution statement were marginally less objective about it than participants who received the geographical statement were about that statement (2.64 vs. 2.87, $t(31.57$, unequal variances$) = 1.99, p <.06$).

13. In all of these cases, the participants said that the other party is surely mistaken (rather than that they themselves might be mistaken and the other person correct).

14. Objectivism was also significantly correlated with strength of agreement *within* the ethical statements, as was also seen in Experiment 1, $r(74) = .53, (p <.001)$, and marginally within the social convention statements, $r(70) = .21, p <.08$, although not for the factual and taste statements.

15. We made one change to the moral self-identity grounding, so that for this experiment it read, "Holding these beliefs is essential to what it means to be a good person."

16. Due to a high correlation with mere belief in God, $r(241) = .64, p <.001$, grounding in God was the only reliable predictor of objectivism concerning the goodness of anonymous donations when belief in God was removed from this analysis ($\beta = .18$, $sr^2 = .12, p <.01$, one-tailed).

REFERENCES

Ayer, A. J. (1936). *Language, truth, and logic*. London: Gollancz.

Baron, J., & Spranca, M. (1997). Protected values. *Organizational Behavior and Human Decision Processes, 70*, 1–16.

Blackburn, S. (1984). *Spreading the word*. Oxford: Oxford University Press.

Brink, D. (1986). Externalist moral realism. *Southern Journal of Philosophy, 24*(Suppl.), 23–42.

Cheng, P. W., & Holyoak, K. J. (1989). Pragmatic reasoning schemas. *Cognitive Psychology, 17*, 397–416.

Cosmides, L. (1989). The logic of social exchange: Has natural selection shaped how humans reason? Studies with the Wason selection task. *Cognition, 31*, 187–276.

Darley, J. M., & Shultz, T. R. (1990). Moral rules: Their content and acquisition. *Annual Review of Psychology, 41*, 525–556.

Forsyth, D. R. (1980). A taxonomy of ethical ideologies. *Journal of Personality and Social Psychology, 39*, 175–184.

Forsyth, D. R. (1981). Moral judgment: The influence of ethical ideology. *Personality and Social Psychology Bulletin, 7*, 218–223.

Forsyth, D. R., & Berger, R. E. (1982). The effects of ethical ideology on moral behavior. *Journal of Social Psychology, 117*, 53–56.

Gabennesch, H. (1990a). The perception of social conventionality by children and adults. *Child Development, 61*, 2047–2059.

Gabennesch, H. (1990b). Recognizing conventionality: Reply to Shweder and Helwig et al. *Child Development, 61*, 2079–2084.

Griggs, R. A., & Cox, J. R. (1982). The elusive thematic-materials effect in Wason's selection task. *British Journal of Psychology, 73*, 407–420.

Haidt, J. (2001). The emotional dog and its rational tail: A social intuitionist approach to moral judgment. *Psychological Review, 108*, 814–834.

Haidt, J. & Graham, J. (2007). When morality opposes justice: Conservatives have moral intuitions that liberals may not recognize. *Social Justice Research*.20, 98–116.

Hare, R. M. (1952). *The language of morals*. Oxford: Oxford University Press.

Harman, G. (1975). Moral relativism defended. *Philosophical Review, 84*, 3–22.

Helwig, C. C., Tisak, M. S., & Turiel, E. (1990). Children's social reasoning in context: Reply to Gabennesch. *Child Development, 61*, 2068–2078.

Hunter, J. (1991). *Culture wars: The struggle to define America*. New York: Basic Books.

Johnson-Laird, P. N., & Byrne, R. M. J. (2002). Conditionals: A theory of meaning, pragmatics, and inference. *Psychological Review, 109*, 646–678.

Johnson-Laird, P. N., Legrenzi, P., & Legrenzi, M. S. (1972). Reasoning and a sense of reality. *British Journal of Psychology, 63*, 395–400.

Kahneman, D., & Lovallo, D. (1993). A cognitive perspective on risk taking. *Management Science, 39*, 17–31.

Kant, I. (1959). *Foundations of the metaphysics of morals* (L. W. Beck Trans.). Indianapolis, IN: Bobbs-Merrill. (Original work published 1786)

Klauer, K. C., Musch, J., & Naumer, B. (2000). On belief bias in syllogistic reasoning. *Psychological Review, 107*, 852–884.

Kohlberg, L. (1969). Stage and sequence: The cognitive-developmental approach to socialization. In D. A. Goslin (Ed.), *Handbook of socialization theory and research*. New York: Rand McNally. 347–480.

Kohlberg, L. (1981). *Essays on moral development (Vol. 1). The philosophy of moral development: Moral stages and the idea of justice*. San Francisco: Harper & Row.

Mackie, J. L. (1977). *Ethics: Inventing right and wrong*. New York: Penguin.

Maio, G. R., & Olson, J. M. (1998). Values as truisms: Evidence and implications. *Journal of Personality and Social Psychology, 74*, 294–311.

Miller, J. B., & Bersoff, D. M. (1988). When do American children and adults reason in social conventional terms? *Developmental Psychology 24*, 366–375.

Nagel, T. (1970). *The possibility of altruism*. Princeton: Princeton University Press.

Newstead, S. E., Pollard, P., Evans, J. St. B. T., & Allen, J. L. (1992). The source of belief bias effects in syllogistic reasoning. *Cognition, 45*, 257–284.

Nichols, S., & Folds-Bennett, T. (2003). Are children moral objectivists? Children's judgments about moral and response-dependent properties. *Cognition, 90*, B23–B32.

Piaget, J. (1965). *The moral judgment of the child*. New York: Free Press.

Railton, P. (1986). Moral realism. *Philosophical Review, 95*, 163–207.

Sayre-McCord, G. (1986). The many moral realisms. *The Southern Journal of Philosophy, 24*(Suppl.), 1–22.

Schwartz, S. H. (1992). Universals in the content and structure of values: Theoretical advances and empirical tests in 20 countries. In M. P. Zanna (Ed.). *Advances in experimental social psychology* (Vol. 25, pp. 1–65). New York: Academic Press.

Shantz, C. U. (1982). Children's understanding of social rules and the social context. In F. C. Serifica (Ed.), *Social cognitive development in context* (pp. 167–198). New York: Guilford.

Shweder, R. A. (1990). In defense of moral realism: Reply to Gabennesch. *Child Development, 61,* 2060–2067.

Singer, P. (1972). Famine, affluence, and morality. *Philosophy and Public Affairs, 1,* 229–243.

Smith, M. (1994). *The moral problem.* Oxford: Blackwell.

Snare, F. (1992). *The nature of moral thinking.* London: Routledge.

Sturgeon, N. (1985). Moral explanations. In D. Copp & D. Zimmerman (Eds.), *Morality reason and truth* (pp. 49–78). Totowa, NJ: Rowman & Allenheld.

Tetlock, P. E. (2003). Thinking the unthinkable: Sacred values and taboo cognitions. *Trends in Cognitive Sciences, 7,* 320–324.

Tisak, M. S., & Turiel, E. (1988). Variation in seriousness of transgressions and children's moral and conventional concepts. *Developmental Psychology, 24,* 352–357.

Turiel, E. (1978). Social regulations and domains of social concepts. In W. Damon (Ed.), *New directions for child development. Vol. 1. Social cognition* (pp. 45–74). New York: Gardner.

Turiel, E. (1983). *The development of social knowledge.* Cambridge, UK: Cambridge University Press.

Turiel, E., Hildenbrandt, C., & Wainryb, C. (1991). Judging social issues: Difficulties, inconsistencies, and consistencies. *Monographs of the Society for Research in Child Development, 56,* v–103.

Williams, B. (1972). *Morality: An introduction to ethics.* New York: Harper & Row.

Williams, B. (1985). *Ethics and the limits of philosophy.*Cambridge, MA: Harvard University Press.

8

Folk Moral Relativism*

Hagop Sarkissian, John Park, David Tien, Jennifer Cole Wright, and Joshua Knobe

Suppose that two individuals are discussing mathematics. One of them claims that the number 2,377 is prime, while the other claims that it is not prime. In a case like this, it is usually assumed that one of the two individuals must be wrong. There is a fact of the matter about whether 2,377 is prime, and anyone who holds the other opinion has to be mistaken.

But now suppose we switch to a different topic. Two individuals are talking about the seasons. One of them claims that January is a winter month, while the other claims that it is a summer month. Faced with this latter case, we might well reach a different conclusion. There is no single objective fact about whether January is a winter month or a summer month. Rather, it can only be a winter month or a summer month relative to a specific hemisphere. So if one of them is talking about the northern hemisphere and the other is talking about the southern hemisphere, they can make seemingly opposite claims but still both be correct.

What about moral claims? Suppose that two individuals are talking about the moral status of a particular action. One claims the action is morally bad, while the other claims it is not morally bad. Must one of these individuals be wrong, or could it turn out that they are both right?

Within the philosophical literature, this question remains controversial. Some philosophers say that there is a single objective truth about whether a particular action is morally bad, so that if two individuals hold opposite opinions, one of them must be mistaken (Railton, 1986; Shafer-Landau, 2003; Smith, 1994). Other philosophers say that moral claims can only be assessed relative to a particular moral framework or set of values, so that different moral claims could be right when asserted by different individuals (Dreier, 1990; Harman, 1975; Pinillos,

2010; Prinz, 2007; Wong, 1984, 2006). The debate between these two views has persisted at least since the ancient Greeks and shows no sign of letting up.

Our aim here is to explore what ordinary people think about this age-old philosophical question. Do people believe in objective moral truth, or do they accept some form of moral relativism?[1]

1. PRIOR WORK

Regardless of the position being defended, the usual assumption within the philosophical literature is that people subscribe to some form of moral objectivism. For example, Michael Smith writes that ordinary folk:

> ...seem to think moral questions have correct answers; that the correct answers are made correct by objective moral facts; that moral facts are wholly determined by circumstances and that, by engaging in moral conversation and argument, we can discover what these objective moral facts determined by the circumstances are. (Smith, 1994, p. 6)

This claim that ordinary folk are moral objectivists enjoys a surprising degree of consensus in moral philosophy, and can be found in the works of a diverse range of moral philosophers with disparate theoretical commitments (e.g. Blackburn, 1984; Brink, 1989; Mackie, 1977; Shafer-Landau, 2003). Of course, philosophers hold very different views about how the study of folk intuitions can contribute to moral philosophy (Appiah, 2008; Kagan, 2009; Kauppinen, 2007; Knobe and Nichols, 2008; Ludwig, 2007), and even about whether folk intuitions have any relevance at all (Singer, 1974, 2005). Yet in spite of these important differences, the claim that the folk believe in some form of moral objectivism is widespread in moral philosophy.

Now, this claim of folk moral objectivism is, on the face of it, an empirical claim—one that is amenable to systematic investigation. Researchers have for some time been exploring this very question, and the traditional philosophical view has enjoyed considerable empirical support. Results of many studies have thus far suggested that people reject relativism about morality, and believe instead in some type of absolute moral truth.

For example, in a pioneering study, Nichols (2004) presented participants with a story about two individuals—John and Fred—who appeared to hold different moral views. John says, 'It's okay to hit people just because you feel like it', and Fred says, 'No, it is not okay to hit people just because you feel like it'. Participants were then asked to choose which of the following options best represented their own views:

1. It is okay to hit or shove people just because you feel like it, so John is right and Fred is wrong.
2. It is not okay to hit or shove people just because you feel like it, so Fred is right and John is wrong.
3. There is no fact of the matter about unqualified claims like 'It's okay to hit or shove people just because you feel like it'. Different cultures

believe different things, and it is not absolutely true or false that it's okay to hit people just because you feel like it.

Approximately 78% of participants chose either the first or second option. In other words, the majority of participants seemed to reject the idea that, e.g., hitting or shoving might be both good and bad—good relative to one person yet bad relative to another. On the contrary, they appeared to suggest that there was some definite fact of the matter as to whether hitting or shoving was morally good or bad, and that anyone who held the opposite opinion must be mistaken.

In a subsequent study, Goodwin and Darley (2008) provided participants with a large number of statements purporting to make claims about how things are in factual matters ('the earth is not at the center of the known universe'), moral matters ('consciously discriminating against someone on the basis of race is morally wrong'), conventional matters ('talking loudly and constantly to the person next to you during a lecture is a permissible action'), and matters of taste ('classical music is better than rock music'). After being asked whether they agreed with these statements, participants were told that none of the statements had, in fact, elicited full agreement; whatever judgment they happened to hold, there was some fellow participant holding the opposite view. Once again, participants were asked how they would interpret such disagreements. This time, the options were:

1. The other person is surely mistaken.
2. It is possible that neither you nor the other person is mistaken.
3. It could be that you are mistaken, and the other person is correct.
4. Other.

In the moral cases, 70% of participants answered that the other individual had to be incorrect in her moral judgments (option 1). For Goodwin and Darley, this suggests that people are highly objectivist about many canonical moral transgressions—indeed, only somewhat less objectivist than they are about factual questions (such as whether the earth is at the center of the known universe).

Importantly, this same result has been found across different age groups. Wainryb and colleagues (2004) presented children aged 5, 7, and 9 with cases of disagreement in a number of domains, including the moral domain. For example, subjects were told that Sarah believes it's okay to hit and kick other children, whereas Sophie believes it is not okay to hit and kick other children. They were then asked whether both Sarah and Sophie could be correct and, if not, which of the two was correct and why. The results strongly supported the view that people are objectivists about morality: 100% of the 5 and 7 year olds and 94% of the 9 year olds thought that, in cases of such disagreement, only one of the individuals could be correct. In fact, children were as objectivist about moral disagreements as they were about purely factual disagreements (e.g. disagreement about whether pencils fall down or shoot up when you drop them).

Across all these studies, the same method has revealed the same result, time and again. It seems that ordinary, pre-philosophical folk reject the notion that moral disagreements can admit of many different answers, each of them correct relative to the person who is making the judgment. Rather, the folk appear to believe that when individuals hold opposite opinions about a moral question, only one of those individuals can be correct.

2. A NEW HYPOTHESIS

In our view, however, the appearances here are deceiving. It is true that existing studies have consistently elicited apparently objectivist responses. However, we will argue that this pattern only arises because of a particular feature of the existing experimental procedures. When the studies are conducted in a slightly different way, a more complex pattern of responses begins to emerge.

To get a better sense of the issue here, consider people's ordinary way of talking about the seasons. Many people understand that at a time of year it can only be said to be a particular season relative to a given hemisphere. So they understand that if individuals from different hemispheres make seemingly opposite claims about the seasons, there is no reason to conclude that one of these individuals has to be wrong. It is always possible that both of them are saying something perfectly true.

Now suppose we decided to study people's attitudes toward the seasons using a fairly straightforward experimental design. Participants would be told that one individual says 'January is a winter month' while another says 'January is not a winter month'. How might participants respond in a case like that? Would they say that one of these individuals had to be wrong, or would they say that both could actually be right?

Well, it depends. Do the participants assume that the two individuals are in different hemispheres, or do they assume that they are both in the same hemisphere? As long as experimental materials are designed in such a way that participants tend to think, e.g., that both individuals are living in the United States, they will presumably conclude that one of the individuals has to be wrong. Yet such a response would not show that people are objectivists about the seasons—that they think there is some objective truth about what season it is at any given time, full stop. Rather, the lesson to draw here is that people's deeper understanding of the relativity about the seasons will only come out clearly if they are encouraged to take a broader view and consider a number of possible perspectives—for example, if they are asked about a case involving both Americans and Australians.

Or consider a more extreme example. Suppose we asked people about the claim that there are twenty-four hours in a day. Faced with a case like this, people might initially think, 'That claim is objectively true, and anyone who holds the opposite opinion must surely be mistaken.' But now suppose we tried to broaden their perspective. Suppose we encouraged them to think about other planets, emphasizing that different planets take different amounts of time to rotate around their axes, with some taking less than twenty-four hours and some taking more. People might then begin to have a different intuition. They might begin to think, 'I guess there just happen to be twenty-four hours in a day on this particular planet, but if there are individuals on other planets, they might be perfectly right to say that the number of hours in a day was higher or lower'.

We want to suggest that a similar effect arises in the domain of morality. People do sometimes display what appear to be objectivist intuitions about morality, but it would be a mistake just to conclude straight away that people are moral objectivists. The more accurate thing to say is that people's intuitions depend on the precise way in which they are thinking of the question. As long as they are thinking only about individuals who are fairly similar to themselves—say, individuals from their own cultural groups—their intuitions might look more or less objectivist. But we will argue that people's intuitions do not always have this objectivist character. On the contrary, people's intuitions undergo a systematic shift as they begin considering different sorts of individuals. So as they come to think more and more seriously about individuals who are deeply dissimilar—individuals with radically different cultures, values, or ways of life—their intuitions move steadily toward a kind of relativism. They gradually come to feel that even if two individuals have opposite opinions on some moral question, it could still turn out that neither one would have to be wrong.

Study 1

As an initial test of this hypothesis, we conducted a study in which participants randomly received either a straightforward case like those used in earlier studies, or a case that specifically encouraged them to consider different cultures and ways of life.

All participants read vignettes that described an agent performing a behavior and other individuals judging that behavior. The difference between conditions lay only in the description of the individuals judging the behavior. Some participants were told that the individuals were Americans much like themselves; others were told that one of the individuals was from a very different sort of society with a radically different form of life. (Instead of simply stating that the individual was from a different society, the stimulus materials were designed to present this other society in as vivid and compelling a way as possible.) The hypothesis was that as people were encouraged to think about ever more distant forms of life, they would come to have ever more relativist intuitions.

Methods

Participants

223 students (112 females) taking introductory philosophy courses at Baruch College voluntarily completed a questionnaire after class.

Materials and Procedure

Each subject was randomly assigned to one of three conditions: *same-culture, other-culture,* or *extraterrestrial.*

Participants in the same-culture condition were asked to imagine a person named Sam. They were told that Sam was a fairly ordinary student at their own college who enjoyed watching college football and hanging out with friends. They were then asked to consider Sam's opinions about two moral transgressions. For one of these transgressions, they were given the sentence:

> Horace finds his youngest child extremely unattractive and therefore kills him.

They were told to imagine that one of their classmates thinks that this act is morally wrong but that Sam thinks that the act is morally permissible. The instructions then were:

> Given that these individuals have different judgments about this case, we would like to know whether you think at least one of them must be wrong, or whether you think both of them could actually be correct. In other words, to what extent would you agree or disagree with the following statement concerning such a case
> *Since your classmate and Sam have different judgments about this case, at least one of them must be wrong.*

Responses to this question were recorded on a scale of agreement from 1 to 7. To test the generality of the effect, we also included a second transgression:

> Dylan buys an expensive new knife and tests its sharpness by randomly stabbing a passerby on the street.

Instructions for this second transgression were exactly the same as for the first. (We did not predict any significant differences between the two transgressions.)

Participants in the other-culture condition were asked to imagine an isolated tribe of people called the Mamilons. They were told that this tribe lives in the Amazon rainforests and has preserved a traditional warrior culture, with quite different values from those of the people in the surrounding society. Participants in this condition then received exactly the same two questions as those received by participants in the same-culture condition, except that they were asked to imagine that the individual regarding the transgressions as morally permissible was a Mamilon.

Finally, participants in the extraterrestrial condition were asked to imagine a race of extraterrestrial beings called Pentars. They were told that the Pentars have a very different sort of psychology from human beings, that they are not at all interested in friendship or love and that their main goal is simply to increase the total number of equilateral pentagons in the universe. These participants then received the two questions, this time with a Pentar as the individual who regards the transgressions as permissible.

Results

The data were analyzed using a mixed-model ANOVA, with condition as a between-participants factor and transgression as a within-subject factor. There was no main effect of transgression and no interaction effect. However, there was a significant main effect of condition, $F(2, 218) = 20.7, p <.001, \eta^2 = .16$.

Ratings for the two transgressions were highly correlated ($r = .82, p <.001$) and could therefore be averaged to form a scale. The mean for each condition is displayed in Figure 1.

Participants in the *same-culture* condition tended to agree that at least one person had to be wrong ($M = 5.4$, SD = 2.15), those in the *other-culture* condition were approximately at the midpoint ($M = 4.4$, SD = 2.05), and those in the *extraterrestrial* condition tended to say that both could actually be right ($M = 3.2$, SD = 2.28). Post-hoc Tukey's tests showed significant differences both between responses in the other-culture condition and the same-culture condition ($p <.05$) and between responses in the extraterrestrial condition and the other-culture condition ($p <.01$).

Discussion

The results of this first experiment allow us to locate the results from earlier studies in a broader framework. Those earlier studies demonstrated that when two individuals hold opposite moral views, people think that at least one of those individuals has to be wrong. The present study replicates that basic finding, but also shows that it only arises under certain quite specific conditions—namely, when the individuals are from the same culture. As the individuals under discussion become ever more dissimilar, people become less and less inclined to agree with the claim that one of them has to be wrong, so that when the two individuals become dissimilar enough, people were far more willing to say that both of them can be right.

Overall, then, the responses we find in the same-culture condition do not appear to reflect any kind of general, across-the-board commitment to moral

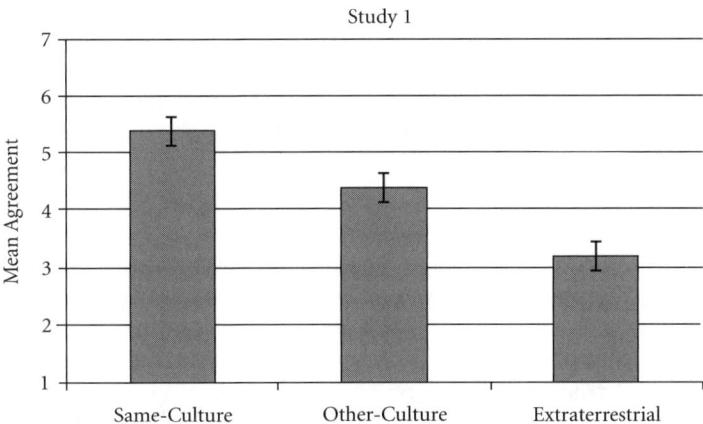

Figure 8.1. Mean agreement with the claim that 'At least one must be wrong' by condition. Error bars show SE mean.

objectivism. On the contrary, it seems that people's intuitions are highly sensitive to the nature of the question posed. The more people are encouraged to consider radically different cultures and ways of life, the more they are drawn to more relativist responses.

But, of course, it would be a big mistake to draw any far-reaching conclusions from just this one experiment. The only way to get a proper understanding of what these results mean is to conduct follow-up studies designed to examine specific hypotheses about the nature of the effect observed here.

Study 2

To begin with, the participants in Study 1 were all American undergraduates. It might therefore be supposed that these initial results are not revealing anything important about the nature of moral cognition per se but are simply showing us something about the idiosyncrasies of contemporary American culture. (For example, American students might think it would be politically incorrect to pass judgments on individuals from other cultures and declare their moral judgments to be wrong.) To address this worry, we conducted a follow-up experiment with a population of subjects from a different culture, one that focuses less on individuals and more on group level, communal norms.

Methods

Participants

151 students (71 females) taking introductory philosophy courses at National University of Singapore voluntarily completed a questionnaire at the start of class.

Materials and Procedure

The materials and procedure were the same as used in Study 1.

Results

A mixed-model ANOVA was run, with culture of the subject as a between-subjects factor and transgression as a within-subject factor. There was a significant main effect of condition, $F(2, 146) = 3.1$, $p = .05$, $\eta^2 = .04$. There was no significant difference between transgressions and no significant interaction effect. The means per condition are reported in Figure 2.

Discussion

The pattern of responses in this Singaporean sample mirrored the pattern of results found with Americans. Here again, the more participants were encouraged to think about individuals with very different cultures or ways of life, the more they were inclined to endorse relativist claims.

Of course, the fact that this same pattern emerged in two different cultures should not be taken as proof that the pattern is some sort of cross-cultural universal. It is possible, and indeed quite likely, that different cultures have

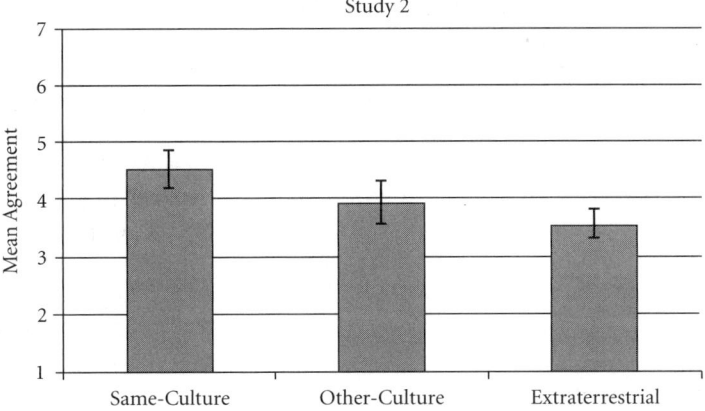

Figure 8.2. Mean agreement with the claim that 'At least one must be wrong' by condition. Error bars show SE mean.

quite different intuitions about the objectivity of moral claims. Still, the present results do provide strong reason to suspect that the pattern obtained here is not simply a reflection of some idiosyncratic feature of contemporary American culture. It appears that we actually are getting at something of importance about moral cognition.

Study 3

In these first two studies, participants gave different responses depending on whether they received the same-culture, other-culture, or extraterrestrial cases. We now wanted to know whether participants would continue to show this effect even if they received all three cases side-by-side. Previous research has shown that in cases where people themselves regard an aspect of their moral judgments as a kind of 'bias' or 'error', differences between conditions disappear when participants are able to see all of the conditions at once (Hsee, Loewenstein, Blount, and Bazerman, 1999). We wanted to know whether a similar pattern would arise here or whether participants would affirm the difference between conditions even when they were presented with all three at the same time.

Methods

Participants

61 students (52 females) taking Introduction to Psychological Science courses at the College of Charleston signed up for the study for research participation credit.

Materials and Procedure

Participants in this study received all three conditions (*same-culture, other-culture,* and *extraterrestrial*) in counterbalanced order (1: Sam/Mamilon/

Pentar, 2: Mamilon/Pentar/Sam, 3: Pentar/Sam/Mamilon). Otherwise, the stories and questions were identical to those used in Study 1. Students signed up for the study and then were sent an online survey link to the questionnaires, which they were instructed to complete on their own in a quiet setting.

Results

The mean responses for each cultural condition are reported in Figure 3.

The data were analyzed using a mixed-model ANOVA, with cultural condition and transgression as within-participant factors and counterbalancing order as a between-participants factor, revealing a significant main effect for culture, $F(2, 116) = 22.3$, $p < .001$, $\eta^2 = .28$. As in Study 1, participants were significantly more likely to give an objectivist response (at least one of the judgments had to be wrong) in the *same-culture* condition ($M = 5.2$, $SD = 2.02$) than in the *other-culture* condition ($M = 4.3$, $SD = 2.11$) and even less likely in the *extraterrestrial* condition ($M = 3.7$, $SD = 1.97$).

Discussion

Even when each participant received all three cases side by side, they continued to offer different responses depending on which sort of individual they were considering. Just as in the two earlier studies, participants were more inclined to reject the claim that at least one individual must be wrong as they moved toward individuals who were more deeply different in their culture or way of life.

These results show us something important about the nature of the effect under study here. It is not just that people respond differently in the different conditions; they seem actually to think that it is *right* to offer these different responses. So, even after they have given a clearly relativist response in one

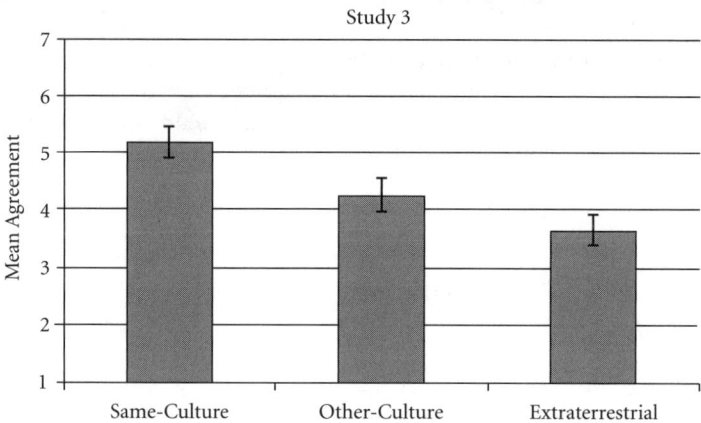

Figure 8.3. Mean agreement with the claim that 'At least one must be mistaken' by condition. Error bars show SE mean.

condition, they are happy to say in another condition that if the two individuals hold opposite opinions, one of them has to be wrong.

Study 4

The experimental results thus far seem to indicate that participants' intuitions change as they begin to consider individuals with radically different cultures or ways of life judging a single moral transgression. However, some might wonder whether important details are left out of the descriptions of the transgressions themselves. After all, there are *two* characters in our vignettes. First, there is the *agent*, the individual who actually commits the moral transgression (e.g. Horace, who kills his own child). Then, second, there is the *judge*, the individual who makes a judgment about whether the agent's action was morally bad or morally permissible (e.g. the Mamilon, an Amazonian tribesman). So far, we've asked people to consider only the latter of these two. But, details with respect to the former could arguably be relevant to people's moral judgments as well. For example, where is Horace located? Might people's judgments change if they are told that Horace is a member of their own culture—perhaps even a peer? Might people hold everyone to the same moral standards when judging an act taking place in their own culture or backyard? Conversely, would people apply very different standards when judging a similar act if took place far away, on another continent and in a different cultural context? Our claim has been that participants' intuitions about the rightness or wrongness of a judgment might actually depend on the identity of the *judge*, so that different judges could rightly arrive at different judgments of the very same agent. But what about the identity of the agent? Could this sway people's intuitions?

To get at this question more directly, we conducted a study in which we independently varied the cultural identity of both the agent and of the judge. Hence, the agent who performed the transgression could be either an American or someone from another culture, and the judge could be either an American, someone from another culture or an extraterrestrial. This design enabled us to clarify what impact the agent's identity might have on people's intuitions (apart from the judge's identity).

Methods

Participants

118 students (91 females) taking Introduction to Psychological Science courses at the College of Charleston signed up for the study for research participation credit.

Materials and Procedure

Participants were given the same within-participants questionnaire as in Study 2 (counterbalancing the three judges: *same-culture, other-culture,* and *extraterrestrial*), only now they were divided into two groups: half received the *local agent transgression* condition, in which the child-killer was represented as being American and the knife-stabber was represented as being a College of Charleston student, and half received the *foreign agent transgression* condition, in which the child-killer was represented as being Algerian and the knife-stabber was represented as being a University of Algiers student.

Results

The data were analyzed using a mixed-design ANOVA, with the identity of the judge (same-culture vs. other-culture vs. extraterrestrial) and transgression as within-participant factors and the identity of the agent (local vs. foreign) as between-participant factors. There was a main effect for the identity of the judge, $F(2,224) = 34.7$, $p < .001$, $\eta^2 = .24$, but no main effect of the identity of the agent. There was also a significant interaction effect, $F(2,224) = 3.1$, $p = .048$, $\eta^2 = .03$.

The means for each condition are displayed in Figure 4. Inspection of these means indicated that the interaction effect arose because participants gave especially objectivist responses when presented with the case involving a local agent and a same-culture judge.

Discussion

Although we found no main effect from our manipulation of the identity of the agent, we did find a main effect from our manipulation of the identity of the judge. In other words, the pattern of intuitions observed here does not seem to be arising simply because people have different reactions to different kinds of agents. Rather, it seems that people can have different reactions to judgments about the very same act, performed by the very same agent, so long as we vary the identity of the judge.

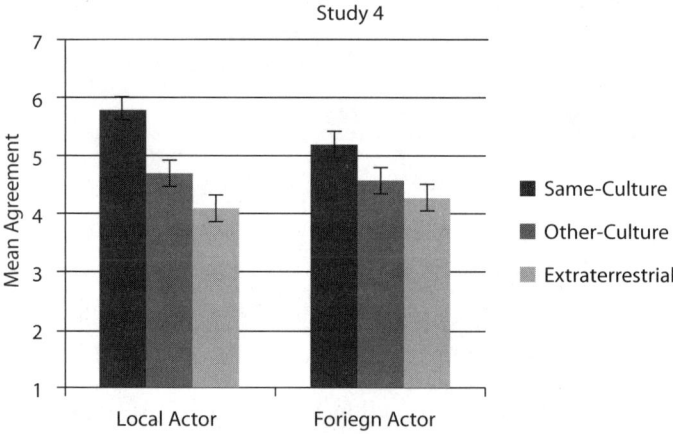

Figure 8.4. Mean agreement with the claim that 'At least one must be mistaken' by condition. Error bars show SE mean.

There was a significant interaction effect, yet this was due, in large part, to the high levels of objectivist responses to the local actor transgression when judged by the two classmates (in the same-culture condition). This result is in line with the hypothesis of this paper. After all, it is made explicit that the agent and the judges are located in the same location and within the same moral framework. When the judges and the actor are all within the same moral framework, it seems reasonable to assume that participants would be least likely to agree with the claim that the differing responses of the judges could both be correct.

It would be more likely to think that in such a situation people should be held to the same standards, that moral norms apply to them all in the same way. When frameworks align in such a fashion, it seems natural for people to assume that there can be an objective fact of the matter as to whether the actor's transgression is permissible—relative to that framework.

This pattern of intuitions suggests that people are evaluating each moral judgment relative to a set of standards that apply specifically to the judge in question, rather than the (potentially different) set of standards that apply to the agents who acted. Such a finding may initially seem a bit puzzling or bizarre, but work in natural language semantics has shown similar sorts of effects in other domains that have nothing to do with morality (Egan, Hawthorne, and Weatherson, 2005; Lasersohn, 2009; MacFarlane, 2007; Stephenson, 2007), and it seems reasonable to suspect that the effects that arise in these other domains might apply in the moral domain as well.

A great deal of controversy remains about how exactly such effects are to be understood, and we cannot hope to resolve those difficult issues here. Nonetheless, the data do seem to be suggesting that the sorts of effects that arise concerning, e.g., judgments of taste can also be found when we turn to moral judgments. People appear to reject the idea that a single absolute standard can be applied to all moral judgments of a given agent and to operate instead with a system that applies different standards to different judges.

Study 5

In studies 1-4 subjects appear to be responding in ways suggesting that they are applying different sets of standards to the persons with differing judgments about the permissibility of a given action. Our hypothesis has been that this is because ordinary folk might be tacitly committed to moral relativism. However, it is possible that subjects in these studies are not expressing a relativistic view about *morality* in particular. Instead, they might be expressing a more general, mad-dog sort of relativism—a relativism that applies not only to moral questions but also to purely descriptive questions, such as those that come up in science, history or mathematics.

In order to ascertain whether the folk really are relativists in this more radical sense, we conducted a follow-up experiment that made it possible to compare intuitions about moral claims with intuitions about non-moral claims.

Methods

Participants

88 students (26 females) taking introductory philosophy courses at Duke University voluntarily completed a questionnaire at the end of class.

Materials and Procedure

Survey materials were distributed for participants to fill out. All participants were presented with the Other-Culture vignette used in Study 1. Participants were then randomly assigned to one of two conditions.

Participants in the *moral* condition were asked to consider the Mamilon's opinions about two moral transgressions. For the first transgression, they were given the sentence: 'Jason robs his employer, the Red Cross, in order to pay for a second holiday for himself.' They were then asked to imagine that one of their classmates believed what Jason did was morally wrong, but that the Mamilon thought what Jason did was not morally wrong. After reading about these different judgments, they were asked the same question as in Study 1—namely, whether they agreed with the statement 'Since your classmate and the Mamilon have different judgments about this case, at least one of them must be wrong'. Participants rated this sentence on a scale from 1 ('disagree') to 7 ('agree'). For the second transgression, participants were given the sentence: 'Emily promises to take Molly's sick child to the hospital for an important surgical procedure but instead decides she'd rather go shopping'. Instructions for this other transgression were exactly the same as for the first. The order of transgressions was counterbalanced.

Participants in the *non-moral* condition were asked to consider the Mamilon's opinion about two non-moral cases. For the first case, participants were told the following: 'A group of individuals are discussing where pasta comes from. Alejandro thinks pasta is made by combining flour, water, and eggs, whereas Marya thinks pasta grows on trees and is harvested by special farmers called "Pastafarians" once every 5 years'. They were then asked to imagine that a classmate agrees with Alejandro, and that a Mamilon agrees with Marya. After reading about these different judgments, they were asked the same question as in the *moral* condition. The second case was as follows: 'A group of individuals are discussing the military strategies of Napoleon Bonaparte. Anita thinks that Napoleon rode into battle on a horse, whereas Fabio thinks Napoleon flew into battle in a helicopter'. They were then asked to imagine a classmate agrees with Anita, whereas a Mamilon agrees with Fabio. Instructions for this other transgression were exactly the same as for the first. The order of transgressions was counterbalanced.

Results

Ratings for the two transgressions were highly correlated, both for the non-moral cases ($r = .67, p < .001$) and for the moral cases ($r = .75, p < .001$), and there were no significant differences between them. They could therefore be averaged to form a scale. The mean for each condition is displayed in Figure 5.

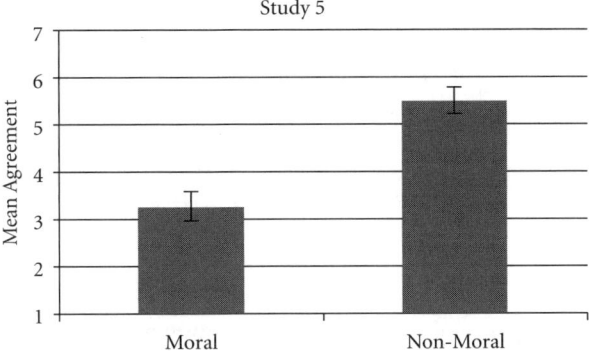

Figure 8.5. Mean agreement with the claim that 'At least one must be wrong' by condition. Error bars show SE mean.

Participants were strongly objectivist when the differing judgments were about non-moral cases ($M = 5.5$, SD = 1.84) but were significantly more inclined to embrace relativism when the differing judgments were about moral cases ($M = 3.3$, SD = 1.99), $t(88) = 5.3$, $p < .001$.

Discussion

Participants showed the usual tendency to endorse relativism about moral questions, but they did not show this same tendency when confronted with non-moral questions. Instead, their responses in the non-moral domain took a more objectivist turn. They tended to agree with the claim that if two individuals held opposite opinions about historical facts, then one of those individuals has to be wrong.

In short, it does not appear that people subscribe to a blanket relativism that applies equally to all issues. People seem instead to be distinguishing between different domains, endorsing relativist claims about morality but not about straightforward matters of fact.

Study 6

Finally, one might worry about how people are interpreting the question they receive in the stimulus materials. Participants in these studies are presented with stories about two judges with seemingly opposite opinions and then asked whether they agree with the claim that at least one of the judges must be 'wrong' or 'mistaken'. But how exactly are participants understanding the words 'wrong' or 'mistaken' in this context? Thus far, we have been assuming that participants understand these words to mean that the opinions of the judges are *not true*. So our assumption has been that when people disagree with the claim, they are saying something like: 'Even though the two judges have opposite opinions, it could be that both of their opinions are true'. This really would be an endorsement of moral relativism.

But it seems that the claim could actually be understood in other, very different ways. For example, one could interpret the words 'wrong' or 'mistaken' to mean something like *not a reasonable inference, given the available evidence.* On this alternative construal, participants are not saying anything deeply controversial about the truth of the judges' opinions. They are simply saying something straightforward of the form: 'Even though the two judges have opposite opinions, it could be that both have good reason to arrive at those inferences, given the available evidence'. Such a statement would not amount to an endorsement of genuine moral relativism. (In the jargon of philosophy, it would be classified as a purely 'epistemic' claim.)

To address this last worry, we conducted a study in which participants were asked both about whether the various judges' beliefs were 'incorrect' and about whether they had 'no good reason' to believe what they did. This method makes it possible to disentangle intuitions about the truth of the judges' opinions from intuitions about whether those opinions were reasonable inferences from the available evidence.

Methods

Participants

Participants were 90 undergraduate students (45 females) taking introductory philosophy courses at Duke University.

Materials and Procedure

Survey materials were distributed for participants to fill out. As in Study 5, all participants were presented with the Other-Culture vignette used in Study 1. Participants were then randomly assigned to one of four conditions in a 2 × 2 design.

Half of the subjects received one of two 'truth' conditions. In these conditions, they were given either two moral cases (the robbing and promise-reneging transgressions used in Study 5) or two non-moral cases (the Napoleon and pasta cases used in Study 5). They were then asked to imagine that a classmate and a Mamilon have differing judgments about whether, for example, the moral transgression was permissible, or whether Napoleon rode a horse or a helicopter, and were asked to what extent they agreed with the following statement: 'Given that your classmate and the Mamilon have these particular beliefs, at least one of their beliefs must be incorrect'. Participants rated this sentence on a scale from 1 ('disagree') to 7 ('agree').

The other half of the subjects received one of two 'justification' conditions. In these conditions, they were given either the same moral or non-moral cases from the 'truth' condition. When told that the classmate and the Mamilon had different judgments about the case, they were given the following question: 'These individuals have different beliefs about this case. We would like to know whether you think only one of them has good reason to believe what he or she does, or whether they both have good reasons'. They were then asked to what extent they agreed with the following statement: 'Given the particular beliefs that your classmate and the Mamilon have, at least one of them must not have good reason to believe as he or she does'. Participants rated this sentence on a scale from 1 ('disagree') to 7 ('agree').

Results

The data were subjected to an ANOVA, with question type (truth vs. justification) and vignette type (moral vs. non-moral) as between-subject factors, transgression as a within subject factor, and gender and number of previous philosophy courses as covariates. There was no main effect of either question type of vignette type. However, there was a significant interaction effect $F(1, 84) = 10.4, p = .002, \eta^2 = .11$.

Inspection of the means revealed opposite patterns of responses for the two question types (see Figure 6). On the question about truth, people tended to reject the claim that at least one of the judges had to be incorrect in the moral cases ($M = 2.93$, $SD = 2.15$) but not in the non-moral cases ($M = 4.67$, $SD = 2.17$), $t(43) = 2.7, p = .01$. By contrast, on the question about justification, people tended to reject the claim that at least one of the judges must not have had good reason in the non-moral cases ($M = 3.0$, $SE = 1.98$) but not in the moral cases ($M = 4.4$, $SD = 2.08$), $t(43) = 2.3, p = .03$.

Discussion

In this final study, participants showed a clear distinction between intuitions about truth and intuitions about justification. On the question about truth, participants showed the same basic pattern of judgments they displayed in Study 5: they were less willing to say that at least one judge had to be 'incorrect' in the moral condition than they were in the non-moral condition. However, on the question about justification, they showed exactly the opposite pattern

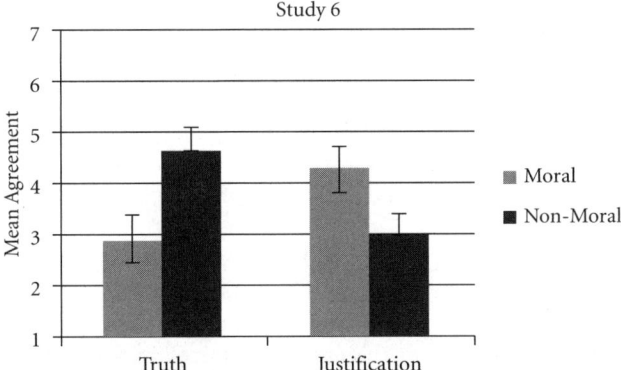

Figure 8.6. Mean agreement with the claim that and 'at least one must be incorrect' (the 'truth question') and 'at least one must not have good reason to believe' (the 'justification question'). Error bars show SE mean

of judgments: they were actually more willing to say that at least one judge had 'no good reason' in the moral condition than in the non-moral condition. In other words, people seem to be willing to grant that people from different cultures may legitimately hold different moral beliefs—that these beliefs need not be considered illicit or false—yet they are not willing to accept that such beliefs are equally justified—that there are equally good reasons supporting them.

Of course, the precise pattern of justification intuitions depends in part on the nature of the vignettes themselves, and we could doubtless have obtained a very different pattern if we had used different vignettes. The important point, however, is simply that participants are drawing a clear distinction between truth and justification. Hence, when we see that participants disagree with the claim that at least one of the beliefs must be incorrect, we have some reason to conclude that they are in fact expressing the relativist view that two judges can make opposite judgments without either of them thinking anything false.

3. GENERAL DISCUSSION

The present studies offer a complex picture of people's intuitions about whether morality is objective or relative. People do have apparently objectivist intuitions in certain cases, but our results suggest that one cannot accurately capture their views in a simple claim like: 'People are committed to moral objectivism'. On the contrary, people's intuitions take a strikingly relativist turn when they are encouraged to consider individuals from radically different cultures or ways of life.

Overall, then, the pattern of people's intuitions about morality appears to resemble the pattern of their intuitions about the seasons. In the course of a typical conversation, people might give little thought to the idea that it can only be winter or summer relative to a given hemisphere. Indeed, people who live in the Northern Hemisphere might ordinarily suppose that a certain time simply *is* winter and that anyone who thinks otherwise must be mistaken. But this pattern of ordinary intuitions would not necessarily make it right for us to draw a conclusion of the form: 'People are committed to seasonal objectivism'. The thing to focus on is people's ability, when suddenly confronted with an individual from another hemisphere, to recognize that a single time might be winter around here but summer somewhere else.

Ordinary intuitions about morality appear to work in much the same way. Day to day, people might give little thought to issues of relativity. It might appear to them, when they witness a typical transgression, that the agent has clearly done something morally bad and that anyone who thinks otherwise must surely be wrong. Yet this pattern of intuitions is not itself sufficient to make them count as moral objectivists. The key question is whether they hold on to that view even in the face of radically different perspectives. The results of the present studies suggest that they do not.

3.1. Relation to Previous Work

It may initially appear that our chief conclusions are opposed to those drawn by earlier researchers. After all, earlier researchers found that most participants were moral objectivists, whereas we are suggesting that many of those participants might actually have had a tendency toward moral relativism.

Our own view, however, is that the disagreement here is only a superficial one and that there is a deeper sense in which our conclusions are actually in harmony with those of earlier researchers. The main goal of research in this area is not to figure out precisely what percentage of people are moral objectivists or moral relativists but rather to reach a better understanding of the psychological processes that can pull people in these different directions. Our claim has been that people are drawn toward moral relativism by one specific type of psychological process: namely, active engagement with radically different perspectives and ways of life. So what we really want to know is whether prior research provides evidence for this same psychological hypothesis.

Though earlier studies found that a majority of participants gave apparently objectivist responses, each of these studies also found a minority who gave relativist responses. Correlational data from these studies can therefore be used to get a sense for the psychological differences between these two groups of participants. The results offer us a remarkably coherent picture. Relativists were higher in the personality trait of openness to experience (Cokely and Feltz, 2010). They scored higher on a measure of 'disjunctive thinking', which is the ability to unpack alternative possibilities when problem solving (Goodwin and Darley, 2010). They were more likely to fall in a particular age range—namely, in their twenties (Beebe and Sackris, 2010). They were more able to explain alternative views (Goodwin and Darley, 2010) and to be tolerant of people with opposite opinions (Wright, Cullum, and Schwab, 2008; Wright, McWhite, and Grandjean, 2010). All in all, these separate studies seem to be converging on a surprisingly unified portrait of relativist participants. Specifically, it appears that the relativists were precisely the people who were *most open to alternative perspectives.*

So perhaps it will be possible to develop a single unified account that explains the full pattern of data. The basic idea would be that people's intuitions are influenced by the degree to which they actively consider alternative perspectives. One factor that leads people to consider alternative perspectives is the wording of the question itself (as in the present studies); another is the personality traits of the participants (as in prior studies). But regardless of the factors that trigger it, the impact of this psychological process is always the same. The more people engage with radically different perspectives, the more they are drawn to moral relativism.

3.2. Relation to Philosophical Metaethics

As noted at the outset of this paper, many philosophers think both that the folk are objectivists about morality and that the folk view bears on the philosophical truth about morality. In the words of Michael Smith, 'the task of the philosopher in meta-ethics is to make sense of ordinary moral practice'—that is, ordinary folk objectivism (Smith, 1994, p. 5). Many philosophers have explicitly tried to fulfill this task.

For present purposes, we can divide the ways in which philosophers have sought to discharge the task into three general categories: 1) affirm that the folk are generally right; 2) explain why the folk are entirely wrong; 3) come with some more complicated interpretation of what the folk are committed to. Each of these represents an attempt to accommodate folk objectivism. We'll explore them in turn.

One way to account for the purported folk view is to say that this view is actually correct: there truly are such things as real, objective moral facts. Philosophers who adopt this 'realist' approach have sometimes claimed that they have a leg up on opposing theories because they can more easily account for the phenomenon of folk objectivism (Brink, 1989; Shafer-Landau, 2003). In the words of Shafer-Landau, only an account of this basic type 'straightforwardly preserves ordinary talk of moral truth' (Shafer-Landau, 2003, p. 23).

A second approach would be to deny the existence of real, objective moral facts. Philosophers who adopt this approach maintain that the sorts of moral properties presupposed by ordinary folk simply do not exist, so the folk err in being objectivists about morality (Joyce, 2001; Mackie, 1977). Mackie (1977, p. 33), for example, argues that such absolute moral properties—'not contingent upon any desire or preference or policy or choice'—are simply nonexistent. Nonetheless, in formulating his theory, Mackie ends up affirming the very same claim about ordinary folk morality. He says that ordinary people tend to 'objectify values', that 'ordinary moral judgments include a claim to objectivity' (1977, p. 35).

Finally, some philosophers have taken a different tack, proposing that we could adopt a more complex interpretation of people's ordinary moral discourse. According to this interpretation, people's ordinary moral claims don't mean precisely what they might appear to mean on first glance. Thus, when people ordinarily make claims like: 'That action is morally bad, and anyone who says otherwise must surely be mistaken', they are not literally saying that there is some kind of objective moral truth in the way that 'moral realists' have supposed (Blackburn, 1984; Gibbard, 1992). Yet even while offering such a complex analysis, these philosophers maintain the usual view about the shape of ordinary folk discourse, suggesting that philosophical theories must endeavor to explain 'why our discourse has the shape it does...to explain, and justify, the realistic-seeming nature of our talk of evaluations—the way we think we can be wrong about them, that there is a truth to be found, and so on' (Blackburn, 1984, p. 180).

Each of these positions tries to accommodate folk objectivism in one way or another: by claiming to best capture it, by dismissing it as riddled with error, or by providing a nuanced interpretation of it. But the results of the present studies raise some questions about whether this task is needed at all. If the folk are not, in fact, moral objectivists, then perhaps there is simply no need to continue engaging in philosophical work aimed at making sense of folk objectivism.

Nevertheless, a task remains. Philosophers are undoubtedly correct in their commitment to make sense of ordinary moral practice; the one mistake was to suppose that people's ordinary moral practice is a straightforwardly objectivist one. So perhaps the real philosophical task here is to make sense of a different sort of practice: one in which people's views differ depending on the extent to which they explore alternative perspectives.

4. CONCLUSION

Recent experimental research has investigated people's intuitions about a whole host of different philosophical questions—free will, moral obligation, personal identity, the nature of knowledge. Even though these questions are in many ways quite different, the outcomes of the various experimental research programs have been surprisingly convergent. Again and again, we find that it is not possible to capture the full pattern of people's intuitions just by constructing a coherent philosophical theory and then claiming that this theory captures the 'folk view'. Instead, it has emerged in each case that people's intuitions show certain kinds of tensions or contradictions, with different psychological processes pulling people in different directions. (For a few representative cases, see Greene, 2008; Nahmias, forthcoming; Nichols and Bruno, 2010; Nichols and Knobe, 2007; Phelan, 2010; Phelan and Sarkissian, 2009; Sinnott-Armstrong, 2008). But perhaps that is exactly what we should have expected. Philosophers do not write about questions where the answer seems obvious; they write about issues that provoke conflict or confusion. What the recent experimental work has done is, in part, to trace such conflict and confusion back to certain tensions within people's ordinary intuitions.

The results of the present studies are very much in line with this general trend. It is, we think, a mistake just to say that ordinary people subscribe to some form of moral objectivism. People do have objectivist intuitions in certain cases, but these intuitions are the product of psychological processes that can, in other cases, lead to strikingly relativist intuitions. Future research might proceed not by asking whether 'people are objectivists' or 'people are relativists' but rather by trying to get a better grip on the different psychological processes at work here and the conflicts and tensions that these processes can create.

NOTES

* We are most grateful to Brad Cokelet, Jamie Dreier, Gilbert Harman, Eric Mandelbaum, Shaun Nichols, Jonas Olson, Mark Phelan, Jonathan Phillips, Ángel Pinillos, Jesse Prinz and David Wong for helpful discussions and comments on this paper.

1. Note on terminology: The word 'relativism' is used in different ways in different disciplines. In moral philosophy, it is used broadly to describe any view according

to which moral claims can only be assessed relative to a particular culture or system of values (e.g. Harman, 1975; Wong, 1996, 2006), whereas in formal semantics, it is used to pick out one very specific way of understanding this relativity (e.g. Lasersohn, 2009; MacFarlane, 2007; Stephenson, 2007). We will be using the term in the broader, non-technical sense in which it appears within moral philosophy and will not be exploring the more specific questions that arise within formal semantics.

REFERENCES

Appiah, K. A. 2008: *Experiments in Ethics*. Cambridge, MA: Harvard University Press.

Beebe, J. R. and Sackris, D. 2010: Moral objectivism across the lifespan. Unpublished Manuscript. University of Buffalo.

Blackburn, S. 1984: *Spreading the Word: Groundings in the Philosophy of Language*. New York: Oxford University Press.

Brink, D. O. 1989: *Moral Realism and the Foundations of Ethics*. New York: Cambridge University Press.

Cokely, E. T. and Feltz, A. 2010: The truth about right and wrong: predicting moral objectivism with a heritable personality trait. Unpublished.

Dreier, J. 1990: Internalism and speaker relativism. *Ethics, 101*, 6–26.

Egan, A., Hawthorne, J. and Weatherson, B. 2005: Epistemic modals in context. In G. Preyer and P. George (eds.), *Contextualism in Philosophy: Knowledge, Meaning, and Truth*. New York: Oxford University Press, 131–170.

Gibbard, A. 1992: *Wise Choices, Apt Feelings: A Theory of Normative Judgment*. Cambridge, MA: Harvard University Press.

Goodwin, G. P. and Darley, J. M. 2008: The psychology of meta-ethics: exploring objectivism. *Cognition, 106*, 1339–1366.

Goodwin, G. P. and Darley, J. M. 2010: The perceived objectivity of ethical beliefs: psychological findings and implications for public policy. *Review of Philosophy and Psychology, 1*, 1–28.

Greene, J. D. 2008: The secret joke of Kant's soul. In W. Sinnott-Armstrong (ed.), *Moral Psychology Volume 3: The Neuroscience of Morality: Emotion, Disease, and Development*. Cambridge, MA: MIT Press.

Harman, G. 1975: Moral relativism defended. *The Philosophical Review, 84*, 3–22.

Hsee, C. K., Loewenstein, G. F., Blount, S. and Bazerman, M. H. 1999: Preference reversals between joint and separate evaluations of options: A review and theoretical analysis. *Psychological Bulletin, 125*, 576–590.

Joyce, R. 2001: *The Myth of Morality*. Cambridge: Cambridge University Press.

Kagan, S. 2009: Thinking about cases. *Social Philosophy and Policy, 18*, 44–63.

Kauppinen, A. 2007: The rise and fall of experimental philosophy. *Philosophical Explorations, 10*, 95–118.

Knobe, J. and Nichols, S. 2008: An experimental philosophy manifesto. In J. Knobe and S. Nichols (eds.), *Experimental Philosophy*. New York: Oxford University Press, 3–14.

Lasersohn, P. 2009: Relative truth, speaker commitment, and control of implicit arguments. *Synthese, 166*, 359–374.

Ludwig, K. 2007: The epistemology of thought experiments: first person versus third person approaches. *Midwest Studies in Philosophy, 31*, 128–159.

MacFarlane, J. 2007: Relativism and disagreement. *Philosophical Studies, 132*, 17–31.

Mackie, J. L. 1977: *Ethics: Inventing Right and Wrong*. New York: Penguin.

Nahmias, E. Forthcoming: Intuitions about free will, determinism, and bypassing. In R. Kane (ed.), *The Oxford Handbook on Free Will*, 2nd ed. New York: Oxford University Press.

Nichols, S. 2004: After objectivity: An empirical study of moral judgment. *Philosophical Psychology*, 17, 3–26.

Nichols, S. and Bruno, M. 2010: Intuitions about personal identity: an empirical study. *Philosophical Psychology*, 23, 293–312.

Nichols, S. and Knobe, J. 2007: Moral responsibility and determinism: the cognitive science of folk intuitions. *Noûs*, 41, 663–685.

Phelan, M. T. 2010: Evidence that stakes don't matter for evidence. Unpublished Manuscript. Yale University.

Phelan, M. T. and Sarkissian, H. 2009: Is the trade-off hypothesis worth trading for? *Mind & Language*, 24, 164–180.

Pinillos, N. Á. 2010: Knowledge and moral relativism. Unpublished Manuscript. Arizona State University.

Prinz, J. 2007: *The Emotional Construction of Morals*. New York: Oxford University Press.

Railton, P. 1986: Moral realism. *The Philosophical Review*, 95, 163–207.

Shafer-Landau, R. 2003: *Moral Realism: A Defence*. New York: Oxford University Press.

Singer, P. 1974: Sidgwick and reflective equilibrium. *The Monist*, 58, 490–517.

Singer, P. 2005: Ethics and intuitions. *The Journal of Ethics*, 9, 331–352.

Sinnott-Armstrong, W. 2008: Abstract + Concrete = Paradox. In J. Knobe and S. Nichols (eds.), *Experimental Philosophy*. New York: Oxford University Press, 209–230.

Smith, M. 1994: *The Moral Problem*. Oxford: Blackwell.

Stephenson, T. 2007: Judge dependence, epistemic modals, and predicates of personal taste. *Linguistics and Philosophy*, 30, 487–525.

Wainryb, C., Shaw, L., Langley, M., Cottam, K. and Lewis, R. 2004: Children's thinking about diversity of belief in the early school years: judgments of relativism, tolerance and disagreeing persons. *Child Development*, 75, 687–703.

Wong, D. B. 1984: *Moral Relativity*. Berkeley: University of California Press.

Wong, D. B. 1996: Pluralistic relativism. *Midwest Studies in Philosophy*, 20, 378–399.

Wong, D. B. 2006: *Natural Moralities: A Defence of Pluralistic Relativism*. New York: Oxford University Press.

Wright, J. C., Cullum, J. and Schwab, N. 2008: The cognitive and affective dimensions of moral conviction: implications for attitudinal and behavioral measures of interpersonal tolerance. *Personality and Social Psychology Bulletin*, 34, 1461–1476.

Wright, J. C., McWhite, C. and Grandjean, P. T. 2010: The cognitive mechanisms of intolerance: Do people's meta-ethical commitments matter? Unpublished Manuscript. College of Charleston.

PART IV

THE IMPACT OF MORALITY ON JUDGMENT

A long tradition of philosophical research has been devoted to understanding the concepts that people ordinarily use to make sense of their world. Some of these concepts appear to involve moral judgments (*right, wrong, blameworthy*), while others appear to be purely descriptive (*causation, intention, knowledge*). A question now arises about the relationship between the moral concepts and the purely descriptive concepts.

Recent work in experimental philosophy has explored the relation between moral judgment and descriptive concepts. A series of experimental studies seem to indicate that people's moral judgments can actually impact their application of the concepts that might at first have seemed purely descriptive. For example, experimental results suggest that people's value judgments can affect their intuitions about what an agent *caused*, whether she acted *intentionally* and even whether she *knew* what she was doing. A surge of recent research has sought to understand why these effects might be occurring and what they might be telling us about the relevant concepts.

Knobe argues that these experimental results point to something fundamental about how people ordinarily make sense of the world. Specifically, the results suggest that moral norms play a role in the basic competence underlying causal cognition and folk psychology. Hence, if we want an accurate theory about people's ordinary understanding, we will need to switch away from a picture of the 'person as scientist' to one that also incorporates the notion of a 'person as moralist'.

Alicke, Rose, and Bloom argue for an alternative hypothesis. On this hypothesis, when people observe a behavior that appears to be a moral transgression, they are motivated to find some way of blaming the agent. This motivation can then lead them to adjust their views about whether the agent caused certain subsequent events. For example, we might explain the impact of people's moral judgments on their causal judgments without assuming any special role for norms in the core processes of causal cognition. The effect can be explained instead in terms of a motivational bias that arises when people enter a mode of 'blame validation'.

Uttich and Lombrozo then suggest a third possible view. They point out that even if moral norms do play a role in people's use of certain concepts, one cannot immediately conclude that people's use of these concepts must be radically unlike anything we find within the sciences. After all, the fact that an agent violated a moral norm might well provide useful scientific information. (It might indicate, for example, that the agent was especially motivated to perform the action.) Uttich and Lombrozo explore this possibility through a series of studies that offer support for a 'rational scientist' model of the role of norms in people's cognition.

SUGGESTED READINGS

Adams, F. & Steadman, A. 2004. "Intentional Action in Ordinary Language: Core Concept or Pragmatic Understanding?" *Analysis 64*, 173–181.

Beebe, J. & Buckwalter, W. 2010. "The Epistemic Side-Effect Effect." *Mind & Language 25*, 474–498.

Guglielmo, S. & Malle, B. F. 2010. "Can Unintended Side Effects Be Intentional? Resolving a Controversy over Intentionality and Morality." *Personality and Social Psychology Bulletin 36*, 1635–1647.

Hitchcock, C. & Knobe, J. 2011. "Cause and Norm." *Journal of Philosophy 106*, 587–612.

Machery, E. 2008. "The Folk Concept of Intentional Action: Philosophical and Experimental Issues." *Mind & Language 23*, 165–189.

Nichols, S. & Ulatowski, J. 2007. "Intuitions and Individual Differences: The Knobe Effect Revisited." *Mind & Language 22*, 346–365.

Pinillos, Á. N., Smith, N., Nair, G. S., Marchetto, P. & Mun, C. 2011. "Philosophy's New Challenge: Experiments and Intentional Action." *Mind & Language 26*, 115–139.

Sloman, S. A., Fernbach, P. M. & Ewing, S. 2012. "A Causal Model of Intentionality Judgment." *Mind & Language 27*, 154–180.

Sripada, C. S. & Konrath, S. 2011. "Telling More than We Can Know about Intentional Action." *Mind & Language 26*, 353–380.

Young, L., Cushman, F. A., Adolphs, R., Tranel, D. & Hauser, M. D. 2006. "Does Emotion Mediate the Relationship between an Action's Moral Status and Its Intentional Status? Neuropsychological Evidence." *Journal of Culture and Cognition 6*, 291–304.

9

Person as Scientist, Person as Moralist

Joshua Knobe

1. INTRODUCTION

Consider the way research is conducted in a typical modern university. There are departments for theology, drama, philosophy... and then there are departments specifically devoted to the practice of *science*. Faculty members in these science departments generally have quite specific responsibilities. They are not supposed to make use of all the various methods and approaches one finds in other parts of the university. They are supposed to focus on observation, experimentation, the construction of explanatory theories.

Now consider the way the human mind ordinarily makes sense of the world. One plausible view would be that the human mind works something like a modern university. There are psychological processes devoted to religion (the mind's theology department), to aesthetics (the mind's art department), to morality (the mind's philosophy department)... and then there are processes specifically devoted to questions that have a roughly "scientific" character. These processes work quite differently from the ones we use in thinking about, say, moral or aesthetic questions. They proceed using more or less the same sorts of methods we find in university science departments.

This metaphor is a powerful one, and it has shaped research programs in many different areas of cognitive science. Take the study of *folk psychology*. Ordinary people have a capacity to ascribe mental states (beliefs, desires, etc.), and researchers have sometimes suggested that people acquire this capacity in much the same way that scientists develop theoretical frameworks (e.g., Gopnik & Wellman 1992). Or take *causal cognition*. Ordinary people have an ability to determine whether one event caused another, and it has been suggested that they do so by looking at the same sorts of statistical information scientists normally consult (e.g., Kelley 1967). Numerous other fields have taken a similar path. In each case, the basic strategy is to look at the methods used by professional research scientists and then to hypothesize that people actually use similar methods in their ordinary understanding. This strategy has clearly led to many important advances.

Yet, in recent years, a series of experimental results have begun pointing in a rather different direction. These results indicate that people's ordinary understanding does not proceed using the same methods one finds in the sciences. Instead, it appears that people's intuitions in both folk psychology and causal cognition can be affected by *moral* judgments. That is, people's judgments about whether a given action truly is morally good or bad can actually affect their intuitions about what that action caused and what mental states the agent had.

These results come as something of a surprise. They do not appear to fit comfortably with the view that certain aspects of people's ordinary understanding work much like a scientific investigation, and a question therefore arises about how best to understand them.

One approach would be to suggest that people truly are engaged in an effort to pursue something like a scientific investigation, but that they simply aren't doing a very good job of it. Perhaps the competencies underlying people's judgments actually are purely scientific in nature, but there are then various additional factors that get in the way of people's ability to apply these competencies correctly. Such a view might allow us to explain the patterns observed in people's intuitions while still holding onto the basic idea that people's capacities for thinking about psychology, causation, and the like, can be understood on the model of a scientific investigation.

This approach has a strong intuitive appeal, and recent theoretical work has led to the development of specific hypotheses that spell it out with impressive clarity and precision. There is just one problem. The actual experimental results never seem to support these hypotheses. Indeed, the results point toward a far more radical view. They suggest that moral considerations actually figure in the competencies people use to make sense of human beings and their actions.

2. INTRODUCING THE PERSON-AS-SCIENTIST THEORY

In the existing literature on causal cognition and theory-of-mind, it has often been suggested that people's ordinary way of making sense of the world is in certain respects analogous to a scientific theory (Churchland 1981; Gopnik & Meltzoff 1997; Sloman 2005). This is an important and provocative suggestion, but if we are to grapple with it properly, we need to get a better understanding of precisely what it means and how experimental evidence might bear on it.

2.1. Ordinary Understanding and Scientific Theory

To begin with, we will need to distinguish two different aspects of the claim that people's ordinary understanding is analogous to a scientific theory. First, there is the claim that human thought might sometimes take the form of a *theory*. To assess this first claim, one would have to pick out the characteristics that distinguish theories from other sorts of knowledge structures and then ask whether these characteristics can be found in ordinary cognition. This is certainly a worthwhile endeavor, but it has already been pursued in a considerable body of recent research (e.g., Carey & Spelke 1996; Goldman 2006; Murphy & Medin 1985), and I will have nothing further to say about it here. Instead, the focus of this target article will be on a second claim, namely, the claim that certain facets of human cognition are properly understood as *scientific*.

To begin with, it should be emphasized that this second claim is distinct from the first. If one looks to the usual sorts of criteria for characterizing a particular knowledge structure as a "theory" (e.g., Premack & Woodruff 1978), one sees immediately that these criteria could easily be satisfied by, for example, a religious doctrine. A religious doctrine could offer systematic principles; it could posit unobservable entities and processes; it could yield definite predictions. For all these reasons, it seems perfectly reasonable to say that a religious doctrine could give us a certain kind of "theory" about how the world works. Yet, although the doctrine might offer us a theory, it does not appear to offer us a specifically *scientific* theory. In particular, it seems that religious thinking often involves attending to different sorts of considerations from the ones we would expect to find in a properly scientific investigation. Our task here, then, is to figure out whether certain aspects of human cognition qualify as "scientific" in this distinctive sense.

One common view is that certain aspects of human cognition do indeed make use of the very same sorts of considerations we find in the systematic sciences. So, for example, in work on causal cognition, researchers sometimes proceed by looking to the statistical methods that appear in systematic scientific research and then suggesting that those same methods are at work in people's ordinary causal judgments (Gopnik et al. 2004; Kelley 1967; Woodward 2004). Different theories of this type appeal to quite different statistical methods, but these differences will not be relevant here. The thing to focus on is just the general idea that people's ordinary causal cognition is in some way analogous to a scientific inquiry.

And it is not only the study of causal cognition that proceeds in this way. A similar viewpoint can be found in the theory-of-mind literature (Gopnik & Meltzoff 1997), where it sometimes goes under the slogan "Child as Scientist." There, a central claim is that children refine their understanding of the mind in much the same way that scientists refine their theories. Hence, it is suggested that we can look at the way Kepler developed his theory of the orbits of the planets and then suggest that children use the same basic approach as they are acquiring the concept of belief (Gopnik & Wellman 1992). Once again, the idea is that the cognitive processes people use in ordinary life show a deep similarity to the ones at work in systematic science.

It is this idea that we will be taking up here. Genuinely scientific inquiry seems to be sensitive to a quite specific range of considerations and seems to take those considerations into account in a highly distinctive manner. What we want to know is whether certain aspects of ordinary cognition work in more or less this same way.

2.2. Refining the Question

But now it might seem that the answer is obvious. For it has been known for decades that people's ordinary intuitions show certain patterns that one would never expect to find in a systematic scientific investigation. People make wildly inappropriate inferences from contingency tables, show shocking failures to properly detect correlations, display a tendency to attribute causation to whichever factor is most perceptually salient (Chapman & Chapman 1967; McArthur & Post 1977; Smedslund 1963). How could one possibly reconcile these facts about people's ordinary intuitions with a theory according to which people's ordinary cognition is based on something like a scientific methodology?

The answer, I think, is that we need to interpret that theory in a somewhat more nuanced fashion. The theory is not plausibly understood as an attempt to describe all of the factors that can influence people's intuitions. Instead, it is best understood as an attempt to capture the "fundamental" or "underlying" nature of certain cognitive capacities. There might then be various factors that interfere with our ability to apply those capacities correctly, but the existence of these additional factors would in no way impugn the theory itself.

To get a rough sense for the strategy here, it might be helpful to return to the comparison with religion. Faced with a discussion over religious doctrine, we might say: "This discussion isn't best understood as a kind of scientific inquiry; it is something else entirely. So if we find that the participants in this discussion are diverging from proper scientific methods, the best interpretation is that they simply weren't trying to use those methods in the first place." This would certainly be a reasonable approach to the study of religious discourse, but the key claim of the person-as-scientist theory is that it would *not* be the right approach to understanding certain aspects of our ordinary cognition. Looking at these aspects of ordinary cognition, a defender of the person-as-scientist view would adopt a very different stance. For example, she might say: "Yes, it's true that people sometimes diverge from proper scientific methods, but that is *not* because they are engaging in some fundamentally different sort of activity. Rather, their underlying capacities for causal cognition and theory-of-mind really are governed by scientific methods; it's just that there are also various additional factors that get in the way and sometimes lead people into errors."

Of course, it can be difficult to make sense of this talk of certain capacities being "underlying" or "fundamental," and different researchers might unpack these notions in different ways:

1. One view would be that people have a *domain-specific capacity* for making certain kinds of judgments but then various other factors intrude and allow these judgments to be affected by irrelevant considerations.

2. Another would be that people have a *representation of the criteria* governing certain concepts but that they are not always able to apply these representations correctly.
3. A third would be that the claim is best understood *counterfactually*, as a hypothesis about how people would respond if only they had sufficient cognitive resources and freedom from certain kinds of biases.

I will not be concerned here with the particular differences between these different views. Instead, let us introduce a vocabulary that allows us to abstract away from these details and talk about this approach more generally. Regardless of the specifics, I will say that the approach is to posit an underlying *competence* and then to posit various additional factors that get in the way of people's ability to apply that competence correctly.

With this framework in place, we can now return to our investigation of the impact of moral considerations on people's intuitions. How is this impact to be explained? One strategy would be to start out by finding some way to distinguish people's underlying competencies from the various interfering factors. Then one could say that the competencies themselves are entirely scientific in nature, but that the interfering factors then prevent people from applying these competencies correctly and allow moral considerations to affect their intuitions. This strategy is certainly a promising one, and I shall discuss it in further detail later. But it is important to keep in mind that we also have open another, very different option. It could always turn out that there simply is no underlying level at which the relevant cognitive capacities are purely scientific, that the whole process is suffused through and through with moral considerations.

3. INTUITIONS AND MORAL JUDGMENTS

Before we think any further about these two types of explanations, we will need to get a better grasp of the phenomena to be explained. Let us begin, then, just by considering a few cases in which moral considerations appear to be impacting people's intuitions.

3.1. Intentional Action

Perhaps the most highly studied of these effects is the impact of people's moral judgments on their use of the concept of *intentional action*. This is the concept people use to distinguish between behaviors that are performed intentionally (e.g., hammering in a nail) and those that are performed unintentionally (e.g., accidentally bringing the hammer down on one's own thumb). It might at first appear that people's use of this distinction depends entirely on certain facts about the role of the agent's mental states in his or her behavior, but experimental studies consistently indicate that something more complex is actually at work here. It seems that people's moral judgments can somehow influence their intuitions about whether a behavior is intentional or unintentional.

To demonstrate the existence of this effect, we can construct pairs of cases that are exactly the same in almost every respect but differ in their moral status.[1] For a simple example, consider the following vignette:

> The vice president of a company went to the chairman of the board and said, "We are thinking of starting a new program. It will help us increase profits, but it will also harm the environment."
>
> The chairman of the board answered, "I don't care at all about harming the environment. I just want to make as much profit as I can. Let's start the new program."
>
> They started the new program. Sure enough, the environment was harmed.

Faced with this vignette, most subjects say that the chairman *intentionally* harmed the environment. One might initially suppose that this intuition relies only on certain facts about the chairman's own mental states (e.g., that he specifically knew his behavior would result in environmental harm). But the data suggest that something more is going on here. For people's intuitions change radically when one alters the moral status of the chairman's behavior by simply replacing the word "harm" with "help":

> The vice president of a company went to the chairman of the board and said, "We are thinking of starting a new program. It will help us increase profits, and it will also help the environment."
>
> The chairman of the board answered, "I don't care at all about helping the environment. I just want to make as much profit as I can. Let's start the new program."
>
> They started the new program. Sure enough, the environment was helped.

Faced with this second version of the story, most subjects actually say that the chairman *unintentionally* helped the environment. Yet it seems that the only major difference between the two vignettes lies in the moral status of the chairman's behavior. So it appears that people's moral judgments are somehow impacting their intuitions about intentional action.

Of course, it would be unwise to draw any strong conclusions from the results of just one experiment, but this basic effect has been replicated and extended in numerous further studies. To begin with, subsequent experiments have further explored the harm and help cases to see what exactly about them leads to the difference in people's intuitions. These experiments suggest that moral judgments truly are playing a key role, since participants who start out with different moral judgments about the act of harming the environment end up arriving at different intuitions about whether the chairman acted intentionally (Tannenbaum et al. 2009). But the effect is not limited to vignettes involving environmental harm; it emerges when researchers use different cases (Cushman & Mele 2008; Knobe 2003a) and even when they turn to cases with quite different structures that do not involve side effects in any way (Knobe 2003b; Nadelhoffer 2005). Nor does the effect appear to be limited to any one particular population: It emerges when the whole study is translated into Hindi and conducted on Hindi speakers (Knobe & Burra 2006) and even when it is simplified and given to 4-year-old children (Leslie et al. 2006a). At this point, there is really a great deal of evidence for the claim that people's moral judgments are somehow impacting their intuitions about intentional action.

Still, as long as all of the studies are concerned only with intuitions about intentional action specifically, it seems that our argument will suffer from a fatal weakness. For someone might say: "Surely, we have very strong reason to suppose that the concept of intentional action works in more or less the same way as the other concepts people normally use to understand human action. But we have good theories of many of these other concepts—the concepts of deciding, wanting, causing, and so forth—and these other theories do not assign any role to moral considerations. So the best bet is that moral considerations do not play any role in the concept of intentional action either."

In my view, this is actually quite a powerful argument. Even if we have strong evidence for a certain view about the concept of intentional action specifically, it might well make sense to abandon this view in light of theories we hold about various other, seemingly similar concepts.

3.2. Further Mental States

As it happens, though, the impact of moral considerations does not appear to be limited to people's use of the word "intentionally." The very same effect also arises for numerous other expressions: "intention," "deciding," "desire," "in favor of," "advocating," and so forth.

To get a grip on this phenomenon, it may be helpful to look in more detail at the actual procedure involved in conducting these studies. In one common experimental design, subjects are randomly assigned to receive either the story about harming the environment or the story about helping the environment and then, depending on the case, are asked about the degree to which they agree or disagree with one of the following sentences:

(1)
a. The chairman of the board harmed the environment intentionally.

    ○   ○   ○   ○   ○   ○   ○

    definitely   unsure   definitely
    disagree   agree

b. The chairman of the board helped the environment intentionally.

    ○   ○   ○   ○   ○   ○   ○

    definitely   unsure   definitely
    disagree   agree

When the study is conducted in this way, one finds that subjects show moderate agreement with the claim that the chairman harmed intentionally and moderate disagreement with the claim that he helped intentionally (Knobe 2004a). The difference between the ratings in these two conditions provides evidence that people's moral intuitions are affecting their intuitions about intentional action.

It appears, however, that this effect is not limited to the concept of intentional action specifically. For example, suppose we eliminate the word "intentionally" and instead use the word "decided." The two sentences then become:

(2) a. The chairman decided to harm the environment.
    b. The chairman decided to help the environment.

Faced with these revised sentences, subjects show more or less the same pattern of intuitions. They tend to agree with the claim that the agent decided to harm, and they tend to disagree with the claim that the agent decided to help (Pettit & Knobe 2009).

Now suppose we make the case a little bit more complex. Suppose we do not use the adverb "intentionally" but instead use the verb "intend." So the sentences come out as:

(3) a. The chairman intended to harm the environment.
    b. The chairman intended to help the environment.

One then finds a rather surprising result. People's responses in both conditions are shifted over quite far toward the "disagree" side. In fact, people's intuitions end up being shifted over so far that they do not, on the whole, agree in either of the two conditions (Shepard 2009; cf. Cushman 2010; Knobe 2004b; McCann 2005). Nonetheless, the basic pattern of the responses remains the same. Even though people's responses don't go all the way over to the "agree" side of the scale in either condition, they are still *more* inclined to agree in the harm case than they are in the help case.

Once one conceptualizes the issue in this way, it becomes possible to find an impact of moral considerations in numerous other domains. Take people's application of the concept *in favor*. Now consider a case in which an agent says:

> I know that this new procedure will [bring about some outcome]. But that is not what we should be concerned about. The new procedure will increase profits, and that should be our goal.

Will people say in such a case that the agent is "in favor" of bringing about the outcome?

Here again, it seems that moral judgments play a role. People disagree with the claim that the agent is "in favor" when the outcome is morally good, whereas they stand at just about the midpoint between agreement and disagreement when the outcome is morally bad (Pettit & Knobe 2009). And similar effects have been observed for people's use of many other concepts: *desiring, intending, choosing,* and so forth (Pettit & Knobe 2009; Tannenbaum et al. 2009).

Overall, these results suggest that the effect obtained for intuitions about intentional action is just one example of a far broader phenomenon. The effect does not appear to be limited to the concept *intentionally,* nor even to closely related concepts such as *intention* and *intending.* Rather, it seems that we are tapping into a much more general tendency, whereby moral judgments impact the application of a whole range of different concepts used to pick out mental states and processes.

3.3. Action Trees

But the scope of the effect does not stop there. It seems also to apply to intuitions about the relations that obtain among the various actions an agent performs. Philosophers and cognitive scientists have often suggested that such relations could be represented in terms of an *action tree* (Goldman 1970; Mikhail 2007). Hence, the various actions performed by our chairman in the help case might be represented with the tree in Figure 1.

Needless to say, ordinary folks do not actually communicate with each other by writing out little diagrams like this one. Still, it seems that we can get a sense of how people are representing the action tree by looking at their use of various ordinary English expressions, for example, by looking at the way they use the expressions "in order to" and "by."

A number of complex issues arise here, but simplifying slightly, the key thing to keep in mind is that people only use "in order to" for relations that *go upward* in the tree, and they only use "by" for relations that *go downward.* Thus, people are willing to say that the chairman "implemented the program in order to increase profits" but not that he "increased profits in order to implement the program." And, conversely, they are willing to say that he "increased profits by implementing the program" but not that he "implemented the program by increasing profits." Looking at people's intuitions about simple expressions like these, we can get a good sense of how they are representing the geometry of the action tree itself.

But now comes the tricky part. Experimental results indicate that people's intuitions about the proper use of these expressions can actually be influenced by their moral judgments (Knobe 2004b, forthcoming). Hence, people are willing to say:

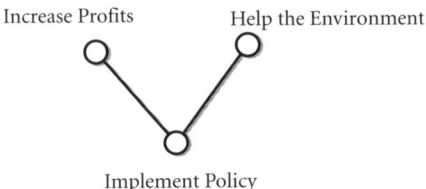

Figure 9.1. Action tree for the help case.

> The chairman harmed the environment in order to increase profits.

but not:

> The chairman helped the environment in order to increase profits.

And, similarly, they are willing to say:

> The chairman increased profits by harming the environment.

but not:

> The chairman increased profits by helping the environment.

One natural way of explaining these asymmetries would be to suggest that people's moral judgments are having an effect on their representations of the action tree itself. For example, suppose that when people make a judgment that harming the environment is morally wrong, they thereby come to represent the corresponding node on the action tree as "collapsing" into a lower node (see Fig. 2).

The asymmetries we find for "in order to" and "by" would then follow immediately, without the need for any controversial assumptions about the semantics of these specific expressions. Although the issue here is a complex one, recent research does seem to be supporting the claim that moral judgments are affecting action tree representations in this way (Knobe forthcoming; Ulatowski 2009).

3.4. Causation

All of the phenomena we have been discussing thus far may appear to be quite tightly related, and one might therefore suspect that the effect of morality would disappear as soon as one turns to other, rather different cases. That, however, seems not to be the case. Indeed, the very same effect arises in people's intuitions about *causation* (Alicke 2000; Cushman 2010; Hitchcock & Knobe 2009 ; Knobe forthcoming; Knobe & Fraser 2008; Solan & Darley 2001).

For a simple example here, consider the following vignette:

> The receptionist in the philosophy department keeps her desk stocked with pens. The administrative assistants are allowed to take pens, but faculty members are supposed to buy their own.

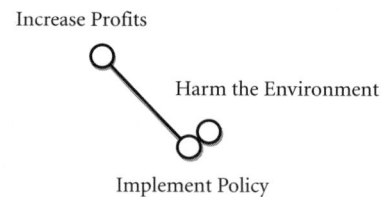

Figure 9.2. Action tree for the harm case.

The administrative assistants typically do take the pens. Unfortunately, so do the faculty members. The receptionist repeatedly e-mailed them reminders that only administrators are allowed to take the pens.

On Monday morning, one of the administrative assistants encounters Professor Smith walking past the receptionist's desk. Both take pens. Later that day, the receptionist needs to take an important message...but she has a problem. There are no pens left on her desk.

Faced with this vignette, most subjects say that the professor did cause the problem but that the administrative assistant did not cause the problem (Knobe & Fraser 2008). Yet, when we examine the case from a purely scientific standpoint, it seems that the professor's action and the administrative assistant's action bear precisely the same relation to the problem that eventually arose. The main difference between these two causal factors is just that the professor is doing something wrong (violating the departmental rule) while the administrative assistant is doing exactly what she is supposed to (acting in accordance with the rules of the department). So it appears that people's judgment that the professor is doing something wrong is somehow affecting their intuitions about whether or not the professor *caused* the events that followed.

Now, looking just at this one case, one might be tempted to suppose that the effect is not at all a matter of moral judgment but simply reflects people's intuitive sense that the professor's action is more "unusual" or "strange" than the administrative assistant's. But subsequent studies strongly suggest that there is something more afoot here. People continue to show the same basic effect even when they are informed that the administrative assistants *never* take pens whereas the professors always do (Roxborough & Cumby 2009), and there is a statistically significant effect whereby pro-life subjects are more inclined than pro-choice subjects to regard the act of seeking an abortion as a cause of subsequent outcomes (Cushman et al. 2008). All in all, the evidence seems strongly to suggest that people's moral judgments are actually impacting their causal intuitions.

3.5. Doing and Allowing

People ordinarily distinguish between actually breaking something and merely allowing it to break, between actually raising something and merely allowing it to rise, between actually killing someone and merely allowing someone to die. This distinction has come to be known as the distinction between *doing* and *allowing*.

To explore the relationship between people's intuitions about doing and allowing and their moral judgments, we used more or less the same methodology employed in these earlier studies (Cushman et al. 2008). Subjects were randomly assigned to receive different vignettes. Subjects in one condition received a vignette in which the agent performs an action that appears to be morally permissible:

Dr. Bennett is an emergency-room physician. An unconscious homeless man is brought in, and his identity is unknown. His organ systems have shut down and a nurse has hooked him up to a respirator. Without the respirator he would die. With the respirator and some attention from Dr. Bennett he would live for a week or two, but he would never regain consciousness and could not live longer than two weeks.

Dr. Bennett thinks to himself, "This poor man deserves to die with dignity. He shouldn't spend his last days hooked up to such a horrible machine. The best thing to do would be to disconnect him from the machine."

For just that reason, Dr. Bennett disconnects the homeless man from the respirator, and the man quickly dies.

These subjects were then asked whether it would be more appropriate to say that the doctor *ended* the homeless man's life or that he *allowed* the homeless man's life to end.

Meanwhile, subjects in the other condition were given a vignette that was almost exactly the same, except that the doctor's internal monologue takes a somewhat different turn:

...Dr. Bennett thinks to himself, "This bum deserves to die. He shouldn't sit here soaking up my valuable time and resources. The best thing to do would be to disconnect him from the machine."

These subjects were asked the same question: whether it would be more appropriate to say that the doctor ended the man's life or allowed it to end.

Notice that the doctor performs exactly the same behavior in these two vignettes, and in both vignettes, he performs this behavior in the hopes that it will bring about the man's death. The only difference between the cases lies in the moral character of the doctor's reasons for hoping that the man will die. Yet this moral difference led to a striking difference in people's intuitions about *doing* versus *allowing*. Subjects who received the first vignette tended to say that the doctor "allowed" the man's life to end, whereas subjects who received the second vignette tended to say that the doctor "ended" the man's life. (Moreover, even within the first vignette, there was a correlation whereby subjects who thought that euthanasia was generally morally wrong were less inclined to classify the act as an "allowing.") Overall, then, the results of the study suggest that people's moral judgments are influencing their intuitions here as well.

It would, of course, be foolhardy to draw any very general conclusions from this one study, but the very same effect has also been observed in other studies using quite different methodologies (Cushman et al. 2008), and there is now at least some good provisional evidence in support of the view that people's intuitions about doing and allowing can actually be influenced by their moral judgments.

3.6. Additional Effects

Here we have discussed just a smattering of different ways in which people's moral judgments can impact their intuitions about apparently non-moral questions. But our review has been far from exhaustive: there are also studies showing that moral judgments can affect intuitions about *knowledge* (Beebe & Buckwalter forthcoming), *happiness* (Nyholm 2009), *valuing* (Knobe & Roedder 2009), *act individuation* (Ulatowski 2009), *freedom* (Phillips & Knobe 2009), and *naturalness* (Martin 2009). Given that all of these studies were conducted just in the past few years, it seems highly probable that a number of additional effects along the same basic lines will emerge in the years to come.

4. ALTERNATIVE EXPLANATIONS

Thus far, we have seen that people's ordinary application of a variety of different concepts can be influenced by moral considerations. The key question now is how to explain this effect. Here we face a choice between two basic approaches. One approach would be to suggest that moral considerations actually figure in the competencies people use to understand the world. The other would be to adopt what I will call an *alternative explanation*. That is, one could suggest that moral considerations play no role at all in the relevant competencies but that certain additional factors are somehow "biasing" or "distorting" people's cognitive processes and thereby allowing their intuitions to be affected by moral judgments.

The first thing to notice about the debate between these two approaches is that we are unlikely to make much progress on it as long as the two positions are described only in these abstract, programmatic terms. Thus, suppose that we are discussing a new experimental result and someone says: "Well, it could always turn out that this effect is due to some kind of interfering factor." How would we even begin to test such a conjecture? As long as the claim is just about the possibility of "some kind of interfering factor," it is hard to know where one could go to look for confirming or disconfirming evidence.

Fortunately, however, the defenders of alternative hypotheses have not simply put forward these sorts of abstract, programmatic conjectures. Instead, they have developed sophisticated models that make it possible to offer detailed explanations of the available experimental data. Such models start out with the idea that people's actual competence includes no role for moral considerations, but they then posit various additional psychological factors that explain how people's moral judgments might nonetheless influence their intuitions in specific cases. Each such alternative explanation then generates further predictions, which can in turn be subjected to experimental test. There has been a great deal of research in recent years devoted to testing these models, including some ingenious new experiments that enable one to get a better handle on the complex cognitive processes underlying people's intuitions. At this point, then, the best approach is probably just to look in detail at some of the most prominent explanations that have actually been proposed and the various experiments that have been devised to test them.

4.1. The Motivational Bias Hypothesis

Think of the way a District Attorney's office might conduct its business. The DA decides to prosecute a suspect and hands the task over to a team of lawyers.

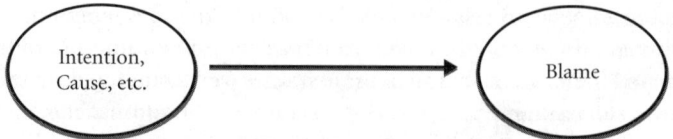

Figure 9.3. Traditional account of the process underlying blame ascription.

These lawyers then begin looking at the case. Presumably, though, they do not examine the evidence with perfectly unbiased eyes. They have been hired to secure a conviction, and they are looking at the evidence with a view to achieving this goal (cf. Tetlock 2002). One might say that they are under the influence of a *motivational bias*.

A number of researchers have suggested that a similar mechanism might be at the root of the effects we have been discussing here (Alicke 2008; Nadelhoffer 2006a). Perhaps people just read through the story and rapidly and automatically conclude that the agent is to blame. Then, after they have already reached this conclusion, they begin casting about for ways to justify it. They try to attribute anything they can—intention, causation, etc. —that will help to justify the blame they have already assigned. In essence, the suggestion is that the phenomena under discussion here can be understood as the results of a motivational bias.

This suggestion would involve a reversal of the usual view about the relationship between people's blame judgments and their intuitions about intention, causation, and so forth. The usual view of this relationship looks something like what's shown in Figure 3.

Here, the idea is that people first determine that the agent fulfilled the usual criteria for moral responsibility (intention, cause, etc.) and then, on the basis of this initial judgment, go on to determine that the agent deserves blame. This sort of model has a strong intuitive appeal, but it does not seem capable of explaining the experimental data reviewed above. After all, if people determine whether or not the agent caused the outcome before they make any sort of moral judgment, how could it be that their moral judgments affect their intuitions about causation?

To resolve this question, one might develop a model that goes more like the one shown in Figure 4.

In this revised model, there is a reciprocal relationship between people's blame judgments and their intuitions about intention, causation, et. As soon as people observe behavior of a certain type, they become motivated to find

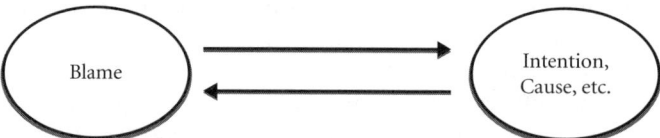

Figure 9.4. Motivational bias account of blame ascription.

some way of blaming the agent. They then look to the evidence and try to find a plausible argument in favor of the view that the agent fulfills all of the usual criteria for responsibility. If they can construct a plausible argument there, they immediately blame the agent. Otherwise, they reluctantly determine that the agent was not actually blameworthy after all. In short, the hypothesis says that people's intuitions about intention and causation affect their blame judgments but that the causal arrow can also go in the other direction, with people's drive to blame the agent distorting their intuitions about intention and causation.

One of the main sources of support for such a hypothesis is the well-established body of theoretical and experimental work within social psychology exploring similar effects in other domains. There is now overwhelming evidence that motivational biases can indeed lead people to interpret evidence in a biased manner (for a review, see Kunda 1990), and, within moral psychology specifically, there is a growing body of evidence suggesting that people often adopt certain views as part of a post hoc attempt to justify prior moral intuitions (Ditto et al. 2009; Haidt 2001). So the motivational bias hypothesis is perhaps best understood as the application to a new domain of a theoretical perspective that is already quite well supported elsewhere.

More importantly, the hypothesis makes it possible to explain all of the existing results without supposing that moral considerations actually play any role at all in any of the relevant competencies. The thought is that people's competencies are entirely non-moral but that a motivational bias then interferes with our ability to apply these concepts correctly. (An analogous case: If John sleeps with Bill's girlfriend, Bill may end up concluding that John's poetry was never really any good—but that does not mean that Bill's criteria for poetry actually involve any reference to sexual behavior.)

All in all, then, what we have here is an excellent hypothesis. It draws on well-established psychological theory, provides a clear explanation of existing results, and offers a wealth of new empirically testable predictions. The one problem is that when researchers actually went out and tested those new predictions, none of them were empirically confirmed. Instead, the experimental results again and again seemed to go against what would have been predicted on the motivational bias view. At this point, the vast majority of researchers working on these questions have therefore concluded that the motivational bias hypothesis cannot explain the full range of experimental findings and that some other sort of psychological process must be at work here (Hindriks 2008; Machery 2008; McCann 2005; Nichols & Ulatowski 2007; Turner 2004; Wright & Bengson 2009; Young et al. 2006).

4.1.1. Neuropsychological studies. The usual way of understanding the motivational bias hypothesis is that reading through certain kinds of vignettes triggers an immediate affective reaction, which then distorts people's subsequent reasoning (Nadelhoffer 2006a). An obvious methodology for testing the hypothesis is therefore to find people who *don't* have these immediate affective reactions and then check to see whether these people still show the usual effect.

Young et al. (2006) did just that. They took the cases of the corporate executive who harms or helps the environment and gave these cases to subjects who had lesions in the ventromedial prefrontal cortex (VMPFC). Previous experiments had shown that such subjects have massive deficits in the ordinary capacity for affective response. They show little or no affective response in situations where normal subjects would respond strongly (Damasio et al. 1990), and when they are presented with moral dilemmas in which most people's answers seem to be shaped by affective responses they end up giving answers that are radically different from those given by normal subjects (e.g., Koenigs et al. 2007). The big question was whether they would also give unusual answers on the types of questions we have been examining here.

The results showed that they did not (Young et al. 2006). Just like normal subjects, the VMPFC patients said that the chairman harmed the environment intentionally but helped the environment unintentionally. In fact, *100 percent* of patients in this study said that the environmental harm was intentional. On the basis of this experimental result, Young and colleagues concluded that the asymmetry observed in normal subjects was not, in fact, due to an affective reaction.

But, of course, even if it turns out that affective reactions play no role in these effects, the motivational bias hypothesis would not necessarily be refuted (Alicke 2008). After all, it is important to distinguish carefully between affect and motivation, and we need to acknowledge the possibility that people are experiencing a motivational bias that does not involve any kind of affect at all. Perhaps people just calmly observe certain behaviors, rapidly arrive at certain moral appraisals, and then find themselves trying to justify a judgment of blame.

This proposal is, I believe, an interesting and suggestive one. To address it properly, we will need to develop a more complex theoretical framework.

4.1.2. Types of moral judgment. To begin with, we need to distinguish between a variety of different types of moral judgment. One type of moral judgment is a judgment of *blame*. This is the type of judgment we have been discussing thus far, and it certainly does play an important role in people's psychology. But it is not the only type of moral judgment people make. They also make judgments about whether an agent did something morally *wrong*, about whether a behavior violated people's moral *rights*, about whether its consequences were *bad*. A complete theory of moral cognition would have to distinguish carefully between these various types of moral judgments and explain how each relates to people's intuitions about intention, causation, and the like.

In any case, as soon as we distinguish these various types of moral judgment, we see that it would be possible for people's intuitions to be influenced by their moral judgments even if these intuitions are not influenced by *blame* in particular. In fact, a growing body of experimental evidence suggests that the process actually proceeds in a quite different way (see Fig. 5).

This model involves a quite radical rejection of the view that people's intuitions about intention, causation, etc., are distorted by judgments of blame. Not

Figure 9.5. Distinct processes of moral judgment.

only are these intuitions not *distorted* by blame, they are not even influenced by blame at all. Rather, people start out by making some other type of moral judgment, which then influences their intuitions about intention and causation, which in turn serves as input to the process of assessing blame.

Though this model may at first seem counterintuitive, it has received support from experimental studies using a wide variety of methodologies. To take one example, Guglielmo and Malle (2010) gave subjects the vignette about the chairman and the environment and then used structural equation modeling to test various hypotheses about the relations among the observed variables. The results did not support a model in which blame judgments affected intuitions about intentional action. In fact, the analysis supported a causal model that went in precisely the opposite direction: it seems that people are first arriving at an intuition about intentional action, and that this intuition is then impacting their blame judgments. In short, whatever judgment it is that affects people's intentional action intuitions, the statistical results suggest that it is not a judgment of blame per se.

In a separate experiment, Guglielmo and Malle (2013) used reaction time measures to determine how long it took subjects to make a variety of different types of judgments. The results showed that people generally made judgments of intentional action *before* they made judgments of blame. (There was even a significant effect in this direction for some, though not all, of the specific cases we have been considering here.) But if the blame judgment does not even take place until after the intentional action judgment has been completed, it seems that people's intentional action judgments cannot be distorted by feedback from blame.

Finally, Keys and Pizarro (unpublished data) developed a method that allowed them to manipulate blame and then look for an effect on intuitions about intentional action. Subjects were given the vignettes about the agent who either helps or harms the environment, but they were also randomly assigned to receive different kinds of information about the character of this agent. Some were given information that made agent look like a generally nice person; others were given information that made the agent look like a generally nasty person. The researchers could then examine the impact of this manipulation on intuitions about blame and about intentional action. Unsurprisingly, people's intuitions about blame were affected by the information they received about the agent's character, but—and this is the key result of the experiment—this information had no significant impact on people's intuitions about intentional action. Instead, intuitions about intentional action were affected only by information about the actual behavior (helping vs. harming) the agent was said to have performed.[2]

In the face of these new results, friends of the motivational bias view might simply retreat to a weaker position. They might say: "Okay, so we initially suggested that people's intuitions were distorted by an affective reaction associated with an impulse to blame, but we now see that the effect is not driven by affect and is not caused specifically by blame. Still, the basic idea behind the theory could nonetheless be on track. That is to say, it could still be that people's intuitions are being distorted by an effort to justify some kind of moral judgment."

4.1.3. Cause and blame. This approach certainly sounds good in the abstract, but as one proceeds to look carefully at the patterns of intuition observed in specific cases, it starts to seem less and less plausible. The difficulty is that the actual patterns observed in these cases just don't make any sense as an attempt to justify prior moral judgments.

For a simple example, consider the case in which the receptionist runs out of pens and people conclude that the professor is the sole cause of the problem that results. In this case, it seems that some kind of moral judgment is influencing people's intuitions about causation, but which moral judgment is doing the work here? One obvious hypothesis would be that people's intuitions about causation are being influenced by a judgment that *the agent deserves blame for the outcome*. If this hypothesis were correct, it would make a lot of sense to suggest that people's intuitions were being distorted by a motivational bias. The idea would be that people want to conclude that the professor is to blame for a particular outcome and, to justify this conclusion, they say that he is the sole cause of this outcome.

The one problem is that the data don't actually suggest that people's causal intuitions are being influenced by a judgment that the agent is to blame for the outcome. Instead, the data appear to suggest that these intuitions are being influenced by a judgment that *the agent's action itself is bad*. So, for example, in the case at hand, we can distinguish two different moral judgments that people might make:

(a) The professor is to blame for the outcome (the receptionist's lack of pens).
(b) There is something bad about the professor's action (taking a pen from the desk).

The key claim now is that it is the second of these judgments, rather than the first, that is influencing people's intuition that the professor caused the outcome.

To test this claim empirically, we need to come up with a case in which the agent is judged to have performed a bad action but in which the agent is nonetheless not judged to be blameworthy for the outcome that results. One way to construct such a case would be to modify our original story by switching the outcome over to something *good*. (For example: the receptionist was planning to stab the department chair's eye out with a pen, but now that all of the pens have been taken, her plan is thwarted, and the department chair's eyes are saved.) In such a case, the professor would still be performing a bad action, but there would not even be a question as to whether he was "to blame" for the outcome that resulted, since there would be no bad outcome for which anyone could deserve blame.

Experiments using this basic structure have arrived at a surprising pattern of results (Hitchcock & Knobe 2009). Even when the outcome has been switched to something good, people continue to have the same causal intuitions. They still conclude that the agent who performed the bad action is more of a cause than the agent who performed the good action. Yet when the outcome is something good, it seems impossible to explain this pattern in terms of a motivational bias. After all, friends of the motivational bias hypothesis would then have to say that people are displeased with the agent who performs the bad action, that their intuitions thereby become distorted by moral judgment, and that they end up being motivated to conclude: "This bad guy must have been the sole cause of the wonderful outcome that resulted." It seems quite difficult, however, to see how such a conclusion could possibly serve as a post hoc justification for some kind of negative moral judgment.

4.1.4. Conclusion. Of course, it might ultimately prove possible to wriggle out of all of these difficulties and show that the data reviewed here do not refute the motivational bias hypothesis. But even then, a larger problem would still remain. This problem is that no one ever seems to be able to produce any positive evidence in favor of the hypothesis. That is, no one seems to be able to provide evidence that motivational biases are at the root of the particular effects under discussion here.

There is, of course, plenty of evidence that motivational biases do in general exist (e.g., Kunda 1990), and there are beautiful experimental results showing the influence of motivational biases in other aspects of moral cognition (Alicke 2000; Ditto et al. 2009; Haidt 2001), but when it comes to the specific effects under discussion here, there are no such experiments. Instead, the argument always proceeds by drawing on experimental studies in one domain to provide evidence about the psychological processes at work in another (see, e.g., Nadelhoffer 2006a). That is, the argument has roughly the form: "This explanation turned out to be true for so many other effects, so it is probably true for these ones, as well."

It now appears that this strategy may have been leading us astray. The basic concepts at work in the motivational bias explanation—affective reactions, post hoc rationalization, motivated reasoning—have proved extraordinarily helpful in understanding other aspects of moral cognition. But moral cognition is a heterogeneous phenomenon. What proves helpful in thinking about certain aspects of it may prove utterly irrelevant in thinking about others.

4.2. The Conversational Pragmatics Hypothesis

Let us turn, then, to a second possible alternative hypothesis. When people are engaged in ordinary discussions, their use of words does not simply serve as a straightforward reflection of the way they apply the corresponding concepts. Instead, people strive to act as helpful conversation partners, following certain complex principles that enable them to provide useful information to their audience. The study of these principles falls under the heading of "conversational pragmatics," and researchers engaged in this study have illuminated many puzzling aspects of the way people ordinarily use language in communication. A number of researchers have suggested that this approach might also serve to explain the phenomena we are trying to understand here (Adams & Steadman 2004a, 2004b; Driver 2008a, 2008b).

To get a sense for this hypothesis, it might be helpful to start out by looking at a potentially analogous case in another domain. Imagine that you have a bathroom in your building but that this bathroom is completely nonfunctional and has been boarded up for the past three years. And now imagine that someone hands you a questionnaire that asks:

Do you have a bathroom in your building?
___Yes ___No

It does seem that your actual concept *bathroom* might correctly apply to the room in your building, but when you receive this question, you immediately have an understanding of what the questioner really wants to know—namely, whether or not you have a bathroom that actually works—and you might therefore choose to check the box marked "No."

With these thoughts in mind, consider what might happen when subjects receive a questionnaire that asks whether they agree or disagree with the sentence:

The chairman of the board harmed the environment intentionally.

O　　O　　O　　O　　O　　O　　O

definitely　　　　unsure　　　　definitely
disagree　　　　　　　　　　　　agree

It might be thought that people's concept of intentional action does not, in fact, apply to cases like this one; but that, as soon as they receive the questionnaire, they form an understanding of what the questioner really wants to know. The real question here, they might think, is whether the chairman deserves to be blamed for his behavior, and they might therefore check the circle marked "definitely agree."

Similar remarks might be applied to many of the other effects described above. Thus, suppose that subjects are asked whether they agree or disagree with the sentence:

The administrative assistant caused the problem.

O　　O　　O　　O　　O　　O　　O

definitely　　　　unsure　　　　definitely
disagree　　　　　　　　　　　　agree

It might be thought that people's concept of causation does apply in cases like this one, but it also seems that subjects might quite reasonably infer that the real point of the question is to figure out whether the administrative assistant deserves blame for this outcome and that they might therefore check the circle marked "definitely disagree."

Before going on any further, it might be helpful to take a moment to emphasize just how different this pragmatic hypothesis is from the motivational bias hypothesis we discussed above. The motivational bias hypothesis posits an error that affects people's understanding of certain morally relevant events. By contrast, the pragmatic hypothesis does not involve any error or even any effect on people's understanding of events. It simply suggests that people are applying certain kinds of conversational rules. The basic idea is that moral considerations aren't actually affecting people's understanding of the situation; it's just that moral considerations do sometimes affect people's view about which particular words would be best used to describe it.

In any case, although the two hypotheses are very different in their theoretical approaches, they have proved remarkably similar in their ultimate fate. Like the motivational bias hypothesis, the pragmatic hypothesis initially looked very promising—a clear and plausible explanation, backed by a well-supported theoretical framework—but, as it happened, the actual empirical data just never came out the way the pragmatic hypothesis would predict. Indeed, the pragmatic hypothesis suffers from many of the same problems that plagued the motivational bias hypothesis, along with a few additional ones that are all its own.

4.2.1. Patient studies. One way to test the hypothesis would be to identify subjects who show an inability to use conversational pragmatics in the normal way, and then to check to see whether these subjects still show the usual effect. Zalla, Machery, and Leboyer did exactly that in a recent study (Zalla et al. 2011). They took the story about the chairman who harms or helps the environment and presented it to subjects with Asperger's syndrome, a developmental disorder characterized by difficulties in certain forms of communication and a striking inability to interact normally with others. Previous studies had shown that subjects with Asperger's display remarkable deficits in the capacity to understand conversational pragmatics, tending instead to answer questions in the most literal possible way (e.g., De Villiers et al. 2006; Surian et al. 1996). If the original effect had been due entirely to pragmatic processes, one might therefore have expected subjects with Asperger's to respond quite differently from neurotypical subjects.

But that is not what Zalla and colleagues found. Instead, they found that subjects with Asperger's showed exactly the same pattern of responses observed in previous studies. Just like neurotypical subjects, people with Asperger's tended to say that the chairman harmed the environment intentionally but helped it unintentionally. This result suggests that the pattern displayed by subjects in earlier studies is not, in fact, a product of their mastery of complex pragmatic principles.

4.2.2. Cancellation. Of course, the study of linguistic deficits in people with Asperger's brings up a host of complex issues, and this one experiment certainly should not be regarded as decisive. The thing to notice, though, is that results from a variety of other tests point toward the same basic conclusion, offering converging evidence for the claim that the effect here is not a purely pragmatic one (Adams & Steadman 2007; Knobe 2004b; Nichols & Ulatowski 2007; for a review, see Nadelhoffer 2006b).

Indeed, one can obtain evidence for this claim using one of the oldest and most widely known tests in the pragmatics literature. Recall that we began our discussion of conversational pragmatics with a simple example. If a person says, "There is a bathroom in the building," it would be natural to infer that this bathroom is actually in working order. But now suppose that we make our example just a little bit more complex. Suppose that the person utters two sentences: "There is a bathroom in the building. However, it is not in working order." Here it seems that the first sentence carries with it a certain sort of pragmatic significance but that the second sentence then eliminates the significance that this first sentence might otherwise have had. The usual way of describing this phenomenon is to say that the pragmatic "implicatures" of the first sentence have been *canceled* by the second (Grice 1989).

Using this device of cancellation, we could then construct a questionnaire that truly would accurately get at people's actual concept of bathrooms. For example, subjects could be asked to select from among the options:

- There is no bathroom in the building.
- There is a bathroom in the building, and it is in working order.
- There is a bathroom in the building, but it is not in working order.

Subjects could then feel free to signify the presence of the bathroom by selecting the third option, secure in the knowledge that they would not thereby be misleadingly conveying an impression that the bathroom actually did work.

In a recent experimental study, Nichols and Ulatowski (2007) used this same approach to get at the impact of pragmatic factors in intuitions about intentional action. Subjects were asked to select from among these options:

- The chairman *intentionally* harmed the environment, and he is responsible for it.
- The chairman didn't *intentionally* harm the environment, but he is responsible for it.

As it happened, Nichols and Ulatowski themselves believed that the original effect was entirely pragmatic, and they therefore predicted that subjects would indicate that the behavior was unintentional when they had the opportunity to do so without conveying the impression that the chairman was not to blame. But that is not at all how the data actually came out. Instead, subjects were just as inclined to say that the chairman acted intentionally in this new experiment as they were in the original version. In light of these results, Nichols and Ulatowski concluded that the effect was not due to pragmatics after all.

4.2.3. Other effects.
Finally, there is the worry that, even if conversational pragmatics might provide a somewhat plausible explanation of some of the effects described above, there are other effects that it cannot explain at all. Hence, the theory of conversational pragmatics would fail to explain the fact that moral considerations exert such a pervasive effect on a wide range of different kinds of judgments.

The pragmatic hypothesis was originally proposed as an explanation for people's tendency to agree with sentences like:

> The chairman of the board harmed the environment intentionally.

And when the hypothesis is applied to cases like this one, it does look at least initially plausible. After all, it certainly does seem that a sentence like "He did not harm the environment intentionally" could be used to indicate that the agent was not, in fact, to blame for his behavior.

But now suppose we take that very same hypothesis and apply it to sentences like:

> The chairman harmed the environment in order to increase profits.

Here the hypothesis does not even begin to get a grip. There simply isn't any conversational rule according to which one can indicate that the chairman is not to blame by saying something like: "He didn't do that in order to increase profits." No one who heard a subject uttering such a sentence would ever leave with the impression that it was intended as a way of exculpating or excusing the chairman.

Of course, one could simply say that the pragmatics hypothesis does explain the effect on "intentionally" but does not explain the corresponding effect on "in order to." But such a response would take away much of the motivation for adopting the pragmatics hypothesis in the first place. The hypothesis was supposed to give us a way of explaining how moral considerations could impact people's use of certain words without giving up on the idea that people's actual concepts were entirely morally neutral. If we now accept a non-pragmatic explanation of the effect for "in order to," there is little reason not to accept a similar account for "intentionally" as well.

4.3. Summary

Looking through these various experiments, one gradually gets a general sense of what has been going wrong with the alternative explanations. At the core of these explanations is the idea that people start out with an entirely non-moral competence but that some additional factor then interferes and allows people's actual intuitions to be influenced by moral considerations. Each alternative explanation posits a different interfering factor, and each explanation thereby predicts that the whole effect will go away if this factor is eliminated. So one alternative explanation might predict that the effect will go away when we eliminate a certain emotional response, another that it will go away when we eliminate certain pragmatic pressures, and so forth.

The big problem is that these predictions never actually seem to be borne out. No one has yet found a way of eliminating the purported interfering factors and thereby making the effect go away. Instead, the effect seems always to stubbornly reemerge, coming back again and again despite all our best efforts to eliminate it.

Now, one possible response to these difficulties would be to suggest that we just need to try harder. Perhaps the relevant interfering factor is an especially tricky or well-hidden one, or maybe there is a whole constellation of different factors in place here, all working together to generate the effects observed in the experiments. When we finally succeed in identifying all of the relevant factors, we might be able to find a way of eliminating them all and thereby allowing people's purely non-moral competence to shine through unhindered.

Of course, it is at least possible that such a research program would eventually succeed, but I think the most promising approach at this point would be to try looking elsewhere. In my view, the best guess about why no one has been able to eliminate the interfering factors is that there just *aren't* any such factors. It is simply a mistake to try to understand these experimental results in terms of a purely non-moral competence, which then gets somehow derailed by various additional factors. Rather, the influence of moral considerations that comes out in the experimental results truly is showing us something about the nature of the basic competencies people use to understand their world.

5. COMPETENCE THEORIES

Let us now try to approach the problem from a different angle. Instead of focusing on the interfering factors, we will try looking at the competence itself. The aim will be to show that something about the very nature of this competence is allowing people's moral judgments to influence their intuitions.

5.1. General Approach

At the core of the approach is a simple and straightforward assumption that has already played an enormously important role in numerous fields of cognitive science. Specifically, I will be relying heavily on the claim that we make sense of the things that actually happen by considering *other ways things might have been* (Byrne 2005; Kahneman & Miller 1986; Roese 1997).

A quick example will help to bring out the basic idea here. Suppose that we come upon a car that has a dent in it. We might immediately think about how the car would have looked if it did not have this dent. Thus, we come to understand the way the car actually is by considering another way that it could have been and comparing its actual status to this imagined alternative.

An essential aspect of this process, of course, lies in our ability to select from among all the possible alternatives just the few that prove especially relevant. Hence, in the case at hand, we would immediately consider the possibility that the car could have been undented, and think: "Notice that this car is dented rather than undented." But then there are all sorts of other alternatives that we would immediately reject as irrelevant or not worth thinking about. We would not take the time, for example, to consider the possibility that the car could have been levitating in the air, and then think: "Notice that this car is standing on the ground rather than levitating in the air."

Our ability to pick out just certain specific alternatives and ignore others is widely regarded as a deeply important aspect of human cognition, which shapes our whole way of understanding the objects we observe. It is, for example, a deeply important fact about our way of understanding the dented car that we compare it to an undented car. If we had instead compared it to a levitating car, we would end up thinking about it in a radically different way.

A question now arises as to why people focus on particular alternative possibilities and ignore others. The answer, of course, is that all sorts of different factors can play a role here. People's selection of specific alternative possibilities can be influenced by their judgments about controllability, about recency, about statistical frequency, about non-moral forms of goodness and badness (for reviews, see Byrne 2005; Kahneman & Miller 1986; Roese 1997). But there is also another factor at work here that has not received quite as much discussion in the existing literature. A number of studies have shown that people's selection of alternative possibilities can be influenced by their *moral judgments* (McCloy & Byrne 2000; N'gbala & Branscombe 1995). In other words, people's intuition about which possibilities are relevant can be influenced by their judgments about which actions are morally right.

For a simple illustration, take the case of the chairman who hears that he will be helping the environment, but reacts with complete indifference. As soon as one hears this case, one's attention is drawn to a particular alternative possibility:

> (1) Notice that the chairman reacted in this way, rather than specifically preferring that the environment be helped.

This alternative possibility seems somehow to be especially relevant, more relevant at least than many other possibilities we could easily imagine. In particular, one would not think:

> (2) Notice that the chairman reacted in this way rather than specifically trying to avoid anything that would help the environment.

Of course, one could imagine the chairman having this latter sort of attitude. One could imagine him saying: "I don't care at all whether we make profits. What I really want is just to make sure that the environment is harmed, and since this program will help the environment, I'm going to do everything I can to avoid implementing it." Yet this possibility has a kind of peculiar status. It seems somehow preposterous, not even worth considering. But why? The suggestion now is that moral considerations are playing a role in people's way of thinking about alternative possibilities. Very roughly, people regard certain possibilities as relevant because they take those possibilities to be especially good or right.

With these thoughts in mind, we can now offer a new explanation for the impact of moral judgments on people's intuitions. The basic idea is just that people's intuitions in all of the domains we have been discussing—causation, doing/allowing, intentional action, and so on—rely on a comparison between the actual world and certain alternative possibilities. Because people's moral judgments influence the selection of alternative possibilities, these moral judgments end up having a pervasive impact on the way people make sense of human beings and their actions.[3]

5.2. A Case Study

To truly spell out this explanation in detail, one would have to go through each of the different effects described above and show how each of these effects can be explained on a model in which moral considerations are impacting people's way of thinking about alternative possibilities. This would be a very complex task, and I will not attempt it here. Let us proceed instead by picking just one concept whose use appears to be affected by moral considerations. We can then offer a model of the competence underlying that one concept and thereby illustrate the basic approach. For these illustrative purposes, let us focus on the concept *in favor*.

We begin by introducing a fundamental assumption that will guide the discussion that follows. The assumption is that people's representation of the agent's attitude is best understood, not in terms of a simple dichotomy between "in favor" and "not in favor," but rather, in terms of a whole *continuum* of different attitudes an agent might hold. So we will be assuming that people can represent the agent as strongly opposed, as strongly in favor, or as occupying any of the various positions in between. For simplicity, we can depict this continuum in terms of a scale running from *con* to *pro*.[4] (See Fig. 6.)

Looking at this scale, it seems that an agent whose attitude falls way over on the *con* side will immediately be classified as "not in favor" and that an agent whose attitude falls way over on the *pro* side will immediately be classified as "in favor." But now, of course, we face a further question. How do people determine the threshold at which an agent's attitude passes over from the category "not in favor" to the category "in favor"?

To address this question, we will need to add an additional element to our conceptual framework. Let us say that people assess the various positions along the continuum by comparing each of these positions to a particular sort of alternative possibility. We can refer to this alternative possibility as the *default*. Then we can suggest that an agent will be counted as "in favor" when his or her attitude falls sufficiently far beyond this default point. (See Fig. 7.)

Figure 9.6. Continuum of attitude ascription.

The key thing to notice about this picture is that there needn't be any single absolute position on the continuum that always serves as the threshold for counting an agent as "in favor." Instead, the threshold might vary freely, depending on which point gets picked out as the default.

To get a sense for the idea at work here, it may be helpful to consider a closely analogous problem. Think of the process a teacher might use in assigning grades to students. She starts out with a whole continuum of different percentage scores on a test, and now she needs to find a way to pick out a threshold beyond which a given score will count as an A. One way to do this would be to introduce a general rule, such as "a score always counts as an A when it is at least 20 points above the default." Then she can pick out different scores as the default on different tests—treating 75% as default on easy tests, 65% as default on more difficult ones—and the threshold for counting as an A will vary accordingly.

The suggestion now is that people's way of thinking about attitudes uses this same sort of process. People always count an agent as "in favor" when the agent's attitude falls sufficiently far beyond the default, but there is no single point along the continuum that is treated as default in all cases. Different attitudes can be treated as default in different cases, and the threshold for counting as "in favor" then shifts around from one case to the next.

Now we arrive at the crux of the explanation. The central claim will be that people's moral judgments affect their intuitions *by shifting the position of the default*. For morally good actions, the default is to have some sort of *pro* attitude, whereas for morally bad actions, the default is to have some sort of *con* attitude. The criteria for "in favor" then vary accordingly.

Suppose we now apply this general framework to the specific vignettes used in the experimental studies. When it comes to helping the environment, it seems that the default attitude is a little bit toward the *pro* side. That is to say, the default in this case is to have at least a slightly positive attitude—not necessarily a deep or passionate attachment, but at least some minimal sense that helping the environment would be a nice thing to do. An attitude will then count as "in favor" to the extent that it goes sufficiently far beyond this default point. (See Fig. 8.)

But look at the position of the agent's actual attitude along this continuum. The agent is not even close to reaching up to the critical threshold here—he is interested in helping the environment only as a side effect of some other policy, and people should therefore conclude that he does not count as "in favor" of helping.

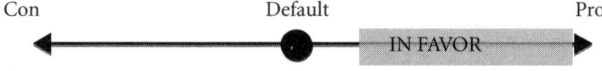

Figure 9.7. Criteria for ascription of "in favor."

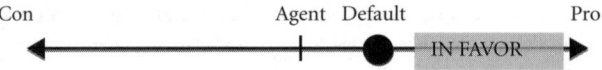

Figure 9.8. Representation of the continuum for the help case.

Now suppose we switch over to the harm case. There, we find that the agent's actual attitude has remained constant, but the default has changed radically. When it comes to harming the environment, the default is to be at least slightly toward the *con* side—not necessarily showing any kind of vehement opposition but at least having some recognition that harming the environment is a bad thing to do. An agent will then count as "in favor" to the extent that his or her attitude goes sufficiently far beyond this default (Fig. 9).

In this new representation, the agent's actual attitude remains at exactly the same point it was above (in Fig. 8), but its position relative to the default is now quite different. This time, the attitude falls just about at the critical threshold for counting as "in favor," and people should therefore be just about at the midpoint in their intuitions as to whether the agent was in favor of harming—which, in fact, is exactly what the experimental results show.

Notice how sharply this account differs from the alternative hypotheses discussed above. On those alternative hypotheses, people see that the agent harmed the environment they want to blame him for his behavior, and this interest in blame then shapes the way they conceptualize or describe various aspects of the case. The present account says nothing of the kind. Indeed, the account makes no mention at all of blame. Instead, it posits a role for an entirely different kind of moral judgment—a judgment that could be made even in the absence of any information about this specific agent or his behaviors. The claim is that before people even begin considering what actually happened in the case at hand, they can look at the act of harming the environment and make a judgment about what sort of attitude an agent could be expected to hold toward it. This judgment then serves as a standard they can use to make sense of the behavior they actually observe.

5.3. Extending the Model

What we have here is a model of the competence underlying people's use of one particular concept. The key question now is whether this same basic approach can be applied to the various other concepts discussed above. In a series of recent papers, I have argued that it can be used to explain the impact of moral judgment on people's intuitions about freedom, knowledge, and causation[5] (Hitchcock & Knobe 2009; Pettit & Knobe, 2009; Phillips & Knobe 2009).

Figure 9.9. Representation of the continuum for the harm case.

But new studies are coming out all the time, and we may soon be faced with experimental results that the model cannot explain. At any rate, one certainly should not expect that this model will turn out to be correct in every detail. Presumably, further work will show that it needs to be revised or expanded in various ways, and perhaps it will even have to be scrapped altogether.

In the present context, however, our concern is not so much to explore the details of this one model as to use it as a way of illustrating a more general approach and the contrast between this approach and the one we saw in the alternative explanations described above. The alternative explanations start out with the idea that the relevant competencies are entirely non-moral but that some additional factor then interferes and allows people's intuitions to be influenced by moral considerations. These explanations therefore predict that it should be possible, at least in principle, to eliminate the interfering factors and examine the judgments people make in the absence of this influence.

By contrast, in the approach under discussion here, moral considerations are not understood as some kind of extra factor that gets added in on top of everything else. Instead, the whole process is suffused with moral considerations from the very beginning. Hence, in this approach, no real sense can be attached to the idea of eliminating the role of morality and just watching the basic process unfold in its pure, non-moral form.

6. CONCLUSION

This target article began with a metaphor. The suggestion was that people's ordinary way of making sense of the world might be similar, at least in certain respects, to the way research is conducted in a typical modern university. Just as a university would have specific departments devoted especially to the sciences, our minds might include certain specific psychological processes devoted especially to constructing a roughly "scientific" kind of understanding.

If one thinks of the matter in this way, one immediately arrives at a certain picture of the role of moral judgments in people's understanding as a whole. In a university, there might be faculty members in the philosophy department who were hired specifically to work on moral questions, but researchers in the sciences typically leave such questions to one side. So maybe the mind works in much the same way. We might have certain psychological processes devoted to making moral judgments, but there would be other processes that focus on developing a purely "scientific" understanding of what is going on in a situation and remain neutral on all questions of morality.

I have argued that this picture is deeply mistaken. The evidence simply does not suggest that there is a clear division whereby certain psychological processes are devoted to moral questions and others are devoted to purely scientific questions. Instead, it appears that everything is jumbled together. Even the processes that look most "scientific" actually take moral considerations into account. It seems that we are moralizing creatures through and through.

ACKNOWLEDGMENTS

For comments on earlier drafts, I am deeply grateful to John Doris, Shaun Nichols, Stephen Stich, and five anonymous reviewers.

NOTES

1. In each of the studies that follow, we found a statistically significant difference between intuitions about a morally good act and intuitions about a morally bad act, but one might well wonder how large each of those differences was. The answers are as follows. *Intentional action*: 33% vs. 82%. (All subsequent results are on a scale from 1 to 7.) *Deciding*: 2.7 vs. 4.6. *In favor*: 2.6 vs. 3.8. *In order to*: 3.0 vs. 4.6. *By*: 3.0 vs. 4.4. *Causation*: 2.8 vs. 6.2. *Doing/allowing*: 3.0 vs. 4.6.

2. Surprisingly, there was also a significant gender x character interaction, whereby women tended to regard the act as more intentional when the agent had a bad character, while men tended to regard the act as more intentional when the agent had a good character. I have no idea why this might be occurring, but it should be noted that this is just one of the many individual differences observed in these studies. Feltz and Cokely (2007) have shown that men show a greater moral asymmetry in intentional action intuitions when the vignettes are presented within-subject, and Buckwalter (2010) has shown that women show a greater moral asymmetry when they are asked about the agent's knowledge. Though not well understood at the moment, these individual differences might hold the key to future insights into the moral asymmetries discussed here. (For further discussion, see Nichols & Ulatowski 2007.)

3. Strikingly, recent research has shown that people's intuitions about intentional action can be affected by non-moral factors, such as judgments about the agent's own interests (Machery 2008; Nanay forthcoming knowledge of conventional rules (Knobe 2007), and implicit attitudes (Inbar et al. 2009). This recent discovery offers us an interesting opportunity to test the present account. If we can come up with a general theory about how people's evaluations impact their thinking about alternative possibilities—a theory that explains not only the impact of moral judgments but also the impact of other factors—we should be able to generate predictions about the precise ways in which each of these other factors will impact people's intentional action intuitions. Such predictions can then be put to the test in subsequent experiments.

4. There may be certain general theoretical reasons for adopting the view that people's representations of the agent's attitude have this continuous character, but the principal evidence in favor of it comes from the actual pattern of the experimental data. For example, suppose that instead of saying that the agent does not care at all about the bad side effect, we say that the agent deeply regrets the side effect but decides to go ahead anyway so as to achieve the goal. Studies show that people then tend to say that the side effect was brought about *unintentionally* (Phelan & Sarkissian 2008; Sverdlik 2004). It is hard to see how one could explain this result on a model in which people have a unified way of thinking about all attitudes that involve the two features (1) foreseeing that an outcome will arise but (2) not specifically wanting it to arise. However, the result becomes easy to explain if we assume that people represent the agent's attitude, not in terms of sets of features (as I earlier believed; Knobe 2006) but in terms of a continuous dimension. We can then simply say that people take the regretful agent to be slightly more toward the *con* side of the continuum and are therefore less inclined to regard his or her behavior as intentional.

5. Very briefly, the suggestion is that intuitions in all three of these domains involve a capacity to compare reality to alternative possibilities. Thus, (a) intuitions about whether an agent acted freely depend on judgments about whether it was possible for her to choose otherwise, (b) intuitions about whether a person knows something depend on judgments about whether she has enough evidence to rule out relevant alternatives, and (c) intuitions about whether one event caused another depend on judgments about whether the second event would still have occurred if the first had not. Because moral judgments impact the way people decide which possibilities are relevant or irrelevant, moral judgments end up having an impact on people's intuitions in all three of these domains.

REFERENCES

Adams, F. & Steadman, A. (2004a) Intentional action in ordinary language: Core concept or pragmatic understanding? *Analysis* 64:173–181.

Adams, F. & Steadman, A. (2004b) Intentional actions and moral considerations: Still pragmatic. *Analysis* 64:268–276.

Adams, F. & Steadman, A. (2007) Folk concepts, surveys, and intentional action. In C. Lumer (ed.) *Intentionality, deliberation, and autonomy: The action-theoretic basis of practical philosophy*. Aldershot: Ashgate Publishers.

Alicke, M. D. (2000) Culpable control and the psychology of blame. *Psychological Bulletin* 126:556–574.

Alicke, M. D. (2008) Blaming badly. *Journal of Cognition and Culture* 8:179–186.

Beebe, J. R. & Buckwalter, W. (forthcoming) The epistemic side-effect effect. *Mind & Language*.

Buckwalter, W. (2010) Gender and epistemic intuition. Unpublished manuscript. City University of New York.

Byrne, R. (2005) *The rational imagination: How people create alternatives to reality*. Cambridge, MA: MIT Press.

Carey, S. & Spelke, E. (1996) Science and core knowledge. *Philosophy of Science* 63:515–533.

Chapman, L. & Chapman, J. (1967) Genesis of popular but erroneous psychodiagnostic observations. *Journal of Abnormal Psychology* 72:193–204.

Churchland, P. (1981) Eliminative materialism and the propositional attitudes. *Journal of Philosophy* 78(2):67–90.

Cushman, F. (2010) Judgments of morality, causation and intention: Assessing the Connections. Unpublished manuscript. Harvard University.

Cushman, F. & Mele, A. (2008) Intentional action: two-and-a-half folk concepts? In: *Experimental Philosophy*, ed. J. Knobe & S. Nichols. Oxford: Oxford University Press.

Cushman, F., Knobe, J. & Sinnott-Armstrong, W. (2008) Moral appraisals affect doing/allowing judgments. *Cognition* 108:353–380.

Damasio, A.R., Tranel, D. & Damasio, H. (1990) Individuals with socio-pathic behavior caused by frontal damage fail to respond autonomously to social stimuli. *Behavioural Brain Research* 41:81–94.

De Villiers, J., Stainton, R. & Szatmari, P. (2006) Pragmatic abilities in autism spectrum disorder: A case study in philosophy and the empirical. *Midwest Studies in Philosophy* 31:292–317.

Ditto, P., Pizarro, D. & Tannenbaum, D. (2009) Motivated moral reasoning. In: *Moral judgment and decision making: The psychology of learning and motivation*, ed. D. M. Bartels, C. W. Bauman, L. J. Skitka, & D. L. Medin. London: Elsevier.

Driver, J. (2008a) Attributions of causation and moral responsibility. In: *Moral psychology volume 2: The cognitive science of morality: Intuition and diversity*, ed. W. Sinnott-Armstrong. Cambridge, MA: MIT Press.

Driver, J. (2008b) Kinds of norms and legal causation: Reply to Knobe and Fraser and Deigh. In: *Moral psychology volume 2: The cognitive science of morality: Intuition and diversity*, ed. W. Sinnott-Armstrong. Cambridge, MA: MIT Press.

Feltz, A. & Cokely, E. (2007) An anomaly in intentional action ascription: More evidence of folk diversity. *Proceedings of the Cognitive Science Society*.

Goldman, A. (1970) *A theory of human action*. Upper Saddle River, NJ: Prentice-Hall, Inc.

Goldman, A. (2006) *Simulating minds: The philosophy, psychology and neuroscience of mindreading*. Oxford: Oxford University Press.

Gopnik, A. & Meltzoff, A. (1997) *Words, thoughts and theories*. Cambridge, MA: MIT Press.

Gopnik, A. & Wellman, H. (1992) Why the child's theory of mind really *is* a theory. *Mind & Language* 7:145–171.

Gopnik, A., Glymour, C., Sobel, D., Schulz, L., Kushnir, T. & Danks, D. (2004). A theory of causal learning in children: Causal maps and Bayes nets. *Psychological Review* 111:1–31.

Grice, H. P. (1989) *Studies in the way of words*. Cambridge, MA: Harvard University Press.

Guglielmo, S. & Malle, B. F. (2009a) Can unintended side-effects be intentional? Solving a puzzle in people's judgments of intentionality and morality. Unpublished manuscript. Brown University.

Guglielmo, S. & Malle, B. F. (2009b) The timing of blame and intentionality: Testing the moral bias hypothesis. Unpublished manuscript. Brown University.

Haidt, J. (2001) The emotional dog and its rational tail: A social intuitionist approach to moral judgment. *Psychological Review* 108:814–834.

Hindriks, F. A. (forthcoming) Intentional action and the praise-blame asymmetry. *Philosophical Quarterly*.

Hitchcock, C. & Knobe, J. (forthcoming) Cause and norm. *Journal of Philosophy*.

Inbar, Y., Pizarro, D. A., Knobe, J. & Bloom, P. (2009) Disgust sensitivity predicts intuitive disapproval of gays. *Emotion* 9:435–439.

Kahneman, D. & Miller, D. (1986). Norm theory: Comparing reality to its alternatives. *Psychological Review* 93:136–153.

Kelley, H. H. (1967)Attribution theory in social psychology. In: *Nebraska Symposium on Motivation*, ed. D. Levine. Lincoln: University of Nebraska Press.

Koenigs, M., Young, L., Adolphs, R., Tranel, D., Cushman, F., Hauser, M. & Damasio, A. (2007) Damage to the prefrontal cortex increases utilitarian moral judgements. *Nature* 446:908–911.

Knobe, J. (forthcoming) Action trees and moral judgment. *Topics in Cognitive Science*.

Knobe, J. (2003a) Intentional action and side effects in ordinary language. *Analysis* 63:190–193.

Knobe, J. (2004) Intention, intentional action and moral considerations. *Analysis* 64:181–187.

Knobe, J. (2003b) Intentional action in folk psychology: An experimental investigation. *Philosophical Psychology* 16:309–324.

Knobe, J. (2004a) Intention, intentional action and moral considerations. *Analysis* 64:181–187.

Knobe, J. (2004b) Folk psychology and folk morality: Response to critics. *Journal of Theoretical and Philosophical Psychology* 24(2):270–279.

Knobe, J. (2007) Reason explanation in folk psychology. *Midwest Studies in Philosophy* 31:90–107.
Knobe, J. & Burra, A. (2006) Intention and intentional action: A cross-cultural study. *Journal of Culture and Cognition* 6:113–132.
Knobe, J. & Fraser, B. (2008) Causal judgment and moral judgment: Two experiments. In: *Moral psychology volume 2: The cognitive science of morality: Intuition and diversity*, ed. W. Sinnott-Armstrong. Cambridge, MA: MIT Press.
Knobe, J. & Roedder, E. (forthcoming) The ordinary concept of valuing. *Philosophical Issues*.
Kunda, Z. (1990) The case for motivated reasoning. *Psychological Bulletin* 108(3):480–498.
Leslie, A., Knobe, J. & Cohen, A. (2006) Acting intentionally and the side-effect effect: 'Theory of mind' and moral judgment. *Psychological Science* 17:421–427.
Machery, E. (2008). The folk concept of intentional action: Philosophical and experimental issues. *Mind & Language* 23:165–189.
Martin, K. (2009) An experimental approach to the normativity of 'natural'. Paper presented at the Annual Meeting of the South Carolina Society for Philosophy, Rock Hill, SC.
McArthur, L. & Post, D. (1977). Figural emphasis and person perception. *Journal of Experimental Social Psychology* 13:520–535.
McCann, H. (2005) Intentional action and intending: Recent empirical studies. *Philosophical Psychology* 18:737–748.
McCloy, R. & Byrne, R. (2000). Counterfactual thinking about controllable events. *Memory and Cognition* 28:1071–1078.
Mikhail, J. (2007) Universal moral grammar: Theory, evidence, and the future. *Trends in Cognitive Sciences* 11:143–152.
Murphy, G. L. & Medin D. L. (1985) The roles of theories in conceptual coherence. *Psychological Review* 92:289–316.
N'gbala, A. & Branscombe, N. R. (1995). Mental simulation and causal attribution: When simulating an event does not affect fault assignment. *Journal of Experimental Social Psychology* 31:139–162.
Nadelhoffer, T. (2005) Skill, luck, control, and folk ascriptions of intentional action. *Philosophical Psychology* 18:343–354.
Nadelhoffer, T. (2006a) Bad acts, blameworthy agents, and intentional actions: Some problems for jury impartiality. *Philosophical Explorations* 9:203–220.
Nadelhoffer, T. (2006b) On trying to save the Simple View. *Mind & Language* 21:565–586.
Nanay, B. (forthcoming). Morality of modality? What does the attribution of intentionality depend on? *Canadian Journal of Philosophy*.
Nichols, S. & Ulatowski, J. (2007) Intuitions and individual differences: The Knobe effect revisited. *Mind & Language* 22:346–365.
Nyholm, S. (2009) Moral judgments and happiness. Unpublished manuscript. University of Michigan.
Pettit, D. & Knobe, J. (forthcoming) The pervasive impact of moral judgment. *Mind & Language*.
Phelan, M. & Sarkissian, H. (2008) The folk strike back; or, why you didn't do it intentionally, though it was bad and you knew it. *Philosophical Studies* 138:291–298.
Phillips, J. & Knobe, J. (2009) Moral judgments and intuitions about freedom. *Psychological Inquiry* 20:30–36.
Premack, D. & Woodruff, G. (1978). Does the chimpanzee have a theory of mind? *Behavioral and Brain Sciences* 1:515–526.

Roese, N. (1997). Counterfactual thinking. *Psychological Bulletin 121*:133–148.
Roxborough, C. & Cumby, J. (2009) Folk psychological concepts: causation. *Philosophical Psychology 22*:205–213.
Shepard, J. (2009) The side-effect effect in Knobe's environment case and the Simple View of intentionality. Unpublished manuscript. Georgia State University.
Sloman, S. (2005) *Causal models: How people think about the world and its alternatives.* Oxford: Oxford University Press.
Smedslund, J. (1963). The concept of correlation in adults. *Scandinavian Journal of Psychology 4*:165–173.
Solan, L. & Darley, J. (2001) Causation, contribution, and legal liability: An empirical study. *Law and Contemporary Problems 64*:265–298.
Surian, L., Baron-Cohen, S. & van der Lely, H. K. J. (1996) Are children with autism deaf to Gricean maxims? *Cognitive Neuropsychiatry 1*:55–71.
Sverdlik, S. (2004) Intentionality and moral judgments in Commonsense Thought about Action. *Journal of Theoretical and Philosophical Psychology 24*:224–236.
Tannenbaum, D., Ditto, P. & Pizarro, D. (2009) Different moral values produce different judgments of intentional action. Unpublished manuscript. University of California, Irvine.
Tetlock, P. E. (2002) Social-functionalist frameworks for judgment and choice: The intuitive politician, theologian, and prosecutor. *Psychological Review 109*:451–472.
Turner, J. (2004) Folk intuitions, asymmetry, and intentional side effects. *Journal of Theoretical and Philosophical Psychology 24*:214–219.
Ulatowski, J. (2009) Action under a description. Unpublished manuscript. University of Wyoming.
Woodward, J. (2004) *Making things happen: A theory of causal explanation.* Oxford: Oxford University Press.
Wright, J. C. & Bengson, J. (2009) Asymmetries in judgments of responsibility and intentional action. *Mind & Language 24*(1):24–50.
Young, L., Cushman, F., Adolphs, R., Tranel, D. & Hauser, M. (2006) Does emotion mediate the effect of an action's moral status on its intentional status? Neuropsychological evidence. *Journal of Cognition and Culture 6*:291–304.
Zalla, T., Machery, E. & Leboyer, M. (2010) Intentional action and moral judgment in Asperger Syndrome and high-functioning autism. Unpublished manuscript. Institut Jean-Nicod.

10

Causation, Norm Violation, and Culpable Control[*]

Mark Alicke, David Rose, and Dori Bloom

Human brains do spectacular things. They solve complex logical puzzles, compose symphonic masterpieces, conceive technological marvels, and create enduring artworks, for starters. But before they can embark on these prodigies, human brains must achieve something that they share in common with all brains—they must evaluate and differentiate which creatures, objects, and conditions will facilitate their prospects and well-being, and which will do them harm. Evaluation is the most fundamental component of human judgment[1] and one of the most important cognitive capacities for survival.

Virtually all meaningful human actions are automatically evaluated.[2] These evaluative reactions intrude on the judgments and attributions that people make about their own and others' behavior. So, when people make focal judgments about the components of a human act, such as whether it caused a particular outcome, whether the outcome was foreseen or foreseeable, whether the action was intentional or involuntary, and whether incapacities or situational constraints excuse or mitigate it, they are influenced by their peripheral evaluative reactions to the actor, the actor's behavior, and the outcomes that ensue.[3] As a result, when people are asked to identify, for example, the primary cause of an event, they accord privileged status to actions that arouse positive or negative evaluations. In this way, causal attributions reflect a desire to praise or denigrate those whose actions we applaud or deride.

At least, that is our story. There are two prominent alternatives to this assumption about the primacy of evaluation, the first fairly implausible in light of the extant data, the second much in favor. The less credible view conflates how action components *should* be evaluated (in accordance with the criteria of Anglo-American jurisprudence and rational prescriptions for justice and fairness) with how people actually evaluate others. These prescriptive models stipulate that blame and responsibility require causation, intention, foresight or foreseeability, and the absence of mitigating or extenuating circumstances.[4] The primary value of such models is to translate fundamental legal and philosophical tenets into normative models of blame. Such models do a reasonable job of predicting blame or responsibility ascriptions under ideal conditions.[5] They falter, however, once the funk and muck of real life events are transported to the judgment task, primarily because, in our view, they fail to account for the contribution of evaluative reactions to the judgment process.[6]

The second alternative pertains specifically to causal judgments rather than to blame and responsibility per se. According to this view, of the various causal influences that compete for recognition, observers will elevate the most unusual or abnormal condition to primary causal status. This view harkens back to Hart and Honoré's classic treatment of causation in the law,[7] was resurrected and further developed in Kahneman and Miller's norm theory,[8] and is the basis of much current thinking and research on counterfactual reasoning.[9] Because an event can have numerous abnormal causes, further refinements are needed, and have been supplied. One view is that people grant privileged status to causal conditions that, if altered, would prevent a harmful or unfortunate outcome.[10] The second, related view is that people favor causes that identify an intervention that would alter the event's outcome.[11] Because people are more likely to imagine interventions that change negative events into positive ones than the reverse, this view is similar to the first in that it entails citing the cause that, if changed, would negate the harmful outcome.

Both of these views, therefore, assume that causal ascriptions are based on a species of counterfactual reasoning. This reasoning highlights interventions that would undo the outcome that occurred, especially when the outcome is harmful or undesirable. In most cases, the prepotent cause will be the one whose negation improves the present state of affairs. Hitchcock and Knobe have explicitly endorsed this intervention approach as an alternative to what we call the *evaluation* (and they call the *blame*) *perspective*.[12] On their view, the causal candidate that deviates most from the normal state of affairs will be identified as the primary cause because it provides the most suitable target for intervention. We refer to their approach and its cognates as the *norm-violation view*.

Before reporting the results of the studies that we conducted to distinguish between our evaluation perspective and Hitchcock and Knobe's norm-violation view, we want to clarify the basis of our disagreement with Hitchcock and Knobe's position to avoid exaggerating the differences in our views and to elaborate the specific assumptions that underlie our position.

1. CLARIFYING THE BASIS OF THE DEBATE

Hitchcock and Knobe's analysis of how laypeople ascribe causation emphasizes the importance of identifying abnormal conditions that, if altered, would restore an event to its more normal state. Discerning such intervention points highlights ways to improve one's own and others' prospects. Hitchcock and Knobe identify three types of norm violations that serve this purpose. First, abnormality in a statistical sense can be informative. Changing the behavior of people who do unusual things effectively restores an event to its normal state, and this capacity to perform statistically abnormal actions enhances their perceived causal potency. Second, Hitchcock and Knobe clearly recognize that moral or ethical transgressions provide a basis for heightened causal ascriptions. Finally, norm violations also include deviations from proper functioning. A malfunctioning machine, for example, would hinder a company's operations. Hitchcock and Knobe assume that the distinctions among these types of norm violations are relatively unimportant and that what ultimately matters is whether altering a particular causal candidate (for example, fixing the machine) restores an event to its normal state and makes a bad situation better.

Because Hitchcock and Knobe clearly recognize that moral or evaluative judgments matter, our main point of contention concerns why they matter. We agree with Hitchcock and Knobe that norm violations are almost certainly the primary determinants of causal citations for events that do not involve human agents. Similarly, we concur that norm violations rule the causal roost for benign events that lack nefarious motives, undesirable or reckless actions, or harmful outcomes. We grant, therefore, that norm violations suffice to explain heightened causal efficacy for some types of events.

But the areas in which we disagree with Knobe and Hitchcock are significant in that they involve the events to which most of their examples apply, namely, those involving undesirable or harmful behavior. The crux of the disagreement concerns the fundamental motivation that drives the ordinary person's construal of social events. Identifying ways to improve things that go wrong has obvious instrumental value and may consciously guide much of people's behavioral analyses. Nevertheless, primitive motives for revenge and retribution weigh heavily in human affairs and can impede rational decision strategies. We assume that blame represents a symbolic form of retribution. Blame expresses disapprobation for the actor's motives or actions and, to borrow Joel Feinberg's terminology, "stains" the actor's character.[13] Because people generally prefer to view themselves as fair and rational, they must support these blame attributions with evidence. Exaggerating an actor's causal role in an event is one way this can be achieved. We elaborate this assumption below in the context of outlining the *culpable-control model of blame*.

2. THE CULPABLE-CONTROL MODEL

The culpable-control model assumes that people generally try to follow cultural prescriptions for ascribing blame. In short, they seek to ascertain whether a person negligently or intentionally caused, or could have caused, harm to another's person or property, and if so, whether situational pressures (for example, coercion or provocation) or personal incapacities (for example, ignorance or mental illness) were sufficient to excuse or mitigate blame. These considerations comprise three linkages (see Figure 1) that represent distinct ways of exerting control during an action sequence: a link from mind to behavior (did the behavior occur on purpose?), from behavior to consequence (how strong was the causal connection between the actor's behavior and the outcomes that occurred?), and from mind to consequence (did the consequences come about as foreseen)?

In addition to assessing actual control, observers also estimate potential control, which involves judging whether the consequences that occurred *should have* been foreseen. Potential control is important in assessing negligent behavior in which harmful consequences are effected unintentionally but irresponsibly. Taken together, these linkages comprise assessments of *behavior control* (acting purposively), *causal control* (causing one or more harmful outcomes), and *outcome control* (causing the outcome in the desired and foreseen manner), and represent the degree of actual or potential control an individual exerted (or could have exerted) over an event.

At the same time that people consciously assess these aspects of control, they also spontaneously evaluate the actor, his or her actions, and the outcomes that occurred. We assume that spontaneous evaluations occur in response to the central elements of control (behavior, causal, and outcome), as well as to peripheral features of the event such as the actor's or victim's race or character, or the degree of harm that occurred. For example, an observer might react unfavorably to the knowledge that an actor spent a long time planning a despicable act (behavior control) or to the fact that the act was committed by someone who belongs to a disliked ethnic or racial group. Some evaluations are virtually endemic to control estimations, especially when assessing potential control. It is difficult, for example, to isolate negative reactions to what someone did or caused from determinations of what they should have done

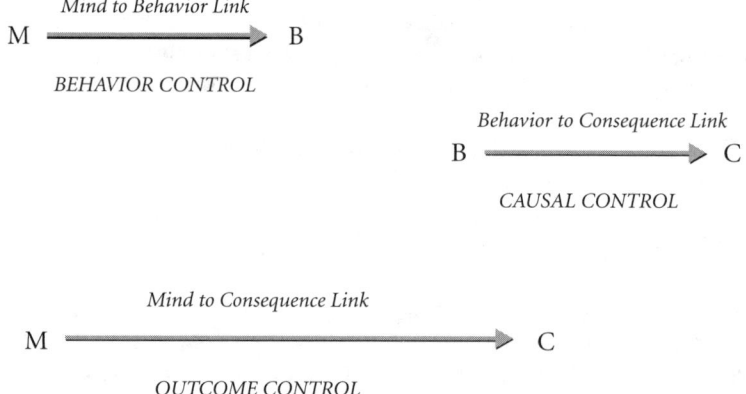

Figure 10.1. Structural Linkages among Mental, Behavioral, and Consequence Elements

or known, especially under highly ambiguous circumstances. When spontaneous evaluations are sufficiently strong, the culpable-control model assumes that the control elements (behavior, causal, and outcome) that observers analyze are processed in a "blame validation" mode. Blame validation entails either exaggerating a person's actual or potential control over an event to justify the desired blame judgment or altering the threshold for how much control is required for blame.

The phrase "culpable control" reflects the fact that the desire to blame or find someone culpable intrudes on assessments of mental, behavior, and outcome control. In a sense, culpability, which is supposed to be the output of the judgment, becomes part of the process of assessing the blame criteria. Much of the current debate on blame and causation is couched in terms of two simple models: blame attributions determine causal attributions (blame → cause), or the reverse (cause → blame).[14] The culpable-control model is usually characterized as endorsing the former relationship. However, a more complete characterization of the culpable control model would be: negative evaluative reaction → initial blame hypothesis → blame validation processing → enhanced causal control → blame. In other words, negative evaluations or spontaneous reactions lead to the hypothesis that the source of the evaluations is blameworthy and to an active desire to blame that source. This desire, in turn, leads observers to interpret the available evidence in a way that supports their blame hypothesis. In the present discussion, the primary avenue for supporting or validating a blame hypothesis is to increase perceptions of causal control, but more generally it can also entail enhancing perceptions of behavior and outcome control.

The ultimate effect of perceived control and negative evaluations on blame is a compensatory one. We assume that some level of behavior, causal, and outcome control is required to blame an actor for an actual or attempted offense. Even extremely prejudiced observers are unlikely to blame someone whose behavior was completely accidental or who was causally unconnected to the harmful consequences. However, given a requisite baseline level of perceived control, strong negative evaluations increase blame ascriptions and alter judgments of the control elements that should, ideally, be assessed independently in ascribing blame. On the other hand, when the control evidence is overwhelming, there is scant opportunity for negative evaluations to skew the blame process.

3. STUDY 1: DOCTORS VIOLATING NORMS FORTUITOUSLY

Our first study was based on one that Hitchcock and Knobe conducted to illustrate their norm-violation position. In this scenario, an intern wants to administer a new drug to a patient with kidney problems but must obtain the signature of the pharmacist and the attending physician. The pharmacist signs off, but the physician realizes that the hospital has banned the drug due to its dangerous side effects. Nevertheless, the physician consents, and the patient recovers with no adverse reactions. When asked to rate the physician's and pharmacist's causal roles in the patient's recovery, participants gave higher ratings to the physician. Since the outcome was favorable, Hitchcock and Knobe argue that the culpable-control model cannot account for the findings, because people do not blame others for favorable outcomes. On their view, heightened causal attributions occur because the physician's behavior is counternormative. As they state it, "Our own account makes no mention of any sort of moral judgment regarding the effect. Instead, it posits a role for judgments about whether the candidate cause was itself a norm violation."[15] Specifically, the physician's deviation from the normal state of affairs, regardless of the outcome of the event, leads people to view it as a suitable target for intervention, which in turn leads them to select him as the primary cause.

We believe that the culpable-control model provides a more compelling account of causal attributions in the physician scenario. Hitchcock and Knobe would agree that the physician's behavior provides a basis for negative evaluations, although they would emphasize the counter-normativeness of the physician's behavior. The culpable-control model, however, assumes that this negative evaluation encourages observers to believe that the physician is blameworthy and that they seek to validate their desire to blame him. The nature of the outcome, rather than being irrelevant, as Hitchcock and Knobe maintain, provides a basis for either justifying the desire to blame the physician or for attenuating that desire. A negative outcome such as the patient's death would fuel the desire to blame, which would be reflected in heightened causal attributions to the physician. On the other hand, a positive outcome such as occurred in Hitchcock and Knobe's scenario would attenuate the physician's perceived causal role. These assumptions could not be tested in Hitchcock and Knobe's scenario, because they included only a positive outcome condition and simply compared the physician's perceived causal influence to that of the pharmacist, whose actions were comparatively normal.

A more complete analysis of causal attributions in Hitchcock and Knobe's scenario requires conditions that vary both the normativeness of the physician's behavior and the nature of the outcome. To this end, we expanded Hitchcock and Knobe's scenario to include conditions in which the physician's behavior was normative (that is, he followed the hospital's policy and refused to administer the drug) or counternormative (that is, he administered the drug, as in Hitchcock and Knobe's scenario) and in which the patient experienced a positive outcome (that is, he recovered with no side effects, as in Hitchcock and Knobe), a negative outcome (that is, death), or no outcome information was provided. We assessed ratings of the physician's causal impact on the patient's outcome as well as positive versus negative evaluations of the physician's decision to administer or to refrain from administering the drug.

In this context, the main difference between the culpable-control and norm-violation views concerns the role of outcome information in causal attributions. Hitchcock and Knobe stipulate that whereas the culpable-control model is based on the goodness or badness of the event's outcomes (since people can only be blamed for bad outcomes), their norm-violation position applies to behaviors rather than outcomes. As the previous discussion of the culpable-control perspective makes clear, this does not characterize the model quite accurately. Positive and especially negative evaluative reactions can occur in relation to the actor's intentions, motives, actions, and outcomes as well as to a host of other features such as his or her race, gender, or personality. Nevertheless, what is most germane for present purposes is that the valences of the outcomes *do* matter in the culpable-control model. Because Hitchcock and Knobe claim that only behavioral norm violations count in causal ascriptions, they would predict no effects due to the event's outcomes.

The culpable-control model, however, makes specific predictions regarding the interplay between the normalcy of the physician's behavior and the outcomes that it produces. When the physician evokes negative evaluations by violating the hospital's policy, the death of the patient counts as a severely aggravating circumstance and raises the physician's perceived causal influence beyond where it would reside if he followed the hospital's policy and produced the same outcome. By contrast, the physician who behaves appropriately by following the hospital's policy is less likely to be penalized for the patient's death. Specifically, there should be a statistical interaction such that the physician who violates hospital policy is seen as more causal when the patient dies than when the patient lives, whereas no such difference should occur for the physician who follows hospital policy.

Results. The findings of Study 1 are illustrated in Figures 2 and 3;[16] the first figure depicts ratings of blame/praise, whereas the second shows causation ratings.

Significant interactions between the drug decision (that is, to violate the norm and administer the drug or to adhere to the norm and refuse the drug) and the outcome of the decision (that is, recovery, death, or no outcome) on evaluations (that is, blame/praise) of the physician's decision, $F(2, 313) = 11.28$, $p < .0001$, and on ratings of his causal involvement, $F(1, 213) = 13.05$, $p < .001$, supported culpable-control predictions. These findings show that when the

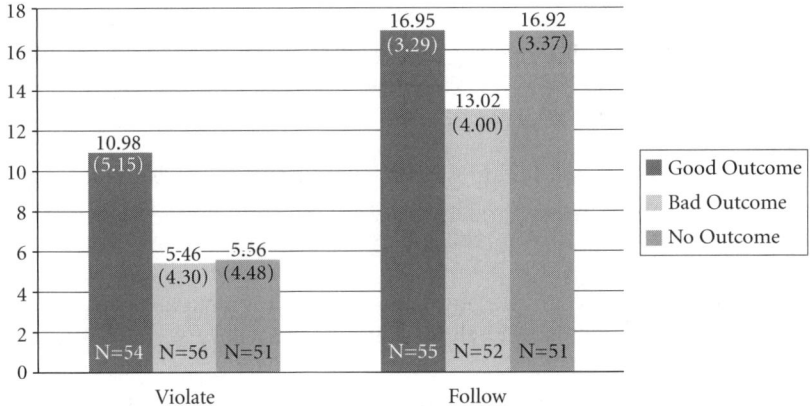

Figure 10.2. Blame/Praise Ratings[17]

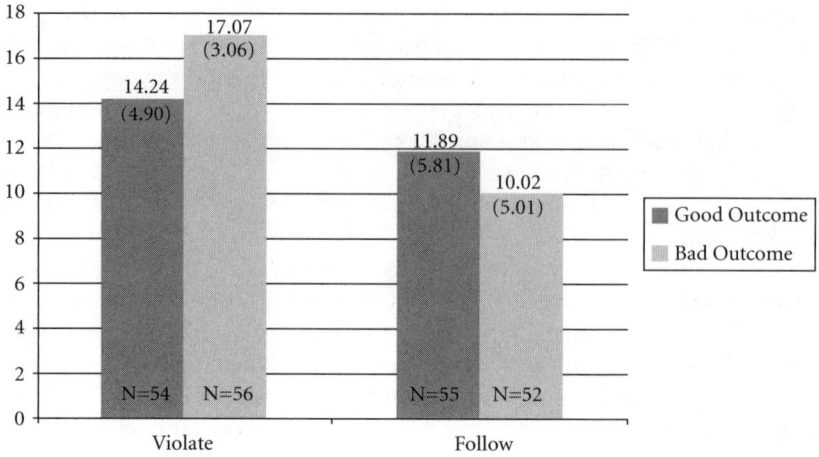

Figure 10.3. Causal Ratings[17]

physician violated hospital policy, he was viewed more negatively when the patient died than when he lived, $F(1, 313) = 48.59$, $p < .0001$, and was viewed as more causal in the former case than in the latter, $F(1, 213) = 9.59$, $p < .01$. When the physician followed hospital policy, evaluations of his decision were relatively favorable regardless of the outcome, although they were significantly reduced by the fact of the patient's death, $F(1, 313) = 23.92$, $p < .0001$.

The pattern of results displayed in Figure 2 shows the importance of positive and negative evaluations of the physician's behavior and the outcome that the patient experiences. First, the physician who violated the hospital's policy but had the fortuitous outcome of the patient recovering (as in Hitchcock and Knobe's scenario) was viewed far more negatively (that is, as relatively more blameworthy) than the physician who respected the hospital's policy and obtained the same outcome, $F(1, 313) = 56.28$, $p < .0001$. In fact, the physician who violated hospital policy and obtained a positive outcome was viewed even more negatively than the physician who followed hospital policy but obtained a negative outcome (that is, the patient's death), $F(1, 104) = 6.38$, $p = .012$. Clearly, violating the hospital's policy is by itself a potent source of blameworthiness in this context.

Comparisons between the no-outcome conditions were also revealing. As we assumed, the physician who violated hospital policy was viewed very negatively, whereas the physician who followed hospital policy was viewed very positively, $F(1, 313) = 188.24$, $p < .0001$. However, the patient's recovery had no corresponding effect when the physician was already evaluated positively, in that favorable evaluations were about equal in the recovery and no-outcome conditions.

In general, therefore, the findings of this study are consistent with the culpable-control model and very difficult to explain from a norm-violation perspective. First, the data support the culpable-control model's assumption that there are two important sources of evaluation in this scenario: the physician's decision to go along with or to violate the hospital's policy, and the patient's death or survival. The results show that the physician in Hitchcock and Knobe's original scenario would have been viewed very negatively if not for the fortuitous outcome of the patient's recovery, and he was not viewed very positively even with this happy consequence. These findings are consistent with the culpable-control assumption that the physician's decision to contravene hospital policy provided a strong initial basis for blame. When the patient died as a result, this negative outcome counted as a severely aggravating circumstance that further elevated the physician's perceived causal role. However, when the physician was viewed positively for following the hospital's policy, he was not viewed as any more causal as a result of the patient's death in comparison to when the patient survived. Since the norm-violation view explicitly disavows the influence of outcomes on causal judgment, it cannot explain this interaction pattern.

4. STUDY 2: A DIRECT TEST OF NORMS VERSUS EVALUATION

The most direct way to adjudicate between the norm-violation and culpable-control views is to implement a design that varies the goodness or badness of an actor's behavior simultaneously with whether it violates or adheres to a norm. We therefore created a story in which a group of students who lived on the same floor of a dormitory obtained a copy of the final exam for their biology class. The students either cheated or did not cheat on the test. One student, John Granger, went along with the group (norm condition) or did not go along with the group (counternorm condition). This design, therefore, included four conditions: (a) Granger follows the local norm and cheats on the test (norm, bad); (b) Granger follows the local norm and does not cheat on the test (norm, good); (c) Granger deviates from the local norm and cheats on the test (counternorm, bad); (d) Granger deviates from the local norm and refuses to cheat on the test (counternorm, good).

The biology class comprises 80 students and is graded on a curve such that 20 people will receive a grade of A, 20 a grade of B, 20 a grade of C, and 20 students will receive a D. Granger's score was the 20th highest score in the class, which means he was the last student to receive a grade of A. The 21st student was a pre-med student who received a B and , as a result, missed the GPA cutoff she needed to get into the medical school she was hoping for by .07 GPA points. Participants were asked to indicate the extent to which they thought Granger was the cause of the student failing to meet the medical-school cutoff and the degree to which he was to blame and also to rate the goodness or badness of his actions.

Results. Our most fundamental prediction was that judgments of causation and blame would be based more on whether Granger's behavior was good or bad than whether it was normative or counter-normative. The results confirmed

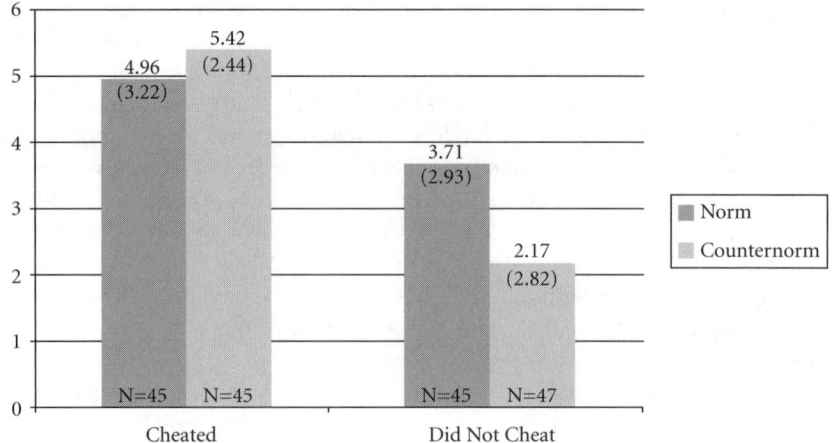

Figure 10.4. Blame Ratings[17]

this prediction. Granger was seen as less causal when his behavior was good ($M = 3.37$) than when it was bad ($M = 5.20$), $F(1, 178) = 17.12$, $p < .0001$, and he was also blamed less when his behavior was good ($M = 2.92$) than when it was bad ($M = 5.19$), $F(1, 178) = 27.98$, $p < .0001$. Overall, there was no main effect of whether his behavior was normative or counternormative on causal ratings, $F(1, 178) = 2.10$, $p < .15$, or on blame, $F(1, 178) = 1.59$, $p < .21$.

However, these findings were qualified by an interaction that revealed the same pattern on causal judgments, $F(1, 178) = 4.24$, $p < .05$; blame judgments, $F(1, 178) = 5.58$, $p < .02$; and evaluative judgments, $F(1, 178) = 38.96$, $p < .001$ (see Figures 4, 5, and 6).

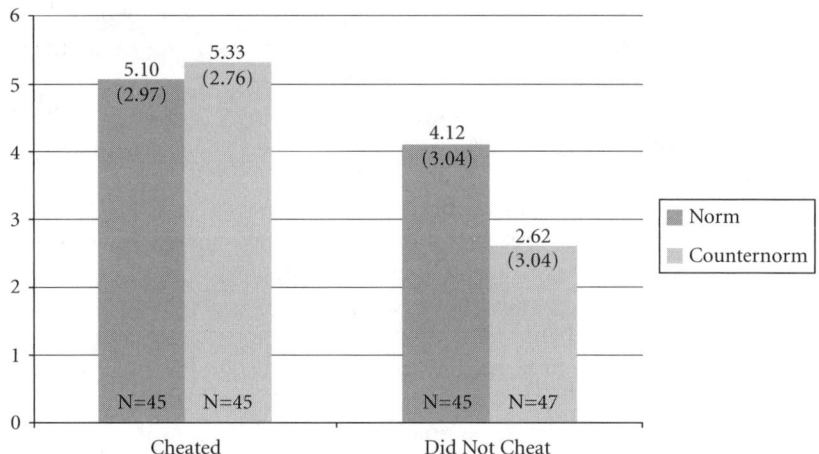

Figure 10.5. Causal Ratings[17]

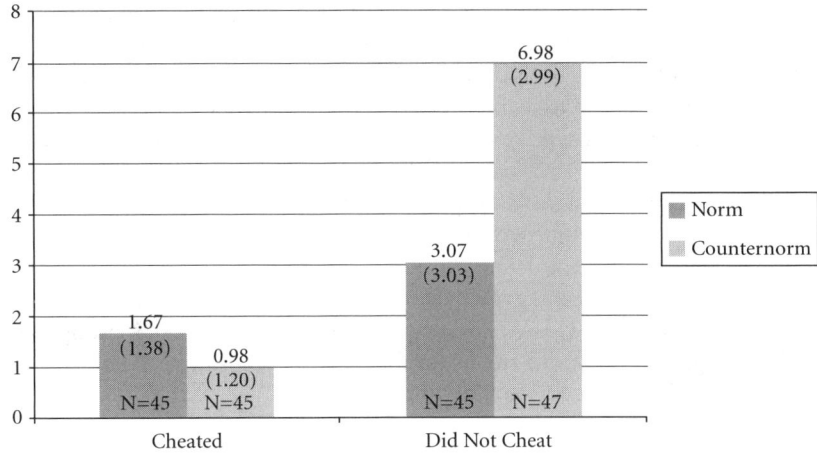

Figure 10.6. Evaluative Ratings[17]

When Granger cheated on the test, his causal impact and blameworthiness were uninfluenced by whether he was the only one who cheated or one of a group of cheaters. However, when he behaved admirably by refusing to cheat, he was seen as less causal and less blameworthy when he was the only one who took the moral high ground than when everyone else also refrained from cheating.

These data show clearly that causal judgments for behavioral outcomes are not determined by norm violations alone. Whether a norm violation influences causal judgment depends on the way it is evaluated. Clearly, people can violate norms by doing good things or bad things. When an actor behaves badly, in this instance by cheating, his perceived causal influence and blameworthiness are maximized regardless of what everyone else did. Essentially, participants apply a deontological principle that states "do not cheat" regardless of what others are doing. However, things are a bit more nuanced for positive behaviors. People who go against the crowd to do the right thing are rewarded by being assigned *less* causal impact and decreased blameworthiness. Specifically, the actor who refused to cheat when everyone else on his floor cheated was seen as less causal and less blameworthy for the prospective medical student's misfortune. In contrast to the norm-violation view, which predicts that actions that violate norms will be seen as *more* causal, we have shown that a person who behaves admirably by violating the norm is seen as less causal and less blameworthy as a result.

It could be argued that there are conflicting norms in the situation that we created. That is, in addition to the local norms within a group of individuals who chose to cheat or not to cheat, there are general social norms that proscribe cheating. One might say that the student who violated local norms by not cheating nevertheless honored general proscriptions against cheating. Indeed, conflicting norms are the rule rather than the exception in evaluating undesirable human actions. In Hitchcock and Knobe's physician scenario, for example, the physician who violated hospital policy by administering a drug that he thought would help the patient could be said to have followed a general norm of "do what is best to help others."

Our point, which is strongly supported by the data we have presented, is that the effects of either local or general norm violations on causal judgments depend upon the evaluative tone (goodness or badness) of the behaviors they entail. The student who violated local norms of cheating was seen as less causal not because he adhered to a general norm per se but because he did something good and praiseworthy, namely, exhibited integrity and independence. However, for the student who cheated either solely or as part of a group, local and general norm violations made no difference to causal attributions, since both violations were equally bad and blameworthy.

5. STUDY 3: BLAME → CAUSE, OR CAUSE → BLAME?

In her comparison of the culpable-control model with Knobe's view,[17] Driver suggests that the culpable-control model entails that blame judgments precede and determine causal ascriptions (that is, blame → cause), whereas Knobe's model stipulates the opposite relationship (that is, cause → blame).[18] As we discussed earlier, the culpable-control assumption is a bit more complex than this (specifically, we have suggested: negative evaluative reaction → initial blame hypothesis → blame-validation processing → enhanced causal control → blame), but we agree with Driver that demonstrating the viability of the blame → cause model would provide further support for the culpable-control position. While resolving this issue will require numerous studies with diverse methodologies, we designed a third study, one purpose of which was to provide preliminary support for the blame → cause argument.

We created a new scenario in which a homeowner shot and killed an intruder who, unbeknownst to the homeowner, turned out to be an innocent and sympathetic victim or a dangerous criminal. The culpable-control model predicts that, with all other things being equal, an actor who harms a likable victim will be seen as more causal than one who harms a dislikable victim. This prediction is based on the assumption that people will react more negatively to someone who harms a likable victim and will therefore augment the actor's perceived causal role to express their disapprobation. Because the norm-violation view explicitly states that outcomes of events do not matter in causal assignment, it would predict no difference between these conditions, since the antecedent event—that of the homeowner shooting a presumed intruder—is identical in both cases.

According to the story (see appendix), the victim, Edward Poole, was either a dangerous ex-convict who broke into a home (negative characterization) or a physician who entered a home at the neighbor's request to feed her cat while she was away (positive characterization). In both cases, Poole was shot by one of the homeowners, John Turnbull (who came home unexpectedly and did not know of his wife's arrangement), who confronted Poole as he was climbing the stairs inside the house. The most basic prediction is that Turnbull will be blamed more, and seen as more the cause of the victim's death, when the victim is characterized positively as opposed to negatively. In addition, we ran a series of statistical tests in order to provide some support for the blame → cause model.

We were also interested in establishing boundary conditions for the hypothesized victim-characterization effect. We assume that effects based on evaluative reactions will be canceled when an actor's causal role is unambiguous, that is, when an actor obviously is, or obviously is not, an important causal contributor to an event. To test this, we created a causal-overdetermination condition in which the external circumstances negated the actor's causal influence. Because people generally do not stray far from the objective evidence, we assume that they will refrain from ascribing heightened causality when the data unequivocally fail to support such a judgment. However, we also contend that this restraint is tenuous. Given even a small degree of ambiguity, evaluative reactions again should exhibit substantial effects on causal assessment.

Three versions of the circumstances surrounding Poole's death were created. In the first, an autopsy revealed that Poole suffered a brain aneurysm virtually at the moment that he was shot by Turnbull. Under these circumstances, even those who have strong reactions to an innocent victim's death will be reluctant to ascribe more causal influence to Turnbull, because his behavior was unnecessary to produce Poole's death in the immediate situation. Accordingly, we expected to obtain uniformly low causal ratings in these conditions regardless of whether Poole was characterized negatively or positively.

Once these constraints on causal interpretation are loosened, however, effects of Poole's negative-versus-positive characterization should be observed. In the second version of the story, participants were told that the autopsy indicated that Poole was seriously ill and would have died from a brain tumor within a few weeks. In contrast to the previous condition, we assumed that the constraint in this condition—that Poole would have died in a few weeks from a brain tumor—would introduce sufficient causal ambiguity to restore positive and negative evaluation effects. Thus, we predicted higher causal ratings in the condition in which Poole was characterized positively than in which he was characterized negatively. In fact, we predicted that these effects would be approximately equal to those in the control condition in which no further information was provided about Poole's medical condition. In sum, we wanted to show that only severe constraints on causal judgment (that is, causal overdetermination), and not moderate ones (that is, the victim would have died in the near future), mitigate effects of positive and negative characterizations on causal assignment. Findings such as these would suggest a pervasive influence of evaluation effects on causal judgment and would show that they are eradicated only when objective information about countervailing causal forces is exceptionally compelling.

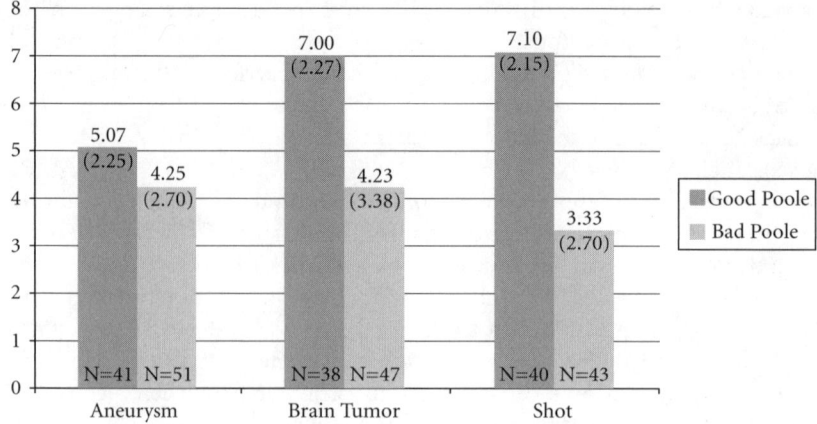

Figure 10.7. Blame Ratings[19]

In addition to asking participants to indicate the extent to which they thought that Turnbull was the cause of Poole's death, we asked them to indicate the extent to which they thought that he was to blame. We expected to find the same pattern of effects on blame as on causation.

Results. As the culpable-control model predicts, the homeowner was both blamed more, $F(1, 254) = 55.22$, $p <.0001$, and seen as more the cause of the victim's death, $F(1, 254) = 13.53$, $p <.0001$, when the victim was characterized positively as opposed to negatively. The more specific contrasts were also consistent with our predictions (see Figures 7 and 8).

The difference between the positive and negative victim-characterization conditions was significant when the victim's death was delayed by two weeks, both on ratings of Turnbull's causal influence, $F(1, 254) = 4.109$, $p <.05$, and

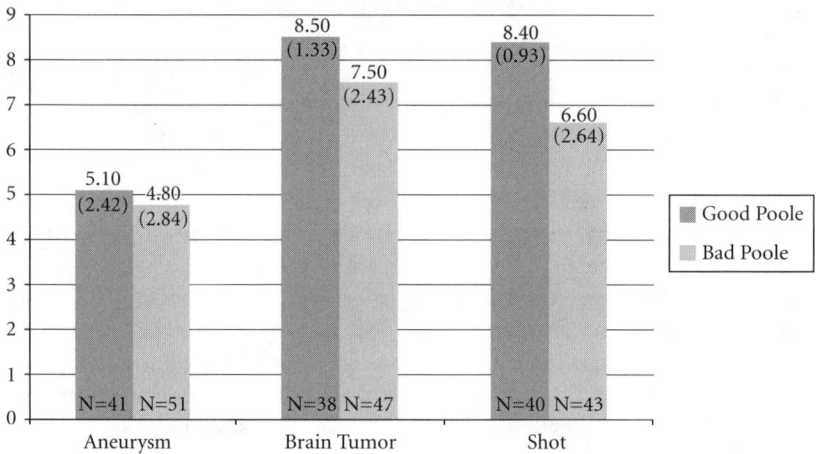

Figure 10.8. Causal Ratings

on his blameworthiness, $F(1, 254) = 4.804$, $p < .01$. These same findings were obtained on ratings of causation, $F(1, 254) = 13.381$, $p < .0001$, and blameworthiness, $F(1, 254) = 41.822$, $p < .0001$, when the victim died immediately after being shot by the actor without any further qualification. As we predicted, however, this effect was not obtained when the victim would have died anyway in the immediate situation due to an aneurysm ($p > .05$).

Finally, we provide two independent statistical arguments for the plausibility of the blame → cause explanation.[19] The first approach was to assess whether blame mediates the effects of Poole's character on causal judgments.[20] A regression model with only Poole as a predictor of causal judgments showed that Poole was a significant predictor of causal judgments (*Beta* = .196, $p = .001$). Additionally, a regression model with Poole as a predictor of blame was significant (*Beta* = .404, $p = .000$). But when blame was added to the model, the effect of Poole's character on causal judgments was eradicated (Blame: *Beta* = .368, $p = .000$; Poole: *Beta* = .048, $p = .449$). A Sobel test[21] shows that the reduction in the effects of Poole's character on causal judgments when blame is added to the model is highly significant ($Z = 4.4913$, $p = .000$). This pattern demonstrates that blame mediates the effects of Poole's character on causal judgments (Figure 9) and provides one source of evidence for the argument that blame → cause.[22]

A separate statistical argument suggesting that blame → cause involves testing whether or not cause is a collider. A collider is produced whenever at least two variables serve as independent inputs into a third variable. Testing whether cause is a collider involves testing whether the mode of the victim's death (aneurysm, brain tumor, shot) is a significant predictor of causal judgments and whether blame judgments for each mode of death (aneurysm, brain tumor, shot) are independent. A regression model with mode of death as a predictor of causal judgments shows that death is a significant predictor of causal judgments (*Beta* = .397, $p = .000$). And an analysis of variance with death as a predictor of blame was nonsignificant, $F(2, 254) = 1.874$, $p = .156$. But most importantly, Bonferroni post hoc tests showed that blame judgments were no different between the aneurysm, brain tumor, and shot conditions (aneurysm versus brain tumor, $p > .05$; aneurysm versus shot, $p > .05$; brain tumor versus shot, $p > .05$). This suggests that death and blame are independent causes of

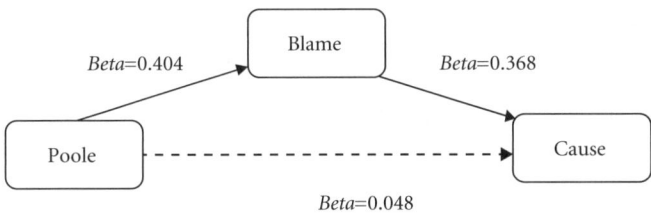

Figure 10.9. Mediation Model[i]

causal judgments, which establishes cause as a collider (Figure 10). This provides a separate source of evidence for the blame → cause argument.

Thus, the two independent statistical arguments we have provided suggest that blame → cause.

6. CULPABLE CONTROL, NORM VIOLATIONS, AND CAUSATION: AN OVERVIEW

We have argued that norm violations are insufficient to account for causal attributions for human events that involve undesirable behavior and/or harm-doing. The data presented in this paper cast serious doubt on whether any evidence has yet been adduced to show that the norm-violation account is a better model of ordinary causal attributions than the culpable-control model. What we have demonstrated is that blameworthiness has a pervasive influence on causal judgment and that it can account for the types of effects that Hitchcock and Knobe describe.

Whereas Hitchcock and Knobe view moral or evaluative considerations as one species of norm violation, we view norm violations as one aspect of evaluative judgment. One might say that we are barking up the same tree but from different sides. Nevertheless, the distinction is a vital one. The norm-violation position depicts causal judgment as a largely rational process whereby people seek to identify actions that, if changed, would improve an undesirable or harmful state of affairs. Moral or evaluative considerations are merely one type of norm violation that can help to identify where interventions would remedy a bad situation. In other words, by emphasizing an actor's wrongdoing as a causal factor, observers disclose how to improve his or her future behavior.

We see three primary limitations to the norm-violation position as Hitchcock and Knobe have stated it. First, like us, they advocate a functional view of causation as it applies to human events, especially harmful ones. However, in promoting interventions as the primary motive in causal assignment, they liken

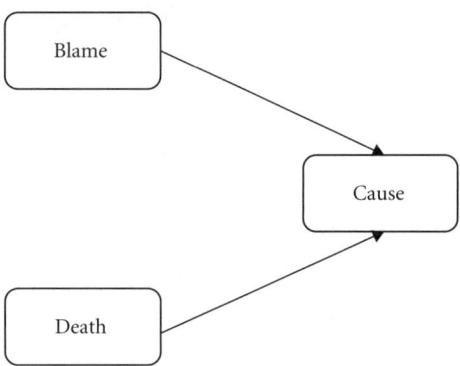

Figure 10.10. Model of Cause as a Collider

people to engineers who appraise nonoptimal situations with an eye toward improving them. In distinguishing among different criteria for assessing causation, Feinberg has referred to this as the "engineering criterion."[23] The engineering criterion is a perfectly apt metaphor for causal analysis when there is no strong basis for positive or negative evaluations, but as we have shown, norm violations alone cannot account for variations in causal ascriptions when a basis for positive or negative evaluation is present. Consider again the scenario in which the physician violated the hospital's norm by recommending a drug that was prohibited. We agree with Hitchcock and Knobe that if interventions could be identified to discourage doctors from violating hospital policies, patients generally would have better outcomes. But as the findings of our second study suggest, if observers had applauded rather than disapproved of the physician's actions, they would have seen him as less, rather than as more, causal for his intervention. In our view, the "person as engineer" metaphor applies best to relatively mundane human actions, rather than to the events that fascinate philosophers, lawyers, psychologists, and other inquiring minds. For more interesting cases of ordinary causal judgment, we would replace the engineering criterion with what Feinberg calls the "stain criterion," thereby transforming the "person as engineer" into the "person as evaluator."

The second limitation of the norm-violation approach as an account of causal judgment in human affairs is the claim that such violations refer only to behaviors and not to other elements of harmful events such as outcomes. This seems like an arbitrary stipulation: most psychological theories of counterfactual reasoning acknowledge that norms apply both to actions and outcomes.[24] Thus, in thinking about how harmful events could have turned out differently, observers consider different paths that could have been taken and different consequences that could have been achieved.

While this weakness can be rectified simply by extending the norm-violation view to encompass outcomes, our third issue with a pure norm-violation approach is that it depicts causal judgment as a highly rational, controlled process. Affective responses have no special role, and evaluations are important only as applied to moral transgressions, which constitute one type of norm violation. Presumably, observers scrutinize an actor's selfish, greedy, or malevolent actions primarily because they contain the blueprints to remedy a harmful event. By contrast, the culpable-control model assumes that evaluative reactions accompany virtually all human events in which good or bad actions or outcomes occur. These evaluative reactions can and do influence causal judgment.[25] Some evaluative reactions are emotionally charged, such as when an actor behaves despicably or produces horrendous outcomes, whereas others may simply entail goodness-or-badness assessments with little emotion. Although affectively charged events are probably more susceptible to bias than comparatively mundane ones, evaluative reactions generally provide the opportunity for pervasive biases in causal judgment.

For a norm-violation approach to have priority over an evaluation-based model, it must provide at least some examples in which the influence of norm violations on causal judgment cannot be explained with reference to the praiseworthiness or blameworthiness of some element of the action sequence. Another example that figures prominently in Hitchcock and Knobe's norm-violation position is a scenario in which administrative assistants and faculty members routinely take pens from a receptionist's desk. The administrators are allowed to take the pens, whereas the faculty members are not. As the story develops, an administrator and a faculty member each take a pen from the receptionist's desk, leaving her penless when an important message arrives. Knobe and Fraser asked participants to rate the extent to which the administrator or the faculty member was the cause of the receptionist's misfortune.[26] Participants gave much higher causal ratings to the faculty member.

Hitchcock and Knobe interpret this as evidence that people accord primary causal status to actions that violate norms. Since moral transgressions are merely one type of norm violation and different types of norm violations are effectively interchangeable, what matters most for them in the pen scenario is that the professor violated a norm, not that he did something blameworthy.

We disagree heartily with this interpretation. In our view, the primary reason for highlighting the faculty member's role in this unfortunate event surely must be that he is a depraved pen pilferer. Again, while we acknowledge that norm violations are important to causal assignment, norm violations that entail undesirable behavior are dignified with special causal status because they support blame attributions. Rather than demonstrating that norm violations identify interventions that improve events, Hitchcock and Knobe have shown that observers express their disapproval of an individual who violates explicitly stated rules by saddling him with heightened causal responsibility.

We ran two small studies to assess our contention that perceptions of the professor's bad behavior underlie causal judgments in this scenario. Consistent with Knobe and Fraser's methodology, we had separate groups of participants ($N = 265$) rate the extent to which they agreed or disagreed that the professor or the administrative assistant caused the secretary's problem (1–7 scale ranging from "totally disagree" to "totally agree"). We then asked participants to explain their causal ratings. A single coder who was blind to the purpose of the study coded the explanations.

The results for causal judgments of the professor and administrative assistant replicated Knobe and Fraser's findings in that the professor was seen as significantly more causal ($M = 4.23$, $SD = 1.69$) than the administrative assistant ($M = 2.68$, $SD = 1.66$), $t(263) = 7.52$, $p < .001$. Codings of the explanations revealed that participants cited the professor as the cause of the secretary's plight 66% of the time; the other 34% of the explanations were scattered among other causes including the administrative assistant, the receptionist, the other faculty members, and the prohibitory rule itself. Of those who cited the professor as the main cause, all but one indicated as their reason the blameworthiness of his behavior. Not a single participant mentioned that he violated a norm. Interestingly, virtually all other causal citations also entailed the blameworthiness of someone's actions. For example, those who cited the receptionist stated that she should have hidden her pens or stood up for herself to prevent the pen thievery. Those who saw the administrative assistant as the main cause explained this by saying that the administrative assistant should have known better and that although taking the pens was permitted, the assistant should have foreseen that this would lead to a shortage. The explanations that participants provided, therefore, support the culpable-control contention that people do not view causation for harmful events merely in terms of norm-violating actions. Rather, when asked to explain their causal judgments, they emphasize that someone did something that warranted blame.

We then conducted one more variation of the penless-secretary scenario ($N = 71$). In addition to asking whether the professor or administrator was more causal, we asked participants to rate the badness or goodness of the professor's behavior on a 7-point scale ranging from "very bad" to "very good." Ratings of the professor's and the administrative assistant's causal influence replicated the findings of the previous study as well as those of Knobe and Fraser in that the professor was seen as more causal ($M = 3.89$, $SD = 1.45$) than the administrative assistant ($M = 2.43$, $SD = 1.46$), $t(70) = 4.27$, $p < .001$. Furthermore, the average rating of the professor's behavior was $M = 3.00$, which was below the scale midpoint, indicating a negative view of his actions. In fact, not a single participant rated the professor's behavior above the scale midpoint. Clearly, therefore, the professor's behavior was viewed as relatively bad and blameworthy in this context. In the realm of offensive or harmful human behavior, blame is the engine that makes norm violations matter.

7. CONCLUDING COMMENTS

We have shown that evaluations are an important component of causal judgments for undesirable or harmful actions, and we have demonstrated that causal judgments, at least in some circumstances, are determined by perceived blameworthiness rather than the reverse. Norm violations are important determinants of perceived causal influence, but they are effective because they indicate whether an actor has done something exceptionally good or exceptionally bad. In fact, ascribing causation is, by itself, rarely the ultimate goal of the layperson's behavioral analysis. From the standpoint of the culpable-control model, causation is but one of the criteria (along with intent, foresight, foreseeability, and mitigating circumstances) that determine the extent to which actors are blamed or praised for the consequences they attempt or achieve. Judgments of these criteria, however, are strongly influenced by observers' evaluative reactions to the people involved in an action sequence, their behavior, and the consequences that occurred or could have occurred. These evaluative influences are not exceptions to an otherwise rational process. They are essential components of lay behavioral analyses, because they stem from observers' most fundamental motives of discerning which objects, events, and people are likely to facilitate their goals and well-being and which endanger their prospects.

APPENDIX

Positive Characterization; Death Imminent (Aneurysm)

(1) Edward Poole was a physician who had recently moved into a new neighborhood.
(2) Poole had become friends with the Turnbulls, who lived on his street.
(3) Mrs. Turnbull asked Poole if he could feed her cat, which stayed in an upstairs bedroom while she and her husband were out of town at separate conferences.
(4) On Nov. 2, 2004, Poole used the key that Mrs. Turnbull had given him and headed upstairs to the room in which the Turnbulls kept the cat.
(5) Neither Poole nor Mrs. Turnbull realized that Mr. Turnbull had returned home after finding out that his conference had been canceled at the last minute.
(6) Poole tripped over one of the children's toys and made a loud nose as he was going up the stairs.
(7) Turnbull heard the noise and took a licensed gun from his drawer.
(8) Turnbull shot at Poole just as he was about to enter the room where the cat stayed.
(9) The bullet hit Poole in the chest and back and killed him almost instantly.
(10) The autopsy conducted on Poole showed that he had suffered a brain aneurysm almost at the same time that he was shot by Turnbull. Thus, Poole would have died even if Turnbull had not shot him.

Positive Characterization; Death Delayed (Brain Tumor)

(1) Edward Poole was a physician who had recently moved into a new neighborhood.
(2) Poole had become friends with the Turnbulls, who lived on his street.
(3) Mrs. Turnbull asked Poole if he could feed her cat, which stayed in an upstairs bedroom while she and her husband were out of town at separate conferences.
(4) On Nov. 2, 2004, Poole used the key that Mrs. Turnbull had given him and headed upstairs to the room in which the Turnbulls kept the cat.
(5) Neither Poole nor Mrs. Turnbull realized that Mr. Turnbull had returned home after finding out that his conference had been canceled at the last minute.
(6) Poole tripped over one of the children's toys and made a loud nose as he was going up the stairs.
(7) Turnbull heard the noise and took a licensed gun from his drawer.

(8) Turnbull shot at Poole just as he was about to enter the room where the cat stayed.
(9) The bullet hit Poole in the chest and back and killed him almost instantly.
(10) The autopsy conducted on Poole showed that he had an advanced, inoperable brain tumor that would have killed him within two weeks. Thus, Poole would have died soon even if Turnbull had not shot him.

Positive Characterization; Shot Dead

(1) Edward Poole was a physician who had recently moved into a new neighborhood.
(2) Poole had become friends with the Turnbulls, who lived on his street.
(3) Mrs. Turnbull asked Poole if he could feed her cat, which stayed in an upstairs bedroom while she and her husband were out of town at separate conferences.
(4) On Nov. 2, 2004, Poole used the key that Mrs. Turnbull had given him and headed upstairs to the room in which the Turnbulls kept the cat.
(5) Neither Poole nor Mrs. Turnbull realized that Mr. Turnbull had returned home after finding out that his conference had been canceled at the last minute.
(6) Poole tripped over one of the children's toys and made a loud nose as he was going up the stairway.
(7) Turnbull heard the noise and took a licensed gun from his drawer.
(8) Turnbull shot at Poole just as he was about to enter the room where the cat stayed.
(9) The bullet hit Poole in the chest and back and killed him almost instantly.

Negative Characterization; Death Imminent (Aneurysm)

(1) Edward Poole was released from prison after serving an 18-year sentence for the rape of an 11-year-old girl.
(2) Poole was living in a neighborhood with an old friend who had also recently been released after serving a 6-year sentence for armed robbery.
(3) On Nov. 2, 2004, Poole broke a window in the house of John Turnbull with a baseball bat and headed upstairs toward the room of his youngest daughter.
(4) Turnbull heard the noise and took a licensed gun from his drawer.
(5) Turnbull shot at Poole just as he was about to enter the girl's room.
(6) The bullet hit Poole in the back and chest and killed him almost instantly.

(7) The autopsy conducted on Poole showed that he had suffered a brain aneurysm almost at the same time that he was shot by Turnbull. Thus, Poole would have died even if Turnbull had not shot him.

Negative Characterization; Death Delayed (Brain Tumor)

(1) Edward Poole was released from prison after serving an 18-year sentence for the rape of an 11-year-old girl.
(2) Poole was living in a neighborhood with an old friend who had also recently been released after serving a 6-year sentence for armed robbery.
(3) On Nov. 2, 2004, Poole broke a window in the house of John Turnbull with a baseball bat and headed upstairs toward the room of his youngest daughter.
(4) Turnbull heard the noise and took a licensed gun from his drawer.
(5) Turnbull shot at Poole just as he was about to enter the girl's room.
(6) The bullet hit Poole in the back and chest and killed him almost instantly.
(7) The autopsy conducted on Poole showed that he had an advanced, inoperable brain tumor that would have killed him within two weeks. Thus, Poole would have died soon even if Turnbull had not shot him.

Negative Characterization; Shot Dead

(1) Edward Poole was released from prison after serving an 18-year sentence for the rape of an 11-year-old girl.
(2) Poole was living in a neighborhood with an old friend who had also recently been released after serving a 6-year sentence for armed robbery.
(3) On Nov. 2, 2004, Poole broke a window in the house of John Turnbull with a baseball bat and headed upstairs toward the room of his youngest daughter.
(4) Turnbull heard the noise and took a licensed gun from his drawer.
(5) Turnbull shot at Poole just as he was about to enter the girl's room.
(6) The bullet hit Poole in the back and chest and killed him almost instantly.

NOTES

* We would like to thank Josh Knobe, Chandra Sripada, and Liane Young for their helpful comments on an earlier draft of this paper. We would also like to thank David Danks for his very helpful discussions.

1. Charles E. Osgood, George J. Suci, and Percy H. Tannenbaum, *The Measurement of Meaning* (Urbana: Illinois University Press, 1954).

2. John A. Bargh and Tanya L. Chartrand, "The Unbearable Automaticity of Being," *American Psychology*, liv, 7 (July 1999): 462–479; Russel H. Fazio, David M. Sabonmatsu, Martha C. Powell, and Frank R. Kardes, "On the Automatic Activation of Attitudes," *Journal of Personality and Social Psychology*, l, 2 (February 1986): 229–238.

3. Mark D. Alicke, "Culpable Causation," *Journal of Personality and Social Psychology*, 63, 3 (September 1992): 368–378; "Culpable Control and the Psychology of Blame," *Psychological Bulletin*, cxxvi, 4 (July 2000): 556–574; "Blaming Badly," in "On Folk Conceptions of Mind, Agency, and Morality," special issue, *Journal of Cognition and Culture*, 8, 1–2 (2008): 179–186.

4. Jean Piaget, *The Moral Judgment of the Child* (London, UK: Routledge, 1932); Kelly G. Shaver, *The Attribution of Blame: Causality, Responsibility, and Blameworthiness* (New York: Springer-Verlag, 1989).

5. Frank D. Fincham and Thomas R. Shultz, "Intervening Causation and the Mitigation of Responsibility for Harm," *British Journal of Social and Clinical Psychology*, 20, 2 (June 1981): 113–120; Marylie Karlovac and John M. Darley, "Attribution of Responsibility for Accidents: A Negligence Law Analogy," *Social Cognition*, 6, 4 (Winter 1988): 287–318; Schultz, Michael Schleifer, and Ian Altman, "Judgments of Causation, Responsibility, and Punishment in Cases of Harm-Doing," *Canadian Journal of Behavioural Science*, 13, 3 (July 1981): 238–253.

6. Alicke, "Culpable Causation"; "Culpable Control and the Psychology of Blame." Also see Alicke and Ethan Zell, "Social Attractiveness and Blame," *Journal of Applied Social Psychology*, 39, 9 (September 2009): 2089–2105.

7. H. L. A Hart and Tony Honoré, *Causation in the Law* (Oxford, UK: Clarendon, 1959).

8. Daniel Kahneman and Dale T. Miller, "Norm Theory: Comparing Reality to Its Alternatives," *Psychological Review*, 93, 2 (April 1986): 136–153.

9. David R. Mandel, Denis J. Hilton, and Patrizia Catellani, *The Psychology of Counterfactual Thinking* (New York: Routledge, 2005).

10. Mandel and Darrin R. Lehman, "Counterfactual Thinking and Ascriptions of Cause and Preventability," *Journal of Personality and Social Psychology*, 71, 3 (September 1996): 450–463.

11. R. G. Collingwood, *An Essay on Metaphysics* (Oxford, UK: Clarendon, 1940).

12. Christopher Hitchcock and Joshua Knobe, "Cause and Norm," *Journal of Philosophy* (September 2001): 2105–2108; Greene and Jonathan Haidt, "How (and Where) Does Moral Judgment Work?" *Trends in Cognitive Science*, 6, 6 (December 2002): 517–523; Haidt, "The Emotional Dog and Its Rational Tail: A Social Intuitionist Approach to Moral Judgment," *Psychological Review*, 108, 4 (October 2001): 814–834; Bryce Huebner, Susan Dwyer, and Marc Hauser, "The Role of Emotion in Moral Psychology," *Trends in Cognitive Science*, 13, 1 (December 2008): 1–6; and David A. Pizarro and Paul Bloom, "The Intelligence of Moral Intuitions: Comment on Haidt," *Psychological Review*, 90, 1 (January 2003): 193–196.

15. Hitchcock and Knobe, op. cit., p. 603.

16. A total of 319 participants (Male = 121, Female = 193, Did Not Indicate = 5) were selected from an introductory psychology course.

17. Knobe, "Folk Psychology, Folk Morality" (PhD diss., Princeton University, 2006).

18. Julia Driver, "Attributions of Causation and Moral Responsibility," in Walter Sinnott-Armstrong, ed., *Moral Psychology, Volume 2: The Cognitive Science of Morality* (Cambridge, MA: MIT Press, 2008), pp. 423–439.

19. Due to the many statistical interactions, there are significant difficulties with using structural equation modeling.

20. We are following the procedure for testing mediation hypotheses outlined in Reuben M. Baron and David A. Kenny, "The Moderator-Mediator Variable Distinction in Social Psychological Research: Conceptual, Strategic, and Statistical Considerations," *Journal of Personality and Social Psychology*, 51, 6 (December 1986): 1173–1182; and Kenny et al., "Data Analysis in Social Psychology," Daniel T. Gilbert et al., eds., *The Handbook of Social Psychology*, vol. 1, 4th ed. (Boston: McGraw-Hill, 1984), pp. 233–265.

21. See Michael E. Sobel, "Asymptotic Intervals for Indirect Effects in Structural Equations Models," in Samuel Leinhardt, ed., *Sociological Methodology 13* (San Francisco: Jossey-Bass, 1982), pp. 290–312.

22. Mediation models usually indicate that only one variable lies between two others. For example, in our case, mediation might be due to (a) Poole → blame → cause or (b) Poole → cause → blame. One might think that there are other models, but since Poole is an exogenous variable it cannot be caused by either blame or cause, and so the only plausible causal models are (a) and (b). We have provided evidence for (a), but we need to rule out (b). To do this we tested whether cause mediated the effects of Poole on blame. In testing this mediation model, a regression model with only Poole as a predictor of blame is significant ($Beta = .404$, $p = .000$). However, adding cause to the regression model does not make Poole independent of blame (Cause: $Beta = .320$, $p = .000$; Poole: $Beta = .341$, $p = .000$). Cause, then, does not mediate the effects of Poole on blame, and so model (b) is ruled out. This provides further evidence that the correct model of the relationship between blame and causation is that blame → cause.

23. Feinberg, *op. cit.*

24. Mandel, Hilton, and Catellani, "Introduction," in *op. cit.*, pp. 1–7.

25. See Alicke, "Culpable Causation"; and Alicke and Zell, "Social Attractiveness and Blame." Also see Alicke, Teresa L. Davis, and Mark V. Pezzo, "A Posteriori Adjustment of A Priori Decision Criteria," *Social Cognition*, 12, 4 (December 1994): 281–308; Alicke, Justin Buckingham, Zell, and Davis, "Culpable Control and Counterfactual Reasoning in the Psychology of Blame," *Personality and Social Psychology Bulletin*, 34, 10 (October 2008): 1371–1381; and Philip J. Mazzocco, Alicke, and Davis, "On the Robustness of Outcome Bias: No Constraint by Prior Culpability," *Basic and Applied Social Psychology*, 26, 2–3 (2004): 131–146.

26. Knobe and Ben Fraser, "Causal Judgments and Moral Judgment: Two Experiments," in Sinnott-Armstrong, ed., *op. cit.*, pp. 441–47.

11

Norms Inform Mental State Ascriptions: A Rational Explanation for the Side-Effect Effect

Kevin Uttich and Tania Lombrozo

1. INTRODUCTION

Consider sitting at a commencement address and thinking, "That speaker must love to wear billowy black gowns." This attribution is odd, because we know that academic norms dictate commencement attire. But upon viewing someone dressed in full regalia at a café, it might be appropriate to infer an underlying mental state, such as a false belief that it is commencement or a desire to look scholarly, because in this situation the academic norm does not apply. These examples illustrate that norms inform mental state ascriptions. More precisely, prescriptive norms provide reasons for acting in accordance with those norms (Searle, 2001), with the consequence that norm-conforming behavior is relatively uninformative about underlying mental states: one need not observe norm-conforming behavior to infer underlying reasons to obey the norm. In contrast, norm-violating behavior is informative about underlying mental states, as there must be a reason behind the norm-violating behavior, and moreover the reason must be sufficiently strong to outweigh the reason(s) to observe the norm.

The capacity to understand and attribute mental states is often characterized as a theory of mind (e.g. Gopnik, 1999; Wellman, 1992). Like a scientific theory, Theory of Mind (ToM) posits unobserved entities (internal states) to support explanation and prediction. Knowing that a man in a café desires to appear scholarly, for example, can explain eccentric attire and supports predictions about whether he is more likely to smoke a pipe or a cigar. But for the commencement speaker, eccentric attire is better explained by appeal to a conventional norm, and smoking habits are better predicted from base rates. These observations suggest that norms *should* inform mental state ascriptions if reasoners are to be effective "intuitive scientists" (Kelley, 1967), and if ToM is to accomplish the functions of predicting and explaining behavior.

This paper explores the relationship between norms and mental state ascriptions by considering the relationship between prescriptive norms—both moral and conventional—and ascriptions of intentional action. Previous work suggests that ascriptions of intention have an impact on moral evaluations (e.g. Malle & Nelson, 2003). For example, an intentional killing is typically judged a murder, while an unintentional killing is considered manslaughter (e.g. California Penal Code). But recent findings suggest that the reverse may likewise hold—that moral evaluations can influence ascriptions of intentional action (Knobe, 2003a, 2006). Specifically, Joshua Knobe has uncovered an intriguing asymmetry in judgments concerning whether actions that brought about morally good versus bad side effects were performed "intentionally," a phenomenon known as the side-effect effect or the Knobe effect. Consider the following vignette, which Knobe presented to participants in his initial studies:

> The vice president of a company went to the chairman of the board and said, 'We are thinking of starting a new program. It will help us increase profits, but it will also harm the environment.'
>
> The chairman of the board answered, 'I don't care at all about harming the environment. I just want to make as much profit as I can. Let's start the new program.'
>
> They started the new program. Sure enough, the environment was harmed.

When participants were asked if the chairman intentionally harmed the environment, 82% said yes. However, when the new program's side effect was to *help* the environment, only 23% of participants said the chairman intentionally helped the environment (Knobe, 2003a). Because the chairman expressed indifference to the side effect in both vignettes, judging either side effect intentional violates previous accounts of intentional action, which identify intent and desire, along with skill and foresight, as prerequisites to intentional action (Malle & Knobe, 1997). Moreover, the harm and help vignettes seem to differ only in the moral valence of the side effect, which suggests that *moral* considerations somehow influence ToM judgments.

The side-effect effect has been replicated with different methodologies (Knobe, 2003a, 2004; Knobe & Mendlow, 2004; Machery, 2008), across cultures (Knobe & Burra, 2006), and with preschool children (Leslie, Knobe, & Cohen, 2006). While a variety of explanations for the effect have been offered (Adams & Steadman, 2004; Knobe, 2006; Machery, 2008; Nadelhoffer, 2004), no single proposal successfully accounts for all the data collected to date (Pettit & Knobe, 2009).

Broadly speaking, responses to the side-effect effect have fallen into two distinct camps, which we call the 'Intuitive Moralist' view and the 'Biased Scientist' view. The Intuitive Moralist view takes the effect as evidence that ToM competencies are shaped by the role ToM judgments play in evaluating behavior, be it in assessing moral responsibility or assigning praise and blame. For example, Knobe writes that "...moral considerations are actually playing a role in the fundamental competencies underlying our use of the concept of intentional action" (Knobe, 2006). This interpretation challenges the idea not only that the influence of ToM judgments on moral judgments is one way but also that the function of ToM is to predict and explain behavior—instead, ToM may be a multipurpose tool partially shaped by its role in moral evaluation.

The Biased Scientist view instead suggests that the effect results from a bias in ToM judgments. On this view, moral evaluations are not contained within ToM judgments but do exert an extraneous influence. For example, conversational pragmatics (Adams & Steadman, 2004), the desire to blame an agent for a negative outcome (Malle & Nelson, 2003; Mele, 2001), or an emotional reaction (Nadelhoffer, 2004) could lead participants to (mistakenly) describe the side effect as having been brought about intentionally. Here ToM capacities are still regarded as the product of an "intuitive scientist," but the particulars of the Knobe scenarios lead to results the intuitive scientist cannot accept. Judgments are consequently altered to generate a more acceptable result. This view preserves the traditional function of theory of mind, adding the claim that moral evaluations can have a biasing effect.

We propose a third way of explaining the side-effect effect and of understanding the relationship between ToM and moral judgment. Perhaps moral judgments inform ToM judgments, but not because moral considerations partially constitute or bias ToM concepts. Rather, as suggested in the introduction, actions that violate norms (e.g. harming the environment) provide a basis for ascribing counter-normative mental states and traits to an agent, whereas actions that conform to norms do not. This asymmetry in ascribed mental states and traits is sufficient to in turn generate the asymmetric judgments that characterize the side-effect effect.

We call our proposal the "Rational Scientist " view to emphasize that inferring mental content on the basis of a behavior's relationship to norms (moral or otherwise) makes sense if the goal of ToM is to support prediction and intervention. We suggest that people can make use of information about the agent being evaluated, situational factors, applicable norms, and so on to draw initial or "baseline" mental state and trait inferences (call them "MST1"). After observing the agent's behavior, mental state and trait ascriptions can be updated, yielding MST2. Whether or not a behavior is considered intentional is a function of MST2. While norm-conformance provides little evidence to change MST2 from MST1, norm-violating behavior suggests mental states or traits strong enough to outweigh reasons to obey the norm, and as a result MST2 will be quite different from MST1. When the CEO knowingly proceeds with a plan that will harm the environment, for example, MST2 may supply the desire or intention component required by Malle and Knobe (1997) model of intentional action (for related arguments about differences in desire across conditions see Guglielmo & Malle, submitted for publication; see also Sripada, in press, for the relationship between disposition and self).

The Rational Scientist view differs from the Intuitive Moralist view in preserving the traditional function of theory of mind: prediction and explanation. Our approach concedes that moral judgments influence ToM, but this influence is seen as *evidential,* not *constitutive.* In other words, moral norms affect ToM ascriptions by influencing mental state ascriptions, but such ascriptions are not inherently evaluative. The Rational Scientist view also differs from Biased Scientist views in regarding the influence of moral judgment on ToM as a rational strategy for achieving the function of ToM, and not as a bias or extraneous pressure. While our view differs from many contemporary explanations for the side-effect effect, it shares important elements with classic ideas in attribution, such as the Correspondent Inference Theory of trait attribution (Jones & Davis, 1965), the cue-diagnosticity approach to trait attribution (Skowronski & Carlston, 1987), and the Covariation ANOVA Model (Kelley, 1967), many of which emphasize the importance of atypical (and hence counter-normative) behavior in guiding judgment (see also Malle & Guglielmo, 2008; Holton, 2010; Sripada, 2010; Sripada & Konrath, 2011.

In this paper we test the Rational Scientist view as a hypothesis about the relationship between moral evaluation and theory of mind. First, we examine whether the asymmetric ascriptions of intentional action in previous demonstrations of the side-effect effect stem from the side effects' *norm status* or their *moral status.* In previous cases, "harm" scenarios involved bad side effects that resulted from norm-violating actions, while "help" scenarios involved good side effects that resulted from norm-conforming actions. Experiments 1 and 2 deconfound moral status and norm status to examine what drives the side-effect effect: norm status, as predicted by the Rational Scientist view, or moral status, as predicted by the Intuitive Moralist and Biased Scientist views. Experiment 1 additionally examines whether effects of norm status are restricted to moral norms or extend to conventional norms. Second, we examine whether norm-violating actions are indeed more informative than norm-conforming actions when it comes to positing mental states and traits that support prediction. This is the focus of Experiment 3.

To preview our results, we find that the asymmetry in the side-effect effect results from the side effects' norm status, that the side-effect effect extends to conventional norms, and that norm-violating behavior supports stronger predictions about future behavior than norm-conforming behavior. These findings offer strong support for the Rational Scientist view and provide a way to understand the relationship between ToM and moral norms.

2. EXPERIMENT 1

In focusing on norm status and mental state inferences, rather than on moral evaluations, the Rational Scientist view makes a few unique predictions. First, because the Rational Scientist view argues that what drives the side-effect effect is the relationship between norms and behavior, not the moral status of behavior or outcomes itself, the Rational Scientist view predicts that judgments of intentional action should vary when the norms in a situation vary, even if a behavior and its outcome remain the same. Second, because the Rational Scientist view argues that the asymmetry in the side-effect effect results from mental state inferences licensed by norm-violations, the Rational Scientist view predicts that the effect should extend to non-moral norms, such as conventional norms. While other studies have provided evidence that the side-effect effect is not limited to moral cases (Machery, 2008), they have not focused on conventional norms or on asymmetries arising from norm conformance versus norm violation.

Experiment 1 investigates both predictions using vignettes in which an agent acts to bring about an intended, main effect with a foreseen side effect. While the agent's action and the side effect are held constant across conditions, norm status is varied by introducing industry standards. For example, one set of vignettes involves a CEO who pursues an action with a 25% chance of causing environmental harm, but where the industry standard for pursuing a plan with environmental risk specifies that the probability of harm must be either 45% or less (making the behavior *norm conforming*) or 5% or less (making the behavior *norm violating*).[1] While norm status varies across conditions, the probability of harm (25%) is held constant, and the environmental harm always occurs. In matched vignettes involving a conventional norm, the CEOs actions will change the color of a manufactured product to black, where the color change is either norm-conforming (the product is conventionally darker than blue) or norm-violating (the product is conventionally lighter than blue). If the Rational Scientist view is correct, participants should judge it more appropriate to say a side effect was brought about intentionally in the *norm-violating* cases than in the *norm-conforming* cases, for both moral and conventional norms, no matter that matched cases involve identical side effects.

2.1. Participants

Participants were 300 University of California–Berkeley undergraduates who received the questionnaire as part of a larger packet completed for course credit. There were 12 conditions with 25 participants in each condition.

2.2. Materials and Procedure

Participants read vignettes involving an agent who acted to bring about a main effect with a foreseen side effect. The side effect could be norm conforming or norm violating , and the relevant norm could be *moral* or *conventional*. To match vignettes as closely as possible, the side effect was held constant across pairs of scenarios, with norm status manipulated by stipulating an industry standard in each vignette. Specifically, the moral vignettes always involved a side effect with a 25% probability of occurring, but the stipulated norm was to proceed when the side effect had less than a 45% chance of occurring, making the action norm conforming, or when the side effect has less than a 5% chance of occurring, making the action norm violating. However, the side effect always in fact occurred. Below are sample vignettes:

> [Moral norm condition] A regulatory agency for the Gizmo industry exists in order to provide environmental standards even though it does not have the authority to ensure compliance with these standards. This regulatory agency has established an environmental standard, which states that a company may only start new programs if the chance of environmental harm due to the program is under 5% [45%].
>
> The vice president of a company in the Gizmo industry went to the chairman of the board and said, "We are thinking of starting a new program. It will help us increase profits, but there is a 25% chance that it will also harm the environment. The industry standard is to only start programs of this type when the chance for harm is under 5% [45%]."
>
> The chairman of the board answered, "I don't care at all about harming the environment. I just want to make as much profit as I can. Let's start the new program."
>
> They started the program. As it happened, the environment was harmed.
>
> [Conventional norm condition] The convention in the Gizmo industry is for Gizmos to be a dark color. Specifically, the convention is to make Gizmos that are colored darker than blue.
>
> The vice president of a company in the Gizmo industry went to the chairman of the board and said, "We are thinking of starting a new program. It will help us increase profits, but it will result in our Gizmos being colored black. The convention is to make Gizmos colored darker than blue, so we would be complying with the convention." [The convention is to make Gizmos colored lighter than blue, so we would be violating the convention.]
>
> The chairman of the board answered, "I don't care at all about the color of the Gizmos. I just want to make as much profit as I can. Let's start the new program."
>
> They started the program. As it happened, the Gizmos were black, colored darker than blue.

Participants were then asked to rate how appropriate it would be to say that the side effect was brought about intentionally, providing ratings on a 1–7 scale, with 1 being "not at all appropriate," 7 "very appropriate," and 4 "neither appropriate not inappropriate." For the sample vignettes above, they were asked: "How appropriate is it to say the CEO intentionally harmed the environment [the chairman of the board intentionally made Gizmos colored darker than blue]?"

In addition to varying the nature of the norm (moral, conventional) and the side effect's norm status (conforming, violating), there were three distinct sets of vignettes, one involving a CEO and included above, one involving a doctor (DR), and one involving a trucking company (TRUCK). There were thus 12 distinct vignettes, with participants randomly assigned to a single vignette.

2.3. Results and Discussion

Participants' ratings of whether it is appropriate to say that the agent brought about the side effect "intentionally" (see Fig. 1) were analyzed using an ANOVA with three between-subjects factors: norm status (2: conforming, violating), norm type (2: moral, conventional), and vignette version (3: CEO, DR, TRUCK). This analysis revealed a main effect of norm status ($F(1, 288) = 12.828, p < .01$), with norm-violating side effects receiving higher ratings than norm-conforming side effects. There was also a main effect of vignette ($F(2, 288) = 11.705, p < .01$), with average ratings in the DR Vignette lower overall. There was no interaction between norm status and norm type ($F(1, 288) = 2.269, p = .133$), suggesting the effect was comparable for both norm types. In all 12 conditions the average ratings for the norm-violating side effects were numerically higher than those for the norm-conforming side effect.[2]

These results suggest that in evaluating whether an outcome was brought about intentionally, participants consider the relationship between behavior and norms, and not merely the behavior or its outcome. Thus the asymmetry observed in the side-effect effect does not depend specifically on a difference between "good" and "bad" actions or outcomes as most versions of the Intuitive Moralist and Biased Scientist views would predict, but rather on the difference between norm-conforming and norm-violating actions. Moreover, the importance of *norm* status as opposed to *moral* status is reinforced by the fact that the effect is also observed when the norms in question are conventional. Like moral norms, conventional norms provide reasons for action, establishing an asymmetry in the mental states one can infer (MST2) on the basis of norm conformance versus norm violation.

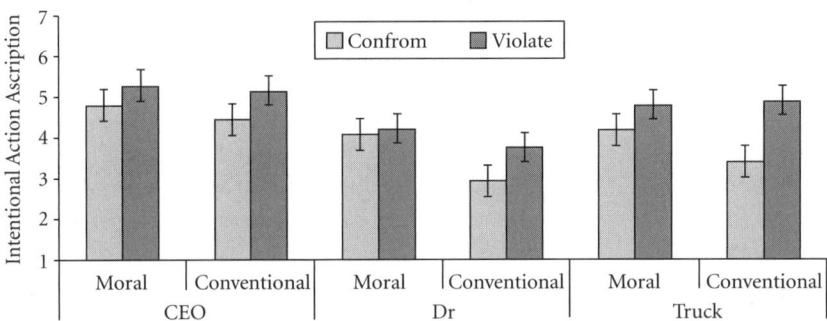

Figure 11.1. Experiment 1 ratings of how appropriate it is to describe an action as having been performed intentionally as a function of norm status and norm type. Ratings were made on a scale from 1 (neither appropriate nor inappropriate to say outcome brought about intentionally) to 7 (appropriate to say outcome brought about intentionally) with 4 (neither appropriate nor inappropriate) as a midpoint.

3. EXPERIMENT 2

While Experiment 1 is consistent with the Rational Scientist view and makes the case that the side-effect effect extends beyond moral norms, other explanations for the data are possible. In particular, an advocate for the Intuitive Moralist or Biased Scientist view could argue that stipulating a norm influences judgments of intentional action by establishing whether a side effect is good or bad, with participants' own evaluations of "goodness" or "badness" ultimately responsible for judgments, not norm status per se. This concern is plausible in light of the fact that the scenarios involved uncertain side effects about which participants had little prior knowledge. Providing norms may have effectively *taught* participants what counts as good and bad in the course of the experiment. While this concern already concedes a role to norms, Experiment 2 replicates the key findings with side effects for which participants have strong, antecedent moral judgments.

Experiment 2 thus employs vignettes with side effects that are likely to generate strong moral evaluations with or without experimental context, and includes an assessment of participants' own evaluations of the moral status of the side effects. To manipulate norm status while keeping the moral status of side effects constant, an agent's actions are embedded in a context with typical moral norms (the "superhero" context) or a context with reversed norms (the "supervillain" context). So, for example, the side effect of accelerating global warming should be norm violating for a superhero and norm conforming for a supervillain but is likely to be judged morally bad by all participants.

Because the Rational Scientist view claims that norm status drives the side-effect effect by determining which mental states are ascribed to an agent, it predicts that changing a vignette's context (superhero versus supervillain), and therefore the norms with respect to which the agent operates, should influence judgments of intentional action. For example, a supervillain who *decelerates* global warming is violating a supervillain norm to cause harm, so one can infer that the supervillain must have had a reason to bring about this (good) outcome that was sufficiently strong to outweigh reasons to conform to supervillain norms. This (good) outcome should therefore support stronger ascriptions of intentional action than a (bad) outcome that conforms to supervillain norms, such as *accelerating* global warming. In contrast, because both alternative views focus on moral status and participants' moral evaluations of the side effects, they would presumably predict that responses will track participants' moral evaluations of the side effects, irrespective of vignette context. That is, an agent who accelerates global warming should be judged to have done so intentionally and one who decelerates global warming should not, irrespective of whether the agents are superheroes or supervillains.

3.1. Participants

Participants were 96 University of California–Berkeley undergraduates who received the questionnaire as part of a larger packet completed for course credit. There were eight participants in each of 12 conditions.

3.2. Materials and Procedure

Participants read a vignette about an agent who acted to bring about an intended main effect and a foreseen side effect, where the side effect was either morally good or morally bad. However, the agent was embedded either in a context with typical norms concerning morally good and bad action (the "superhero" context) or in a context with reversed norms (the "supervillain" context). Participants were asked to take the perspective of an assistant to a superhero or supervillain and to evaluate the actions of an agent who was being considered for a promotion. Below is an example of a vignette from the supervillain condition, involving a harmful side effect:

> There is a Supervillain that has a group of evil henchmen who work for him. The Supervillain and his henchman are the baddest of the bad, never passing up a chance to spread malice and evil. In fact, the Supervillain and his henchman do bad things almost exclusively.
>
> You are the assistant to the Supervillain. Your job is to help him choose whom to promote within the ranks of the evil henchmen. The job of the evil henchmen is to do maximum evil at every opportunity. To make your decision, you've planted secret microphones and video cameras to observe the henchmen in action. Below is an episode that you've learned about concerning Bob, a henchman eager to move up the ranks whom you will be asked to evaluate:
>
> A rookie henchmen said to Bob: "Sir, we have a plan to rob a bank by releasing neurotoxins in the air, temporarily causing anyone in the vicinity of the bank to be incapacitated. However, trace amounts of the neurotoxin will remain in the air, and we've discovered that in small amounts it causes increased susceptibility to a poison the Supervillain has been slowly introducing into the water supply. Exposure to the neurotoxin will cause even more people in town to become ill from the water and the reactions will be more severe. It will greatly harm the town's quality of life."
>
> Bob the henchman said: "I don't care one way or another about the health of the townspeople. I just want to steal as much money as I can. Let's go ahead with the plan."
>
> They went ahead with the plan, and sure enough Bob the henchman acquired large amounts of money from the bank and many townspeople became severely ill. The health of the townspeople was thus harmed.
>
> Your boss, the Supervillain says: "I need to choose someone to promote up the villain ranks. I have a lot of henchman to choose from. All of them have proven that they are capable of doing bad, but I want someone who is truly evil. What about Bob? I heard he robbed a bank, acquired a large amount of money and made a bunch of townspeople ill."

The corresponding vignette for the superhero condition involved stopping a bank robbery by using the neurotoxins, and as a side effect harming the health of the townspeople. For both the superhero and supervillain conditions, in the corresponding "help" side effect condition participants were told: "Exposure to the neurotoxin will cause fewer people in town to become ill from the water and the reactions will be less severe. It will greatly increase the town's quality of life." As in the harm cases, the agent claimed not to care about the foreseen helpful side effect, and the effect always occurred as expected. The other two sets of vignettes involved destroying the UN (supervillain's goal) or a supervillain's compound (superhero's goal) using a giant mirror and thereby accelerating (harm) or decelerating (help) global warming, and blowing up a dam (supervillain's goal) or building a dam (superhero's goal) with negative (harm) or positive (help) consequences for the town's fishing industry.

Participants were asked to maintain the perspective of the assistant to the supervillain (superhero) and were told to "respond to the following questions as if the supervillain (superhero) asked you." They were then asked, "How appropriate is it to say Bob intentionally harmed the health of the townspeople?" and provided ratings on a 1–7 scale as in Experiment 1. Participants made additional judgments (see Table 1) to examine whether the context manipulation effectively altered judgments concerning the agent's behavior, and to examine the inferences participants drew about the agent on the basis of the context and side effect. To verify that participants' own norms corresponded to the superhero context, with the "help" side effect judged good and the "harm" side effect judged bad, participants were asked to respond to additional questions "from your own personal perspective (as if you were telling a friend about Bob instead of responding to the supervillain as his assistant)" (see Table 1).

Participants were randomly assigned to one of 12 conditions, the result of crossing side effect moral status (2: harmful, helpful), context (2: superhero, supervillain), and vignette version (3: bank robbery, global warming, fishing).

3.3. Results and Discussion

The critical dependent measure was participants' evaluation of whether it is appropriate to say that the agent brought about the side effect "intentionally." We analyzed ratings using an ANOVA with three between-subjects factors: side effect valence (2: harmful, helpful), context (2: superhero, supervillain), and vignette version (3: bank robbery, global warming, fishing). This analysis revealed a main effect of side effect valence ($F(1, 83) = 7.17, p < .01$), with harmful side effects receiving higher ratings than helpful side effects, as well as the predicted interaction between side effect valence and context ($F(1, 83) = 20.91, p < .01$; see Fig. 2). There were no other significant effects. In the superhero context, the results replicated past demonstrations of the side-effect effect, with the harmful side effect receiving higher ratings for intentional action than the helpful side effect. However, this pattern was not observed for the supervillain context; in fact, the ratings for the helpful side effect were numerically higher than those for the harmful side effect. Judgments about whether the main effect was intended were uniformly high (5.84, s.d. = 1.52), and did not vary as a function of condition.

Findings involving the remaining dependent measures are summarized in Table 1, which indicates the means for each judgment as a function of SE valence and context, as well as significant main effects and interactions. First, consider the judgments made from the perspective of the assistant to the superhero or

Table 1.1 Judgments from Experiment 2 as a function of context and side-effect valence. Means are followed in parentheses by standard deviations. The patterns of shading highlight significant differences across conditions. Main effects and interactions are also indicated in the right-hand portion of the table, with a single asterisk (*) indicating a significant effect at the $p < .05$ level, and a double asterisk (**) indicating a significant effect at the $p < .01$ level.

Question	Superhero		Supervillain		Main effects			Interactions		
	Good SE	Bad SE	Good SE	Bad SE	SE valence	Context		SE valence × Context	Context × vignette	3-way
Questions from superhero or supervillain perspective										
(a) Which do you think Bob is more likely to do in the future, [good or bad SE]? (7 = likely to [good SE])	4.08 (1.31)	3.67 (1.44)	3.17 (1.66)	3.12 (1.42)		*				
(b) Which do you think Bob is more likely to do in the future, [good or bad main effect]? (7 = likely to [good ME])	5.71 (1.20)	5.88 (1.30)	1.42 (.88)	1.79 (1.25)		*		*		
(c) In comparison to Steve [an average candidate], do you think Bob is more or less likely to [bad SE]? (7 = more likely)	4.17 (1.27)	4.83 (1.09)	4.46 (1.50)	4.17 (1.01)						*
(d) In comparison to Steve, do you think Bob is more or less likely to [good SE]? (7 = more likely)	4.21 (1.38)	3.50 (1.18)	3.46 (1.02)	4.25 (1.03)				**		
(e) Was [SE] good or bad? (7 = definitely good)	6.33 (1.05)	2.42 (1.10)	4.04 (2.26)	4.29 (2.49)	**			**		
(f) Is Bob a good or bad person? (7 = definitely good)	4.83 (1.34)	4.12 (1.26)	1.87 (.74)	2.37 (1.35)		**		*		**
(g) Should Bob be blamed or praised? (7 = praised)	4.92 (1.21)	3.29 (1.04)	4.25 (1.51)	4.83 (1.71)				**		
(h) How does observing Bob's effect on [SE] impact your recommendation to the supervillain? (7 = recommend promotion)	3.37 (1.28)	2.83 (1.71)	3.04 (1.27)	4.08 (1.79)				*		
Questions from personal perspective										
(i) Do YOU think [SE] was good or bad? (7 = good)	6.29 (1.08)	2.17 (1.24)	6.21 (1.25)	1.62 (1.25)	**					*
(j) Do YOU think Bob is a good or bad person? (7 = good)	4.67 (1.20)	3.96 (1.12)	1.96 (.96)	1.83 (1.13)		**				
(k) Do YOU think Bob should be blamed or praised? (7 = praised)	4.79 (1.29)	3.12 (.99)	2.67 (1.66)	1.79 (1.14)	**	**				*

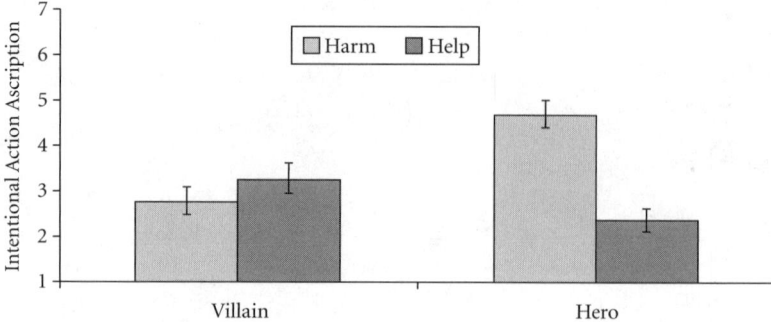

Figure 11.2. Experiment 2 ratings of how appropriate it is to describe an action as having been performed intentionally as a function of norm status and context. Presented on a scale from 1 (not appropriate to say outcome brought about intentionally) to 7 (appropriate to say outcome brought about intentionally), with 4 (neither appropriate nor inappropriate) as a midpoint.

supervillain. The fact that participants rated heroes more likely than villains to bring about good effects in the future (a and b) confirms that participants understood the intended, typical behavior for agents in each community. More reassuring, the significant interaction between SE valence and context for judgments about the side effect, the agent, blame versus praise, and promotion (e, f, g, and h) all suggest that participants effectively adopted the intended perspective and were able to evaluate the agent with respect to the stipulated norms.

The questions about the agent's future behavior in relation to an average candidate (c and d) were intended to test the hypothesis that norm-violating behavior is more informative than norm-conforming behavior in the sense that it provides evidence to alter predictions from baseline, which should correspond to the predictions for an average agent (4 on the 7-point scale). That is, MST2 should differ more from MST1 for norm violation than for norm conformance. This predicts that agents who conform to norms (a helping hero or a harming villain) should generate judgments very close to 4, while agents who violate norms (a harming hero or a helping villain) should differ from 4, with harming heroes more likely to harm and less likely to help in the future and helping villains less likely to harm and more likely to help. While this pattern of results was obtained for the heroes, it was not for the villains. It may be that some participants assumed that a norm-violating agent would compensate for the norm violation—for example, that a supervillain who helped would make up for the help with future harm. Because these findings are difficult to interpret, Experiment 3 examines the influence of norm violation and norm conformance on future prediction more directly.

Finally, consider the judgments that were made from the perspective of the participant. Unsurprisingly, participants judged good side effects good and bad side effects bad; heroes good and villains bad; and praised heroes more than villains, with greater praise for bringing about good side effects. These findings reinforce that participants' own moral evaluations were consistent across conditions, and that differences in ascriptions of intentional action stemmed from the relationship between an agent's behavior and the norms with respect to which that behavior was evaluated, not the moral "goodness" or "badness" of the actions or outcomes themselves.

While these additional dependent measures serve principally to confirm background assumptions, they also provide an opportunity to examine the relationship between these judgments and ascriptions of intentional action. Ratings for whether the side effect was brought about intentionally correlated significantly with the valence of the side effect from the perspective of the vignette ($r = -.39$, $p < .001$), with higher ratings for intentional action corresponding to ratings that the side effect was more negative. However, an equivalent relationship was not observed from participants' own perspective ($r = -.17$, $p = .12$), again suggesting that participants' own moral judgments played little role in ascriptions of intentional action.

These results provide evidence for the Rational Scientist view over alternatives. While the superhero cases replicate previous findings, reversing the norms with a supervillain context had a corresponding effect on ascriptions of intentional action. This reversal is predicted by the Rational Scientist view. While a participant's norms and an evaluated agent's norms may often be the same—especially if participants consult their own norms as a default—the two can diverge when there's evidence that an agent subscribes to different norms, as in our supervillain context. The norms attributed to the agents in turn determine mental state ascriptions, because only norms that apply to an agent can supply that agent with a reason to act in accordance with the norm, and hence generate the evidential asymmetry that we suggest drives the side-effect effect. In contrast, because the Intuitive Moralist view, as well as most versions of the Biased Scientist view, suggest that participants are tracking moral status or are influenced by their own moral understanding, these views predict that ascriptions of intentional action should track a participant's own moral evaluations, not those of an arbitrarily stipulated context within which the evaluated agent is operating.

Additionally, Experiment 2 addresses a potential concern about Experiment 1: that judgments in Experiment 1 were influenced only by norms because participants did not have a prior basis for making an evaluation about the valence of the side effect. In Experiment 2, participants had clear judgments about the moral status of the side effect, and these judgments were not influenced by context.

Experiments 1 and 2 thus make the case for the role of norm status rather than moral status in generating the side-effect effect. However, there are two potential concerns in using our findings to make sense of prior research on the side-effect effect. The first is that compared with previous demonstrations of the effect, the differences between the norm-conforming and norm-violating conditions in Experiment 1 are modest, and the "reverse" side-effect effect in the supervillain context from Experiment 2 is numerically smaller than that in the more typical, superhero context. A second potential concern is that while we find systematic differences in ascriptions of intentional action across our scenarios, it's not always the case that a majority of participants provide "intentional" ratings in the norm-violating cases (i.e. ratings above the scale midpoint) and a majority provide "unintentional" ratings in the norm-conforming cases (i.e. ratings below the scale midpoint), as has been found in the past for the CEO vignette, among others.

In evaluating these concerns it's important to note that our vignettes were designed such that the actions and outcomes were identical across scenarios that varied in norm status. The fact that *any* differences were observed across matched vignettes supports a role for norm status. Moreover, it's likely that norms other than those the vignettes manipulated influenced the absolute ascriptions of intentional action, if not the differences across matched cases. For example, in the CEO vignette from Experiment 1, participants presumably applied the norm that environmental harm is bad in both the norm-conforming and norm-violating conditions, generating ratings that were typically above the midpoint in both conditions. Finally, our vignettes required participants to accept a stipulated norm rather than employ their own norms, requiring non-trivial perspective taking. This is especially apparent in Experiment 2. It's impressive that norm status had a reliable effect above and beyond the effects of other norms that operated in the vignettes, participants' own norms, and additional factors that may contribute to ascriptions of intentional action.

4. EXPERIMENT 3

In Experiment 3, we turn to another prediction of the Rational Scientist view: that asymmetries in mental state ascriptions should track differences in predictions of future behavior. According to the Rational Scientist view, theory of mind serves the function of predicting and explaining behavior. It follows that mental state terms should track aspects of behavior that support prediction. Experiment 3 examines this aspect of the Rational Scientist view by considering whether *norm-violating* behavior, which supports a stronger ascription of intentional action than does *norm-conforming* behavior, also supports stronger predictions. More precisely, we suggest that background information supports mental state and trait inferences (MST1) that are updated in light of what an agent says and does (yielding MST2). In the case of norm-conforming behavior, MST2 will be very similar to MST1. In the case of norm-violating behavior, MST2 may differ substantially from MST1. If mental states and traits are posited to support predictions about future behavior, then norm-violating behavior should lead to predictions that deviate more from baseline predictions than does norm-conforming behavior.

To test these predictions, we consider three conditions. In the norm-conforming and norm-violating conditions, agents bring about good or bad side effects, respectively. In the *baseline* condition, agents do not perform actions or bring about side effects. Then, in all conditions, instead of having participants judge whether a side effect was brought about intentionally, they make two predictions about the agent in the vignette's future behavior. The *specific* prediction considers whether the agent is more likely to engage in a norm-conforming or norm-violating behavior in the future. The *general* prediction concerns the agent's broader adherence to norms and thus examines whether the inferred properties of the agent are restricted to the specific outcome in the vignette (e.g. harming the environment) or generalize more broadly (e.g. harming in general). The baseline condition should track the predictions supported by MST1; the norm-conforming and norm-violating conditions should track the predictions supported by MST2, where MST2 will differ across conditions in light of the agent's norm-conforming or norm-violating behavior.

The Rational Scientist view predicts that participants who learn about the agent who generates a norm-violating side effect will make predictions about the agent's future behavior that differ more from baseline predictions than will participants who learn about the agent who generates a norm-conforming side effect. In contrast, the Intuitive Moralist and Biased Scientist views focus primarily on the role of evaluative considerations in ascriptions of intentional action, and do not explicitly bear on the relationship between such ascriptions and predictions about future behavior. While the views could potentially be modified or supplemented to generate a prediction, they do not do so in their current forms.

4.1. Participants

Participants were 156 University of California–Berkeley undergraduates who participated for course credit.

4.2. Materials and Procedure

Participants were randomly assigned to one of three conditions: *baseline*, *norm conforming*, or *norm violating*. Participants in the *norm-conforming* and *norm-violating* conditions were presented with two short vignettes, the CEO vignette (Knobe, 2003a) from the introduction as well as the analogous DR vignette:

> DR Vignette:
> A team of doctors is treating a patient. One doctor on the team came to the senior doctor and said, "We are thinking of starting a treatment. It will lower the patient's blood pressure but it will also help [hurt] the patient's stomach problems."
> The senior doctor answered, "Stomach problems are not our concern. I just want to lower the patient's blood pressure as much as I can. Let's start the treatment."
> They started the treatment. Sure enough the patient's stomach problems were helped [hurt].

After each vignette participants were asked to make two ratings about the future actions of the agent in the story, a *specific* prediction and a *general* prediction. These questions are below, with the text for the CEO vignette in brackets:

> Specific prediction:
> In the following month the doctor [chairman] will make another decision that results in either:
>   A. An action that has a positive consequence beyond what the doctor is treating. [that helps the environment]
>   Or **B.** An action that has a negative consequence beyond what the doctor is treating. [that harms the environment]

Which decision do you think the doctor [chairman] will make?
General prediction:

> The next month the doctor [chairman] will make another decision that results in either:
>   A. Exceeding ethical standards.
>   Or **B.** Violating ethical standards.

Which decision do you think the doctor [chairman] will make?
Participants rated the likelihood of each event on a scale from 1 to 7, where 1 indicated "very likely to choose A," 4 "equally likely to choose A or B," and 7 "very likely to choose B."

Participants in the *baseline* condition were introduced to the agents (e.g. "There is a chairman of the board who makes the final decisions for his company") and made all four prediction judgments, but were given no information about the agents' past behavior.

The order of story presentation (CEO first or DR first) and the direction of the 7-point scale (from conforming to violating or vice versa) were counterbalanced across participants.

4.3. Results and Discussion

To examine whether participants' prediction ratings varied across conditions, the data were first reverse-coded for participants who received a 7-point scale with higher values indicating a greater probability of acting to bring about a positive side effect. Thus for all participants, higher ratings correspond to a higher subjective probability that the agent will act to bring about a negative side effect. We then conducted an ANOVA with condition as a between-subjects variable (*baseline, norm conforming, norm violating*), vignette as a within-subjects variable (CEO, DR), prediction question as a within-subjects variable (specific, general), and prediction rating as the dependent variable. This revealed a main effect of condition ($F(2, 153) = 14.36, p < .001$), as well as a main effect of vignette ($F(1, 153) = 83.43, p < .001$). Overall, participants rated negative actions more probable in the *norm-conforming* condition than in the *baseline* condition, and in the *norm-violating* condition than in the *norm-conforming* condition (see Fig. 3). Ratings in the *norm-conforming* condition may have been more negative than in the *baseline* condition because failing to endorse a fortuitous side effect (e.g. helping the environment) is itself a norm violation (see Mele & Cushman, 2007). The main effect of vignette resulted from the fact that predictions concerning the CEO were generally more negative than those concerning the doctor.

The key hypothesis that predictions in the *norm-violating* condition should differ more from baseline than do those in the *norm-conforming* condition can be examined by looking for significant differences across these conditions, as both yielded ratings more negative than those in the *baseline* condition. An ANOVA like that above but restricted to the *norm-violating* and *norm-conforming* conditions reproduced the main effect of vignette ($F(1, 102) = 50.86$, $p < .001$) and revealed a main effect of condition ($F(1, 102) = 8.75$, $p < .01$) as well as a three-way interaction between vignette, prediction, and condition ($F(1, 102) = 4.80$, $p < .05$). With post hoc t-tests, the *norm-conforming* and *norm-violating* conditions differed significantly on both CEO predictions (specific: $t(102) = 3.43$, $p < .001$; general: $t(102) = 2.18$, $p < .05$), and were marginal for the general DR predictions (specific: $t(102) = 1.11$, $p = .271$; general: $t(102) = 1.91$, $p = .059$).[3] These findings confirm the prediction that relative to baseline, norm-violating behavior provides more information about an agent's future behavior than norm-conforming behavior.

Although our task did not require participants to report the mental states ascribed to the agents in each vignette, the nature of their predictions provides some evidence concerning these mental state ascriptions. Recall that participants made two kinds of predictions: a specific prediction about the same norm-violation in the future, and a general prediction about norm-violation in general. The fact that the predicted pattern of results was obtained for both kinds of predictions suggests that participants not only ascribed the agents in each vignette with a specific attitude concerning the violated norm (e.g. that the CEO does not value the environment or that the DR is insensitive to patients' overall well-being), but also ascribed the agents with a more general trait (e.g.

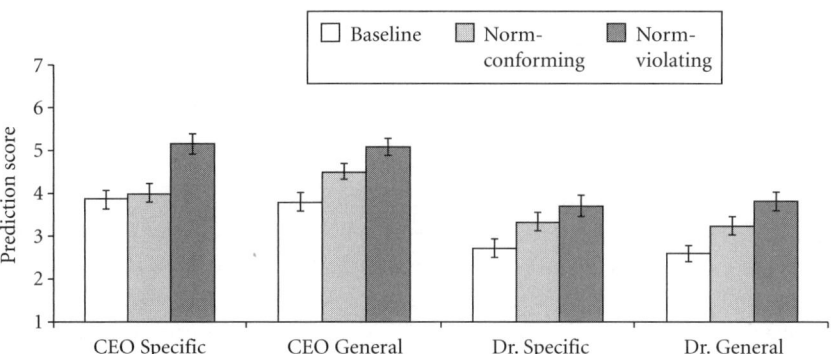

Figure 11.3. Prediction scores from Experiment 3 on a scale from 1 (good side effect likely in future) to 7 (bad side effect likely in future).

the CEO is evil) or a general attitude towards norms (e.g. the DR thinks he can ignore the rules).

Of the views that have been proposed, only the Rational Scientist view provides an explanation for why norm-violating behavior would support stronger predictions than norm-conforming behavior. Accordingly, only the Rational Scientist view predicts the findings from Experiment 3. However, the Intuitive Moralist and Biased Scientist views could be modified to accommodate these findings. In particular, the Intuitive Moralist view could stipulate that the valence of an outcome influences mental state ascription in general (beyond ascriptions of intentional action), with consequences for prediction, and one of the most recent formulations (Pettit & Knobe, 2009) does extend beyond ascriptions of intentional action. Similarly, Biased Scientist models could build in a mechanism by which judgments of praise or blame bias all mental state ascriptions, which in turn influence predictions. So while the findings from Experiment 3 are specifically predicted by the Rational Scientist view, the greatest contribution of Experiment 3 may be to highlight the intimate relationship between mental state ascriptions and prediction.

5. GENERAL DISCUSSION

The three studies presented suggest that norm status is sufficient to produce a side-effect effect, and that moral status is not necessary. In particular, the findings demonstrate that norm status can generate a side-effect effect when moral status is controlled (Experiments 1 and 2), that conventional norms can also generate a side-effect effect (Experiment 1), and that norm-violating behavior has a greater influence on future predictions than does norm-conforming behavior (Experiment 3). These findings are predicted by the Rational Scientist view, according to which norms influence mental state ascriptions because norm-violating behavior supports the ascription of counter-normative mental states, which in turn influence ascriptions of intentional action, predictions of future behavior, and other judgments relevant to theory of mind.

According to the Rational Scientist view, mental states and traits (MST1) are ascribed to novel agents on the basis of context, norms, and other available information. After observing a behavior—such as a CEO denying an interest in the environment or proceeding with a risky plan—observers update ascribed mental states and traits (generating MST2), with the behavior's relationship to norms as a source of evidence concerning the agent's mental states. In particular, moral (and other prescriptive) norms provide a reason for behaving in accordance with the norm, so a behavior that deviates from the norm suggests the existence of a conflicting reason for action—one sufficiently strong to outweigh the reason to conform to the norm. Positing such conflicting reasons may involve mental state ascriptions (e.g. "dislikes the environment," "is evil") that in turn generate different judgments.

So while there does seem to be an influence of moral evaluation on theory of mind judgments, the relationship may be best described as *evidential*. That is, the status of a behavior with respect to norms provides *evidence* about underlying mental states, but norm status need not be constitutively tied to folk psychological concepts like "intentional action." Instead, the judgment that an outcome was or wasn't brought about "intentionally" is a function of the mental states and traits ascribed to the agent (MST2), with information about the outcome and the agent's causal contribution to its occurrence also likely to play a role.

Why would the mental state ascriptions licensed by norm-violating behavior lead participants to judge that a side effect was brought about intentionally? One possibility is that participants ascribe the mental states required by Malle and Knobe's (1997) account of intentional action. According to this account, the folk concept of intentional action involves five components: desire, belief, intention, awareness, and skill. In Knobe's original CEO vignette and in those in the current experiment, the agents believe their actions will produce the outcome in question, they perform actions with this awareness, and they have the requisite skills. This leaves "desire" and "intent" as components of intentional action that are not explicitly specified by the vignette, but that participants may infer in the norm-violating case. In particular, instances of norm violation provide a relative ranking of what the agent values. When the CEO violates an environmental norm, for example, one can infer that he values (desires) profit more than he values the aspect of the environment that will be harmed. But in the norm-conforming condition there is no equivalent information about how the CEO values the environment relative to profits. While in both cases the agent expresses no concern for the side effect, the agent's actions provide unambiguous mental state information in the form of a relative value only when a norm is violated. It may be that the low relative value of the environment in norm-violating cases is sufficient to satisfy the "desire" and "intent" requirements of Malle and Knobe's (1997) account of intentional action, even if the agent does not actively desire that the environment be harmed.

Another possibility is that people's understanding of intentional action centers on choice, with an action judged intentional when there are alternative options apparent to the agent (James, 1890/1981; Miller, Galanter, & Pribram, 1960; Tolman, 1925). Along these lines, some have suggested that intent is particularly clear when the agent makes the "hard choice by following a previously nondominant alternative" (Fiske, 1989). Perhaps participants ascribe intent in cases of norm violation because they involve a clear (and dominant) alternative.

5.1. Relationship to Previous Accounts

While other accounts of the side-effect effect can be modified to accommodate our findings, the Rational Scientist view has the advantage of specifically predicting the observed pattern of results. Moreover, the Rational Scientist view can accommodate several cases in the literature that have proved difficult for other accounts of the side-effect effect. We briefly review these cases and alternative theories, and then consider the role of norms in theory of mind more broadly.

Most accounts of the side-effect effect have focused on the influence of moral valence (good or bad) or moral evaluation (blameworthiness or praiseworthiness) on judgments of intentional action (e.g. Knobe, 2003a, 2003b, 2006; Nadelhoffer, 2004; Wright & Bengson, 2009). However, subsequent studies using similar vignettes have produced examples that counter these accounts. For example, Phelan and Sarkissian (2006) generated vignettes for which side effects were judged intentional but neither bad nor blameworthy as well as others for which side effects were *not* judged intentional despite being judged bad. In one case, participants evaluated vignettes (from Knobe & Mendlow, 2004) in which the president of a corporation maximized company-wide sales but as a side effect either decreased sales in one particular division or increased the prominence of one division relative to another. Most participants judged that the president had intentionally performed both side effects but did not judge the side effects to be either bad or blameworthy. In a vignette demonstrating the opposite pattern, a city planner reluctantly decides to implement a plan that increases joblessness as a side effect of cleaning up pollution. Participants rated the side effect as bad but did not endorse the claim that it was brought about intentionally.

These results are difficult to accommodate with an account that focuses exclusively on moral valence or responsibility. However, the Rational Scientist view can explain these results. Because information about mental states is inferred from norm violations, the Rational Scientist view does not require side effects to be bad or blameworthy, only to be norm-violating. In the context of a corporation, a president operates under a norm to improve the corporation. The fact that the president is willing to incur a cost in the form of decreased sales in one division provides evidence that there must be a compelling reason to engage in the action—one sufficiently strong to outweigh a standing reason to increase sales. In the language of the Rational Scientist view, the baseline MST1 says that the president wants sales in all divisions to increase or stay the same. As in the CEO vignette, the action tells us about relative value: that the value assigned to sales in that division is lower than that assigned to the principle aim, in this case maximizing company-wide sales. This is evidence that MST1 does not provide a satisfactory picture of the president's mental states, suggesting a change to MST2 is necessary. This evidence about relative value may in turn influence ascriptions of intentional action.

In the case of the city planner, there is extra information about the agent's mental state. The city planner is choosing between adhering to two conflicting norms, one to decrease joblessness and another to clean up pollution. The city planner states that he "feel[s] awful" about the side effect. Because participants are told about the city planner's attitude towards the side effect (and they have no reason to doubt what they are told), they have no need to infer a desire or other mental state that could support an ascription of intentional action. (For a similar point see Guglielmo & Malle, submitted for publication.)

Machery (2008) proposes an account of the side-effect effect called the trade-off hypothesis that does not involve moral valence or responsibility. In his studies, participants evaluated non-moral situations, such as one in which an agent orders the largest smoothie available and as a side effect either pays an extra dollar or receives a free cup. Most participants judged that the agent paid the extra dollar intentionally but that he did not receive the free cup intentionally. Machery suggests that the extra dollar is conceptualized as a cost incurred as a means to a benefit and that costs are considered intentional. Because the free cup is not a cost that trades-off with the benefit, it is not judged intentional. However, Mallon (2008) provides examples of the side-effect effect that offer *prima facie* evidence against the trade-off hypothesis. The key vignettes involve agents who would not consider a "bad" side effect a cost. In one case, a terrorist intends to harm Americans and as a side effect either hurts Australians or helps orphans. According to the terrorist both side effects are good, so neither is a cost incurred for a greater benefit. However, participants responded that harming Australians was intentional but helping orphans was not, which Mallon argued was evidence against the trade-off hypothesis, since participants were willing to call a bad side effect intentional even when the agent did not view it as a cost.

We see the trade-off hypothesis as similar in spirit to the Rational Scientist view, but the Rational Scientist view is more general and can more easily accommodate examples like Mallon's. Conceptualizing costs in terms of norms and norm-violation can help explain both what is considered a cost and why a cost might be considered intentional. The fact that an agent is willing to incur a cost provides evidence that the agent has a reason to perform the action that is sufficiently strong to outweigh the cost—we can infer that according to the agent, the benefit outweighs the cost. Costs thus play a similar evidential role to norm violations.

Given the similarities between the trade-off hypothesis and the Rational Scientist view, Mallon's "no trade-off" terrorist cases pose a potential challenge. In particular, why don't the terrorist cases generate a side-effect effect reversal, as in the supervillain context from Experiment 2? First, because the Rational Scientist view suggests that key mental states and traits are inferred on the basis of norm violations, it's difficult to know how to evaluate the terrorist cases without explicit guidance on the norms with respect to which the agent is operating. Although the terrorist does not consider harming Australians to be a cost, taking this statement at face value requires participants to suspend their own norms—precisely what Experiment 2 attempts to accomplish with the supervillain cover story by being *very* explicit about the agent's norms. Even if participants succeed in considering the vignette from the perspective of the terrorist, participants may have reasonably inferred a reason to harm Australians that outweighed a universal norm such as "do not harm for no reason." In the supervillain context, we aimed to eliminate such background norms by stipulating that the supervillains are the baddest of the bad, look for every opportunity to cause harm, and so on. In contrast, there is no norm against helping orphans, so the same asymmetry as in the CEO problem emerges. (A similar argument can be made for interpreting the results of the Nazi identification problem used in Knobe, 2007.)

Additionally, the terrorist case only presents one side of the 2 × 2 design used in our Experiment 2 (superhero or supervillain context × helpful or harmful side effect). Reducing or eliminating a trade-off for all or some participants should have reduced the asymmetry in the side-effect effect, but this reduction wouldn't be apparent without conditions featuring a typical agent (i.e. a non-terrorist context) for comparison. Finally, the terrorist case differs from our own supervillain cases in the agent's expressed attitude towards the side effect. The terrorist acknowledges that the side effect would be a good thing in both conditions; the agents in our supervillain context claim indifference, but operate amidst norms that would dictate a positive attitude towards bad side effects (such as harming Australians) and a negative attitude towards good side effects (such as helping orphans).

Other accounts of the side-effect effect have been offered, but most have the characteristics of the accounts we have considered: they invoke a notion like moral valence or moral responsibility, or they appeal to a more general (non-moral) notion of goodness and badness. Because the Rational Scientist view emphasizes the relationship between an action and norms, involves tracking mental states, and allows for multiple sources of predictive information, it is equipped to address the kinds of cases that have proved problematic for such accounts, and provides a more complete explanation of the side-effect effect.

More recently, some have offered accounts suggesting that the side-effect effect is multiply determined (Sloman, Fernbach, & Ewing, 2012; see also Guglielmo & Malle, 2010; Sripada, 2010, for views that emphasize other factors). While we have argued that the Rational Scientist view is sufficient to explain observed asymmetries in judgments of intentional action, it is certainly possible that the factors highlighted by these accounts play an additional role in generating judgments.

5.2. Norms in Theory of Mind

The Rational Scientist view preserves the traditional functions of ToM, prediction and explanation, though additional functions are certainly possible. However, the Rational Scientist view also emphasizes a role for information about norms in prediction and explanation (see also Kalish, 2006; Wellman & Miller, 2006, 2008). Specifically, norms play a critical role in establishing baseline mental state and trait inferences (MST1) and in determining how observations influence subsequent mental state and trait inferences (MST2). In the absence of evidence that an agent has counter-normative mental states or traits, norms may support prediction and explanation directly—without being mediated by explicit mental state attributions.

Developmental research has suggested that for children under the age of four, moral and conventional norms are an important basis for explaining and predicting behavior (Kalish, 1998). For example, young children predict that an agent will conform to a norm, even if the norm is unknown to the agent or conflicts with the agent's own preferences. However, older children and adults predict that when norms and preferences conflict, preferences will often win out (Kalish &

Cornelius, 2007; Kalish & Shiverick, 2004). Even in adults, not all belief inferences are automatic (Apperly, Riggs, Simpson, Chiavarino, & Samson, 2006); it's possible that norms directly support many everyday predictions and explanations, with the corresponding mental state inferences drawn only as needed.

Recognizing a role for norms in mental state ascriptions raises a number of important questions. For example, is the influence of norms on mental state ascriptions restricted to prescriptive norms, such as the conventional and moral norms considered here? We suspect a similar relationship holds for statistical "norms" or generalizations. A behavior that violates a statistical norm is not "expected" and hence provides information about the agent's underlying mental states that may lead to a change from MST1 to MST2. If most people conform to a norm to drink coffee black, for example, observing someone drink black coffee is relatively uninformative: the behavior could have been predicted from the statistical norm. On the other hand, observing an agent violate this norm by adding cream and sugar *is* informative: rather than ascribing default mental states, we can ascribe an atypical attitude towards coffee. (See Lucas, Griffiths, Xu, & Fawcett, 2009, for a similar argument.)

As with prescriptive norms, this makes sense if the function of ToM is to track information that supports prediction and explanation.

A related question concerns the interactions between multiple norms. While many moral norms are also statistical norms, there may be cases in which norm conformance is rare, placing a moral norm in conflict with a statistical norm. How are mental state ascriptions made under such conditions? These cases may be uncommon because a moral norm would presumably be the statistical norm unless conformance had a cost. But as an illustrative example, consider the low-cost behavior of agreeing to donate one's organs in case of accidental death. Though it is generally believed that organ donation is morally good (*morally norm conforming*), actual organ donor rates in the US are not very high (*statistically norm violating*) (Sheehy et al., 2003). In this case, it may be possible to see a reversal of the typical side-effect effect, where the morally good behavior (organ donation) is more informative and judged intentional.

6. CONCLUSION

While we have contested Knobe's (2003a, 2003b, 2006) interpretations of the side-effect effect as a challenge to the traditional functions of theory of mind, our findings support the underlying claim that moral (and other) norms influence mental state ascriptions. The key lesson from our arguments and findings is that sensitivity to norms is central to the ability to predict and explain behavior.

ACKNOWLEDGMENTS

We thank Joshua Knobe and Edouard Machery for comments on an earlier draft, Lori Markson, Jennifer Cole Wright, Bertram Malle, and Steven Sloman for relevant conversations and the Berkeley Moral Psychology group and Child

Cognition Lab for helpful feedback. Finally, we'd like to thank Jesse van Fleet and the other members of the Concepts and Cognition lab for feedback and help with data collection.

NOTES

1. Each scenario involves multiple behaviors, some of which could potentially be considered norm violating in the norm-conforming condition (e.g. stating a lack of care for the environment) or norm conforming in the norm-violating condition (e.g. pursuing a plan that will increase profits). Because the scenarios were designed to test particular norms (e.g. one should not harm the environment without sufficient reason), we continue to refer to the scenarios as simply "norm conforming" or "norm violating" depending on whether the agent's behavior violates the norm that varies across paired vignettes.

2. Because the CEO vignette involving a moral norm has been the focus of so much debate, we ran a post hoc t-test comparing intentional action ratings as a function of norm status for just this vignette, revealing a non-significant effect (4.8 versus 5.2, $t(48) = -.91$, $p = .37$). However, a replication restricted to this condition with 431 participants revealed that those in the *norm-violating* (5%) condition generated significantly higher ratings of intentional action (4.96, sd = 1.66) than did those in the *norm-conforming* (45%) condition (4.42, sd = 1.73; $t(429) = -3.28$, $p <.01$).

3. To verify that the DR vignette generates a side-effect effect, a different group of 72 participants was randomly assigned to either the CEO or the DR vignette in a condition involving either a helpful or a harmful side effect. On a 7-point scale, participants judged whether it was appropriate to say that the agent *intentionally* brought about the side effect. This experiment revealed a main effect of condition ($F(1, 68) = 121.5$, $p <.001$) as well as an interaction between condition and vignette ($F(1, 68) = 9.82$, $p = .003$). The help/harm asymmetry was smaller for the DR (2.3 for help versus 4.5 for harm) than for the CEO (1.4 for help versus 5.3 for harm), but even the DR vignette involved a significant effect of condition ($t(34) = 5.13$, $p <.001$).

REFERENCES

Adams, F., & Steadman, A. (2004). Intentional action in ordinary language: Core concept or pragmatic understanding? *Analysis, 64*, 173–181.

Apperly, I. A., Riggs, K. J., Simpson, A., Chiavarino, C., & Samson, D. (2006). Is belief reasoning automatic? *Psychological Science, 17*, 841–844.

Cal. Penal Code, Section 187. Fiske, S. T. (1989). Examining the role of intent. In J. S. Uleman & J. A. Bargh (Eds.), *Unintended thought* (pp. 253–283). New York: The Guilford Press.

Gopnik, A. (1999). Theory of Mind. In R. Wilson & F. Keil (Eds.), *The MIT encyclopedia of the cognitive sciences* (p. 838). Cambridge, MA: MIT Press. Guglielmo, S., & Malle, B. F. (submitted for publication). Can unintended side-effects be intentional? Solving a puzzle in people's judgments of morality and intentionality.

Holton, R. (2010). Norms and the Knobe effect. *Analysis*.

James, W. (1890/1981). *The principles of psychology (2 vols.)*. Cambridge, MA: Harvard University Press. (Original work published 1890)

Jones, E. E., & Davis, K. E. (1965). From acts to dispositions: The attribution process in person perception. In L. Berkowitz (Ed.), *Advances in experimental social psychology* (Vol. 2, pp. 219–266). New York: Academic Press.

Kalish, C. W. (1998). Reasons and causes: Children's understanding of conformity to social rules and physical laws. *Child Development, 69,* 706–720.

Kalish, C. W. (2006). Integrating normative and psychological knowledge: What should we be thinking about? *Journal of Cognition and Culture, 6,* 191–208.

Kalish, C. W., & Cornelius, R. (2007). What is to be done? Children's ascriptions of conventional obligations. *Child Development, 78,* 859–878.

Kalish, C. W., & Shiverick, S. M. (2004). Children's reasoning about norms and traits as motives for behavior. *Cognitive Development, 19,* 401–416.

Kelley, H. H. (1967). Attribution theory in social psychology. In D. Levine (Ed.), *Nebraska symposium on motivation* (Vol. 15, pp. 192–240). Lincoln: University of Nebraska Press.

Knobe, J. (2003a). Intentional action and side effects in ordinary language. *Analysis, 63,* 190–193.

Knobe, J. (2003b). Intentional action in folk psychology: An experimental investigation. *Philosophical Psychology, 16,* 309–324.

Knobe, J. (2004). Intention, intentional action and moral considerations. *Analysis, 64,* 181–187.

Knobe, J. (2006). The concept of intentional action: A case study in the uses of folk psychology. *Philosophical Studies, 130,* 203–231.

Knobe, J. (2007). Reason explanation in folk psychology. *Midwest Studies in Philosophy, 31,* 90–107.

Knobe, J., & Burra, A. (2006). Intention and intentional action: A cross-cultural study. *Journal of Culture and Cognition, 6,* 113–132.

Knobe, J., & Mendlow, G. (2004). The good, the bad, and the blameworthy: Understanding the role of evaluative considerations in folk psychology. *Journal of Theoretical and Philosophical Psychology, 24,* 252–258.

Leslie, A., Knobe, J., & Cohen, A. (2006). Acting intentionally and the side-effect effect: "Theory of Mind" and moral judgment. *Psychological Science, 17,* 421–427.

Lucas, C., Griffiths, T. L., Xu, F., & Fawcett, C. (2009). A rational model of preference learning and choice prediction by children. *Advances in Neural Information Processing Systems, 21.*

Machery, E. (2008). The folk concept of intentional action: Philosophical and experimental issues. *Mind and Language, 23,* 165–189.

Malle, B. F., & Knobe, J. (1997). The folk concept of intentionality. *Journal of Experimental Social Psychology, 33,* 101–121.

Malle, B. F., & Guglielmo, S. (2008). The Knobe artifact? Lessons in the subtleties of language. Paper presented at the pre-conference workshop on experimental philosophy, society of philosophy and psychology 34th annual meeting, Philadelphia, PA.

Malle, B. F., & Nelson, S. E. (2003). Judging mens rea: The tension between folk concepts and legal concepts of intentionality. *Behavioral Sciences and the Law, 21,* 563–580.

Mallon, R. (2008). Knobe vs. Machery: Testing the trade-off hypothesis. *Mind & Language, 23,* 247–255.

Mele, A. (2001). Acting intentionally: Probing folk notions. In B. F. Malle, L. J. Moses, & D. Baldwin (Eds.), *Intentions and intentionality: Foundations of social cognition.* Cambridge, MA: MIT Press.

Mele, A. R., & Cushman, F. (2007). Intentional action, folk judgments, and stories: Sorting things out. *Midwest Studies in Philosophy, 31,* 184–201.

Miller, G. A., Galanter, E., & Pribram, K. H. (1960). *Plans and the structure of behavior.* New York: Holt, Rinehart and Winston.

Nadelhoffer, T. (2004). Praise, side effects, and intentional action. *The Journal of Theoretical and Philosophical Psychology, 24*, 196–213.

Pettit, D., & Knobe, J. (2009). The pervasive impact of moral judgment. *Mind and Language, 24*, 586–604.

Phelan, M., & Sarkissian, H. (2006). The folk strike back; or, why you didn't do it intentionally, though it was bad and you knew it. *Philosophical Studies, 138*, 291–298.

Searle, J. R. (2001). *Rationality in action*. Cambridge, MA: MIT Press.

Sheehy, E., Conrad, S. L., Brigham, L. E., Luskin, R., Weber, P., Eakin, M., et al. (2003). Estimating the number of potential organ donors in the United States. *New England Journal of Medicine, 349*, 667–674.

Skowronski, J. J., & Carlston, D. E. (1987). Social judgment and social memory: The role of cue diagnosticity in negativity, positivity, and extremity biases. *Journal of Personality and Social Psychology, 52*, 689–699.

Sloman, S. A., Fernbach, P. M., & Ewing, S. (submitted for publication). A causal model of intentionality judgment.

Sripada, C. S. (in press). The deep self model and asymmetries in folk judgments about intentional action. *Philosophical Studies*.

Sripada, C. S., & Konrath, S. (submitted for publication). Telling more than we can know about intentional action.

Tolman, E. C. (1925). Purpose and cognition: The determiners of animal learning. *Psychological Review, 32*, 285–297.

Wellman, H. M. (1992). *The child's theory of mind*. Cambridge, MA: MIT Press.

Wellman, H. M., & Miller, J. G. (2006). Developing conceptions of responsive intentional agents. *Journal of Cognition and Culture, 6*, 27–55.

Wellman, H. M., & Miller, J. G. (2008). Including deontic reasoning as fundamental to theory of mind. *Human Development, 51*, 105–135.

Wright, J. C., & Bengson, J. (2009). Asymmetries in judgments of responsibility and intentional action. *Mind & Language, 24*, 24–50.

PART V

MISCELLANEOUS

One of the most exciting developments within recent work in experimental philosophy is the way experimental methods are now being applied in an increasingly diverse array of different areas. There are now active experimental research programs in everything from philosophy of logic and formal semantics to political philosophy and the philosophy of art. This final section offers a small taste of this diversity, presenting a single paper on each of a number of different philosophical issues.

Griffiths, Machery, and Linquist use experiments on people's ordinary intuitions to explore a difficult question in the philosophy of science—how to understand the concept of *innateness*. They argue that this apparently scientific concept is actually rooted in folk biology. Specifically, they suggest that the concept of innateness is connected with people's folk-biological essentialism—their sense that each organism has an 'inner nature' that can in some way determine its observable traits. This hypothesis is then tested experimentally. The results indicate that people's intuitions about innateness are indeed impacted by precisely the criteria one would expect to find if people were guided by essentialist assumptions.

Buckwalter and Stich use the methods of experimental philosophy to explore the role of gender in philosophy as an academic discipline. They begin by noting that women are dramatically underrepresented in contemporary philosophy departments (with far fewer women working as professors of philosophy than as professors in related disciplines). They then introduce the hypothesis that this underrepresentation might be due, at least in part, to gender differences in philosophical intuitions. In a series of studies, they put this hypothesis to the test, showing that there are in fact systematic differences between the intuitions of men and women regarding some of the most well-known thought experiments in philosophy.

Finally, **Schwitzgebel and Cushman** examine the differences between the intuitions of ordinary people and those of philosophy professors. They find that both ordinary people and philosophy professors suffer from certain cognitive biases when evaluating philosophical thought experiments. However, they also find an important difference between the two groups. In the results for ordinary people, there are biases in judgments about individual cases, but these biases do not affect judgments about broader philosophical principles. By contrast, since the philosophy professors tend to make sure that their judgments about the principles cohere with their judgments about the cases, the biases they show on the individual cases end up influencing their judgments about the broader principles.

SUGGESTED READINGS

De Brigard, F. 2010. "If You Like It, Does It Matter If It's Real?" *Philosophical Psychology*, 23: 43–57.

May, J., Sinnott-Armstrong, W., Hull, J. & Zimmerman, A. 2010. "Practical Interests, Relevant Alternatives, and Knowledge Attributions: An Empirical Study." *Review of Philosophy and Psychology*, 1: 265–273.

Phelan, M. 2010. "The Inadequacy of Paraphrase is the Dogma of Metaphor." *Pacific Philosophical Quarterly*, 91: 481–506.

Pinillos, N. 2012. "Knowledge, Experiments and Practical Interests." In J. Brown & M. Gerken (eds.), *New Essays On Knowledge Ascriptions*. Oxford: Oxford University Press, 192-219.

Ripley, D. 2011. "Contradictions at the Borders." In Rick Nouwen, Robert van Rooij, Uli Sauerland & Hans-Christian Schmitz (eds.), *Vagueness in Communication*. Springer, 69-188.

Scholl, B. 2007. "Object Persistence in Philosophy and Psychology." *Mind & Language*, 22: 563–591.

Sripada, C. 2012. "What Makes a Manipulated Agent Unfree?" *Philosophy and Phenomenological Research*, 85(3), 563-593.

12

The Vernacular Concept of Innateness

*Paul Griffiths, Edouard Machery, and Stefan Linquist**

1. INTRODUCTION

It is a truism that the term 'innate' is vague and ambiguous. According to ethologist Patrick Bateson, '[a]t least six meanings are attached to the term: present at birth; a behavioral difference caused by a genetic difference; adapted over the course of evolution; unchanging throughout development; shared by all members of a species; and not learned.... Say what you mean (even if it uses a bit more space) rather than unintentionally confuse your readers by employing a word such as innate that carries so many different connotations' (Bateson, 1991, pp. 21–2; see Mameli and Bateson, 2006 for further argument). The rejection of the term 'innate' on these grounds has a long and distinguished history in behavioural biology (Lehrman, 1953; Hinde, 1968; Tinbergen, 1963), although some biologists think that the harm done by these ambiguities has been exaggerated (Marler, 2004, pp. 25–33).

The term 'innate' nevertheless remains popular in psychology and cognitive science. Some philosophers have proposed that in these contexts it is primarily a device to say 'not my department—ask a biologist' (Cowie 1999; Samuels, 2002). But many philosophers continue to propose analyses of the concept of innateness which purport to show that there is a single, coherent notion of innateness that either does or should underlie the use of the term in the sciences of the mind (recent examples include Mallon and Weinberg, 2006; Ariew, 2006; Khalidi, 2007). These analyses are typically subject to intuitively compelling counterexamples from the proponents of alternative analyses (see Section 5).

Our aim in this article is to show that these philosophical analyses of the concept each pick out one feature of the vernacular concept of innateness but ignore other equally real features. This fact explains both the intuitive appeal of these analyses and their vulnerability to equally intuitive counterexamples. We further argue that this undermines these attempts to defend the coherence and continuing value of the notion of innateness. Our argument is supported by some new evidence which we provide about the pre-scientific or 'vernacular' understanding of innateness. As Mameli and Bateson (2006, p. 156) note, despite the long-standing debate over the meaning of 'innate' there has been no previous empirical examination of what ordinary English speakers understand by this term.

Here is how we proceed. In Section 2, we outline some ideas about 'folk biology', and in Section 3 we make a specific proposal about the structure of the vernacular innateness concept based on these ideas. Section 4 reports two 'experimental philosophy' studies testing this proposal. In Section 5, we argue that our results explain the intuitive appeal of many of the existing analyses of the concept. They simultaneously explain why all such analyses are subject to compelling counterexamples. In Section 6, we conclude with some reflections on what philosophers can and should be trying to achieve when analysing the concept of innateness. In particular, we argue against using philosophical analysis to defend the concept of innateness against the standard biological critique we have just described.

2. INNATENESS AND FOLK BIOLOGY

The vernacular concept of innateness finds its home in a broader folk biology. It is closely related to other concepts such as instinct and human nature. These are all part of pre-scientific efforts to describe and reason about the living world, efforts that are often described as making up a folk theory. 'Folk theory' is a fancy name for the views that non-scientists hold, either explicitly or implicitly, on topics that are also topics of scientific inquiry. For example, there is a folk physics of heat, according to which heat is a physical quantity more or less directly measurable by the intensity of subjective sensations of heat. In this conception of heat, the wooden handle of a snow shovel is warmer than the metal shovel itself, and the marble slab in a fishmonger's shop is cooler than the wooden stand on which it rests. These beliefs give rise to the (correct) advice to hold the shovel by the handle and the (incorrect) advice that food will stay fresh longer if kept on the marble slab. The folk physics of heat served people fairly well until they developed technologies that required distinctions between temperature, quantity of heat and conductivity, and the folk theory persists today alongside the scientific theory. To use another example, folk dynamics is the body of beliefs which people unreflectively hold about the movement of three-dimensional, medium-sized objects. People tend to explain the movement of an object that has been thrown by ascribing to it some kind of impetus (Clement, 1983; McCloskey, 1983). Needless to say, impetus-like forces have no place in either Newtonian or post-Newtonian physics.

Just as there are commonsense ideas about heat and dynamics, there are commonsense ideas about biology. Prominent amongst these is the idea that some traits are expressions of the inner nature of animals and plants, whilst other traits result from the influence of the environment. For example, dogs are bred for their coat and for their temperament, both of which are presumed to be part of their nature and thus inherited, but they are not bred for their attachment to a particular family, which is presumed to be the result of experience. The idea that living things have inner natures that make them the kind of organism that they are is intimately linked to the very idea of heredity. The hereditary traits of an animal are those that are passed on as part of its nature. Natures also explain the stability of some traits within a single lifetime—we do not expect a black sheep to grow white wool after shearing, because the colour of its wool is part of its nature.[1] Like the folk theory of heat, folk-biological ideas work reasonably well for hunting, farming, and traditional stockbreeding. They are not adequate, however, for the purposes of scientific biology. The ecological and evolutionary trajectories of populations cannot be understood with a folk theory of heredity, and it is not possible to understand development using the folk theory of inner natures.

For over 20 years, psychologists and anthropologists have investigated the structure and development of folk biological concepts across a range of different cultures.[2] Although many key issues remain unresolved, a consensus has emerged that a core set of biological beliefs is commonly held by non-scientists in a wide range of cultures. We briefly outline the aspects of folk biology that, we suggest, are the likely source of people's vernacular concept of innateness.

One widely documented feature of folk biological categories is that they are hierarchically structured (Berlin, Breedlove, and Raven, 1973; Atran, 1990; Berlin, 1992). People everywhere identify (at least) three general levels of biological classification: a 'generic species' category (e.g. dogs and cedars), a super-ordinate category of biological domains (e.g. animals and plants), and a subordinate category of species varieties (e.g. particular breeds or strains). From a cognitive point of view, not all levels of this taxonomy are equally significant. The generic species rank is of particular importance. Membership in a generic species is associated with what psychologists call 'psychological essentialism' (Medin and Atran, 2004). People are psychological essentialists when they believe that membership in a biological kind is associated with a particular *causal essence* or *inner nature*—that is, some property or set of properties that define membership in a kind and cause members of the kind to possess kind-typical properties (Medin and Ortony, 1989; Atran, 1990; Gelman, 2003). The hypothesis that people are unreflectively essentialist is associated with at least two closely related beliefs that have been identified across a wide range of cultures.[3] First, adults believe that membership in a species is a permanent property of an organism that is inherited by descent and that is not affected by changes to its appearance. For example, when asked to imagine a raccoon that has been surgically modified to look and smell like a skunk, adults maintain that the animal is still a raccoon (Keil, 1989; see also Rips, 1989; Atran et al., 2001 with Yukatek adults; Sousa, Atran, and Medin, 2002 with Brazilian adults). Second, and most important for our purposes, people believe that the development of species-typical traits does not depend on environmental influences. For example, when asked to imagine a cow that has been raised by a family of pigs, adults assume that the cow will display the normal bovine traits (e.g. mooing instead of oinking) (Atran et al., 2001; Sousa, Atran, and Medin, 2002). In addition to psychological essentialism, Scott Atran (1995) has also proposed that folk biology has another core feature: the tendency to explain traits teleologically. That is, people tend to explain the traits possessed by animals and plants by asserting that these traits have a purpose.

The suggestion that humans share a core set of folk biological beliefs raises a host of controversial issues. There is some debate over the exact point in development at which these beliefs emerge, for example, and the extent of their cross-cultural similarity remains a matter of ongoing investigation.[4] There is also a lingering question about the nature of the underlying psychological mechanism. Some argue that psychological essentialism and the tendency to explain traits teleologically are generated by a domain-specific module (Atran, 1995), whilst others attribute the formation of psychological essentialism to a more general-purpose reasoning ability (Gelman and Hirschfeld, 1999) and yet others attribute the formation of the tendency to explain traits teleologically to our disposition to provide intentional explanations (Kelemen, 1999, 2004). Importantly, none of these more controversial issues bear on the hypothesis being investigated here. What is important for our purposes is that early on and across cultures, people believe that organisms possess inherited 'inner natures' that [1] cause them to possess species-typical properties, [2] whose development is resistant to environmental influences, and [3] that are functional (they have a purpose). Following Griffiths (2002), we hypothesize that the vernacular concept of innateness has its origin in these folk biological beliefs. That is, when the folk believe a trait is innate, what they believe is that it is an expression of an organism's inner nature, and hence that the trait will possess all or some combination of the three features of species typicality, developmental fixity, and purposive function (hereafter: 'Typicality', 'Fixity', and 'Teleology').

3. THE THREE-FEATURE THEORY OF INNATENESS

According to Griffiths (2002, p. 71), it is part of folk biology that three features are particularly associated with traits that are expressions of the inner nature that organisms inherit from their parents. These features are:

1. Fixity—the trait is hard to change; its development is insensitive to environmental inputs in development; its development appears goal directed, or resistant to perturbation.
2. Typicality—the trait is part of what it is to be an organism *of that kind*; every individual has it, or every individual that is not malformed, or every individual of a certain age, sex or other natural subcategory.

3. Teleology—this is how the organism is *meant* to develop; to lack the innate trait is to be malformed; environments that disrupt the development of this trait are themselves abnormal.

Griffiths described these three features in such broad terms in order to capture shared themes in the very different ideas about the inner natures of living things that are found in different human societies.[5] Consider, for example, the feature that we have called 'Teleology'. Darwinists will understand this as evolutionary design, whereas creationists will understand it as God's intention. Each seeks to make sense in their own terms of an intuitive sense that an organism is *meant* to be a certain way whether or not it actually turns out that way. In the 17th century, the anatomist William Harvey dealt with the same fundamental intuition within an Aristotelian framework by supposing that the 'idea or form' of the organism provided by the male parent is sometimes misinterpreted by the 'formative faculty' of the female parent's womb (Harvey, 1989, p. 578). It is the underlying intuition shared by all three theorists that we regard as an expression of folk biology, and in particular of the folk-biological conception of inner natures.

We cannot sufficiently stress that we are *not* proposing to define innateness with a set of necessary and sufficient conditions called Typicality, Fixity, and Teleology. The three-feature theory has a similar status to accounts of other concepts developed by psychologists and cognitive anthropologists. It treats the vernacular concept of innateness as a cognitive structure (or a mental representation) that has its origin in folk biology. If the three-feature theory is correct, then the cognitive structure that underpins the use of the term 'innate' is an implicit theory that views organisms as having inner natures which are expressed in traits that are likely to be Typical, Fixed, and Teleological.

The aim of the present study is to test the three-feature theory by examining how people actually apply the concept of innateness. The three-feature theory makes claims about folk biology, not about the ideas that people derive from scientific biology. Thus, the study asks specifically whether *non-scientists* use the innateness concept in the manner predicted by the three-feature theory. If innateness judgments are indeed influenced by these three features in the way we have suggested, then two predictions should follow:

1. The association of each of the three features with a trait increases the likelihood that participants will identify that trait as innate.
2. All three features will contribute *independently* to participants' judgments about whether a trait is innate.

Note that prediction two is stronger and more risky than prediction one. It is a direct consequence of our hypothesis that the three features in question (Typicality, Fixity, and Teleology) contribute *additively* to judgments about whether some trait is innate. Suppose that we are wrong, and that people only take one feature—Fixity, for example—to be characteristic of traits which express inner natures. But, suppose also that people use the other two features as suggestive cues for whether the defining feature is present (perhaps because they believe that the corresponding properties tend to co-occur). This alternative to the three-feature theory predicts an interaction among the three features. Direct evidence that the trait is not Fixed will reduce the influence of evidence that the trait is Typical or Teleological on the final judgment about its innateness. An analogy may make this point clearer: seeing a Prada logo on a handbag strongly influences the judgment that it is a Prada handbag. But independent evidence that it is *not* a Prada bag—for example, the fact that it is being sold in a street market in Jakarta for the equivalent of one US dollar—reduces the influence of the logo on judgments about the brand. Prediction two says that evidence about the three features of innate traits will not interact in this way.

We should also stress that we are not proposing that only three, simple cues affect judgments of innateness. It seems clear, for example, that being present at birth and not being learnt are cues which people use to identify traits as innate. But we suggest that these and many other specific cues can be understood in terms of the three broad intuitive aspects of innateness which we have identified. The significance of presence at birth and not being learnt, for example, is that they provide evidence that the trait is insensitive to the environment and is developing as if guided by some internal goal—that is, evidence that the trait has the folk-biological feature that we have labelled 'Fixity'.

4. TESTING THE THREE-FEATURE THEORY OF INNATENESS

4.1. Study 1: Materials

To test the prediction that Fixity, Typicality, and Teleology are additive factors positively affecting judgments of innateness, we studied whether people judge eight examples of birdsong to be innate behaviours. We chose birdsong because it offers the opportunity to find real, or at least realistic, examples of the eight possible combinations of the three factors under consideration (Table 1). There are over nine thousand species of birds and song learning has been the focus of intense investigation since the groundbreaking work of William Thorpe and Peter Marler in the 1950s (for an accessible introduction, see Marler and Slabbekorn, 2004). Although the participants in our experiment had no expertise in biology or in any behavioural science, we hope to use these materials in later studies with scientists and feedback from scientists involved in other 'experimental philosophy' studies suggests that they are unwilling to devote time and effort to thinking about unrealistic cases (Griffiths and Karola Stotz, personal communication).

In four cases, we used a bird which is known to acquire its song in a manner corresponding exactly to one of the boxes in Table 1. We failed to find a bird for the remaining four cases. For these remaining cases we used a speciose genus where some species are known to acquire their song in a manner very close to what we required. We invented a new species of that genus which fitted our requirements, and made up plausible common and scientific names for that species. One of our species is the Pale-Headed Thornbird *(Phacellodomus*

Table 12.1 The eight possible combinations of fixity, typicality, and teleology

	Typical		Atypical	
	Functional	Non-functional	Functional	Non-functional
Fixed	Grey-Throated Antwren	Eastern Phoebe	Alder Flycatcher	Pale-Headed Thornbird
Plastic	Black-Capped Chickadee	Archer's Grasshopper Warbler	Chaffinch	Sarkar's Sparrow

pallida). Unless you are a keen birder with expertise in the relevant region, we doubt that you can tell whether this is one of the real species.

The eight probes describing the examples of birdsong have the same structure. The probe begins with a standard paragraph about research on birdsong, designed to convince participants that there is a wealth of well-established scientific knowledge about birdsong. The next paragraph begins with one or two sentences naming a specific bird and providing some neutral information about it. This is designed to convince participants that this is a real animal. The remainder of this paragraph states whether the song of the male of this species is Fixed, Typical, Teleological or their opposites, using one of each of these pairs of statements:

Fixed/Plastic
0. Studies on _____ show that the song an adult male produces depends on which songs they hear when they are young.
1. Studies on _____ show that the song an adult male produces does not depend on which songs they hear when they are young.

Typical/~Typical
0. Studies also show that different males in this species sing different songs.
1. Studies also show that all males of this species sing the same song.

Teleology/~Teleology
0. Close observations of these birds reveal that the males' song is not used to attract mates or to defend territories. Scientists therefore agree that this feature of the bird has no real function, like the appendix in humans.
1. Close observations of these birds reveal that the males' song attracts mates and helps to defend their territory. Scientists therefore agree that this feature of the bird has a real function, like the heart in humans.

To control for order effects, we presented the information about Typicality, Fixity, and Teleology in three different orders—Typicality-Fixity-Teleology (order 1), Teleology-Typicality-Fixity (order 2), Fixity-Teleology-Typicality (order 3)—resulting in 24 different probes.[6]

To illustrate, the probe describing a species of bird in which birdsong is not-Typical, is Fixed, and has a Function, with the items presented in order 1, read as follows:

Birdsong is one of the most intensively studied aspects of animal behaviour. Since the 1950s scientists have used recordings and sound spectograms to uncover the structure and function of birdsong. Neuroscientists have investigated in great detail the areas of the brain that allow birds to develop and produce their songs. Other scientists have done ecological fieldwork to study what role song plays in the lives of different birds.

The Alder Flycatcher (*Empidonax alnorum*) is a migratory neo-tropical bird which breeds in southern Canada and the northern USA. Studies on the Alder Flycatcher show that the song an adult male produces does not depend on which songs they hear when they are young. Studies also show that different males in this species sing different songs. Furthermore, close observations of these birds reveal that the males' song attracts mates and helps to defend their territory. Scientists therefore agree that the bird's song has a real function, like the heart in humans.

On a 7-point scale, 1 meaning strongly disagree and 7 meaning strongly agree, how would you respond to the following statement?

'The song of the male Alder Flycatcher is innate.'

It should be noted that a substantial amount of interpretation is involved in reducing the three hypothesized features associated with innateness to these three information items. Our interpretation of Fixity reflects the general tenor of the birdsong literature, in which the songs of sub-oscine passerine birds are traditionally described as 'innate' because, unlike the oscine passerines, their development does not depend on exposure to correct song. Our interpretation of Typicality ignores the idea that a variable song might be an evolved polymorphism like eye colour. Our interpretation of Teleology as having a 'real function' was driven by the need to remain neutral between evolutionary and creationist conceptions of teleology. The examples of organs that have and do not have a 'real function' (respectively, heart and appendix) were included to ensure that participants interpreted 'real function' in the sense we intended. It seems plausible that typical North American participants will be familiar with these two examples.

4.2. Study 1: Participants and Procedure

Two hundred fifty-five individuals taking classes at the University of Pittsburgh took part in the experiment. Ten participants were not native speakers of English, and 1 subject did not specify whether she was a native speaker of English. These 11 participants were removed from the data set, resulting in a sample of 244 participants (mean age: 20.9; range: 18–40; 50.8% males).

In classroom settings, participants were randomly assigned to one of the 24 probes. They were asked to answer the innateness question by circling a numeral on a 7-point scale, anchored at 1 with 'totally disagree' and at 7 with 'totally agree'. Participants were also asked to fill a short demographic questionnaire. This asked for their education level in biology and in psychology as well as for their general propensity to favour 'biological' over 'environmental' explanations of human behaviour. We found no meaningful relation between either our participants' education level in biology and in psychology or their propensity to favour biological over environmental explanations and their answer to the innateness question.

4.3. Study 1: Results

To exclude outliers, we eliminated seven data points whose values deviated from the mean of the relevant probes by at least two standard deviations. Table 2 summarizes our results.

To test the three-feature theory of innateness, we used an ANOVA with Fixity, Typicality, and Teleology as between-participants factors. As expected, we found a main effect of Fixity (Fixed > Plastic, $F(1, 229) = 47.39, p < .001$, partial $\eta^2 = .17$) and Typicality (Typical > Atypical, $F(1, 229) = 10.24, p = .002$, partial $\eta^2 = 04$), and a marginal effect of Function (Functional > Non-functional, $F(1, 229) = 3.16, p = .08$, partial $\eta^2 = .01$). Importantly for our purposes, there was no significant interaction (see Figure 1).

Together, our three predictors explain around 22% of the total variance (see Figure 2).

4.4. Study 1: Discussion

The three-feature theory of innateness is supported by the results of Study 1. As we expected, people are more likely to agree that a trait is innate when it is fixed than when it is plastic, when it is typical than when it is atypical, and when it is functional rather than when it is non-functional. Together, Typicality, Fixity, and Teleology explained more than 20% of the variance in participants' answers to the innateness question. Finally, as we also expected, the influence of each of these three factors on people's judgments about innateness does not depend on the other factors.

Fixity turned out to be a more important factor than Typicality. Typicality alone explained only 4% of the variance in participants' answers to the innateness question, while Fixity explained 17% of the variance. Thus, when people decide whether a trait is innate, the Fixity of a trait matters more than its Typicality. Teleology significantly influenced participants' answers to the innateness question, but its influence was limited, since it explained only 1% of the variance.

Study 1 is limited in two main respects. First, the effect of Teleology on participants' answer to the innateness question was only marginally significant and Teleology explained only a very small portion of total variance. Thus, though relevant, the functional significance of a trait does not seem to be clearly an important factor when people decide whether this trait is innate. We see three mutually exclusive explanations of this result. First, we may simply be wrong in assuming that the function of a trait is one of the cues that people use to decide

Table 2 Mean answers (and standard deviations) for the eight combinations of factors

	Typical		Atypical	
	Functional	Non-functional	Functional	Non-functional
Fixed	5.86 (.86)	5.57 (1.16)	5.39 (1.17)	4.52 (2.03)
Plastic	4.40 (1.77)	4.03 (1.87)	3.64 (1.41)	3.75 (1.67)

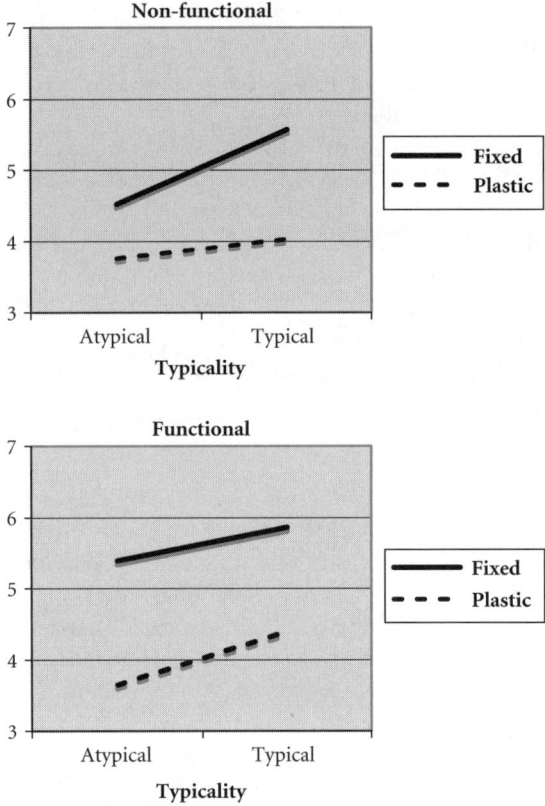

Figure 12.1. Participants' mean answer to the innateness question as a function of Typicality, Fixity, and Teleology (Function).

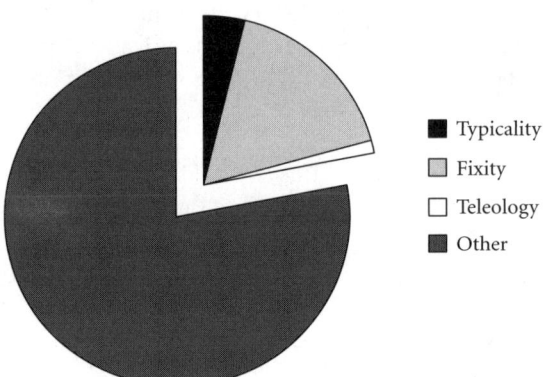

Figure 12.2. Proportion of the variance independently predicted by Fixity, Typicality, and Teleology.

whether this trait is innate. In support of this first explanation, one might follow some psychologists (Kelemen, 1999, 2004) in arguing that in contrast to the folk tendency to categorize a trait as innate if it is either canalized or species typical, the folk tendency to explain teleologically biological traits does not originate in folk biology. If folk biology is the source of the vernacular concept of innateness, function might then not be relevant when the folk decide whether a trait is innate.

A second, alternative explanation is that, while it is part of folk-biology that innate traits are how organisms are 'meant to be' (Teleology), this is not adequately expressed by the claim that innate traits have a function. Griffiths's (2002) original proposal was inspired by the widespread assumption that an organism which fully expresses its inner nature is somehow better than one which does not and that only ill effects can come from interfering with the expression of an organism's true nature. The original meaning of 'monster' (*terata*) is, after all, an organism in which the form of the species has failed to impress itself on recalcitrant matter. These ideas may simply not be adequately represented by the information we provided about whether a trait has a function.

There is a third, simpler explanation that is also consistent with the three-feature theory of innateness. In our probes, when we gave information about the functional significance of birdsong, we compared birdsong to a biological organ *both* when birdsong was functional (the heart) *and* when it was not (the appendix). Now, if participants believed that the heart and the appendix are both innate traits of humans, our probes inadvertently suggested that function was not important for deciding whether a trait was innate. This explanation can be tested, by eliminating the comparisons from our current probes. We intend to do this test in a follow-up study.

The second limitation of our study is that our three predictors taken together explain 22% of the variance in participants' answer to the innateness question, corresponding to a medium effect size (Cohen, 1992). One might wonder why they do not explain a larger part of the variance if the three-feature theory of innateness is true.

We hypothesized that the limited proportion of variance captured by each factor (Fixity, Typicality, Teleology) is mostly due to the noise introduced by the between-subject design. Because individual participants likely differ in their background beliefs about whether birdsong, or animal behaviour generally, is innate, it is unlikely that each subject made the same use of the 7-point scale, resulting in a substantial amount of variance not explained by our three factors. We thus predict that the proportion of variance explained by each factor would substantially increase in a within-subject design. Study 2 was designed to test this prediction.

4.5. Study 2: Replication

The goal of Study 2 was to extend the findings of Study 1, by circumventing some of its limitations. Specifically, we attempted to better evaluate the influence of our three factors on intuitive judgments about innateness by reducing the noise produced by between-subject differences. To achieve this we used a within-subject design: each subject was presented with all of the probes.[7]

Thirty-eight individuals at the University of Guelph (Canada) took part in the experiment in exchange for a small monetary compensation. One subject was not a native speaker of English and was removed from the data set, resulting in a sample of 37 participants (mean age: 22; range: 18–50; 43.2% males).

Instead of counterbalancing the order of the three factors, as we did in Study 1, we used the following order: Fixity, Typicality, Teleology. Participants read the eight resulting probes and were asked to answer the innateness question on a 7-point scale after each probe. The order of the probes was counterbalanced across participants.

Table 3 summarizes our results.

To test the three-feature theory of innateness, we performed a repeated-measures ANOVA with Typicality, Fixity, and Teleology as within-subject factors, resulting in a main effect of Fixity (Fixed > Plastic, $F(1, 36) = 16.48$, $p < .001$, partial $\eta^2 = .31$), a main effect of Typicality (Typical > Atypical, $F(1, 36) = 15.80$, $p < .001$, partial $\eta^2 = .31$), and a main effect of Teleology (Functional > Non-functional, $F(1, 36) = 3.33$, $p = .07$, partial $\eta^2 = .09$). No interaction was significant, as can be seen on Figure 3.

Together, our three factors explained around 70 percent of the variance (Figure 4).

4.6. Study 2: Discussion

Study 2 extends the findings of Study 1, providing further support for the three-feature theory of innateness. We found again that people are more likely to agree that a trait is innate when it is fixed than when it is plastic, when it is typical than when it is atypical, and when it is functional rather than when it is non-functional. Together, Typicality, Fixity, and Teleology explained around 70% of the variance in participants' answers to the innateness question—a large increase in explained variance in comparison to Study 1. Finally, we found again that the influence of each of these three factors on people's judgments about innateness does not depend on the other factors.

Typicality and Fixity explained a large part of the variance in participants' answers to the innateness question (Fixity slightly more than Typicality). Teleology explains a smaller part of the variance than Typicality and Fixity, but

Table 12.3 Mean answers (and standard deviations) for the eight probes of study 2

	Typical		Atypical	
	Functional	Non-functional	Functional	Non-functional
Fixed	5.54 (.30)	5.12 (.30)	4.62 (.35)	3.95 (.32)
Plastic	4.46 (.33)	4.11 (.28)	3.60 (.30)	3.11 (.26)

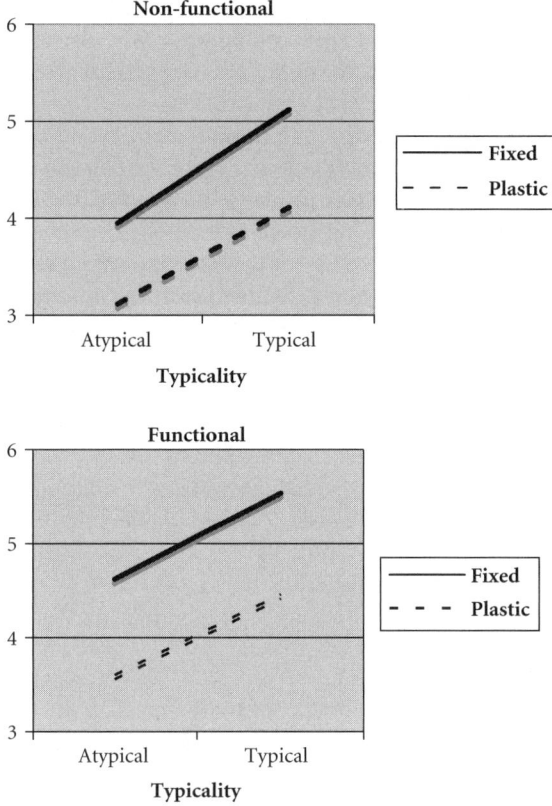

Figure 12.3. Participants' mean answer to the innateness question as a function of Typicality, Fixity, and Teleology.

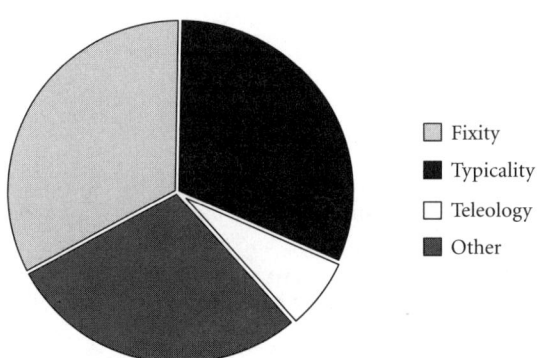

Figure 12.4. Proportion of the variance explained by Fixity, Typicality, and Teleology.

one that is markedly larger than in Study 1. We conclude that controlling for the noise introduced by the diverse use of the scale in Study 1 reveals the strong influence of Fixity and Typicality on people's judgments about innateness as well as the weaker but real influence of Teleology.

It is noteworthy that Studies 1 and 2 lead us to refine Griffiths' original hypothesis about the vernacular concept of innateness. As we saw, Griffiths proposed that folk judgments about the innateness of a trait depends on whether this trait is typical, on whether it is fixed, and on whether it serves a function. Our findings allow us to specify the relative importance of these three factors. Whether a trait is judged to be innate depend primarily on its fixity and on its typicality and, to a lesser extent, on its functionality. Its fixity seems to matter a little bit more than its typicality.

Finally, this study is a first step toward examining our hypothesis cross-culturally. One might indeed wonder whether innateness is conceptualized similarly across cultures.[8] Although Canada and the USA are culturally similar, Study 2 at least suggests that people think similarly about innateness in these two countries. Further studies should investigate further the cross-cultural generality of our hypothesis.

5. ACCOUNTING FOR THE EXISTING ANALYSES OF INNATENESS

Philosophers have proposed several intuitively appealing analyses of the concept of innateness, but these analyses are typically subject to intuitively compelling counterexamples, resulting in some kind of stalemate. We now argue that our results explain this aspect of the philosophical literature on innateness. Each analysis fixes on one or two aspects of the vernacular concept of innateness, leaving itself open to counterexamples which appeal to intuitions derived from the other aspects.

5.1. Analyses of Innateness Based on Typicality[9]

In his seminal paper 'The idea of innateness' (1975), Steven Stich examined a number of suggestions about the structure of the concept. One is that a trait is innate if and only if a person will manifest it in the normal course of human development. The intuitive appeal of this analysis is confirmed by the fact that some scientists have used the term 'innate' to refer to any feature which is characteristic of an entire species (Bateson, 1991). Stich himself immediately offered a counterexample to this analysis: universally held beliefs, such as the belief that water quenches thirst, will count as innate on this analysis whereas intuitively they are acquired (Stich, 1975, p. 9). André Ariew has offered another counterexample: it is part of the normal course of human development to develop the typical gut flora that allows us to digest our food, but Ariew finds it counterintuitive to call these bacterial communities an innate feature of human beings (Ariew, 1999, p. 133). Ariew has suggested that Stich's analysis derives its plausibility from the unspoken assumption that if a trait is species-typical, then there is some mechanism that ensures its presence (Ariew, 2006, p. 10).

The proposal that a trait is innate just in case it is typical of normal development appeals to the folk biological idea that traits which express an organism's inner nature will typify that species. Our results show clearly that judgments of innateness are influenced by information about Typicality, so it is unsurprising that suitably chosen thought experiments evoke intuitions that favour this analysis. However, our results also show that judgments of innateness are influenced by information about Fixity, so it is equally unsurprising that the thought experiments listed above, both of which make salient the dependence of typical traits on interaction with the environment, evoke intuitions hostile to the analysis.

5.2. Analyses of Innateness Based on Teleology

Another popular analysis of innateness suggests that a trait is innate if its development is guided by 'inherited information' rather than 'environmental information'. This idea was suggested by Stich (1975, pp. 13–16) and has been defended at length by Muhammad Ali Khalidi (2002, 2007). Its most prominent defender, however, was the ethologist Konrad Lorenz (1965).[10] The key question facing an account of this kind is how to measure 'information'. Lorenz identified information in this context with adaptive fit. An adaptive trait fits some environments better than others and hence can be said to contain information about the environment. If a person has calluses on their palms rather than on the backs of their hands, then these calluses contain information about where their skin gets rubbed.[11] If they form calluses on their palms more easily than on the backs of their hands (or if, like the ostrich, they are born with calluses in useful places), and if these traits fit their future environments, then those traits contain information about those future environments. This anticipatory information, Lorenz argues, must have been in the genome and must have been absorbed from ancestral environments.

Lorenz's analysis can readily be expressed in information-theoretic terms, with the environment as the signal source and the organism as the receiver. Organisms need to reduce their uncertainty about what demands the environment will place on them and to develop in a way that meets those demands. There are two ways to do this. One is to gather information during development. The water flea *Daphnia pulex* monitors chemical traces of predators as it develops and grows defensive armour if predators are indicated. The information about the environment inherent in the armour was collected by the individual as it developed. The other way is to inherit information from your ancestors. The sickle cell allele, a costly trait which survives only because it also confers resistance against malaria, carries information about the prevalence of malaria in the ancestral environment and thus, probably, in the environment of the organism which inherits it. The information about the environment inherent in the sickle cell allele was collected by the individual's ancestors through natural selection. To the extent that the functional adjustment of a trait to its environment is explained by 'inherited information' of this kind, Lorenz argued, the trait is innate.

Stripped of its colourful language, the 'inherited information' analysis amounts to the claim that a trait is innate if its fit to the environment can be explained only by evolutionary adaptation (or by intelligent design, if you swing that way). An organism is *innately* suitable for a particular kind of environment, if it is designed in advance to fit that environment. The intuitive appeal of this analysis can readily be explained if it is part of folk biology that traits which reflect an organism's inner nature are design features, representing how the organism is intended to develop. Our data showed a significant effect for Teleology (though weaker than for Typicality and Teleology) in driving judgments of innateness, suggesting that this explanation is correct. Moreover, despite its intuitive appeal the analysis is open to counterexamples based on Typicality and/or Fixity, just as we would predict on the basis of our results. For example, the massively overgrown jaw typical of the inbred Hapsburg royal family was innate—the Hapsburgs were innately hideous—but this was neither an evolutionary adaptation nor an instance of intelligent design.

5.3. Analyses of Innateness Based on Fixity

A third class of analyses identifies innateness with Fixity: innate traits are those like the Hapsburg jaw which are hard to change. This view has been ably defended by Andre Ariew, who argues that traits are innate to the extent that they exhibit environmental canalisation (Ariew, 1996, 1999, 2006; for discussion, see Griffiths and Machery, 2008). The concept of canalisation derives from the mid-20th century embryologist and theoretical biologist Conrad H. Waddington. A trait is genetically canalised to the extent that it will develop despite variations in the organism's genome. It is environmentally canalised to the extent that it will develop despite variation in the organism's environment. It is canalised *simpliciter* to the extent that both of these are true (Griffiths, 2006). Innateness-as-canalisation is a matter of degree. A trait is more innate the more environmental parameters its development is buffered against and the wider the range of variation in those parameters against which it is buffered.

Our data suggest that intuitions about innateness respond more strongly to information about Fixity than to information about Typicality or Teleology. Innateness-as-canalisation should therefore fit people's intuitions about innateness better than other analyses.[12] Despite this, however, analyses which identify innateness with Fixity remain subject to intuitive counterexamples that trade on intuitions derived from those other features. Consider the penile reflexes of the rat. Celia Moore (1992, 1984) has shown that the spinal cord nuclei of male rats differ from those of female rats in ways that allow the male to use his penis during copulation. These neural differences result from differences in gene expression in the developing spinal cord of the rat pup, which in turn result from differences in the amount of licking of the genital area by the mother, which in turn results from greater expression of a chemical that elicits maternal licking in male pups. According to innateness-as-canalisation, these experiments show that the rat's ability to copulate is not innate:

Distinguish between two reasons why the trait appears invariantly in an environmental range: the first, because an environmental condition is developmentally required yet is found everywhere the system develops; the second, because the system develops independently of the environmentally condition. Innateness should be identified with the second sort of invariance, not the first. (Ariew, 2006, p. 10)

We do not think that intuitions about the penile reflex case follow this prescription. Our data support this hunch. One of our examples of birdsong is the Black-Capped Chickadee *(Parus atricapillus)* (Table 2). Despite the wide geographic range of the chickadee, its morning 'fee-bee' song is invariant throughout the species. But males must be exposed to species-typical song in order to acquire that song themselves. With this probe we gave participants exactly the evidence Ariew takes to show that a trait is not innate—'an environmental condition is developmentally required yet is found everywhere the system develops'—but our participants regard the song as innate. The modal answer in Study 1 was 5 on our 7-point scale, while the modal answer in Study 2 was 7 on the same scale.

6. WHAT, IF ANYTHING, CAN CONCEPTUAL ANALYSIS OF INNATENESS ACHIEVE?

We showed in Section 4 that people rely on the typicality of a trait, on its universality, and (to a lesser extent) on its teleology (functionality) to decide whether it is innate. In Section 5 we have shown that the main proposed analyses of the concept have focused on one of these three features. As a result, they are left open to counterexamples that elicit intuitions about innateness derived from the other two features. We argue in Section 6.1 that this shows traditional philosophical analysis is not a good tool for studying the vernacular concept. In Section 6.2 we argue that philosophical analysis should not be used to sidestep the criticisms advanced by the many scientists involved in the study of behavioural development who regard the concept of innateness as fundamentally confused. Finally, in Section 6.3 we consider the use of philosophical analysis to understand the use of the innateness concept by specific scientific communities.

6.1. Conceptual Analysis and the Vernacular Conception of Innateness

Traditional philosophical analysis is not a good tool for studying the vernacular concept. The thirty-year tradition of philosophical analysis of the innateness concept discussed in this section has yet to produce an analysis that comes close to being successful. In fact, each major analysis picks only *one* of the three features that the ordinary speakers actually use to assess innateness. Some more recent analyses seem to draw on *two* features, which probably increases their intuitive adequacy (e.g. Mallon and Weinberg, 2006). However, a successful analysis of the vernacular concept of innateness—one that would not fall prey to intuitive counterexamples—would have to include (at least) all three features discussed in this article—viz. Fixity, Typicality, and Teleology.

Moreover, if philosophers truly want to characterize the vernacular concept of innateness, they should renounce the methods that were used to develop the existing analyses. An accurate characterization would not just *include* all three features but would give them appropriate *weights* and specify the pattern in which the features *interact*. Our two empirical studies suggest that, though relevant, Teleology matters less than Fixity and Typicality. Our studies also suggest that they interact additively, when they could equally well have exhibited complex interaction effects, with one taking on more or less significance in the light of the others. It is not plausible that the lower weighting of Teleology, or the fact that the various features interact additively, could have been discovered by comparing putative analyses of the concept of innateness with an unsystematic set of counterexamples, as philosophers traditionally do. At most this traditional, informal approach might suggest hypotheses for testing. Thus, if philosophers really wanted to characterize the vernacular concept of innateness, they should undertake empirical studies of the kind described in this article.

6.2. Conceptual Analysis and the Scientific Critique of Innateness

Many philosophers see themselves as reforming, rather than analysing, the folk notion of innateness in order to make this notion more useful role for science. Ariew (2006) is particularly explicit about this. He proposes to identify innateness with environmental canalization because such a reformed concept of innateness would be useful in biology and psychology. These reformist 'explications' of innateness are supposed to sidestep criticism of the innateness concept as vague and confused by providing a clear account of what 'innate' *could* be used to mean. In this section we argue that philosophical analysis should not be used in this way to sidestep scientific criticisms of the concept.

The data from our two empirical studies bolsters the standard scientific criticism of the concept, which is that it conflates a number of different ideas and leads to fallacies of ambiguity (e.g. Lehrman, 1953; Hinde, 1968; Tinbergen, 1963; Johnston, 1987; West and King, 1987; Bateson, 1991; Oyama, 1990; Ford and Lerner, 1992; Michel and Moore, 1995; Gottlieb, 1997; Meaney, 2001; for a good introduction, see Moore, 2001). We have shown that Typicality, Fixity, and Teleology have an *independent influence* on folk judgments about innateness. This means that people need not know whether a trait is fixed or has a function to decide whether it is innate on the basis of evidence about typicality (and vice versa). Thus, if they are told that a trait is species-typical, people may well infer that it is innate. But all three features are involved in vernacular conceptions of the innate. Having judged that it is innate, people are likely to infer that it is fixed—that its development does not depend on its environment. Or if they are told that a trait has a function, people may infer on that basis alone that it is innate. Having judged that it is innate, they are likely to conclude that it is species-typical (and so on). The problem is that traits that are species-typical are not necessarily fixed, traits that are functional are not necessarily species-typical, and so on.

At this point, some philosophers will object that whilst the inferences just described may technically be fallacious, this is not important because as a matter of fact, when a trait is species-typical, it is usually also canalized and functional (and vice versa). In our experience, philosophers presented with the standard critique of the concept of innateness from behavioural biology are unimpressed because it seems intuitively obvious to them that the various aspects of innateness, whilst theoretically separable, are always found together in nature. But this intuition is merely an expression of the folk theory of inner natures which philosophers, as much as anyone else, make use of in their everyday lives. In fact, the literature just cited contains many well-researched examples of disassociations between Fixity, Typicality, and Teleology, disassociations that from a folk-biological point of view appear paradoxical. It was these discoveries, rather than a desire for conceptual precision, that led the many students of behavioural developmental listed above to reject the idea of innateness.

There are also sound theoretical reasons for rejecting the presumption that Typicality, Fixity and Teleology will go together, however intuitive this presumption may appear. First, natural selection has no particular bias towards producing traits that are species-typical (monomorphic). Many important traits in humans and other organisms are genetically maintained polymorphisms, either as a result of frequency dependent selection, or as a response to variation in the environment across the species' range (ecotypes). Natural selection also frequently produces phenotypic plasticity, in which the developmental system responds to the environment with a range of traits, as in the example of the water flea *Daphnia pulex* given above. Second, natural selection does not select for mechanisms which buffer traits against variation in the environment unless variation of that kind has posed a significant problem in the past. In fact, any buffering mechanism which is not actively being used will tend to decay by mutation. The human ascorbic acid synthesis pathway was disabled by mutation during the long period in which our fruit-eating primate ancestors had no chance of developing vitamin C deficiencies (Jukes and King, 1975). As Terence Deacon has nicely put it, in evolution organisms become 'addicted to' innumerable aspects of their environments, from ascorbic acid to gravity to social interactions (Deacon, 1997). In less colourful terms, the development of evolved traits assumes the presence of an 'ontogenetic niche' (West and King, 1987) which supports and enables the normal expression of the genome. Thus, on theoretical grounds, we should expect many evolved adaptations to be polymorphic, many to exhibit plasticity, and many, including those which are monomorphic and show no plasticity in natural environments, to nevertheless depend on the details of a 'developmental niche'.

Reformists like Ariew respond to the scientific critique of the innateness concept by stipulating that the term 'innate' be used to express only one, clear idea. He suggests 'innate' be used to express fixity, and he makes the idea of fixity as precise as possible by identifying it with the biological concept of 'environmental canalisation'. This is supposed to provide a useful concept for scientific research. But scientists already have such a concept, namely the concept of canalisation, and they already have a word that expresses that concept, namely, 'canalised.' As Bateson (1991) and Griffiths (2002) each remarked, if your goal is to mean canalised when you say 'innate', why not just say 'canalised'? Furthermore, our findings show that by 'innate', the folk do not merely mean 'canalised'. By using the term 'innate' instead of 'canalised', biologists who follow Ariew's reformist suggestion would systematically increase the risk of miscommunication between themselves, other biologists, and the public at large. When Robin Andreasen (1998) and Philip Kitcher (1999) proposed to reform the concept of race so that the word 'race' would become synonymous with the word 'clade' or with the expression 'breeding population', Joshua Glasgow (2003) and others were quick to note that since the term 'race' as used by the folk has specific connotations, this proposal would lead to dangerous misunderstandings among the lay consumers of science. A similar argument applies to reformist proposals for 'innate', although the anticipated danger is obviously less immediately catastrophic.

6.3. Analysing the Scientific Use of the Innateness Concept

We are more sympathetic to a third proposed aim for philosophical analyses of the innateness concept. A philosophical analysis can aim to make clear how innateness is conceptualised by some specific group of scientists. For example, Samuels (2002) describes his project as an attempt to analyze the concept of innateness used by cognitive scientists, particularly in the controversies spurred by Chomsky's poverty of stimulus argument. Work of this kind could make a valuable contribution to assessing the scientific value of different innateness constructs, as urged by Mameli and Bateson (2006).

But if this is the really the project Samuels and others are engaged in, their methods suffers from serious shortcomings. Philosophers like Samuels (2002) and Mallon and Weinberg (2006) still use thought experiments that tap into their own or the folk's intuitions. If the goal really is to analyze scientists' concept of innateness, this traditional methodology should be abandoned. Neither philosophers' nor the folk's judgments about innateness provide strong evidence about how, say, generative syntacticians think about the innateness of generative syntax. These philosophers also regularly make use of outlandish thought experiments, such as the spontaneous acquisition of the capacity to read or understand Latin after having ingested the famed Latin pill (Fodor 1975; Samuels 2002; Mallon and Weinberg 2006). It seems highly unlikely that the intuitions (if any) triggered among scientists by these thought-experiments would derive from a specific, technical understanding of innateness that plays a role in their scientific work.

When they are not dealing with intuitions elicited by thought experiments, philosophers assume that their analysis of a scientific concept is supported if it casts light on some scientific debate involving that concept or on some body of scientific literature (e.g. the writings of some prominent scientist). For instance, an analysis of the concept of innateness in cognitive science is supported if it casts some light on the debates spurred by Chomsky's poverty of stimulus argument or on Chomsky's writings. This is the obvious way to determine how a particular scientist or research community thinks about innateness: find a way of thinking about innateness that makes sense of their scientific practice and of what they say. But it can be usefully supplemented by empirical methods. The method we used in this article to study the folk concept of innateness can be readily extended to study scientists' concept(s) of innateness (for discussion, see Stotz and Griffiths, 2008). Scientists' judgments can be surveyed in the same way that we surveyed folk judgments. Unlike exegetical efforts to cast some light on scientific debates or on specific scientific texts, these methods can systematically examine the factors that influence those scientists' judgments. We are in the process of designing research that will examine the judgments of psychologists, behavioural biologists, linguists, and others.

7. CONCLUSION

We have shown experimentally that judgments of innateness are strongly and independently influenced by Fixity and Typicality, with the former weighted somewhat more heavily than the later, and that they are independently influenced to a lesser extent by Teleology. This data provide some support for our hypothesis of a folk-biological, implicit theory of animal 'natures' of which the idea of innateness is one expression. We have argued that existing philosophical analyses of the innateness concept are inadequate because they try to make do with only one of these three features and ignore the weighting issue. We concluded with some reflections on the aims and methods of 'conceptually analysing' innateness. If conceptual analysis aims to capture the concept used by the folk or by some specialist community, empirical methods are more powerful than the traditional method of counterexamples, which is best regarded as a source of hypotheses. Empirical methods are also a powerful supplement to the exegesis of scientific texts, although we accept that this is a valuable approach to understanding scientific concepts. Alternatively, the aim of analysis may be to replace the existing concept of innateness with a more coherent, partly stipulative, explication of that concept for use in one or more areas of scientific research. In that case, the traditional philosophical method of counterexamples has at best a minor role to play and attention should focus on showing that the proposed explication meets a significant scientific need. Moreover, we doubt it is wise to use the term 'innate' to express any such explication, since the vernacular understanding of the term is so deeply entrenched.

NOTES

* Griffiths and Linquist were supported by Australian Research Council grant FF0457917. We thank Patrick Bateson, Ron Mallon, and Matteo Mameli for helpful comments on an earlier draft.
1. It may be that an organism's nature can, ultimately, be altered by the environment in which it finds itself. Lamarckian theories of heredity which make this assumption seem to be highly intuitive. But this is a special, deep kind of alteration different in kind

from the usual ways in which organisms are affected by the environment. Certain deeply ingrained habits become 'second nature' to people. In a typical Lamarckian theory, like that of Darwin (1872), it is only behaviours which are deeply ingrained for several generations that eventually become part of an organism's hereditary nature.

2. See, particularly, Carey, 1985; Keil, 1989; Atran, 1990; Medin and Atran, 1999, 2004; Astuti, Solomon, and Carey, 2004; Inagaki and Hatano, 2006.

3. Some have challenged the claim that postulating a belief in causal essences was necessary to explain these phenomena (Strevens, 2000; Rips, 2001; Ahn et al., 2001). Be that as it may, the psychological phenomena themselves—a belief in a persistent species membership and a belief in inherited properties whose development is impervious to external influences—are not controversial.

4. On developmental and cultural issues, see Keil (1989), Gelman and Wellman (1991), Atran et al. (2001), Sousa, Atran, and Medin (2002), and Astuti, Solomon, and Carey (2004).

5. In his 2002 paper Griffiths referred to the three features as 'developmental fixity', 'species nature', and 'intended outcome'. In this paper we use the handier terms 'Fixity', 'Typicality', and 'Teleology', and we reserve the term 'nature' for the broader idea that organisms have an underlying nature of which innate traits are an expression.

6. Probes and full data sets are available at http://philsci-archive.pitt.edu.

7. The full data set is available at http://philsci-archive.pitt.edu.

8. We are grateful to one of our reviewers for pressing us on this point.

9. Recall that the capitalized terms Typicality, Fixed, and Teleological refer to the elements of folk-biological theory discussed in Sections 2 and 3 and are being used here strictly in this stipulated sense.

10. This account of innateness replaced Lorenz's much criticized 1937 account based on the deprivation experiment. For more on Lorenz's (1965) theory, see Browne (2007).

11. Stich and Khalidi both restrict their account to cognitive traits, presumably because they think it will be easier to measure the information content of cognitive traits. Lorenz's analysis suggests that this restriction is unnecessary. This avoids the difficult problem of defining 'cognitive.' Khalidi counts birdsong as 'cognitive', but why is singing more 'cognitive' than walking or biting?

12. We believe that this reveals something important about the concept of innateness vis-à-vis other concepts that reflect the underlying folk-theory of biological natures, such as the concepts of instinct and of human nature. These concepts may place different weightings on the three aspects of the folk-conception of biological natures which we described above. The readiness with which people speak of diseases as 'innate' already suggests that Teleology is not as heavily weighted in innateness as it is in instinct or human nature. It would seem perverse to express a strongly hereditarian view of autism, for example, by saying that autistic behaviours are 'instinctive.' If this suggestion about alternative weightings is correct it should be possible to demonstrate this in future research by comparing the application of the different concepts to the same set of examples. We intend to study this issue in future research.

REFERENCES

Ahn, W.-K., Kalish, C., Gelman, S., Medin, D., Luhmann, C., Atran, S., Coley. J. and Shafto, P. 2001: Why essences are essential in the psychology of concepts. *Cognition*, 82, 59–69.

Andreasen, R. O. 1998: A new perspective on the race debate. *British Journal of Philosophy of Science*, 49, 199–225.

Ariew, A. 1996: Innateness and canalization. *Philosophy of Science*, 63, S19–S27.
Ariew, A. 1999 : Innateness is canalization: In defense of a developmental account of innateness. In V. G. Hardcastle (ed.), *Where Biology Meets Psychology: Philosophical Essays*. Cambridge, MA: MIT Press.
Ariew, A. 2006 : Innateness. In M. Matthen and C. Stevens (eds.), *Handbook of the Philosophy of Science*. Dordrecht: Elsevier.
Astuti, R., Solomon, G. E. A. and Carey, S. 2004: *Constraints on Conceptual Development: A Case Study of the Acquisition of Folkbiological and Folksociological Knowledge in Madagascar*. Oxford: Blackwell.
Atran, S. 1990: *Cognitive Foundations of Natural History: Towards an Anthropology of Science*. Cambridge: Cambridge University Press.
Atran, S. 1995: Causal constraints on categories. In D. Sperber, D. Premack and A. J. Premack (eds.), *Causal Cognition: A Multi-Disciplinary Debate*. Oxford: Clarendon Press.
Atran, S., Medin, D., Lynch, E., Vaparansky, V., Edilberto, U. E. and Sousa, P. 2001: Folkbiology doesn't come from folkpsychology: evidence from Yukatek Maya in cross-cultural perspective. *Journal of Cognition and Culture*, 1, 3–42.
Bateson, P. 1991 : Are there principles of behavioural development? In P. Bateson (ed.), *The Development and Integration of Behaviour: Essays in Honour of Robert Hinde*. Cambridge: Cambridge University Press.
Berlin, B. 1992: *Ethnobiological Classification*. Princeton, NJ: Princeton University Press.
Berlin, B., Breedlove, D. and Raven, P. 1973: General principles of classification and nomenclature in folk biology. *American Anthropologist*, 74, 214–242.
Browne, D. 2007: Konrad Lorenz on instinct and phylogenetic information. *The Rutherford Journal: The New Zealand Journal for the History and Philosophy of Science and Technology*, [cited 23rd March 2007]. Available at http://www.rutherfordjournal.org/article010104.html.
Carey, S. 1985: *Conceptual Change in Childhood*. Cambridge, MA: MIT Press.
Clement, J. 1983 : A conceptual model discussed by Galileo and used intuitively by physics student. In D. Gentner and A. L. Stevens (eds.), *Mental Models*. Hillsdale, NJ: Erlbaum.
Cohen, J. 1992: A power primer. *Psychological Bulletin*, 112, 155–159.
Cowie, F. 1999: *What's Within? Nativism Reconsidered*. Oxford: Oxford University Press.
Darwin, C. 1872: *The Expressions of Emotions in Man & Animals*. New York: Philosophical Library.
Deacon, T. W. 1997: *The Symbolic Species: The Coevolution of Language and the Brain*. New York: W.W. Norton.
Fodor, J. 1975: *The Language of Thought*. Cambridge, MA: Harvard University Press.
Ford, D. H. and Lerner, R. M. 1992: *Developmental Systems Theory: An Integrative Approach*. Newbury Park, CA: SAGE.
Gelman, S. 2003: *The Essential Child: Origins of Essentialism in Everyday Thought*. New York: Oxford University Press. Gelman, S. and Wellman, H. 1991: Insides and essences: early understandings of the non-obvious. *Cognition*, 38, 213–244.
Gelman, S. A. and Hirschfeld, L. A. 1999: How biological is essentialism? In D. L. Medin and S. Atran (eds.), *Folkbiology*. Cambridge, MA: MIT Press.
Glasgow, J. M. 2003: On the new biology of race. *The Journal of Philosophy*, 9, 456–474.
Gottlieb, G. 1997: *Synthesizing Nature-Nurture: Prenatal Roots of Instinctive Behavior*. Hillsdale, NJ: Lawrence Erlbaum Assoc.
Griffiths, P. E. 2002: What is innateness? *The Monist*, 85, 70–85.

Griffiths, P. E. 2006: The Baldwin Effect and genetic assimilation: contrasting explanatory foci and gene concepts in two approaches to an evolutionary process. In P. Carruthers, S. Laurence, and S. Stich (eds.), *The Innate Mind: Culture and Cognition*. Oxford: Oxford University Press.

Griffiths, P. E. and Machery, E. 2008: Innateness, canalisation and 'biologicizing the mind'. *Philosophical Psychology*, 21, 397–414.

Harvey, W. 1989: *The Works of William Harvey*, trans. R. Willis; ed. A. P. Fishman. *Classics in Medicine and Biology*.Philadelphia: University of Pennsylvania Press.

Hinde, R. A. 1968: Dichotomies in the study of development. In J. M. Thoday and A. S. Parkes (eds.), *Genetic and Environmental Influences on Behaviour*. New York: Plenum.

Inagaki, K. and Hatano, G. 2006: Young children's conception of the biological world. *Current Directions in Psychological Science*, 15, 177–181.

Johnston, T. D. 1987: The persistence of dichotomies in the study of behavioural development. *Developmental Review*, 7, 149–182.

Jukes, T. H. and King, J. L. 1975: Evolutionary loss of ascorbic acid synthesizing ability. *Journal of Human Evolution*, 4, 85–88.

Keil, F. C. 1989: *Concepts, Kinds and Cognitive Development*. Cambridge, MA: Bradford Books/MIT Press.

Kelemen, D. 1999: Functions, goals and intentions: children's teleological reasoning about objects. *Trends in Cognitive Sciences*, 12, 461–468.

Kelemen, D. 2004: Are children 'intuitive theists'? Reasoning about purpose and design in nature. *Psychological Science*, 15, 295–301.

Khalidi, M. A. 2002: Nature and nurture in cognition. *British Journal for the Philosophy of Science*, 53, 251–272.

Khalidi, M. A. 2007: Innate cognitive capacities. *Mind & Language*, 22, 92–115.

Kitcher, P. 1999: Race, ethnicity, biology, culture. In L. Harris (ed.), *Racism*. Amherst, NY: Humanity.

Lehrman, D. S. 1953: Critique of Konrad Lorenz's theory of instinctive behavior. *Quarterly Review of Biology*, 28, 337–363.

Lorenz, K. 1965: *Evolution and Modification of Behavior*. Chicago: University of Chicago Press.

Mallon, R. and Weinberg, J. 2006: Innateness as closed-process invariantism. *Philosophy of Science*, 73, 323–344.

Mameli, M. and Bateson, P. 2006: Innateness and the sciences. *Biology and Philosophy*, 22, 155–188.

Marler, P. 2004 : Science and birdsong: the good old days. In P. Marler and H. Slabbekorn (eds.), *Nature's Music: The Science of Birdsong*. Dordrecht: Elsevier.

Marler, P. and Slabbekorn, H. (eds.) 2004: *Nature's Music: The Science of Birdsong*. San Diego: Elsevier.

McCloskey, M. 1983: Intuitive physics. *Scientific American*, 248, 122–130.

Meaney, M. J. 2001: Nature, nurture, and the disunity of knowledge. *Annals of the New York Academy of Sciences*, 935, 50–61.

Medin, D. and Atran, S. (eds.) 1999: *Folk Biology*. Cambridge, MA: MIT Press.

Medin, D. and Atran, S. 2004: The native mind: biological categorization and reasoning in development and across cultures. *Psychological Review*, 111, 960–983.

Medin, D. and Ortony, A. 1989: Psychological essentialism. In S. Vosniadou and A. Ortony (eds.), *Similarity and Anological Reasoning*. Cambridge: Cambridge University Press.

Michel, G. F. and Moore, C. L. 1995: *Developmental Psychobiology: An Interdisciplinary Science*. Cambridge, MA: MIT Press.

Moore, C. L. 1984: Maternal contributions to the development of masculine sexual behavior in laboratory rats. *Developmental Psychobiology*, 17, 346–356.

Moore, C. L. 1992: The role of maternal stimulation in the development of sexual behavior and its neural basis. *Annals of the New York Academy of Sciences*, 662, 160–177.

Moore, D. S. 2001: *The Dependent Gene: The Fallacy of 'Nature versus Nurture'*. New York: W.H Freeman/Times Books.

Oyama, S. 1990: The idea of innateness: effects on language and communication research. *Developmental Psychobiology*, 23, 741–747.

Rips, L. J. 1989 : Similarity, typicality, and categorization. In S. Vosniadou and A. Ortony (eds.), *Similarity and Analogical Reasoning*. Cambridge: Cambridge University Press.

Rips, L. J. 2001: Necessity and natural categories. *Psychological Bulletin*, 127, 827–852.

Samuels, R. 2002: Nativism in cognitive science. *Mind & Language*, 17, 233–265.

Sousa, P., Atran, S. and Medin, D. 2002: Essentialism and folkbiology: further evidence from Brazil. *Journal of Cognition and Culture*, 2, 195–223.

Stich, S. P. 1975 : The idea of innateness. In S. P. Stich (ed.), *Innate Ideas*. Los Angeles: University of California Press.

Stotz, K. and Griffiths, P. E. 2000: Biohumanities: Rethinking the relationship between biosciences, philosophy and history of science, and society. *Quarterly Review of Biology*, 83, 37–45.

Strevens, M. 2000: The naive aspect of essentialist theories. *Cognition*, 74, 149–175.

Tinbergen, N. 1963: On the aims and methods of ethology. *Zietschrift für Tierpsychologie*, 20, 410–433.

West, M. J. and King, A. P. 1987: Settling nature and nurture into an ontogenetic niche. *Developmental Psychobiology*, 20, 549–562.

13

Gender and Philosophical Intuition*

Wesley Buckwalter and Stephen Stich

In recent years, there has been much concern expressed about the underrepresentation of women in academic philosophy in the English-speaking world. A full explanation of this troubling phenomenon is likely to be quite complex since there are, almost certainly, many factors that contribute to this gender disparity. Our goal in this paper is to call attention to a cluster of phenomena that may be contributing to the underrepresentation of women in philosophy, though until now these phenomena have been largely invisible. The findings we review indicate that when contemporary American and Canadian women and men with little or no philosophical training are presented with standard philosophical thought experiments, in many cases their intuitions about these cases are significantly different. We suspect that these differences could be playing a significant role in shaping the demography of the profession. But at present this is *only* a hypothesis, since we have no evidence that bears directly on the causal relation between the gender gap in academic philosophy and the facts about intuition that we will recount. In future work, we plan to focus on that causal link. However, we believe that the facts we report about gender differences in philosophical intuitions are both important and disturbing, and that philosophers (and others) should begin thinking about their implications both for philosophical pedagogy and for the methods that philosophers standardly use to support their theories. It is our hope that this paper will help to launch conversations on these issues within the philosophical community and beyond.

Here is how we plan to proceed. In section 1 we briefly review some of the data on the underrepresentation of women in academic philosophy. In section 2 we explain how we use the term 'intuition', and offer a brief account of how intuitions are invoked in philosophical argument and philosophical theory building. The third section is the longest and most important.

It is in that section that we set out the evidence for gender differences in philosophical intuition.[1] We also mention some evidence about gender differences in decisions and behaviors that are (or at least should be) of considerable interest to philosophers. In the fourth section, our focus switches from facts to hypotheses. In that section we explain how differences in philosophical intuition might be a hitherto neglected part of the explanation for the gender gap in philosophy. The fifth section is a brief conclusion.

1. SOME DATA ON THE GENDER GAP IN ACADEMIC PHILOSOPHY

In a powerful and much discussed paper about the challenges confronting women who pursue academic careers in philosophy, Sally Haslanger (2008) included a table indicating the number and percent of women faculty in the top twenty American philosophy departments, as ranked by the *Philosophical Gourmet Report* (more commonly known as the *Leiter Report*).[2] Using data reported by Leiter, Haslanger computed that 19.5% of the tenured and tenure track faculty in these departments were women. Checking and updating Leiter's data, Haslanger found that the percentage of women faculty was actually a bit lower: 18.7%. Since these data were collected in 2006, we thought it would be interesting to see if things had changed. Using Leiter's rankings in the 2009 *Philosophical Gourmet Report* and current philosophy department websites, we found that the situation has changed very little (Table 1).[3] Using the same method, we looked at the top four Leiter-ranked philosophy departments in Canada and the top four in Australasia. By our count there are 216 regular faculty in these eight departments, 55 of whom (25.4%) are women.[4] The numbers cited thus far are from highly ranked philosophy departments. For a more comprehensive measure, we turned to the report on women in philosophy in the UK by Professors Helen Beebee and Jennifer Saul (2011), written for the British Philosophical Association and the Society for Women in Philosophy joint committee for women in philosophy. According to the figures provided by 38 Heads of Department (including the largest departments) in response to a questionnaire, there are 448 permanent staff (Lecturers, Senior Lecturers, Readers and Professors) in these 38 departments, 24% of whom are women.

For a different kind of data, we consulted the *PhilPapers* internet survey of philosophers conducted by David Chalmers, David Bourget, and associates in November 2009.[5] The survey was taken by 3226 respondents, including 1803 philosophy faculty members and/or PhDs and 829 philosophy graduate students. Though respondents were based in over 29 countries, about 79% of those who indicated a 'country of primary affiliation' were based at institutions in the USA, the UK, Australia, Canada, and New Zealand. Among the respondents, 3013 specified their gender. There were 2525 males and 488 females. So in the *PhilPapers* survey, 16.2% of respondents who indicated their gender were women. Though there is room for debate about which of these measures is most informative or most useful, the general picture is quite clear. Women are seriously underrepresented in academic philosophy.

Table 13.1. Gender Ratios in Tenure-Track Positions by Faculty Rank in United States Philosophy Departments Ranked 1–20 in the 2009 Leiter Report as of March 2010.

Department	Women	Total	Percentage	Full Professor			Associate			Assistant		
				W	T	%	W	T	%	W	T	%
NYU	5	30	17%	1	24	4%	1	2	50%	3	4	75%
Rutgers	5	33	15%	3	25	12%	2	8	25%	0	0	NA
Princeton	4	23	17%	0	12	0%	1	4	25%	3	7	43%
Pittsburgh	3	22	12%	1	17	6%	0	2	0%	2	3	67%
Michigan	4	23	17%	2	15	13%	1	3	33%	1	5	20%
Harvard	5	19	26%	5	13	39%	0	1	0%	0	5	0%
MIT	4	16	25%	3	11	27%	0	3	0%	1	2	50%
Yale	8	24	33%	5	17	29%	1	1	100%	2	6	33%
Stanford	5	23	22%	2	14	14%	3	8	37%	0	1	0%
Berkeley	5	21	24%	3	13	23%	1	5	20%	1	3	33%
UCLA	3	18	17%	2	12	17%	1	4	25%	0	2	0%
UNC	3	19	16%	3	13	23%	0	4	0%	0	2	0%
Columbia	7	26	27%	5	20	25%	0	1	0%	2	5	40%
Arizona	6	23	26%	1	11	9%	5	11	45%	0	1	0%
CUNY	12	48	25%	10	42	24%	2	6	33%	0	0	NA
Notre Dame	6	39	15%	2	24	8%	2	8	25%	2	7	29%
Brown	4	17	24%	3	12	25%	0	1	0%	1	4	25%
Cornell	4	15	27%	1	8	13%	2	5	40%	1	2	50%
USC	3	21	14%	1	13	8%	2	6	33%	0	2	0%
UT–Austin	3	29	10%	2	21	10%	0	4	0%	1	4	25%
USA Total	99	489	19.8%	55	337	16.3%	24	87	27.6%	20	65	30.7%

2. WHAT ARE PHILOSOPHICAL INTUITIONS AND WHAT ROLE DO THEY PLAY IN PHILOSOPHICAL ARGUMENT?

There is a lively debate in the philosophical literature on the use of intuitions as evidence in philosophy (Bealer 1998; Devitt 2006, 2009; Gendler 2007; Goldman 2007; Jackson 1998; Kornblith 1998; Ludwig 2007; Sosa 2007, 2009; Stich 2009; Weinberg, Nichols & Stich 2001; Weinberg 2007; Williamson 2004, 2007). In this debate there are, broadly speaking, two families of views about how intuitions should be characterized. One family uses the terms 'intuition' and 'philosophical intuition' quite inclusively. For authors who adopt this view, intuitions are whatever contemporary philosophers have in mind when they use the term 'intuition' reflectively. Writers in the other family propose much narrower definitions, which require that philosophical intuitions have quite restrictive phenomenological, epistemic, or psychological properties. The second family is significantly more quarrelsome than the first, and the definitions proposed often pick out what appear to be quite different classes of psychological phenomena. In this paper, we will adopt the terminological strategy endorsed by the first family; we will use the terms 'intuition' and 'philosophical intuition' quite liberally. On this terminological issue, we share the view expressed by Timothy Williamson: 'Although we could decide to restrict the term "intuition" to states with some list of psychological or epistemological features, such a stipulation would not explain the more promiscuous role the term plays in the practice of philosophy' (Williamson 2007, 218).

Appeal to intuition has played a central role in Anglo-American philosophy over the last 50 years. In a typical episode, a philosopher will describe a real or (more commonly) an imaginary situation and ask whether some of the people or objects or events in the situation described exhibit some philosophically interesting property or relation:

- Is the action described *morally wrong*?
- Does the person described *know* that he won't win the lottery?
- When the speaker in the story uses the word 'water' does the word *refer* to H_2O?
- Does the "Chinese Room" really *understand* the story?

When things go well, both the philosopher and his audience will agree that the answer is intuitively obvious, and that will be taken to be *evidence* for or against some philosophical thesis. Readers acquainted with contemporary 'analytic' philosophy will have encountered many examples of this practice; readers who are unfamiliar with this literature will find lots of examples in section 3. However, it is worth noting that while using the term 'intuition' as a label for people's spontaneous responses to philosophical thought experiments is a relatively new phenomenon,[6] the practice itself goes all the way back to the beginnings of Western philosophy. In a famous passage in Plato's *Republic,* Cephalus proposes an account of justice on which what justice requires is speaking the truth and paying one's debts. Socrates responds with a thought experiment and a question: 'Suppose that a friend when in his right mind has deposited arms with me and he asks for them when he is not in his right mind, ought I to give them back to him?' He then proceeds to answer his own question: 'No one would say that I ought to or that I should be right in doing so, any more than they would say that I ought always to speak the truth to one who is in his condition.'[7] Cephalus agrees. In contemporary terminology, Socrates' thought experiment is designed to elicit the intuition that returning the weapons and speaking the truth is not morally required in this situation, and it succeeds admirably both for Cephalus and for many modern readers.

In many traditional and contemporary philosophical projects, when an intuition is invoked it is assumed that the *propositional content* of the intuition is likely to be true, and thus that the proposition can be used as evidence. Philosophical theories that are compatible with the content of the intuition are supported, and philosophical theories that are incompatible with the content of the intuition are challenged. So, for example, if we have the intuition that a character in a Gettier thought experiment does not know that p (where p is a true proposition that he believes and is justified in believing), this is evidence against the justified-true-belief account of knowledge (Gettier 1963; for an example see section 3). Similarly, in a Magistrate and the Mob thought experiment (Smart 1973; for an example see section 3), if we have the intuition that it would be morally impermissible for the Chief of Police to frame an innocent man to stop a riot, that is evidence against some versions of act utilitarianism. Though a few recent writers have denied that philosophical intuitions are used as evidence in this way (Ichikawa 2008; Deutsch 2010; Cappelen 2013), they are very much in the minority. Far more common is the view voiced by Kripke (1980):

> Some philosophers think that something's having intuitive content is very inconclusive evidence in favor of it. I think it is very heavy evidence in favor of anything, myself. I really don't know, in a way, what more conclusive evidence one can have about anything, ultimately speaking. (P. 42)

In contemporary philosophy, the explicitly stated goal of many projects is conceptual analysis. In these projects, intuitions play a somewhat different role. Rather than assuming that the content of the intuition is likely to be true, it is typically assumed that intuitions are evidence about the nature of the concept being analyzed. One version of this assumption has been stated very clearly by Alvin Goldman (2007):

> [T]he evidential status of application intuitions is of the constitutively grounded variety.[8] It's part of the nature of concepts (in the personal psychological sense) that possessing a concept tends to give rise to beliefs and intuitions that accord with the contents of the concept. If the content of someone's concept F implies that F does (doesn't) apply to example x, then that person is disposed to intuit that F applies (doesn't apply) to x when the issue is raised in his mind. (P. 4)

Though there is much more to be said about the ways in which intuitions are used as evidence in philosophy, for our purposes this brief discussion should suffice. The bottom line is that in philosophy intuitions are often taken to be evidence relevant either to the truth or falsity of a philosophical theory that purports to characterize some philosophically important phenomenon (like knowledge or reference or moral permissibility) or to an account of some philosophically important concept.[9]

3. SOME EVIDENCE FOR GENDER DIFFERENCES IN PHILOSOPHICAL INTUITION

We first became interested in gender differences in philosophical intuition after learning of a study in which Christina Starmans and Ori Friedman (2009) found dramatic differences in the intuitions reported by undergraduate men and women on Gettier-style thought experiments. Intrigued by these data, we set out to determine whether they were isolated results or whether there are other gender differences in philosophical intuition. However, this is a challenging task because researchers who study philosophical intuitions often do not collect or analyze demographic variables such as gender. So our strategy was threefold. First, we contacted a number of researchers who had done work on philosophical intuition and asked whether they were aware of published or unpublished data that could throw light on the existence and scope of gender differences in response to philosophical thought experiments. In addition to sending us references and copies of papers in press, several of the colleagues we contacted reported that while they had collected gender data, they had not bothered to analyze it. At our request, they agreed to do so. Second, Buckwalter reanalyzed the data of an earlier study he had conducted with James Beebe to see if there was a gender effect that they had not noticed, and ran an additional follow-up experiment in a neighboring domain. Third, we launched a series of new studies to determine whether there are gender differences in intuitive responses to some well-known philosophical thought experiments for which gender data had not previously been collected. We will report our findings in the order just recounted.

3.1. Starmans and Friedman: Gettier Cases

Starmans and Friedman presented undergraduate participants at the University of Waterloo in Canada with a number of pen-and-paper, Gettier-style thought experiments. In one study, participants ($N = 140$; 84 men, 56 women) read the following vignette:

> Peter is in his locked apartment, and is reading. He decides to have a shower. He puts his book down on the coffee table. Then he takes off his watch, and also puts it on the coffee table. Then he goes into the bathroom. As Peter's shower begins, a burglar silently breaks into Peter's apartment. The burglar takes Peter's watch, puts a cheap plastic watch in its place, and then leaves. Peter has only been in the shower for two minutes, and he did not hear anything.

After reading the text, participants were presented with three comprehension check questions to determine whether they understood and recalled the details of the story. They were then asked the test question:

> Does Peter really know that there is a watch on the table, or does he only believe it?

where they could respond with either 'really knows' or 'only believes'. To provide a basis for comparison, a control group of participants were given the same vignette, but were instead asked the test question about the book rather than the watch. Though there were no significant gender differences when participants were asked whether Peter knows that there is a book on the table (a large majority of both genders said that he really knows) there was a huge gender difference when participants were asked about the watch. Only 41% of the male participants said that Peter really knows that there is a watch on the table, while 71% of the female participants said that Peter really knows ($p < 0.05$, Fisher's exact test). Concerned that the gender of the protagonist might be playing a role in generating these results, Starmans and Friedman ran another study using a slightly different vignette in which the central protagonist was female. In this version, the objects involved were a wedding ring and a fork. Once again, the results were striking: 36% of male participants said the female protagonist really knows in the Gettier condition, while 75% of the female participants said that she really knows ($N = 112$, 54 men, 58 women, $p < 0.01$, Fisher's exact test). These results indicate that, at least in some groups of undergraduates, intuitive responses to Gettier cases can be highly variable and that men and women students can respond very differently to some prototypical Gettier-style thought experiments.

Since their original study, Starmans and Friedman (personal communication) have conducted a number of additional experiments using different Gettier vignettes and different populations of participants, including people recruited in public places in New York City. Among that latter group, they found that roughly half of both male and female participants attributed knowledge to the protagonists in their Gettier vignettes. We are currently conducting a series of further studies of Gettier intuitions in both student populations and in the general public. Preliminary results show a bewildering pattern in which some vignettes evoke gender differences in some groups and some do not. It is clear that there is still a lot to learn.

3.2. Holtzman: Compatibilism, Physicalism, and Dualism Cases

When we notified colleagues that we were interested in gender differences, the first researcher we heard from was Geoffrey Holtzman who had been conducting a series of online studies of philosophical thought experiments (Holtzman 2013).[10] In one of these studies, he elicited participants' intuitions ($N = 192$; 102 men, 90 women) about the following compatibilism thought experiment:

> Suppose Scientists figure out the exact state of the universe during the Big Bang, and figure out all the laws of physics as well. They put this

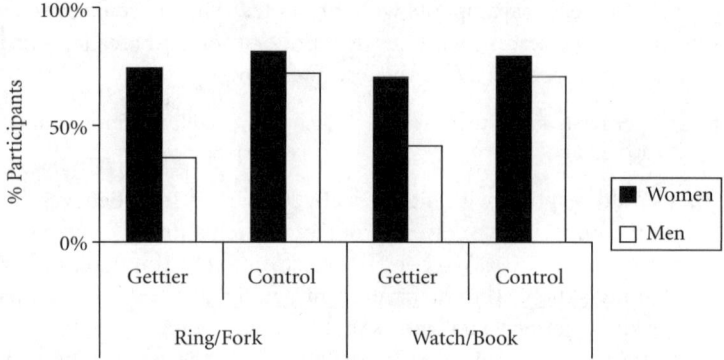

Figure 13.1. Percent of participants attributing knowledge in Gettier Study.

information into a computer, and the computer perfectly predicts everything that has ever happened. In other words, they prove that everything that happens, has to happen exactly that way because of the laws of physics and everything that's come before. ***In this case, is a person free to choose whether or not to murder someone?***[11]

As shown in Figure 2, Holtzman found a very substantial difference between the responses of men and women participants (Holtzman, under review, a). While 63% of women responded that a person in the situation described is free to choose whether or not to murder someone, only 35% of men gave that response ($d = 0.58$, $p < 0.0005$, Fisher's exact test, all experiments two-tailed).

In a second study ($N = 195$; 93 women, 102 men), Holtzman asked participants to read an intuition probe inspired by Frank Jackson's famous "Mary" case (Jackson 1982, 1986):

> Suppose you meet a man from the future who knows everything there is to know about science. He tells you that he doesn't like apples, and says that though he has never eaten one, he has figured out what apples taste like

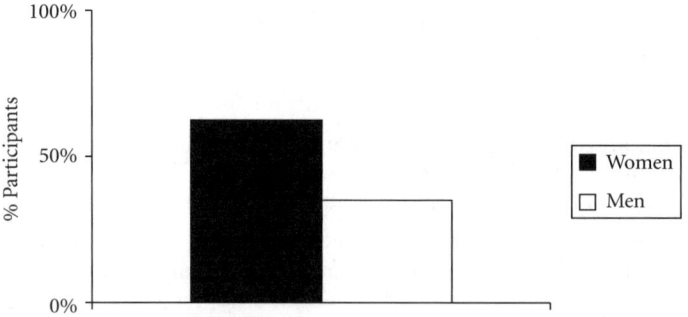

Figure 13.2. Percent answering 'yes' in Compatibilism Study.

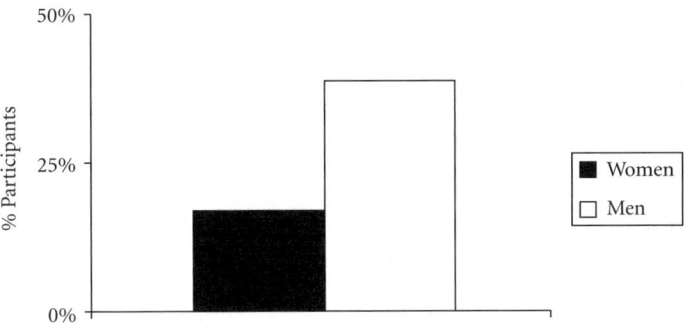

Figure 13.3. Percent answering 'yes' in Physicalism Study.

just by studying the relevant science. **Could he know what apples taste like without ever having eaten one?**

Among male participants, 39% said 'yes', but among female participants, only 17% said 'yes' ($d = 0.50$, $p < 0.005$, Fisher's exact test).

Participants in a third study ($N = 185$; 87 women; 98 men;) were presented with a version of a well-known 'dualism' thought experiment (Holtzman, under review, b):

> Suppose neurologists are able to identify every part and every connection in the human brain. Working with a team of computer scientists, they then build a robot that has a complete electronic replica of the human brain. **Could this robot experience love?**

Here Holtzman found a smaller, but significant difference. Among male participants, 79% said 'yes'; among female participants, 62% said 'yes' ($d = 0.37$, $p = 0.016$, Fisher's exact test).

It is important to note that Holtzman also collected data on participants' intuitions about a number of other philosophical thought experiments and found no significant gender differences.[12]

3.3. Cushman: The Violinist and 'Magistrate and the Mob Cases

Fiery Cushman was one of the researchers who agreed to look for gender effects in data he had collected online in collaboration with Liane Young. One study in which he found them used a version of one of contemporary philosophy's most famous thought experiments, the 'Violinist' case first introduced into the literature by Judith Jarvis Thomson (1971) in a widely discussed paper on abortion. In this experiment, Cushman and Young presented participants ($N = 298$; 176 men, 122 women) with the following vignette:

> Jill wakes up one morning and finds a strange man next to her in bed, plugged into her kidney. A man from the Society for Music Lovers introduces himself and explains to Jill that she has been plugged into a famous

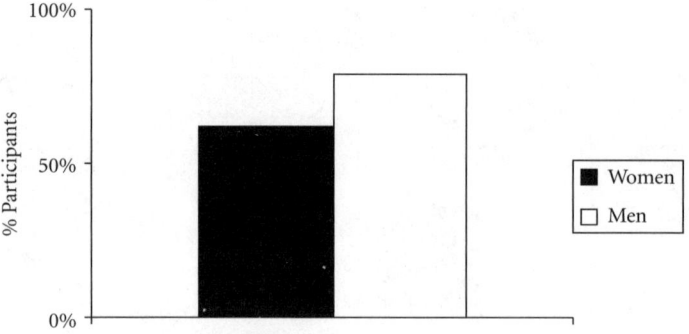

Figure 13.4. Percent answering 'yes' in Dualism Study.

violinist who is dying of kidney failure. Without Jill's help, the violinist will die. The man from the Society explains that Jill must stay plugged into the violinist for 9 months in order for him to recover and survive. Jill pulls the plug and the violinist dies.

Jill's pulling the plug was:

Participants were asked to respond on a scale from 1 to 7, with 1 labeled 'forbidden', 4 labeled "permissible", and 7 labeled "obligatory". What Cushman found was that men were more likely to say that Jill's pulling the plug was permissible, while women tended to consider this action forbidden.[13] The surprising results are depicted in Figure 5.

A second case in which Cushman found a significant gender effect was a version of the 'Magistrate and the Mob' thought experiment made prominent by Smart (1973). Participants ($N = 529$; 380 men, 149 women) read the following:

> Steve is the police chief of a large city. A particularly volatile political situation has erupted into violence with the assassination of a candidate, and citizens are rioting in the streets, demanding an arrest be made. The

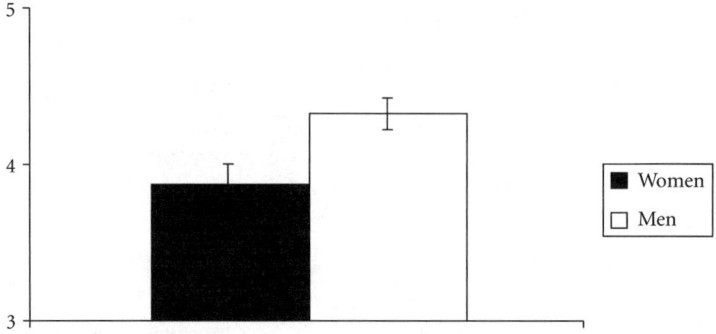

Figure 13.5. Mean judgment in Violinist Study (the scale ran from 1 to 7).

situation will worsen unless Steve can produce a perpetrator; people have already looted numerous stores, overturned cars, brutally attacked bystanders, and set fire to a government building. The police department has Steve's 14-year-old brother in custody for petty theft and drunkenness. He could easily fabricate sufficient evidence against his young brother to satisfy the public and stop the riots. Steve chooses not to frame his teenage brother and the violent attacks escalate.

The choice Steve made was:

Participants were asked to respond with a horizontal sliding bar, where the leftmost side was anchored with 'good' and the rightmost side was anchored with 'bad'. Numerical scores were then assigned to those responses on a scale from −225 to +225. This means that lower scores indicate that participants thought the action was good, while higher scores indicate that participants thought the action was bad. As can be seen in Figure 6, while both groups tended to think that Steve's choice was a good one, the results suggest that men judged it was better for Steve *not* to have framed his teenage brother than women did.[14]

Like Holtzman, Cushman also reported that there were a number of cases in which gender differences were not found.

3.4. Zamzow and Nichols: A Trolley Case

A third colleague who responded to our inquiry was Shaun Nichols, who provided a copy of a recently published paper co-authored with Jennifer Zamzow (Zamzow & Nichols 2009). The paper includes a report of a pen-and-paper study in which undergraduate participants were presented with a bystander version of the trolley dilemma in which five people can be saved if a train is diverted to a sidetrack where it will kill a different innocent person. Some participants were told that the individual on the side track was 'a stranger'; others were told that it was 'a 12-year-old boy'. The text of their vignettes were as follows:

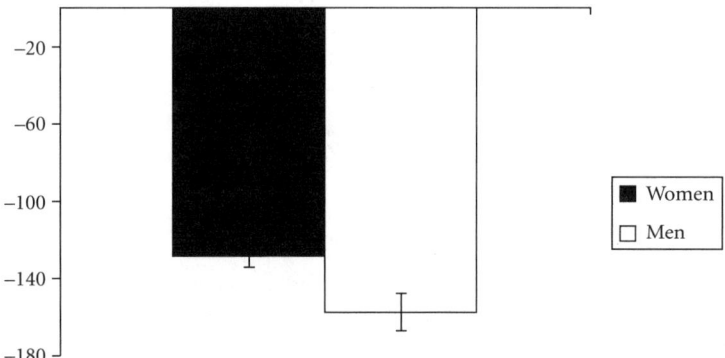

Figure 13.6. Mean Judgment in Magistrate and Mob Study (the scale ran from −225 to +225).

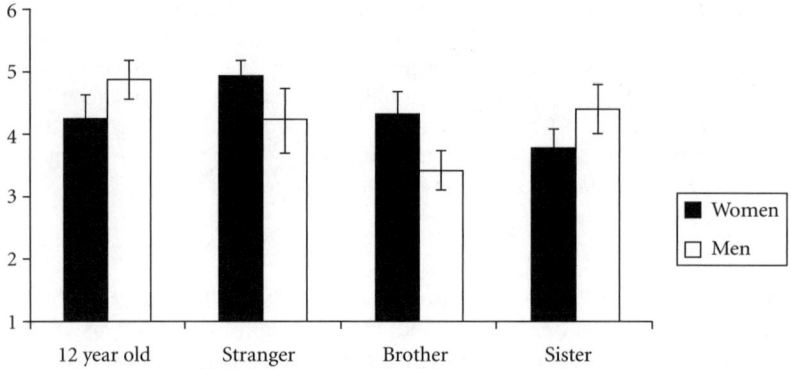

Figure 13.7. Mean agreement in Trolley Study (the scale ran from 1 to 7).

> You are taking your daily walk near the train tracks and you notice that the train that is approaching is out of control. You see what has happened: the driver of the train saw five people working on the tracks and slammed on the brakes, but the brakes failed and the driver fainted. The train is now rushing toward the five people. It is moving so fast that they will not be able to get off the track in time. You happen to be standing next to a switch, and you realize that the only way to save the five people on the tracks is to throw the switch, which will turn the train onto a side track, thereby preventing it from killing the five people. However, there is a stranger [or, in the other vignette, a 12-year-old boy] standing on the side track with his back turned, and if you proceed to throw the switch, the five people will be saved, but the person [boy] on the sidetrack will be killed.

Participants, each of whom saw only one version of the vignette, were asked the extent to which they agreed with several statements including: *'It is morally acceptable for me to pull the switch.'* Responses were collected on a 7-point scale with 1 labeled 'strongly disagree' and seven labeled 'strongly agree'. Zamzow and Nichols found that men judged that the killing of a stranger is *less* morally acceptable than did women.[15] However, when the person on the side track was described as a 12-year-old boy, this pattern was reversed. In that case, men tended to judge that the killing was *more* morally acceptable than women did.[16] Zamzow and Nichols also explored participants' judgments about trolley cases in which the person on the side track is described as either a brother or a sister of the participant. They found that men judged killing one's brother to be less morally acceptable than did women but that women judged that killing one's sister is less morally acceptable than did men.[17]

Interestingly, Zamzow and Nichols also asked participants what they *would do* when confronting this dilemma and found *no* significant difference between males and females.

3.5. Pizarro, Uhlmann, and Bloom: Moral Responsibility and Causal Deviance

Yet another colleague who responded to our inquiry about gender differences was David Pizarro, who reported that on reanalyzing some of the data that he and colleagues had collected (Pizarro et al. 2003) he found an intriguing gender difference that they had not previously noticed. To understand the motivation for this experiment, a bit of background is needed. In typical cases of intentional action, an agent forms the intention to accomplish a goal, comes up with a plan for doing it, and then carries out that plan. But many philosophers have been intrigued by another sort of case, where the agent forms the intention to bring about a goal, and does bring it about, but not in the way the agent planned. Rather, in these cases, the agent's intention causes a chain of events quite different from those the agent had planned. Cases of this sort are sometimes said to exhibit 'causal deviance' (Searle 1983). Pizarro and colleagues were interested in whether people's intuitions about the *moral* properties of an action would be affected if the action were causally deviant. To find out, participants in this experiment read each of the four vignettes below, counterbalanced for order. The first two describe a morally positive action, the second two a morally negative action. In each pair, the link between the intention and the action is normal in the first vignette and 'deviant' in the second.

> *Positive Normal*: Tom is walking in the park when he sees a man choking on a sandwich. Tom, full of nervousness because of his intention to save the man's life, runs over and performs the Heimlich maneuver. The man coughs up the sandwich he had been choking on and his life is saved.
>
> *Positive Deviant*: Tom is walking in the park when he sees a man choking on a sandwich. Tom, full of nervousness because of his intention to save the man's life, runs over to perform the Heimlich maneuver. However, Tom's nervousness leads him to have an epileptic seizure. (Had Tom not had the epileptic seizure, he would have carried out the Heimlich maneuver and saved the choking man's life.) By chance, the epileptic fit happens to lead Tom's arms to squeeze on the man's chest, causing the man to cough up the sandwich and saving his life.
>
> *Negative Normal*: Tom lies in wait for his enemy, who had stolen his life savings. As soon as his enemy appears, Tom, nervous because of his intention to kill the man, pulls out a gun and shoots his enemy dead.
>
> *Negative Deviant*: Tom lies in wait for his enemy, who had stolen his life savings. As soon as his enemy appears, Tom, nervous because of his intention to kill the man, pulls out a gun. However, Tom's nervousness triggers an epileptic seizure. (Had Tom not had an epileptic seizure, he would have shot his enemy dead.) By chance, the epileptic fit leads Tom to squeeze the trigger, and the bullet happens to hit and kill his enemy.

After each vignette, participants were asked to judge (1) how moral or immoral the agent was, (2) how much blame or praise the agent should receive for his actions, and (3) how positively or negatively the agent should be judged. Responses were assessed on a 9-point scale ranging from −4 to +4. In the blame question, −4 was labeled 'extreme blame', 0 was labeled 'neither blame nor praise', and +4 was labeled 'extreme praise'. The labels for the other questions were similar. Scores for the negative actions were multiplied by −1. Thus while higher numbers in the positive cases mean that participants judged those agents to be more praiseworthy, etc., higher numbers in the negative cases mean that participants judged the characters more blameworthy. Since within-subjects responses to the three questions that were asked about each of the four cases were highly correlated, they were averaged to create a 'moral sanction index'.

As Pizarro and colleagues had predicted, in both the positive and the negative cases, responses were less extreme in the deviant cases than in the normal cases. Participants thought that the action in the Positive Normal case was better than the action in the Positive Deviant case, and they thought the action in the Negative Normal case was worse than the action in the Negative Deviant case.[18] What Pizarro and colleagues did not predict, and had not noticed until we asked about gender effects, was that 'the discounting of blame for the Negative Deviant act is driven by the women, and the discounting of praise for the Positive Deviant act is driven by the men' (Pizarro, personal communication).[19] The reanalyzed data that Pizarro provided are represented in Figure 8. (Recall that higher scores in negative cases represent a higher blameworthiness index, while higher scores in positive cases represent a higher praiseworthy index.)

3.6. Beebe and Buckwalter: The Epistemic Side-Effect Effect

Intrigued by some of the findings we have been recounting, Buckwalter decided to reanalyze the data he and James Beebe had collected, which had demonstrated a surprising extension of the side-effect effect discovered by Joshua Knobe (Beebe & Buckwalter 2010). While Knobe's original studies focus on attributions of intention, Beebe and Buckwalter's study explores attributions of

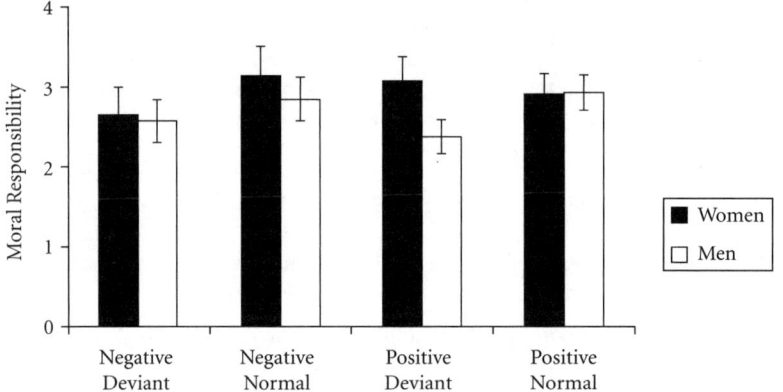

Figure 13.8. Moral sanction indexes in Causal Deviance Study.

knowledge. Knobe (2003) constructed a pair of vignettes which described the circumstances of a chairman of a company receiving some news from a subordinate about a new program they could adopt to increase profits. However, instituting this program has a side effect: in one case it will harm the environment, and in another case it will help the environment. In both cases, the chairman does not care about any possible side effect to the environment; his only concern is profit. So in both cases the chairman tells his subordinate to start the new program, and in each case the environment is affected as predicted. Knobe's surprising finding was that when asked about the actions of the chairman in the harm case, 82% of participants agreed that the chairman intentionally harmed the environment, whereas in the help case 77% of subjects denied that the chairman intentionally helped the environment. The result suggests that people are more likely to say that an agent brought about a side effect *intentionally* when that side effect is bad than when it is good. This asymmetry in participant responses has been widely replicated (Knobe 2010).

Beebe and Buckwalter wanted to know whether moral considerations like those invoked in Knobe's studies affect people's intuitions about whether people have knowledge. To investigate this question, they conducted a pen and paper experiment to see if the original side-effect effect asymmetry persisted when participants were asked about what the chairman knows. Their hypothesis was that given the same evidence in these cases, participants would be less likely to say an agent knows that an action will bring about a specified side effect when the side effect is good, and more likely to attribute knowledge when the side effect is bad. Using a between-subjects experimental design, undergraduate participants ($N = 749$) were given either the help or harm version of the following vignette:

> The vice president of a company went to the chairman of the board and said, 'We are thinking of starting a new program. We are sure that it will help us increase profits, and it will also (*help/harm*) the environment.' The chairman of the board answered, 'I don't care at all about (*helping/harming*) the environment. I just want to make as much profit as I can. Let's start the new program.' They started the new program. Sure enough, the environment was (*helped/harmed*).

On a seven -point scale from –3 to 3 (where –3 was anchored with 'the chairman didn't know' and 3 was anchored with 'the chairman knew'), participants were asked, **'Did the chairman know that the new program would (*help/harm*) the environment'?** The result was that the degree to which participants attribute knowledge to the chairman was significantly different between conditions.[20] Even though there is equally strong evidence in both help and harm conditions that the chairman's action would bring about a certain side effect, participants were significantly less likely to agree that the chairman knows an action will bring about that side effect when the effect is good, and more likely to attribute that knowledge when the side effect is bad. Beebe and Buckwalter call this asymmetry between knowledge attribution in help and harm conditions 'the epistemic side-effect effect' .[21]

One might think that the interesting thing about the epistemic side-effect effect finding is not that knowledge attribution is close to ceiling in the harm condition but rather that participants are much less willing to attribute knowledge in the help condition. However, when Buckwalter re-analyzed the data he found that that men (405 participants) and women (340 participants) answer differently in the help condition and that much of the difference between the harm and the help condition can be attributed to this gender difference. The mean differences between the way men and women responded between conditions is represented in Figure 9; women were more likely than men to say that an agent *does not know* an action will bring about the side effect when that effect is good. This study of the epistemic side-effect effect reveals another significant gender effect in epistemic intuitions.

3.7. Buckwalter: Absence Causation

Intuitions about intention and knowledge are not the only ones that exhibit Knobe's side-effect effect. Similar results have been reported for a wide range of intuitions, including intuitions about causation (Hitchcock & Knobe 2009; Knobe & Fraser 2008; for reviews see Knobe 2010 and Knobe et al. forthcoming). However, none of this work has tried to determine whether the gender effect on knowledge judgments recounted in the previous section generalizes to other sorts of intuitions. To explore the issue, Buckwalter designed an experiment focused on people's intuitions about cases in which an agent's failure to act facilitates either a positively valenced or a negatively valenced outcome (Buckwalter manuscript 2013a, 2013b). Cases like this are sometimes described as examples of 'absence causation'.

In a between-subjects 2 × 2 experimental design, each participant (N = 415; 251 female, 160 male, 4 unreported) received one of four vignettes that are similar in structure to Knobe's chairman cases. The vignettes differed in a pair of ways. First, two of them make it explicit that the protagonist's failure to act is intentional, while in the other two the protagonist's failure to act is not

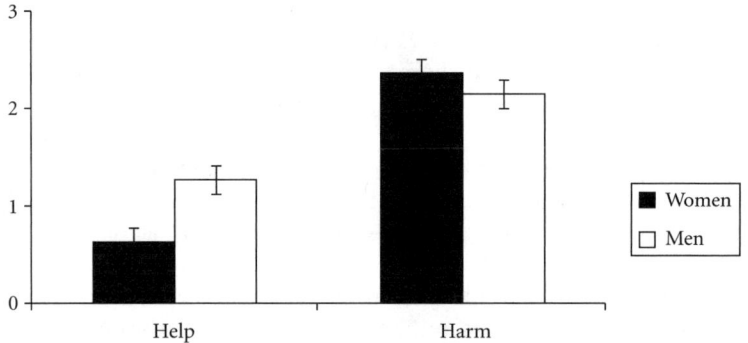

Figure 13.9. Mean judgment in epistemic side-effect Effect Study (the scale ran from −3 to +3).

intentional. Second, in two of the vignettes the outcome is positively valenced, while in the other two the outcome is negatively valenced. These are the two vignettes in which the protagonist's failure to act is intentional:

> *Intentional-Help*: P&G has just purchased all of the utility companies in a small, rural community. The previous owner neglected the power plants, and many of the pipes are leaking a certain chemical into the local town's water supply. This chemical is full of natural nutrients for plants, and will surely double the harvest. *When the president of P&G found out about the leaks he thought to himself, 'This is great! If I don't fix the leaks, all of the local crops will flourish.' In hopes that it would help the crops, he decides to do nothing.* Sure enough, the crops flourished and the harvest was doubled.
>
> *Intentional-Harm*: P&G has just purchased all of the utility companies in a small, rural community. The previous owner neglected the power plants, and many of the pipes are leaking a certain chemical into the local town's water supply. This chemical is toxic to plants, and will surely cut the town's harvest in half. *When the president of the company found out about the leaks he thought to himself, 'This is great! If I don't fix the leaks, all of the townspeople's crops die, and they will have no choice but to buy all their food from us. Think of all those profits.' In hopes that it would harm the crops, he decides to do nothing.* Sure enough, the crops died, and the townspeople lost half of the harvest.

In the other two vignettes, *Unintentional-Help* and *Unintentional-Harm*, the information about the president's mental states is omitted, and the italicized text is replaced by the following sentence: *The president of P&G had no idea about the leaks and no idea about how the chemical might affect the townspeople's crops.* After reading the vignettes, participants were asked a pair of questions. The first question was:

> How much (*praise/blame*) does the president of P&G deserve?

Participants responded on a seven-point scale anchored by 'Not at all Blameworthy/Praiseworthy' and 'very blameworthy/praiseworthy'. In the second question, they were asked to indicate their level of agreement with the following statement:

> By not fixing the pipes, the president of P&G is a cause of the (improved/diminished) harvest.

Participants responded on a seven -point scale, anchored by '*strongly disagree*' and '*strongly agree*'.

Not surprisingly, participants judged that the president deserved a lot of blame in the harm conditions, but deserved much less praise in the help conditions. They also attributed more praise or blame in the intentional conditions than in the unintentional conditions.[22] The responses to the causation question exhibited a similar pattern. Participants were much more likely to treat the president as a cause when the outcome was bad than when it was good, and when it was intentional rather than unintentional.[23] But what makes this study important for our purposes is that there is a significant gender difference in responses to the causation question. Women were much more likely than men to agree that the president was a *cause* of the outcome when that outcome was bad and more likely to disagree that the president was a cause when the outcome was good.[24] The results, displayed in Figure 10, are remarkably similar to the pattern of results in the epistemic side-effect effect study displayed in Figure 9.[25]

3.8. Buckwalter and Stich: 'Brain in the Vat', 'Twin Earth', 'Chinese Room', and 'Plank'

We have now completed a series of experimental studies looking at other familiar philosophical thought experiments. This research was conducted on the Internet using Amazon's Mechanical Turk, recruiting participants from across the United States.[26] In all of the studies we discuss in this section, participants were presented with the text of a thought experiment, asked a comprehension check question and a test question, and then were asked to fill out a short, eight-item demographic questionnaire.[27] Importantly, one of the items included on the demographic questionnaire asked about previous philosophical training. In the results we discuss below, we focus on the data from people who reported that they have taken no philosophy courses. The reason for this will become clear in section 4.[28] What we have found reinforces the observation we made earlier: in this population of American participants there are quite significant gender differences in responses to philosophical thought experiments in some cases, while in other cases there aren't.

The first case we'll discuss is a version of the old philosophical chestnut, the 'Brain in the Vat' (Brueckner 2008). The text of the scenario we used was borrowed from an earlier study in which Nichols, Stich, and Weinberg (2003) found a substantial difference between the intuitions of participants who had taken few or no philosophy courses and participants who had taken three or more. This is the vignette participants were asked to read:

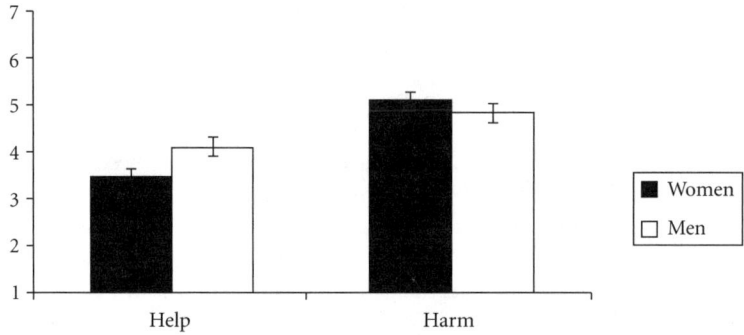

Figure 13.10. Mean agreement in Absence Causation Study (the scale ran from 1 to 7).

George and Omar are roommates, and enjoy having late-night 'philosophical' discussions. One such night Omar argues, 'At some point in time, like, the year 2300, the medical and computer sciences will be able to simulate the real world very convincingly. They will be able to grow a brain without a body, and hook it up to a supercomputer in just the right way so that the brain has experiences exactly as if it were a real person walking around in a real world, talking to other people. The brain would believe it was a real person walking around in a real world, except that it would be wrong. Instead it's just stuck in a virtual world, with no actual legs to walk and with no other actual people to talk to. And here's the thing: how could you ever tell that it isn't really the year 2300 now, and that you're not really a virtual-reality brain? If you were a virtual-reality brain, after all, everything would look and feel exactly the same to you as it does now'! George thinks for a minute, and then replies: 'But, look, here are my legs'. He points down to his legs. 'If I were a virtual-reality brain, I wouldn't have any legs really, I'd only just be a disembodied brain. But I know I have legs, just look at them! So I must be a real person, and not a virtual-reality brain, because only real people have real legs. So I'll continue to believe that I'm not a virtual-reality brain'. George and Omar are actually real humans in the actual real world today, and so neither of them is a virtual-reality brain, which means that George's belief is true.

After answering a comprehension check question designed to be sure that they had understood the story, participants saw the sentence:

George knows that he is not a virtual-reality brain.

They were then asked to indicate their agreement or disagreement on a seven-item scale, with the leftmost anchor labeled 'Completely Disagree', the midpoint labeled 'In between', and the rightmost anchor labeled 'Completely Agree'. The result, shown in Figure 11, was that women were significantly more likely than men to agree that George knows that he is not a virtual-reality brain.[29]

'Twin Earth' scenarios, first used by Hilary Putnam (1973), have been become a staple of debate in the philosophy of mind and the philosophy of

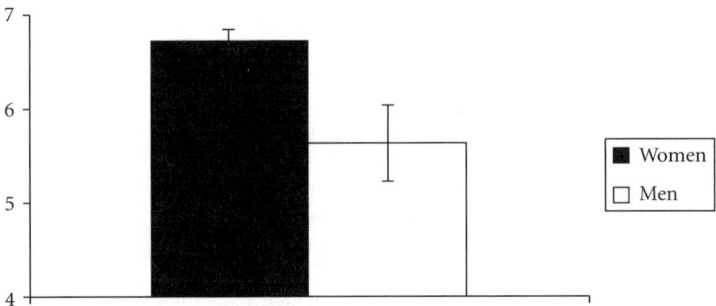

Figure 13.11. Mean agreement in Brain in Vat Study (the scale ran from 1 to 7).

language (Pessin & Goldberg 1996). This is the version that we presented to participants:

> Suppose that elsewhere in the universe there is a planet called 'Twin Earth'. Twin Earth looks exactly like our Earth in virtually all respects. It is populated by twin equivalents to every person and thing here on our Earth, and even revolves around a star that appears to be exactly like our sun.
>
> Oscar grows up here on our Earth, while someone exactly like Oscar, who we can call 'Twin Oscar', lives on Twin Earth. Oscar and Twin Oscar both go through life having the same experiences, and both perceive their environment in exactly the same way. They look and act completely alike and even experience the same emotions.
>
> In fact, there is only one difference between these two planets. The difference is that on Earth the stuff that fills the lakes and rivers and that people and animals drink is H_2O, while on Twin Earth, the stuff that fills the lakes and rivers and that people and animals drink is another chemical compound, XYZ, that to the naked eye looks completely indistinguishable from the H_2O on Earth. H_2O and XYZ also taste exactly the same, and both have the ability to quench thirst and to sustain life.
>
> However, Oscar and Twin-Oscar both live before the development of modern science, and they have no idea about chemistry or molecular composition. When they go for a swim, both Oscar and Twin Oscar point to the liquid in the lake and call it 'water' even though on Earth that liquid is made up of H_2O, and on Twin Earth it is made up of XYZ.

Again, there was a comprehension check question, and then participants were asked:

> When Oscar and Twin Oscar say 'water' do they mean the same thing or different things?

Responses were solicited on a seven-point scale, the leftmost anchor labeled 'they mean different things', the midpoint labeled 'in between', and the rightmost anchor labeled 'they mean the same thing'. The result was that women were more likely to give the Putnamian answer that Oscar and Twin Oscar mean different things when they say 'water (Figure 12).[30]

Searle's 'Chinese Room' thought experiment (Searle 1980) has been widely discussed in the philosophy and cognitive science literature and has found its way into a number of introductory textbooks. In our study, we asked participants to read the following version of the Chinese Room scenario.

> Jenny is a native English speaker who can speak only English. She is locked in a room full of boxes of Chinese symbols, together with an instruction manual written in English for manipulating the symbols. People from outside the room send in notes on pieces of paper with Chinese symbols written on them, which unknown to Jenny, are questions in Chinese. Jenny's job is to look through her manual until she finds the symbols that look exactly like the ones written on the pieces of paper. When she finds that string of symbols, the manual will tell her what new string of symbols to write down, and send to the people outside the room.

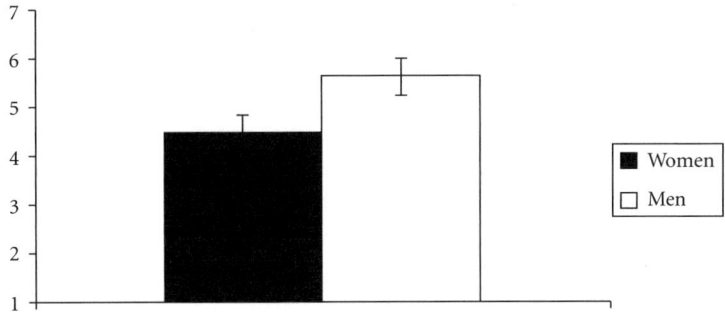

Figure 13.12. Mean judgment in Twin Earth Study (the scale ran from 1 to 7).

> By following the instructions in the manual, Jenny is able to give the correct answers to the questions. The system consisting of Jenny and the instruction manual that she is using can be thought of as an unusual sort of computer. Jenny gets so good at following the instructions in the manual, that from the point of view of any one outside the room who speaks Chinese, her responses are absolutely indistinguishable from those of Chinese speakers.

After responding to a comprehension question participants were asked whether they agreed with the following statement:

> The computational system consisting of Jenny and her instruction manual understands the Chinese written on the notes.

As in the Brain in the Vat case, responses were on a 7-item scale with the leftmost anchor labeled 'Completely Disagree', the midpoint labeled 'In between', and the rightmost anchor labeled 'Completely Agree'. The result, shown in Figure 13, was that men were more likely than women to agree that the computational system understands the Chinese written on the notes.[31]

In a fourth study, we looked at participants' moral intuitions, using a version of the 'Plank of Carneades' thought experiment. Participants saw the following vignette:

> There are two shipwrecked sailors, Jamie and Ricki. They both see a small plank that can only support one of them and both of them swim desperately towards it. Jamie gets to the plank first. Ricki, who is stronger and is going to drown, pushes Jamie off and away from the plank and, thus, ultimately, causes Jamie to drown. Ricki gets on the plank and is later saved by a rescue team.

After responding to a comprehension question participants were asked:

> How morally blameworthy is Ricki for what he did?

Participants answered on a seven-item scale, with the leftmost anchor labeled 'not at all blameworthy', the midpoint labeled 'in between', and the rightmost anchor labeled 'extremely blameworthy'. The result was that while both groups

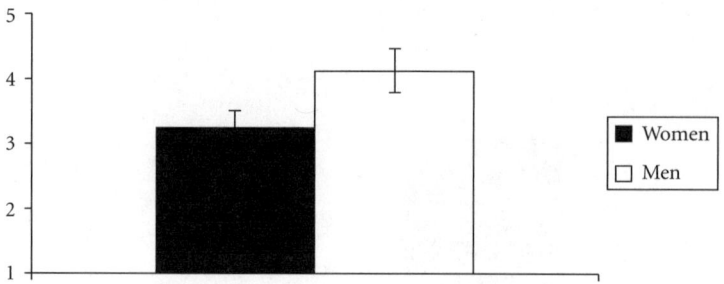

Figure 13.13. Mean judgment in Chinese Room Study (the scale ran from 1 to 7).

were above the midline, on average women judged the character in the vignette more morally blameworthy (Figure 14).[32]

3.9. Similar Findings in Social Psychology and Experimental Economics

Our theme in section 3 has been that in the Americans and Canadians who participated in the experiments we have reviewed there are indeed gender differences in intuitive responses to many philosophical thought experiments, some of which are large, unexpected, and dramatic—though as we have noted repeatedly, there are also a number of studies of philosophical intuitions that do not find gender differences. To the best of our knowledge, there is currently no good way of predicting where these gender differences will be found. It has been our experience that philosophical audiences often find results indicating gender differences in intuition to be quite surprising. But perhaps they shouldn't. For the picture we have been sketching is broadly consistent with a substantial body of research in psychology (Eagly 1995; Halpern 2011) and experimental economics (Croson & Gneezy 2009; Eckel & Grossman 2008a, 2008b) that has reported gender differences in studies of a number of preferences, decisions, and behaviors that are (or should be) of considerable interest

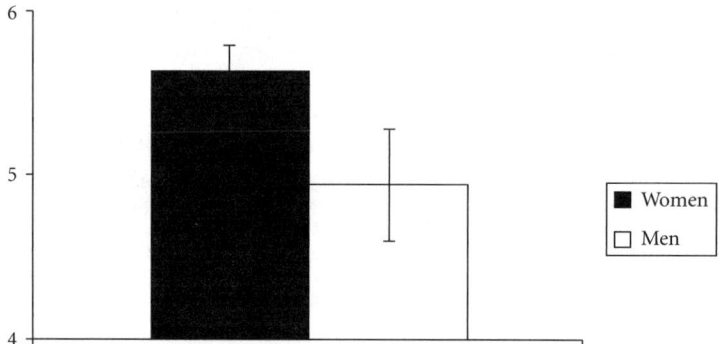

Figure 13.14. Mean judgment in Plank Study (the scale ran from 1 to 7).

to philosophers. Though this is not the place to review this literature in detail, a single example may help to convey its interest and importance.

Several studies of prosocial behavior have shown that women are considerably more generous than men in double-blind dictator games. In these games, one person (the "dictator") must choose how to divide a fixed amount of money between himself and an anonymous recipient. A common finding is that female dictators give recipients about twice as much as male dictators (Eckel & Grossman 1998; Vesterlund 2006; Rigdon et al. 2009). But there is an important exception to this rule. If there is even the slightest hint that participants are being observed, the gender disparity disappears. In one fascinating study, Rigdon et al. presented participants ($N = 113$; 51 men, 62 women) with either the 'face' or the 'control' version of the task displayed in Figure 15.[33]

Figure 16 shows the percent of participants who transferred a dollar or more in each condition. Though the manipulation had no significant effect on the women, it had a powerful effect on the men. In the control condition, only 37% of men transferred $1.00 or more, but in the presence of a weak social cue—three dots arranged to look like a face—79% of men transferred $1.00 or more to the 'Receiver' they had been paired with ($p = 0.006$). Rigdon et al. also found that the three dot "face" dramatically increases the average amount that male participants give—from $1.41 in the control condition to $3.00 in the face condition, while having no significant effect on female participants who gave $2.12 in the face condition, and $2.79 in the control condition).[34]

Money Allocation Sheet

You have received $5 for showing up on time.

You now have an additional $10 to allocate between you and the Receiver you are paired with in the other room (in $1 increments). Please record how much money you will keep for yourself, and how much you will allocate to the Receiver

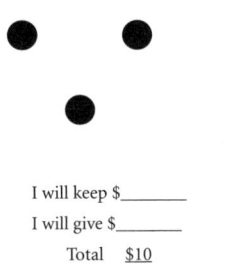

I will keep $_____
I will give $_____
Total $10

"Face" from Rigdon et al.

Money Allocation Sheet

You have received $5 for showing up on time.

You now have an additional $10 to allocate between you and the Receiver you are paired with in the other room (in $1 increments). Please record how much money you will keep for yourself, and how much you will allocate to the Receiver

I will keep $_____
I will give $_____
Total $10

"Control" from Rigdon et al.

Figure 13.15. Stimuli in Dictator Game Study.

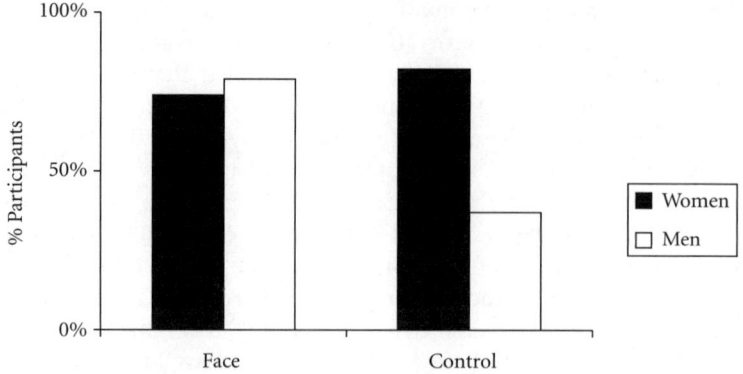

Figure 13.16. Percent transfer (> $1) in Dictator Game Study.

3.10. Conclusions, Caveats, and Further Questions

Our central claim has been that in the North American populations that have been studied there are significant differences between men and women in intuitive responses to some philosophically important thought experiments. While much work remains to be done, we believe we have made a reasonably persuasive case for this conclusion. In section 3.8, we saw that there are also significant differences between the genders in some philosophically interesting behaviors and choices, like those studied in various economic games. It is important to note that in a variety of other domains psychologists have either failed to detect gender differences or have detected only very weak gender differences.[35] However, we do not think that the absence of strong gender differences in many areas of mental processing provides plausible grounds to doubt the variation in philosophical intuitions that has been our concern. Instead, we think, it shows that the differences between men and women are subtle, complex, and—for the moment, at least—often quite unpredictable.

A natural question to raise at this point is: What is the *explanation* for the gender differences in philosophical intuition? On our view, however, it would be premature to venture an answer. We will need to know much more about gender differences in intuition (and behavior and choices) before making a serious attempt to explain them. One of the most important questions that remains unanswered is whether these differences in intuition are a culturally local phenomenon. As we have taken pains to emphasize, all the participants in the studies we have discussed were located in North America, and many of them were university students. This is not at all unusual. In a recent and very influential paper, Henrich, Heine, and Norenzayan (2010) point out that a substantial majority of experimental participants in recent behavioral science experiments are Americans, and a majority of these are university students. Indeed, 'a randomly selected American undergraduate is more than 4,000 times more likely to be a research participant than is a randomly selected person from outside the West' (ibid., 63). However, Henrich and colleagues go on to show that when cross-cultural data are available it often turns out that Americans are outliers, and American university students are outliers among the outliers! So without data from cross-cultural studies, we think it would be unwise to assume that the intuition differences we have reported would be found in European participants and even more unwise to assume that they would be found in Asians or Africans or other groups around the globe. Moreover, when cross-cultural studies of philosophical intuitions are done, there is no reason to suppose they will all turn out the same way. It is entirely possible that some gender differences we have recounted are pan-cultural while others are culturally local.

There are many other important questions that also remain unanswered. Do some gender differences in intuition reflect deep cognitive or affective differences between the genders, or do they all arise from relatively superficial semantic factors, or pragmatic factors, or local norms of self-presentation—or from something else entirely? Here again the answer is that we do not know. Are there different explanations for the gender differences in intuition in different parts of philosophy? Is the explanation for the gender differences in moral intuitions different from the explanation for the gender differences in metaphysical intuitions? Indeed, is the explanation for the gender differences in one sort of moral intuition different from the explanation for the gender differences in another sort of moral intuition? Once again, we do not know. We believe that all of these questions are addressable using the techniques of contemporary cognitive science, and that this sort of experimental philosophy should be high on the agenda of philosophers interested in understanding their own discipline and explaining why men and women sometimes have different philosophical intuitions. Much more work will be needed before we understand gender differences in philosophical intuition.

Another question raised by the finding that men and women sometimes have significantly different philosophical intuitions is: What implications do these gender differences have for philosophical methodology and philosophical pedagogy? We believe that the implications are both important and pervasive. But defending that view requires a long, careful, and systematic argument that will have to be postponed for another occasion.[36]

4. HOW GENDER DIFFERENCES IN PHILOSOPHICAL INTUITION MIGHT HELP TO EXPLAIN THE GENDER GAP IN ACADEMIC PHILOSOPHY

In this section, we turn from facts to hypotheses. Our goal is to outline a series of conjectures about ways in which the sorts of gender differences in philosophical intuition that we have been exploring, and differences in intuition that may not be associated with gender, might be part of the explanation for the gender gap in academic philosophy. Along the way, we will present some evidence that is compatible with these hypotheses, though much more evidence will be required before we can have confidence that the hypotheses are correct. Before beginning, we want to make it very clear that if hypotheses like those we will discuss turn out to be true, it most definitely would not follow that differences in intuition are the *only* factor leading to the gender gap in philosophy. Quite to the contrary, we think that historical, sociological, and economic factors are also very likely to be part of the explanation and that gender based discrimination and sexist attitudes and behavior are also important contributing factors (Haslanger 2008; Saul forthcoming). All of this would be fully compatible with our hypotheses. We have chosen to focus our research on differences in philosophical intuition not because we think it is the only factor involved, or the most important, but because until very recently these differences were almost entirely unrecognized. Moreover, as we will argue in this section, when combined with one of the standard methods invoked in doing and teaching analytic philosophy, they have the potential to generate *unconscious* and *unintentional* biases against women. If we are to develop efficacious strategies for combating the underrepresentation of women that is rampant in our profession, it is crucial that we understand how these biases might arise, assess how large their impact has been, and begin to think about ways to lessen their influence.

We will start with a brief elaboration of a point made in section 2. When a philosopher invokes a philosophical intuition in a philosophical argument, the intuition (or, more accurately, the propositional content of the intuition) is typically being used as *evidence*. Philosophers rarely argue that the propositional content of an intuition they are invoking is true. Rather, they take the propositional content of the intuition to be *obvious*, and they use the proposition as a premise in the argument they are constructing. So, for example, while philosophers (and philosophy instructors) can and do offer arguments from the intuitively supported *premise* that the protagonist in a Gettier-style thought experiment does not know that p, to the conclusion that the justified-true-belief account of knowledge is false, philosophers rarely even attempt to argue that the protagonist does not know that p. If an interlocutor were to deny that the premise is true and insist that the protagonist *does* know that p, the philosopher might take steps to ensure the interlocutor has understood the story and has not ignored or forgotten some of the crucial details. But if the interlocutor has understood the vignette and has not ignored important details, it is far from clear what else the philosopher could say to convince him, since philosophers generally assume that it is obvious that the Gettier protagonist does not know that p.[37] In this respect, as Sosa (2007) has noted, the role of philosophical intuition is similar to the role of observation or perception in providing evidence for scientific theories.

> [T]he way intuition is supposed to function in epistemology and in philosophy more generally ... is by analogy with the way observation is supposed to function in empirical science. Empirical theories are required to accord well enough with the deliverances of scientific observation.[38] (P. 107)

But now consider the predicament of a young woman in a philosophy class, who (like 71–75% of women in the Starmans and Friedman study) does not find it obvious that the characters in Gettier vignettes do not have knowledge of the relevant proposition. Rather, her intuitions tell her that the Gettier characters *do* have knowledge, though her instructor, whether male or female, as well as a high percentage of her male classmates, clearly think she is mistaken. Different women will, of course, react to a situation like this in different ways. But it is plausible to suppose that some women facing this predicament will be puzzled or confused or uncomfortable or angry or just plain bored. Some women may become convinced that they aren't any good at philosophy, since they do not have the intuitions that their professors and their male classmates insist are correct. If the experience engenders one or more of these alienating effects, a female student may be less likely to take another philosophy course than a male classmate who (like 59–64% of the men in the Starmans and Friedman study) has the 'standard' intuitions that their instructor shares. That male student, unlike the majority of his female classmates, can actively participate in, and perhaps enjoy, the project of hunting for a theory that captures 'our' intuitions.

If these speculations are on the right track, then as students in philosophy courses are repeatedly exposed to the practice of using intuitions as evidence, we should expect to find enrollments of women dropping off. The more courses a woman takes, the more likely it is that she will be exposed to thought experiments on which her intuitions and those of her instructor diverge—and the more likely it is that she will decide not to take another course. Is this the case? Though gender coded enrollment data are not readily available, we have been able to obtain reliable data on the gender ratios in philosophy courses during a recent 10-year period at Rutgers University, a large state university with a highly ranked philosophy department.[39] As can be seen in Figure 17, in the 100-level introductory courses, the percent of female and male students is almost equal: 46.2% female and 53.8% male.[40] But at *each* higher level, the percent of women goes down: 40.38% at the 200 level, 36.50 at the 300 level, 29.31 at the 400 level, and 26.2% in 500- through 800-level graduate courses.[41]

Of course, the hypothesis we are urging is plausible only if students are, often enough, exposed to thought experiments that tend to evoke different intuitions in men and women. Are they? One way to address this question is to look at the most widely used philosophy textbooks. This is easier said than

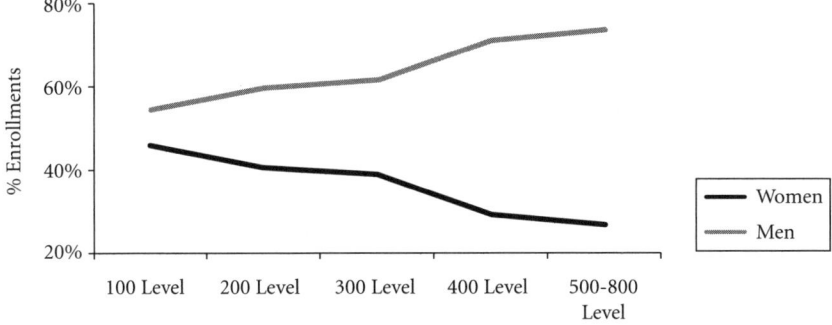

Figure 13.17. Percent Enrollment in undergraduate philosophy courses at Rutgers, The State University of New Jersey, from Spring 1999 to Spring 2010.

done, since most major textbook publishers treat their sales data as proprietary information that is not publicly available. As a workaround, we contacted the philosophy textbook editor of a leading publishing house and asked him to provide his professional opinion about which texts published by both his firm and his competitors had the largest sales. We then examined these texts to see which philosophical thought experiments were most common.[42] The five most common, in decreasing order, were versions of (or close relatives of)

1. The Violinist
2. The Brain in the Vat
3. Compatibilism (thought experiments about free will in a deterministic universe)
4. Physicalism (inspired by Jackson's Mary case)
5. The Chinese Room

This was a relatively crude exercise, to be sure, but the results are suggestive nonetheless. Note that gender differences in intuition have been found in versions of all of the philosophical thought experiments on this list. So there is reason to conclude, albeit tentatively, that many students are indeed exposed to these thought experiments and that the more philosophy courses they take the more philosophical thought experiments they encounter.

What we are suggesting is that part of the gender gap in academic philosophy can be explained as a *selection effect*. Students come to philosophy with somewhat different intuitions about many standard philosophical thought experiments, and as we have shown, in many cases there are statistically significant differences between women's intuitions and men's. However, most of the faculty members who get to say which intuitions are correct (and 'obvious') are now, and always have been, men. So women students are more likely than men students to find that their intuitions about the thought experiments discussed in their philosophy classes are at odds with those of their instructor. If it is indeed the case that students (of either gender) are less likely to continue in philosophy if their intuitions do not accord with those of their instructor, then all the elements of a powerful and cumulative selection effect are in place—a selection effect which "filters out" a greater proportion of women than of men.

We are not the first to suggest the existence of an intuition-based selection effect in philosophy, though, to the best of our knowledge, it has not previously been linked to gender. In his well-known paper "Reflection on Reflective Equilibrium," Robert Cummins (1998) wrote:

> The Putnamian take on these [Twin Earth] cases is widely enough shared to allow for a range of thriving intramural sports among believers. *Those who do not share the intuition are simply not invited to the games.* This kind of selection allows things to move forward, but it has its price.... We must take care that such agreement about intuitions as there is not merely a selection effect. This is easier said than done, since it is all too easy for insiders to suppose that dissenters just do not understand the case. *If we are honest with ourselves, I think we will have to confront the fact that*

selection effects like this are likely to be pretty widespread in contemporary philosophy. (P. 116, emphasis added)

What we would add to this is that, more often than not, those who are filtered out by these intuition-based selection effects are women.

One concern about our selection effect hypothesis that has been raised frequently by philosophical colleagues with whom we have discussed our work is that in a number of the cases of gender difference that we report in section 3, it is not clear that it is the women who have the intuitions that most professional philosophers take to be incorrect. What fuels this worry is that, while there is substantial data showing gender-linked variation in non-philosophers' intuitions about various philosophical thought experiments, there is little or no reliable data concerning professional philosophers' intuitions in these cases. If the differences in non-philosophers' intuitions are going to be part of the explanation of why women are more inclined than men to stop taking philosophy classes, then the female intuitions in these studies should be more likely than the male intuitions to diverge from the consensus among professional philosophers. However, since there is relatively little data about the intuitions of professional philosophers, it is not clear that the evidence assembled in section 3 exhibits this pattern.

While there is little data available indicating how professional philosophers might respond to the specific thought experiments discussed in section 3, many colleagues have offered conjectures. Most of them agree that the women's intuitions reported in the Gettier, Violinist, and Magistrate and Mob cases are at odds with the dominant intuitions of professional philosophers in these cases. Though they are less confident, a number of colleagues are also inclined to think that the women's intuitions differ from those professional philosophers would have in the Dualism and Epistemic Side-Effect Effect experiments. However, in three of the cases presented in section 3—Compatibilism , Brain in the Vat, and Twin Earth—most of the colleagues we have spoken with speculate that the women's intuitions in the studies are *more* consistent with the dominant view among professional philosophers and the men's intuitions are less consistent.

This is an important challenge.[43] But, for two very different reasons, we are not persuaded that it undermines our selection effect hypothesis. The first is that, as already noted, in most cases we really do not know what the dominant intuition is among professional philosophers. It has been suggested that the *PhilPapers* survey cited in section 1 could help to shed light on this matter. However, that survey asked about respondents' philosophical *views* rather than about their intuitions in response to specific thought experiments. So, for example, the Free Will question in the *PhilPapers* survey simply asked, 'Free will: compatibilism, libertarianism, or no free will'? Results indicated that 59% 'accepted or leaned toward' compatibilism, 13.7% libertarianism, 12.2% no free will, 14.9% other. We doubt that information of this sort gives us a reliable way of predicting what participants in the *PhilPapers* survey would have said in response to any detailed compatibilism thought experiment. For, as the burgeoning experimental philosophy literature exploring intuitions about free will and responsibility makes clear, people's intuitions in this area are exquisitely sensitive to subtle features of the vignette. With a relatively small and apparently inconsequential change in wording, a vignette that evokes mostly compatibilist intuitions will sometimes evoke mostly incompatibilist intuitions.[44] Moreover, to assess the selection effect hypothesis, what we really need to know is not which intuitions are dominant among professional philosophers but which intuitions are dominant among the subset of professional philosophers (and philosophers-in-training) who teach the first few philosophy courses to which students are exposed. And since there are typically many quite different thought experiments used to gather evidence for or against a philosophical theory, we need to know which versions are actually used in the classroom. So, contrary to what our critics have suggested, it is far from clear that the men in the studies reviewed in section 3 often have intuitions that are incompatible with those they are likely to encounter from their philosophy instructors.

Clearly, the response we have just offered is a two-edged sword. If we do not have adequate information about which intuitions are favored by people teaching philosophy courses, it undercuts the plausibility of the objection we have been considering, but it also undercuts the plausibility of our claim that an intuition-based selection effect contributes to the gender disparity in philosophy. However, our second response suggests that one edge of the sword is significantly sharper than the other. The core idea of our second response is that difference in intuitions can interact with a cluster of other factors in ways that will make it more likely that women will be discouraged from continuing in philosophy. The factors we have in mind have been a main focus of the widely discussed work of Carol Dweck and her associates.[45]

The story starts with the finding that there is an important difference in the way people, both children and adults, think about intelligence and intellectual ability. Dweck and colleagues have used a variety of terms for this distinction. In a recent book aimed at a popular audience, she calls them the 'fixed mind-set' and the 'growth mind-set'. People with the fixed mind-set view intellectual ability in general and more focused abilities in specific subjects as 'a gift—an ability that you simply have or you don't' (Dweck 2006, 3). Those with the growth mind-set view both general intelligence and ability in specific subjects as malleable and cultivatable—'something that builds on an initial ability and expands through practice and dedication' (ibid.). The distinction is important because it correlates with a surprising range of additional phenomena, particularly in the domain of education (Dweck 2000). The most important of these, for our purposes, is that 'viewing intellectual ability as a gift (a fixed entity) led students to question that ability and lose motivation when they encountered setbacks. In contrast, viewing intellectual abilities as qualities that could be developed led them to seek active and effective remedies in the face of difficulty' (Dweck 2006, 3). In an experiment reported in Licht and Dweck (1984), it was found that inducing confusion, by including some intentionally puzzling text in an otherwise straightforward series of written lessons, had a major impact on the success of fixed mind-set 5th graders in mastering the remaining, sensible, material. But inducing confusion had no impact on the success of growth mind-set children in mastering the rest of the material. This, and a number of similar findings, some of them involving university students (Grant & Dweck 2003) indicate that fixed mind-set individuals do not deal well with material that engenders puzzlement or confusion.

What makes all of this relevant to our current concerns is that there is also a substantial body of evidence indicating that the fixed mind-set view of intellectual ability is significantly more common in females than in males (Dweck & Gilliard 1975; Dweck & Bush 1976). So if, as we have suggested, having philosophical intuitions that one's instructor takes to be obviously mistaken (though he typically does not and cannot explain why) engenders puzzlement and confusion, and if fixed mind-set individuals react to this by becoming convinced that they are not good at philosophy and losing their motivation to pursue it, then we would expect fixed mind-set individuals to drop out of philosophy more frequently than growth mind-set individuals, when they find that they have what their instructors take to be the wrong intuitions. And the majority of these fixed mind-set individuals will be women. Thus even if it is the case that women and men are about equally likely to have intuitions that are at odds with those of their instructors, women are more likely than men to conclude that they are no good at philosophy.

To make matters worse, Dweck and her colleagues have also found that the debilitating effect of puzzlement and confusion interacts with IQ differently in males and females. Among males, those with higher IQs did better when confronted with confusing material than those with lower IQs. But among females, the pattern was reversed. The brighter they were, the more likely they were to be negatively impacted by confusing material (Licht & Dweck 1984, 634). So the impact of having intuitions that clash with those of one's instructors may tend to selectively discourage *bright women*. Thus when intuitions play a significant role in philosophical education, as the level of the course and the difficulty of the material increases, we might expect the men to excel, to get more encouragement from their instructors, and thus to be more inclined to continue in philosophy, while the women will be more inclined to look elsewhere. If this story, or even a substantial part of it, is more or less on the right track, then differences in philosophical intuition will play a role in unleashing a cascade of events that increasingly skews the gender distribution in philosophy courses toward men and away from women.

The goal of this section has been to develop some hypotheses about ways in which differences in philosophical intuition—both those that are associated with gender and those that are not—might play a role in explaining the underrepresentation of women in philosophy. Here is how we see the state of play. It is plausible to assume that students who have intuitions that conflict with those of their instructor often find the experience puzzling, confusing, and alienating. If so, then in those cases where the majority of women have intuitions that are in conflict with the intuitions of the majority of philosophy instructors (and the majority of males in their classes), a straightforward selection effect would lead to more women deciding not to continue in philosophy. If cases like this predominate in contemporary philosophical education, then a simple selection effect hypothesis might be all we need to link differences in philosophical intuition with the underrepresentation of women. But since we have relatively little reliable data about the intuitions of philosophy instructors, it is not clear that women have intuitions that are inconsistent with those of their instructors significantly more often than men in thought experiments that are commonly invoked in philosophy classes. However, even in the cases where more men than women have the professionally disparaged intuition, the data assembled in section 3 suggest that there will still be *lots* of women who have the that disparaged intuition. Indeed, one of the most striking facts about the data we have presented is how much *disagreement* there is in intuition, not just between the genders but within them.[46] Dweck's work suggests that when more men than women have the intuition that their instructors take to be mistaken, it is still the case that more women may be driven from philosophy, since when confronted with confusing or puzzling material women are more likely than men to conclude that they have little ability in that domain, and the brighter a woman is, the more likely it is that she will be susceptible to this effect. As the acute reader will have noticed, what are doing the work in our Dweck-inspired hypotheses are not *gender* differences in intuition but *differences* in intuition tout court.

This might lead one to wonder whether philosophical practice and philosophical education should rely so heavily on undefended, and typically undefendable, intuitions that *some* people take to be *obviously* true while many others do not. We think this is an excellent question which one of us has tried to address elsewhere.[47]

5. CONCLUSION

In this paper, we have had a pair of goals. The first was to call attention to a fact about the sorts of intuitions that philosophers have relied on as evidence from antiquity to the present. In some cases—or perhaps in many—men and women in our culture tend to have different philosophical intuitions. Until the recent blossoming of experimental philosophy, these differences had been almost entirely unrecognized. Though there are now more than a dozen studies in which gender differences in philosophical intuitions have been found, there is no obvious pattern in these findings and no good way to predict where gender differences will be found in the many cases that have not yet been studied. Much work remains to be done before we have an accurate account of the contours of gender differences in philosophical intuition and a good explanation of why they exist.

Our second goal was to propose a cluster of hypotheses about how differences in intuition, both those that are associated with gender and those that are not, might play a role in explaining the egregious underrepresentation of women in philosophy. We have set out several ways in which differences in philosophical intuition, along with the practice of using intuitions as evidence, might lead to unconscious and unintentional bias against women. Bias of this sort, if it exists, is surely not the only factor contributing to the underrepresentation of women in philosophy, though it might well amplify and exacerbate some of the other causes of the gender gap in philosophy. In order to develop effective strategies for combating the gender disparity, we need to know whether the hypotheses we have proposed are true and, if they are, how large a role the bias they generate is playing in generating and sustaining the lamentably skewed demography of academic philosophy. In research currently underway, we hope to make some progress toward answering these questions.

NOTES

* We are very grateful to Helen Beebee, Fiery Cushman, Carrie Figdor, Ori Friedman, Joshua Greene, Geoffrey Holtzman, Jonathan Livengood, Edouard Machery, Shaun Nichols, Molly Paxton, Jennifer Saul, Christina Starmans, Justin Sytsma, Valerie Tiberius, and Liane Young, all of whom shared their data with us and provided clear and careful answers to our many questions about their work. Special thanks to our research assistant, Michael Sechman. We would also like to thank Louise Antony, Helen Beebee, Michael Bishop, Ned Block, Paul Bloom, Tamar Gendler, Joshua Knobe, Tania Lombrozo, Brian Leiter, Edouard Machery, Ron Mallon, Shaun Nichols, Richard Nisbett, Jesse Prinz, Jennifer Saul, Christina Starmans, Valerie Tiberius, Virginia Valian, and Jonathan Weinberg as well as members of the MERG (Metro Experimental Research Group) lab, the Moral Psychology Research Group, and the Society for Philosophy and Psychology for insightful comments on earlier versions of this material.

1. More accurately, what the evidence indicates is that there are gender differences in philosophical intuitions *among contemporary residents of the USA and Canada*. As we emphasize in section 3.9, whether these differences exist in other groups is currently unknown. Since repeating the italicized phrase makes for awkward prose, we will often omit it. But the reader should keep in mind that the qualification is always intended.

2. http://www.philosophicalgourmet.com/.

3. The websites of the philosophy departments mentioned in this section were accessed on various days from March 8 through March 19, 2010. In assembling Table 1, we made no attempt to correct the information we found on departmental websites, though in several cases we had good reason to believe that the websites did not accurately reflect the current department membership. In a number of cases, we had to make decisions about whether to count people who had various sorts of split or part-time appointments. We consulted with Professor Haslanger and tried to apply the same rules of thumb that she had employed. But, inevitably, this table reflects a number of 'judgment calls'.

4. Here again we had to make quite a few 'judgment calls'. The people we counted were on lists with a variety of labels including 'permanent faculty', 'main faculty', 'continuing positions', and 'academic staff'.

5. Available at http://philpapers.org/surveys/.

6. Hintikka (1999) notes that the use of the term 'intuition' in contemporary philosophy became much more common as philosophers became acquainted with Chomsky's work in linguistics where 'intuition' is used as a label for spontaneous judgments about the grammatical properties of sentences that speakers are asked to consider.

7. Plato (1892), I, 331, p. 595.

8. 'Application intuitions' is Goldman's term for 'intuitions about how cases are to be classified'.

9. Though intuitions clearly play an important role in contemporary philosophy, they are *not* the only source of evidence for philosophical theories, and some contemporary philosophers make little or no use of them.

10. Holtzman used SurveyMonkey for these experiments, a commercially available Web-based survey tool.

11. In all of the Holtzman studies we discuss, participants were asked to reply either 'yes' or 'no'. Only participants who reported that they had taken no philosophy courses were considered.

12. In Holtzman's studies, the three cases we have discussed were presented along with six other vignettes for which no significant gender differences were found. See Holtzman (2013) for details on these six vignettes. With the exception of the dualism study, significance values in the experiments we have recounted remain at the $p < 0.05$ level after correcting by a factor of 9.

13. For male participants the mean was 4.32, $SD = 1.39$; for female participants the mean was 3.86, $SD = 1.57$, $(d = 0.31)$. An independent samples t-test reveals a significant difference between these two groups, $t(296) = 2.65, p < 0.01$.

14. For male participants the mean was −158, $SD = 120.39$, and for female participants the mean was −129, $SD = 108.36$, $(d = 0.25)$. A significant main effect was obtained for gender, $F(1,521) = 7.40, p < 0.01$.

15. In the stranger case, the mean response among male participants was 4.21, $SD = 1.93$, and the mean among female participants was 4.95, $SD = 1.07$, $(d = 0.50)$.

16. In the 12-year-old boy case, the mean response for male participants was 4.87, $SD = 1.71$, and the mean for female participants was 4.26, $SD = 1.79$, $(d = 0.35)$. A two-way between-subjects analysis of variance was conducted to evaluate the effect of condition (either stranger or 12-year-old boy) and gender on participant responses. The interaction of these two factors approached significance $F(1, 85) = 3.46, p = 0.07$.

17. In the killing your brother case, the mean judgment for male participants was 3.41, $SD = 1.67$, and the mean for female participants was 4.33, $SD = 1.35$, $(d = 0.59)$. In the killing your sister case, mean judgments for male participants was 4.40, $SD = 2.13$, and the mean for female participants was 3.78, $SD = 1.58$, $(d = 0.33)$. A two-way between-subjects analysis of variance reveals a significant interaction effect between these two factors $F(1, 95) = 4.45, p < 0.05$.

18. Pizarro et al. (2003) provide the following technical details: 'In order to test the hypothesis that individuals discounted responsibility for causally deviant actions, a 2 (causal condition: deviant vs. normal) × 2 (positive vs. negative act), repeated measures ANOVA was conducted. As predicted, there was a main effect for experimental condition, $F(1, 25) = 18.13, p < 0.001$, such that individuals discounted moral responsibility for acts that were causally "deviant".'

19. For women: Negative Deviant ($M = 2.67, SD = 1.00$), Negative Normal ($M = 3.17, SD = 1.05$); paired-sample t-test, $t(13) = -2.88, p = 0.01$. Positive Normal ($M = 2.93, SD = 0.80$), Positive Deviant ($M = 3.10, SD = 0.85$); $t(13) = -1.53, p = 0.15$. For men: Negative Deviant ($M = 2.58, SD = 1.19$), Negative Normal ($M = 2.86, SD = 1.23$); $t(11) = -1.39, p = 0.19$. Positive Normal ($M = 2.94, SD = 1.01$), Positive Deviant ($M = 2.39, SD = 0.86$); $t(11) = -3.35, p = 0.01$.

20. In the help condition the mean response was 0.91, $SD = 2.09$; in the harm condition the mean was 2.25, $SD = 1.50$. An independent samples t-test reveals a significant difference between these two groups, $t(747) = -10.126, p < 0.001$.

21. For more on the epistemic side-effect effect, see Schaffer and Knobe (forthcoming) and Beebe and Jensen (forthcoming).

22. A two-way between-subjects analysis of variance was conducted to evaluate the effect of intentionality and valence. A significant main effect was obtained for intentionality, $F(1, 410) = 63.92, p < 0.001$. The main effect for valence was also significant, $F(1, 410) = 230.86, p < 0.001$.

23. Means and standard deviations for *causal agreement*: Intentional-Help ($M = 3.89$, $SD = 1.88$), Intentional-Harm ($M = 5.50, SD = 1.59$), Unintentional-Help ($M = 3.51$, $SD = 1.97$), Unintentional-Harm ($M = 4.50, SD = 1.71$). A significant main effect was obtained for intentionality, $F(1, 411) = 15.17, p < 0.001$. The main effect for valence was also significant, $F(1, 411) = 54.83, p < 0.001$.

24. Women (Help $M = 3.48, SD = 1.87$, Harm $M = 5.11, SD = 1.67$) and men (Help $M = 4.1, SD = 1.98$, Harm $M = 4.83, SD = 1.79$). A two-way between-subjects analysis of variance was conducted to evaluate the relationship between gender and valence on participant responses in the causation cases. A significant interaction was found between these factors $F(1, 407) = 6.11, p < 0.05$.

25. For further discussion of the relation between these two sets of findings, see Buckwalter (manuscript a).

26. $N = 1836$; 715 men, 1090 women, 37 unreported; 48% under 30 years of age; 78% self-identified as white non-Hispanic; 50% reported that they hold less than a bachelor's degree.

27. Our eight-item demographic questionnaire collected information about gender, age, education level, philosophical training, native language, race, religiosity, and income level.

28. In addition to excluding data from participants who have taken one or more philosophy courses, participants were also eliminated if they did not select English as their native language, if they completed the studies in less than 30 seconds, or if they did not correctly answer simple comprehension check questions. Participants whose IP address indicated that they were not located in the United States were excluded from participation.

29. $N = 63$; 24 men, 39 women. The mean response from male participants was 5.62, $SD = 1.97$, the mean for female participants was 6.72, $SD = 0.76$, ($d = 0.81$). An independent samples t-test reveals a significant difference between these two groups, $t(61) = -3.12; p < 0.01$.

30. $N = 84$; 35 men, 49 women. The mean response for male participants was 5.63, $SD = 2.21$, the mean for female participants was 4.49, $SD = 2.42$, ($d = 0.49$). An independent samples t-test reveals a significant difference between these two groups, $t(82) = 2.21, p < 0.05$.

31. $N = 127$; 54 men, 73 women. The mean response for male participants was 4.13, $SD = 2.47$, the mean for female participants was 3.25, $SD = 2.36$, ($d = 0.37$). An independent samples t-test reveals a significant difference between these two groups, $t(125) = 2.05, p < 0.05$.

32. $N = 110$; 37 men, 73 women. The mean response for male participants was 4.95, $SD = 2.07$, the mean for female participants was 5.64, $SD = 1.35$ ($d = 0.42$). An independent samples t-test reveals a significant difference between these two groups, $t(108) = -2.13, p < 0.05$.

33. 'Face' stimuli like those used in Rigdon et al. (see figure 15) have been shown to activate the fusiform face area (FFA) of the brain (Bednar & Miikkulainen 2003).

34. Rigdon et al. report that they conducted a logit analysis to see the extent to which gender influences the amount transferred in the face condition. Regressing the amount (where amount = 1 if transfer > average transfer) on gender (where gender = 1 if male),

they found that males are 3.35 times more likely than females to fall in this category ($p = 0.048$). The difference in average transfers by female participants across treatments is not significant ($p = 0.1592$); the difference in proportion of female participants who send $1.00 or more is not significantly different across the treatments ($p = 0.4223$).

35. See, for example, Hyde's (2005) paper, 'The Gender Similarity Hypothesis', which offers a meta-analysis in defense of the claim that on many different psychological variables men and women are quite similar.

36. See Stich (in preparation).

37. As Ned Block reminded us, not all that long ago it was a common practice for philosophers to dismiss people who didn't share their intuitions by saying that they have 'a tin ear'.

38. The analogy, as Jonathan Weinberg (2007) notes, is rather too favorable toward intuition, since in the case of perceptual disagreements there are often well-established procedures for adjudication.

39. Our thanks to Barry Qualls, vice president for undergraduate education at Rutgers, and Kenneth Iuso, the Rutgers University registrar, for making these data available.

40. Students at Rutgers are not required to take an introductory philosophy course.

41. Percentages calculated from 79,904 enrollments (47,013 men, 32,891 women) during the target period. Though we claim that these enrollment data are *consistent* with our hypothesis, we want to be very clear that we do not claim that they support our hypothesis over a variety of other hypotheses that might be offered about the causal mechanisms responsible for the underrepresentation of women in philosophy. At the 2011 meeting of the Society for Philosophy and Psychology, Molly Paxton, Carrie Figdor, and Valerie Tiberius presented data from an ongoing study that are broadly consistent with this pattern. They found that the largest statistically significant drop in the proportion of women in philosophy occurs between taking an introductory class in philosophy and declaring a major in philosophy. For details of this valuable and sophisticated study, see Paxton et al. (in preparation). Additional data from the University of Minnesota, provided by Valerie Tiberius, confirmed that there is a precipitous drop in the proportion of women taking philosophy courses between introductory-level courses, where about 45% of the students are women, and intermediate-level courses, where only about 28% are women. Tiberius also provided University of Minnesota enrollment data for 11 other departments: anthropology, biology, computer science, electrical engineering, English, history, journalism, mechanical engineering, political science, psychology, and sociology. None of them exhibited the pattern found in philosophy. Obviously *something* is discouraging women students from continuing in philosophy beyond the introductory level, and whatever it is is not present in many other disciplines.

42. We searched over 25 leading introduction to philosophy, introduction to ethics, contemporary moral issues, philosophy of mind, philosophy of language, epistemology, and metaphysics textbooks and readers published by Cengage, McGraw Hill, Oxford University Press, and Pearson Press.

43. Our thanks to the many colleagues who have proposed versions of this challenge. Special thanks to Michael Bishop for a particularly clear and detailed statement of the argument.

44. See, for example, Nahmias, Coates, and Kvaran (2007) and Feltz, Cokely, and Nadelhoffer (2009).

45. We are indebted to Tania Lombrozo for calling Dweck's work to our attention. For an excellent—though now slightly dated—overview of Dweck's work, see Dweck (2000). For a more recent overview, aimed at a wider audience, see Dweck (2008).

46. Arguably, the existence of widespread disagreement in philosophical intuitions is the single most consistent finding to emerge from a decade of work in experimental philosophy. For some further discussion of this point, see Mallon et al. (2009).

47. Stich (in preparation).

REFERENCES

Bealer, G. (1998). Intuition and the autonomy of philosophy. In M. DePaul and W. Ramsey (eds.), *Rethinking Intuition: The Psychology of Intuition and Its Role in Philosophical Inquiry*. Lanham, MD: Rowman and Littlefield, 201–239.

Beebe, J. and Buckwalter, W. (2010). The epistemic side-effect effect. *Mind and Language*, 25: 474–498.

Beebe, J. and Jensen, M. (forthcoming). Surprising connections between knowledge and action: The robustness of the epistemic side-effect effect. *Philosophical Psychology*.

Beebee, H. and Saul, J. (2011). Women in Philosophy in the UK: A Report. http://www.bpa.ac.uk/policies.

Bednar, J. and Miikkulainen, R. (2003). Learning innate face preferences. *Neural Computation*, 15: 1525–1557.

Buckwalter, W. (unpublished manuscript, a). *Gender and epistemic intuition*. City University of New York, Graduate Center.

Buckwalter, W. (unpublished manuscript, b). *Solving the puzzle of causation by absence: Experiments in metaphysics*. City University of New York, Graduate Center.

Brueckner, T. (2008). Brains in a Vat. *The Stanford Encyclopedia of Philosophy (Fall 2008 Edition)*, Edward N. Zalta (ed.). http://plato.stanford.edu/archives/fall2008/entries/brain-vat/>.

Cappelen, H. (forthcoming). *Philosophy without Intuitions*. Oxford: Oxford University Press.

Croson, R. and Gneezy, U. (2009). Gender differences in preferences. *Journal of Economic Literature*, 47: 448–474.

Cummins, R. (1998). Reflections on reflective equilibrium. In M. DePaul and W. Ramsey (eds.), *Rethinking Intuition: The Psychology of Intuition and Its Role in Philosophical Inquiry*. Lanham, MD: Rowman and Littlefield, 113–127.

Deutsch, M. (2010). Intuitions, counter-examples and experimental philosophy. *Review of Philosophy and Psychology*, 1: 447–460.

Devitt, M. (2006). Intuitions. In V. Gomez Pin, J. Galparaso and G. Arrizabalaga (eds.), *Ontology Studies Cuadernos de Ontologia: Proceedings of VI International Ontology Congress*, 169–176.

Devitt, M. (2009). On determining what there isn't. In D. Murphy and M. Bishop (eds.), *Stich and His Critics*. Oxford: Blackwell, 46–61.

Dweck, C. and Gilliard, D. (1975). Expectancy statements as determinants of reactions to failure: Sex differences in persistence and expectancy change. *Journal of Personality and Social Psychology*, 32: 1077–1084.

Dweck, C. and Bush, E. (1976). Sex differences in learned helplessness: I. Differential debilitation with peer and adult evaluators. *Developmental Psychology*, 12: 147–156.

Dweck, C. (2000). *Self-Theories: Their Role in Motivation, Personality, and Development*. New York: Psychology Press.

Dweck, C. (2006). Is math a gift? Beliefs that put females at risk. In S. Ceci and W. Williams, (eds.), *Why Aren't More Women in Science? Top Researchers Debate the Evidence.* Washington, DC: American Psychological Association. Also available at: https://www.stanford.edu/dept/psychology/cgibin/drupalm/system/files/cdweckmathgift.pdf. Page references in the text are to the website version.

Dweck, C. (2008). *Mindset: The New Psychology of Success.* New York: Ballantine Books.

Eagly, A. (1995). The science and politics of comparing women and men. *American Psychologist, 50*: 145–158.

Eckel, C. and Grossman, P. (1998). Are women less selfish than men? Evidence from dictator experiments. *Economic Journal, 108*: 726–735.

Eckel, C. and Grossman, P. (2008a). The difference in the economic decisions of men and women: Experimental evidence. In C. Plott and V. Smith (eds.), *Handbook of Experimental Economics Results.* Amsterdam: North-Holland/Elsevier, 509–519.

Eckel, C. and Grossman, P. (2008b). Sex and risk: Experimental evidence. In C. Plott and V. Smith (eds.), *Handbook of Experimental Economics Results.* Amsterdam: North-Holland/Elsevier, 1061–1073.

Feltz, A., Cokely, E. and Nadelhoffer, T. (2009). Natural compatibilism versus natural incompatibilism: Back to the drawing board. *Mind and Language, 24*: 1–23.

Gendler, T. (2007). Philosophical thought experiments, intuitions, and cognitive equilibrium. *Midwest Studies in Philosophy, 31*: 68–89.

Gettier, E. L. (1963). Is justified true belief knowledge? *Analysis 23*: 121–123.

Goldman, A. (2007). Philosophical intuitions: their target, their source, and their epistemic status. *Grazer Philosophiche Studien, 74*: 1–26.

Grant, H. and Dweck, C. (2003). Clarifying achievement goals and their impact. *Journal of Personality and Social Psychology, 85*: 541–553.

Halpern, D. (2011). *Sex Differences in Cognitive Abilities,* 4th ed. Florence, KY: Psychology Press, Taylor & Francis.

Haslanger, S. (2008). Changing the ideology and culture of philosophy: Not by reason (alone). *Hypatia, 23*: 210–223.

Henrich, J., Heine, S. and Norenzayan, A. (2010). The weirdest people in the world? *Behavioral and Brain Sciences, 33*: 61–83.

Hintikka, J. (1999). The emperor's new intuitions. *Journal of Philosophy, 96*: 127–147.

Hitchcock, C. & Knobe, J. (2009). Cause and norm. *Journal of Philosophy, 106*: 587–612.

Holtzman, G. (2013). Do personality effects mean philosophy is intrinsically subjective? *Journal of Consciousness Studies,* 20: 27-42.

Holtzman, G. (under review, a). Personal is universal: Why women's judgments of moral agency are more reliable than men's.

Holtzman, G. (under review, b). Neuroessentialism, neuropluralism, and normative gender differences in the judgment of violent psychopaths.

Hyde, J. S. (2005). The gender similarities hypothesis. *American Psychologist, 60*: 581–592.

Ichikawa, J. (2008). *Imagination and Epistemology,* Ph.D. dissertation, submitted to the Graduate School of Rutgers University, Chapter 5.

Jackson, F. (1982). Epiphenomenal qualia. *Philosophical Quarterly, 32*: 127–136.

Jackson, F. (1986). What Mary didn't know. *Journal of Philosophy, 83*: 291–295.

Jackson, F. (1998). *From Metaphysics to Ethics: A Defence of Conceptual Analysis.* Oxford: Clarendon Press.

Knobe, J. (2003). Intentional action and side effects in ordinary language. *Analysis, 63*: 190–193.

Knobe, J. (2010). Person as scientist, person as moralist. *Behavioral and Brain Sciences,* 33: 315–329.
Knobe, J. and Fraser, B. (2008). Causal judgment and moral judgment: Two experiments. In W. Sinnott-Armstrong (ed.), *Moral Psychology,* vol. 2: *The Cognitive Science of Morality: Intuition and Diversity.* Cambridge, MA: MIT Press.
Knobe, J., Buckwalter, W., Nichols, S., Robbins, P., Sarkissian, H. and Sommers, T. (forthcoming). Experimental philosophy. *Annual Review of Psychology.*
Kornblith, H. (1998). The role of intuition in philosophical inquiry: An account with no unnatural ingredients. In M. DePaul and W. Ramsey (eds.), *Rethinking Intuition: The Psychology of Intuition and Its Role in Philosophical Inquiry.* Lanham, MD: Rowman and Littlefield, 129–141.
Kripke, S. (1980). *Naming and Necessity.* Cambridge, MA: Harvard University Press.
Licht, B. and Dweck, C. (1984). Determinants of academic achievement: The interaction of children's achievement orientations with skill area. *Developmental Psychology,* 20: 628–636.
Livengood, J., Sytsma, J., Feltz, A., Scheines, R. and Machery, E. (forthcoming). Philosophical temperament. *Philosophical Psychology.*
Ludwig, K. (2007). The epistemology of thought experiments: First vs. third person approaches. *Midwest Studies in Philosophy, Philosophy and the Empirical,* 31: 128–159.
Mallon, R., Machery, E., Nichols, S. and Stich, S. (2009). Against arguments from reference. *Philosophy and Phenomenological Research,* 79: 332–356.
Nahmias, E., Coates, D. and Kvaran, T. (2007). Free will, moral responsibility and mechanism: Experiments on folk intuition. *Midwest Studies in Philosophy,* 31: 214–242.
Nichols, S., Stich, S. and Weinberg, J. (2003). Meta-skepticism: Meditations on ethno-epistemology. In S. Luper (ed.), *The Skeptics.* Aldershot, UK: Ashgate Publishing, 227–247.
Paxton, M., Figdor, C. and Tiberius, V. (in preparation). Quantifying the gender gap: An empirical study of the underrepresentation of women in philosophy.
Pessin, A. and Goldberg, S. (eds.) (1996). *The Twin Earth Chronicles: Twenty Years of Reflection on Hilary Putnam's 'The Meaning of Meaning'.* Armonk, NY: M.E. Sharpe.
Plato (1892). *The Republic* in *The Dialogues of Plato,* Vol. I (B. Jowett, Trans.). New York: Random House.
Pizarro, D., Uhlmann, E. and Bloom, P. (2003). Causal deviance and the attribution of moral responsibility. *Journal of Experimental Social Psychology,* 39: 653–660.
Putnam, H. (1973). Meaning and reference. *Journal of Philosophy,* 70: 699–711.
Rigdon, M., Ishii, K., Watabe, M. and Kitayama, S. (2009). Minimal social cues in the dictator game. *Journal of Economic Psychology,* 30: 358–367.
Saul, J. (forthcoming). Unconscious influences and women in philosophy. In F. Jenkins and K. Hutchison (eds.), *Women in Philosophy: What Needs to Change?*
Schaffer, J. and Knobe, J. (forthcoming). Contrastivism surveyed. *Nous.* doi: 10.1111/j.1468-0068.2010.00795.x
Searle, J. (1980). Minds, brains and programs. *Behavioral and Brain Sciences,* 3: 417–457.
Smart, J. (1973). An outline of a system of utilitarian ethics. In J. Smart and B. Williams (eds.), *Utilitarianism: For and Against.* Cambridge: Cambridge University Press, 3–47.
Sosa, E. (2007). Experimental philosophy and philosophical intuition. *Philosophical Studies,* 132: 99–107.
Sosa, E. (2009). A defense of the use of intuitions in philosophy. In M. Bishop and D. Murphy (eds.), *Stich and His Critics.* Oxford: Blackwell, 101–112.

Starmans, C. and Friedman, O. (2009). Is knowledge subjective? A sex difference in adults' epistemic intuitions. Poster presented at the 6th Biennial Meeting of the Cognitive Development Society, San Antonio, TX, October 16–17. Abstract available at http://www.cogdevsoc.org/prog2009/CDS09Program.pdf.

Stich, S. (2009). Reply to Sosa. In M. Bishop and D. Murphy (eds.), *Stich and His Critics*. Oxford: Blackwell, 228–236.

Stich, S. (in preparation). Experimental philosophy and the bankruptcy of the great tradition.

Thomson, J. (1971). A defense of abortion. *Philosophy and Public Affairs, 1*, 1: 47–66.

Vesterlund, L. (2006). Why do people give? In R. Steinberg and W. Powell (eds.), *The Nonprofit Sector*, 2d ed. New Haven, CT: Yale University Press.

Weinberg, J. (2007). How to challenge intuitions empirically without risking skepticism. *Midwest Studies in Philosophy, 31*: 318–343.

Weinberg, J., Nichols, S. and Stich, S. (2001). Normativity and epistemic intuitions. *Philosophical Topics, 29*: 429–460.

Williamson, T. (2004). Philosophical intuitions and skepticism about judgment. *Dialectica, 58*: 109–153.

Williamson, T. (2007). *The Philosophy of Philosophy*. Oxford: Blackwell.

Zamzow, J. and Nichols, S. (2009). Variations in ethical intuitions. *Philosophical Issues 19*: 368–388.

14

Expertise in Moral Reasoning? Order Effects on Moral Judgment in Professional Philosophers and Non-Philosophers

Eric Schwitzgebel and Fiery Cushman

1. INTRODUCTION

Moral judgment is sometimes claimed to arise mostly from automatic processes that depend little on conscious reasoning from general principles (Haidt, 2001; Mikhail 2009). Recent work in moral psychology suggests that people can have trouble explaining the bases of their moral judgments (Cushman, Young, and Hauser, 2006; Haidt and Hersh, 2001; Wheatley and Haidt, 2005) and that moral judgments are influenced by factors most people would deem irrelevant, such as the presence of an odor (Schnall, Haidt, Clore, and Jordan, 2008), the presence or absence of direct physical contact (Cushman et al., 2006), or the order in which hypothetical moral scenarios are presented (Lombrozo, 2009; Petrinovich and O'Neill, 1996). On the basis of such considerations it is sometimes claimed that, when participants are asked to describe the general principles underlying their moral judgments, they are engaged mostly in post hoc rationalization disconnected from the real psychological bases of their judgments (Ditto and Liu, in press; Haidt, 2001). Psychologists have by no means reached consensus on this point, however, with others arguing that moral reasoning does often influence moral judgment (Bartels, 2008; Cushman et al., 2006; Paxton and Greene, 2010; Pizarro and Bloom, 2003; a view also reflected in Kohlberg, 1984).

Because of their extensive training, professional philosophers are a 'best-case' population for the skillful use of principled reasoning to influence moral judgment, and they have occasionally been explicitly described as such by psychologists (e.g. Haidt 2001, pp. 819 and 829). Indeed, professional ethicists sometimes describe themselves as experts at moral reasoning (Crosthwaite, 1995; Føllesdal, 2004; Singer, 1972). And in reaction to critiques by Jonathan Weinberg and others (e.g. Weinberg, Gonnerman, Buckner, and Alexander, 2010), a number of philosophers have recently asserted that their professional training helps protect them from unconscious and unwanted biases in their domain of expertise (Grundmann, 2010; Hofmann, 2010; Horvath, 2010; Williamson, 2011; Wright, 2010).

There is some empirical cause for optimism about philosophical expertise in moral reasoning. Rest (1993) found that people with graduate training in philosophy responded with more sophistication than did non-philosophers to moral dilemmas, like Kohlberg's (1984) famous 'Heinz' dilemma about stealing a drug to save a life. Kuhn (1991) found that philosophy graduate students treated evidence and argument, in general, more skillfully than did other groups. Livengood and colleagues (2010) found that philosophers were more likely than non-philosophers to succeed at the Cognitive Reflection Test, a series of conceptually tricky but computationally simple math problems (Frederick, 2005).

It remains possible, however, that philosophers' apparent skill at moral argumentation is mostly skill at the post-hoc rationalization of judgments driven by automatic processes that would not necessarily be endorsed upon explicit reflection. Recent evidence suggesting that professional ethicists behave similarly to others of similar social background (e.g. in voting rates, in courtesy at conferences, in rates of charitable giving, in rates of National Socialist party membership during the Nazi era, and in peer-evaluated overall moral behavior) may support the post-hoc rationalization view, if we assume that non-rationalizing philosophical moral reflection would tend to precipitate changes in behavior (Leaman, 1993; Schwitzgebel and Rust, 2009, 2010, in preparation; Schwitzgebel, Rust, Moore, Huang, and Coates, in press).

We test whether philosophical expertise enhances stable reasoning from moral principles by examining order effects on moral judgments about hypothetical scenarios and also on the endorsement of general moral principles. We compare these effects among professional philosophers, non-philosopher academics, and non-academics. We assume that few people—philosophers or non-philosophers—think that one ought to judge case A worse than case B when judged in the order A-B but not when judged in the order B-A. Similarly, we assume that few people think that such variations of presentation order ought to subsequently affect the endorsement of a general principle governing cases A and B. Thus, to the extent moral judgment derives from stable general principles, it should be insulated from such order effects.

Ordinary non-philosophers do show order effects upon their moral judgments (Lombrozo, 2009; Petrinovich and O'Neill, 1996). Our question is whether professional philosophers are any less subject to such order effects. If so, it might warrant optimism about philosophical expertise and support a model of moral cognition on which skill at explicit moral reasoning can help protect people from unwanted influences on their moral judgments. If not, it would suggest a more pessimistic view about the power of explicit moral reasoning to protect against unwanted sources of bias, even in a best-case population. It would also raise a practical concern about the security of the intuitions that ground philosophical inquiry.

We targeted three moral principles drawn from the philosophical literature, chosen because they are well known among philosophers and also exhibited in non-philosophers' moral judgments. According to the *doctrine of the double effect*, it is worse to harm a person as a means of saving others than to harm a person as a side-effect of saving others (Foot, 1967; McIntyre, 2004/2009; Thomson, 1985). This principle is illustrated by the famous 'trolley problem': Many people consider it morally worse to throw somebody in front of a train as a means of stopping it from hitting five others (the 'push' case) than to divert a train away from five people with the side-effect that it hits one person instead (the 'switch' case) (Hauser et al., 2007; Mikhail, 2000; Petrinovich and O'Neill, 1996).

According to the principle of *moral luck*, we can be morally assessable for outcomes partly outside our control (Nagel, 1979; Nelkin, 2004/2008; Williams, 1981). For example, a reckless driver who kills a pedestrian may deserve more punishment than one who does not, even if the difference in outcome was a matter of chance. Non-philosophers' moral judgments often accord with moral luck (Cushman, 2008; Cushman, Dreber, Wang, and Costa, 2009; Gino, Shu, and Bazerman, 2010; Young, Nichols, and Saxe, 2010).

A third principle targeted the difference between killing versus letting die—for example, causing someone to drown versus not saving her from drowning. Such cases have been invoked to support a moral principle distinguishing between *action and omission* or doing and allowing (Bennett, 1998; Howard-Snyder, 2002/2007; Quinn, 1989), again reflected in ordinary people's judgments (Baron and Ritov, 2004; Cushman et al., 2006; Spranca et al., 1991).

We presented participants with hypothetical scenarios varying along the dimensions indicated by these moral principles, varying the order of presentation between subjects. If participants are stably applying (or declining to apply) the three moral principles, their response patterns should reflect (or fail to reflect) those principles independently of order of presentation. Finally, we asked participants whether they endorsed each of these principles in general form. If participants stably embrace general principles rather than merely recruiting general principles post-hoc to rationalize prior judgments, the order of presentation of the scenarios should have little influence on subsequent endorsement of the general principles.

2. METHODS

2.1. Participants

We surveyed participants using the Moral Sense Test website (http://moral.wjh.harvard.edu), recruiting through direct emails to philosophy and non-philosophy departments at 25 major research universities with well-ranked PhD programs in philosophy (a minority of participants were recruited through academic blogs). Our usable sample comprised 324 'philosophers' (completed MA or PhD in philosophy), 753 'academic non-philosophers' (completed Master's or PhD not in philosophy), and 1389 'non-academics' (no Master's or PhD in any field) tested between October 2008 and July 2009. Among philosophers, 221 (68%) claimed an area of specialization or competence in ethics and 91 of those also claimed a PhD ('ethics PhDs').

We excluded 66 respondents who stated that they had previously taken some version of the Moral Sense Test and 25 more with apparently frivolous demographic responses (age < 11 or > 97, residence in Antarctica, or graduate degree obtained before age 20). We also excluded individual responses when the reading and response time was under 4 seconds (2% of responses).

2.2. Questionnaire Design

The survey consisted of several demographic questions (age, gender, education level, etc.), then 17 hypothetical scenarios, each requiring a moral judgment, followed by 5 questions about general moral principles. The Supplementary Online Material contains the full text (see http://moral.wjh.harvard.edu/methods/order.html).

Double effect scenarios. Questions 1 and 2 involved judgments about saving five lives at the expense of one. A Push-type scenario involved killing one person through direct physical contact as a means of saving five people. A Switch-type scenario involved one person's dying, without direct physical contact from the agent, as a side effect of an action to save five. There were four versions of each scenario type, differing in context: a runaway boxcar, a fire, a boat, and a hospital. Questions 1 and 2 comprised one Push and one Switch scenario drawn from the same scenario context, in random order. Respondents rated the hypothetical action on a seven-point scale from (1) 'extremely morally good' to (7) 'extremely morally bad' with the midpoint (4) labeled 'neither good nor bad'.

Questions 14–17 also included double effect scenarios. In addition to the Push and Switch scenarios, we presented two other types expected to receive intermediate responses but which are not targets of the present analysis. We presented the four scenario types in random order, always in a different scenario context than had appeared in Questions 1-2.

Questions 3–5 concerned killing one to save many (e.g. in an epidemic), were unvaried in order, and are also not targets of the present analysis.

Action–omission scenarios. Questions 6–9 involved judging actions versus omissions. The 'Vest' scenario pair involved snatching a life vest from a drowning person to increase one's own safety ('Take' Action) or failing to offer one's life vest ('Not Give' Omission). The 'Oxygen' scenario pair involved either taking away a troubled diver's oxygen line for one's own use ('Take') or failing to sacrifice one's own oxygen line ('Not Give'). Order of presentation was counterbalanced between participants, either AOOA or OAAO. Responses employed the same scale as in the double effect scenarios. Half of the respondents saw a version of the Vest scenarios in which the drowning victim is described in the second person, as 'you', rather than as 'a man'. Order effects were consistent across both phrasings, so we merged both types in the analyses below.

Moral luck scenarios. Questions 10–13 concerned moral luck. In one scenario pair, a drunk driver passes out and discovers either that he has hit a tree (Good Luck) or that he has killed a girl (Bad Luck). Another scenario pair involved a negligent construction worker either killing or not killing a pedestrian below. Order of presentation was counterbalanced between participants, either GBBG or BGGB. The order of the moral luck scenarios was yoked to the order of the action-omission scenarios so that GBBG was always paired with AOOA and BGGB was always paired with OAAO. Responses were on a 7-point scale from (1) 'not at all morally blameworthy' to (7) 'extremely morally blameworthy', with the midpoint labeled 'substantially morally blameworthy'.

Endorsement of principles. The test ended with several questions about abstract principles. Question 18 concerned moral luck:

> Suppose two people do the exact same thing, with the exact same frame of mind. Then, due entirely to matters of chance beyond their control, one of them produces a very bad outcome, but the other does not. Should they receive different amounts of punishment or the same amount of punishment?

Response options were 'same' or 'different'. Question 19 concerned the action–omission principle:

> Sometimes you can save several people by actively and purposefully killing one person whom you could have let live. Other times you can save several people by purposefully allowing one person to die whom you could have saved. Is the first action morally better, worse, or the same as the second action?

Response options were 'better' 'worse' or 'same'. Question 20 concerned the doctrine of the double effect:

> Sometimes it is necessary to use one person's death as a means to saving several more people—killing one helps you accomplish the goal of saving several. Other times one person's death is a side-effect of saving several more people—the goal of saving several unavoidably ends up killing one as a consequence. Is the first morally better, worse, or the same as the second?

Response options were 'better' 'worse' or 'same'. Questions 21 and 22 concerned the moral relevance of physical contact and general normative ethical stance (deontological, consequentialist, or virtue based) and are not targets of the present analysis.

We recognize that much can turn on exactly how the above principles are stated; we aimed for simple statements comprehensible to non-specialists. For example, we recognize that the action–omission distinction may look different depending on whether one's motive is self-interest or charity and that one might endorse moral luck concerning punishment but not blameworthiness. For this reason among others, endorsement or rejection of the various general principles is consistent with a variety of responses to the scenario types. Our analyses do not test for consistency between scenario ratings and principle endorsements, but rather test whether variation in presentation order of the scenarios affected endorsement of the general principles. We did find the expected associations between scenario judgments and endorsements of related principles (e.g. respondents who rated the Good Luck and Bad Luck scenarios inequivalently were more likely to endorse the principle of moral luck), but these patterns are not informative for present purposes because such relationships might reflect either a pattern of principled moral reasoning from the outset or a pattern of post hoc rationalization of prior scenario judgments.

2.3. Analysis

Our main analysis asks, for each scenario pair, whether the participant gave the same numerical response to each scenario ('equivalent' judgment) or rated the scenarios differently ('inequivalent' judgment) in the direction predicted by the relevant principle: double effect, action-omission principle, or moral luck. We excluded cases in which the participant rated the scenarios differently in the non-predicted direction (5% of double effect cases, 8% of action–omission cases, and 1% of moral luck cases). So, for example, if a respondent rated a Push and a Switch scenario both as 5's on our 7-point scale, she rated the two scenarios equivalently; if she rated Push 6 and Switch 5 (thus, Push worse, the predicted direction), she rated the scenarios inequivalently; and if she rated Switch 7 and Push 6 (thus, Switch worse), the pair is excluded from the equivalency analysis. Similarly, our analysis of the endorsement of principles excluded cases in which the participant indicated that harmful omissions were *worse* than harmful actions (8%) or that harmful side-effects were *worse* than harmful means (7%), and also cases in which the participant's prior scenario judgments targeting the relevant principle had been excluded due to low reaction time.

We also examined order effects on mean scenario ratings. However, we emphasize the equivalency analysis for four reasons. (1) The equivalency analysis is less subject to scaling concerns due to participants' using early cases to 'anchor' key points on the scale. (2) The doctrine of the double effect, action–omission distinction, and principle of moral luck are principles that directly concern the equivalency or inequivalency of different actions rather than the goodness or badness of those actions, so our focus on equivalency matches the focus of the philosophical literature. (3) Equivalency of response is more comparable across scenarios types. (4) For some scenarios median response was at ceiling, problematizing parametric analysis of means. However, the overall results of our analysis are similar whether we examine equivalency or means.

3. RESULTS

3.1. Double Effect Scenarios

In Questions 1–2, respondents were more likely to rate the Push and Switch scenarios equivalently when Push was presented before Switch (70% versus 54%, $Z = 8.1$, $p < .001$). All three participant groups showed similar effect sizes (Figure 1a), and for each the effect was statistically significant (Table 1).

Questions 14–17 showed order effects similar to those in Questions 1–2. When Push was presented before Switch among the four scenario types, 73% of respondents rated the two equivalently, versus 60% when Switch was presented before Push ($Z = 6.27$, $p < .001$). The order effect size was smaller for philosophers (Table 1), but not significantly (binary logistic regression, $Z = -1.3$, $p = .21$).

Analysis of means shows a similar pattern in order effect size among the groups (Table 2). Push was rated better when presented after Switch than when presented first, and Switch was rated worse when presented after Push than when presented first. Thus, respondents tended to assimilate their responses to the second scenario to their responses to the first scenario. However, Switch responses were considerably more labile than Push responses, explaining the higher rates of equivalency in scenario ratings when Push was presented first.

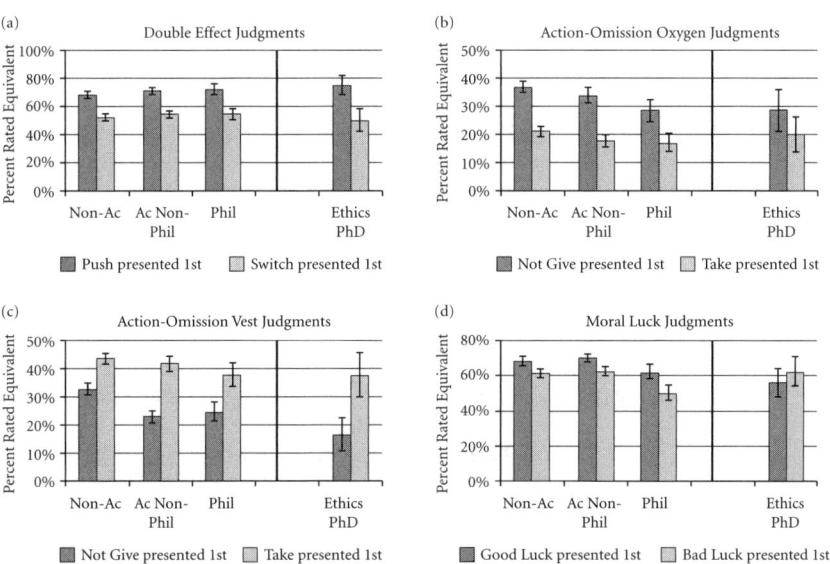

Figure 14.1. Effect of presentation order on percentage of scenarios rated equivalently across four types of scenarios: (a) double effect cases for Q1–Q2, (b) the action–omission oxygen case for Q6–10, (c) the action–omission Vest case for Q6–10 and (d) moral luck cases for Q11–12. Ethics PhD is a subset of Phil.

Table 14.1 Effect of presentation order on percentage of scenarios rated equivalently for six types of scenarios, comparing across participant groups.

Group		Percent rated equivalent	95% CI of difference in proportions	Z	p	Effect size h
			Switch First/Push First			
Double Effect: Q1–Q2	Non-Ac	53%/68%	10%–21%	5.8	<.001	0.31
	Ac Non-Phil	55%/71%	10%–24%	4.7	<.001	0.33
	Phil	54%/73%	8%–29%	3.4	.001	0.40
	Eth PhD	50%/75%	0.5%–45%	2.4	.02	0.52
			Switch First/Push First			
Double Effect: Q14–Q17	Non-Ac	56%/72%	10%–21%	5.4	<.001	0.34
	Ac Non-Phil	62%/74%	5%–19%	3.3	.001	0.26
	Phil	68%/74%	−6%–17%	1.0	.32	0.13
	Eth PhD	70%/78%	−13%–29%	0.8	.45	0.18
			Take First/Not Give First			
Act vs. Omit: Oxygen	Non-Ac	21%/37%	10%–21%	5.8	<.001	0.36
	Ac Non-Phil	18%/34%	9%–23%	4.6	<.001	0.37
	Phil	17%/29%	1%–21%	2.2	.03	0.29
	Eth PhD	20%/29%	−11%–28%	0.9	.39	0.21
			Take First/Not Give First			
Act vs. Omit: Vest	Non-Ac	44%/33%	5%–16%	3.8	<.001	0.23
	Ac Non-Phil	42%/23%	12%–26%	5.4	<.001	0.41
	Phil	38%/25%	2%–24%	2.4	.02	0.28
	Eth PhD	38%/17%	2%–40%	2.2	.03	0.48
			Good Luck First/Bad Luck First			
Moral Luck: Q10–Q11	Non-Ac	68%/62%	1%–12%	2.3	.02	0.13
	Ac Non-Phil	70%/63%	0.2%–15%	2.0	.04	0.15
	Phil	62%/50%	0.1%–24%	2.0	.048	0.24
	Eth PhD	56%/63%	−29%–16%	−0.6	.58	−0.14
			Good Luck First/Bad Luck First			
Moral Luck: Q12–Q13	Non-Ac	61%/66%	−11%–1%	−1.7	.09	−0.10
	Ac Non-Phil	67%/67%	−8%–7%	−0.1	.89	−0.00
	Phil	50%/59%	−21%–3%	−1.5	.14	−0.18
	Eth PhD	63%/62%	−21%–25%	0.2	.88	0.02

Table 14.2 Effect of presentation order on scenario mean ratings, all groups combined

Target Principle	Case	Mean when first	Mean when second	Difference (philosophers' difference)
Double Effect	Q1–Q2: Push	4.37	4.13	.24*** (.21)
	Q14–Q17: Push	4.51	4.37	.14 (.16)
	Q1–Q2: Switch	3.38	3.88	−.50*** (−.52**)
	Q14–Q17: Switch	3.71	4.12	−.41*** (−.35)
Act/Omit	Take Oxygen	5.82	5.29	.53*** (.39*)
	Not Give Oxygen	4.53	4.02	.51*** (.49***)
	Take Vest	5.61	5.88	−.27*** (−.20)
	Not Give Vest	4.74	4.71	.03 (−.05)
Moral Luck	Q10–Q11: Good Luck	5.61	5.46	.15* (.11)
	Q10–Q11: Bad Luck	6.25	6.21	.04 (.09)

*T-test p values: * $p < .05$, ** $p < .01$, *** $p < .001$.

3.2. Action–Omission Scenarios

The Vest and Oxygen scenarios showed opposite order effects—the Vest cases showed greater equivalency for the action–omission order, while the Oxygen cases showed greater equivalency for the omission–action order. Thus, we analyzed order effects separately for the Vest and Oxygen cases. As with the double effect scenarios, the direction and magnitude of the order effects were similar among the groups (Figures 1b and 1c; Tables 1 and 2).

3.3. Moral Luck Scenarios

We also found order effects for the moral luck cases, and again these were comparable across the three major participant groups (Figure 1d; Tables 1 and 2), although absent for the ethics PhD subset.

Considering only the first presented scenario pair, participants were more likely to rate the Good Luck and Bad Luck cases equivalently when a Good Luck scenario was presented first (68% versus 60%, $Z = 3.6$, $p < .001$). Ethics PhDs trended in the opposite direction (figure 1d and Table 1), but a binary logistic regression predicting equivalency from Good Luck–Bad Luck order and ethics PhD (versus all others) found no significant interaction effect ($Z = 1.3, p = .21$), so it is not clear whether the lack of a similar effect among the ethics PhDs was due to chance.

The second Good Luck–Bad Luck scenario pair showed a marginally significant order effect in the opposite direction (62% versus 66%, $Z = −1.9, p = .06$). Because scenarios were counterbalanced GBBG or BGGB, the observed reverse equivalency effect for the second pair may have reflected order effects carrying over from the first pair. For example, having judged the two drunk driver cases equivalently (hitting the tree versus hitting the girl), participants may have been more likely to judge the subsequent pair of construction worker cases equivalently (killing a pedestrian versus not killing a pedestrian) and vice versa for judgments of inequivalency.

Two-proportion analyses revealed no order effects on equivalency from one scenario type to any later scenario type (e.g. from double effect order to action–omission judgments) or between the order of presentation of the Push and Switch cases in Q1–Q2 and Push–Switch equivalency in Q14–Q17.

3.4. A Summary Measure of Order Effects on Equivalency Judgments

We aggregated equivalency order effects across all scenarios into a single summary statistic for each participant, facilitating an overall comparison of the magnitude of equivalency order effects between participant groups (Figure 2). The dependent variable was the number of scenario pairs (0 to 6) that the participant rated as equivalent. We included all scenario pairs analyzed above, including only participants whose data were included in all six analyses. The predictor was a variable indicating the number of scenario pairs (0 to 6) the participant viewed in the order favoring equivalency responses. These two variables were correlated ($r = .22, p <.001$), and to a similar extent for all groups: non-academics ($r = .21, p <.001$), academic non-philosophers ($r = .19, p <.001$), philosophers ($r = .29, p <.001$), ethics PhDs ($r = .35, p = .007$). Indeed, philosophers trended towards showing larger order effects than did the reference group of academic non-philosophers in a general linear model ($t = 1.8, p = .08$), including after controlling for age and gender ($t = 1.9, p = .07$).

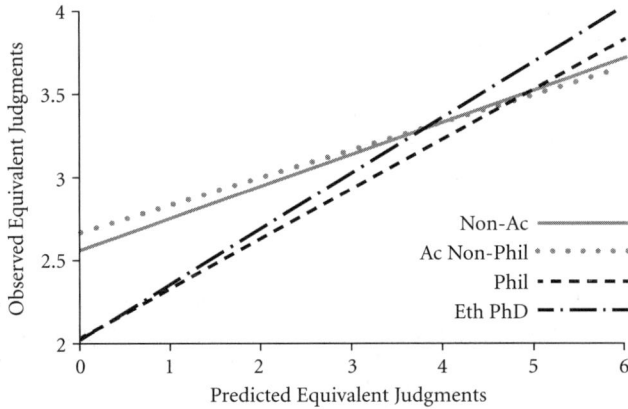

Figure 14.2. Linear regression trend lines for the number of scenario pairs rated as equivalent as a function of number of scenario pairs presented in an order favoring equivalent judgment. Greater slope indicates stronger equivalency order effects on moral judgment.

3.5. Order Effects on Endorsements of Moral Principles

The order of presentation of the scenarios showed little influence on non-philosophers' endorsements of moral principles. Non-philosophers who saw Bad Luck first were no more likely to endorse the principle of moral luck than those who saw Good Luck first (non-academics, 20% versus 20%, $Z = 0.1$, $p = .95$; academic non-philosophers 18% versus 18%, $Z = 0.3$, $p = .78$; Figure 3a). Those who saw Switch first were no more likely to endorse the doctrine of the double effect, and in fact less likely (non-academics, 46% versus 53%, $Z = -2.2$, $p = .03$; academic non-philosophers, 51% versus 55%, $Z = -1.1$, $p = .30$; Figure 3b). Given the scenario ratings results, the endorsement of the action–omission distinction should be favored when the first-presented scenario is Take Oxygen or Not Give Vest (as opposed to Not Give Oxygen or Take Vest). In this case, there was a moderate effect on endorsement (non-academics, 52% versus 44%, $Z = 2.6$, $p = .01$; non-philosopher academics, 59% versus 53%, $Z = 1.6$, $p = .11$; Figure 3c).

In contrast, the order of presentation of the scenarios substantially influenced philosophers' subsequent endorsements of two of the three abstract moral principles. Philosophers were much more likely to endorse the principle of moral luck if they received a Bad Luck scenario first: 45% versus 29% ($Z = 2.7$, $p = .006$); and they were also more likely to endorse the doctrine of the double effect if they saw Switch first: 62% versus 46% ($Z = 2.4$, $p = .02$).

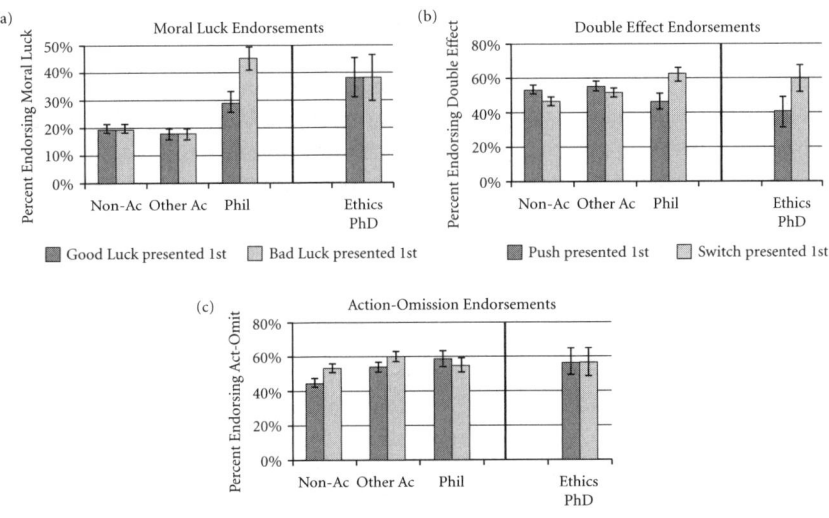

Figure 14.3. Percentage of participants endorsing (a) the principle of moral luck depending on the order of presentation of moral luck scenarios, (b) the doctrine of the double effect depending on the order of presentation of first double effect scenarios, and (c) the action–omission distinction depending on order of presentation of the action–omission scenarios. Ethics PhD is a subset of Phil.

However, philosophers who viewed Take Oxygen or Not Give Vest first were not more likely to endorse the action–omission distinction than the remainder who viewed Not Give Oxygen or Take Vest first, trending slightly in the opposite direction 54% versus 58% ($Z = -0.7, p = .49$).

Turning to the ethics PhD subset of philosophers, for the doctrine of the double effect, endorsements differed by a degree similar to other philosophers: 59% versus 40% ($Z = 1.6, p = .12$). However, this effect did not achieve statistical significance and must be interpreted cautiously due to the small sample size. As described above, ethics PhDs did not exhibit an equivalency order effect for their moral luck judgments, and therefore would not be predicted to exhibit a corresponding rationalization effect on endorsement. Indeed, order of presentation did not significantly influence ethics PhDs' endorsement of the principle of moral luck (38% versus 38%, $Z = 0.0, p = .96$). Similarly to philosophers as a group, ethics PhDs were not significantly more likely to endorse the action-omission distinction when viewing Take Oxygen and Not Give Vest first (56%) than when viewing Not Give Oxygen and Take Vest first (56%; $Z = 0.0, p = .99$).

Across all participant groups, willingness to endorse one moral principle (e.g., moral luck) was correlated with willingness to endorse other moral principles (e.g. double effect). This was apparently due in part to a sequential endorsement effect: Endorsing one moral principle earlier in a sequence made participants more likely to endorse another moral principle later in that sequence. Philosophers who viewed the Bad Luck case first, and who were thus more likely to endorse moral luck, were significantly more likely than those who viewed the Good Luck case first to endorse the doctrine of double effect (64% versus 44%, $Z = 3.2, p = .001$) and the action-omission distinction (63% versus 49%, $Z = 2.1, p = .03$), endorsement choices that were presented *after* moral luck endorsements. There was no effect of double effect scenario order on moral luck or action–omission endorsements, endorsement choices presented *before* double effect endorsements.

We took advantage of the sequential endorsement effect to measure the maximum influence of scenario order on endorsement by comparing philosophers' endorsement of the doctrine of the double effect among participants who viewed both the Switch case and Bad Luck case first to those who viewed both cases second. Among all philosophers, 70% who viewed both cases first endorsed the doctrine of the double effect, compared with 28% who viewed both cases second ($Z = 4.7, p < .001$). Among ethicists, 62% who viewed both cases first endorsed the doctrine of the double effect, compared with 28% who viewed both cases second ($Z = 2.0, p = .049$).

3.6. A Summary Measure of Order Effects on Endorsement of Principles

We aggregated order effects on endorsement across all three principles into a single summary statistic for each participant in order to compare of the overall magnitude of those effects between participant groups (Figure 4). Our dependent variable was the number of principles (0 to 3) that the participant

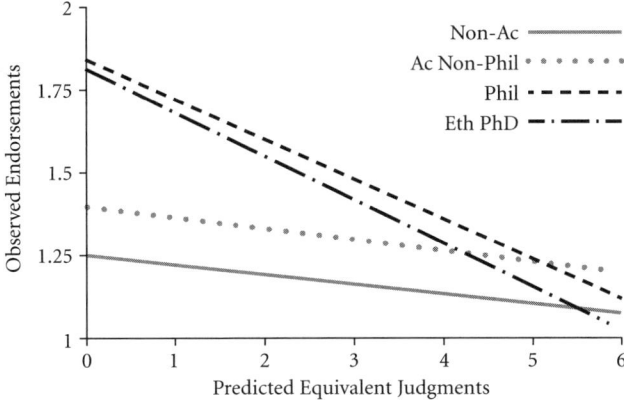

Figure 14.4. Linear regression trend lines for the number of moral principles endorsed that favor inequivalency as a function of number of scenario pairs presented in an order favoring equivalent judgment. Greater slope with negative sign indicates larger order effects on the endorsement of general principles.

endorsed. We used the same predictor as in our aggregate analysis of equivalency order effects during scenario judgment: the number of scenario pairs (0 to 6) the participant viewed that had been presented in the order favoring equivalency responses. We predicted that participants who viewed cases in the order favoring equivalency would be less likely to endorse moral principles favoring inequivalency between the cases. As predicted, these two variables were negatively correlated, though only slightly ($r = -.07, p = .006$). This relationship was largest and statistically significant for philosophers ($r = -.17$, $p = .009$), with the largest effect size for ethics PhDs ($r = -.20, p = .11$). Smaller trends were evident but non-significant for non-academics ($r = -.05, p = .15$) and academic non-philosophers ($r = -.05, p = .23$). A comparison of the effect between philosophers and non-philosopher academics in a general linear model was marginally significant ($t = -1.7, p = .08$; and $t = -1.8, p = .07$ after controlling for gender and age; coincidentally, the same rounded p-values as the GLM in 3.4).

4. DISCUSSION

To the extent that judgments about individual scenarios are driven by stable moral principles, those judgments should not be affected by order of presentation of the scenarios. And to the extent that people choose to endorse or reject moral principles for stable, consistent reasons, those decisions should not be strongly influenced by the order in which several previous judgments were made. Philosophers—especially ethics PhDs at well-ranked research departments—should seemingly be particularly resistant to order effects on their scenario judgments and endorsements of principles, due to prior familiarity with the principles and general types of scenarios. However, even this 'best-case' group of participants showed substantial order effects on their judgments about moral scenarios and their endorsement of moral principles. Our analysis found no support for the view that philosophical expertise enhances the stability of moral judgment against order effects; it suggests, instead, that philosophical expertise may actually enhance post-hoc rationalization.

4.1. Order Effects on Judgments about Particular Scenarios

Both philosophers and non-philosophers showed significant order effects for all three types of scenario. In our summary measure of order effects across all scenario judgments, philosophers and ethics PhDs trended marginally higher than the comparison groups. Thus, philosophers showed no greater tendency than non-philosophers to use the consistent application of moral principles to reduce order effects on their scenario judgments. Of course, there may be contexts in which philosophers will excel at the application of explicit principles, for example, in evaluating the validity of a proposed deductive syllogism. Philosophers may also more skillfully apply general moral principles to specific moral cases, but this is difficult to assess in a way that unambiguously distinguishes principled reasoning from post hoc rationalization. It is precisely this methodological challenge that motivated our use of order effects as a metric for the consistent application of principled reasoning. It is particularly striking that philosophical expertise did not reduce order effects for cases intended to target the doctrine of the double effect, the action-omission distinction, and the principle of moral luck, given that these philosophical principles are widely discussed in terms of hypothetical scenario comparisons very much like those we presented to our participants.

Our experiment was not designed to clarify the psychological basis of the order effects on scenario judgments, and the order effects we observed were variable in size and direction. For instance, our two pairs of action–omission cases produced opposite effects. However, it is likely that order effects between closely matched pairs of hypothetical scenarios reflect a general desire to maintain consistency in judgment (see also Lombrozo, 2009). For example, having judged that it is morally bad to push a man in front of a train to save five others, some participants may resist the apparent inconsistency in judging that it is permissible to flip a switch that produces the same consequences. Accordingly, we suggest that order effects arise from an interaction between intuitive judgment and subsequent explicit reasoning: The intuition elicited by the first case becomes the basis for imposed consistency in the second case (Lombrozo, 2009). When the intuition elicited by one case is 'stronger'—that is, more resistant to revision by explicit reasoning—than the intuition elicited by the complementary scenario, this would lead to the asymmetric equivalency effects that we report here. When the stronger case comes first, it would exert a relatively larger influence on the subsequent judgment of the weaker case, making it more likely for the cases to be judged equivalently, but when the weaker case comes first, it would exert a lesser influence on the stronger case, leading to more inequivalent judgments. To take the familiar example of the trolley problem, it has been proposed that the 'Push' version engages an automatic, affective response that the 'Switch' case does not (Cushman, Young, and Greene, 2010; Greene et al., 2001, 2009). This may explain why judgments of the switch case are apparently more malleable under the influence of prior push judgments, whereas push judgments are comparatively stable. The simplest interpretation of our findings is that this interaction between automatic processes and explicit reasoning, as well as the general desire to impose consistency between judgments, operates similarly in philosophical experts and novices.

An alternative explanation for the order effects we have identified is that certain cases presented new information or highlighted new considerations relevant to the judgment of the other cases. For instance, the Push version of the trolley problem might highlight the rights of a single victim against harmful intervention, consequently exerting an influence on the judgment of the Switch version. Participants viewing the cases in different orders would then have access to identical information after, and only after, both cases have been presented. If this alternative explanation of the order effects is correct, order of presentation should not have any influence on the subsequent endorsement of a moral principle that distinguishes the cases: By the time of endorsement, all participants would have seen (for example) the rights-highlighting case. Yet we did find order effects on the endorsement of principles, and we turn next to consider this finding.

4.2. Order Effects on Endorsements of Abstract Moral Principles

Professional philosophers who viewed the first pair of double effect or moral luck scenarios in an order favoring inequivalent judgment were more likely to subsequently endorse the doctrine of the double effect and the principle of moral luck—principles favoring inequivalent treatment of the scenarios. For these scenario types we observed no corresponding effect among non-philosophers. Conversely, for the action–omission principle we did not find the predicted effect of order on endorsement among philosophers, but we did identify a small effect for non-philosophers. Aggregating across all three principles we found a significant order effect on philosophers' endorsements of general moral principles that was three times larger than the corresponding, non-significant effect for non-philosophers.

Thus, it appears that a factor that we assume philosophers would deem irrelevant—order of presentation of cases—can exert a large influence on professional philosophers' judgments about abstract moral principles, presumably without their awareness. This effect is particularly striking because, regardless of the order of presentation, all philosophers had viewed and judged the same pairs of cases by the time they were asked about the general principles. The effect sizes are also striking: For example, the joint effect of the order of presentation of the moral luck and double effect cases was to shift philosophers' rates of endorsement of the doctrine of the double effect from 28% to 70%, including 28% to 62% for ethics PhDs—a very large change considering how familiar and widely discussed the doctrine is within professional philosophy.

Rationalization, as we use the term, occurs when automatic, intuitive processes drive moral judgments and explicit moral reasoning is recruited only after the fact to justify those judgments, normally proceeding without introspective access to the original processes driving the judgments. Perhaps the simplest interpretation of our results is that philosophers' skill at moral reasoning is most effective during post hoc rationalization. That is, philosophical expertise provides no protection against unwanted order-effect biases on moral judgments about particular scenarios, and philosophers' labile subsequent reasoning about abstract moral principles follows where their judgments about particular scenarios lead. However, even if we accept this interpretation, the magnitude of such rationalization remains to be determined. The effect sizes we report, though large, are consistent with the possibility that a majority of philosophers adhere consistently to principles.

It is notable that non-philosophers' endorsements of moral principles appear to be substantially less influenced by the order of presentation of the particular scenarios. We suggest two complementary hypotheses that would account for this result. First, non-philosophers might have lacked the conceptual resources necessary to recognize the relationship between their initial judgments and their subsequent endorsements of abstract principles. This explanation seems particularly likely for the doctrine of the double effect, which involves a non-obvious conceptual distinction between harm intended as a means and harm as a foreseen side effect. However, it seems less likely for the principle of moral luck, which deals with the more familiar concepts of recklessness, accidents, and punishment. Second, philosophers might be more motivated to impose consistency between their judgments about specific cases and their endorsements of abstract principles. On the first explanation, philosophers are more *able* to rationalize; on the second, they are more *motivated* to rationalize.

5. CONCLUSION

The method of philosophy is often characterized as a matter of reconciling intuitive judgments about particular cases with plausible general principles (Bealer, 1998; Fischer and Ravizza, 1992; Rawls, 1971). While the psychological basis of ordinary people's judgments about particular moral cases may often be very different from the principles they invoke to rationalize those judgments (Carlsmith, Darley, and Robinson, 2002; Cushman et al., 2006; Haidt, 2001; Hauser et al., 2007), it has been unclear to what extent this is also true of professional philosophers. Our results suggest that even professional philosophers' judgments about familiar types of cases in their own field can be strongly and covertly influenced by psychological factors that they would not endorse upon reflection, and that such unwanted influences can in turn strongly influence the general principles those philosophers endorse.

REFERENCES

Baron, J. and Ritov, I. 2004: Omission bias, individual differences, and normality. *Organizational Behavior and Human Decision Processes*, 94, 74–85.

Bartels, D. 2008: Principled moral sentiment and the flexibility of moral judgment and decision making. *Cognition*, 108, 381–417.

Bealer, G. 1998: Intuition and the autonomy of philosophy. In M. R. DePaul and W. Ramsey (eds.), *Rethinking Intuition: The Psychology of Intuition and Its Role in Philosophical Inquiry*. Lanham, MD: Rowman & Littlefield.

Bennett, J. 1998: *The Act Itself*. Oxford: Clarendon Press.

Carlsmith, K., Darley, J. and Robinson, P. 2002: Why do we punish? Deterrence and just deserts as motives for punishment. *Journal of Personality and Social Psychology*, 83, 284–299.

Crosthwaite, J. 1995: Moral expertise: a problem in the professional ethics of professional ethicists. *Bioethics*, 9, 361–379.

Cushman, F. A. 2008: Crime and punishment: distinguishing the roles of causal and intentional analyses in moral judgment. *Cognition*, 108, 353–380.

Cushman, F. A., Dreber, A., Wang, Y. and Costa, J. 2009: Accidental outcomes guide punishment in a 'trembling hand' game. *PLOS One*, 4, e6699. doi:6610.1371/journal.pone.0006699.

Cushman, F. A., Young, L. and Greene, J. D. 2010: Multi-system moral psychology. In J. Doris, G. Harman, S. Nichols, J. Prinz, W. Sinnott-Armstrong and S. Stich (eds.), *The Oxford Handbook of Moral Psychology*. Oxford: Oxford University Press.

Cushman, F. A., Young, L. and Hauser, M. D. 2006: The role of conscious reasoning and intuitions in moral judgment: testing three principles of harm. *Psychological Science*, 17, 1082–1089.

Ditto, P. and Liu, B. In press: Deontological dissonance and the consequentialist crutch. In M. Mikulincer and P. R. Shaver (eds.), *Social Psychology of Morality: The Origins of Good And Evil*. Washington, DC: APA Press.

Fischer, J. M. and Ravizza, M. 1992: *Ethics: Problems and Principles*. New York: Holt, Rinehart and Winston.

Føllesdal, A. 2004: The philosopher as coach. In E. Kurz-Milcke and G. Gigerenzer (eds.), *Experts in Science and Society*. New York: Kluwer.

Foot, P. 1967: The problem of abortion and the doctrine of double effect. *Oxford Review*, 5, 5–15.

Frederick, S. 2005: Cognitive reflection and decision making. *Journal of Economic Perspectives*, 19 (4), 25–42.

Gino, F., Shu, L. and Bazerman, M. 2010: Nameless + harmless = blameless: When seemingly irrelevant factors influence judgment of (un)ethical behavior. *Organizational Behavior and Human Decision Processes*, 111, 93–101.

Greene, J. D., Cushman, F. A., Stewart. L. E., Lowenberg, K., Nystrom, L. E. and Cohen, J. D. 2009: Pushing moral buttons: the interaction between personal force and intention in moral judgment. *Cognition*, 111, 364–371.

Greene, J. D., Sommerville, R. B., Nystrom, L. E., Darley, J. M. and Cohen, J. D. 2001: An fMRI investigation of emotional engagement in moral judgment. *Science*, 293, 2105–2108.

Grundmann, T. 2010: Some hope for intuitions: A reply to Weinberg. *Philosophical Psychology*, 23, 481–509.

Haidt, J. 2001: The emotional dog and its rational tail: A social intuitionist approach to moral judgment. *Psychological Review*, 108, 814–834.

Haidt, J. and Hersh, M. A. 2001: Sexual morality: the cultures and emotions of conservatives and liberals. *Journal of Applied Social Psychology*, 31, 191–221.

Hauser, M. D., Cushman, F. A., Young, L., Jin, R. and Mikhail, J. M. 2007: A dissociation between moral judgment and justification. *Mind & Language*, 22, 1–21.

Hofmann, F. 2010: Intuitions, concepts, and imagination. *Philosophical Psychology*, 23, 529–546.

Horvath, J. 2010: How (not) to react to experimental philosophy. *Philosophical Psychology*, 23, 447–480.

Howard-Snyder, F. 2002/2007: Doing vs. allowing harm. In E. N. Zalta (ed.), *Stanford Encyclopedia of Philosophy* (Spring 2010 edition).

Kohlberg, L. 1984: *The Psychology of Moral Development*. Cambridge, MA: Harper and Row.

Kuhn, D. 1991: *The Skills of Argument*. Cambridge: Cambridge University Press.

Leaman, G. 1993: *Heidegger im Kontext*. Hamburg: Argument-Verlag.

Livengood, J., Sytsma, J., Feltz, A., Schemes, R. and Machery, E. 2010: Philosophical temperament. *Philosophical Psychology*, 23, 313–330.

Lombrozo, T. 2009: The role of moral commitments in moral judgment. *Cognitive Science*, 33, 273–286.

McIntyre, A. 2004/2009: Doctrine of double effect. In E. N. Zalta (ed.), *Stanford Encyclopedia of Philosophy* (Spring 2010 edition).

Mikhail, J. M. 2000: *Rawls' linguistic analogy: A study of the 'generative grammar' model of moral theory described by John Rawls in A Theory of Justice*. PhD dissertation in philosophy. Cornell University, Ithaca, NY.

Mikhail, J. 2009: Moral grammar and intuitive jurisprudence: a formal model of unconscious moral and legal knowledge. *Psychology of Learning and Motivation*, 50, 27–100.

Nagel, T. 1979: *Mortal Questions*. Cambridge: Cambridge University Press.

Nelkin, D. K. 2004/2008: Moral luck. In E. N. Zalta (ed.), *Stanford Encyclopedia of Philosophy* (Spring 2010 edition).

Paxton, J. M. and Greene, J. D. 2010: Moral reasoning: hints and allegations. *Topics in Cognitive Science*, 2, 511–527.

Petrinovich, L. and O'Neill, P. 1996: Influence of wording and framing effects on moral intuitions. *Ethology and Sociobiology*, 17, 145–171.

Pizarro, D. A. and Bloom, P. 2003: The intelligence of the moral intuitions: comment on Haidt (2001): *Psychological Review*, 110, 193–196.

Quinn, W. S. 1989: Actions, intentions, and consequences: the doctrine of doing and allowing. *The Philosophical Review*, 145, 287–312.

Rawls, J. 1971: *A Theory of Justice*. Cambridge, MA: Harvard University Press.

Rest, J. R. 1993: Research on moral judgment in college students. In A. Garrod (ed.), *Approaches to Moral Development*. New York: Teachers College Press.

Schnall, S., Haidt, J., Clore, G. L. and Jordan, A. H. 2008: Disgust as embodied moral judgment. *Personality and Social Psychology Bulletin*, 34, 1096–1109.

Schwitzgebel, E. and Rust, J. 2009: The moral behaviour of ethics professors: peer opinion. *Mind*, 118, 1043–1059.

Schwitzgebel, E. and Rust, J. 2010: Do ethicists and political philosophers vote more often than other professors? *Review of Philosophy and Psychology*, 1, 189–199.

Schwitzgebel, E. and Rust, J. In preparation: The moral behavior of ethics professors.

Schwitzgebel, E., Rust, J., Moore, A., Huang, L. and Coates, J. In press: Ethicists' courtesy at philosophy conferences. *Philosophical Psychology*.

Singer, P. 1972: Moral experts. *Analysis*, 32, 115–117.

Spranca, M., Minsk, E. and Baron, J. 1991: Omission and commission in judgment and choice. *Journal of Experimental Social Psychology*, 27, 76–105.

Thomson, J. J. 1985: The trolley problem. *The Yale Law Journal*, 94, 1395–1415.

Weinberg, J., Gonnerman, C., Buckner, C. and Alexander, J. 2010: Are philosophers expert intuiters? *Philosophical Psychology*, 23, 331–355.

Wheatley, T. and Haidt, J. 2005: Hypnotic disgust makes moral judgments more severe. *Psychological Science*, 16, 780–784.

Williams, B. 1981: *Moral Luck*. Cambridge: Cambridge University Press.

Williamson, T. 2011: Philosophical expertise and the burden of proof. *Metaphilosophy*, 42: 215–229.

Wright, J. 2010: On intuitional stability: the clear, the strong, and the paradigmatic. *Cognition*, 115, 491–503.

Young, L., Nichols, S. and Saxe, R. 2010: Investigating the neural and cognitive basis of moral luck: it's not what you do but what you know. *Review of Philosophy and Psychology*, 1, 333–349.

Author Index

Abell, F. 113
Adams, F. 16, 36, 37, 214, 216, 254, 255
Aiken, H. 22
Alexander, J. 1, 5, 25, 34, 46, 51, 52, 348
Alicke, M. 193, 204, 208, 210, 213
Allen, J. 157
Andreasen, R. 300
Apperly, I. 275
Appiah, K. 170
Appleton, J. 70
Arico, A. 76, 86, 117, 131
Ariew, A. 281, 294–300
Arkes, H. 66
Astuti, R. 302, 303
Atran, S. 283, 284, 302
Audi, R. 51
Augustine 111, 129
Ayer, A. 139

Balthazard, C. 70
Bargh, J. 251
Baron, J. 140, 156, 349
Baron, R. 252
Baron–Cohen, S. 79
Bartels, D. 347
Bartsch, K. 51
Bateson, P. 281, 282, 294, 298, 300, 301
Bazerman, M. 177, 349
Bealer, G. 51, 52, 310, 362
Bednar, J. 341
Beebe, J. 187, 206, 312, 320, 321, 340
Beebee, H. 308, 339
Bengson, J. 70, 209, 272
Bennett, J. 349
Bennett, M. 92
Berger, R. 140
Berlin, B. 283
Bersoff, D. 158
Betsch, C. 70
Betsch, T. 70
Blackburn, S. 27, 139, 170, 188
Block, N. 75, 82–84, 101, 108, 128, 339, 342
Bloom, P. 47, 84–85, 129, 319, 347
Blount, S. 177

Boghossian, P. 26
Bonjour, L. 51, 52
Bowers, K. 70
Bowler, D. 113
Brandom, R. 25
Branscombe, N. 219
Breedlove, D. 283
Brink, D. 27, 139, 170, 188
Brown, J. 51
Browne, D. 302
Brueckner, T. 324
Bruno, M. 129, 133, 189
Buckingham, J. 252
Buckwalter, W. 206, 224, 279, 312, 320–322, 324, 341
Burra, A. 201, 254
Bush, E. 337
Byrne, R. 157, 218, 219

Cappelen, H. 26, 311
Carey, S. 197, 302
Carlsmith, K. 362
Carlston, D. 256
Carruthers, P. 129, 131
Casullo, A. 51
Catellani, P. 251, 252
Chaiken, S. 118
Chalmers, D. 25, 82, 101–103, 105, 133, 308
Chapman, J. 198
Chapman, L. 198
Chartrand, T. 251
Cheng, P. 157
Chiavarino, C. 275
Choi, I. 52
Chomsky, N. 42, 70, 300, 339
Christensen, D. 35
Churchland, P. M. 112, 196
Churchland, P. S. 101
Claxton, G. 51
Clement, J. 282
Coates, D. 342, 348
Cohen, A. 254
Cohen, J. 106, 291
Cokely, E. 187, 224, 342
Collingwood, R. 251

367

Conrad, S. 296
Cornelius, R. 275
Cosmides, L. 157
Costa, J. 349
Cowie, F. 281
Cox, J. 157
Crick, F. 83
Croson, R. 328
Crosthwaite, J. 348
Cullum, J. 64, 187
Cumby, J. 205
Cummins, R. 38, 51, 52, 334
Cushman, F. 200, 202, 204–206, 269, 279, 315–317, 339, 347, 349, 361, 362

Damasio, A. 210
Dancy, J. 51
Danks, D. 105, 250
Darley, J. 137, 140, 156, 171, 187, 204, 362
Darwin, C. 302
Dasser, V. 113
Davidson, J. 4, 70
Davis, K. 256
Davis, T. 252
De Villiers, J. 215
Deacon, T. 299
Denes–Raj, V. 51, 52
Dennett, D. 77, 79, 83, 85, 86, 101
Derose, K. 3
Descartes, R. 112
Deutsch, M. 311
Devitt, M. 70, 310
Ditto, P. 209, 213, 347
Dorfman, J. 51, 70
Dreber, A. 349
Dreier, J. 169, 189
Dreyfus, H. 70
Dreyfus, S. 70
Driver, J. 214, 240, 251
Dweck, C. 336–338, 343
Dwyer, S. 42, 251

Eckel, C. 328, 329
Egan, A. 181
Einhorn, H. 66
Elga, A. 35
Epstein, S. 51, 52
Erickson, J. 125, 126, 129
Estes, D. 84
Evans, J. 129, 157
Ewing, S. 274

Farvolden, P. 70
Fawcett, C. 275
Fazio, R. 251
Feldman, R. 35
Feltz, A. 187, 224, 342
Fernbach, P. 274
Fiala, B. 76, 128, 133
Figdor, C. 339, 342
Fincham, F. 251

Fischer, J. 362
Fiske, S. 271
Fodor, J. 24, 127, 300
Folds–Bennett, T. 140
Føllesdal, A. 348
Foot, P. 349
Ford, D. 298
Forsyth, D. 140
Fraser, B. 204, 205, 246, 247, 252, 322
Frederick, S. 348
Friedman, O. 312, 313, 332, 333, 339

Gabennesch, H. 140
Galanter, E. 271
Gelman, S. 37, 283, 284, 302
Gendler, T. 51, 52, 310, 339
German, T. 47
Gettier, E. 6, 10, 25, 37, 311–314, 332, 333
Gibbard, A. 188
Gilliard, D. 337
Gino, F. 349
Glasgow, J. 33,46, 300
Glucksberg, S. 132, 164
Gneezy, U. 328
Goldberg, R. 76, 131
Goldberg, S. 326
Goldman, A. 32, 33, 70, 101, 112, 113, 197, 203, 310, 311, 339
Goodwin, G. 137, 171, 187
Gopnik, A. 112, 195–197, 253
Gottlieb, G. 298
Graham, G. 112
Graham, J. 155
Grandjean, P. 187
Grant, H. 337
Gray, H. 75, 84, 85, 86, 107, 115, 116, 117
Gray, K. 75, 115
Greene, J. 34, 42, 129, 189, 251, 339, 347, 361
Grice, H. P. 16, 17, 26, 28, 216
Griffin, D. 70
Griffiths, P. 46, 279, 284–5, 286, 291, 294, 296, 300, 301, 302
Griffiths, T. 275
Griggs, R. 157
Grossman, P. 328, 329
Grundmann, T. 348
Guglielmo, S. 211, 256, 272, 274

Hacker, P. 92
Haidt, J. 51, 70, 140, 155, 156, 209, 213, 251, 347, 348, 362
Halpern, D. 328
Hammond, K. 70
Hare, R. 22, 25, 139
Harman, G. 5, 25, 42, 139, 169, 189, 190
Harris, P. 112
Hart, H. 230
Harvey, W. 285
Haslanger, S. 308, 332, 339
Hatano, G. 125, 126, 302
Hauser, M. 42–44, 47, 251, 347, 349, 362

Author Index

Hawthorne, J. 4, 181
Heider, F. 113, 115, 118, 127, 130, 132
Heine, S. 330
Helwig, C. 140
Henrich, J. 330
Hersh, M. 347
Herz, R. 96
Hildenbrandt, C. 143
Hill, C. 112
Hilton, D. 252
Hinde, R. 281, 298
Hindriks, F. 209
Hintikka, J. 52, 70, 339
Hitchcock, C. 204, 213, 222, 230, 231, 233–237, 240, 244–246, 322
Hofmann, F. 348
Hogarth, R. 66
Holstein, C. 51
Holton, R. 256
Holtzman, G. 313–315, 317, 339, 340, 344
Holyoak, K. 157
Honoré, T. 230
Horvath, J. 348
Howard–Snyder, F. 349
Hsee, C. 177
Huebner, B. 86, 108, 129, 131, 133, 251
Huemer, M. 51
Huh, E. 51
Hunter, J. 140, 141, 159
Hyde, J. 342
Hyslop, A. 112

Ichikawa, J. 311
Inagaki, K. 125, 126, 302
Inbar, Y. 224

Jack, A. 85, 86, 95, 102, 104, 107, 116, 129
Jackson, F. 3, 5, 25, 32, 33, 51, 52, 310, 314, 334
James, W. 271
Jensen, M. 340
Johnson, K. 46
Johnson, S. 113–114, 118, 132, 133
Johnson–Laird, P. 157, 164
Johnston, T. 298
Jones, E. 256
Joseph, C. 51
Joyce, R. 188
Jukes, T. 299

Kagan, S. 170
Kahneman, D. 52, 66, 70, 128, 158, 218, 219, 230, 251
Kalish, C. 274, 275
Kant, I. 139
Kardes, F. 251
Karlovac, M. 251
Kauppinen, A. 1, 46, 170
Keil, F. 125, 126, 283, 302
Kelemen, D. 284, 291
Kelley, H. 196, 197, 254, 256
Kelly, T. 35, 251
Kenny, D. 252

Khalidi, M. 281, 295, 302
Kilstrom, J. 51
King, A. 298, 299
King, J. C. 26
King, J. L. 299
King, L. 70
Kitcher, P. 300
Klauer, K. 157
Klein, G. 66
Klienmutz, B. 70
Knobe, J. 5, 8, 9, 16, 24–28, 33–42, 52, 85, 86, 105, 107, 116, 117, 129–131, 137, 170, 189, 193, 200–205, 207, 213, 216, 222, 224, 230, 231, 233–237, 240, 244–247, 250–252, 254, 255, 267, 270–273, 275, 320–322, 339, 340
Koenigs, M. 210
Kohlberg, L. 140, 156, 347, 348
Konrath, S. 256
Kornblith, H. 51, 310
Korsgaard, C. 130
Kripke, S. 11, 12, 25, 26, 311
Krosnick, J. 58
Kuhn, D. 348
Kunda, Z. 209, 213
Kvaran, T. 129, 342

Laio, M. 52
Lawrence, S. 4
Leaman, G. 348
Leboyer, M. 215
Legrenzi, M. 157
Legrenzi, P. 157
Lehman, D. 251
Lehrer, K. 52
Lehrman, D. 281, 298
Lepore, E. 26
Lerner, R. 298
Leslie, A. 47, 201, 254
Levin, J. 83
Levine, J. 101, 104
Lewis, D. 33
Lipson, A. 51
Liu, B. 347
Livengood, J. 105, 339, 348
Loewenstein, G. 70, 177
Lombrozo, T. 194, 339, 343, 347, 349, 360
Lorenz, K. 295, 296, 302
Lovallo, D. 158
Lucas, C. 275
Ludwig, K. 170, 310

MacFarlane, J. 181, 190
Machery, E. 5, 33–37, 52, 70, 75, 86, 108, 117, 129, 131, 209, 215, 224, 254, 257, 272, 273, 275, 279, 296, 339
Mackie, J. 139, 170, 188
Macnamara, J. 51
Maio, G. 140, 141, 156
Malle, B. 211, 254–256, 266, 271, 272, 274, 275
Mallon, R. 1, 33, 35, 46, 47, 52, 273, 281, 297, 300, 301, 339, 343

Mameli, M. 281, 282, 300, 301
Mandel, D. 251, 252
Mandelbaum, E. 189
Marcus, M. 38
Margolis, E. 4, 24
Marler, P. 281, 286
Marr, D. 38, 39
Martin, K. 207
Mascalzoni, E. 130
Mates, B. 26
Mazzocco, P. 252
McArthur, L. 198
McCann, H. 202, 209
McCloskey, M. 132, 282
McCloy, R. 219
McDowell, J. 26
McIntyre, A. 349
McWhite, C. 187
Meaney, M. 298
Medin, D. 197, 283, 284, 302
Mele, A. 24, 200, 255, 269
Melnyk, A. 130
Meltzoff, A. 112, 196,197
Mendlow, G. 254, 272
Mermigis, L. 70
Michel, G. 298
Miikkulainen, R. 341
Mikhail, J. 42, 43, 203, 347, 349
Mill, J. 111, 112, 129
Miller, A. 26
Miller, D. 218, 219, 230
Miller, G. 271
Miller, J. B. 158
Miller, J. G. 274
Miller, V. 70
Monsay, E. 70
Moore, C. 296, 298
Murphy, G. 197
Musch, J. 157

N'gbala, A. 219
Nadelhoffer, T. 36
Nagel, J. 51
Nagel, T. 81, 82, 104, 139, 349
Nahmias, E. 5, 24, 26, 33, 46, 189, 342
Nanay, B. 224
Naumer, B. 157
Nelkin, D. 349
Nelson, S. 254, 255
Newstead, S. 157
Newton, N. 93, 95
Nichols, S. 5, 7, 9, 15, 17, 25, 27, 33, 34, 37–42, 46, 52, 70, 76, 105, 112, 113, 140, 170, 189, 209, 216, 224, 310, 317, 318, 324, 339, 349
Nisbett, R. 52, 339
Norenzayan, A. 52, 330
Nyholm, S. 207

O'Neill, P. 34, 347, 349
Olson, J. 140, 141, 156, 189

Opfer, J. 125, 126, 133
Ortony, A. 283
Osbeck, L. 51, 52, 70
Osgood, C. 250
Oyama, S. 298

Papineau, D. 83
Pargetter, R. 112
Parsons, C. 51
Paxton, J. 347
Paxton, M. 339, 342
Peng, K. 52
Perner, J. 112, 113
Pessin, A. 326
Petrinovich, L. 34, 43, 49, 347, 349
Pettit, D. 202–203, 222, 254, 279
Pettit, P. 3, 13, 25
Petty, R. 58
Pezzo, M. 252
Phelan, M. 189, 224, 272
Phillips, J. 189, 207, 222
Piaget, J. 84, 140, 156, 251
Pinillos, N. 169, 189
Pizarro, D. 211, 319–320, 340, 347
Plato 310, 339
Plessner, H. 70
Pollard, P. 157
Post, D. 198
Powell, M. 251
Premack, D. 79, 197
Pribram, K. 271
Prinz, J. 85, 86, 107, 116, 117, 129–131, 170, 189, 339
Pust, J. 32, 33, 51, 52, 70
Putnam, H. 25, 325

Quine, W. 35–37
Quinn, P. 349

Railton, P. 139, 169
Raven, P. 283
Ravizza, M. 362
Rawls, J. 362
Reber, A. 70
Regehr, G. 70
Reid, T. 111, 129, 130
Rest, J. 348
Rigdon, M. 329, 341
Riggs, K. 275
Rips, L. 283, 302
Ritov, I. 349
Robbins, P. 85, 86, 95, 102, 105, 116, 129
Robinson, P. 362
Roedder, E. 5, 27, 207
Roxborough, C. 205
Rust, J. 348
Ryle, G. 14

Sabonmatsu, D. 251
Sackris, D. 187
Samson, D. 275

Sarkissian, H. 133, 137, 189, 224, 272
Saul, J. 308, 332, 339
Schaffer, J. 340
Schleifer, M. 251
Schnall, S. 347
Scholl, B. 45, 47, 113, 118
Schwab, N. 64, 187
Schwartz, S. 141
Schwitzgebel, E. 46, 105, 279, 348
Searle, J. 82, 253, 319, 326
Seung, T. 70
Shafer–Landau, R. 23, 27, 169, 170, 188
Shafir, E. 52, 63
Shames, V. 51
Shantz, C. 140
Shaver, K. 251
Sheehy, E. 275
Shepard, J. 202
Shimizu, Y. 114
Shiverick, S. 275
Shu, L. 349
Shultz, T. 140, 156, 251
Shweder, R. 140
Siegler, R. 126, 133
Simmel, M. 113, 115, 118, 127, 130, 132
Simpson, A. 79, 275
Singer, P. 159, 170, 348
Sinnott–Armstrong, W. 189
Skowronski, J. 256
Slabbekorn, H. 286
Sloman, S. 51, 70, 118, 196, 274, 275
Smart, J. 311, 316
Smedslund, J. 198
Smith, E. 132
Smith, M. 3, 23, 25, 27, 139, 141, 144, 169, 170, 188
Snare, F. 140, 141, 144, 160
Soames, S. 13
Solan, L. 204
Solomon, G. 302
Sosa, D. 52
Sosa, E. 51, 52, 310, 332
Sousa, P. 284, 302
Spelke, E. 197
Sperber, D. 43
Spranca, M. 140, 156, 349
Sripada, C. 250, 256, 274
Stanley, J. 26
Stanovich, K. 42, 118
Starmans, C. 312, 313, 332, 333, 339
Steadman, A. 16, 36, 37, 214, 216, 254, 255
Stephenson, T. 181, 190
Sternberg, R. 70
Stevenson, C. 21, 22, 27
Stotz, K. 46, 286, 301
Strevens, M. 302
Sturgeon, N. 139
Suci, G. 250

Surian, L. 47, 215
Swain, S. 5, 25, 34, 46, 52–54, 57, 64, 66, 67
Sytsma, J. 75, 86, 108, 117, 129, 131, 135, 339
Szabo Z. 26

Tannenbaum, D. 200, 203
Tannenbaum, P. 250
Tetlock, P. 140, 156, 208
Thompson–Schill, S. 131
Thomson, J. 349
Tiberius, V. 339, 342
Tisak, M. 140
Tolman, E. 271
Tremoulet, P. 113, 118
Trope, Y. 118
Turiel, E. 140, 141, 143, 147, 158
Turing, A. 77, 79
Turner, J. 209
Tversky, A. 52, 70
Tye, M. 83

Ubel, P. 70
Uhlmann, E. 34, 319
Ulatowski, J. 33, 37, 204, 207, 209, 216, 224

Vesterlund, L. 329, 346

Wainryb, C. 143, 171
Wallace, R. 23
Wang, Y. 349
Weatherson, B. 181
Wegner, D. 75, 115
Weinberg, J. 1, 5, 15, 24, 25, 27, 34, 46, 51–53, 281, 297, 300, 310, 324, 339, 342, 348
Wellman, H. 84, 112, 113, 195, 197, 253, 274, 302
West, M.
West, R.
Wheatley, T. 347
White, R. 35
Williams, B. 139, 140, 349
Williamson, T. 25, 46, 51, 52, 310, 348
Winston, J. 96
Wittgenstein, L. 11, 26, 45
Wong, D. 170, 189, 190
Woodruff, G. 79, 197
Woodward, A.
Woodward, J.
Wright, C.
Wright, J.

Xu, F. 275

Young, L. 209, 210, 250, 315, 339, 347, 349, 361

Zalla, T. 215
Zamzow, J. 70, 317, 318
Zell, E. 251, 252

Subject Index

Action trees 203–4
Agency 115–117
Agency dimension 78–79, 84, 115–6
Agency model 117–9, 122–4, 127–9
Argument from analogy 111–112
Authority of Reflection 21–24

Bias 21, 40, 44, 177, 279, 332, 339, 348–9
    Biased Scientist view 254–6, 259–60, 265, 267, 270
    Impact of moral considerations as a 193, 199, 207–15, 245,
    In connection with order effects 52–53, 57, 64–67, 362, 349
Belief strength 61–6
Best explanation and other minds 112
Blame 13–18, 36, 193, 208–217, 222, 255, 263–4, 270, 272, 323, 327–8, 351–2
    Connection to causal judgment 229–252, 212, 319–320
Bodily sensations 83, 87–89
Brain in a vat thought experiment 324–5, 334–5
British Philosophical Association 308

Canalization 291, 298–9
Causation 36, 112, 115, 118, 127, 271, 284, 319–320
    Impact of moral considerations 193, 195–8, 201, 204–205, 208–215, 220, 222, 224, 229–252, 323–324
    Causal essence 283, 301
Chinese Room thought experiment 310, 324–8, 334
Compatibilism 40, 42, 313–14, 334–5
Competence, semantic 5–6, 9–12, 15
Competence/performance distinction 38–41, 199, 217
Concept individuation 36–38
Conceptual analysis 3–6, 297–301
Confidence 57, 64–66
Counterexamples 4, 10, 12, 20–23, 27, 281–2, 294–8, 301
Culpable control 229–252

Defaults 33, 220–2, 265, 275
Dialogue 19–24
Dictator game 329–30

Disagreement 17–18
Doctrine of double effect 349–352, 357–8, 360–2
Dual process models 128
Dualism 84–85, 129, 133, 313–16, 335, 340
Emotions 78, 81–85, 93–101, 107, 116, 131
    Impact on judgments 40, 217, 245, 255
Epistemic side–effect effect 320–4, 335, 340
Essentialism 37, 279, 283–4
Ethical disagreement 139
Experience 115–117
Experience dimension 78–79, 84, 115–6
Expertise 33, 70, 347–365
Explanatory gap 101–4
Explication 301
Extramentalism 32–33

Fixed mind–set 336–7
Folk dualism 129

Gender differences 53, 59, 224, 279, 307–346
Gettier cases 6, 10, 25, 37, 311–14, 332–5
Grounding of ethical judgments 148–9, 158–9
Group agency 85–6, 116–7
Growth mind–set 336–7

Hard problem 82, 101–4

Ideal conditions 12–13, 16
Inherited information 295–6
Innate 43–44, 130, 281–305
    Concept of innateness 33, 279
Inner nature 279, 283–5, 291, 295–6, 299
Insects and attribution of consciousness 119–121, 129
Intentional action 5, 8, 16–17, 26–27, 33, 35–36, 199–203, 211, 215–17, 231, 253–278, 319–22
Intentional agent 114–115
Intuitional stability 52–3, 57–8, 64–67
IQ 337

Levels of explanation 39
Life model 124–7
Linguistic analogy 42–3

373

Magistrate and the Mob thought experiment 311, 315–17, 335
Mary thought experiment 314–15, 334
Mentalism 33–34, 35–38
Mind perception 77–79
Modularity 127–8, 284
Morality 78–79
    Moral dilemmas 43, 70, 210, 317–18, 347–365
    Moral/conventional distinction 141
    Moral judgment internalism 7, 21–24
    Moral luck 349, 351–62

Nation of China example 128–9
Normativity 6, 10–12, 15–17
Norm violations 141, 194, 205, 230, 229–252, 253–278

Objectivity 140–2
    Objectivity and cultural difference 169–191
    Objectivity judgments and religious belief 153–4, 159
    Objectivity judgments variation with ethical domain 145–7, 153, 157
    Objectivity operationalized 144–5, 150–1
Omissions 22
    Act/omission (doing/allowing) 205–206, 224, 349–361
Order effects 52, 287, 347–365

Paradigmaticity 63–6
Perceived consensus 58, 63–4
Perceptual experience 83, 88–93, 95
Person as scientist theory 193–9
    Rational scientist theory 253–278
Phenomenal consciousness 82, 83, 85–6, 89–92, 100–4

Phenomenal stance 85
Philosophical Gourmet Report ('Leiter Report') 308–9
PhilPapers 308, 335
Physicalism 313, 315
Plank of Carneades thought experiment 327
Plants and attribution of consciousness 119–121, 123–7
Pragmatic considerations 13–14, 213–217, 255, 331
Principled reasoning 27, 348, 352, 360,
Problem of other conscious minds 111–2
Problem of other minds 113–115
Proper domain problem 41–44

Rationalization 213, 347–9, 352, 358, 360, 362
Reflective equilibrium 4, 334
Relativism 44–45, 169–191
Rutgers University 311, 333, 342

Selection effect hypothesis 334–7
Society for Women in Philosophy 308
Subjective experience, chapter 5 *passim*

Teleology 126, 133, 281–305
Trolley problem 42–44, 317–18, 349, 361
Twin Earth thought experiment 324–7, 334–5
Typicality 43,
    Connection to mental state attribution 256, 260–1, 264, 266, 275
    Connection to innateness 281–305

Valence 95–104
    Moral 235, 254, 262–5, 270, 272, 274, 322–3
Violinist thought experiment 315–16, 334–5